EUROPEAN COMPETITION LAW ANNUAL 2004:

The Relationship Between Competition Law and the (Liberal) Professions

EUROPEAN COMPETITION LAW ANNUAL: 2004

The Relationship Between Competition Law and the (Liberal) Professions

Edited by

Claus-Dieter Ehlermann

and

Isabela Atanasiu

OXFORD – PORTLAND OREGON
2006

Published in North America (US and Canada) by
Hart Publishing
c/o International Specialized Book Services
920 NE 58th Avenue, Suite 300
Portland, OR 97213-3786
USA

Tel: +1 503 287 3093 or toll-free: (1) 800 944 6190
Fax: +1 503 280 8832
E-mail: orders@isbs.com
Web Site: www.isbs.com

Hart Publishing, Salters Boatyard, Folly Bridge, Abingdon Rd, Oxford, OX1 4LB Telephone: +44 (0)1865 245533 Fax: +44 (0) 1865 794882
email: mail@hartpub.co.uk
WEBSITE: http//:www.hartpub.co.uk

British Library Cataloguing in Publication Data
Data Available

ISBN 13: 978-1-84113-612-7 (hardback)
ISBN 10: 1-84113-612-3

Typeset by Hope Services Ltd, (Abingdon), Oxon
Printed and bound in Great Britain by
Biddles Ltd, Kings Lynn, Norfolk

PERMANENT SPONSORS OF THE ANNUAL EUI COMPETITION WORKSHOPS

Blake, Cassels & Graydon LLP
Contact: *Calvin S. Goldman, QC*
Commerce Court West
199 Bay Street
Toronto, Ontario
Canada
M5L 1A9
Tel: 416 863 22 80
Fax: 416 863 26 53
E-mail: cal.goldman@blakes.com

Cleary, Gottlieb, Steen & Hamilton
Contact: *Prof. Mario Siragusa*
Rome Office
Piazza di Spagna 15
I-00187 Rome
Tel: (06) 695 221
Fax: (06) 692 00 665
E-mail: msiragusa@cgsh.com

Hengeler, Müller, Weitzel, Wirtz
Contact: *Jochen Burrichter*
Trinkausstrasse 7
D-40213 Düsseldorf
Germany
Fax: 00 49 211 83 04 222
E-mail: jochen.burrichter@hengeler.com

Howrey Simon Arnold & White
Contact: *James Rill Esq.*
1299 Pennsylvania Ave., NW
Washington, DC 20004
Tel: (001 202) 383 65 62
E-mail: rillj@howrey.com
Fax: (001 202) 383 66 10

Martinez Lage & Asociados

Contact: *Santiago Martínez Lage*
Claudio Coello 37—28001 Madrid
Tel (34) 91 426 44 70 –
Fax (34) 91 577 37 74
E-mail: smlage@m-lage.es

Skadden, Arps, Slate, Meagher & Flom L.L.P.

Contact: *Prof. Barry Hawk*
Brussels Office
523 Avenue Louise
B-1050 Brussels
Tel: (32 2) 639 03 00
Fax: (32 2) 639 03 39
E-mail: bhawk@skadden.com

White & Case/Forrester Norral & Sutton

Contact: *Prof. Ian Forrester*
Brussels Office
62, rue de la Loi
B-1040 Brussels
Tel: (32 2) 219 16 20
Fax: (32 2) 219 16 26
E-mail: forreia@brussels.whitecase.com

Wilmer Cutler Pickering Hale and Dorr LLP

Contact: *John Ratliff*
Bastion Tower
Place du Champ de Mars/Marsveldplein 5
B-1050 Brussels, Belgium
Tel: (32 2) 285 49 08
Fax: (32 2) 285 49 49
E-mail: john.ratliff@wilmerhale.com

CONTENTS

TABLE OF CASES

1.EC Courts:

2. EC Commission:

3. France:

4. Ireland:

5. Spain:

5. The Netherlands:

6. US Cases:

7. Canada:

INTRODUCTION

This volume includes the written contributions presented at the ninth edition of the Annual EU Competition Law and Policy Workshop, held on 11-12 June 2004 at the Robert Schuman Centre for Advanced Studies of the European University Institute (EUI) in Florence, as well as the (edited) transcripts of the debate that took place at the event.

Background. The Annual EU Competition Law and Policy Workshop was set up in 1996, at the Robert Schuman Centre for Advanced Studies of the EUI, by Law Professors Giuliano Amato and Claus-Dieter Ehlermann. The Workshop brings together every year top-level EU and international policy-makers, academics and legal practitioners to discuss in an informal environment topical issues of EC competition law and policy.

The objective of the 2004 edition of the Workshop was to examine some of the economic, legal and institutional/political aspects of the relationship between EC competition law and the regulation of the liberal professions, in the context of the ongoing public debate on the modernization of professional regulation in the EU Member States.[1] 'Liberal professions' are usually defined as occupations requiring special training in the arts or sciences–including, for example, lawyers, notaries, accountants, architects, engineers, pharmacists, doctors, etc. Liberal professions and the rules governing their functioning have

[1] Some information about earlier editions of the Annual EU Competition Law and Policy Workshop and the corresponding volumes in the *European Competition Law Annual* series might be useful to the readers of the present publication.

The first Workshop (June 1996) examined problems of implementation of competition law and policy in a 'federal' context (see Claus D. Ehlermann and Laraine L. Laudati, eds. (1997): *The Robert Schuman Centre Annual on European Competition Law 1996*, Kluwer Law International, London).

The second Workshop (June 1997) discussed the objectives of competition law and policy in general (see Claus D. Ehlermann and Laraine Laudati, eds. (1998): *European Competition Law Annual 1997: Objectives of Competition Policy,* Hart Publishing, Oxford and Portland Oregon).

The third Workshop (June 1998) concentrated on the application of competition policy in the evolving communication and information markets (see Claus D. Ehlermann and Louisa Gosling, eds. (2000): *European Competition Law Annual 1998: Regulating Telecommunications*, Hart Publishing, Oxford and Portland Oregon).

The fourth Workshop (1999) studied three groups of problems in the field of EU state aid control: the economic justifications for granting state aid, state aid in the banking sector, and the possibilities for a decentralised approach to the control of state aid in the EU (see Claus D. Ehlermann and Michelle Everson, eds. (2001): *European Competition Law Annual 1999: State Aid Control in the European Union–Selected Problems*, Hart Publishing, Oxford and Portland Oregon).

The fifth Workshop (June 2000) examined the European Commission's proposal to modernize and decentralize EC antitrust enforcement, as published in the 'Modernization White Paper' of May 1999, and the public reactions provoked by it (see Claus D. Ehlermann and Isabela Atanasiu, eds. (2001): *European Competition Law Annual 2000: The Modernization of EC Antitrust Policy*, Hart Publishing, Oxford and Portland Oregon).

become of interest for EC competition law enforcement since the early Nineties, and they have been the subject of a series of Commission decisions and judgments of the European Courts. The regulation of liberal professions is also a matter of concern from the perspective of the freedom of services in the Internal Market.

In recent years, the modernization and decentralization of EC antitrust enforcement, on the one hand, and the Lisbon Agenda on the other, have generated a perceived need to reconsider and better define the relationship between EC competition law and professional regulation in the Member States. Regulation 1/2003 empowered the competition authorities of the Member States and national courts to apply EC competition rules in full, including in the area of the liberal professions. In 2000, in Lisbon, the European Council set out the ambitious objective of transforming the EU into the most competitive and dynamic knowledge-based economy of the world by 2010. Professional services are important in this context, as they represent a key sector of the European economy (both in terms of the employment they generate and their business turnover - it is estimated that in 2001 professional services created approximately 600 billion Euro of total value added in the EU15[2]) and a significant input to a wide range of other sectors of the economy (the Italian Antitrust Authority has estimated that in Italy an average of 6% of the costs of exporting firms are due to professional services[3]). However, in Europe the liberal professions have traditionally been characterized by a high level of regulation, which is often a mix of state regulation, self-regulation, custom and practice. The concern is that a high degree of restrictive regulation in this area can have knock-on effects on the competitiveness of other economic sectors, and on employment and growth in general.

The 2004 edition of the Annual EU Competition Law and Policy Workshop took place at an important stage of the ongoing public debate on the reform of professional regulation in the Member States, i.e., a few months after the publi-

The sixth Workshop (2001) carried further the debate on the Commission's modernization project by examining the conditions for effective private enforcement of EC competition law (see Claus D. Ehlermann and Isabela Atanasiu, eds. (2003): *European Competition Law Annual 2001: Effective Private Enforcement of EC Antitrust Law*, Hart Publishing, Oxford and Portland Oregon).

The seventh Workshop (June 2002) concluded the series devoted to the modernization of EC antitrust enforcement by discussing the conditions for the set up and effective functioning of the European network of competition authorities (ECN) (see Claus D. Ehlermann and Isabela Atanasiu, eds. (2005): *European Competition Law Annual 2002: Constructing the EU Network of Competition Authorities*, Hart Publishing, Oxford and Portland, Oregon).

The eighth Workshop (June 2003) explored the legal and economic issues arising in the enforcement of EC competition rules against abuses of a dominant position (see Claus D. Ehlermann and Isabela Atanasiu, eds. (2006): *European Competition Law Annual 2003: What Is an Abuse of a Dominant Position?*, Hart Publishing, Oxford and Portland, Oregon.

Further information about the Workshop, as well as non-edited versions of the written contributions prepared starting with the 2000 edition, are available at http://www.iue.it/RSCAS/Research/Competition/CompetitionLawPolicy.shtml.

[2] See European Commission (2004): *Report on Competition in the Professional Services*, COM(2004) 83 final, of 9 February 2004, at p. 8.

[3] *Idem*, at p. 8.

cation of the European Commission's *Report on Competition in the Professional Services*.[4] The Report is the outcome of a 'stock-taking' exercise launched in March 2003 by DG Competition, under the leadership of Mario Monti, who was at that time the Commissioner responsible for competition. The exercise involved consulting the interested parties (professionals, professional bodies, consumers and consumer associations) in order to identify restrictive professional regulation in the Member States and evaluate its justification and effects. In a nutshell, the Report contains the main findings of this consultation process and invites public authorities in the Member States to screen restrictive professional regulation on the basis of a proportionality test.

First, the Report identifies five main categories of potentially-restrictive regulation in the EU with respect to the liberal professions: 1) price-fixing; 2) recommended prices; 3) advertising restrictions; 4) entry requirements and reserved rights; and 5) rules governing business structure and multi-disciplinary practices.

Second, the Report acknowledges that regulation may be necessary in order to address certain problems that arise in the area of the liberal professions, including asymmetry of information between customers and service providers, externalities (or the impact of services on third parties) and the need to ensure the provision of certain 'public goods' that are of value to society as a whole. At the same time, the Report suggests that certain traditional restrictive regulatory tools aimed at solving these issues should be replaced by more pro-competitive mechanisms.

Third, the Report maps out the conditions under which EC competition rules are applicable to restrictive professional regulation in the Member States, in accordance with the relevant case law of the European Court of Justice (including the judgments in *Arduino*, *Wouters* and *Fiammiferi*[5]). The Report distinguishes between the liability of the Member States and that of professional bodies, and points out that the case law of the ECJ does not solve all enforcement issues arising in this area.

Finally, the Report invited the regulatory authorities in the Member States as well as professional bodies to review existing professional regulation on the basis of a proportionality test according to which professional rules must be: (i) objectively necessary in order to pursue a clearly articulated and legitimate public interest objective, and (ii) the least restrictive way to attain that objective.

Structure of the Workshop. Against this background, the objective of the 2004 EU Competition Law and Policy Workshop was to examine some of the issues raised by the Commission's *Report on Competition in Professional Services*. **Panel 1 (Economic Aspects)** discussed the following main issues: 1)

[4] *Idem.*

[5] C-35/99 *Arduino* [2002] ECR I-1529; Case C-309/99 *Wouters* [2002] ECR I-1577; Case C-198/01 *Consorzio Industrie Fiammiferi* [2003] ECR I-8055.

whether professional services are characterized by specific market failures justifying a different treatment under EC competition rules; 2) the contribution of economic theory and analysis to defining and assessing the public interest objectives pursued by professional regulation; and 3) the economics perspective on the costs and benefits of different regulatory models applicable in this area. **Panel 2 (Legal Issues)** focused on the following issues: 1) whether the standards resulting from the ECJ's case law for assessing the legality of anticompetitive professional regulation are adequate and sufficiently well articulated; 2) similarities and differences between the EU and US approach in the application of competition rules to restrictive professional regulation; and 3) the application of the proportionality test in the context of the 'state action' doctrine. **Panel 3 (Institutional/Political Issues)** concentrated on three main groups of issues: 1) complementarity between the enforcement of EC competition rules with respect to restrictive professional regulation, the Commission's competition advocacy initiatives supporting the modernization of professional regulation and the Commission's legislative and enforcement interventions in the area of professional regulation in the context of the freedom to provide services in the Internal Market; 2) the role played by national competition authorities (NCAs) in the screening of restrictive professional regulation in the context of the recent modernization and decentralization of EC antitrust enforcement; and 3) lessons to be learned from the experience of competition authorities in the US and other international jurisdictions (particularly Australia and Canada) in terms of institutional arrangements and doctrines/concepts that affect the quality of antitrust interventions in the area of professional regulation.

The Workshop proceedings opened with an **introductory exposé** by Mario Monti, then-Commissioner responsible for competition. Commissioner Monti started his speech by underlining the importance of liberal professions in the EU economy, in terms of the value added and employment generated, and as an input to the activity of several other economic sectors. The quality, competitiveness, growth and occupational potential of the professional services thus has significant spillover effects on the rest of the economy. The objective of the Lisbon Agenda brought into the spotlight the traditionally high level of professional regulation in Europe. Outdated and over-restrictive regulation is a matter of concern insofar as it leads to either excessive prices or poor quality of services, removes the incentives for improvement, and generates macroeconomic allocative distortions - the extraction of excessive prices favours rent-seeking behaviour, and thus distorts the allocation of human capital.

Next, Commissioner Monti outlined DG Competition's initiatives in the area of professional services, as undertaken within the framework of the European Competition Network (ECN). The Commissioner emphasized the fact that DG Competition does not advocate the total deregulation of professional services. To the contrary, the Commission acknowledges that certain characteristics of professional services, such as information asymmetries and externalities, may need to be addressed with regulatory tools. The question is, rather, whether the current regulatory mix is the most efficient possible. For example, some of the regulatory means that were traditionally used in order to tackle information asymmetries, such as the setting of tariffs and restrictions on advertisement, no longer correspond to the present reality, where consumers are more educated and better organized for defending their interests. Nowadays, consumers appear to prefer to reduce information asymmetries by increasing the information available as to the nature, quality and availability of professional services.

By launching in March 2003 the stock-taking exercise which led to the publication in February 2004 of the Commission's *Report on Competition in the Professional Services*,[6] DG Competition acted as the initiator of a public debate on the efficiency of the current professional regulatory mix in the Member States. DG Competition invited European professional bodies to bilateral meetings to discuss the scope for modernizing existing regulation. Similar bilateral consultation exercises were scheduled to take place between the national competition authorities and national professional bodies. The purpose of this consultation process is to assess the justifications for and effects of professional regulation on the basis of a proportionality test: rules must be objectively necessary to achieve a clearly articulated and legitimate public interest objective, and must be the least restrictive means to that end.

At the same time, the Commission is well aware that the simple elimination of restrictive professional rules is not sufficient to bring about more competition in this sector. This is why DG Competition and DG Health and Consumer Protection liaised and consulted with European consumer organizations in order to identify other pro-competitive supporting measures–for example, the monitoring of professional services by consumer associations, the collection and publication of information by independent organizations, etc.

In addition to the application of EC competition rules in this area and besides advocating the screening of current professional regulation on the basis of the proportionality principle, the Commission also supports the modernization of professional regulation through Internal Market legislative initiatives. For example, the draft *Directive on Services in the Internal Market*,[7] which also covers professional services, is a mixture of mutual recognition, administrative cooperation, harmonization where strictly necessary, and encouragement of self-regulation. The **Directive on Recognition of Professional Qualifications (adopted in September 2005)**[8] is another example in this regard.

Commissioner Monti concluded his intervention by underlining the important role played by the national competition authorities (NCAs) in the area of liberal professions. Regulation 1/2003 empowers the NCAs and national courts

[6] See *supra* n. 2.

[7] The Commission's original proposal, dated January 2004, as well as the European Parliament's First Reading Legislative Resolution of February 2006 and the Commission's amended proposal of April 2006, are available at http://europa.eu.int/comm/internal_market/services/services-dir/proposal_en.htm.

[8] *Directive 2005/36/EC of the European Parliament and of the Council on the Recognition of Professional Qualifications*, OJ L 255 [2005].

to apply Article 81 EC in full, and the NCAs are very often the best placed to act in cases of anticompetitive professional regulation. Most NCAs have in fact pursued actions in this area (the most frequent cases involve price-fixing, discriminatory rules on access to the professions, boycotts, and advertising restrictions). By the time of the Workshop, several NCAs (including, for example, those in Denmark, Ireland, The Netherlands, Finland and the UK) had also undertaken general programmes of action to bring about the modernization of professional regulation in their countries.

Panel 1: Economic Aspects. The first general issue addressed by the participants under this Panel was whether the professional services are characterized by specific market failures that justify a different treatment under EC competition rules. From this perspective, the written contributions tackled four distinct problem areas: asymmetric information on quality; asymmetric information on demand; the problem of so-called 'credence goods' (i.e., where consumers do not know how to evaluate the consumed services); and externalities (in the sense that in the area of professional services there are often wider social interests to consider than those of the directly interested parties).

From the discussion it became clear that all agree on the existence of market failures in the area of liberal professions. At the same time, some of the participants emphasized that market failures are present in other economic sectors as well. Information asymmetries are generally present in markets where customers' purchases are less frequent - in other words, the information asymmetry problem is common among non-frequent purchasers, who are usually individuals and households as opposed to firms. From an economic perspective, repeated purchases also weaken the case for qualifying professional services as credence goods.

Some of the participants argued that, considering the features of the modern economy, including information and technological developments, information asymmetries no longer justify special treatment for any of the liberal professions. The case of externalities is different: from an economic perspective, it does not make sense to liberalize and at the same time ask the professions to produce positive externalities. The original question could therefore be rephrased, to ask instead whether in the modern economy it still makes sense to impose competitive constraints in order to derive positive externalities.

It therefore appears that externalities remain the strongest argument for regulation of the professions. However, economists recommend that it must first be determined whether the markets could solve the problem themselves before it can be decided whether to intervene through regulation. Another important policy suggestion that emerged from the debate is that, when speaking of market failures, both regulators and competition law enforcers should seek to identify and define the specific markets at stake rather than discussing the profession in general–for example, within the legal services there are several distinct markets to be considered. By the same token, regulators and competition law enforcers should also look at the specificities of the markets from the perspective of differences between consumers. As already mentioned, corporations and/or repeat customers do not face the same kind of information asymmetry problems as non-frequent individual consumers. In other markets, the problem of information asymmetry faced by non-frequent individual consumers was solved through the creation of new types of contracts (e.g., leasing) or quasi-contracts (i.e., informal contracts between the service provider and the customer). In fact, professional regulation that limits entry, diminishes price competition, establishes price caps or prohibits advertising is an imperfect attempt to establish a sort of 'global quasi-contract'.

The experience of competition authorities that have been active in the area of professional services shows that, if the intervention is not precisely calibrated for the actual problems that occur in a specific market, the outcomes may be less welcomed by the consumers. To avoid adverse effects, the intervention of the competition law enforcer to eliminate restrictive professional rules should be preceded or accompanied by other measures destined to make competition workable - for example, it should facilitate access to information, provide independent mechanisms for the assessment of the quality of services, etc.

Another interesting and topical argument brought forward in the debate was that, from an economic perspective, restrictions on organizational forms imposed through professional regulation can actually be detrimental in terms of the information asymmetry problem. Larger organizations can generate a reputation more easily than individual professionals, and in multi-professional organizations that reputation can be transferred across markets. Thus, restrictions on multi-professional organizations prevent the reputation mechanism from ameliorating the information asymmetry problem.

Economic theory can also be helpful in defining the public interest at stake in the area of professional services. What is generally understood by 'public interest' is the social interest that governments take responsibility for protecting or providing. One of the difficulties that arises in defining the public interest protected/promoted by professional regulation is that market failures, such as information asymmetries, or the fact that the goods are not produced, usually produce 'complex negative external effects', in the sense that several diverse interests are involved and affected, and it is not straightforward how to balance them. From an economic perspective, there are three broadly-defined public interests at stake in the area of the liberal professions: quality, accessibility (physical or financial), and macro-affordability (e.g., in health care, the need to establish a standard for the services provided that can be sustained by the state at macro-level).

Once the public interest at stake is identified and defined, the question that arises is: who is better placed to protect/promote it - public authorities, professional bodies, or a combination of the two? And how may less restrictive and more effective regulatory tools be chosen? The participants discussed in particular the advantages and disadvantages of self-regulation by professional bodies, and weighed its efficiency against that of alternative regulatory models, such as competitive self-regulation and 'co-regulation'–the latter being understood as a mix of self-regulation and public oversight and/or monitoring.

Among the arguments in favour of self-regulation, the most convincing appears to be the one that professional bodies are best placed to produce efficient regulation because they have insight and information advantages over public regulators. The argument that self-regulation is more flexible than state regulation is considered less convincing, especially when self-regulation is abused to increase the rents extracted by the members of the profession. Economic theory has in fact demonstrated that it is difficult to change self-designed rules, even after the excessive rents have been dissipated among the professionals (a situation that economists define as 'the transitional gains trap'). Finally, the argument that self-regulation is more advantageous because its costs are borne by the members of the profession and not by the taxpayer is not valid in cases where self-regulation is used to extract excessive rents–in such cases the costs are actually passed on to consumers.

The main possible disadvantages of self-regulation are, first, the risk that professional bodies may use their regulatory power in order to restrict competition, and second, a certain 'democratic deficit', in the sense that consumer interests may not be sufficiently well represented in this regulatory framework. It was underlined, however, that the results of empirical research on the risk of abusing self-regulatory powers to restrict competition are mixed. In addition, a good part of the restrictions identified in the Commission's *Report on Competition in the Professional Services*[9] were set by public authorities, and not by professional bodies.

The participants also discussed possible modalities to minimize the disadvantages of self-regulation. One of the suggested possibilities was switching from *ex ante* to *ex post* self-regulation coupled with external regulation. Another possibility is making room for competitive self-regulation, which could be either inter-professional or intra-professional.

Ex post self-regulation implies, in essence, setting up incentives for good behaviour through the threat of punishment for professionals who breach rules and commitments. The main components of an *ex post* self-regulatory regime are: 1) explicit rules of conduct and service commitments, set up by a professional regulatory body; 2) a mechanism for monitoring compliance–for example, customer complaints, random audits, external monitoring of average performance; and 3) a punishment regime with an efficient deterrent effect. The main benefits of adding elements of external regulation to supplement the basic regulatory mechanism are to reduce the risk of regulatory capture and to have minimum quality standards set externally.

The draft *EC Directive on Professional Services*[10] encourages the step towards a mix of self-regulation and public regulation, as Member States are

[9] See *supra* n. 2.
[10] See *supra* n. 7.

called on to justify the extent to which their rules satisfy public interest goals. EC competition law also indirectly supports such a regulatory mix, as *Arduino*[11] indicates that only restrictive measures established outside the umbrella of the state action doctrine may be subject to competition scrutiny based on Article 81 EC.

In the context of **Panel 2: Legal Issues**, the debate concentrated principally on the standards for applying EC competition rules to anticompetitive professional regulation in the Member States in light of the relevant case law of the ECJ.

The main principle resulting from *Arduino*, *Wouters* and *Fiammiferi*[12] is that the state action doctrine, i.e., whether the state assumes full responsibility for the restrictive measure by clearly articulating the public interest pursued and actively supervising its implementation, excludes the application of Article 81 EC to anticompetitive professional regulation. There was also agreement on the point that the current approach needs to be further refined in several respects.

First, the 'active supervision' test has not yet been sufficiently articulated by the Court.

Second, the 'constitutional' underpinning of the current EU approach to anticompetitive state regulation may also need to be further clarified. There is no Treaty provision expressly prohibiting anticompetitive state measures that is comparable to the prohibition of anticompetitive agreements between undertakings laid down in Article 81 EC, and it is not clear under what circumstances Articles 3(1)(g) and 10(2) EC apply in this context. It was therefore suggested that the principles set forth in *GB-INNO-BM*[13] might need to be revised in light of *Arduino*.

Third, once an anticompetitive rule fails the 'state action' test, the criteria for assessing the measure under Article 81 EC are not yet clearly spelled out. The view of one of the participants is that, once an anticompetitive rule fails the 'state action' test, the justification of the restrictive measure comes into question, but that the conditions of Article 81(3) EC should be applied instead of proceeding with an evaluation of the public interest at stake. This opinion appears to be in agreement with the observation, made by other participants, that the Commission cannot infer the existence of a proportionality test from *Arduino;* in this judgment, the Court only recognized that Article 81 EC does not apply to anticompetitive measures covered by the 'state action' defence.

Also relevant in this context is the observation that, in the context of the application of Article 10 EC to restrictive professional regulation, the ECJ has proven hesitant to question the public interest objectives articulated by public authorities in the Member States. Furthermore, in *Wouters* the Court established that restrictive rules adopted by professional bodies outside the 'state

[11] See *supra* n. 5.

[12] See *supra* n. 5.

[13] Case 13/77 *GB-INNO-BM v. ATAB* [1997] ECR 2115.

action' umbrella may still fall outside the scope of application of Article 81 EC where they are adopted in the public interest.

Wouters is considered by many commentators to be a regrettable error, and there is fear that this judgment may lead to the importation of non-competition considerations into the competition analysis under Article 81(3) EC, thus spoiling the 'purity' of this provision. However, some of the participants argued that in this judgment the Court intentionally set out a margin of discretion for national professional bodies, recognizing that certain matters are best regulated at the national level and allowing for diversity between the Member States in defining the notion of public interest. One participant interestingly suggested that *Wouters* to some degree counteracts the risk arising from *Arduino* that the professions may lobby for state regulation in order to be shielded from the application of EC competition law behind the state action doctrine.

The participants questioned whether the Court's hesitance to apply a proportionality test in the context of the state action doctrine will be sustainable in the future. One of the possibilities suggested was to introduce a sort of generic 'exception for non-EC public interest reasons' in the application of Article 81(3) EC, so as to allow scrutiny of anticompetitive professional regulation and prevent possible abuses. This suggestion is not likely to meet the support of the (many) supporters of maintaining the purity of competition analysis. Another proposal was to refine the *Wouters* criteria by better targeting them on market failures, and on true, rather than false, matters of public interest. One of the arguments to support this view is that a global approach, such as that in taken in *Wouters,* does not make it possible to distinguish between the problems faced by frequent and non-frequent service customers.

In the context of the same Panel, the participants also discussed the similarities and differences between the EU and US approaches on the application of competition rules in the area of the liberal professions. One of the main differences is that in the US the public interest defence is not considered in antitrust cases, whereas in Europe it is the main defence invoked in cases involving anticompetitive measures. In the US, self-regulation of the professions can in theory be problematic, to the extent that in the absence of a clearly articulated state policy and active state supervision neither the state action doctrine nor public interest can be invoked as a defence. At the same time, interestingly, the First Amendment of the US Constitution can be used to strike down self-regulation. In US practice, what are usually referred to as 'second order restraints' (e.g., price advertising) are subject to closer scrutiny than state regulation.

Second, the US courts accept rather easily the information asymmetry theory–in *California Dental*,[14] the US Supreme Court relied on this theory in order to give more latitude to professional self-regulation.

[14] *California Dental Association v. FTC*, 128 F.3d 720, *vacated and remanded*, 526 U.S. 756 (1999).

Third, the current US approach is that antitrust analysis should take into account the structure and circumstances of each specific market, including the applicable regulatory rules -.an approach that is best reflected in *Trinko*.[15]

Fourth, several cases involving restrictive regulation of the professions have played an important role in shaping the analytical framework for dealing with horizontal restraints in general. In the US, private action has played a crucial role in the development of the jurisprudence in this area. It is hoped that a similar trend will start to develop in Europe as well, following the decentralization of EC competition law enforcement, as Regulation 1/2003 entitles the NCAs and national courts to apply Article 81 EC in full, including in the area of professional services. However, in this context some of the participants underlined an important drawback of the European system: in cases that are not initiated by the Commission, and therefore arrive before the ECJ as requests for preliminary rulings from the national courts, the Court is limited mainly to interpreting EC rules, and is not formally competent to apply them directly in the factual context of the cases. This is a severe limitation in the area of professional services, where the factual circumstances are important to the competition analysis in ways that have already been mentioned.

Fifth, the participants noted a convergence between the EU and US on the standards for the application of the state action doctrine. In this context, the US participants warned their EU counterparts about the danger of allowing the Member States to implicitly set aside EC competition rules in the area of restrictive professional regulation by invoking that doctrine.

Finally, in spite of the differences of constitutional setting, standards and approach, the outcomes of competition cases in the area of the professions appear to be very similar.

The first group of issues discussed by the participants under **Panel 3–Institutional/Political Issues** concerned the complementarity between the enforcement of EC competition rules with respect to restrictive professional regulation, the Commission's competition advocacy initiatives in support of the modernization of professional regulation, and the Commission's legislative and enforcement interventions in the area of professional regulation within the broader field of the freedom to provide services in the Internal Market.

In this context, the participants discussed the Commission's competition advocacy initiatives in the area of professional regulation, as evidenced in the ongoing stock-taking exercise launched by the Commission in this area since March 2003, and the path of reform suggested in the *Report on Competition in the Professional Services* of February 2004. Commission representatives emphasized that the real reform work needs to be done at the level of the Member States, while the Commission's role should be to continue to facilitate the reform through consultative means. After the publication of the Report, DG Competition organized bilateral meetings with the European professional

[15] *Communications Law Offices of Curtis v. Trinko*, 124 U.S. 872 (2004).

bodies to discuss and assess the justification for the main categories of restrictive professional rules identified in the Report. In the course of this consultation process, DG Competition asked for written detailed comments from the professional bodies whenever it was not entirely convinced of the justification for certain restrictions. Similar bilateral consultation meetings were to take place at the level of the Member States, between the national competition authorities (NCAs) and national professional bodies. European professional bodies and NCAs were asked to relay the Commission's concerns to the public and private bodies concerned at the national level.

In the same context, DG Competition advocates and encourages the adoption of pan-European Codes of Conduct for the various professions, to include the deontological rules whose uniformity at EU level is considered strictly necessary. In the Commission's view, the adoption of such codes could be a helpful point of reference in the review of professional regulation on proportionality criteria. Some of the participants, however, expressed concerns with respect to the usefulness or consequences of adopting such codes. For example, it was suggested that one of the risks is that such an initiative could lead to a codification of standards based on the lowest common denominator. One the other hand, such codes could be useful if conceived in a manner that allows for competition between national regulatory systems and the comparison of best practices.

DG Competition also advocates the undertaking of independent reviews of professional regulation in the Member States - similar to the independent review of the regulation for the legal professions in England and Wales, an exercise that produced interesting outcomes and recommendations which were presented in some detail at the Workshop. However, the participants underlined that such exercises can only succeed in bringing about the proposed reforms if there is real political willingness at the level of national public authorities and professional bodies.

Another DG Competition advocacy initiative is to bring into discussion the impact of past deregulation experiences in the Member States. Since some of the past experiences have not been entirely positive (for example, the deregulation of notary activities in the Netherlands has raised the cost of these services for non-frequent customers, as the distributional effects of deregulation were not taken into account) this exercise can be a useful source of reference for future reforms.

In parallel with consultations with the professional bodies on the justification for restrictive professional rules, DG Competition initiated a useful process of consultation with European consumer organizations. This initiative generated some interesting conclusions. First, the consumers do not appear to be very concerned about whether the professions are regulated or not - their main concern lies with the quality and accessibility of the services provided. Second, consumers confirm that in this area there are information asymmetry problems: basically, it is difficult to choose among different service providers. Consumers do not have sufficient information to be able to make an informed choice in this respect, and lifting restrictions on advertising is not enough to resolve existing problems. Third, consumers find it difficult to identify professional mistakes or negligence, and it is difficult to gather evidence of malpractice. Fourth, consumers want to have *ex ante* information concerning costs made available to them, and currently there are few provisions on how this information could be better supplied.

The Commission's competition advocacy initiatives in the area of liberal professions are complemented by enforcement and legislative actions in the area of the freedom to provide services in the Internal Market. In this sense, in *Wouters* the Court only re-confirmed a principle established long ago in the EC case law, according to which EC Treaty provisions on the freedom to provide services are applicable to public and private professional regulation.

The draft *Directive on Services in the Internal Market*[16] contains provisions that specifically address regulatory barriers to entry in the area of the liberal professions. On the one hand, the Member States would be obliged to remove prohibitive requirements such as nationality, residence authorizations, prohibitions on being enrolled in professional bodies in more than one Member State, etc. On the other hand, Article 15 of the draft Directive concerns other kinds of restrictions that might be justified under the ECJ test on the general interest objective and proportionality of the measure. Member States would be required to review professional regulation under this test and to draft comprehensive reports on the basis of that review. The reports will be subject to public comments and evaluation, in a sort of benchmarking exercise comparing best practices. On the basis of these national reports and the comments received, the Commission will produce a synthesis report, proposing specific action measures and possibly even some harmonization measures where deemed strictly necessary. Finally, the draft Directive also encourages the professions to develop Codes of Conduct at European level, as a useful instrument for diminishing regulatory differences between the Member States and reducing barriers to entry.

With respect to the role played by the NCAs in the reform and modernization of professional regulation, one of the essential aspects to consider is that the modernization and decentralization of EC antitrust enforcement has fundamentally changed the preceding paradigm in three principal ways.

First, Regulation 1/2003 empowers NCAs to apply in full Articles 81(1) and 81(3) EC, including in the area of liberal professions. Since in cases involving anticompetitive professional regulation the centre of gravity is usually within one Member State, the role of NCAs in the enforcement of EC competition rules in the area of liberal professions is expected to increase (although some NCAs have been very active in this area even in the past, and some, such as the French competition authority, have even proven to be more active that the Commission itself in this domain).

[16] See *supra* n. 7.

Second, *Fiammiferi*[17] requires the NCAs to disapply national rules, including rules of professional regulation, that are incompatible with EC competition rules. It is hoped that this power will support the NCAs in the review of professional regulation on the merits. Some of the participants warned, however, that there are still ambiguities about the NCAs' exact powers in this respect, and many NCAs have not had the opportunity to test how it works in the context of national institutional and legal arrangements.

Third, the modernization of EC competition law enforcement has fundamentally changed the relationship between the NCAs and the Commission, and Regulation 1/2003 has put in place clear mechanisms of vertical and horizontal cooperation within the European Competition Network.

Several participants argued that, in spite of this change of paradigm due to the decentralization of EC competition law enforcement, NCAs still have many difficulties to overcome in their interventions in the area of professional regulation. For example, some consider that the Commission's *Report on Competition in the Professional Services*[18] is not very helpful in this respect, insofar as it does not distinguish very well between the NCAs' tasks in the area of enforcing EC competition rules with respect to restrictive professional regulation and their competition advocacy tasks. The lack of a proportionality test in EC competition law generates difficult enforcement issues for the NCAs. Furthermore, shortage of resources can be a serious obstacle to an effective competition advocacy in this field. In addition, NCAs sometimes face institutional and political obstacles in performing their competition advocacy role. In this respect, the participants suggested that the adoption of national rules formalizing the competition advocacy functions of the NCAs would be helpful. One interesting example comes from the Australian experience, where restrictive professional rules that are by law exempt from antitrust scrutiny need to be reviewed by an independent body every two years, and the Australian competition authority has the possibility to express competition-related concerns in the process.

Finally, US participants highlighted some interesting and useful lessons from the US experience in this area in terms of institutional arrangements and doctrines/concepts that affect the quality of antitrust intervention in the area of professional regulation.

First, the US experience shows that, ironically, the more successful the antitrust agencies become with litigation against restrictive professional rules, the more aggressive the claims are by professional organizations for dispensation from the application of antitrust rules. The important lesson to be learned in this respect is that focusing only on enforcement is not the most advisable strategy–competition authorities should also engage in active competition advocacy through various means, including the preparation of guidelines, the formulation of advisory opinions, the publication of detailed market studies and surveys.

[17] See *supra* n. 5.

[18] See *supra* n. 2.

Second, the building of a solid knowledge base is essential for the success of the competition authorities' interventions before courts and legislative bodies. One way to build this knowledge base is through empirical research. Courts usually demand from the competition authorities 'precedents', which do not necessarily have to be exclusively case law, but may also usefully include market studies that advance empirically-tested arguments. Another way to build the knowledge base is to perform *ex post* assessments of how antitrust decisions taken in this area have actually been implemented, and with what effects, including in other jurisdictions. Furthermore, the FTC's activities demonstrate that there are increasingly important links between antitrust functions and consumer protection.

Third, the US experience indicates that the failure to make progress with deregulation or the elimination of ineffective regulation is due to the combination of three main factors: the strong incentives of the professions to pursue rent-seeking activities, including through regulation; the spread of the state action doctrine, which shields most anticompetitive professional rules from antitrust scrutiny; and the fact that in the US courts and antitrust agencies are somewhat reluctant to challenge restrictive professional rules even where they are not covered by the state action doctrine. These problems can be addressed through vigorous antitrust enforcement, the limitation of the scope of the state action doctrine, and determined competition advocacy.

Finally, one of the distinctive features of the US experience is the important role played by individuals and private litigation in the development of the jurisprudence on the application of antitrust rules to restrictive professional regulation. It is hoped that the modernization of EC competition law enforcement will contribute to stimulating similar development in the EU. While some doubt that the preliminary reference mechanisms can be very effective under the current paradigm, where the ECJ is limited to interpreting the EC rules and cannot formally rule on the factual contexts of cases, others argue that private action can still be the most promising way to achieve the reform of professional regulation in the Member States through the development of EC jurisprudence–an illustrative example being the enormous contribution of the preliminary reference mechanism in the area of the free movement of workers.

Conclusions and policy recommendations. The debate that took place at the ninth edition of the EU Competition Law and Policy Workshop on the relationship between EC competition law and the regulation of the liberal professions produced a number of significant conclusions and policy recommendations, which are of high relevance in the context of the ongoing public debate on the reform and modernization of professional regulation in Europe. These can be summarized as follows.

First, the simple elimination of anticompetitive professional regulation is not sufficient to bring about more competition and better regulation in the area of the liberal professions. Such measures need to be accompanied by other pro-competitive accompanying mechanisms (including, for example, the monitoring of professional regulation and performance by consumer organizations and/or independent supervisory bodies, the publication of systematic information and surveys by independent sources, etc.) and by vigorous competition advocacy in the context of the review of professional regulation in the Member States.

Second, from an economic perspective, when speaking of market failures that justify and require the regulation of the professions, it is necessary to identify and define the specific markets at stake instead of discussing categories of professions in general. It is equally important to look at market failures from the perspective of differences between types of consumers: non-frequent and individual consumers face different information asymmetry problems than frequent customers and large industrial or professional clients. Regulatory instruments need to be specifically tailored to take into account this distinction.

Third, again from an economic perspective, the primary objective of regulation is how to ensure that positive externalities are generated while at the same time diminishing complex negative externalities. In this sense, a clear definition of the public interest at stake becomes of paramount importance, and economic theory and evidence can contribute in this respect.

Fourth, economic theory has important contributions to make when it comes to choosing the most effective and efficient models of regulation. The empirical evidence regarding the benefits of self-regulation is mixed, but this does not necessarily mean that state regulation is a better option. There are means of mitigating the disadvantages of self-regulation while preserving its advantages, for example by adding elements of external regulation and supervision to a basic self-regulatory mechanism. In that regard, external regulation is not the exclusive prerogative of public authorities, as the same functions can be carried out by independent bodies, consumer organizations, etc.

Fifth, the current approach to the application of the EC competition rules in the area of professional regulation needs to be further clarified and refined in several respects. These include the refinement of the 'state supervision' criterion established by the case law of the ECJ, the clarification of the constitutional underpinnings of the current enforcement approach, the setting of criteria for the competition assessment of professional regulation falling outside the scope of the state action doctrine, and the identification of the possible means by which a proportionality test in the context of the state action doctrine may be applied.

Sixth, NCAs have a fundamental role to play in the ongoing process of reforming European professional regulation. Competition law enforcement needs to be complemented with vigorous competition advocacy activities. Also, experience shows that combining competition and consumer protection functions is a fruitful and illuminating approach. At the same time, the absence of the proportionality test in EC competition law poses serious difficulties for the NCAs in the enforcement of EC competition rules. Insofar as their competition advocacy role is concerned, it would be recommendable to adopt specific national rules to affirm their functions in this respect.

Several of the foregoing points are confirmed in the Commission's *Follow-Up Report on Competition in the Professional Services* of September 2005,[19] which assesses the progress made by the Member States in the elimination of professional restrictions that fail the proportionality test and puts forward recommendations for the continuation of the review process. For example, in the context of the debate on defining the public interest pursued through professional regulation, the Follow-Up Report stresses the importance of distinguishing between the problems faced by individual and non-frequent consumers and those of frequent consumers and large clients. One of the interesting findings of this Follow-Up Report is that most progress has been achieved in those Member States (e.g., Denmark, the Netherlands and the UK) that have embarked on a structured programme of regulatory reform in this field, involving close cooperation with and the participation of the national competition authorities.

Isabela Atanasiu
April 2006, EUI Florence

[19] Communication from the Commission to the Council, the European Parliament, the European Economic and Social Committee and the Committee of the Regions: *Professional Services–Scope for more reform. Follow-up to the Report on Competition in Professional Services*, COM(2005) 405 final. See also the Annex, *Progress by the Member States in reviewing and eliminating restrictions to competition in the area of professional services,*

PANEL ONE

ECONOMIC ASPECTS

1

PANEL DISCUSSION

PARTICIPANTS:

Allen Fels
Amelia Fletcher
Benito Arruñada
Calvin Goldman
David Clementi
Frank Stephen
Frédéric Jenny
Hans Gilliams
Harald Herrmann
Ian Forrester
James Venit
John Cooke
John Fingleton
Lowri Evans
Luc Gyselen
Marc Hameleers
Mario Monti
Rafael Allendesalazar Corcho
Roger van den Bergh
Santiago Martínez Lage
William Kolasky
William Kovacic

Panel One: Economic Aspects

► John Fingleton

Our Workshop opens with an exposé by the Commissioner responsible for competition. Mario Monti has presided over DG Competition for almost five years now, at a time of unprecedented changes, and raised the profile of competition policy in Europe, including through competition advocacy and by exposing EC competition policy to public debate. This holds particularly true in the area of professional services, where DG Competition has articulated a strong policy.

► Mario Monti

It is always a pleasure to take part in this Workshop, and I am delighted that the subject under discussion this year is the interface between the regulation of (liberal) professions and competition law. The choice of this subject probably has to do with the fact that recently DG Competition has been quite active in this area. I believe that the public debate stirred by this activity is very useful.

In March 2000 the European Council in Lisbon adopted the very ambitious objective of transforming the EU into the most dynamic and competitive knowledge-based economy in the world by the year 2010. Obviously this objective does not regard exclusively liberal professions, but certainly attaining this objective in a knowledge-based economy brings the spotlight also onto the liberal professions. The liberal professions are depositories of large knowledge, and their quality and competitiveness, their growth and occupational potential have important spill over effects on the rest of the economy.

Liberal professions are occupations requiring special training in the arts or sciences. One of the distinguishing features of this sector is the usually high level of regulation, in the form of either state regulation, or self-regulation by professional bodies. This regulation is often at least half a century old—in some cases the current system can be traced back to medieval guilds, and I believe that Florence is an appropriate place for putting this in historical perspective. . . . We have to ask ourselves whether the current regulatory mix is the most efficient possible. It is clear that there are some sensitive issues in this sector concerning public interest, and we certainly do not advocate deregulation 'across the board'. Rather, the issue here is whether there is a need for better regulation, which is more adapted to the conditions of the modern economy, and which can spur growth, rather than hinder it. When I speak of more efficient regulation, I refer both to the benefits for the final consumer of professional services, and to the economy as a whole. Indeed, professional services can be seen as a final product, but also as an input to so many other outputs.

Allow me to start with some remarks on consumers and professional services. Consumers are normally the lenses through which competition experts look at things. For the foreseeable future, competition within professionals services will continue to take place mainly at the local level. Greater choice in the range of services available and in terms of prices empowers consumers to choose the combination of price and quality which best suits their needs. An essential characteristic of professional services is the asymmetry of information between customers and service providers. Professional services require their practitioners to display, and hopefully to effectively have, a high level of technical knowledge. Consumers may not have this knowledge, and therefore find it difficult to judge the quality of the services purchased. Therefore professional services are credence goods, the quality of which cannot easily be judged by prior observation and/or by consumption/use.

In relation to information asymmetry, I would refer to the written contribution prepared by Prof Frank Stephen for this Workshop, which attempts to put some flesh around the information asymmetry concept, and also—at least, it seems to me—largely demystifies it. Information asymmetries do not exist only in the area of professional services, but are inherent to many other service areas in a knowledge-based economy. To give you an example, we might be able to judge the quality of service in a restaurant, but whenever we run into problems with the PC software, or we try to get our car repaired, the situation changes. It is important to emphasise that professional services are not the exclusive holders of asymmetrical information.

The question is, how to deal with the negative effects of asymmetrical information? The answer is quite straightforward: by trying to reduce it. The principal modality for reducing information asymmetry is to limit access to the profession to individuals who have passed a qualification examination or are members of a professional association. The premise is that being a member of a professional association not only gives rights, but also some obligations in terms of integrity and ethical behaviour. Therefore, belonging to a professional association should be a signal to the market. The Commission certainly does not oppose these kind of measures.

Another method used to reduce asymmetric information is to set tariffs, which can be binding or not, usually accompanied by advertising prohibitions. What is the message given to the client with this method? It is something like: 'You cannot understand, so let us take care of it.' This rather paternalistic attitude of the professions does not necessarily coincide with the interests of consumers. Consumers are nowadays more educated, consumer protection bodies have emerged, and such a top-down attitude is not anymore fruitful or possible. The Services Directorate at DG Competition, headed by Lowri Evans, has recently intensified contacts with consumer organisations. The general idea that emerges from these contacts is that, from the standpoint of the consumers, information asymmetries can be reduced more effectively by increasing the information available. More precisely, consumers would like to have available a better definition of the role of professionals, of what they can or cannot do, of how much a specific service can cost on average, and what a higher or a lower price means in terms of the quality of the service provided. Naturally, consumers also want to be informed on the different supply options, and on the relationship between quality of the service and cost, in order to make a learned choice. This goes towards more freedom for professionals and greater transparency towards consumers. It appears that consumers are more demanding in countries where tariffs are free and there is greater freedom of information. I have no difficulty believing this. As we all know, freedom implies responsibility. A greater responsibility on behalf of consumers implies a greater professionalism and greater attention to the client on behalf of the professions.

I will return now to the role of professional services as an input to the economy as a whole. Professional services have a very important role to play in improving the competitiveness of the European economy. They are indeed inputs for companies in the rest of the economy, and their quality and competitiveness have substantial spill over effects. for example, the Italian antitrust authority has estimated that in Italy an average of 6% of costs of exporting firms are related to professional services.[1] This is more than, for example, the costs of energy or financial services. The analysis of the Italian authority specifically showed how sectors that are untouched by international competition enjoy rents and act as a deadweight for the rest of the economy, which is exposed to international competition. I believe that this kind of analysis could be repeated in other EU countries and arrive at broadly similar conclusions. It is, after all, the underlying theory and philosophy that led Europe to set up a common market in the first place.

It is a fact that some of the national regulations on professional services are outdated, and no longer adapted to the current needs of the internal market. This leads not only to excessive prices or poor quality of the services offered by unscrupulous practitioners, but more strikingly, it removes the incentives for improvement, it hinders organisational efficiencies and service innovation. High prices, lack of quality, and slowness in innovation act as an extra cost to other business sectors. From a macroeconomic perspective, one should also consider the allocation issues: indeed, the extraction of excessive rents creates a rent-seeking behaviour, and therefore a distortion in the allocation of resources, namely human capital. A recent comparative study showed that, for examplwe, in Ireland, since studying pharmacy is extremely selective, the brightest Irish students usually want to study pharmacy, whereas in Italy students do not prefer scientific subjects—almost everybody rushes to study law. . . . Now, that may not always be the case, but there is some empirical evidence of such a tendency. In the new economy, the

[1] Autoritá Garante della Concorrenza e del Mercato (1997): *Indagine conoscitiva IC15–Settore degli ordini e dei collegi professionali*, full text (in Italian) available at http://www.agcm.it.

Member States should aim at improving the allocation of resources, both financial and human.

After these background observations, I would like to make a few general comments regarding the Commission's actions in this area, taken within the framework of the European Competition Network (ECN)—which, as you all know, was set up following the modernisation of EC competition law enforcement. My colleague Lowri Evans will give you further details on this subject tomorrow.

On 9 February 2004, we adopted a quite innocuous—but not necessarily considered as such by some of the professional organisations in Europe—Report on competition in the professional services,[2] with the purpose of laying out our thinking about the scope for reform and modernisation of specific professional rules. The Report identifies five main categories of potentially-restrictive professional regulation in the EU: price fixing, recommended prices, advertising regulations, entry requirements and reserved rights, and, finally, regulation governing business structure and multi-disciplinary practices. As far as the application of EC competition rules is concerned, the Report builds on the indications set out by the European Court of Justice in *Arduino*,[3] *Wouters*[4] and *Fiammiferi*[5]—judgments that will be discussed in some detail during this Workshop.

The Report distinguishes clearly between the potential liability of professional bodies and that of Member States. When a professional body regulates the economic behaviour of its members, the regulations adopted is a decision of an association of undertakings within the meaning of Article 81 EC. However, regulations that are objectively necessary in order to guarantee the proper practice of a profession fall outside the scope of the prohibition in Article 81 EC. State regulation that imposes or favours anticompetitive conduct or reinforces its effects infringes Articles 3(g), 10(2) and 81 EC. Whenever a Member State delegates policy-making attributions to a professional association without clearly indicating the public interest objective to be attained, and without retaining the power to adopt 'last resort' decisions to preserve the public interest and to control their implementation, the Member State can also be held liable for infringement of the Treaty provisions.

In our view, the ECJ jurisprudence to date does not solve all the enforcement issues arising in this respect. In his written contribution for this Workshop, Hans Gilliams suggested that the careful approach adopted so far by the ECJ is defensible, since it is delicate for a court to set aside measures adopted by public authorities. A court should not second-guess the reasons

---

[2] *Commission Report on competition in the professional services*, COM (2004) 83 final, available at www.europa.eu.int/comm/competition/liberal_professions/final_comm_en.pdf.

[3] Case C–35/99 *Arduino* [2002] ECR I–1529.

[4] Case C–309/99 *Wouters* [2002] ECR I–1577.

[5] Case C–198/01 *Consorzio Industrie Fiammiferi* [2003] ECR I–8055.

of the state for imposing measures that have an anticompetitive effect. The Commission believes that, in all scrutiny of professional regulation, a proportionality test should be applied—and this is an aspect that the Court has not yet had the opportunity to examine properly. In simple words, rules must be objectively necessary to attain a clearly-articulated and legitimate public interest objective, and be the least competition-restrictive way to achieve that objective. If these conditions are met, the rules then serve the interest of users and the professionals alike.

In preparing this Report, the Commission performed its role of initiator of the debate, placing the issues on the table and encouraging the different parties involved to come together and discuss their respective points of view. DG Competition is inviting European professional bodies of lawyers, notaries, accountants, tax consultants, architects and pharmacists within the EU to bilateral meetings for discussing the justification for the existing regulation and the scope for their modernisation. These bilateral meetings enable the Commission to clarify which restrictions appear to be excessive and therefore need to be eliminated or changed. They provide an opportunity for the European professional bodies to explain their understanding of the public interest objectives in their domain, and to discuss with the Commission whether more pro-competitive regulatory mechanisms could be implemented in order to achieve the same objectives. The European professional bodies have been asked to relay the Commission's concerns to the relevant national professional organisations, and national competition authorities are doing the same where possible. For example, the Italian antitrust authority has started a series of systematic meetings with the professional orders in this country, where discussions centre on the proportionality test and take into account the ideas emerging from the Commission's report on professional services. I know that similar exercises have either started or are in the pipeline in other Member States.

Experience of past modernisation attempts in the field of professional services in some Member States shows that a simple elimination of anticompetitive mechanisms may not be enough to bring about more competition in this sector. For this reason, DG Competition and DG Health and Consumer Protection are liaising with consumer organisations, to learn their views on the restrictions identified and on the ways in which professions could best be organised so as to take into account consumer interest. It has been agreed that there is a need for pro-competitive accompanying mechanisms, which increase transparency and enhance consumer empowerment. Such mechanisms could include, for example, active monitoring by consumer associations, collection and publication of server-based historical data by independent organisations, or public announcements of the abolition of tariffs.

Moreover, as you all know, since the coming into force of Regulation 1/2003 on 1 May 2004, the national competition authorities (NCAs) can apply Article 81 EC in full. In most competition cases involving liberal professions, the NCAs are often the best placed to apply EC competition law. This competence has been reignited by *Fiammiferi,*[6] and indeed, some NCAs (including in the new Member States) are becoming particularly active in this area. (As a parenthesis, I found it very interesting to note that, since 1 May 2004, when the Commissioners' table became larger, our colleague Commissioners from the new Member States are actually more liberal and targeted on the objectives adopted by the European Council in Lisbon than some of their colleagues from the older Member States, at least when it comes to issues bordering on antitrust and state aid control. . . .) Almost all NCAs have by now carried out enforcement actions in this area. The most common cases are those involving price-fixing by professional associations, discriminatory conditions of access to the professions, boycott practices, and advertising restrictions. Five NCAs (those of Denmark, Ireland, The Netherlands, Finland, and the UK) have undertaken, or are working on, general programmes of action to bring reform to this sector, and in particular to forbid price-fixing arrangements or recommended tariffs.

I will conclude with some remarks on recent developments in the national legislation on liberal professions. In various Member States, some professional bodies have already started to reconsider the existing regulation and improve the information supply to consumers. For example, in the UK, an ongoing process involving the independent review of legal services aims to identify the most appropriate regulatory framework for promoting competition, innovation, and the public and consumer interests alike. Sir David Clementi will offer more details about this tomorrow. The German government has proposed to eliminate a provision granting exclusivity on offering legal advice to professional lawyers, and to limit the scope for practicing fixed tariffs. In Italy, the various proposals on reform of liberal professions pending before the Parliament have been consolidated in a single text, which is currently under examination. These developments also concern the new Member States, and the Commission is currently proceeding with fact-finding concerning their rules and regulations affecting liberal professions.

Of course, DG Competition and the NCAs can only address typical anti-competitive behaviour such as price-fixing and advertising restrictions. However, the Commission as a whole has at hand legal instruments for improving market structure in general. Indeed, the whole exercise of creating a single market for goods and services can be viewed as a supply-side experiment, which involves changing the structure of the markets. In the field of professional services, another instrument for changing market structures is the internal market legislation. The internal market strategy for services is a key part of the Lisbon programme. In this context, the Commission has adopted (following a lively debate) the draft of a directive on services in the

---

[6] See *above* n 5.

internal market,[7] also covering professional services, which is a mix of mutual recognition, administrative cooperation, harmonisation where strictly necessary and encouragement of self-regulation. As far as the regulated professions are concerned, this proposal complements the proposal for a directive on recognition of professional qualifications,[8] which consolidates and improves the current regime on the mutual recognition of professional qualifications, covering a range of parallel issues, including the simplification of cross-border provisional services. I would underline the strong complementarity between all the mentioned Commission initiatives. When the directive on services in the internal market comes into force, it will increase competition between professionals coming from different Member States. Thus, it will complement the initiatives of DG Competition towards creating a level playing field in each Member State.

I do not have time to comment on developments outside the EU in this field, but I think it will be extremely interesting to compare problems and experiences with those of our colleagues from the US and Canada present around this table. My colleague Luc Gyselen has prepared for this Workshop a written contribution in this sense. I think that a comparative study will give us further ideas on how to go forward in this exercise of combining competition advocacy and enforcement action. Finally, I am delighted that we are here debating this subject: the fact that the European University Institute considers it worth discussing is usually a guarantee for good progress.

► CALVIN GOLDMAN

My question, which is related especially to the integration of the new Member States, is whether EU law contains anything similar to the US doctrine on the state action exemption. In Canada, and I believe other common law jurisdictions as well, we ended up with a similar 'scope of judicial review' interpretation related to statutes that give to the professions specific mandates on regulating aspects such as the scope for advertising, etc. In the US and Canada, the clash between such statutes and antitrust law often ends up in courtrooms, where judges are called on to determine which of the two public interests at stake is prevailing. I wonder how is this conflict of laws solved in the EU, and is there are special circumstances regarding enlargement?

► MARIO MONTI

On this, I do not think that the situation of the new Member States is any different from that of the older Member States. Perhaps my colleague Luc Gyselen could develop further on the legal aspects of this. My personal perception is that, likewise to what happens in the US and Canada, these

[7] COM(2004) 2 final/3, of 5.3.2004.

[8] COM(2002) 119, of 12.3.2002, as amended on 20.4.2004 (see COM(2004)317).

issues ultimately tend to go to court for clarification. As to the instruments available under the Treaty, I think that the Commission should put them all to use in order to challenge incompatible state regulation—Articles 10, 81 and 86 EC can offer the basis for examining the justification of exclusive rights and state measures favouring or enforcing anticompetitive agreements.

► LUC GYSELEN

I can only confirm this view: to my knowledge, in Europe, similar to the situation in US and Canada that you described, most of the cases end up in court for clarification on these aspects. Typically, there would be a national piece of legislation that somehow restricts competition or the free movement of goods or services, or that grants exclusive rights to certain entities, and someone would go to a national court and raise the issue of its compatibility with EC law. These cases would then be sent to the ECJ for a preliminary ruling. For example, such a case, concerning the pharmacies' monopoly to sell certain para-pharmaceutical products in Sweden, is currently pending before the ECJ.[9] The cases raises the issue of whether a state-imposed monopoly over the distribution of pharmaceutical products is allowed under EC law, and whether that pharmaceutical monopoly can be extended to products which are not strictly speaking pharmaceutical. This raises issues of interpretation of Article 86 EC, as well as of the interface between freedom of services and competition, which is our topic of today.

► WILLIAM KOLASKY

A short comment on the means by which these issues might be brought before the courts, and about the usefulness of private action. In the US, a striking number of the formative cases involving the professions and the resulting jurisprudence have originated from private litigation whereby a private service provider, seeking to practice in the profession, and feeling aggrieved by the existent limitations, brought a suit seeking to enjoin the restrictions in question. So, this is an area in which private action can be quite useful. Moreover, for the most part, these lawsuits were not brought for obtaining damages, so they did not carry the 'negative baggage' of treble damages that US private action usually carries. Finally, these were instances in which public authorities perhaps felt reluctant or ambivalent about acting themselves, because of concerns about the distribution of authority. The service provider did not feel these inhibitions, and this was the motivating force for bringing the matter to the courts. I find it an interesting example of private action applying pressure to the existing regulatory scheme. It has of course been complemented with public intervention, but this is an instance in which

[9] Case C–438/02 *Åklagaren v Krister Hanner*, at the time of the event pending before the ECJ (Opinion of Advocate General Léger delivered on 25 May 2004).

private action is very important for bringing regulatory matters to court for clarification.

► John Fingleton

The one or two cases that I do know of where private parties brought such actions to court in Ireland have not been successful. But maybe that is just an exception, and the US experience can be repeated in the European jurisdictions.

► Marc Schechter

Not long ago, in a conversation with Tim Murris [former Chairman of the FTC] we were noting with some admiration that in the European legal system the protection of competition is a constitutional principle. We thought that, based on this premise, national authorities would have—in principle at least—a very limited scope for pre-empting competition in favour of some other regulatory objective. The problem that we have in the US—and I think this is going to become more evident as we compare our experiences in this area—is that our federal system allows the states to establish clearly defined policy areas where competition is replaced by regulation. It is within their competence to take such decisions, which grossly complicates the ability of federal antitrust authorities to deal with issues like competition in the professions. In the end, we would have to basically persuade the state authorities that competition is a good idea. I think this is a very significant difference.

► Allen Fels

In Australia, we had a Trade Practices Act prohibiting anticompetitive behaviour in the area of the professions. A state government can override this law by its own legislation, but the central government had the power to override a state law of this kind. However, this power has never been used. Following a review of this framework, we adopted a different approach, whereby state law that restricted competition was subjected to a public, transparent, independent review as to its justification and possible, less anticompetitive means to attain the same objectives. This review procedure is interesting: first of all, there is an independent review; the matter then goes to the state government, which decides to implement or not its recommendations—although it usually tends to implement them. If the state government does not implement the recommendations of the independent review, or, if for some reason the results of the review are not found to be genuine, then the Competition Commission verifies whether the review has been done properly. If not, a quite high financial penalty will be imposed upon the state in question. So, the basic objective was not to get the courts involved in second-guessing the justifications of legislation and making judgements about the public interest are concerned.

On the issue of competition advocacy, I just wanted to mention that it is always disappointing to see that the competition authorities have to humbly go around and try to get some results in this area. It always seemed to me that, politically, it is a lot better if there is some mechanism to put pressure on governments not to issue such regulation in the first place—I am thinking of financial constraints, or something like that.

► MARIO MONTI

First, I find experiences from Australia very telling and interesting, and I was particularly interested in the review procedure described by Allen Fels.

Second, William Kolasky's remark in the sense that in the US a striking number of cases in this area have originated in private actions brings me to reflect on the fact that the modernised competition law enforcement regime in place since May 2004 in Europe probably will help us in the area of competition and the liberal professions in three respects. One is that, as far as public intervention is concerned, the reform will enhance the role of the national competition authorities (NCAs), which is the level where most of the problems actually lie. The second is that the reform will provide the NCAs with the synergies and mutual encouragement derived from seeing closer what happens in other Member States. And third, concerning private action, one consequence of the reform is an enhanced role for the national courts in applying EC competition law. We see the involvement of national courts as a way to foster private action in competition cases across Europe, including those involving professional services.

Third, in relation to Mark Schechter's observation about the constitutional status of competition principles in the EU, I wanted to note that there was a risk, on the occasion of the debate on the EU constitution, that this position might have been lost. Some people apparently believe that values such as the internal market and competition, which were given a prominent role in the Treaty of Rome to begin with, where slightly outdated, and no longer necessary as explicit components of a constitutional text for Europe now that the single market was mostly achieved. This view coupled with a more politically-astute tendency to downgrade or eliminate altogether references to the internal market and competition, because often times their application—just think of state aid control—creates politically-difficult situations. Now, if the text of the Constitution is adopted as it now stands, competition not only remains in, but its status comparative to other policy objectives is even somewhat enhanced. This may seem nothing more than an aesthetic detail, but I am told by lawyers that this will have a sensible influence before the European courts.

► JOHN COOKE

Having read the Commission's draft Report on competition in the liberal professions of February 2004,[10] and having listened to the Commissioner's remarks this morning, I am tempted to ask: how seriously does the Commission believe that it is indeed feasible, in practical terms, to formulate the necessary criteria and conditions for a genuine and coherent application of EC competition principles to the professions? In his introductory exposé, Prof Monti mentioned that, according to the Commission, a so-called 'proportionality test' should be applied to regulatory restrictions in the professions. But the question is: whose proportionality? One thing that emerges from the Commission's draft Report is the sheer diversity of ways which particular aspects, such as prices, barriers to entry, and so on, are dealt with in different Member States and for different professions.

If one reads Ian Forrester's written contribution for this Workshop, and in particular his *exposé* of the Swedish pharmaceutical monopoly case,[11] and also considers the various other examples mentioned in other written contributions, it becomes quite clear that there are a whole variety of services that in some Member States will be regarded as 'professional services', while in other Member States not. Moreover, there is diversity among the categories entrusted with performing a given service. For example, in common law countries, land transactions are dealt with by solicitors; in other countries these are dealt with by notaries. The basic transaction, or service, is exactly the same, but there is an enormous cultural diversity in the way that the Member States regulate these services and the conditions under which they should be made available to the public. One of the things that struck me about the *Wouters* case[12] was that the Court found that the ban established by the Dutch Bar on multi-disciplinary practices was justified because it was reasonable for the Dutch Bar to consider that this ban formed an inherent part of the organisation of the legal profession. This seems to me to be a judgement on proportionality, made not at Community level, but by the Dutch Bar. So, I wonder, is this not an almost-seminal area, in which the feasibility of applying Community-wide appreciations comes up against the now-recognised latitude of the Member States to organise crucial services regarded as being of public interest in that Member State but not necessarily in others?

► MARIO MONTI

I can see the difficulty of applying a Community-wide proportionality test, but my question is, how much do we really need a Community-wide proportionality test? The Commission's approach actually relies very much on actions by the NCAs. Of course, there is a role for the Commission, but that

[10] See above n 2.
[11] See above n 9.
[12] See above n 4.

role, I believe, is largely of an advocacy nature. Following your intervention, Judge Cooke, I would like myself to find out from my lawyer colleagues at the Commission what is the minimum indispensable requirement for a Community-wide proportionality test.

▸ John Fingleton

I also think that these issues will be to a large extent tackled domestically, by the individual Member States, as it is already happening in Ireland, the UK and other countries. I think that what we are going to see happening is a balance between either court decisions in the Member States or re-regulation, whereby governments change the law. *Wouters* and other decisions of the Court in this area should in principle increase the pressure on the Member States to look at these questions seriously. In many cases, these issues have not yet been examined within the Member States, or if they have, it was quite a long time ago, and things have moved on since then.

▸ James Venit

I think that Judge Cooke pointed to a very critical issue, which is the interaction between a centralising-legislative function of the Commission and the courts' function of individual review. It is possible to proceed in both ways in parallel, but Judge Cooke put his finger on a sensitive issue: with the existent level of diversity among national systems, is it possible to deal with these issues legislatively, at the Community level, or will the process be resolved much more slowly, through the court system? I think this is a fascinating question.

▸ Hans Gilliams

I think that it was very useful for the Commission to make a comparison between different kinds of regulation of liberal professions across the EU. What emerged is an enormous diversity, across national jurisdictions, but also across professional bodies. What is interesting, of course, is to try to determine whether there is some kind of 'minimum level of regulation' necessary to ensure a well-functioning economy. I can imagine that this issue has to be coupled with the debate on public interest. And defining what is the public interest is mainly a political question, so it should be the legislative branch to do it. Now, it could well be that, for instance, in Italy the scope of the concept of 'public interest' is somewhat different than in the Netherlands. So be it. So, it could well be that the professions in Italy are regulated differently than in the Netherlands. A few days ago, I was speaking with someone from the Dutch Bar association about the regulation of their profession, and he mentioned that, at this moment, large multinational companies demand a separation between services of lawyers and accountants, etc, and so the Dutch Bar was right at the time to rule in this sense. But if the market solves the problem itself, then the ruling of the professional bodies is not necessary. So, I think that what the Commission proposes in essence is to enhance the dynamism of these markets through lesser regulation.

► JOHN FINGLETON

Before moving into the first session, I wanted to make a few introductory comments. Liberal professions is a subject that, so far, has been debated by economists mainly from a competitiveness perspective. In other words, as many professional services provide the necessary 'lubricant', so to speak, for the good functioning of other markets, the concern that arises is whether the legal system allows incentives to work in that direction. Another issue of interest for the economists is the allocation of talent in the knowledge-based economy. Here the basic idea is that, as long as in the liberal professions the rents extracted by practitioners are high, mainly as a result of regulatory barriers to entry, then human talent will be attracted into his area, whereas it would perhaps be better employed in other, more productive areas of the economy. A famous economics paper of the early 1990s[13] compared growth rates in economies where the brightest people went on to become lawyers, and respectively engineers, and found growth rates to be higher in economies where most talents went on to become engineers. There are also issues of access to justice, fairness, social preferences, when it comes to health care for example, that I think competition specialists don't often meet when dealing with 'pure' competition cases.

While reading through the written contributions prepared for this Panel, I identified four distinct problem areas: 1) asymmetric information on quality; 2) asymmetric information on demand; 3) the question of credence goods—or, otherwise put, the fact that when we consume something we do not know how to evaluate; and 4) the question of externalities—namely the fact that, in many professional areas, there are wider social interests to consider besides those involved between the parties in question. There seems to be a good deal of agreement on the existence of market failure in the market of professions. I hope that our speakers today will address the question of the rationale for enhancing competition in the professions, and of whether the argument of market failure is well made in this area of competition policy. George Stigler, the famous Chicago economist, said once that we know so little about how markets work that whenever we observe a market failure, our instinct is to think that market power is the problem. This may not always be the case. His plea was to look at whether the market may solve the problem itself, before deciding for regulatory intervention. But there are not always 'easy wins': some regulatory changes may bring benefits for all consumers; in other cases there may be a trade-off. This leads to very difficult issues of balance. If we

[13] KM Murphy, A Schleifer and RW Vishny 'The Allocation of Talent: Implications for Growth' (1991) 106 *Quarterly Journal of Economics* 503.

think, for example, of high price, high quality services versus lower price, lower quality services, a regulatory move from the second to the first would benefit rich people, who prefer the higher quality, high price services. When regulatory reform is solely about bringing about this type of redistribution, we are less sure of what the overall welfare effects will be.

Thus, one of the questions that I would like to see addressed today is, are there clear strategies for the competition authorities that are a 'win-win' for all consumers, as opposed to strategies that benefit only to certain groups? Sometimes consumer groups are opposed to the reform of professional services, even if the reform might actually be a 'win-win' for all consumers. Are there examples of cases where reform is a 'win-win' for everybody? Do they exist across all professions, or are they only confined to some of them? Another question that I think it would be very useful to address is numerical restrictions to entry and limitations on price competition: are there market failures for which numerical restrictions on entry and on price competition are the best regulatory solutions? Next, we could discuss about 'second-tier' restrictions: demarcation restrictions, multi-disciplinary practice-type of restrictions, advertising restrictions, and so on. Do such restrictions solve market failure, and when? In other words, I would like to see if, at the end of this debate, everybody around this table agrees that there should be no numerical restrictions on entry and on price competition.

► William Kolasky

I think it would be very helpful to also address the question of whether liberal professions have characteristics justifying a different treatment under competition rules from that applicable to other professions. Market failures that are observed in the context of liberal professions may actually also be found in many other areas (as I have just undertaken major renovation of my home, I am painfully aware that the same market failures are present in the selection of a homebuilder, never mind an architect, or a construction engineer . . .). With the move towards an information economy, virtually every service acquires the same elements that are traditionally associated with the 'liberal professions': it undoubtedly requires as much education and experience to be a good investment banker or a good software engineer as it does to be a lawyer or an accountant and, frankly, these days, perhaps even to be a good auto mechanic. So, the question is, are these issues common to all service industries, and not just to the liberal professions, and if so, why should liberal professions be treated any different?

► Benito Arruñada

In order to understand professionals and regulate the professions, we need to understand their 'technology', in particular externalities are being produced, and whether professionals are capable of producing them. Having been involved personally in public service management—which, by the way, I consider to be a total failure—I noticed there is a tendency to put forward the category of 'professionals' in order to solve problems of public management. In my opinion, nowadays, information asymmetries do not justify special treatment for the liberal professions', whatever the sector or industry involved. We should simply forget about information asymmetries, because in the 21st Century there are firms which are created to be efficient and overcome problems of information asymmetries. We should ask ourselves: does it make sense to have competitive constraints that motivate efficient production of externalities? I think this is the only valid rationale for regulating professional services in the 21st Century.

In this line, we are often falling into a contradiction: in Europe, as in the US, we are increasingly talking about liberalising all professions, but at the same time we are asking them to produce externalities, without realising that this is in contradiction with the freedom to compete (think of the increased role of auditing, for example). Furthermore, in my opinion it does not make much sense to talk about professions in general: we should talk about specific professions but also about specific outputs. Many of the answers to our questions will not be generally valid; they will depend on what we actually want each individual profession to produce in each of their outputs. Different professions produce different services in different countries.

In my written contribution for the Workshop I briefly discussed two professions that, in my opinion, should be further liberalised namely, conveyanars and pharmacists. I argue that in today's society their demand has diminished drastically because of institutional and market transformations. Institutional transformation has to do with the development of titling systems. Throughout history, three main systems for enforcing property rights have developed, which are privacy, recording, and registration. Under the privacy system, which was dominant in Europe until the 19th Century, notaries (or property conveyancers) had a highly valuable function, as they had first to perform a search on the chain of property titles on a real estate asset in order to identify which parties held or continued to hold conflicting property rights on it. Given that property rights survive irregular transactions, the buyer wants to make sure that no conflicting property rights will emerge in relation to his purchase. Second, there was substantial demand for developing sophisticated title guarantees, making the seller liable in case there was a fault with the title. Third, given that the chain of titles was the main abstract evidence of titling, conveyancers developed a private record or protocol of the transactions made before them. Fourth, the conveyancers played an important role in authenticating the contract.

In the 19th Century, the state started to develop public recording systems. Since then, priority of property rights is established according to the date of filing. This public recording system has radically changed the demand for conveyancers. First, the demand for deposit of the titles disappeared. Second, the demand for title guarantees substantially diminished. Third, the demand for searches changed substantially, depending on the nature of the recording system in different jurisdictions. In the US, the introduction of the public record system triggered the development of title insurance. In France, given that public recording is relatively well organised, examination of the record is more simple, and therefore the search is a less demanding job.

The third stage started with the introduction of a registration system, which further reduced demand for conveyance services. There is no more need to search certificates, because the register provides them, and there is a cleaning of the title with each transaction, therefore no more demand for guarantees. About authenticating documents—clerks or registrars can do it as well.

Changes in the market produce the same result, but at a different level, and this is in general valid for other services as well. Information asymmetry between the parties can now be safeguarded privately. Transactions become standard, and in good part organised by mandatory law, therefore the demand for contract design diminishes.

In the case of pharmacists, something very similar has been happening, as we also observe institutional and market changes. The institutional change occurs in terms of regulation of drugs and market changes overcome information asymmetry. Thinking for a moment of removing the packaging of medicines easily reveals that most guarantees of quality are now provided by the manufacturer, not the pharmacist.

► Marc Hameleers

Prof Arruñada's intervention made me remember that some 600 years ago Bocaccio wrote the *Decameron*, about a group of people meeting on the hills of Florence to tell each other stories. The first story was actually about a notary famous for false statements, perjury, and practicing high prices. So you see, notaries have been the subject of debate for more than 600 years now. . . . Some things have changed since the *Decameron*, yet more could still be done.

I wanted to make three main points: one is that, in evaluating the regulation and functioning of liberal professions, we should take into account the economic perspective, based on a clear definition of 'public interest'. I think that the economists can help define the public interest. Two questions are of relevance here: what are the public interests involved, and how should they be protected/safeguarded? The second point is about the consumers' perspective and the need for pro-competitive measures. The third point is about transition: we should realise that we are going through a large transition process.

As John Fingleton mentioned before, we all seem to agree that market failure is at the heart of the problem. Normally, markets should deliver the services that the consumers demand and at the price that reflects supply and demand. This also goes for the liberal professions. Market failures such as information asymmetry, market dominance, or the fact that goods are not produced, generate what the economists call 'complex negative external effects'. Because there are several interests involved/affected, it could be more efficient for government to step in and counteract the market failures—in other words, to intervene by regulating these markets. Governments may also have other reasons to regulate besides counteracting the effects of market failure, for example, they may seek to attain objectives of wealth redistribution. Government intervention is, in general, motivated by either efficiency or paternalistic considerations. But governments can also fail—for instance, government officials may be rent-seeking, or influenced by the lobby of professionals, or simply inefficient.

At any rate, the starting point should be not to think of who is going to regulate the market, but what the public interest at stake is. I think that 'public interest' is social interest that the government takes the responsibility for protecting/providing. Transposed to our context, the questions to ask are, what are the public interests at stake in the area of liberal professions, and how to make sure that these interests are met. As to the first question, I already mentioned the complex negative external effects that derive when too many players are involved in compensating negative transactions. Another problem to consider is free riding—in simple words, cases where two make a transaction and other people derive a benefit without paying. In such cases, one may want to intervene so as to spread the benefits and costs among all parties involved.

Regarding liberal professions, we can identify three broadly-defined public interests at stake: one is quality, the second is accessibility, and the third one is the so-called 'macro-affordability'. Accessibility could be physical—for instance, you may want to have a general medical practitioner in every neighbourhood—or financial—for instance, people with low wages should also be guaranteed access to certain professional services. (That is the reason why, for instance, although in the Netherlands we have more or less completely liberalised notary services, for people with low wages there is a fixed price ensuring access.) As to what we call 'macro-affordability', I will give you a practical example to understand the concept: the exploding costs of the health care system are in part generated by the medical professions, so we want to have some kind of public interest standard in health care that can be sustained by the state at macro-budgetary level.

So far we have identified three broadly-defined public interests at stake in the area of liberal professions: quality, accessibility and macro-affordability. The next question is, how to protect them? The answer entails considering two distinct aspects: one is who should do it, and the other is, which instruments should be used? As to 'who should do it', the choice is between government regulation, regulation by the professional bodies, and a mix of the two—in other words a kind of co-regulation. If regulation is done by professional bodies, there should be some kind of external democratic control.

As to the regulatory instruments, the Commission's draft Report[15] makes a very useful distinction between instruments designed to address market conduct and those designed to address market entry. What we need to do next is seek to determine which instruments of intervention are 'less heavy', or less intrusive, and most appropriate for securing each of the public interests at stake. Since the definition of public interest is dynamic (because it is essentially political), the choice and use of regulatory instruments should also be dynamic. Ideally, one should always opt for the least intrusive regulatory instruments.

Two concluding remarks. First, about consumers: I think it is important that, within this deregulation or re-regulation process concerning liberal professions, we should give a more active voice to consumers. This could be done through pro-competitive measures. Prof Monti already mentioned some of the possibilities in this respect. We should also think about transparency-enhancing measures, feedback mechanisms (for instance, allowing consumers to comment on a website about the quality of the services provided by individual professionals), information and education about consumer rights and professionals' obligations. We could also consider measures designed to allow new entrants, possibly serving consumer organisations—it would be interesting to see how that works.

Second, on the transition: if we want to liberalise the liberal professions, we must realise that this is a very complex process. The lesson we learned in the Netherlands is that a successful liberalisation process requires taking into account three components. One is to make sure that there is political urgency to liberalise. The fact that the Commission is showing increased interest in this area indicates that there is an international political urgency to this. Second, do the first step in a short period of time, or use 'the pressure cooker method'. Third, within the 'pressure cooker' approach, all parties concerned should be invited to debate together. The following steps are about implementation. I must admit that, in the Netherlands, the first steps were very good, but the implementation was not so. Good implementation takes time, needs attention, and advance planning. The process should be divided into stages, following a logical order and connection. The government should periodically review the implementation process. To conclude, I think that it is important to take public interests at the heart of the debate and be keen on organising the liberalisation process in a coherent way.

► HARALD HERRMANN

In my written contribution for this Workshop, I reviewed recent developments in the sphere of organisations of the learned professions to observe a

---

[15] See above n 2.

certain convergence, that I want to talk about in economic terms. To summarise my findings: first, I detected some infringements of Article 81 EC in regulations issued by organisations of the liberal professions. One example in this sense is the interdiction on solicitation. In my written contribution, I examined in some detail why this is in conflict with Article 81(1) EC. Next, I considered how the Commission could act in relation to this and to other similar infringements of Article 81 EC. My conclusion is that a simple interdiction addressed to professional organisations in Germany or other Member States would not be sufficient. Something is needed to replace the incompatible rules, and we should find out how to incentivise the liberal organisations to produce substitute that are in agreement with EC competition principles. When looking at the development of the organisational structures of those organisations, one observes the emergence of a kind of 'systems competition'.

This leads me to my second point: this sort of 'systems competition' takes professional organisations away from the old ethics model towards the more open and competitive one of professional governance, as derived from the development of corporate governance systems. My main interest here was to determine to what extent new professional organisation structures fit with corporate government structures. Astonishingly, I found a good amount of proof going in this direction. In the third part of my written contribution, I come back to legal analysis in a narrow sense, looking at ways in which the Commission can integrate some incentives for these developments within the decision making in relation to infringements of Article 81 EC in the area of liberal professions.

Very briefly on infringements of Article 81 EC: I already mentioned advertising for mandate, and in my written contribution I mentioned two rules issued by very important professional organisations in Germany, governing the activity of tax consultants and auditors. German law already contained an interdiction of solicitation, but these organisations were free to interpret this provision so as to accelerate and/or sharpen the interdiction of the organisation itself. The case of tax consultants is the most impressive: the organisation stipulated that illegal solicitation should be interpreted to comprise every specially-addressed offer of services to persons who seem to have special need for it. This is clearly too far-reaching, because all advertisements usually touch upon special needs of the customers. Several German commentators—including myself—criticised this narrow-minded approach. A similar case is that of the auditors, which for reasons of shortage of time I will not discuss now.

My second point, which is the most important one, is about the development of professional governance structures. Some years ago I published a monograph on this subject, covering developments in Europe and the United States,[16] where I empirically identified new governance structures and some kind of conver-

[16] H Herrmann, Recht der Kammern und Verbände Freier Berufe in der Europäischen Union und den USA, (Nomos, Baden-Baden, 1996).

gence on certain aspects. One is, no compulsory membership: for example in Germany, the new liberal professions chambers do not function on the basis of compulsory membership, but rather, individuals who want to use a special professional title join as members. Second, I observed interesting developments in the field of inter-professional cooperation. In the monograph that I mentioned before you will not find a discussion on elements of professional governance. This is work in progress, but in my written contribution I anticipated some of my hypotheses on these elements of professional governance. Governance systems are not restricted to listed stock operations, but also comprise organisational systems of the liberal professions. I found such elements in some countries—Australia, Canada, the UK—especially in the area of medical professions. So, close membership systems are still predominant in some countries of continental Europe, like Germany and France, but open organisations with interprofessional and interdisciplinary organisational structures have started to emerge in others, like the UK and the Netherlands. As I mentioned earlier, there is a convergence tendency between these two models, and if one reflects on the causes of this convergence, one necessarily arrives at the theory of systems competition. I do not have the time now to explain systems competition, but the economists around this table may confirm in our debate that this is a modern theoretical framework for explaining competitive developments pushing the regulators to act in a certain direction.

To conclude, I believe that the Commission can contribute to accelerate the development of professional governance by integrating into its competition-related decision-making incentives for the professional organisations to integrate elements of professional government in their structures. Regulation 1/2003, which allows the acceptance of commitments from the parties involved, provides a useful instrument for proceeding in this direction.

► AMELIA FLETCHER

John Fingleton spoke earlier about market failures lying at the heart of the problem in the area of liberal professions. I will not touch upon this again, but I just wanted to add that I agree with William Kolasky, in that the professions are not a special case in this respect. There are several other markets in which some, if not all, of these problems arise (and home renovation is obviously a classic example . . .). For this reason, what I am going to say should not be entirely viewed as specific to the liberal professions. In fact, at the moment the OFT promotes the adoption of self-regulatory codes also in markets other than the liberal professions. In the UK we now apply a code-approval regime, designed to reap the benefits of self-regulation while hopefully avoiding the restrictive consequences of self-regulation, in a wider range of markets, including the professions.

I think that, broadly speaking, there is agreement around this table on the idea that there are failures in the markets of liberal professions and these failures need to be regulated. There is however far less agreement on the forms in which to regulate. Self-regulation does have advantages: by joining together, members of a profession or market may have more incentives to ensure that quality of the service provided is maintained that any individual would have, because the reputation of the profession in general is more observable than the reputation of any given individual. However, so far there has been a very strong emphasis on *ex ante* self-regulation, where the profession itself sets prescriptive rules on who can act in the market, what activities they can engage in, and how they should carry out these activities. This includes rules on entry, demarcation restrictions, pricing rules, advertising rules, and restrictions on corporate forms. These rules can bring benefits for consumers, most obviously in terms of qualification of the professionals offering a service—you would not want to be operated on by someone who has not been trained for this, for example. But they can also go beyond what consumers mostly need. The self-regulatory body will have an incentive to set restrictions higher, in order to create monopoly rents for its members. This is also a very indirect way of achieving an end, because it boils down to attempting to control your own inputs in order to affect your outputs, which is what consumers really want.

In my written contribution I discussed whether there is a case for changing the regulatory balance, specifically for the liberal professions, by switching the emphasis from *ex ante* self-regulation towards *ex post* self-regulation and/or external regulation. By *ex post* regulation I mean in this context incentives for good behaviour created by the threat of punishment for professionals who breach professional rules or service commitments. So far there has really not been that much of this in the area of professions, at least not much in the way of redress and punishment as one might have expected.

Very briefly on what *ex post* regulation involves. First of all, a regulatory board has to set out explicit rules of conduct and service commitments, which members of the profession are expected to adhere to. The first, and most important thing in designing these rules is that they should permit detecting non-compliance—otherwise people cannot be punished for not complying with them. It is difficult to design such rules, but not impossible.

Second, a part of any *ex post* self-regulatory system should be some form of monitoring compliance, so that breaches of the rules and commitments may be detected. One method for carrying out such monitoring—and this is a method that we very much encourage within the OFT codes-approval regime—is to rely on complaints from customers. Including a redress mechanism within the regulatory regime may be a good way of achieving this. If consumers can gain recompense for any damages they incur as a result of poor quality service, this should give them an incentive to complain about such behaviour. Such a redress mechanism would also further benefit the profession, to the extent that such protection gives consumers more confidence in buying their services. Obviously, some of these goods are credence goods—meaning that it may be difficult for consumers to observe poor quality. In such situations, more sophisticated performance measures are needed. One could think of random audits on the performance of players in the market, or to actually monitor average performance so as to get a feel for how average performances work. (You may have heard of Harold Shipman, a family doctor in England who managed to polish off 200 old ladies. Now, if one old lady goes to a doctor and then dies, no one really thinks of bringing a case against that doctor—old ladies do die, it is in the nature of things. However, the fact that 200 old ladies died shortly after visits to Harold Shipman should probably have been picked up earlier than it was. . . .) In designing such performance measures it is important to guard against providing adverse incentives for practitioners, and in particular, against the risk that they may make practitioners overly 'risk-averse' in terms of their willingness to take on what might be termed as 'difficult cases'. For example, in the US, post-operative mortality rates for surgeons are published. The result is that surgeons will be rather unwilling to take on difficult patients, who obviously particularly need the operation. Such problems do not mean, though, that performance measures of this sort are impossible. It just means that they need to be carefully designed. It may also be advisable not to publish them.

The third element of *ex post* self-regulation is a good punishment regime. This needs to be carefully designed, to ensure that professionals have the incentives to behave in accordance with the rules of conduct and the service commitments. In designing such a regime it is necessary to calculate not only the benefits that a professional can derive from a breach, in terms of extra profits or an easier life, but also the proportion of breaches that are likely to come to the notice of the professional organisation. The parallel with cartel deterrents is obvious here. And, as we manage to uncover only some cartels, we have to punish those that we do uncover in an exemplary way. As for cartels, optimal deterrence requires the availability of a range of different sanctions, from criminal sanctions to 'name and shame' procedures, having in between the full range of monetary punishments available. Now, it is also important to note that the appropriate level of redress in any one case, which compensates the consumer for his/her damages, is unlikely to also provide an appropriate punishment for the misconduct in terms of providing the right incentives for the professional. Within litigation systems we sometimes have class action and treble damages to address this problem, but this is a very *ad hoc* solution. A benefit of self-regulation, or generally *ex post* regulatory schemes, is that they can include punishment regimes specifically targeted to achieve the incentive effect that is desired.

I am quite in favour of *ex post* regulation, as you may tell—I think it can be a very useful complement to *ex ante* self-regulation. I am not saying it should completely overtake *ex ante* self-regulation, but that it can be used to complement the latter, and that it should also facilitate the removal of some of the more detrimental restrictions imposed by the latter. However, there still remains a risk that a self-regulator whose primary interest is in serving its members may not always act in the best interest of consumers, but rather set service commitments too high, or fail to punish firms effectively even though they have breached the rules, because they are members of the club. In many situations, this problem can be reduced by enhancing the role played by external regulation. There are of course several pros and cons in relation to external regulation, which have been much discussed. But I am not talking about substituting self-regulation for external regulation, but rather of using a mixed, 'co-regulation' approach, which draws on the benefits that both can bring.

The ways in which external regulation may correct the incentives of the self-regulator to be overly-restrictive include the threat of external regulation if self-regulation does not work properly. We have seen that to be very effective in the UK with the Press Complaints Commission. A second approach may be for the external regulator to stipulate the rules on how a self-regulatory body should function, but without itself becoming involved in the determination of the rules on entry and conduct that this body sets up. I think that one of the models suggested by Sir David Clementi for the UK legal profession, as set out in his consultation paper, goes in this direction. A third approach is for the external regulator to actually stipulate the rules of conduct that the members of a market must follow. For example, in the UK, and I think in other Member States, there are rules with respect to misleading advertising by the professionals. In the UK, the Advertising Standards Authority—a self-regulator—actually imposes the rules externally set, although an external regulator also has concurrent powers to ensure that it can do that properly. The final benefit of external regulation—and this fits very well with our self-regulatory codes in the UK—is to have minimum quality standards set externally for cases where people could be very severely hurt by—for example, fraudulent activities or poor quality of service. In such cases it is furthermore important to make sure there are not going to be any breaches. So one may have external rules, and then use self-regulation to encourage quality on top of those rules. In that sense, you want to have voluntary self-regulation, and not compulsory self-regulation, to give consumers a choice between the absolute basic and the slightly better self-regulatory member's quality. Within such a framework you might also be able to construct competition between self-regulatory organisations. For example, a customer may rather go to this architectural group, which is good in this way, rather that the other architectural group, which is good in another way. To conclude, I argue that, with a careful design, an increased role for both *ex post* and external regulation can improve the effectiveness of *ex ante* self-regulation, whilst reducing the need for overly-restrictive *ex ante* rules and bringing about benefits for both competition and consumers.

► JOHN FINGLETON

It occurred to me to ask—but this is for the general discussion later on—whether you think that *ex post* regulation, combined with the type of minimal external regulation that you talked about, would also address the more general concern expressed by Prof Benito Arruñada earlier about technology, and whether dynamic change is more assisted in that model than in the *ex ante* regulatory model.

► ROGER VAN DEN BERGH

The title of my written contribution ('Towards Efficient Self-Regulation in Markets for Professional Services') suggests that there might be efficient self-regulation, but we have not yet developed the architecture to fully profit from its advantages while minimising its disadvantages. The paper includes a short overview of the literature on advantages and disadvantages of self-regulation. Next, it focuses on a number of suggestions that have been made in the law and economics literature in order to achieve efficient self-regulation in the sense mentioned before.

One argument in favour of self-regulation is that self-regulatory agencies have information advantages. A second argument is that self-regulation may be more flexible than state regulation. A third argument is that the costs of self-regulation are borne by the profession, and not financed by taxpayers. I think that, out of these three arguments, only the first one is really convincing. It cannot be denied that regulatory authorities cannot acquire and maintain specialised knowledge of each profession. Self-regulation will minimise the information costs for the formation and interpretation of quality standards thanks to the information advantages of self-regulatory agencies. Also, monitoring and enforcement costs will be reduced. This is particularly important in areas where it is difficult to give a precise definition of the desired behaviour, such as is the case, for instance, with rules on advertising.

The second argument, of greater flexibility, is somewhat less convincing, especially when self-regulation is abused to increase the rents extracted by professionals. The economic literature has forcefully argued that it is extremely difficult to change self-regulatory rules, even after the rents have been dissipated among the practitioners. This is what Gordon Tullock has called 'the transitional gains trap'[17]: politicians do not have incentives to change rules on licensing and fees as long as the number of new entries into a profession generates a flow of political rents from the restrictions of competition, gains exceeding the one-time gains that would be derived from eliminating the restrictions on competition. We all know that ultimately it takes a revolution to change certain rules. The revolution, in this case, would be the case law of the European Court of Justice and the policy initiatives of the European Commission.

[17] G Tullock, 'The Transitional Gains Trap' (1975) 6 *The Bell Journal of Economics and Management Science* 671.

As far as the argument about costs is concerned, it has been argued that the costs of self-regulation are borne in the markets in which rules are imposed. However, we have to also consider that these costs may be passed on to consumers, certainly to the extent that demand elasticity will allow it.

The most important argument against self-regulation is well known: there is, on the one hand, the information advantage, but on the other hand there is a possibility that professions will abuse their powers to restrict competition. I do not have to elaborate on this argument. I would like only to point out that, even though the argument about restrictions of competition is very strong from a theoretical point of view, the empirical evidence in the economic literature is somewhat mixed, and probably does not always support the strong policy conclusions of the competition authorities.

Another disadvantage of self-regulation is its lack of democratic legitimacy: consumer interests are not sufficiently represented within professional associations.

All this considered, the question that arises is how to preserve the advantages of self-regulation while at the same time minimising its disadvantages. On the one hand, there is the quite strong information argument, and on the other hand there is the argument about restriction of competition and reduction of overall welfare. I will not discuss here all options, but just contrast two of them. One is what I would call 'co-regulation', and the other is competitive self-regulation. As far as the first option is concerned, I think it is fair to say that the legal framework in a number of Member States and also European law already provide some building blocks of co-regulation, even though the overall architecture is not yet finished. By contrast, competitive self-regulation seems to be less liked by regulators. In my view, some recent changes in certain Member States have been rather counterproductive with respect to the goal of achieving competitive self-regulation.

Co-regulation is a system whereby self-regulatory bodies adopt rules that are then over sighted or ratified by public authorities. We should realise that transferring all regulatory power to the state would be unwise, because vesting regulatory powers in governmental agencies would undo the information advantages of the professions. Therefore, the option of co-regulation seems preferable: regulatory power remains with the professional bodies, but their activity is over sighted by the state. As I already mentioned, there are elements in the legal systems of some Member States and in EC law to support such an approach. For instance, the Commission's proposal for a directive on professional services,[18] which will be discussed tomorrow, is a clear example of what I would call co-regulation. Member States will have to justify why certain rules regulating professional services are kept in place, and to what extent they satisfy public interest goals. EC competition law also provides some incentives to make use of co-regulation, but only in an indirect way. The

[18] See above n 8.

competition-related EC case law makes clear that the Member States may not facilitate cartel agreements. The *Arduino* judgment[19] establishes that the delegation of regulatory powers setting the parameters of competition can be challenged. This is an indirect way of stimulating co-regulation.

There are, however, a number of drawbacks to co-regulation. One problem is that such a system offers no guarantee that public authorities will be fully informed about the rules enacted and implemented by the professional bodies. Another problem is that the scope of the cartel prohibition may be too narrow. I will not discuss at length *Wouters*,[20] but in seems clear to me that this judgment has limited the scope for co-regulation by giving to the professions the power to enact rules necessary for a proper practice of the profession. Obviously, there is a difference between justifying rules based on public interest goals formulated as widely as 'guaranteeing the proper practice of a profession', and a full efficiency analysis. The latter would only have been possible under Article 81(3) EC, and then independence would have been one in a series of advantages and disadvantages to be balanced in relation to partnerships between lawyers and accountants. I will not go into further detail, but I just wanted to make clear that this obviously limits the effectiveness of co-regulation. Finally, another problem of co-regulation is that the monopoly of the professions in the field of enforcement is left unchanged. If we want to address this problem, we need a system of enforced self-regulation, which means that governmental agencies would have to negotiate with individual practitioners rules concerning the practice of the profession.

Moving on to the option of competitive self-regulation: first of all, what does this concept mean? Simply put, we are talking about competition between professional bodies. Why should there be, for example, only one order of attorneys at a certain Bar? Why not have twelve, fifteen, sixteen or even more different professional associations, which will all develop their own rules? This is not as uncommon as you may think. When you compare self-regulation that emerges spontaneously in other markets and guarantees optimal performance with self-regulation in the area of the professions, the crucial difference is the delegation of regulatory powers by the state to a monopoly body of professionals. That is the problem. For the case of self-regulatory rules that emerged in other markets, my favourite example is the EC Directive on the 'cooling off period'.[21] The 'cooling off period' concept was created by businesses operating through mail orders. Because their services were considered to be less reliable, they came up with a rule establishing that the consumers would have the possibility to cancel their purchase within a period of seven days. This rule was then taken over by the European Commission. It is one example of self-regulation that proved to be an efficient solution.

---

[19] See above n 3.

[20] See above n 4.

[21] Directive 97/7/EC of the European Parliament and of the Council of 20 May 1997 on the protection of consumers in respect of distance contracts, OJ L 144 [1997].

The problem with self-regulation in the sector of the professions is the delegation of the regulatory powers to professional bodies that actually become regulatory monopolies. The solution seems to be to eliminate the monopolies of the self-regulatory bodies by forcing them to compete with each other. This solution maintains the information advantages, and the professional bodies would still be able to fix quality standards, but in competition with each other. This competition could take two forms. One is what I call 'inter-professional competition', which is competition between different professions that offer the same service. The other is what I call 'intra-professional competition', a concept similar to intra-brand competition, which would stimulate competition within a single profession.

There are examples of inter-professional competition in the UK. One is the abolition of the monopoly of solicitors over real estate transactions and the introduction of the new category of 'licensed conveyancer'. Another example is the possibility for solicitors to also get right of audience in higher courts—although this example is not as straightforward as the first one, because in the latter case a state structure will consult with the Commission and decide whether rights of audience are grounded. So this is competitive self-regulation, but with elements of state supervision. In my own view, this additional supervision by the state is not always indispensable.

As far as intra-professional competition is concerned, I could identify no examples. For instance, in the Netherlands there are two professional associations of real estate agents, but that will not be sufficient to describe the situation as 'competitive'. More professional bodies would be needed to make sure there is actual competition, but anyway, this is a first step towards intra-professional competition. What is striking is that in a number of professions this road is blocked by regulation. Again I would refer to the Netherlands for an example. When the legal profession was deregulated in this country, one of the issues raised was that self-employed lawyers should also be allowed to provide services. Eventually they were compelled to become members of the order of attorneys. So nowadays the Dutch bar has to admit self-employed lawyers as members, and this is where the reform ends. The appropriate solution would have been to allow competition between professional associations of self-employed lawyers, preferably ten or fifteen of them, and other professional associations of lawyers. I think that this point has not been considered so far very thoroughly, even though literature on competitive self-regulation is abundant.

To conclude, the aim should be to profit from the advantages of self-regulation and minimise its disadvantages. So far we saw the first building blocks of efficient self-regulation emerge, but the construction is still far from finished.

▶ JOHN FINGLETON

The Irish competition authority has recently taken a case before the High Court—not in the area of professions, but credit unions—where one of our arguments is that the organisation's monopoly over the representation of its members raises a barrier to entry in the market for representation and prevents the establishment of another body that might represent the members' interests. How the High Court will decide in this case is important for professional services in general, as for the whole question of whether there are markets for representational services distinct from regulatory services. Sometimes these are both done by organisations.

▶ FRANK STEPHEN

To begin with I wanted to set my remarks 'in context': first, over my thirty years of teaching economics and industrial organisation, I spent most of the time talking about market failures, so I do not really come to discuss our topic with the view that markets work perfectly. My view is that markets are actually very prone to failure. Second, I have carried out empirical research on the regulation, and particularly the deregulation, of professions in the UK, and particularly on the legal profession. But I do not want to spend much time talking about these issues, though I will pass through them very quickly. As an academic, I see one of my roles as being that of someone who questions prevailing orthodoxy.

In my written contribution for this Workshop I intended above all to raise questions about issues on which there has been so far a widespread consensus. I want to spend a bit of time talking about information asymmetries, largely because I think it has been oversold, and in fact this issue has emerged in a couple of the points that have been made in the discussion so far. We heard about the credence good nature of professional services, and that is very important. One of the things that I think is curious—but I have not dwelled on it in the written contribution—is that the adverse selection and moral hazard arguments arise in different directions when it comes to regulation. We begin by talking about information asymmetry, in saying that there is an adverse selection problem if quality standards are not set, and you will have a 'lemons market'. So, the presumption is that the members of the profession are likely to undersell on quality. But the moral hazard argument, from a policy-maker's point of view, runs in the other direction, which is that the professional has an incentive to oversell on quality, so as to induce a demand that goes beyond the real need of the consumers. This is not discussed in the paper, it is just something that occurred to me during the discussion, that there is a strange tension in this theoretical proposition. A good part of the economics literature, particularly the North American one, on the professions and competition in the professions, does not consider the externality argument. By the time I had finished thinking about these issues, I started to wonder whether the externality argument is not perhaps the strongest argument in favour of a certain degree of regulation. But we will come back to that later.

Prof Roger van den Bergh mentioned that the evidence on a number of these issues is not as strong as economists and policy-makers would have expected it to be. I agree with this. The main issue at stake here is information asymmetry. My observations related to the legal profession in the UK seem to be in agreement with other economics literature on the subject: the information asymmetry problem is not exclusive to the professional services, but also manifests itself in other markets where customers' purchases are not frequent. (This point was raised back in the 1980s by researchers at the University of Toronto, but since then it somehow drifted out of the debate.) In other words, the information asymmetry problem is inherent to non-frequent purchasers, who are usually individuals and households, as opposed to businesses and public bodies. This issue came back to my attention while participating in a Scottish review exercise on the legal profession similar to that currently performed by Sir David Clementi in England. (Indeed, the Scottish legal system is different from the English legal system, including in this area.) What struck my attention in the course of this exercise was that we were frequently asked questions about information asymmetry and market failure in the market for legal services. When I started to think about this, I realised that there is no 'market for legal services', but rather, there are several markets for distinct legal services. Accordingly, when we talk about market failure, we should look at these distinct markets, and not at the legal profession as a whole. Indeed, professional services in general are provided in highly segmented markets, where dominant consumer groups like businesses and public bodies are frequent purchasers.

Looking at things from this perspective, the next question that arises is, are professional services credence goods? I certainly accepted in the past that they were so. However, once there are repeated purchases in the market, the case for regulation becomes weaker. There are also issues of professional reputation to consider. I think that repeated purchases also generate reputation. This happens with many professional services, in the UK and in other jurisdictions. In many cases, professional services interact with public bodies. Take for example the enforcement of criminal law. In the UK, criminal lawyers are for the most part paid from public funds, and in fact the public bodies providing these funds are now demanding standards of professional performance that go beyond those set by self-regulated bodies. The Legal Aid Board in Scotland and the Legal Services Commission in England have devised protocols on the handling of cases, to which criminal lawyers have to adhere, that demand more in terms of skills than what the legal professional bodies will demand. Similarly, in the area of health care, because insurance companies cover a good part of health care costs, they set their own standards on health care services and have their own lists of providers. Of course, there may be conflicts of interest arising here, but it does seem to me that we have to think more carefully about the role of third parties—or what I call 'repeat purchasers'—in terms of assuring the quality of services that in the past were left to the professional bodies to secure.

What policy conclusions should be drawn from this? The first is that, when talking about market failure, we should be looking at specific markets, and not at the professions in general. Judge Cooke spoke earlier about different professions performing the same services in different European jurisdictions, and about some activities being qualified as 'professional' in some jurisdictions, while in others not. This is the way of viewing the problem from the legal perspective. From the economic perspective, we merely target on markets and the possibility of market failure. I am suggesting that we should test the existence and degree of information asymmetry in traditional professional markets and seek for alternative ways to deal with the asymmetry problem rather than regulation. This would help in avoiding what I call 'regulatory creep', whereby the professions, because of their privileged position, extend their influence and control into areas that are not directly related to their professional functions. I could give you some examples in this sense later during the debate. Of course, the externality and public goods justifications remain separate from this. Thus, my main suggestion to the competition authorities is to focus on the markets, and not on the professions themselves, because by focusing on the profession they actually place the professional bodies in a privileged position that suppliers in other markets do not usually enjoy.

► Frédéric Jenny

The French Competition Council has been quite active in the area of the liberal professions. Among those sanctioned: the French Academy of Architecture, a group of more than ten bar associations (price fixing) and pharmacies (for restrictions on advertising). The paradox is that this activism in the area of professional services has actually alienated the consumer bodies even further. . . . This fact can be interpreted in two ways: one would be to say that consumer advocates do not know what they are talking about, and where the interest of the consumers lie, and thank God the competition enforcers exist to know this better. The second would be that, maybe, the competition enforcer missed something.

I agree with what Prof Stephen said before, but would also try to explain why consumer organisations have been so negative towards any attempt to introduce competition in the area of professional services. I also believe we should focus on the markets rather than on the professions as such. This brings me back to the issue of information asymmetry. I think that there are four issues to be considered when one talks about dysfunctional markets. One, and possibly the most important, is the inability of consumers to know about their own demand: what kind of legal service do I need? What kind of accounting service do I need? What kind of medical service do I need? The second—which was very much at the centre of our discussion this morning—is the inability to judge the quality of the services provided. The third is risk aversion. The reason here is that professional services are usually part of a wider project. For example, if you get the wrong architect, your house may fall down, even if the house builders performed their services according to the plans. More than fifteen of the cases that the French Competition Council brought against local bar associations in France were initiated upon a complaint from one single man, a shepherd in the Alps who lost his divorce trial, his house and the custody of his children, and decided to get even with the legal profession. Well, he succeeded very well. . . . He did not get anything out of this except for the pleasure of getting even with the legal profession, but I think that sometimes the fact that some of these services are incorporated into a larger project is the reason for a particular aversion to risk on the part of consumers. Fourth, the fact that competition law does not necessarily aim only at promoting efficiency, but fairness considerations are also often involved in its enforcement—in Europe at least. Fairness could be an aspect of the problem because professionals services are typically non-standardised, and there is wide variety in the quality or design of the service provided.

Having said this, there is a wider range of activities besides professionals services where these four features can be encountered. The typical response to these problems has been the creation of new types of contracts, such as the leasing of cars, for example. But leasing is not feasible for a lot of the professional services, unless one reinstates slavery. . . . So, a second solution was the creation of *quasi*-contracts. Before starting my intervention, I was thinking of asking everybody around this table to raise their hand if they thought that they had a good dentist. I have done this experiment in other occasions, and almost everybody always raised their hand. This means that, either the qualification restrictions to entry in this profession are very good, or we are suffering here from a severe case of information asymmetry. Actually, what we do with our dentist is similar to what we do with our car mechanic, which is to make a sort of informal arrangement along the following lines: 'If you are not going to cheat me too much, I'll be your faithful customer'. This is a *quasi*-contract attempting to reduce the effect of the asymmetry.

Now, where there is no repeat buying, of course, the solution of *quasi*-contracts is not available. In other words, a company seeking legal advice on antitrust matters is probably not going to be victim of information asymmetry, but the shepherd that I was talking about before may very well have been the victim of information asymmetry. For such cases, the professions have typically established a kind of 'global *quasi*-contract' limiting entry, diminishing price competition, and prohibiting advertising. They basically make it difficult for consumers to switch from one service provider to another, and at the same time limit competition to quality aspects, so as to ensure a reasonable level of quality of the particular service in general. On top of this, they may also establish a price cap, so that customers do not get cheated on the price.

This is a very imperfect way to respond to the four concerns that I mentioned before, and I am not arguing that it should be the only one. I think that one of my difficulties with the Commission's draft report on professional services[22]—and this draws on my personal experience—is that one cannot go beyond self-regulation by simply saying 'we want more competition.' One of the fundamental assumptions behind the competitive model is lacking here, since people do not know what their demands actually are and cannot select the 'good' providers. So there is no reason to believe that competition in itself will lead to an efficient or positive result. What we actually need here—and I think this has been the direction of our discussion since this morning—is some kind of positive intervention from the public authorities, establishing the pre-conditions for competition to work out. The main difficulty is separating the diagnosis from the provision of the service, which is something that professional bodies typically do not do, and this allows them to oversell or offer services of excessively high quality. I think that the state should make it easier for the consumers to obtain information about exactly what they need. Second, there should be an independent assessment of the quality of the different service providers. I do not think that such information providers are going to be spontaneously generated by the market if there is more competition in the professional services. Rather, it will go the other way around. Only once these two pre-conditions are satisfied does it become useful to promote competition. If, to the contrary, one goes straight to promoting competition, then consumers become very upset, because they think that competition is not going to work to their benefit. I was reading the assessments on the Commission's proposal for a Directive on services in the internal market,[23] and I found the following sentence: 'In particular, consumers would be in a better position to make informed choices as a result of a new obligation, firstly on service suppliers, to provide information on themselves and the quality of their service, and secondly, on Member States to provide assistance to consumers.' This is indeed the key issue: promoting competition can be useful, but only if there is also a plan to provide assistance to consumers, and even a requirement to establish the practical means for doing it. Consumer policy and competition policy must literally come together and reinforce each other for either of them to be successful in this field.

► JOHN FINGLETON

In Ireland, the engineering profession is incredibly lightly regulated. There is no obvious market failure, and no consumer call for extra regulation, but there has been a huge demand for extra regulation coming from the engi-

---

[22] See above n 2.

neering profession itself, justified as a means to protect consumers. I wonder if there is a sort of asymmetry here, in the sense that consumers do not go for changing much of the current state of play: if there is no regulation, they will not push for more of it, and if there is regulation, they will probably resist it being removed.

▶ WILLIAM KOLASKY

I think that this whole issue of market failures is indeed important. If you look at the US Supreme Court's decision in *California Dental*,[24] it begins with a discussion of potential market failures in the markets for dental services, citing a famous economics study on the 'lemons market',[25] which clearly showed that information asymmetry and the potential for market failures also exist in as prosaic a market as the one for the sale of used cars. If you think about the four types of market failure that John Fingleton outlined—asymmetric information, customers not knowing what or how much they need, customers having difficulty evaluating the quality of the services, and externalities, especially reputation externalities—these categories of market failure are almost ubiquitous in all markets for differentiated services, and the only question is to what degree they are manifest in each. One point that has been made by several speakers, and on which I agree completely, is that this is an issue that has to be examined market by market, even within a profession, such as the legal profession. Then, the potential for market failure is greater when an individual hires a lawyer to defend him/her against a criminal charge, especially murder, than when firms such as Microsoft or Coca-Cola are hiring a law firm. Those are very different markets, and the potential for market failure is very different in each. On the other point raised by John Fingleton, namely the degree of risk: my point is that a fault in the software used to fly an aircraft has at least as much potential for catastrophic damage as most of the mistakes that would be made by a lawyer or an accountant. So, I do not think it is accurate to say that professionals expose their clients to more serious and irreversible risks than other service providers.

▶ JOHN FINGLETON

I reflected on that point since the break: initially it sounds very compelling. But it is also true that a software programme is a very expensive system put

---

23 Commission Proposal for a Directive on services in the internal market, COM (2004)2. The text of the proposal, as well as the comments submitted during the consultation process and an independent impact evaluation study, are all available at http://europa.eu.int/comm/internal_market/en/services/services/.

24 *California Dental Assn v FTC,* 526 US 756; 128 F3d 720 (1999), vacated and remanded.

25 The concept was introduced in 1970 by George A Akerlof in his Nobel Award-winning paper 'The Market for "Lemons": Quality Uncertainty and the Market Mechanism' (1970) 84 *Quarterly Journal of Economics* (3), 488.

in place to deal with a specific risk. When dealing with everyday activities by a lot of individuals, we could put such systems against risk in place, but it could be very expensive to apply them for every transaction and every medical treatment. Medical insurance systems show that sometimes ensuring this degree of safety at the level of individual operations can be very expensive.

► CALVIN GOLDMAN

One of the areas where the Canadian competition law arguably had greater impact is related to the profession of real estate agents. When I came into office [at the Canadian Competition Bureau] our enforcement was focusing on the existence of cartel-like activities by the real estate boards operating under the—misguided, or perhaps very carefully instructed—belief that they were entitled by governing statutes to prescribe price levels for the sale of homes. Anyone selling below the prescribed levels discovered not to be able to use the multiple listing or other essential services necessary in order to sell. The Competition Bureau brought an action against nine real estate boards across Canada, and the impact of that decision is arguably the most significant in the history of Canadian competition law enforcement from the point of view of real impact on customers' lives. Moreover, this action had an educational sort of impact for other professions and for our judges as to the value of preserving competition.

► JOHN FINGLETON

This is an example of a win-win situation, but I would be interested to learn also about cases where price competition is bad for quality or for the public interest.

► HARRY FIRST

The question that got us started is whether professions are different from other markets. Prof Frank Stephen pointed out that we should be talking about specific markets, rather than professions in general. I think that the first question—whether professions are different—is asked by economists thinking about efficiencies, rather than by antitrust lawyers, who instinctively react in terms of market analysis. Now, I am not an economist, but I will do what the economists did earlier, which is to talk about law, so I will also say something about economics. . . . It seems to me that we tend to generalise on this information asymmetry argument that sounds so clever. Profs Frank Stephen and John Fingleton mentioned externalities, in the sense that there are wider consequences than between the individual customer and the service provider when something goes wrong in the area of professions. Health care was mentioned as an example, as well as legal assistance in criminal law proceedings. Alright, there are externalities in this area, but there are also externalities when airplanes explode because of negligence, or when cars fail and people die. I am not so sure that the professions are so different from other markets in this respect.

Every time I hear about information asymmetries, I tend to think that this is about someone knowing more than someone else. But in reality, in some of the professional services actually nobody knows more. . . . I used to change my dentist very often. Whenever I went to a new dentist, they would tell me how awful my previous dentist must have been. But in time I learned they will always say that. . . . The fact of the matter is that there are always limits to our knowledge, and sometimes it is hard to judge the quality of services received. Amelia Fletcher suggested that we could deal with this problem by establishing quality standards, and that is what repeat buyers might try to do, but even those cannot help much if they are not easy to apply. They also might have 'incentivising' effects, when people tend to 'move down' towards those standards. We saw that happening in the US in a different area, with the 'No Child Left Behind' standards for education, which eventually ended up by leaving behind the smarter children. There is a great system of *ex post* regulation, besides antitrust, for dealing with these issues, which is tort law. And sometimes the criminal justice system can also solve part of the problems: if two hundred persons die in the hands of the same doctor, the criminal justice system hopefully gets involved at a certain point. . . .

A final point on the notion of market failure: every time policy-makers hear about market failures, they tend to react by thinking that the state should intervene. But the real question is, what sort of public intervention is more suitable? I found it very interesting when Frédéric Jenny said—or at least this is what I understood—that the competition authorities are perhaps too willing to use antitrust law as an instrument for dealing with these issues. I think that this point sort of comes through our discussion here so far, along with the idea that one should consider the best possible way of regulating these professions. My instinct is to think first about how markets could best resolve those issues themselves. My impression is that Europe is more prone to regulatory intervention in this area than the US. There are also interesting institutional differences between Europe and the US in this area, and I think it would be quite interesting to discuss them later on.

► WILLIAM KOVACIC

I think one of the main implications for public policy coming out of this debate is the importance of enforcement targeted against restrictions on information flows. I think there are a number of instances in which private initiative has had an important role in providing information that helps users to both identify their needs and to assess quality. Even if short of solving the ultimate question of the regulatory framework, there still is an undeniable benefit for competition policy measures aimed to stop the professions from restricting information flows. Professions would usually try to restrict information in two ways. One is by placing direct limits on advertising. To give you a simple example, there was an early formative FTC case involving a physician in the Miami area who, in addition to placing his name in an advertisement, added the words 'se habla español'. The Florida medical society challenged him for illegal advertising on that. Clearly, the process of consultation and discussion to identify needs is facilitated if you can understand what your physician is saying. It is a simple case, but a basic example of a professional restriction on information flows that gets in the way of trying to solve the information problem.

Another one of our formative cases at the FTC dealt with third party information. The Indiana federation of dentists had decided not to allow insurance companies to see the X-rays taken during treatment in order to verify the quality of the service provided. We won this case in front of the US Supreme Court, and this judgment is an example of how to encourage the flow of information through third parties, who can act as agents on behalf of the users. A third example: there is a publication in the US that evaluates law schools, called *US News and World Report*. They do a survey and rank law schools according to a set of standards they have developed. Before this survey was established there were approximately 50 US law schools that claimed to be 'among the ten best in the US'. This survey is, admittedly, imperfect, but I attended many meetings of the Professional Association of American Law Schools in which one Law School dean after another stood up and said 'Let us refuse to participate in the survey. Do not give them the information.' This happened while I was at the FTC, and in an informal and quiet manner, I told a few of these deans that I did not think it would be a good idea if the Association of Law Schools adopted this attitude as a policy. As a matter of fact there are huge information asymmetries in this area. Law students have only some idea of what they really need, which is not only a law degree. This survey was admittedly imperfect, and a purely private initiative, but you certainly do not want the service providers to be able to collectively decide that such information cannot be gathered and published.

A last consideration: the situation in the legal services that Prof Frank Stephen just described did not exist thirty years ago. Back then, there were mostly locked-in relationships with law firms, which had almost legacy-type relationships with their clients. Switching from one law firm to another was uncommon. Within the law firms themselves there was no such mobility as nowadays, when lawyers change about six law firms throughout their career. Then, roughly about thirty years ago, private organisations started to publish information about fees, compensation rates, articles about what clients ought to do to monitor the performance of their lawyers, including turning in-house legal departments from sinecures into really top-quality law offices. This change, for the most part, happened without regulatory intervention. Private service providers started to provide information about quality that helped people identify their needs and evaluate quality. Again, I think that an interesting area in which competition policy can do a good job is to police efforts by the interested bodies to prevent such developments and the restriction of the information flow.

► JOHN FINGLETON

I was always struck by the fact that, while in general the US Supreme Court tends to dismiss the asymmetric information argument, *California Dental*[26] is largely based on this argument.

► WILLIAM KOLASKY

I think that this case was correctly decided, in the sense that the analytical framework laid out by the Court—requiring the FTC not to presume competitive injury in the case of restraints on potentially false or misleading advertising, but rather to prove such injuries with empirical evidence—is correct. It is another issue whether Justice Breyer (who wrote the dissent) was right about the facts, namely that there was in fact sufficient empirical evidence to show an anticompetitive effect of those restraints. I know that the 9th Circuit, on remand, ended up ruling against the FTC, and I would not necessarily defend this decision. The point is simply that the FTC may well have been right to bring the case, but they did not prove the case to the satisfaction of the US Supreme Court.

► WILLIAM KOVACIC

I will explain in tomorrow morning's discussion why I think *California Dental* is a bad decision. But William Kolasky's point about proof and the sort of economic precedents that should be brought forward in this context is very important. It highlights an important consideration, that we have not spoken about yet, which is as follows. Let us assume there is market failure and a set of controls are imposed to deal with it. An important point for the competition law enforcer is to determine whether the specific regulatory solution chosen by the profession actually fits the problem identified both in theory and in practice. My impression is that, quite often, such a correlation does not exist.

► DAVID CLEMENTI

I have two comments, one is about information asymmetries, and the other is about Prof van den Bergh's comments on co-regulation.

I have little doubt that information asymmetries do exist in almost all service industries, and they are certainly prevalent in the financial services

[26] See above n 24.

industry for many of the financial products offered. One of the four statutory objectives of the Financial Services Authority in the UK is to promote public information and understanding about these products. Therefore, the question that I address in my review of this topic is not whether asymmetries do exist, but rather, what is the responsibility of the regulator in this sense, and furthermore, what do we want done in this respect by the subjects of regulation (financial services providers). Should it be one of the attributions and obligations of the regulator to address the information asymmetry?

On co-regulation, I understood that Prof van den Bergh thought the choice was between competitive self-regulation and co-regulation. Competitive self-regulation is an extremely interesting area, on which I will try to say something tomorrow. But I do not see it as a matter of choice between the two; rather, I see them as co-existing. If there is only competitive self-regulation, who will give accreditation to these competing bodies, and insurance against the risk of a regulatory race to the bottom, and ensure minimum quality standards? Prof Monti said this morning that the protection of public interest is a state function, and that this function may also be delegated, but not without some degree of accountability. In my view, competitive regulation by professional bodies should coexist with co-regulation.

► ALLEN FELS

Having headed the Australian Competition and Consumer Protection Authority for years, I sometimes also wrestled with these problems, and I would like to add a few comments to the discussion.

First, and going back to one point mentioned earlier, an important part of our discussion is the issue of restraints on entry, or the exclusive reservation of certain work for professionals. For example, if I want to be given a simple injection, why cannot I go to my pharmacist for that? What criteria determine these kinds of limitations on entry?

Secondly, about the asymmetry issue, I wanted to add a couple of remarks. Any serious discussion about consumer protection has to take into account the vast number of disadvantaged and vulnerable consumers—that is, people with low IQ, people with mental illnesses (which account for 3% of the population in most countries), people who have language problems, people who have poor education, and children. For these categories of people, the standard calculations regarding 'the rational consumer' just do not work. And this is where many of the problems lie in consumer protection. Also, I wanted to remind you that there is an increasing body of economic literature about decision-making and how poor a guide the 'rational consumer' model with limited information is. This really gives us a very different picture of the realities of consumer protection. Another thing that I think should be emphasised a bit more by the economists who are working on this issue is that many problems arise in relation to actual legal remedies: if there is some problem with a professional service and the client seeks legal remedy—through tort law, or whatever—he will come against a wall of problems: costs, delay, uncertainty, and also bias on professional matters in the courts. For example, the courts in my country, and I believe elsewhere as well, are biased when it comes to questions about the regulation of the legal profession.

This brings me to another point: so far I have not heard much from the European speakers around this table about the professional area where the largest problems arise, which is the medical profession. Problems with lawyers? Fine, we can have a bit of fun talking about that, but the serious issues are really within the medical profession, and there we face quite a number of difficult issues. I do not think that I would be very happy to have a discussion about the medical profession just coming off the paradigm of asymmetrical information. There are so many other policy questions there, about access, equity, etc, and not in the least, we all have a very different attitude when it comes to matters affecting people's health. In other words, if someone says that the solution is to give patients enough information so that they can make informed judgments about the quality of the medical services, I would not agree that this is enough.

Some suggested that one way or another we should somehow 'activate' the consumers' side, by giving them more information and maybe getting consumer organisations more involved in the regulation of professions. But of course everyone knows that consumer organisations are chronically weak and under-funded, and this leads me to the conclusion that I have reluctantly reached over the years, that the government itself has to get into funding consumer research and set up some of its own consumer bodies—a bit like in the UK with the National Consumer Council. Admittedly, there are a lot of problems to face in doing that, but I believe it has to be done.

On the question of whether we should be looking at professions or at specific markets, I feel I should make one 'historical' point, which is that, on the one hand, the professions are being pushed to be competitive, and on the other hand, for decades in most of our countries we promoted collective bargaining by unions as a matter of policy. This is a very interesting divergence between promoting competition in some markets and collective bargaining being heavily promoted in other markets, and about where to draw the line between the two.

On the question of self-regulation, I had a lot of experience with this in Australia, because if there is self-regulation, it invariably involves some anti-competitive behaviour. We have a system whereby professions have to apply to the Competition Commission to allow anticompetitive behaviour by way of exemption, and in this way the competition authority has a window of control over their behaviour.

▶ RAFAEL ALLENDESALAZAR CORCHO

John Fingleton asked for an example where price limitation may be useful. I remember a case some time ago where the Spanish competition authority sanctioned the plumbers' association in a small region of Spain for publishing guidance prices. I remember that, as a consumer, I was thinking, well, why are guidance prices so awful? If, on Sunday evening, pipes in my house start dripping on my neighbour's house and I have to look urgently for a plumber, I want to know if it reasonable for the plumber coming on Sunday evening to charge me 10 or 100 Euro. I think that this is a case where some kind of price guidance may be reasonable and useful.

▶ JOHN FINGLETON

You articulated very well one of the main concerns that consumer associations raise in the area of professions. Consumers see price restrictions as ensuring lower prices for consumers, whereas the competition law enforcers see them as bringing about higher prices for the consumers. Maybe there is an element of truth in both.

▶ IAN FORRESTER

I would like to draw your attention to a different kind of asymmetry that seems to be affecting us this morning. We seem to be proceeding in this debate on the basis that private restrictions are to be treated with the greatest suspicion whereas public regulation is to be treated with great deference and respect—I am exaggerating a bit here, of course, but just to get the point through, I voice a suspicion. I suspect that the state does all kinds of stupid things in every country in the world. For example, I am a consumer of financial services, in the sense that I have insurance policies and mortgages and so on. Now, in the UK the financial sector is intensely regulated at present, following various scandals and dramas. There is a very heavy burden of reporting, and I am sure many people would tell me that this made financial services more transparent. However, I am of the belief that all the warnings and reminders and cautions that I get are simply a nuisance. I do not think that the quality of the services that I get is any higher. Furthermore, I am told that one of the consequences of this orgy of corporate purity that has been launched for the financial services is that now there is a new profession in Wall Street, known as the 'chaperone', that is a person who sits in the presence of certain kinds of financial activities to make sure that nothing filthy is being done. It is a complete waste of time, and everyone knows it. I believe that the best kind of regulation is that emerging in good faith and from a thorough knowledge of the industry. Now, I am ready to believe that private sector regulators sometimes do ridiculous things, and it is easy to make fun of them, but I do not think we should assume that the state would certainly do better.

► JAMES VENIT

I found the example of needing information about law schools to eliminate information asymmetries fascinating, because I believe law schools do have entrance exams, or require certain qualifications from people they will admit. Thus, in a certain sense, they self-select and establish their own reputation through this selection. So, the notion that there would be a larger information gap between the user of that service and the provider struck me as odd. I think that is an example of where the market may actually be functioning quite well, because the provider of the service is imposing requirements on those to whom it is willing to provide the service.

► MARK SCHECHTER

Earlier in the morning, Judge Cooke raised a particularly interesting and important question. As I understood it, I think he asked whether the EC institutions, and the EC courts in particular, could be expected to devise overall objective rules to apply to the professions, given that there are significant differences among Member States as to, in particular, what we hope to get out of the professions, and their obligations to the public. As the discussion proceeded, it became clearer to me that the answer is, absolutely not: 'overall objective rules' are not feasible. I think that what came out of the debate so far is that we cannot devise an overall analytical framework to situations that may be quite diverse from one jurisdiction to another. Prof Frank Stephen's comments on information asymmetry were most interesting and helpful. They suggest that, in order to devise such an overall analytical approach, one has to clearly define the problem that is thought to be addressed by a proposed regulation. And indeed, if the problem is to protect corporate purchasers of legal services, for example, then regulation might be pretty unnecessary. So the problem has to be well defined, and the solution has to be narrowly tailored to address that specific problem. And it may be the case that, in the end, the costs of the solution can be found to exceed the magnitude of the problem, once the latter is carefully and well defined.

I have to say that, as an American, I was quite surprised by the lack of analysis in terms of a definition of the problem and of the solution in *California Dental*.[27] In my view, what comes out of that decision is a fairly unintelligible rule of law which sounds something like: 'If the state does it, it is okay, as long as that is what they really intended to do.' I think that Europe has the possibility to live by a much higher standard than that.

A second point: during my many years spent at the US Department of Justice, one of my responsibilities was to oversee an airline price-fixing case, where airlines exchanged information about their future pricing intentions. Their principal defence was that consumers would like to know in advance

[27] See above n 26.

if prices are going up, so as to have an opportunity to book in advance. I received about 750 letters from travel agents invoking that argument, purportedly on behalf of the consumers they represented. We responded of course that, clearly, consumers would like to know in advance if prices are going to go up, but if the cost of having that information is to increase substantially the likelihood that the prices will go up, then also clearly, the consumers are better off not having this kind of information.

▸ SANTIAGO MARTÍNEZ LAGE

This morning Prof Arruñada asserted that, nowadays, there is zero demand for public notaries in Europe. I was astonished to hear that, as probably also several others of you coming from countries in continental Europe, where the so-called Roman model of law prevails. I think that what Prof Arruñada said can only be sustainable in Spain, which is quite a unique case in this area. In Spain, to assure the security of a real estate property transaction, two different liberal professionals intervene: public notaries and public registrars. This second element is what makes the Spanish system unique, because public registrars in Spain are liberal professionals, and not civil servants as in other countries. They are purely liberal professionals, in the sense that they are paid by customers individually on each transaction. There is an overlap with public notaries, and the system is not quite efficient, but in my opinion, the solution should be to have the public registrar services organised as in other European countries, through civil servants, and then have them compete with the public notaries in what they do, which is to control the legality of the transaction. I do not think it is correct to state that there is zero demand for public notaries in Europe. I agree, however, that introducing more competition, as was done in the UK when allowing also solicitors to perform real estate transactions, could help to increase competition in this sector.

▸ LOWRI EVANS

Just one contextual remark, which I think has been slightly forgotten during the discussion: the Commission has stated in the draft Report on the liberal professions[28] that many of the restrictions identified are actually set up in state legislation, and not by the professional bodies. This is a known fact, and we are tending to discuss here restraints as if professional bodies are responsible for them. They may sometimes be, but it is indirect causality, I think.

The second point is that there are indeed—and this cannot be underlined too much—huge differences among the Member States in this area. I would like us to keep in mind which are the most 'legislative' Member States, because I think it is interesting to compare the situation in those countries. Italy is the heaviest regulated Member State, followed by Austria, Germany

---

[28] See above n 2.

and Luxembourg—this being a group where you could see some common cultural background. At the other extreme, that of the least regulated countries, is Ireland. When the first draft of our study came out and we described Ireland as 'very low regulated', I remember that John Fingleton [Chairman of the Irish competition authority] was quite in disagreement, because from his perspective Ireland is a highly regulated Member State, and he wants to see further deregulation. . . . I think it is very interesting to compare this reaction with that of the Italian legislators, who obviously do not feel that Italy is over-regulated.

The point is that if we talk about public interest and externalities from a legislative perspective, I think it is legitimate, in the context of the Lisbon agenda, to ask the legislator to better specify the externalities and public interest objectives addressed by legislation. Since all Member States signed up to the Lisbon agenda, we all presumably agree that there are efficiencies to be gained from competition in this area, subject to the analysis of possible trade-offs. But before we can embark on such analysis, we have to understand what public interest means in each Member State, and so far this remains unclear.

▸ Frédéric Jenny

One quick point on the question of degree: so far, we said that the same failures will arise in other markets, and therefore it's only a question of degree. Somebody referred to buying used cars. To me, the main difference here is that I know when I want to buy a used car. Then I may have difficulties assessing the quality of the used cars that I find on the market. But I do not know if I need an eye operation, or what kind of legal service I need. I think that one important dimension of this 'degree' is the self-assessment of demand, and this is where advertising is not going to help. Advertising may give some information on the quality of the services, but it is not going to solve this other problem.

▸ David Clementi

Just a couple of quick points. First, I think I have been misinterpreted in what I said. I certainly would not argue that the market should be allowed to do all the regulation. What I would argue for is that the degree of regulation should be sensitive to the context. I think one of the problems economists have—and it has been exemplified several times during this morning's discussion—is that they generalise too much. It seems to me to be unhelpful in this context to talk about 'the professions' in general, because what people in Germany regard as a liberal profession is not necessarily regarded as such in the UK, and so on. Or indeed, to talk in general about consumers and their interest: consumers are different in different markets. Large multinational corporations are not the same as the individual wanting to get advice on buying an insurance policy or whatever; there is a major difference. Context is very important, and unfortunately, context is something that economists never think about.

I also thought there is a shortage here of participants from those parts of the EU where there is a significant degree of de-regulation, particularly in the legal services area. It would have been interesting to hear about how legal markets—to use that generalisation—work in Finland, where there is no restriction at all in operating and giving legal advice, besides having a title.

► Roger van den Bergh

This allows me to elaborate a bit further on how I see competitive self-regulation, which in my view is really distinct from co-regulation. If there is a role for the state in competitive self-regulation, it will be very limited. In the case of co-regulation, the state will recognise standards. In the case of competitive self-regulation, the idea is that the professions themselves develop the set of standards, and through competition between different bodies these will evolve towards the optimum. This idea builds on the economic literature regarding the benefits of regulatory competition. The two major benefits of regulatory competition are that it makes it possible to satisfy more preferences and it enables learning processes. Both points are really crucial in the market for professional services. On the other hand, economists are sceptical about regulatory competition when it could lead to a race to the bottom. Whenever such outcomes could happen, the state should fix a minimum standard. But in this case the role of the state will be more limited than in the case of co-regulation

► Benito Arruñada

First, a clarification on the issue of demand for notaries. Whether the notaries system is working or not does not mean anything in this respect, because in most countries the demand is mandated by law. There is nothing in my paper grounded specifically on the Spanish case—actually, all arguments are supported by international evidence, for instance the sixteen US states where lawyers by law still have exclusivity over real estate transactions. Therefore, the argument is completely applicable to notaries or to other cases. I think that Santiago Martinez Lage has misunderstood my argument. Indeed, the Spanish land registers are civil servants, but they are paid with the residual profit of their office, this is their only peculiarity. This is a 19th Century structure, which is working quite ineffectively. Probably UK participants around this table can understand this very well, considering that, the UK attempted to reform the national healthcare system by transforming general practitioners into fund-holders in the context of the internal market. This has to be well understood: there is no overlap at all between the role of notaries and the role of land registrars. The land registrar takes care of the interests of third parties, while the notaries take care of the interests of the parties to the contract.

▸ Harald Hermann

I simply wanted to make sure how close my own arguments are to the ones of other speakers. Prof van den Bergh spoke about competitive self-regulation, which seems quite close to what I said about systems competition. As far as I see, we both talk about competition between regulatory bodies, with the difference that Prof van den Bergh looks at regulatory or self-regulatory organisations within the same member state, whereas I look at competition between such bodies across the boundaries of the member states. In the latter case, the results of competition are having the benefits of the 'better' regulatory or self-regulatory system.

I listened with interest to Ms Amelia Fletcher talking about *ex ante* and *ex post* regulatory systems. I just wanted to underline that, even within *ex ante* regulatory systems, there are differences, as I pointed out earlier, between those regimes of an older type, so to speak, and the more open minded professional governance systems.

▸ Amelia Fletcher

First, a brief point on notaries: you may all be interested to know that I actually had to ask someone the other day what a notary did, because there are so few of them left in the UK—which shows that we can do without them. . . . On *ex ante* regulation: John Fingleton had asked us before to think about price guides and quantitative restrictions. I think that it is also worth talking very briefly about comparative advertising and restrictions on organisational form. I took in William Kovacic's point on comparative advertising. I think that we need to be really careful with *ex ante* regulation when it prevents the market from actually starting to help overcome some of these asymmetric information problems that we talked about. His dentist example illustrates very well how limitations on comparative advertising can be really detrimental in terms of solving the information asymmetry problem. What I wanted to add—perhaps more controversially—is that I think restrictions on organisational form can have a very similar effect. Essentially, we heard earlier that, within bigger organisations, you can generate reputation in a way that individuals cannot generate. If you have multi-professional organisations, you can transfer that reputation across markets as well, and therefore, by putting restrictions on organisational form, I think there is a risk that you could actually prevent the reputation mechanism for improving some of these adverse asymmetric information problems.

▸ John Fingleton

I think that after this discussion I might have even more questions than at its beginning. In terms of what we seem to all agree on: first, nobody argued that numerical entry restrictions were a justified regulatory instrument. Second, on price control, the point was made that maybe consumers might find it useful for some purposes, even though competition law enforcers consider this might keep price levels too high. Third, nobody seemed to disagree with William Kovacic's point that we should vigorously tackle restrictions on the dissemination of information. This also answered my second question, which was whether there are win-win strategies. From my own point of view, looking at some of the issues we are dealing with in Ireland, I think that sometimes entry restrictions are clearly disproportionate. The pharmaceutical market is an example in this sense. So there are win-win cases, but we are discussing the very frequent cases that are not a win-win, without realising there are some really substantial gains to be made there. We had a heated debate about the insurance market in Ireland, and in this context it turned out that about 42% of the funds from insurance premiums charged to people actually goes to the legal profession. Some of that is undoubtedly a transaction cost, but a large part of it is just a tax. This is not necessarily a competition problem but a systemic problem with how the market works.

This leads me to Allan Fels's point about health care—where personally I think that the gains from reform would be spread across other professions. Very often the competition issues we are dealing with in this area are part of a much larger framework, with hidden costs and hidden benefits to consider. And economists and competition specialists are well trained in looking at hidden costs and benefits. If we can bring these aspects into the wider public debate on the liberal professions, it is very useful. Allocation of talent is a very good example of a hidden cost to society that somebody thinking exclusively from the point of view of access to justice or fairness would not necessarily pick up. I think that competition experts, and economists in particular, need to realise what their comparative advantage is, but this has to happen within a wider context.

Finally, I do not think I got an answer to my question of why the professions should be different from other services. David Clementi brought in the example of financial services, others mentioned the examples of software and air traffic control, but then Ian Forrester seemed disagree. So I was left confused as to whether there really are good examples of other markets outside the professions that have this cumulative credence good on top of asymmetric information characteristics, with the add-on of externalities, and where we see competition or lighter regulation or competitive co-regulation working well. But maybe this question will surface again this afternoon and tomorrow morning.

PANEL ONE

ECONOMIC ASPECTS
2

WORKING PAPERS

I

Benito Arruñada[1]

Managing Competition in Professional Services and the Burden of Inertia

I. Introduction

Professional services require certain organisational patterns in order to avoid information asymmetries and external effects. These same patterns are used within production structures involving various degrees of monopoly. However, competitive restraints are justified today only when substantial external effects are clearly present, whereas information asymmetries hardly justify such restraints because reputation investments have become widespread in the economy and are relatively efficient in overcoming such asymmetries. As a consequence, innovation in the production of externalities can make competitive constraints unnecessary.

The rest of this work is divided into two parts. The first one discusses the problems of professions generally and the second focuses on two specific cases. Thus, Section 2 identifies the characteristic situation of professional services, which is caused by the presence of information asymmetries when private services are offered, the presence of, or desire for, external effects and the reduction in costs that arises when the same professional provides both types of service. Section 3 argues that in order to resolve the problems of information asymmetry, it is usually necessary to adopt a series of organisational patterns: deferred and variable compensation in line with the professional's and others' conduct, and self-selection of professionals having ideal characteristics. Section 4 outlines a scheme for assessing the situation of professions from the point of view of economic policy.

The second part encompasses Sections 5 and 6, which analyse the situation of two professions—pharmacies and conveyaners—which are now the most highly regulated in Europe, perhaps because they are also the oldest (Monti,

[1] Department of Economics and Business, Universitat Pompeu Fabra (Trias Fargas, 25; E–08005–Barcelona. E-mail: benito.arrunada@upf.edu). The author thanks Jürgen Backhaus, Cándido Paz-Ares, Frank Stephen and participants at several academic meetings, including the Ninth EU Competition Law and Policy workshop, for their comments to previous versions of this work. Usual disclaimers apply. This project has received financial support from the MCYT, an agency of the Spanish Government, through grants SEC99–1191 and SEC2002–04471 –C02–02.

2003, 2). A similar conclusion is reached in both cases, namely, that historical justification for a corporatist organisation of these services is no longer valid and that, as a consequence, both professions now offer inappropriate services for the current situation of demand and technology. Liberalisation is therefore advisable, especially for the most standard services.

II. Nature of Professional Services

Professional services have two properties: information asymmetry between providers and customers and the production of external effects. Many other goods and services share these two properties but their extent in professional services leads to special problems which can only be resolved by adopting special organisational formulas.

1. Information Asymmetry

Production of professional services suffers from serious information asymmetries for two reasons. Firstly, such services often involve application of the professional's human capital in order to judge individual cases. Secondly, results are extremely difficult to assess. Professional work can therefore be seen as the application of specialised human capital to the solution of individual cases, leading to a product that is difficult to evaluate. Each of these elements—assessment, a personalised product that is difficult to observe and intense human capital—involve specific contractual problems. The fact that they come together compounds the difficulties which characterise professional services.

Moreover, transactions are often non-repetitive and atypical. Many professional services present 'search' attributes, the quality of which might be known prior to purchase or consumption, as well as 'experience' attributes, whose quality can only be appreciated during or after consumption, as with many other services (Nelson, 1970). In addition, the most outstanding characteristic is the presence of 'credence' attributes, whose quality can never be fully appreciated (Darby and Karni, 1973).

Other complications relate to the heterogeneity of demand, the high degree of specific human capital, and the presence of professional judgment.

a) *Heterogeneous demand.* Professional services are individual to the extent that each customer demands and receives different services. Even when cases share certain elements, these usually appear in different combinations, so that service standardisation is often impossible or at least unadvisable. Although to some extent the development of routines and protocols assists in standardisation, this is often a source of problems as it affects quality as perceived by the customer.[2] Control can only exist in the form of evaluation of the productive process rather than of its results, using implicit motivation mechanisms through moral indoctrination, *quasi*-rents and self-selection.

b) *Specific human capital.* Essentially, professionals have to invest now in knowledge needed to resolve problems in the future. As a result, their decisions must not be seen as if they were just supplying labour, in the neo-classical sense. They have to be seen instead as investors. Furthermore, not only is compensation deferred but also investments are *specific* because professional knowledge has practically no value outside the profession. As a result, expected returns and the risk of expropriation play important roles in the long term and must be taken into account when professional activities are regulated or managed.

c) *Professional judgment.* An essential part of professional work involves judging individual cases, often urgently, and using information which is imperfect but can be improved at an additional cost in time and money. This judgement is mostly individual, with each professional taking decisions alone. Even when the production processes of many professional services involve teams in which there is a degree of mutual control, a large degree of individual discretion is applied.

All these circumstances create a situation in which there are substantial information asymmetries amongst those providing, organising, regulating and using professional services, making it very difficult to contain conflicts of interest among them. For example, it is difficult for professionals to guarantee the optimal level of quality. When a professional does not provide optimal quality, she will obtain a short-term gain in exchange for an uncertain possibility of a future sanction. Supervision of service quality is difficult for other participants, whether they are customers, regulators, professional associations or other professionals, even within a single firm. Any subsequent review of quality will be, for instance, subject to the typical problem involved in assessing decisions taken in a context of uncertainty and imperfect information. The decision being assessed might have been right with the information available, although information gathered subsequently shows that it was wrong under the actual circumstances. (There is, as a consequence, a

---

[2] Standardisation is curbed not only by technological but also by psychological considerations. This was learned several decades ago by non-professional service firms which pioneered 'service industrialisation'. Many management experts supported this wave of industrialisation, following Levitt (1972, 1976), *until the limitations of this 'manufacturing' approach in service management became clear* (Sullivan, 1982).

substantial risk of falling into the traps of hindsight bias[3]). A main problem of this type of service is therefore that of creating mechanisms for safeguarding or ensuring quality under unfavourable circumstances because verification of contractual performance by third parties and even by the interested parties themselves is often only possible in the long term.

2. External Effects

So far we have considered the problem of the information asymmetry that exists between the suppliers and customers of private services. This is a typical bilateral agency relationship in which the supplier acts as agent for a principal who is the customer. In fact, however, it is more complex than this. Not only because there are usually other individuals involved, such as partners, regulators, informers, assessors, etc, reducing the bilateral nature of the transaction, but also because the provision of private services usually goes together with external effects or, in other words, with the provision of public services. Hence, the relationship becomes a multilateral one, involving greater complexity and potential for conflict.

These externalities stem from both the nature of the private services and from political decisions which oblige certain private service providers to also provide certain public services. The underlying economic rationale is the same in both cases—the production of private and public services by a single professional implies economies of scope or joint production. In other words, it is less costly if a single professional produces both private and public services on the same cases. The reason lies in the use of joint informational and contractual resources. On the one hand, the provision of private and public services usually requires the same information, both general—the human capital or general knowledge to be applied—and specific—relating to the customer or the case in question. On the other hand, similar problems arise with both types of service regarding contractual safeguards. It is necessary and costly to ensure that the professional fulfils the contract. Such problems require the use of safeguard mechanisms which, being costly, should be used to ensure fulfilment over the widest possible range of services.

Professional services result in a wide variety of external effects with an element of so-called 'gatekeeping'. This gatekeeping entails authorising a third party to provide services—the gatekeeper, who has other functions, in this case the provision of private services, and who is free to refuse to cooperate

---

[3] Evidence on hindsight bias, a phenomenon first described by Fischhoff (1975), has been accumulating over time (Christensen-Szalanski and Willham, 1991).

and, by doing so, will prevent or curb unlawful conduct.[4] The concept is a broad and imprecise one. For Kraakman, examples of gatekeepers include accountants and lawyers in securities transactions, doctors, pharmacists, employers' vicarious liability, bouncers, sellers of firearms, advertising agencies, insurance companies in environment regulation, common law duties of lenders and corporate directors, tax preparers and practitioners, and chaperones. Most lawyers, including civil law notaries, carry out a dual role which involves not only the provision of private services but also acting as gatekeepers in this sense. English barristers, for example, act as agents for the courts.[5] Gatekeeping is not the only type of external effect, however. For example, litigation lawyers contribute substantially to judicial rulings and the quality of their services is therefore important in the creation of case law.

Assigning the production of externalities to professionals reaches economies of scope but poses a serious problem in that, in principle, the professional has no incentives to produce the externalities, as these are services for which she is not paid and for which she might even have to incur a certain cost. As a gatekeeper, the professional is an agent for two principals (her customer and society) whose interests are often in conflict. In order to resolve this satisfactorily, there must be strong incentives to make the professional *independent* from the customer who is paying her even considering that, if the services are refused, she risks losing the customer. Achieving sufficient incentives for such a high degree of independence will be costly. In particular, it will require suppressing or restraining competition. The efficiency and cost of standard organisational patterns, as described in the next section, must be evaluated in this context.

III. Organisational Patterns

Because of the characteristics analysed in the previous section, professional services have to be produced and sold within organisational formulas—such as professional associations, professional firms or hybrids, such as health maintenance organisations—which are quite different from those of

[4] This figure of the gatekeeper as a guardian of law has been described by Kraakman (1986), who defines his liability as

> liability imposed on private parties who are able to disrupt misconduct by withholding their cooperation from wrongdoers.
>
> Gatekeeper liability is distinguished by the duty that it imposes on private 'gatekeepers' to prevent misconduct by withholding support. This support—usually a specialized good, service, or form of certification that is essential for the wrongdoing to succeed—is the 'gate' that the gatekeeper keeps (Kraakman, 1986, 53–54).

[5] See, for example, Posner (1995) for an argument along these lines.

neoclassical abstractions of firms and markets. In addition, these formulas are similar in liberal professions and professional firms, another reason why competition policy should focus more on professional firms than on traditional professions.

1. Common Patterns

The common organisational structure for all professional activities, whether in competition or not, is characterised by incentives for the professionals themselves and by the process of self-selection which such incentives generate. Three basic features are present: (a) a deferred compensation system, with high penalties in case of non-compliance with professional standards; (b) variability in earnings, promoting productivity and mutual control; and (c) a process of self-selection introducing a certain degree of automatic control.

a) *Quasi-rents*. Professionals are paid above their highest opportunity earnings during the most important stage of their career, with the professional or the firm receiving a quality premium or '*quasi*-rent',[6] which compensates for prior investments. This type of compensation motivates individual professionals and firms to comply, provided there is a positive probability of losing the *quasi*-rents in case of non-compliance. In the absence of competition, such *quasi*-rents are structured in the form of professional entry barriers—entry examinations, hierarchies, and apprenticeships—which require a large initial investment. On the other hand, in firms that compete with others in providing professional services—as in consulting, auditing, law, investment banking, or even higher education[7]—these *quasi*-rents result from organisational decisions on personnel selection, task allocation, promotions and compensation profiles.[8] In both cases, however, compensation is below opportunity earnings during the initial period and above it afterwards.
b) *Variable compensation*. The fact that earnings vary positively with the professional's conduct in aspects in which competition is accepted and negatively with the conduct of colleagues in areas in which it is prohibited (basically with their bad conduct) favours the achievement of some

[6] Studies on how the expectation of receiving a flow of *quasi*-rents in the future automatically encourages producers to preserve the quality of the products or services they provide, which go back to Becker and Stigler (1974), were developed by Klein and Leffler (1981), Williamson (1983) and Shapiro (1983) and applied to labour in models on deferred compensation (Lazear, 1979) and efficient wages (Shapiro and Stiglitz, 1984).

[7] See, amongst many others, Fama and Jensen (1983a, 315–17; and 1983b, 334–7), Gilson and Mnookin (1985), and Carr and Mathewson (1990).

[8] One remuneration system that has these properties is that of federal judges in the US, whose payment is deferred in the form of a generous pension. See Posner (1995, 109–44).

efficiency objectives in two ways. Firstly, it promotes productivity in areas in which there is competition. Secondly, it encourages mutual control so that competition is restricted to such areas.

c) *Self-selection.* Finally, the presence of such incentives usually leads to a process of self-selection of a certain type of person, those who appreciate working under such restrictions and with such payment patterns. Mainly, deferred compensation encourages entry by people having a low subjective discount rate. To the extent that preferences differ amongst individuals and are constant throughout their lives, this self-selection favours the entry of professionals having preferences that are well suited for rejecting temptations of bad professional practice, which often bring benefits in the short term only, with possible penalties being paid only in the future.

Revealingly, the structure of such incentives is similar, whether they result from an internal decision by organisations which compete freely in the provision of professional services (auditing, consultancy, law firms) or from the competitive constraints faced by liberal professionals practicing independently as individuals. When competing firms provide the services, such incentive patterns are not seen as restrictions to competition but as professional 'careers' in a sort of internal labour market. In many cases this distinction is more legal than economic, as with the treatment of vertical restrictions when the distinction depends on whether distributors are vertically integrated with the producer or not.

In practice, however, there is more often a radical difference. While producers and distributors of non-professional goods usually compete with other producers and distributors—this being a necessary condition if the vertical restrictions are to be considered favourably—professional associations almost always act as monopolies. Economic justification for the restrictions in the latter case therefore requires two additional conditions. First, the existence of substantial external effects as produced by the incentive structure created by the restrictions, because the problems of information asymmetry can be resolved using contractual safeguards that are freely drawn up by competing private organisations.[9] Second, it must be less efficient to produce such external effects under an alternative regime of regulated competition between firms whose employees and partners are motivated according to the standard professional patterns.[10] This might be the case where such a regime requires

[9] An example are the contracts being used in the US health sector in the form of Health Maintenance Organizations or 'HMOs'. This unusual type of franchise uses various organisational patterns such as contracts for assistance from a closed list of doctors, supervision of doctors and vertical integration. Some of the serious conflicts of interest between doctors, patients and insurance companies have led to this sector being considered as full of 'market faults'. See Feldstein (1988, 314–18) for an introduction.

[10] This may be the situation of financial auditors who compete both through professional associations and through firms and as individual professionals. See especially Watts and Zimmerman (1979; 1986, 179–99 and 222–43), and Arruñada (1999a, 2000).

a high degree of supervision and regulation and where public administrations are not capable of providing it efficiently.

2. The Power of Competition between Professional Firms

Much of the discussion on professional regulation would be more relevant for policymaking in the 19th than in the 21st century because this discussion ignores the fact that professional services are (or in the absence of competitive restraints would be), provided through professional firms. The presence of professional firms redefines the problems, provides effective solutions and requires a broader regulatory perspective for professional services.

Firstly, professional firms are better able to safeguard their transactions with reputation, repetition and a longer horizon. Secondly, agency problems between the firm and both its professionals and its customers become the key issue.[11] Thirdly, the presence of firms combines the issue of professionals' regulation with the more basic matter of freedom of contract.

This last point requires a short digression. The commonality of organisational patterns within traditional liberal professions and professional firms freely competing in the market also holds an important lesson for competition policy in this field. One of the main problems of self-regulation amongst professionals is that there is no competition between self-regulatory structures, as each profession enjoys a monopoly over a certain market. The use of organisational devices to avoid information asymmetries and control quality indicates that professional firms are also self-regulatory structures and thus, when competing with each other, they in fact create competition between regulatory frameworks.

The legal environment does not always help firms to solve the agency problems, mainly because during the 20th century judges have been increasingly allowed to regulate contracts (Arruñada and Andonova, 2004), impeding the development of private legal orders by firms. Without this constraint, professional firms would work more as private and competitive jurisdictions, providing the most viable form of *competitive self-regulation*, with each firm acting as its own self-regulator each time it changes its internal rules or its product guarantees. For example, if competitive firm *A* provides a service to client *B*, in order to motivate itself and to control its professionals, the firm could promise full satisfaction or the money back. Depending on the legal system, the mechanism may be allowed to function under second party enforcement or may be mandatory supervised by the courts. This defines two

[11] On the other hand, competition between firms should not be a particular problem in professional services, because, being intensive in human capital and being human capital mobile, restructuring and entry is relatively easy.

situations for cases in which a customer *B* claims to be unsatisfied and provider *A* rejects the claim because he thinks *B* is abusing the guarantee and acting opportunistically. If the case is subject to a court decision (mandatory third party enforcement) and the judge rules for *B*, this may hinder the development of private legal orders, in which firms would act as judges, controlled by reputation and competition. The tendency of judges to intervene in all areas irrespective of the contractual assignment of decision rights (in which *A* is granted the right to freely decide on the merits of *B*'s claim) thwarts competition between private legal orders which could otherwise provide the most effective solutions for such difficult relationships. In sum, the main issue is to what degree firms should be allowed to act as judges within relational contracting structures, and how this competition among contractual frameworks could be made easier, or at least not be hampered, by legal institutions.[12]

IV. Assessment of Competitive Restraints in the Professions

The use of similar organisational patterns by firms providing professional services in competitive markets, by professional associations, and even by some civil service systems indicates that such patterns are likely to be efficient or at least, to some degree, adaptive. It also justifies a case-by-case analysis of the possible benefits and monopoly costs present in the various types of institution and market structures in the professional service sector. Such an analysis must be based on its own merits, like the type of analysis which is increasingly being carried out on the vertical restrictions between producer and distributor. For vertical restrictions, both the economic literature and, increasingly, antitrust authorities, prefer to study each case separately, applying a *rule of reason* and rejecting rigid, *per se* exclusion of certain general patterns, such as territorial exclusivity. In the professions, it is also best to adopt a case-by-case approach, analysing each profession separately. A study of each of these institutions must take into account the possible existence of external effects and the cost of alternatives for dealing with them as well as problems of information asymmetry, considering how they can be mitigated or resolved both now and in the future within the new framework being considered. In other words, on the one hand policy-makers have to define which services they want professionals to produce and which services they

[12] This kind of judicial activism is not the only barrier. Another example are the barriers on multidisciplinary practice, epitomised in Europe by the *Wouters* ruling of the European Court of Justice, which allows national rules forbidding lawyers working with auditors to protect the proper practices of the legal profession, and which been followed by the *Proposal for a directive on professional services in the internal market* (COM (2004) 2). On multidisciplinary practice, see Arruñada (1999b).

want regulators and civil servants to produce. On the other hand, they have to consider achieving a transition that will avoid unintentionally increasing entry barriers and creating uncontrolled regulatory bodies, while encouraging the development of spontaneous, contractual safeguards for problems of information asymmetry.

Ideally, economic policy should not only examine the situation in the appropriate professional sector but should also compare its efficiency with alternative formulas. Both tasks are difficult, however, as shown by the following analysis.

1. A Checklist for Analysing a Profession

Analysis of regulation of a specific profession should include at least a thorough review of the objectives of the profession regarding information asymmetry and external effects, its real efficiency in achieving such objectives and the cost of achieving them.

Efficient analysis of the attributes or nature of the service requires an understanding of the productive and contractual technology involved. Initially, the attributes of information asymmetry and quality in the professional field might be considered of secondary importance today to external effects, because modern markets have been shown to have greater capacity than the State for resolving problems of information asymmetry, partly because of durable firms with considerable reputation investments. In other words, restricting competition within a profession makes more sense to the extent that the profession provides public services involving external effects. The possible costs of such patterns caused by the restriction of competition may be negligible in comparison with the greater costs that would be generated if such services were provided by civil servants or even by professional firms in a highly regulated environment.

Secondly, study of the efficiency with which the service is provided within a real or hypothetical organisational formula will generally focus on the incentives created by the collection of *quasi*-rents through deferred payment and rents, variability of earnings and the consequent processes of self-selection. In this set-up, it is especially important to assess whether the sanctioning mechanisms needed to make *quasi*-rent incentives really effective actually work; whether variability of earnings is sufficient to promote cost reduction and mutual quality control; and whether the process of self-selection favours the entry of the type of personnel most suitable for the functions in question and for the development of corporate control patterns.

Finally, the costs generated by competitive restrictions must be considered. This assessment must include the loss of welfare caused by the higher prices and the resulting lower quantities; the increase in costs caused by competitive restrictions, which becomes more marked when innovation is restricted and, finally, rent seeking costs which largely depend on how the entry mechanism is designed. Of fundamental importance are indications on effective elasticity of demand, which will be low when there are legal restrictions making consumption compulsory; the rate of return on the whole professional career, with the data on annual earnings being of little consequence; and the design of mechanisms for taking decisions on price-fixing and entry controls. It is also important to determine to what extent the regulator is 'captured', whether there is sufficient separation between regulators and the regulated and whether citizens are correctly informed.[13] Finally, it is important to analyse entry mechanisms and the costs of rent seeking, at both the entry and rent distribution stages.

2. Comparing Organisational Possibilities

It is difficult to compare possible solutions because there are certain aspects about which little is known. Three main problems are: too narrow a focus on one of the dimensions of competition, with price fixing or freedom of entry often being considered the only relevant competitive variable; the invisibility of solutions that have not surfaced because they require technological innovations that are inaccessible within the current corporative structures; and the need to reach a certain equilibrium between the risks of regulatory capture and regulatory opportunism.

2.1 Emphasis on One Dimension of Competition

Many deregulating proposals do not attempt to understand the nature of the services and just focus on one of the variables that may be useful in institutional design—either the intensity of price competition or freedom of entry. A focus on price competition often disregards its implications for the nature of the service that can be produced in a specific institutional order and the concentration process that is often generated. Similarly, freeing entry under fixed prices (as sometimes occurs and has often been proposed for pharmacies) disregards substantial costs (such as those related to dissipation of rents used to keep marginal pharmacies open and thus fully cover a given territory).

However, legislators may change not only the intensity of competition but also its dimensions, as well as product definition and the degree of integration.

[13] For instance, when professionals act as tax collectors, information asymmetries often lead citizens to incorrectly value professionals' earnings.

Explicit consideration should be given to these possibilities in order to avoid the risk of adopting adventurous reforms which may have doubtful results and may end up in situations that are regulated in an even more deficient way.[14] Otherwise, the exclusion of external effects from the professional's task usually means that production or control has to be carried out by new regulations and regulators whose organisation is by no means totally efficient. The costs of these new regulations are usually underestimated, despite the tendency of deregulation measures to quickly end up as just a different way of regulating an economic sector.

2.2 Dynamic Analysis: the Relativity of Technological Determinants

The discussion so far has assumed a given technology and has analysed the influences it creates. But technology in any industry changes as a consequence of innovation. In this dynamic context, the technological restrictions analysed in the second section should be partially seen as the result and not only the cause of the competitive restrictions present in markets for professional services. It is no coincidence that typical restrictions in professional sectors remove incentives for innovation (Arruñada, 1992), in order to protect professionals' *quasi*-rents and to recover investments in human capital. These systems involve a certain cost in terms of slow, limited innovation.

This lack of innovation can be expected to vary greatly from activity to activity and the technological gap with the rest of the economy to widen as external innovation increases. There are clear signs that this may be a problem, with potential technology being applied slowly due to the organisation of some professional sectors. And this is applicable to both production and contractual technologies. In the case of medicine, for example, an increasing number of therapeutic and diagnostic techniques now require knowledge that is not strictly medical but doctors are still required for using them.

This is also true for contractual technologies because, as argued above, greater development of brands and commercial names makes it possible for free action in the market to resolve the problems of information asymmetry between the professional and the customer. The justification for competitive restrictions based on information asymmetry was clearer in the past, when the participants in commercial transactions were mostly individuals.[15] In many new sectors, the free market has now shown its capacity for resolving more serious information asymmetries than those existing in many sectors that

[14] On the mixed results of liberalisation efforts, see, for example, Evans, Laurila and Paserman (2004, 11–12).

[15] See, for similar conclusion, Stephen (2004), who emphasises how in many markets customers are repeat purchasers and public bodies.

were traditionally professional.[16] For example, compare the design, production and sale of automobiles and buildings.

Consequently, there seems to be a substantial degree of inertia in the assignation of competitive or corporate organisational patterns to different sectors depending on their situation in the past. In many cases, corporate patterns seem to be little more than a historical remnant for which there is little justification today. The cognitive problem in such cases, however, is complex. Although, ideally, public policy should apply reforms allowing for the evolution of corporate sectors in line with new possibilities for market operation which have opened up but are mostly unknown, such reforms run the risk of destroying the efficiency of the traditional system. The transition therefore becomes risky and may even cause a reaction towards new restraints on competition.

2.3 The Need for Balance between Regulatory Capture and Opportunism

In any of the organisational possibilities—from the regulation of private suppliers to management by civil servants—preserving the long-term incentives which are characteristic of professional services requires balancing two opposing dangers: opportunism by regulators (or managers) against professionals; and the capture of regulators by professionals.

a) Opportunism takes the form of imprudent or self-interested regulatory or managerial changes which, by bringing down prices, freeing entry, changing operating methods, skipping promotions, reducing salaries, forcing early retirement, and so on, may expropriate earnings above what is obtainable outside the profession or the firm (the '*quasi*-rents' which compensate for investments made in the past). The risk is especially great when there is poor knowledge about the nature of the *quasi*-rents, which are often seen, especially by the general public, as a surplus salary or pure rent when they might be a return on a prior investment in human capital. Furthermore, expropriation decisions can result from the short-sighted horizon of regulators and managers, inclining them to destroy the system of deferred payment, altering or introducing uncertainty into expectations of future remuneration and removing incentives for future investments, even when such a system is efficient.
b) There may also be capture of regulators and managers by professionals. This phenomenon may result in price rises or freezing of the supply with the resulting generation of rents or distribution amongst a smaller number

[16] I understand 'the market' here as an institutional reality, not as the neoclassical abstraction used in some economic analysis. In particular, controlling professionals in order to solve the problem of information asymmetry often requires creating a professional service firm.

of senior professionals. Wealth is thus transferred from customers and junior professionals to senior professionals, output falls, and possible candidates waste more resources in their attempts to enter the profession. It is difficult to find a perfect solution to these problems because, while the introduction of greater self-regulation protects professionals' investments, it causes a greater risk of regulatory capture. However, it is important to provide guarantees that deferred compensation will be received in the future. Note that professional firms display several features that act as safeguards when using systems of this type. For instance, the recipients of *quasi*-rents are also the main decision-makers, as the longest-serving professionals are often partners in their firms. In the public area, we should therefore learn to consider this positive aspect of self-regulation, accepting some degree of regulatory capture to safeguard specific investments in human capital.

3. International Comparisons

A final word of caution is in order regarding the use of international comparisons, because of the interconnections between services provided by professionals and other institutions in the public sector.[17] Professionals in different countries may be providing different services which require different organisational structures—that is, different competitive restraints.[18] Evidence on differential regulation would therefore support a private interest explanation only if such differences in regulation are shown to be inconsistent with the different services being provided. Sections V and VI below analyse the cases of pharmacies and conveyancers.

V. Pharmacies

Like many other human activities, health care has undergone gradual specialisation. A single individual, who often also acted as priest, once cared for the sick. Over the centuries, a range of specialists grew up—doctors, pharmacists, producers of medicines, nurses. Pharmaceutical service underwent two

[17] This problem plagues the ambitious 'law and finance' research program and its related initiatives, such as the World Bank's *Doing Business* (2004). See Arruñada and Andonova (2004, 239–246) for a detailed critical analysis.

[18] These interconnections limit the value of arguments based on the differential constraints imposed on the same professions across a given set of countries, as in Monti (2003), and Paterson, Fink and Ogus (2003).

basic transformations. The first, when medical care was separated from the production of medicines, took place in ancient Egypt but the second, when the production of medicines was separated from distribution, only took place after the First World War.[19]

This historical sequence suggests that the survival of a profession devoted to dispensing might well be an anomaly. Perhaps what was regulated at the time was not so much the activity of distribution as that of production by pharmacies. Yet medicines are no longer produced by hand in pharmacies but industrially in factories and laboratories, in processes that are also subject to substantial regulation. Medicines on sale also need to be safe and effective, but the role of pharmacies is now insignificant in this area as they only prepare a small number of prescribed formulae. For most medicines, control is achieved by industrial production, with the incentives provided by manufacturers' reputations, and regulation which includes the authorisation of new medicines.

All the same, in most developed countries, pharmacies have retained a professional status, with entry barriers and organisational controls that depart substantially from a free market regime. Justification of this professional status is usually based on three types of objective: (1) use of the right medicines in each individual case; (2) availability of the necessary medicines; (3) gatekeeping, either in the control of certain drugs or, more recently, some type of economic optimisation. With the exception of use, the other objectives are associated to externalities. Let us briefly examine these objectives to see to what extent they are justified in today's economy.

1. Services

1.1 Health Advice

In their traditional form, pharmacies have always supplied customers with a wide range of information, including the diagnosis of minor complaints that can be treated with over-the-counter medicines, and advice on the proper dosage and use of medicines. Obviously, the quality of these information services is of vital importance and users find it difficult to evaluate such quality. Furthermore, it is widely believed that the increasing strength, variety and cost of medicines has made proper selection and control more important.

However, it is unclear whether the dual control of prescriptions by both doctors and pharmacies is really efficient and, if not, who should carry out

[19] For more detail on the arguments developed in this section, see Arruñada (2001).

this control. Furthermore, even if this doubt were resolved in favour of pharmacists, it would still be necessary to determine what type of pharmacy would be required to provide such advisory services and how they should be provided. It is possible that pharmacies as we know them today are no longer necessary and that the production of information should be carried out separately from the physical distribution of medicines. This debate on the design of pharmacies links up with the possibilities of providing pharmaceutical services via the Internet, which would dilute the importance of the economies of scope that perhaps still exist amongst the logistical and advisory functions of conventional 'brick and mortar' pharmacies.

In addition, health care experts insist that modern pharmacies should have more human and physical resources than is often the case. Examples of such resources are the constant presence of at least one qualified pharmacist, users' clinical data bases integrated with those of the rest of the health system, and enough space to guarantee confidentiality for users. In many European countries, traditional pharmacies find it difficult to meet these requirements because regulations impede them from reaching economies of scale.

1.2 Availability

Most countries have given priority to nationwide provision of pharmaceutical services. They have therefore regulated the opening of new pharmacies and have manipulated prices and margins in order to guarantee profitability for even the most remote pharmacies and therefore their survival. This has led to serious imbalances because there has been no adaptation to changes in demand and in technology caused by urbanisation and new means of transportation.

As a result of such changes and of the difficulties of regulation, in most of Europe pharmacies are often too small and their density is excessive. Furthermore, this fragmentation of pharmacies disregards the fact that the lower costs of public transport have drastically altered the size of the relevant markets. If it is efficient for many rural users to travel 40 or 60 km to receive primary health care, it is difficult to understand why the organisation and the cost of a pharmaceutical distribution system should be manipulated so that the same rural (and, increasingly, old town) consumers have access to a pharmacy near their home.

The way in which distribution is carried out for unregulated and widely consumed products provides a useful empirical comparison, of special interest for showing the opportunities which are missed by the current system. All over Europe, small towns are visited—on at least a weekly basis—by distributors of fruit, meat, frozen goods, fresh bread and other foods who, having invested in suitable vehicles, make a living from running such mobile shops. Such travelling services would not be sufficient to meet urgent needs but would at least meet the demand of those towns which today have no pharmaceutical service at all, let alone an emergency service. Territorial coverage, if necessary, could therefore be achieved by using a number of methods, such as mobile sales points, mail orders, the Internet and setting up dispensaries, and not necessarily by keeping small pharmacies open. Such methods would serve not only rural users but all people who are unable to travel, and would so without sacrificing any possible gatekeeping.

Physical pharmaceutical distribution is a necessary condition for obtaining access to medicines. It is therefore logical for such distributors to carry out certain public gatekeeping functions to ensure that access complies with the law. In particular, pharmacies have traditionally been assigned the task of controlling access to dual-purpose substances, such as narcotics and stimulants, which can be used not only as medicines but also for other purposes that are considered improper.

In a similar way, pharmacies can be used to contain the moral hazard inherent in controlling pharmaceutical expenditure by carrying out financial control of prescriptions, either by dispensing substitutes for costly prescriptions or forcing doctors to prescribe generics. The aim is that only the drugs that are necessary should be consumed for each complaint, avoiding the tendency to consume unnecessarily costly medicines, especially when a third party pays the bill, or ones that might generate negative externalities, such as the use of antibiotics that are too powerful.

2. Policy

This analysis of the nature and evolution of pharmaceutical retailing leads to the conclude that there are two relevant aspects—private and public. With private services, the essential element is the substitution that has taken place throughout the 20th century regarding quality guarantees. Professional safeguarding of quality has become less important with the development of industrial drugs and wider access to medical prescription.

With regard to public services, modern methods of communication have made the need for physical presence unnecessary in achieving territorial coverage.

The current structure of the sector is, therefore, defective in many European countries because it still aims to avoid private information asymmetries and to guarantee territorial coverage, leading to inefficient fragmentation. If there is any justification for restricting competition, it should be based on the objective of achieving public services associated with the sequential control of health activity, especially from an economic point of view.

To avoid the inefficiencies seen in the sector today and to promote the public service objectives, it would be necessary to renovate the regulations, which should aim to promote larger pharmacies and allow the use of distance-service technologies, both by mail and online. With respect to control and gatekeeping functions, there is no apparent reason why the control exerted by a distance or online pharmacy should be less effective than that performed by a conventional pharmacy. On the one hand, the larger size of the former makes them easier to supervise and gives them a greater incentive to comply with the law. On the other hand, control of both the doctor giving the prescription and the purchaser could be more effective than in conventional pharmacies in which, for example, purchases are often made on behalf of the patient. In addition, computerisation of prescriptions would reduce the current risk of forgeries.

A case in point is that of the European policy on online pharmacies.[20] The European Commission and most governments declare that they are committed to promoting innovation in this field but they do not adopt effective measures. On the contrary, concern over consumer safety is used as the argument against liberalisation of online sales of medicines. Meanwhile, sales by rogue sites keep increasing, given the difficulties for effective enforcement. The end result is that prohibition hinders the existence of reliable online operations and not only protects conventional pharmacies but also, indirectly, rogue sites, as an increasing number of customers use them to buy legal medicines that could be provided by reliable online operators. A report on competitiveness commissioned by the European Commission concluded that 'the diffusion of cost-effective ways of dispensing drugs could be encouraged, relying on mail-order pharmacies and on the potential gains in productivity that are associated with the new Information and Communication Technologies' (Gambardella, Orsenigo and Pammolli, 2000, 61). The sector is almost undeveloped in Europe, however, because only three countries (Denmark, Netherlands and the UK) allow distance selling of medicines. Furthermore, the pioneer online pharmacies established in these countries are in theory allowed to sell to buyers from other countries of the EU by the e-commerce directive (Bordoni, 2001, 2). National authorities are increasingly constraining such practice, however, as shown by the DocMorris.com case (Zwick, 2001).[21] Meanwhile, the EU is busy devising grand plans and implementing costly infrastructures of doubtful value, such as the 'eEurope An Information Society for All' initiative (European Commission, 1999, 14; 2001). In summary, it seems that European governments are striving to facilitate e-commerce by all means except, in the case of e-pharmacy, for removing the regulatory constraints that make it still impossible in most of the EU.

---

20 See on this Arruñada (2004).

21 The case has been ruled in favour of Doc. Morris by the European Court of Justice in its judgment of 11 December 2003 (Case C–322/01 *Deutscher Apothekerverband eV v 0800 DocMorris NV and Jacques Waterval* [2003] ECR I–14887). As a consequence, national law may not prohibit mail-order sales of to non-prescription drugs.

VI. Conveyancers

Intervention by various kinds of lawyers is legally required to contract real estate in many countries. In other cases, including 16 states in the USA, there is no such legal requirement but lawyers are the only professionals allowed to help in writing such contracts. Notaries public enjoy similar monopoly all over Europe, with the exceptions of Ireland, the UK and Scandinavia but including former Socialist countries, as well as in Latin America. Their position is grounded on the legal requirement of notarisation to file all sorts of documents in public registers and is protected by a full set of restrictions, including a closed number of notaries, fixed prices and prohibitions on advertising and organisation of notary offices.

Various international initiatives have recently argued that mandatory intervention by civil law notaries is inefficient. In its *Doing Business 2004*, the World Bank suggested that notaries are the main culprits for the greater cost and longer duration of company incorporations in civil law countries (World Bank, 2004, 26–27). Together with pharmacies, notaries figured prominently as the most regulated profession in the study commissioned by the European Union Competition DG on the liberalisation of professions (Monti, 2003, 2; Paterson, Fink and Ogus, 2003, 51–57).

Both initiatives made a good case but also forgot two key points. By focusing on notaries, the *Doing Business* report disregards the fact that a similar argument can be made about lawyers when their intervention is still *de jure* or *de facto* mandatory. By paying insufficient attention to the nature of the service in question, the EU risks advancing costly reforms that might perpetuate many of the current inefficiencies, as shown by the mixed results of liberalisation efforts. For instance, the Netherlands liberalised most notaries' prices since 1999 and allowed some freedom of entry by notaries into each other's reserved markets, but results have been poor (Kuijpers, Noailly and Vollaard, 2005; and Nahuim and Noailly, 2005).

Instead of partial liberalisations of dubious effects, what is needed is to adapt public policy to current circumstances. The starting point is to evaluate under which titling systems and for which transactions mandatory intervention by notaries and other lawyers is still necessary.

The demand for conveyance services has changed substantially with the development of land titling systems and the radical transformations that have taken place in the parties, technology and transactions of the conveyance market. Such changes in both institutions and markets have made intervention by law professionals less necessary, especially in standard residential transactions. Let us briefly explain why.[22]

[22] This is based on Arruñada (2003).

At the institutional level, states have developed titling systems which effectively make property contracts or property rights public, reducing the threat that hidden property rights previously posed to acquirers. This destroyed most of the demand for those conveyance services that, to some extent, provided a substitutive service, avoiding title conflicts, designing title guarantees and acting as title depositories. Public titling systems made these services unnecessary with respect to rights held by third parties. The recording of deeds made lawyers and notaries redundant as depositories of deeds and reduced their demand for designing title guarantees. And registration of rights fundamentally modifies their role in gathering the consent of affected third parties, given that under registration courts adjudicial rights by applying a rule of liability (Arruñada, 2003), parties tend to encourage conveyancers and title examiners to disguising before the register instead of preventing such title conflicts, a change that further reduces the former gatekeeping function of these professionals. More recently, information technologies are competing with notaries as document authenticators.

At the market level, the emergence of large firms in mortgage lending, real estate development and mediation of property transactions has reduced the comparative advantage of conveyancers because such firms are in a good position to guarantee quality to their customers and to reach economies of scale and lower costs in the preparation of contracts. A similar consequence has resulted from changes in the nature of transactions, which have become more standardised with the development of mass markets and mandatory legislation, both of which reduce the demand for tailoring contracts to individual needs.

In sum, public titling systems have made qualified conveyancers less useful with respect to rights held by third parties. At the same time, large, reputable parties and standardised transactions have made such professional conveyance less necessary and effective for protecting parties to private contracts as against each other. Mandatory intervention by law professional should therefore be abolished where still in force, especially for standard contracts. Alternative procedures for entering individual contracts and other standard documents in land and company registers should be established. These should include steps for checking parties' identities and capacities more effectively and should cover the use of electronic documents. The State may also play a greater role in drawing up standard-form default contracts for real estate conveyance, mortgage loans and company registration.

Recent reforms and trends are moving in this direction, with lawyers being used only in transactions in which they are really needed. In most of the US, lawyers do not intervene in most residential transactions and mortgages, and title companies, through lay employees, search the title, prepare the documents and close the transaction. These tasks have also been performed in England by licensed conveyancers since 1986. The fact that the US uses the recording of deeds and England the registration of rights suggests that these changes are viable under both systems of public titling.

VII. Conclusion

Professional services are characterised by information asymmetries, economies of scope and externalities. To resolve conflicts of interest, they require special organisational formulas, based on deferred and variable compensation, self-selection and, when positive externalities are necessary, competitive restraints. In principle, a set of criteria and organisational design patterns could be used for assessing, managing and regulating all types of professional organisation, whether public or private, competitive or monopolistic. Competitive restraints, however, entail substantial risks, one of the main ones being that they tend to outlast their useful life. This point has been illustrated here by examining pharmacists and conveyancers, two professions for which the existing restraints may today be dysfunctional to the extent that the services that might have made such restraints necessary are now in fact provided by other public and private agents. Greater liberalisation is therefore advisable, especially for standard services, and not only from a public service perspective but also from the private interest perspective of the professions themselves. If my argument is correct, liberalization would encourage professionals to quit providing trivial services and focus on those which make efficient use of professionals knowledge and add greater value to users, which nowadays seems to be the only strategy in a dynamic society.

II

Dr Amelia Fletcher[1]

The Liberal Professions—Getting the Regulatory Balance Right[2]

I. Introduction

Regulation within the professions can take many forms. There has traditionally been a strong focus on *ex ante* self-regulation, whereby the profession itself sets prescriptive rules as to who can act in the market, what activities they can engage in and how they should carry out these activities.

Ex ante self-regulation has some clear advantages, but the incentives of self-regulatory organisations (SROs) can also diverge from those of consumers, with resulting detrimental implications for competition. This paper explores whether there may be a case for changing the regulatory balance for the liberal professions, putting less emphasis on *ex ante* regulation and more on *ex post* regulation and on external regulation. Under *ex post* regulation, incentives for good behaviour are created by the threat of punishment for professionals who breach professional rules or service commitments. An enhanced role for external regulation can alter the incentives of an SRO such that they are better aligned with those of consumers.

The paper argues that, with careful design, an increased role for these alternative forms of regulation has the potential to improve the effectiveness of *ex ante* self-regulation whilst reducing the need for overly restrictive *ex ante* rules. This should have benefits for both competition and consumers. Competition between regulatory forms may also bring advantages. In addition, the paper argues that professional organisations should be wary of taking on a representative function, on behalf of the profession, alongside their self-regulatory function, since this can give rise to conflicting incentives. These functions are better carried out by separate organisations.

---

[1] Chief Economist, Office of Fair Trading. All views expressed are personal and are not necessarily the views of the OFT. This paper was co-written by Peter Lukacs. Comments were also gratefully received from Grahame Horgan and John Vickers.

[2] This is a topical issue in UK as the structure of regulation of legal services is the subject of a current review. As the OFT has already given its response to that review last week, and as the chairman of the review, Sir David Clementi, will talk later I do not plan to address that review directly, although the subject matter of this paper is clearly relevant to parts of the review. See 'Consultation on the future regulatory framework for legal services in England and Wales: Response from the Office of Fair Trading', June 2004, available at http://www.oft.gov.uk.

II. The Different Functions of Self-Regulatory Organisations

It is useful to distinguish two types of self-regulation that may be carried out by professional organisations: *ex ante* and *ex post* regulation.

Ex ante regulation involves the prescription of rules that govern the members of a profession. These are the 'who, what and how issues' such as entry restrictions, behavioural restrictions, demarcation restrictions and restrictions on organisational form. It is in this form of regulation where most of the competition concerns arise, as discussed below.

Ex post regulation involves the proactive monitoring of quality, handling of complaints, obtaining redress for consumers, punishing miscreants. Such regulation does not in itself usually raise substantial competition concerns.

In addition, many professional organisations act as a representative body, lobbying for the interests of members. This representative function is distinct from the regulatory function although it is often performed by the same body. For example in England and Wales the Bar Council decides upon the professional rules that barristers abide by, enforces those rules and also acts as the representative body for barristers.

This representative function may be likened to the role of a trade union, and when acting purely in its role as advocate for its members a professional organisation is unlikely to raise competition concerns. To argue the case for an interest group is a healthy part of democracy. It is when those private interests become enshrined in rules and regulations that problems may be created.

However, this representative role may raise concerns if carried out alongside the self-regulatory role. There would seem to be a real risk that the regulator's judgement might be swayed (or at least appear to be swayed) by putting the interest of members above those of consumers. Perhaps for this reason, doctors in Britain are represented, and represented highly effectively, by the British Medical Association (BMA) while they are regulated by and their performance is accountable to the General Medical Council (GMC).

III. The Pros and Cons of *Ex Ante* Self-Regulation

It is widely accepted that the characteristics of the liberal professions imply a greater need for regulation than for other kinds of occupations or types of business. Asymmetric information, which characterises many types of goods and services, is more severe because consumers are frequently not in a position to either assess what services they require or assess the quality of provision even after it has been provided. The professions often supply what are known as credence goods. The possibility of supplier induced demand[3] combined with the severity of losses to the consumer if problems arise[4] can certainly justify some eligibility criteria and conduct rules.

The core rationale for self-regulation is, at its most basic, that the profession as a whole has an incentive to ensure that quality of service is maintained. Whilst any one member of the profession might have an incentive to 'cheat' by supplying poor quality or over-providing service, or by offering a service he or she is not competent to carry out, it is clear that the reputation of the profession would in the end be harmed if all of its members were to behave in this way. As such, self-regulation can be seen as a solution to a 'free rider' problem. Each member of the profession would individually like to cheat, but if all members cheat, then they will all be worse off. The setting of professional rules will be in the interest of all members if it can prevent (or at least restrict) such cheating and ensure that consumers receive the service levels that they are paying for.[5]

1. *Ex Ante* Entry Restrictions

Ex ante regulation can take various forms. The most prevalent are entry restrictions based upon quality or training. These can act to raise service quality in at least three ways. Firstly, they can alleviate the risk of parties offering services they are not competent to carry out by ensuring that the professional's knowledge is appropriate to the services offered. Secondly, such restrictions can reduce the incentives to cheat by lowering the cost of providing good quality. A highly trained professional needs to put in less effort in order to do a good job, and thus the benefits of shirking are lower. Thirdly, they can reduce the incentives to cheat by raising the cost of being 'struck off'. When a substantial investment is required in order to gain entry to a profession, the returns to membership will be high, and thus the cost of losing membership will also be high.

However, entry rules can also restrict competition. Where such rules are set by a self-regulatory organisation, this body may have an incentive to set the

[3] Where a professional induces an uninformed consumer to demand more of a service than is necessary.

[4] For example, loss of liberty in case of legal error, or death or serious injury in case of medical or architectural error.

[5] In addition to this core rationale, other rationales for self-regulation include (i) the fact that an SRO will tend to be better informed about what is going on in its own industry than will an external regulator, (ii) the fact that self-regulatory codes can be more flexible and readily changed in response to changes in the industry than external regulation and (iii) the fact that external regulation itself has a variety of potential problems and costs associated with it, including the risk of regulatory capture.

entry hurdle higher than is strictly necessary to achieve the beneficial objectives described above, in order to create monopoly rents for its members. Alternatively, it might have an incentive to design the entry hurdle specifically to restrict competition. For example, in the Glasgow Solicitors' Property Centre case in 2003, the OFT intervened to prevent GSPC from operating membership criteria that were not objective and transparent in circumstances where there was a strong suspicion that vague criteria were being employed by GSPC to exclude a potential member who might compete 'too vigorously'.[6]

2. Demarcation Restrictions and Restrictions on Organisational Form

Demarcation restrictions and restrictions on organisational form are intended to act in a different way. Some demarcation restrictions can be justified on the same grounds as entry restrictions more generally. For example, the differing levels of training for dentists and dental hygienists can (to some extent) explain the different functions they are allowed to carry out. However, a second rationale for demarcation restrictions[7] and restrictions on organisational form is that if professionals are allowed to engage in different types of activity, or combine in business with those who do, a conflict of interest can arise which could compromise their judgement. As such these restrictions are again an *ex ante* method of dealing with an *ex post* problem. In order to prevent the moral hazard problems of supplier induced demand or poor quality advice the professional's hands are tied in advance.

This second rationale is not entirely convincing. Without wishing to cast aspersions on any professional group, it seems possible that even a professional successfully closeted away in his or her narrow professional confine, and untainted by vile external commercial pressures, might have a private interest that differs from his or her client.

Indeed, the creation of larger corporate entities could arguably even reduce the incentives to provide poor quality service or induce unnecessary demand. For example, a professional working in a large firm will receive only a share of the profits (if anything) from any extra demand he or she induces from the client, whereas a professional working as an individual receives the full benefit of induced demand and thus presumably has raised incentives to engage in such behaviour. Likewise, one of the most common market-based methods of solving asymmetric information issues is the creation of a reputation. This is

[6] See: http://www.oft.gov.uk/news/press+releases/2003/pn154-03.htm

[7] Such as the Bar Council rule that Barristers at the independent bar cannot conduct litigation, despite the fact that they have easily undergone sufficient training to do so.

arguably easier for a corporate body than for an individual and once a corporate reputation has been established, the business will have a strong incentive to control the behaviour of its staff such that this reputation is not tarnished.

These restrictions can also damage competition, and in particular the development of new forms of competition. For example, in its 2003 study of private dentistry in the UK,[8] the OFT found that, while it was appropriate to have some demarcation restrictions between dentists and other 'professions complementary to dentistry' (or PCDs),[9] it was inappropriate that PCDs should be prevented from selling their services directly to the consumer. The OFT also challenged restrictions on corporate form that limited any dentistry business to engage only in dentistry (or ancillary business) and to have a majority of directors that are registered dentists. These restrictions were viewed as limiting the range and type of businesses which can enter the market, to the detriment of consumers.

IV. The Balance between *Ex Ante* and *Ex Post* Regulation

As described above, *ex ante* self-regulation is primarily designed to ameliorate the incentives that members might otherwise have to offer poor quality service or induce unnecessary demand. However, the mechanisms by which these various *ex ante* restrictions achieve this are both indirect and have detrimental implications for competition.

Is there an argument, then, for reviewing the role played by *ex post* regulation within the liberal professions? Under *ex post* regulation, incentives for good behaviour are created by the threat of *ex post* punishment for professionals who are found to have breached professional rules or service commitments. Arguably, SROs have been in the past long on *ex ante* regulation and short on *ex post* regulation. If this balance could be shifted, then there may be an opportunity for gains to competition, due to a relaxation of restrictive *ex ante* rules, alongside a regulation system that is more directly targeted at the incentive problems that the SRO aims to overcome.

Three elements are required for effective *ex post* self-regulation. First, the SRO must set out explicit rules of conduct and service commitments, which its members are expected to adhere to. Second, there needs to be some form of monitoring regime, such that breaches of these rules and commitments may be observed. Third, a punishment regime for breaches is required. Each of these elements needs to be designed with care, as described below.

---

8 See http://www.oft.gov.uk/Business/Market+studies/dentistry.htm

9 These comprise dental hygienists, dental therapists and dental technicians.

1. Rules of Conduct and Service Commitments

In designing rules of conduct and service commitments, the most important element will be ensuring that non-compliance with these rules and commitments is both observable and verifiable. Otherwise, it will not be possible to impose punishments for non-compliance.

As for *ex ante* regulation, there is a risk that an SRO will have an incentive to increase their service commitments to a higher level than consumers want, in order to restrict output and increase its members profits. One benefit of *ex post* regulation, however, is that it may be easier to tell whether such rules are proportionate. For example, it is difficult to assess whether hospital consultants really need a total of 12 years of training (as they currently receive in the UK) before they should be fully qualified. It may be easier to determine whether the quality standards set for particular medical procedures in a hospital are reasonable.

Nevertheless, the fact that there remains an incentive for setting standards too high provides a rationale for further complementing such regulation with an increased role for external regulation, and possibly greater competition between regulatory systems, as discussed further below.

2. Monitoring Regime

If *ex post* regulation is to work effectively, the quality of members needs to be monitored in some way to ensure that rules and commitments are adhered to.

One method for carrying out such monitoring is to rely on complaints from consumers. Including a redress mechanism within the regulatory regime may be a good way of achieving this. If consumers can gain recompense for any damages they incur as a result of poor quality service, this should give them an incentive to complain about such behaviour. Such a redress mechanism would have a further benefit to the profession to the extent that such protection gives consumers more confidence in purchasing its services.

It could be argued that formal complaints and redress procedures are unnecessary when consumers have the right to undertake litigation against a professional. However litigation has weaknesses as a mechanism for gaining redress, and consequently also as a mechanism for monitoring service quality. Firstly, litigation is only possible where laws have been infringed. Thus litigation will only work to promote service quality where either these service commitments are embodied in law or they are specified within the contract between the professional and the customer. Secondly, the risks and costs of the legal process can lead to insufficient litigation occurring to provide an effective monitoring mechanism.[10] This tendency for insufficient litigation to occur is exacerbated by the fact that it can confer positive externalities. Other potential victims of the miscreant can benefit from the litigation but do not incur the costs.

For this reason, a formal complaints procedure may be a useful element of *ex post* self-regulation. One difficulty with relying on complaints, however, is that consumers are not always able to tell whether they have received poor quality service, or it may be hard to prove this in any individual case. For example, in many markets the outcome of a professional's work will be dependent not only on the service provided by that professional but also on a variety of other factors, both observable and unobservable.

In such cases, more sophisticated performance measures may be needed for whether a professional is meeting his or her service commitments than relying on any individual case. For example, the fact that one old lady dies following a visit to her family doctor is unlikely to justify disciplinary procedures against the doctor. The fact that 200 old ladies died following visits to Harold Shipman, a family doctor in England, should have raised alarm bells rather sooner than it did, and would probably have done so had patient mortality rates been monitored on a more formalised basis.

In designing such performance measures, however, it is important to guard against providing adverse incentives for practitioners, and in particular the risk that they might make practitioners overly risk averse in terms of their willingness to take on 'difficult' cases. For example, in the US, post-operative mortality rates for surgeons are now published. The result: surgeons can be unwilling to take on 'difficult' patients.[11]

Such problems do not mean that performance measures of this sort are impossible, but it does mean that they need to be carefully designed. SROs may be well-advised not to publish them, and also need to ensure that they do not place more weight on them than they deserve. Nevertheless, such measures may be useful even if they are not primarily used to prove malpractice, but rather to identify members that may warrant further investigation.

---

[10] The risk of 'false negatives' (ie, where professionals are wrongly cleared of breaches) can act as a strong disincentive to litigation, even for customers with genuine grievances. Even with 'no win, no fee', the customer may have to pay the legal costs of the professional if the litigation fails.

[11] This is an example of a more general problem, the problem of generating 'false positives' (ie, where professionals are wrongly found guilty of breach). Following the 'Rodney King' incident in Los Angeles, the LAPD put in far stronger punitive measures to combat poor behaviour on the part of its police. The result: its police stayed clear of 'difficult' areas, to avoid the risk of being found guilty even where trying to perform properly. Crime rates in these areas soared. See C Prendergast, 'Selection and Oversight in the Public Sector, with the Los Angeles Police Department as an Example', February 2002.

3. Punishment Regime for Breaches

If *ex post* self-regulation is to be effective, the punishment regime needs to be carefully designed to ensure that SRO members have an incentive to behave in accordance with the SRO's rules of conduct and service commitments. In designing such a regime, it is necessary to calculate not only the benefits that a professional can derive from a breach (in terms of extra profits or an easier life) but also the proportion of breaches that are likely to come to notice of SRO.

Ideally, punishments would vary according to the severity of the breach and the likelihood of being caught. Punishments might range, for example, from criminal procedures or being 'struck off', at one end of the scale, to being 'disqualified from directorship' or 'name and shame' procedures, at the other end, with a full range of monetary punishments available between these extremes.

It is important to note that the appropriate level of redress in any one case—which compensates the consumer for his or her damages—is unlikely to provide an appropriate punishment for the misconduct, since only a proportion of customers are ever likely to make claims under redress procedures. In certain legal systems, class actions and triple damages are designed to overcome this problem to some extent, but they necessarily work in an *ad hoc* way (and also have other problems associated with them). A benefit of self-regulation is that it can design punishment regimes specifically to achieve the incentivisation required for its members.

If appropriate incentives are to be provided, the SRO also needs to consider the extent to which punishments should relate to businesses and the extent to which they should relate to the individuals actually engaged in the breach. If the onus is placed upon the individual, then managers may put employees under pressure to engage in misconduct, but then escape responsibility themselves.[12] On the other hand, if the onus is placed on the business, it may be possible for bad practitioners simply to dissolve one business and start a new one. A mixed approach might therefore be best.

One possible problem with an SRO designing its own punishment regime is that it may not have the right incentive to set appropriate levels of punishment or redress. Clearly where there are public examples of misconduct the need to safeguard the reputation of the profession requires that punishment of offenders is seen to be appropriate. However, if one considers a professional organisation as a form of 'club', it is equally clear that there may be an

---

[12] Such behaviour can in turn be used as a justification for restrictions on corporate form. If regulation relates to individuals, rather than businesses, then (it is argued) professionals need to be managed by other members of the same profession, so that they are all covered by the same code. This argument would seem to collapse if regulation relates to businesses as well as individuals.

incentive to be lenient with 'old boy' members if possible. By contrast there may be an incentive to be harsh on those mavericks, the Mr Wouters of this world, who threaten internal stability.[13]

This may justify the use of independent directors in monitoring and regulating any codes of conduct or service commitments. For example, in the UK there is a voluntary self regulatory Banking Code. Independent directors are in a majority overlooking the Code. Likewise, under the UK 'Consumer Codes Approval Scheme', whereby the OFT will place its stamp of approval on industry codes which meet certain criteria, a key condition is that 'Code sponsors shall have independent disciplinary procedures available to deal effectively with cases of non-compliance'.

As part of this, the OFT expects there to be at least 50% independent representation on any board or committee that deals with disciplinary procedures.[14]

V. The Balance between External Regulation and Self-Regulation

With appropriate design, *ex post* self-regulation can thus be a useful complement to *ex ante* self-regulation and should facilitate the removal of some of the more detrimental restrictions imposed by *ex ante* self-regulation. However, there remains a risk that a self-regulator—whose primary interest is in serving its members—may not always act in the best interests of consumers. In many situations, this problem could potentially be reduced by enhancing the role played by external regulation.

The pros and cons of external regulation versus self-regulation have been much discussed. The key pros of external regulation include independence and a focus on the public interest. The key cons include a lack of understanding about the market, inflexibility, cost and inefficiency, regulatory capture, and the need to avoid political interference/capture. Here, however, I am not advocating the substitution of one form of regulation for another, but rather a 'mixed' regulatory approach, which draws on the benefits that both self-regulation and external regulation can bring.

---

[13] Or the French Notaire who is being threatened with exclusion by his professional body for the heinous offence of providing advice 'en dehors de son cabinet' (ie, at the premises of the client rather than at his own premises). This case has been referred back to the regional court by the French Cour D'Appel on procedural grounds, and is likely to make its way back to the Cour D'Appel before it is resolved.

[14] See OFT, *Consumer Codes Approval Scheme: Core Criteria and Guidance* (2004), available at at http://www.oft.gov.uk/business/codes. Codes approved under this scheme are free to advertise themselves as such.

An increased role for external regulation can take a variety of forms. One useful approach may be to use the threat of external regulation to condition the behaviour of a self-regulatory body. This will work well only if the threat is a credible one. Arguably, a good example where the threat of external regulation is both credible and works passably well at constraining self-regulation is the UK Press Complaints Commission, which regulates the behaviour of the UK press.

A second approach might be for an external regulator (or legislator) to stipulate rules relating to how a self-regulatory body must function, but without itself becoming involved in the determination of rules of entry and conduct. The framework criteria set out under the OFT's 'Consumer Codes Approval Scheme' are again good example of this. In the specific area of the legal profession, the Courts and Legal Services Act (1990) requires consideration of the competition implications of amendments to rules of the Law Society or Bar Council, via advice from the OFT.[15] One of Sir David Clementi's suggested models for the UK legal profession, as set out in his consultation paper, proposes developing this role for external regulation, while leaving the core regulatory function within the professions.[16]

As discussed above, one especially useful area where external legislation could play a role is in regulating the composition of self-regulatory boards to include both insiders who can provide expertise and outsiders who can provide an independent view. Such outsiders can also confer legitimacy in the eyes of the general public who may otherwise see the decisions of a SRO as self serving.

A third approach may be for external legislation to actually stipulate the rules of conduct that members of an SRO must follow, even though the SRO then takes the primary role in ensuring compliance with these rules. This approach may also require that an external body has parallel powers, if the SRO is to carry out its own function effectively. An example of this regulatory model within the UK relates to legislation on misleading advertising. The Control of Misleading Advertising Regulations (1988) are primarily enforced by a self-regulator, the Advertising Standards Authority. However, the OFT has a role (together with local trading standards departments) in also enforcing breaches of regulations on misleading advertising, where the ASA is unable to get appropriate assurances from non-compliant members.

---

[15] While this is a welcome form of oversight, it has a weakness that it is restricted to the examination of new proposals brought forward and does not enable proactive consideration of existing rules.

[16] See the draft *Review of the Regulatory Framework For Legal Services In England And Wales: A Consultation Paper*, as presented by Sir David Clementi at this Workshop. His 'Model B+' involves leaving much of the regulatory function within professional bodies, while giving oversight function to a new 'Legal Services Board'.

VI. Competition Between Forms of Regulation

A final approach to enhancing the role of external regulation may be for external regulation and self-regulation to work alongside each other, but with slightly different emphases, such that there is a degree of competition between them. One option here is to use legislation to set absolute minimum standards, which avoid the worst problems associated with the industry (for example, fraudulent activities or activities that threaten health and safety). The role of an SRO would then be to set higher standards for its members above this statutory minimum.

This approach to dual regulation can be effective where different consumers with different needs may value the resulting choice between 'cheap and cheerful' non-SRO members and paying a premium for the higher quality SRO members. The competition between the regulatory forms may also limit the incentives of the SRO to behave anti-competitively, not least because such an approach would clearly require that membership of the SRO was not compulsory in order to function in the market.

Under such a framework, it should also be possible to allow for the existence of multiple SROs. In principle, competition between SROs should further limit the incentives of any one SRO to act anti-competitively by setting over-restrictive membership rules, but rather increase the incentives of SROs to act efficiently to ensure that members offer consumers what they want.

Such a framework might also encourage the development of market-based mechanisms for overcoming some of the quality problems that arise within the liberal professions. For example, the use of referrals might potentially allow an experienced and sophisticated customer of a profession[17] to provide useful direction for less experienced customers about where to go for good service. So long as the experienced customer has a reputational incentive to provide good direction, the use of referrals may to some extent overcome the asymmetric information problem between professional and consumers.

'Mixed' forms of regulation of this sort again need to be designed with care. Potential disadvantages of competition between regulators include the duplication of resources involved with creating a competing regulator and the fact that consumers may find multiple competing standards of quality confusing. If this means that consumers are unable to evaluate the merits of the respective regulators, then such confusion would in turn damage the incentives of the SROs to provide what consumers want.

Nonetheless, it would seem appropriate to experiment further with such mixed regulation, given the aim of reducing the anti-competitive implications of self-regulation while gaining the benefits that self-regulation has to offer in the area of the liberal professions.

---

[17] For example a trade union, bank, or automobile association.

III

Marc Hameleers, Jeroen van den Heuvel Rijnders and Sander Baljé[1]

Towards a Smarter Protection of Public Interests in the Liberal Professions

I. Introduction

The Dutch economy currently recovers slowly from the sharpest downturn in its economic cycle since the early 1980s. A matter of concern is that because of an underlying structural weakness the Netherlands is still not benefiting enough from the recovery in the global economy. The Dutch government has therefore drawn up an agenda for reform, entitled 'Choosing for growth: prosperity for now and later'. This agenda, which fully reflects the challenge of the Lisbon agenda, provides a perspective of a more favourable development of prosperity.[2] The main aim of the agenda is threefold: strengthening the competitive position, smarter working and activating people.[3] In order to strengthen the competitive position, the 'Choosing for growth' agenda devotes specific attention, as does the Lisbon agenda, on the liberal professions.

This focus on the liberal professions is not surprising when viewed from a number of angles of approach:

- Those in the liberal professions, such as notaries, lawyers and pharmacists, have traditionally played an important role in our society. Citizens come into contact with them on all kinds of generally important occasions: when buying a house, being involved in litigation before the courts or undergoing medical treatment. Citizens experience problems with the services of the liberal professions. Well-known problems are the lack of (price) competition within the notary and legal professions, a substandard quality of

[1] Marc Hameleers MPA, and SH Baljé are at the Competition Directorate of the Dutch Ministry of Economic Affairs—Marc Hameleers as manager, and Sander Baljé as senior policy advisors. Sander Baljé currently works at the Directorate for Economic Policy. Jeroem van den Rijnders currently works at the Energy Authority NMa/DTe. For questions or useful contributions to this subject, please contact to m.a.h.m.hameleers@minez.nl.

[2] Ministry of Economic Affairs and Ministry of Social Affairs and Employment (2004).

[3] In March 2000 the European Council of Ministers met in Lisbon to discuss welfare and social cohesion in Europe in the near future. The Council concluded that Europe had good economic prospects, but it felt that the EU needed to change direction to become a more knowledge-based economy. Against this background, the Lisbon Summit set itself the goal of making the European Union the world's most dynamic and competitive economic region by 2010.

accountants, insufficient insight into the quality of doctors and general practitioners, and an inadequate number of medical specialists.

- Liberal professions provide input for the restructuring of other industries. Companies on average spend 6% of their costs on services provided by the liberal professions. In some cases this can rise to as much as 9%.[4]
- There are still barriers obstructing the functioning of the (internal) market for professionals.[5] For example, the OECD concluded in the *2004 Economic Survey* that a number of restrictive rules and barriers of entry still maintain in the liberal professions.[6] The consequences of these barriers are that individual consumers and entrepreneurs are both literally and metaphorically paying the price for the sub-optimal operation of such markets.

The central aim of this paper is to discuss how public interests in the liberal professions can be protected more intelligently so that the ambitions set out in 'Choosing for growth' can be fulfilled. Part II discusses—from an economic perspective—which public interests can play a role in the services of the liberal professions. In chapter III, a link is made between these potential public interests and the structure of the regulatory model, focusing particular attention on the crucial role played by consumers in achieving the benefits of smarter regulation. Parts II and III elaborate on the policy framework developed by the Ministry of Economic Affairs that policy advisors can use in their search for an ideal form of regulation of the liberal professions. The proper protecting of public interests also means proper implementation management. Part IV sets out a number of lessons for successful implementation. Part V ends with a number of conclusions and with an overall presentation of the policy framework.

II. Public Interests in an Economic Perspective

1. The Concept of Public Interests

Public interests are involved if the government takes upon itself to protect *social* interests in the belief that these interests will otherwise not properly be protected. Public interests are therefore a sub-collection of social interests.[7]

---

[4] Monti (2003b, 3).

[5] Commercial services represent 70% of EU GDP but only 20% in terms of cross border trade (Monti, 2003a). Approximately one-third of the employment and added value by the commercial services can be attributed to the liberal professions (European Commission, 2003).

[6] OECD (2004).

[7] WRR (2000) and Teulings, Bovenberg and van Dalen (2003). An English manual of the second report is available: KCOV (2004).

The starting point is an economic analysis of (trans)actions on a market without government intervention. Public interests are at stake when transactions between market players or the actions of one market player do not take into account the consequences for other stakeholders who are not involved in that transaction or action. In other words: this is a case of free rider behaviour. As a consequence, private interests served by that (trans)action do not coincide with social interests (eg, complex external effects).[8] In this case, the transaction mechanism does not function well ('missing market').[9] Then, the government can use statutory or other measures to compel stakeholders to compensate third parties for possible negative external effects. The purpose of this is efficiency. The comparative advantage to the government compared to the market is obvious: as the only party, the government can use public compulsion to force all interested parties to participate.

Efficiency, incidentally, is not the only reason for the government to intervene. Realising a politically acceptable distribution of income is also a public interest. Redistribution is not achieved without public compulsion. The individual interests of people of society, with for example high illness risks or low incomes, outweigh the interests of society as a whole.

The use of compulsion also comes with (substantial) transaction costs. Ultimately the value of the public interest must be weighed up against the transaction costs of political intervention.[10]

2. Public Interests in Relation to Liberal Professions

This line of thinking can easily be transposed to (trans)actions in markets where services offered by liberal professions play a role, so that it's possible to identify the specific public interests at stake. The starting point is a situation whereby no specific regulatory framework exists concerning the liberal professions. When consumers call in a liberal professional, they frequently have problems assessing the quality of the services on offer, not only just before paying for the services but often afterwards as well. Professionals usually have access to more information than their customers. As a result, consumers tend to compare the cost, rather than the quality, of the services they are offered. This can reduce quality and can lead to a counterproductive selection (adverse selection) generating external effects.

---

8 Only a few parties are involved in simple external effects: these can be internalised by the parties themselves through negotiations. See Teulings, Bovenberg and Van Dalen (2003).

9 Complex external effects and free rider behaviour arise from (1) economies of scale, which can result in market power; (2) asymmetric and incomplete information; (3) collective goods and externalities; and (4) fundamental insecurity. See Teulings, Bovenberg and Van Dalen (2003).

10 Useful and detailed contributions to this subject are Stephen (2004) and Dutch Ministry of Economic Affairs (2004b).

Transactions between consumers, without mediation by a liberal profession, could also result in those complex external effects. For example, it could lead to undesirable effects if a notary has not established ownership rights properly and the seller is not the lawful owner of a house. If a general practitioner uses an incorrect treatment, this has consequences not only for the patient, which is serious enough in itself, but also for employers and premium-paying citizens due to the greater burden placed on social security and the healthcare sector.

If such effects actually occur in a market, it may be desirable for the government to define a public interest focused on protecting sufficient quality. Minimum quality levels will therefore result in consumer trust affecting the economy positively. The 'quality of the service' public interest could encompass the expertise and independence of the professional, satisfactory complaints handling and the added value of the service for the customer and for society as a whole. In some cases the physical accessibility of the service (eg, accessibility in terms of time and location, and convenient opening hours) could also be elements of the 'quality of the service' public interest.

As already mentioned, in addition to public interests resulting from the poor functioning of markets (aim: to increase efficiency), government intervention could also be prompted by political conviction to bring about a more equitable distribution of income. In the liberal professions, this translates into the second category of public interest: *financial accessibility of the service*. Examples in the liberal professions include access to justice (legal aid) and maximum fees for the service offered by medical professionals.

Concluding, there are two categories of public interests at stake in the liberal professions, namely quality of the service and financial accessibility of the service.

3. Social Interests in Relation to Liberal Professions

Clearly, social interests may also be at stake with the liberal professions, without this constituting a public interest. A good example concerns the quality of Dutch real estate agents, which is indeed a social interest but which is not (not any longer) considered a public interest, as the Dutch government withdrew its involvement with real estate agents in 1999. The profession itself and countervailing powers such as the Association of Homeowners (*Vereniging Eigen Huis*) and the Dutch Consumers' Association (*Consumentenbond*) were considered perfectly capable of guaranteeing sufficient quality without government interference. In the words of Section II–1: complex external effects have been changed over time into simple external effects that have been internalised by the interested parties themselves. Incidentally, the nature and extent of the external effects that could play a role in the service provided by real estate agents also played a role when considering deregulation.

The stages described in this paper in order to define public interest are summarised in Box I below.

Box I: Policy Framework: Stages 1 and 2

Stage 1: Is there an indication for protection?

- Study the indicators which suggest the presence of market or regulatory failure.

A suspicion of the existence of market failure or regulatory failure has to be a starting point in determining whether to change the way a market is regulated. These suspicions can be based on complaints received from consumers, entrepreneurs or other professionals, on the results of legal evaluations or on other studies or reports in the media.

Stage 2: What is the nature and extent of the problem?

- Define the transaction (what service is being delivered?) and identify its specific characteristics.
- Analyse the supply and demand-sides of the market on which this transaction takes place.
- Identify what kind of market failure exists (or could occur) and the extent of it (eg, complex external effects and free riders).
- Define precisely what public interests are at stake.

See Box IV for stages 3 and 4 of the policy framework.

III. Protection of Public Interests in the Liberal Professions

After defining the public interests the next steps deal with protecting these public interests as intelligently as possible, which means as efficiently and effectively as possible. This concerns defining the exact role of the government and defining which instruments to use.

1. Pros and Cons of Regulatory Instruments

A range of regulatory instruments can be used in order to protect public interests.[11] The European Commission distinguishes between instruments that regulate market entry and market conduct.[12] In Table I public interests are

[11] This paragraph is based on Dutch Ministry of Economic Affairs (2004b, 83).

[12] Paterson, Fink and Ogus (2003).

related to regulatory instruments. This table shows at a glance which instrument is preferred for each public interest and which ones are best not applied.[13]

This table may create the impression that one or more regulatory instruments have to be used to protect each potential public interest, which could lead to an accumulation of laws and rules. This is not the intention. Preference should be given to the lightest possible role for the government.

In general, an efficient and effective protection of public interests will mainly be achieved by encouraging supply on a particular market (less market entry regulation). The 'lighter' the instrument, the more freedom will be given to both customers and professionals. In most cases, the better this will be for the realisation of efficient prices and quality and in the end for the protection of the *quality* and *financial accessibility* public interests.[14] 'Heavy' instruments such as capacity restraints, domain monopolies, advertising conditions or tariff regulations should therefore be used sparingly. However, substantial external effects or the quality of essential services (eg, surgery) could be arguments to impose those instruments.

Finally, it is crucial to present several alternatives for the desired protection of public interests. One has to bear in mind that there are transaction costs attached to government interventions. These costs can be higher than those attached to market failure and to those of non-competition. If quantitative cost-benefit analyses are difficult to make, policy makers still have the opportunity to analyse costs and benefits qualitatively.

Two examples illustrate how to use Table I.[15] First, let 'a satisfactory, fast and honest handling of complaints' be an example of the 'quality' public interest. For protecting this public interest, preference is given via a good professional practice, which could mean mandatory membership in an arbitration committee, a liability insurance or disciplinary procedures. A domain monopoly or other barriers limiting access to the market can work counterproductively, as they could lead to a closed shop.

Second, let 'financial accessible service for everybody' be a public interest. Preference is given to encouraging supply by reducing or removing entry barriers and by using as few regulatory instruments as possible. In addition, vouchers for a selected group of persons (for example: 'low income' households) could also be used if encouraging supply does not adequately protect the public interest. Tariff regulation is a stringent instrument and should therefore be used very sparingly.

---

[13] The quality of regulation will improve if policy makers use the OECD 'principles on high quality regulation' (OECD, 1999, 4).

[14] Fewer regulations do not by definition produce a lower quality of service (Paterson, Fink and Ogus, 2003).

[15] Dutch Ministry of Economic Affairs (2004a, 7).

*Table I: Public Interests and Regulatory Instruments**

		Expertise	Independence	Complaints Handling	Added value	Accessibility	Opening hours	Financial accessibility (micro)
Market conduct	Capacity restrictions			–		– –	– –	– –
	Conditions governing location			–		– –	+/–	– –
	Personal preconditions	+	+			–	–	–
	Qualification requirements	++				–	–	–
	Title protection	+/–		–		–	–	–
	Oath-taking		+	+				
	Domain monopoly	+/– –		– –		– –	– –	– –
Market entry	Tied customers				++/– –			
	Tariff regulation (maximum/minimum)	–				+/– –		++/– –
	Vouchers (for consumers) or subsidies (for liberal professions)**					+/–		++/–
	Advertising conditions	–						
	Good professional practice		+	++				
	Requirements governing professional practice		++				+/–	
	Requirements governing intra-professional cooperation.	+/–	+/–				++/–	
	Requirements governing inter-professional cooperation.		+/–					
	Inspection committees, bench-marking, user surveys, fault reports, etc.**	+	+	+	++			

*) ++ highly positive; + positive; +/– positive, but also disadvantages; +/– positive, but major disadvantages; ++/– highly positive, but also major disadvantages; –negative; –highly negative.
**) Not part of the classification as adopted by the European Commission.

Using the analysis of Table I in the profession of Dutch notaries, the reader will observe that there are still rather high barriers of market entry and market conduct (see Box II). Therefore, a more intelligent protection of public interests in the profession of notaries seems possible.

Box II: Challenges in the Profession of Notaries

The barriers of market entry in the notary profession are still high. For example, a notary practice is obliged to offer a full range of services (under the terms of 'ministerial duty'): notaries are not allowed to specialise and to provide services in only one area of expertise. Nor are notaries permitted to employ other notaries, and there is a high element of goodwill when a notary's practice is sold off. Finally, notaries are obliged to join a notary pension fund. These barriers to entry restrict (the dynamics of) supply, which can lead to the passing on of relatively high charges to consumers.

2. Pros and Cons of Self-regulation

The government, professionals and professional bodies can have different roles in the protection of public interest. The concept of self-regulation is very useful in the liberal professions.[16] Self-regulation means that social players are themselves to some extent responsible for drafting and/or implementing and/or enforcing regulations, if necessary within a statutory framework.[17] The fact that players are *to some extent themselves responsible* indicates that there are various forms of self-regulation in which the government has a different role in each instance.

The following roles can be identified, moving from minor to major forms of government intervention:

- *Full or 'pure' self-regulation.* The initiative in this case lies fully with the stakeholders. The government stands to one side and takes a neutral stance, provided the regulations that have been agreed do not conflict with the general statutory regulations (such as competition law). Examples include licensing regulations.
- *Replacement self-regulation.* Here too the initiative lies with the stakeholders, but the government reserves the right to step in with its own legislation if self-regulation does not lead to the envisaged results. The government therefore operates a 'stick behind the door' approach.
- *Conditioned self-regulation.* The government co-authors the self-regulation: it defines the limiting conditions governing the results that must be obtained or the procedure that must be followed, eg, in the form of a covenant.

---

[16] See, for example the contributions by Amelia Fletcher, Sir David Clementi and Roger van den Bergh at this Workshop.

[17] SEO Amsterdam Economics (2003).

- *Legally conditioned self-regulation.* The government drafts specific statutory regulations setting out the limiting conditions that the results of self-regulation must abide by.

However, self-regulation in the liberal professions comes with pros and cons (see Box III).

Box III: Pros and Cons of Self-regulation[18]

Pros:

- Information lead among market players
- Lower transaction costs of regulation
- Better match with outlook of the market
- More flexibility
- Reduces burden on the government
- Involvement of society
- Suitable in cases where the government is reluctant to regulate due to the risk of undermining fundamental rights (eg, the media and freedom of expression)

Cons:

- Danger of misuse due to information lead
- Higher transaction costs for third parties and/or passing on of costs to the consumer
- Risk of 'one-way traffic'
- Risk of competitive distortion
- Regulations are difficult to enforce
- Here also danger for lobby groups
- Single approach risk (difficult to diverge from a particular path once it has been taken)

Finally, self-regulation can be organised either unilaterally or bilaterally. Unilateral self-regulation means that the private sector alone is involved in drawing up the regulations. Bilateral or multilateral self-regulation also involves groups representing the other side of the market, such as for example the government or consumer organisations.

---

[18] SEO Amsterdam Economics (2003).

3. Dealing with the Specific Position of Consumers

In choosing the set of instruments, specific attention should be given to the position of the consumer as the user. In fact, consumers play a crucial role in innovation concerning supply. Without consumer pressure, professionals may not be given enough incentives to adopt efficient and innovative practices. However, consumers do not use the services of the liberal professions regularly. Together with the characteristics of the service (in this case, a matter of experience and trust) this ensures that in practice consumers often have inadequate countervailing power towards the organising professionals. For professional users such as companies, municipalities and housing corporations, the situation is different. They employ the services of those in the liberal professionals more frequently and to a greater extent. The reputation mechanism works better for these users ('repeat purchasers') than for consumers ('one-off consumers').[19] There are two ways of increasing consumer pressure on liberal professions.

First, increasing transparency[20] and reducing the costs of switching to alternative professionals are important ways of increasing the countervailing power of consumers. Social organisations such as the Dutch Consumers' Association can play an important role in increasing this transparency. These organisations could function as intermediary organisations which bundle the demand for specific services in order to get a more demand-driven services provision.[21] Bulk purchasing by private parties results in a shift of power towards the demand side of the economy. For example, clients of the Dutch Postbank may employ a notary for a fixed price which is highly competitive in the recently liberalised notary market. Finally, consumers can set up their own organisations, such as client councils, in order to create the necessary transparency in the market.

Second, the government too can play a role in increasing the countervailing power of consumers. Prohibiting or restricting advertisement regulation for the liberal professions is in many cases a step in the right direction. The regulation could possibly make a distinction between 'one-off consumers' and repeat consumers. Indeed, there is a risk that, despite being adopted on the basis of a paternalistic viewpoint (ie, to 'protect the consumer'), regulation is introduced that is in fact unnecessary for parties such as professional users. An analysis of the relevant transactions in each relevant market could possibly lead to some interesting results in this respect.

---

[19] See also the contribution of Stephen (2004).

[20] See Dutch Ministry of Economic Affairs (2002) for a policy framework of introducing transparency.

[21] See Dutch Ministry of Economic Affairs (2003) for a checklist when (not) to apply demand-driven service provision.

Concluding, specific attention should be given to the position of consumers of liberal services, especially during a transition period of market reform. The stages described in this chapter in order to protect public interest are summarised in Box IV.

Box IV: Policy Framework: stages 3 and 4

Stages 1 and 2 (see Box I) will result in public interests. Stages 3 and 4 are necessary to determine the institutional and instrumental protection of these public interests.

Stage 3: What are the possible solutions?

- Define the potential roles of the government.
- Define the regulatory instruments that could be deployed.
- Estimate the extent of the transaction costs of political intervention (government failure).
- Carry out a national and international comparison.

Stage 4: What is the most suitable solution?

- Compile a social costs-benefits analysis.

All stages of the policy framework are enlisted in Box VI, including brief guidelines for using this framework.

IV. Improving the Success of Regulation

Liberalising a sector is a very complex process. Introducing incentives means changing relations between the market players involved: hierarchical relations are diverted into market relations. These changes take place under political, juridical and economical uncertainties. The transition design plays a key role in reaching the desired market design. To be credible as a government and to gain trust from citizens and businesses, the government should maintain firm managerial control over complex social processes. This means that the government should implement, evaluate and justify its policy and actions. This results in a transition process which is still manageable as the government keeps control and the probability of success of the liberalisation increases. In short, effective change management is vital for a smarter protection of public interests. However, in the past two decades attention has mainly been given to policy making mainly, not to implementing policy. Therefore, the Dutch Ministry of Economic Affairs set up four recommendations for effective change management.

1. Organise the Process as MDW Projects

A useful way of dealing with future changes is the process of Competition, Deregulation and Legislative Quality projects (MDW projects[22]). These projects, eg, on real estate agents and medical specialists, were very successful because of political urgency, a short time period and a working group consisting of all the market players and public bodies involved with a shared goal. Ideally, the four stages of the policy framework play a role in such a working group.

2. Design the Transition Process in an Implementation Plan

An implementation plan should be set up during the process of policy making. This plan describes the step-by-step method used to get to the desired market design. The transition process is divided into sub-processes with a logical and necessary timing and phasing. This results in implementing policies in a careful way and ensuring that (potential) market players, eg, consumers, professionals, professional bodies and trade unions know exactly what to expect from the government. See box IV–1 for an example of Dutch real estate agents.

Box V: Timing and Phasing of Real Estate Agents

The market of Dutch real estate agents was liberalised in 1999. This liberalisation process started with a report of an MDW working group. The cabinet agreed with the reforms suggested by the working group. These reforms were implemented step by step: first by withdrawing the title protection of real estate agents, then by stimulating certification rules via self-regulation (in order to inform consumers on quality) and finally by defining qualification standards and installing an arbitration committee.[23]

3. Review Periodically Potential Strategic Behaviour of market players

In general, introducing competition and freedom of choice is contrary to the interests of present market players. These market players will anticipate and

---

22 In Dutch: 'Marktwerking, Deregulering en Wetgevingskwaliteit' projects.
23 MDW (1998).

react to decisions of others in order to secure their market shares: they will behave strategically. Because of the presence of experience and credence goods in the liberal professions there is a good chance of such behaviour by professionals. One way to deal with this is to review periodically the roles, powers and interests of (potential) market players. Another way is to stimulate professionals to comment on consultation documents or to organise consultation meetings. Both forms will give the government insight into strategic behaviour.

4. Organise the Collection of Relevant Data

Availability of information during the transition process is essential: without information it is almost impossible for the government to stay in control. Correct information enables the government to act and react to unwanted developments. Since October 1999, there has been a new Act on notaries in The Netherlands. The government installed a three–year transition period in order to get a smooth transition form tariff regulation to completely free tariffs for real estate transactions. During this transition period the gap between minimum and maximum tariffs was widened step by step. The so-called Commissie Monitoring Notariaat investigated the effects of each step and published a useful annual report.[24] This was an excellent way for the government to gain useful data about the impact of this deregulation programme.

V. Summary and Conclusions

Since 1994, considerable attention has been given in The Netherlands to problems of market entry, the position of consumers, deregulation and liberalisation in the liberal professions. As a result, The Netherlands is ahead of other EU Member States regarding the number of regulations *without* performing worse.[25] Despite the success of the MDW programme there are still challenges for improving the functioning of markets of liberal services. It is therefore not surprising that the Dutch government, in its reform agenda 'Choosing for growth: prosperity for now and later', is devoting explicit attention to the liberal professions.

---

[24] Commissie Monitoring Notariaat (2003).

[25] Paterson, Fink and Ogus (2003).

More intelligent regulation of the liberal professions demands at any rate a clear definition of the public interests. This limits the scope for lobbying behaviour by the profession, which is usually aimed at maintaining or strengthening its existing position. Regulation must dovetail with these public interests.

A critical analysis of the liberal professions based on the policy framework developed by the Ministry of Economic Affairs is necessary (see Box VI below). This analysis should focus first and foremost on the liberal professions in the health care and legal sectors. Smarter regulation of these professions must result in more scope being created in the liberal professional market for entrepreneurship, to ensure better service towards the consumer. This is also essential in order to achieve the Lisbon objectives.

Box VI: Policy Framework for Protecting Public Interests in the Liberal Professions

This policy framework is divided into four stages which are sub-divided into a total of ten specific priorities for the protection of public interests in the liberal professions. These stages are sequential. However, the priorities *within* each stage influence each other and must therefore be considered together: this is an iterative process

The policy framework can be useful not only when evaluating whether certain measures are or are not justified (argument based on *existing* regulation) but also when considering how markets for the liberal professions could be regulated in future (argument based on *new* regulation).

The policy framework will help economists and policy makers to prevent the government or politicians from being diverted into applying *ad hoc* policy, possibly in response to exaggerated coverage by the media.

Stage 1: Is there an indication for protection?

- Study the indicators which suggest the presence of market or regulatory failure.

Stage 2: What is the nature and extent of the problem?

- Define the transaction (what service is being delivered?) and identify its specific characteristics.
- Analyse the supply and demand-sides of the market on which this transaction takes place.
- Identify what market failure exists (or could occur) and the extent of it (eg, complex external effects and free riders).
- Define precisely what public interests are at stake.

Stage 3: What are the possible solutions?

- Define the potential roles of the government.
- Define the regulatory instruments that could be deployed.
- Estimate the extent of the transaction costs of political intervention (government failure).
- Carry out a national and international comparison.

Stage 4: What is the most suitable solution?

- Compile a social costs-benefits analysis.

Finally, decide on the most suitable role for the government and the most appropriate regulatory instruments to apply to protect public interests.

IV

*Harald Herrmann**

Antitrust Law Compliance and Professional Governance: How Can the European Commission Trigger Competitive Self-regulation?

I. Introduction

The history of learned professions in all Western countries shows strong anticompetitive features.[1] It could even be argued that most of the restraints on competition brought about in the past by self-regulatory organisations (SROs) were constitutive for the development of the liberal professions as such, if one only thinks of the barriers to entry which have been effected by the educational self-regulations, or of the strong price cartels resulting from the minimum fee schedules of the bars or medical associations. The existence of strict supervisory powers, which finally could result in market exclusion, is also anticompetitive, and is typical for learned professions bodies as such.[2] Instead of a competitive market organisation, a framework of cooperative professional associations is typical of this area.

Despite this tradition, nowadays it becomes more and more of a prevailing opinion in Europe that both forms of market organisation should be established. The notion of generating as much competition as possible, and that the supervisory powers of state authorities or professional chambers must be kept down to the lowest feasible level, is making itself room in EC law. This is especially relevant in the area of antitrust exemptions. The ECJ, in the leading cases *Arduino*[3] and *Wouters,*[4] laid down strict conditions for exempting price-fixing and other restrictive professional regulation from the prohibition established by Article 81(1) EC, and the Commission clearly announced that it will not accept the high level of anticompetitive regulation existent in some of the Member States—drawing on the famous so-called 'Vienna study'[5] showing that others do well with less regulation.[6]

---

* University of Erlangen-Nürnberg, Germany.

[1] Waddington I (1992) 388 *et seq;* overview in H Herrmann (1996) 56 *et seq*.

[2] See, as basic for the German developments, the typology of V Deneke (1956); for more recent aspects, see H Herrmann (1996) 44 *et seq*.

[3] Case C–35/99 *Arduino* [2002] ECR I–1529.

[4] Case C–309/99 *Wouters* [2002] ECR I–1577.

[5] I Paterson, M Fink and A Ogus (2003).

[6] See European Commission (2004) 6: 'The Commission will [. . .] continue to carry out casework where appropriate. A coherent application of Arts 81 and 82 will be guaranteed through

Nevertheless, a clear concept of pro-competitive self-regulation is still missing in European law. So far there seems to be consent only on the fact that that chambers or associations of liberal professions are necessary for protecting a high level of quality of services and independent activities on the markets.[7] If the principle of self-regulation is to remain untouched, it does not make too much sense to simply prohibit an antitrust violation or to declare its effects null and void. Rather, the Commission should use legal instruments to trigger better self-regulation. For this purpose, the modern concepts of law compliance by meta-regulation should be taken into consideration. This paper attempts to contribute on this subject by focusing on the German professional chambers (SROs).

The following issues will be discussed in this article: first, some major antitrust violations by the German SROs, which the Commission would have the power to prohibit under Articles 81 and 82 EC, will be identified (II). This will be followed by a theoretical overview of recent research on compliance and the concept of competitive self-regulation follows, focusing on the aspects of responsive regulation and professional governance (III). Next, the paper lays out some empirical and practical remarks on the development of chamber law and the traditional law of professional guilds to professional governance structures in the EC Member States, and in some members of the Anglo-American law family (IV). Finally, we analyse a few types of legal actions through which the Commission can trigger self-regulatory antitrust compliance of the German SROs (V).

II. Selected Antitrust Violations by the German Professional Chambers

1. Restraint of Trade

Some of the most important antitrust offences by German professional chambers occur in the field of advertising regulations. Most of the statutory regulation on liberal professions contain prohibitions of solicitation, which is

---

co-ordination in the European Competition Network.' See also the European Commission's recent decision prohibiting a minimum price schedule of the Belgian chamber of architects (Commission Press Release IP/04/800 of 24 June 2004).

[7] See above n 6, at p 5: 'While the Commission acknowledges that some regulation in this sector (school of liberal professions) is justified, it believes that in some cases more pro-competitive mechanisms can and should be used instead of certain traditional restrictive rules.'

called 'Werbung um Praxis'.[8] While the Federal Chamber of Attorneys has renounced more concrete regulation, the chambers of tax consultants and of auditors have promulgated additional rules. The definition of illegal solicitation applies to any offer of services that is specifically addressed to persons who seem to be in special need of it:

- §10 Codes of Ethics of Tax Consultants (CETC):[9] illegal solicitation shall be every specially-addressed offer of services to persons who seem to have special need of them.
- §35 Code of Ethics of Auditors:[10] illegal solicitation shall be every specifically addressed offer that the client has not asked for.

Both rules mentioned above can be considered decisions of associations restricting competition in the sense of Article 81(1) EC if they go beyond the statutory law of §57a StBG, 52 page 2 WPO, and if the part of the respective rule of the association which is not overlapped by the Statute has competition-restraining effects. This could be denied with respect to the highlighted words 'specially addressed', since the statutory term of 'solicitation' also comprises advertisements which are not published by the mass media and addressed to the general public, but are directed to single individuals. Examples in this sense are all kinds of postal sending of information, circular letters and e-mails, but also invitations to evening lectures or expositions, etc.

A different view, however, could be taken with respect to the wording '... seem to have special needs' in §10 CETC. Section 57a Steuerberatungsgesetz can be interpreted in a narrower sense, and there are strong arguments supporting such an interpretation.[11] A leading decision of the Federal Constitutional Court dating from 1987[12] held that advertisements of learned professions are allowed in principle, reasoning that the basic right of free practice of professions in Article 12 I of the German Federal Constitution must not be restricted more than is necessary and proportionate. Since advertisements essentially aim to special needs of the consumer, an interpretation of §57a Steuerberatungsgesetz in this sense would come too close to a general prohibition of advertising activities of the liberal professions.[13]

The Civil Supreme Court has held that, for the application of §43b BRAO, two circumstances which must be proved additionally: the knowledge of

[8] §43 b Federal Attorney Statute (Bundesrechtsanwaltsordnung, BRAO); 57a Federal Tax Consultant Statute (Steuerberatergesetz, StBG); 52 s 2 Federal Auditors Statute (Wirtschaftsprüferordnung, WPO).

[9] Of 6/2/1997 in the version of 10/24/2001, *Deutsches Steuerrecht* of December 2002, p 518 *et seq*, reprinted in M Kleine-Cosack (2004) 301 *et seq*.

[10] Of 6/11/1996 in the version of 3/11/2002, BAnz. 2002, 789; reprinted in M Kleine-Cosack (2004) 303 *et seq*.

[11] For the following, see BGH NJW 2001, 2087, 2089 'Anwaltswerbung II'; see also M Kleine-Cosack (2004) 105 *et seq*, No 346–50.

[12] BVerfGE 76, 171, 184 *et seq*.

[13] See again M Kleine-Cosack (2004).

special needs of the client *and* a particular exploitation of situations of limited choice, in which the client is, at the time of the advertising activity. The client must be left free to select the attorney of his choice.[14] Extreme examples are the cases of so-called 'ambulance chasing': tow-away or repair enterprises offer their services at the place of an accident without having been asked by the parties.[15] A similar case was decided by the professional tribunal of attorneys (Ehrengerichtshof) of Lower Saxony in 1991.[16] Section 57a Steuerberatungsgesetz has exactly the same meaning. Hence, one can generalise and treat advertisements of learned professions as illegal only in cases in which they appear as impertinent, as in the examples of 'ambulance chasing'.[17]

Section 52 sentence 2, Code of Ethics of Auditors must also be interpreted narrowly. Section 35 Code of Ethics of Auditors, providing that the client has not asked for such an advertisement, goes even further than §10 CETC. This provision seems to be based on the case law of telecom advertisements: telephone calls, faxes and e-mails are illegal if the sender has not been asked to make such communications by the customer. The customer must be protected in his private sphere. This reasoning, however, is not an adequate solution to the problem of advertisements of learned professions. As pointed out above, the possible restraint of free decisions of the client is at stake here, and not the protection of the private sphere.

Accordingly, the rules of the German chambers of liberal professions are substantially more restrictive than the statutory prohibitions of solicitation, and hence restrain competition. They are decisions of associations within the meaning of Article 81(1) EC, despite their legal nature of public law organisations.[18] They restrict competition in the relevant market because they do not only repeat the state regulation or transpose it, but also fix a strict interpretation of it, although a less strict interpretation would be possible. No justification for this can be derived from EC case law, and especially not from the recent decision of the ECJ in *Wouters,*[19] because the binding principles of necessity and proportionality of Article 81(1) EC are violated.

2. State Action Exemption?

The self-regulations of German chambers of liberal professions may also be exempted from EC antitrust law, as was the case for the Italian price sched-

---

14 BGH NJW 2001, 2087, 2089 'Anwaltswerbung II'; *cf* OLG Stuttgart, NJW-RR 1995, 1269, also stressing the argument of freedom of decision making.

15 See BGH NJW 1975, 689, 690 and *ibid.* 691; NJW 1980, 1690, 1691; NJW 2000, 586; see also M Kleine-Cosack (2004) 110; and R Lorz (2002) 169.

16 EGH Celle, BRAK-Mitteilungen 1991, 168.

17 For further examples, see again M Kleine-Cosack (2004) 111.

18 See above n 3..

19 See above n 4.

ules for attorneys in the recent *Arduino* case.[20] The Italian law only regulates the procedure of fixing honoraries by providing that a national committee of elected attorneys ('CNF') has to assemble every two years for deciding on certain adaptations and supplements based on the value of the matter being litigated, without being bound to special provisions of public interest. An Italian court doubted whether the CNF violated Article 81(1) EC and referred the case to the ECJ for a preliminary ruling under Article 234 EC. The ECJ exempted the case from the scope of Article 81 EC, but set forth the following strict conditions for the application of such an exemption:

- First, the ECJ confirmed the decision concerning the Italian schedule of charges for customs carriers, which held that an advisory board of an SRO is a business association within the meaning of Article 81(1) EC, if its decisions are not bound to precise standards of general welfare.
- However, the mentioned decision-making process keeps a public character when the professional association only prepares the decision and the competence of the ultimate decision is assigned to a state body. The ECJ held that this was the case with the reservation of ministerial approval for the above-mentioned price schedules for attorneys, reasoning that their validity depended entirely on the ministerial approval, thus enabling the minister to reach every change of the CNF proposal.[21]
- According to the ECJ, the joint action of the minister with the State Council and the CNF was aimed at safeguarding general welfare, which was another reason why the fixing of charges by the CNF could not be judged to violate Article 81(1) EC.

German legal authors standing close to professional chambers have concluded from this decision that the antitrust exemption already takes effect when the professional association is subject to a governmental supervision which is committed to the general welfare.[22] For example, since the BRAK (Bundesrechtsanwaltskammer, German Federal Chamber of Attorneys) is, according to §176 Section 2 sentence 2 Bundesrechtsanwaltsordnung (BRAO), supervised by the Federal Minister of Justice, decisions of the former that are incompatible with Article 81 EC are considered to be exempted from the application of this provision. Against this background, it would be necessary to apply corresponding rules to the professional chambers of tax advisers and accountants, as after all, the state supervision is intended to ensure that any chamber decisions contrary to competition rules can be corrected according to the criteria of general welfare. Especially the regulatory purpose of supervisory law as a preventive shield against dangers is taken to support the applicability of the antitrust law exemption, since it enables the

---

[20] See above n 5.
[21] See above, p 40 *et seq*.
[22] See H Eichele and E Happe (2003) 1216 *et seq*.

supervisory body to become active already in the case of reduced danger of abuse. From this it is concluded that finally every chamber decision is potentially subject to regulatory measures.

The opposite view builds especially upon the fact that the German supervision of professional chambers is concerned only with questions of law, not with other aspects (eg, §176 Section 2 sentence 2 BRAO). It is thereby reasoned that the influence of the state is therefore limited and cannot be understood as full competence of the ultimate decision within the meaning of the *Arduino* ruling.[23] According to past experience, the influence of the state was too weak to effectively play a steering role in the sense of an ultimate decision.[24] The ECJ has so far apparently made no further distinction as to the necessary extent of the intensity of the governmental influence.

For this purpose, it appears helpful to compare the antitrust exemption of *Arduino* with the question of justification, related to which the ECJ also recently rendered a decision in *Wouters.*[25] This latter case dealt with prohibitions by a Dutch chamber of lawyers concerning professional partnerships between lawyers and notaries. The following points made in the judgment are to be emphasised:[26]

- The chamber decisions are to be regarded as decisions of an association of undertakings within the meaning of Article 81(1) EC, since the state has not reserved the competence of the ultimate decision.
- The organisational form of the chamber as a public law body is irrelevant, since according to the constant case law of the Court, it is not the legal form that is decisive, but rather the fact that the members of the Bar, by offering services on a payment basis, operate on markets where competition is possible (so-called functional interpretation of the term 'enterprise').
- The prohibition of professional partnerships can constitute a significant restraint of competition, as it 'limits production and technical development' in the sense of Article 81(1)(b) EC.[27] The reason is that modern services offered by lawyers increasingly require—especially in the context of giving advice and representing interests in international large-scale mergers—co-operation with accountants, which cannot be served in the way of one-stop shopping if the prohibition applies.[28]
- However, the prohibition in question is justified, even without needing to be covered by an exemption under Article 81(3) EC, if its 'purpose' is an adequate reason for the restraint and competition is not restricted more than 'necessary'.

---

23 See only M Kilian (2003) 256; V Römermann and K Wellige (2002) 637; M Kleine-Cosack (2004) 145 *et seq.* with further references.
24 M Kleine-Cosack (2004) 145 *et seq.*
25 See above n 4.
26 For the following, see above n 25, p 56 *et seq*
27 *Ibid,* p 90.
28 *Ibid,* p 87.

- As accountants under Dutch law are neither subject to a strict professional secrecy nor obliged to independence, the creation of an interdisciplinary professional partnership would lead to situations in which 'a lawyer is possibly no longer able to represent his client independently and safeguard a strict professional secrecy'.[29]

Comparing these criteria with those of the *Arduino* decision, the latter case was concerned the application of the antitrust rules to a single decision, whereas *Wouters* deals with an abstract/general conflict of rules. It is not the governmental competence to intervene in the sense of a right to speak the final word that is to be judged here, but a conflict of rules between antitrust law, on the one hand, and the respective provisions about the maintenance of secrecy by lawyers and accountants, on the other hand. At the same time, this implies a further distinction. While the right to determine the ultimate decision can claim absolute priority, the conflict of two abstract/general regimes of rules demands a strict examination of proportionality. The decision in *Wouters* has therefore been rightly compared with the US case law on the rule of reason, which already at a former stage found a certain acceptance in European antitrust law,[30] and which also recognises the category of anticompetitive rules (so-called ancillary restraints). Here a possible priority of the provision being caught by antitrust law is again only to be considered if specified criteria relating to expedience, necessity, and proportionality are maintained. However, prerogatives by the non-competitive legislator as to the estimation of these aspects are also acknowledged to a certain extent.

A legal in-depth discussion on this subject is beyond the purposes of this paper. Therefore questions regarding how to 'least interfere with competition' have to be left open. But already the above-mentioned aspects of the comparison speak clearly against seeing the German rules on the supervision of professional bodies as provisions for an ultimate decision in the sense of the *Arduino* ruling of the ECJ. A much greater similarity is to be observed to the *Wouters* case, particularly as it dealt with an SRO comparable to the German chambers of the liberal professions. Resulting from this, an absolute exemption from the applicability of the cartel prohibition is not to be considered, but only reasons for a justification can take effect as far as the limits of necessity and proportionality are maintained.

3. Lack of Justification

The question of justification is, as it has already been shown, of essential importance when the restraint of competition by the professional chamber

29 *Ibid*, p 105.

30 See T Ackermann (1997); but compare V Emmerich (2001) 397 *et seq*.

remains within the limits of necessity and proportionality. As to necessity, it is especially doubtful whether the principle of applying the least restrictive means is satisfied. According to some German authors,[31] it would be quite sufficient to provide for a prohibition of 'ambulance chasing', rendering it illegal to exploit the special situation of dependence of the market counterpart in a way which leaves the latter's freedom of decision impaired. As both above-mentioned cases of provisions formulated by professional associations exceed this limit to a significant extent,[32] the resulting impact on competition goes beyond the least restrictive alternative, and the limit of justification is thus exceeded.

According to the opposite view, the prohibition of solicitation must be justified because the respective statutory law not only aims at protecting the freedom of decision of the client, but also at the functionality of the administration of justice, the tax system or auditing system, by safeguarding the traditional professional honour and the reputation of the profession of the tax adviser, accountant, etc.[33]

Other authors lay more stress upon the conservation of the confidential relationship characteristic of the liberal professions, which would be incompatible with the aggressive methods of advertising applied by the commercial economy.[34] However, the BVerfG (the German Federal Constitutional Court), which has been followed by the legislator of the new BRAO, points out in its decision concerning the BRAO professional guidelines[35] that the former reasoning with the traditional position of the profession of attorneys as part of the jurisdiction ('Organ der Rechtspflege') is in conflict with the basic right of free professions in Article 12(1) GG, and thus is to be overruled.[36] Since only aspects of consumer protection can be accepted as justifications for restrictions of the constitutional freedom, any reasoning based on the reputation of the status of attorneys is insufficient.[37]

As to consumer protection, it is indeed true that the confidence specific to the liberal professions is fed primarily by signals of the professional associations, since a direct orientation towards the quality of the performance is not possible as a result of the classification as 'experience goods'.[38] However, this cannot be taken to justify every formation of confidence, particularly where it has adverse effects on competition. Therefore, it is undisputed that not

---

31 See M Kleine-Cosack (2004) 106, point 348 *et seq*. with further references.

32 As show above—see above Section II Point 1.

33 See P Jähnke (1988) 1891; see also R Stürner and J Bormann (2004); for general concepts on alternatives to the race-to-the-bottom phenomenon, like the so-called 'California effect', see D Murphy (2004).

34 See H Löwe (1988) 547; M Henssler and H Prütting (1997), para 43 b, no 10 s, confirming this.

35 See the references in M Henssler and H Prütting (1997), para 43 b, no 10.

36 BVerfGE 76, 171, 191.

37 See above, p 192 *et seq*.

38 More, below Section III, Point 1.

every individual advertisement can be prohibited.[39] But it comes at least close to this if one understands solicitation in the sense of §10 Section 3 CETC, ie, as comprising every exploitation of specific needs. Every advertisement does this, and it is almost a characteristic feature of promotion that it appeals to specific needs of the addressee of the advertising message.

For similar reasons, §35 CE of Auditors also goes too far, since it declares every active individual advertisement to be prohibited. The differentiation between active and passive advertising activities refers obviously to the court decisions in the field of advertising by telephone, according to which calls for advertising purposes are only admissible if asked for by the customer. The intention is to protect the customer in his domestic sphere of privacy. However, this parallel does not fit for the promotion of liberal professions, since here the protection of the private sphere of the market counterpart is not concerned. Instead, constraining liberal professions to passive forms of advertising would leave them with only such restricted promotion possibilities, so that one could no longer speak of a real opening by reference to the total prohibition.

Thus, the prohibitions of advertising for professionals, as laid down in §10 Section 3 CETC and §35 CE of Auditors, are to be regarded as unjustified violations of Article 81(1) EC. Unfortunately, this is not the only antitrust offence: there is a whole line of decisions and recommendations of SROs of the learned professions contrary to antitrust law which cannot be examined in detail here. However, attention should be drawn to the numerous attacks launched by the chambers against price advertising activities, which finally to a large extent were only struck down by individual case decisions by the higher courts.[40] The same is true for the—ultimately unsuccessful—attacks against advertising with turnover figures[41] and ratings.[42] All these cases deal at least with decisions of associations aiming at a prohibition of the respective behaviour. Therefore, one misses as a consequence of the liberalising court decisions the corresponding reversal decisions by the chambers and associations which lost the proceedings—for only by this would it be shown to the members of the profession at large that the self-governing organisations no longer adhere to the exceeding restraints on publicity.

[39] See above Section II, Point 1.

[40] See BGH NJW 2003, 819 *et seq,* 'Anwalts-Hotline'; H Herrmann (2003).

[41] See BayObLG, NJW 1995, 199 'Rechtsanwalts-GmbH'; see also M Kleine-Cosack (2004) 76, arguing that §6II1 BORA cannot prohibit publications which are compelled by §325I2 HGB.

[42] BVerfG NJW 2003, 277 (JUVE-Handbuch), striking down the opinion of OLG München NJW 2001, 1950; *cf* BGH NJW 1997, 2679 (Die Besten I und II).

III. Theoretical Concepts

1. Antitrust Compliance and Competitive Self-regulation

Simple prohibition decisions by the Commission itself or by national antitrust authorities, taken on the basis of Articles 7(1) and 11(1) of Regulation 1/2003,[43] would not seem to have sufficient effects in terms of consumer protection, nor would such prohibitions be in harmony with the well-established principle of self-regulation of the ethics of liberal professions. They would only abandon the respective anti-advertising rule; they would not provide for a better regulation. The consequences do not seem to be favourable when thinking of Akerlof's famous 'lemon market' model:[44] there would not be enough protection against the dangers of adverse selection on the markets of liberal professions. In other words, the SROs should go on to restrict certain advertising and price competition activities of professionals, but they must do so within stricter limits of necessity and proportionality. The problem can be seen as self-regulatory antitrust compliance.[45] The doctrine on this issue, until now, has not focused on the questions of the learned professions, but they do have some aspects in common with the concepts of competitive self-regulation. Therefore, as an initial matter it will be useful to present a brief overview of these concepts.

While the theory of competitive self-regulation has been developed by Ogus, Faure and van den Bergh,[46] the basic concept can be found in the research of Akerlof on information asymmetries in markets for experience goods.[47] Akerlof has already found that the development of associations of liberal professions is not monopolistic or anticompetitive, but serves as a compensation for competition deficiencies, ie, an indirect function of competition. According to Akerlof, the associations and chambers of learned professions serve the purpose of showing signs of quality to the consumer (signalling), since professional services are not search goods but experience goods, the quality of which cannot be evaluated by the consumer in advance. Since indirect information compensating for such asymmetry, such as educational certificates and additional qualifications, labels of independent practice, etc, is supplied by the associations, Akerlof can be understood as a definite initiator of the concept of competitive self-regulation.

---

[43] OJ L 1 (2003).

[44] GA Akerlof (1970) 488 *et seq*.

[45] See the compliance strategies of some US antitrust courts, as cited in the written contribution for this volume by Mark Schechter.

[46] References follow.

[47] See GA Akerlof (1970) 488 *et seq*.

Akerlof, however, left open the question whether the professional associations as such should be in competition to attract members with the best service quality. Nevertheless, the consequence is obvious, if one considers the indications for the demand side of the market. As the signalling effects for the consumer become more intensive, the better the members of the associations perform their business. Hence, a competitive selection of members by the associations seems to follow.

It is the merit of Ogus[48] to have developed the first fully-fledged concept of competitive self-regulation in the mid–1990s. While his work on the rethinking of self-regulation was based on the theory of information asymmetries, just as Akerlof's research, Ogus proposed the abolition of the monopolies held by the Orders of Attorneys at the Bars in Great Britain. According to Ogus, several Orders should be allowed to compete with each other within the jurisdiction of the same Bar. In his view, the main function of this kind of competition was to eliminate rent-seeking activities by the Orders without giving up the advantages of the self-regulation as such. Van den Bergh[49] made a distinction between certain kinds of intra- and inter-professional competitive self-regulation, and classified the proposals made by Ogus as intra-professional. A different development has taken place in the Netherlands, where the Order of Attorneys has been forced to admit employed lawyers,[50] a reform by which the monopoly has remained untouched and its control power was even broadened. Looking at the British example of intra-professional competition, one would rather have allowed different Orders for self-employed and for employed lawyers.[51]

A good example of inter-professional competitive self-regulation is the abandonment of the monopoly of English solicitors in the markets for conveyance services.[52] Since the profession of conveyancers was opened for non-solicitors by means of a deregulation program implemented in the mid–1980s, some competitive activities—and even price competition—became possible. Conveyancers still have to be licensed, but the licensing powers were taken away from the former monopoly of the Orders of Attorneys, a reform which resulted in a kind of inter-professional competitive self-regulation.

Van den Bergh deems this phenomenon to be similar to the well-known regulatory competition of different state legislators (also called 'systems competition'). The legislators, especially self-regulators, compete with different regulatory regimes for attracting citizens/members. One can assume that the

[48] See A Ogus (1995).

[49] R van den Bergh (2000) 435, and also his contribution in this volume. For a similar distinction see H Herrmann (1996) 476 *et seq*, 544 *et seq*.

[50] See JR Cohen (1996) 233.

[51] For this option see R van den Bergh's contribution in this volume.

[52] See R van den Bergh's contribution in this volume; and F Stephen, J Love and A Paterson (1994) 102.

best set of rules will prevail because of a 'learning process' in which market forces decide on the best quality of the competing regimes.[53] However, the danger of an opposite development, the so-called 'race to the bottom', must be carefully analysed, as is done in the context of systems competition.[54] Finally, the lowest level of regulation, rather than the best set of rules, could prevail. Van den Bergh argues that the risk of this adverse selection is relatively low, since 'the markets for professional services are mostly local [. . .] and location decisions of professionals may depend more on family ties and cultural differences than on the contents of self-regulatory regimes'. At least some retarding effects can be expected to develop from these particularities of self-regulatory competition. Once there is no real race to the bottom, there is enough time to learn from the experiences in the 'laboratory of Europe'.[55]

To summarise, one can say that there is a well-reflected discussion on competitive self-regulation which could be linked to the analysed problems of antitrust law compliance. However, the relevant German literature seems far away from the acceptance of such concepts.[56] One reason for this could be seen in the fact that the research referred to is based on developments in Great Britain, the Netherlands and Belgium, the comparability of which to the German situation may be doubted. The particular problems of antitrust law compliance have also not been discussed by the scholars mentioned. For these issues, reference should be made to two further fields of research: the general doctrines of law compliance and the concepts of responsive regulation.

While law compliance theory is based to a certain extent on former research on prudent legislation,[57] its focus must be understood as primarily in contradiction with the latter. Formerly, the main interest was to analyse the legislative material purposes, and how the norm had to be shaped for best expectations to reach the intended goals. Here, questions of socio-economic welfare were fundamental, prevailing over managerial aspects. The compliance research focuses, rather, on regulatory failures and on questions of de-/and re-regulation. Additionally, the reactions of the subjects addressed by legal norms and the pre-conditions of the intended intra-organisational decision-making process are analysed. Sociological and socio-economic methods prevail. Some feedback to the legislation, and even to the interpretation of the legal norms, comes into the perspective of the compliance literature too. In this respect one can speak of a meta-regulation and of regulations of regulation.[58] Methods of traditional interpretation of case law, statutes, etc, are used here.

---

53 See R van den Bergh's contribution in this volume.

54 See the comprehensive study of EM Kieninger (2002) 99 *et seq.*

55 See R van den Bergh's contribution in this volume.

56 See the fundamental critique of R Stürner and J Bormann (2004); see also—although from a somewhat different perspective—M Kleine-Cosack (2003).

57 See P Noll (1973) and H Schneider (1991).

58 See C Parker (2002) 26 *et seq;* M Dreher (2004) 1 *et seq.*

As for European law, from the mod 1980s this approach led to the emergence of the so-called 'technical harmonisation and standardising' concept, which was a reaction to the difficulties of regulating technical details at the centre—the European legislator restrained to the promulgation of principles and 'cornerstones', and left the regulation of the technical details to the Member States.[59] Moreover, the development of the general European subsidiarity principle belongs to this development,[60] since—as in the new concept of technical regulation—general preference is left to the decentralised legislative entities. Particular attention is given to the advantages of self-regulation and to the minimum extent of state regulation. While the details are left to the SROs and to their more flexible and better informed self-regulation, some basic rules as to the legal purposes and the elementary principles are left to Parliament.[61]

If the relevant norms are not addressed to single persons but to collective entities, like corporations, authorities and non-profit associations, the so-called responsive regulation comes into play. The meta-regulatory analysis focuses on certain relations between the internal and the external system functions of the relevant organisation. From such functional reactions, one expects much greater compliance effects than from simple schemes of order and obedience.

One example of such responsive regulation is the connection of legal liability and disclosure standards by tying them 'to incentives for, and guidance on, appropriate standards for self-regulation processes'.[62] One can also combine the 'private justice of the internal management system . . . (with) the public justice of legal accountability, . . . public debate and dialog'.[63] Such system-functional norms have been enacted in Germany by the Statute to Improve Transparency and Control (Gesetz zur Verbesserung der Transparenz und Kontrolle, KonTraG) of 1998, which made the installation of risk management systems compulsory for all corporations in the legal form of Aktiengesellschaft (AG), and which has to be supervised by the supervisory body (Aufsichtsrat).[64] Further supervision is made a mandatory task for all auditors of listed AGs,[65] and the auditors' certificate, which is part of the public announcement in the Bundesanzeiger (BAnz), must provide substantial information on the correctness of the respective risk management system. In other words, the details of risk management are left to the corporation itself,

---

[59] See European Commission (1985) paras 57, 67 *et seq*; also C Joerges, *et al*, (1988) 305 *et seq*; H Herrmann (1989a) 596 *et seq*.

[60] See R van den Bergh (2000) 435.

[61] See BVerfGE 33, 125 *et seq* (Facharztbeschluss, 1975); BVerfGE 76, 171, 184 *et seq* and 191, 205 *et seq* (Bundesrechtsanwaltskammer, 1987).

[62] C Parker (2002) 246.

[63] *Ibid.*

[64] §§91 sec 2, 111 sec 1 AktG; see also H Herrmann (2004), vol 1, p 175 *et seq*.

[65] §317 sec 4 HGB.

but its proper installation has to be made transparent for the public through a particular public announcement.

2. Corporate and Professional Governance: Mechanisms and Principles

The examples already mentioned indicate that there are close relations between the concepts of law compliance and responsive regulation and the theories of corporate governance (CG) and professional governance (PG). Since the CG movement is much better known and acknowledged in Germany, we begin with its essentials. The famous book of *Berle* and *Means* on 'The Modern Corporation and Private Property' of 1932[66] is fundamental. It makes the assumption that the chief executives of the big US-based corporations do not act in the interest of their shareholders, but in their own interest, eg, by maximising their own salaries, gaining economic power or higher social reputation. While the notion of the separation of capital investment interests from those of the corporate management was not new at that time, it came to be understood as a problem of legitimisation by market functions. As far as the interests are separated, the governing effects of the competition functions of the capital markets do not seem to be working as well. For establishing stricter feedbacks of the shareholder interests, different CG theories were developed, some relating more on improvements of the forces of the capital markets and the labour markets (especially the well-known Chicago School), while others emphasised the methods of regulation. In the recent work in this field, there is a unanimous opinion that these perspectives are not mutually exclusive and that each has its advantages and disadvantages and must therefore be related to the other.

For this purpose of correlated governance by market forces and regulatory influences, the following procedural mechanisms most often come into play:

- establishment of semi-public commissions[67] with representatives of related state authorities, scientific experts, representatives of interest groups of the most important branches, and of consumers and employees;
- promulgation of codes of conduct or ethics,[68] which are directed partially to the internal control of the management (supervisory boards, etc.) and partially to the external control by market forces;

---

[66] See AA Berle and GC Means (1968).

[67] See P Hommelhoff and M Schwab (2003) 59 *et seq*; P Hommelhof and M Schwab (2001) 693 *et seq*; more generally G Teubner G (1978) 221 *et seq*; H Herrmann (1984) 63.

[68] For the following, see A von Werder (2003) 12 *et seq*.

- all groups of shareholders and stakeholders have the possibility to participate in the corporation or to terminate this relationship by selling their shares or cancelling credit given, etc. (voice or exit[69]);
- the codes can either be understood as non-binding recommendations[70] or as minimum standards[71] (voluntary compliance, but public announcement of the relevant decision: comply or explain).

From these mechanisms, different principles of CG can be developed.[72] The following have been found to be typical:[73]

- separation of powers;
- transparency;
- reduction of interest conflicts; and
- motivation for value-oriented action.

As to the separation of powers, CG concepts try to assign rights to take decisions to different bodies within the corporation, for thus organising a system of checks and balances. The dangers of misuse by choices of opportunistic options are thus reduced. The decisions of the chief executive manager, eg, can be supervised by the members of the external board respectively the supervisory board of the corporation. CG tries to compensate information asymmetries, which exist between the different interest groups of the corporation, by making use of the principle of transparency. As shareholders do not know about the profit of the corporation, the return of investment, etc, the management has to give account and publish this information annually. The idea that opportunistic behaviour is more likely to be detected as an expectation which will have further preventive effects. Interest conflicts arise between shareholders and the top management, as analysed classically by Berle and Means, and as theoretically worked out in the principal–agent concept. CG rules can prohibit the management from taking advantage of the business opportunities of the corporation. Stock option programs can give them incentives to act in harmony with the interests of the shareholders. Further interest conflicts may become relevant when managers of banks, who are creditors of a corporation, become members of the latter's supervisory board. Furthermore, other members of the supervisory board, auditors and rating agencies can have conflicting interests. 'Value orientation' generally means incentives to maximise the capital market value of the corporation. However, it is also a governance principle in some cases, eg, when the management has an interest in preventing damages because risks of personal liability seem too high.

---

69 AO Hirschmann (1979); especially on the corporate governance concept, see A von Werder (2003) 12.

70 See H-M Ringlieb, *et al*, (2003) 22 *et seq*.

71 See P Hommelhoff and M Schwab (2003) 59.

72 See A von Werder (2003) 12 and 14.

73 *Ibid.*

In a next step of theoretical analysis, one can try to make a general statement about the application of the CG mechanisms and principles to the concept of PG. In this respect, unfortunately, nearly no preparatory research is available in the literature published so far. Even the term 'PG' is not as common as 'CG'. However, it can clearly be understood as an equivalent to CG in the markets for learned professions. Of course, there are some essential differences between corporations as target entities of CG, and chambers or non-profit associations as the targets of PG, which undoubtedly result in different PG structures, but do not necessarily have the consequence that the governance structure is inadequate as such.

First of all, a major difference lies in the fact that SROs do not have to react to developments in the capital markets. It is a general notion that the structure of CG is not restricted to listed corporations and their relations to formally regulated capital markets, but can be generalised for closed corporations (GmbHs) as well as for non-profit organisations, as long as they participate directly or through their members in markets where competition is working. Due to this, the only question that is relevant so far is the degree to which the SROs or their members are involved in a working competition. To answer that question, one has to draw on theories of competitive self-regulation. Insofar as such regulating structures have been developed, an introduction of competition-oriented elements of PG can be taken into consideration. However, there are additional reasons for undertakings of that kind, because members of organisations are always participating in a competitive environment which encloses the liberal professions. This fact has to be kept in mind when designing the PG principles.[74]

IV. Practical Developments

1. Recent Results of Applying Systems Competition Theory

Further useful examples of self-regulation in conformity with competition rules can be found by comparing more recent developments in the EC Member States. We made reference above to the English amendment of the law of solicitors and conveyancing, which led to a whole line of empirical works examining the functionality of the systems competition in the area of liberal professions. After the abolishing of the monopoly of English solicitors on legal advice concerning real-estate transactions and the adoption of a new law governing the profession of the licensed conveyancer in the mid–1980s,

---

[74] For more about the practical developments, see below Section IV Point 2.

initially an intense competition developed between these neighbouring professions. These effects were, however, not examined with a view at the systems competition between individual professional organisations, but with regard to price competition between professional groups. In the beginning, considerable price-cuts could be observed where solicitors and conveyancers were active on the same markets.[75] Later studies showed, however, that the new competitive prices changed again in a rising trend, and even exceeded prices in markets without inter-professional competition.[76] It is assumed that duopolistic competition deficits play a role in such developments.[77] As to the rivalry of Bars and the associations of conveyancers, competitive self-regulation can develop quite differently, since it concerns much more heterogeneous services than the recording of sales of real estate.[78]

In Germany, comparable processes have been noticed on the markets for tax advising services. Tax advice can be offered by tax advisers as well as by lawyers and persons who hold both professional qualifications. As the markets for tax advising services are to a high degree able to expand, there is intense competition between these groups of professions. Due to strict regulation by price schedules in both professions, price competition is to a large extent excluded. Nevertheless, this obviously does not impede competition for market shares, where considerable shifts towards the tax advisers are observed.[79]

Although competition between both chamber regimes for good self-regulation has not yet been examined closely, it is known that there have been significant influences on competition with deregulating effects. This regards, eg, the abandonment of the prohibition of the limited liability company (GmbH) for lawyers, a prohibition which had never applied to tax advisers in this form. Admittedly, this development was finally enforced by court decisions and not in the way of competition between the chamber systems, but there were also impulses from the side of the German Attorneys' Association (DAV) and finally also within the Federal Chamber of Attorneys (BRAK), which can be traced back to experiences in applying the law governing tax advising. The same holds true for the abolition of the prohibition on inter-local professional partnerships and mutual partnerships.[80] Yet these developments do not seem to lead one-sidedly to deregulation tendencies. For example, it has been demanded in the relevant German literature to enforce also for tax advisers the legal position of organ of justice administration.[81]

[75] A Paterson, *et al*, (1988).
[76] *Ibid*, p 102.
[77] See the written contribution of Roger van den Bergh in this volume.
[78] *Ibid.*
[79] See W Strobel (1988) 307 *et seq*.
[80] H Herrmann (1989b) 373.
[81] Speech given by M Seliger at the Nürnberger Steuergespräche 1999.

Hence, one can not talk of a 'race to the bottom',[82] as was feared from many sides.[83]

Similar learning effects can be observed in systems competition at the international level. This trend concerns firstly the emergence of legal rules for the liberal professions as such. A social-historic comparison of developments in this area in the main industrial nations shows that the development of regulation for the professions has not only taken a very similar course (despite some important differences), but also that competitive causes were decisive in this context. This is illustrated by a variety of legal comparative comments in the history of the liberal professions.

Accordingly, there are not only considerable similarities between the rules for the liberal professions in the EC Member States, but also there are elementary differences, and more recently, there are convergence trends. In what follows we discuss the trend towards 'softer' chamber rules and address the question of the causes for their development in the so-called 'systems competition'. In large part, it appears that in the past this mainly concerned impulses for state regulation. However, the emancipation of self-administration and self-regulation can also be traced back to international systems competition.

In more recent times, further trends towards deregulation and liberalisation can be noticed in the laws on learned professions in Europe as well as in the US. While the chamber systems as such does not seem to be on the way to being abandoned, a European-wide trend towards reducing the anticompetitive effects of professional regulation can be noticed.[84] New professional chamber systems in Germany, for example, no longer impose membership to all market participants, but only to those who want to use a certain title, such as counselling engineer, psychotherapist, etc. Existing chambers accept organisational requirements of inter-professional cooperation in cases of special public interest decisions, such as black lists for pharmaceuticals or the acknowledgement of new liberal professions which are closely related to the traditional ones. One could define these developments as a weakening of the chambers system.[85]

Similar phenomena have been observed in the field of CG regimes, which seem to converge throughout Europe and even worldwide. Some interesting empirical research has been conducted lately in the field of corporate governance systems, which used to be very different in the US and in Europe, but seem to converge to a certain extent because of the regulators' competitive strategies for attracting foreign capital investments. Thus, shareholder- and stakeholder-value systems appear likely to converge up to a certain extent.[86]

---

[82] See the written contribution by R van den Bergh in this volume.

[83] R Stürner and J Bormann (2004).

[84] H Herrmann (1996) 470 *et seq*; see also, despite the different focus of the Vienna Study, A Paterson, M Fink and A Ogus (2003); H Herrmann (2003), and M Kleine-Cosack (2003).

[85] See H Herrmann (1996) 470 and 489 *et seq.*

[86] See P Witt (2000) 159 and 163 and M Siems (2005), 325 *et seq.*

2. Professional Governance Developments

CG patterns are is not only acknowledged worldwide, but have also been enacted by the EU in the Directive on Takeovers of 2004[87] and in many Member States' company laws—as has been the case in Germany since 2002.[88] Since the EU Takeover Directive is more recent, it is useful to summarise its main features that are relevant in terms of CG patterns: Articles 9 and 11 of the Directive establish obligations of neutrality for the board of the targeted corporation and prohibit so-called takeover restrictions such as golden shares, restricted voting rights, etc. However, these relatively strict provisions are not fully binding for the EC Member States or the corporations operating on their territory, as the former are given the possibility to 'opt out' of their sphere of application following a public announcement in this sense. In case of such an opt-out, the Member State in question will be rated as a 'class B' country (as opposed to a 'class A' country, which chooses to comply with the relevant provisions of the EC legislation). If a corporation operating in a 'class B' country wants to be classified individually as 'class A', it simply has to declare that it will comply with Articles 9 and 11 of the EC Takeover Directive. This is clearly another kind of systems competition and of competitive self-regulation. By making such a declaration, the corporation can avoid being punished by the capital market for the political decision of its home country.

Next to the rules for CG appear those for PG. In the US, Canada and Australia, PG rules have been tested in some regimes for liberal professions, and in this context they have been referred to as 'professional governance'. In anticipation of a broader empirical evaluation,[89] it can be said that approximately 34% of the institutions referred to as 'professional governance' bodies operate in the field of liberal professions. About 40% belong to teaching and health professions, including the pharmaceutical liberal professions, and to the trainers working mainly in the psychological field. However, only somewhat less than half of these[90] are organised as associations or non-governmental organisations. The rest are formed by state institutions, or institutions depending on them. In Belgium some recommendations on 'Corporate Governance Dans Les Societés Non Cotées' were published in 2001 by the Fédération des Entreprises de Belgique.[91] The following elements seem to be comparable to the basic structure of CG referred to above:

---

[87] OJ L 142 [2004]; for details, see H Herrmann (2004) ch 6, Section III3.

[88] See §161 AktG as amended through the Gesetz zur weiteren Reform des Aktien- und Bilanzrechts, Transparenz und Publizität (19 July 2002) BGBl I, p 2681 *et seq*; Deutscher Corporate Governance Kodex (7 November 2002), version of 21 May 2003 available at www.corporate-governance-code.de.

[89] Research on 571 internet websites of entities using the term 'PG' as their name or for explanation of their activities. The following is based on a pilot study of a sample of the first 100 sites.

[90] 15% of all.

[91] Brochure available at www.feb.be.

CG (as reported, No.III.2)	PG
establishment of a semi-governmental commission comprising representatives of related state authorities, scientific experts, and interest group representatives of the most important branches and of consumers and employees;	establishment of a semi-governmental commission[92] comprising representatives of related state authorities, scientific experts, and interest group representatives of *neighbour branches*;
promulgation of codes of conduct or ethics which are directed partially to internal control of the management (supervisory board, etc.) and partially to external control by market forces;	promulgation of codes of conduct or ethics which are directed partially to internal controls of the management (*member assembly/board of representatives of elementary associations or chambers*) and partially to external control by market forces;
all groups of shareholders and stakeholders have the alternative of participating or giving up relations with the corporation by selling their share, cancellation of credit, etc. (voice or exit)	all groups of shareholders and stakeholders have the alternative of participating or giving up relations with the corporation by *cancellation of membership without being excluded from the market (but excluded from titles given by the SRO* (voice or exit)
the codes can either be understood as non-binding recommendations or as minimum standards (voluntary compliance, but public announcement of the relevant decision: comply or explain)	same

The details of these competitive PG regulations have not yet been fully worked out, but will be discussed in a more comprehensive study due to be published in Spring 2005. The study will be based on a statistical internet research, examining 571 web sites of entities using in their title or explaining their activities by using the words ‘professional governance’. A sample of 100 sites shows that about 34% of these entities conduct governance activities for learned professions, but only around 15% are organised as associations or similar non-government organisations. Approximately 40% belong to the professions of teachers and trainers and to the health professions.

The EU Code of Conduct for Lawyers–despite some significant similarities–cannot be seen as a step towards PG.[93] The CCLEU was enacted by the

[92] See list of the brochure mentioned above, at p 16.

[93] Therefore the German translation of the headline correctly uses the word ‘Standesregeln’, which means rules of (traditional) status. See the publication of M Henssler and H Prütting (1997), Annex, p 1435.

Council of the Bars and Law Societies of the European Union (CCBE) in 1988, and is effective today in its version of December, 2002.[94] The CCBE is a mere interest group, which already existed in 1960, long before the governance-movement was initiated. The CCBE has been officially recognised by the EU Commission as a representative organisation of about 700,000 European lawyers, and the group enjoys consultative status.[95] However, that does not mean an empowerment by the agency in charge, as has been given to the CG commissions in Germany and other countries. Finally, the rules are mainly focused on 'the statement of common rules which apply to all lawyers from the European Economic Area whatever Bar or Law Society they belong to in relation to their cross-border practice' (No 1.3.1). The intention, however, is not to reach a harmonisation for the aim of international transparency, but rather to create legal certainty for lawyers involved with international activities. For this purpose, the code often simply refers to the applicable regulations of the national SROs (No 1.2.2; 2.4; 2.6.1 Section 2). These references especially include competition rules (No 2.6.1) and rules on the calculation of fees (No 3.4.2).

However, the CCLEU contains some rules similar to PG. Here, a special emphasis is put on the voluntary character of the compliance with the norms according to No 1.2.1: 'Rules of professional conduct are designed through their willing acceptance by those to whom they apply'. Furthermore, certain common basic values have been formulated, and the code deems them to be 'based on the same values and in most cases demonstrate a common foundation'. (No 1.2.2, Section 2.) Among them is the 'absolute independence, free from all other influence, especially such as may arise from his personal interests or external pressure'. (No 2.1.1.) Regulation concerning confidentiality (No 2.3), 'incompatible occupations' (No 2.5) and 'conflict of interest' (No 3.2.1) seem to be based on a common foundation. Still, the code does not attempt to severe the link to the ethical traditions of the respective profession, but rather re-confirms them on several occasions (especially No 2.2: 'Relationship of trust can only exist if a lawyer's personal honour, honesty and integrity are beyond doubt. For the lawyer these traditional virtues are professional obligations'). Despite manifold references to national rules for the professions, there is no indication for a competitive regulation that is based on the new regulatory settings.

[94] Available at http://www.ccbe.org.

[95] See the information of the homepage as indicated.

V. How Can the European Commission Trigger Competitive Self-regulation?

1. Is Article 81(3) EC Directly Applicable?

In this section some alternatives of legal reaction by the Commission to illegal rules of chambers of liberal professions will be discussed. First of all, the concept of *ipso jure* exemptions under Regulation 1/2003 has to be described and analysed from the perspective of its compatibility with EU primary law. Article 1(1) Regulation 1/2003 provides that agreements, decisions and concerted practices caught by Article 81(1) EC which do not satisfy the conditions of Article 81(3) shall be prohibited, no prior decision to that effect being required. *Vice versa*, Article 1(2) of the new Regulation *ipso jure* allows such actions if they are in accordance with Article 81(3) EC. Hereby the traditional concept of legalisation by single case decisions of the Commission (so-called legalisation monopoly) has been abandoned. Instead it shall be the matter of the enterprises and trade associations themselves to decide whether the conditions of Article 81(3) are given or not. They have a sort of self-assessment power.

It is quite disputed whether the new system of *ipso jure* legalisation is in compliance with EC primary law. One part of the literature denies the question.[96] Hence one cannot exclude that the ECJ will overrule the Regulation 1/2003. The central reason[97] fort this is that Articles 1 and 6 of Regulation 1/2003 provide for the direct application of Article 81(3) EC despite the fact that the conditions of that article are vague and therefore linked to a decision of a public authority with discretionary power. Also the wording seems to require that a 'declaration' of the Commission is necessary, and that prognoses of contributing 'to promoting . . . economic progress' and of 'consumers . . . fair share of the resulting benefit' shall be made by decisions of an authority with special expert knowledge.[98] Also the power of self-assessment would enable enterprises and trade associations to take unjustified advantages from eventual violations of Article 81(1) EC, despite the fact that the cartel interdiction implies a presumption of illegality.[99]

However, the Commission and the further protagonists of Regulation 1/2003 have stressed the point that Article 81(3) EC does not at all gives a gen-

[96] E-J Mestmäcker and H Schweitzer (2004), §13 No 11 *et seq*.

[97] The further allegation, Reg 1/2003 would be a return to the misuse principle, as opposite to the principle of interdiction (see E-J Mestmäcker (1999) 525), does not seem to be reiterated, see GK-*Schütz*, 2003 Einführung, No 28.

[98] E-J Mestmäcker (1999) 523 *et seq*; E-J Mestmäcker and H Schweitzer (2004), §13 No 15.

[99] W Fikentscher (2001) 448 and 450.

eral discretionary power to enterprises and trade associations.[100] Especially the interdiction on abusing market power in Article 82 EC would be based on significant legal uncertainties in terms of market exclusion dangers, market access impediments etc, notwithstanding the unanimous opinion that the provisions are applicable *ipso jure*.[101] Also, the strictness of Article 81 EC would not be weakened, but intensified, because the enterprises were obliged to assess on their own risk whether a violation of the cartels prohibition is in harmony with Article 81(1) EC.[102]

The author's own position to this discussion is based on a comparison with the US approach of the rule of reason which also provides for a legalisation of violations of the interdiction of cartels of Section 1 of the Sherman Act, and which has been developed by the case law.[103] The scope of application partially is narrower, partially broader, but even in its broader part the rule has been accepted by the ECJ,[104] as discussed above. Also questions of prognosis essentially belong to the rule of reason concept, which are comparably vague as the ones in connection with Article 81(3) EC. However, the reasonability test has never been doubted as violation of the rule of law in the US antitrust law discussion.

Further on, no real legal or economic advantages for the illegally acting enterprises and trade associations are to be seen in the new system of legal exemptions. It is unquestioned that they have to bear the burden of proof for all circumstances conditioned in Article 81(3) EC. One can hence speak of a presumption of illegal actions as far as Article 81(1) EC is violated. An equivalent of the US antitrust law only can be seen in the *per se* doctrine, the reasonability test still is left to directly exempt from the cartel interdiction of Section 1 in the Sherman Act, without a pre-test of an administrative authority. Nevertheless, one can not generally evaluate the rule of reason as an insufficiently effective antitrust law instrument. Hence the better reasons speak for the assumption that Regulation 1/2003 is in compliance of primary EC law.

2. Theory of Discretion and Public Functions of Professional Chambers

In addition, the Commission undoubtedly had a certain power of discretion when deciding on exemptions from the cartel interdiction. While this is

[100] European Commission, *Proposal For a Council Regulation implementing Arts 81 and 82 of the Treaty*, COM (2000)582 final, at Section IIB.

[101] C-D Ehlermann (2000) 557.

[102] European Commission, *29th Competition Report*, Point 30 *et seq*; *cf* Gemeinschaftskommentar-*Schütz*, 2003, Einführung, No 41.

[103] The leading case is *Chicago Board of Trade v US*, 246 US 231, 38 SCt 242 (1918); for further developments see the comparative analysis of Ackermann T (1997) 17 *et seq*.

[104] See above n 4.

abandoned to a far-reaching extent by the new system, it has been questioned that an equivalent discretion power must be given to the enterprises and trade associations, which nowadays have the task of self-assessment and the risk of damages liability, when misjudging the conditions of Article 81(3) EC.[105] The main argument for this assumption is again the vagueness of the prognostic assessments required by this Article, and that it would be unfair if the enterprises and associations had to bear the risk of misinterpreting such unclear legal provisions. Shifting the traditional discretionary power to the competitors themselves is thus considered to be the only fair solution of the problem.

Opponents to this discretion concept have stressed the argument that enterprises and associations would become 'judges in their own affairs', which would be much more unjust than the hardship of vague antitrust law provisions.[106] Also the general shift of discretionary powers seems not to be in harmony with the state action doctrine and reasonability test, as far as they apply to associations with public tasks and functions, and to which some discretionary power is given.[107] The ECJ has confirmed this view in *Arduino*, providing that a state authority must have a right of last word.[108] The discretion concept, in its general form, would be in conflict with this case law, as no presumption of public tasks and state authority supervision would be necessary any more, if the general power of discretion were shifted to every enterprises and trade associations.

On the other hand, the systematic comparison with the traditional exemption tests of reasonability and of state action show that there is a concept of discretionary powers given to institutions other than specified antitrust authorities. Within these provisions it also is generally accepted that the respective entities can—to a certain extent—be judges in their own affairs. The legitimisation for that can be seen in the requirement of public tasks of these organisations which have to be recognised by formal statutory law. Comparing this to the former discretionary powers of the Commission one must add some provisions of essential organisation tasks in respect of competition functions. The tasks of the Commission under the notification and prior authorization system were clearly bound to competition policy, despite the fact that extra-competitive aspects were also considered. If one gives equivalent powers to specialised organisations with state accepted public functions, comparable tasks of competition policy must be evident from the legal basis on which they are built up.

Finally the relation to the state action doctrine seems to be crucial, since—as shown above—this rule does not allow discretionary power in balancing

---

[105] See M Dreher and S Thomas (2004) 8, 16 *et seq*.

[106] A von Wagner (2003), 66; Gemeinschaftskommentqar-*Schütz*, (2003), No 18 and Art 23, No 16.

[107] H Herrmann (1994) 232, 319 *et seq*.

[108] C–35/99 *Arduino* [2002] ECR I–1529; on the discretionary power given by the ECJ, see H Eichele and E Happe (2003) 1214.

competitive and non-competitive public interests. However, this seems to be a pseudo-contradiction. Regarding the state action concept the discretion power would allow for general discretion in questions of evaluation of necessity and reasonability of restraints of competition, which have to be balanced with the plenty of tasks and functions of the trade associations. The ECJ has held that a strong interpretation of necessity and reasonability shall be required. By difference, the discretion concept of Article 81(3) EC only means that the application of this rule of law, to a certain extent, is left to the self-judgement of the public organisations.

In more concrete terms one can draw the following consequences: The German BRAK and further chambers of liberal professions which have stated the analysed interdictions of solicitation are serious candidates for discretionary powers under Article 81(3) EC, but until now they fail the relevant test. While they are based on statutory legal basis and underlie relatively strong state supervisory powers, the requirement of essential competition policy tasks, being analysed above, is not fulfilled. On the one hand, it cannot be contested that the rules on the chambers of law attorneys in §§60 *et seq* BRAO have some competitive intents, especially after a certain degree of price competition at the level above the statutory minimum honoraries has been allowed by §3(1) BRAGO, and after several interdisciplinary cooperation and advertisement of specialisation became admissible under §§42a *et seq*, 59a/b BRAO. However, too many aspects of general scepticism against competitive professional governance still can be found in the BRAO, BRAGO, etc. This issue can not be considered in detail here, but first of all, the above-analysed interdiction of solicitation not only shows that it goes far beyond the borderline of competition law, but also deeply relies on the traditional concept of guildes' honors.

In the future this can may change, as well as it happened with the above mentioned provisions of the BRAO and BRAGO, and as it occured in the British law regarding solicitors and conveyancers.[109] The only thing necessary would be to add to the BRAO a paragraph providing that the professional interests and the tasks of the chamber shall be effectuated 'within the framework of possible competition'. Despite the fact that the chance of such an amendment of the BRAO or another statute of liberal professions in Germany is not very good, an incentive for that could be the consequence under cartel law which has been analysed here: the respective SRO would be given discretionary power in relation to the legal exemption under Article 81(3) EC.

Of course, the consequence of such a discretionary power would not be that the federal chamber of attorneys could promulgate an anti-advertisement rule for protecting the traditional honour of the profession, and that a ruling like that would be exempted from Article 81(1) EC. However, a positive example

[109] See above Section III Point 1.

of a possibly exempted competition restraint would be a rule prohibiting the opening of law offices of attorneys in integrated spaces of discount markets. This would violate Article 81(1) EC, since such restrictions go beyond the above-mentioned borderlines of prohibited solicitation. But one can be of a different opinion about the economic consequences of such law discounting. Chances of cost reduction being caused by focussing on simple cases of everyday life stand against dangers of over-specialisation. It follows from the possible discretionary power of the chamber promulgating such a rule that the discounting prohibition would be exempted from EC competition law by Article 81(3) EC.

3. The Instrument of Accepting Commitments under Regulation 1/2003

For the compliance purposes that have been discussed, the procedural instrument consisting of accepting commitments for closing investigations on the basis of Article 9(2)(a) of Regulation 1/2003, may be a further good approach. Such commitments can give the SROs an opportunity to issue less restrictive anti-advertisement rules which can be justified under a rule of reason approach in the application of competition law. The discussed rule against solicitation, for example, could be designed more narrowly, prohibiting only attempts to take advantage of the actual difficulties of the client.[110] Such rule could also be harmonised with the rules of further professional organisations,[111] which can be heard by the Commission[112] despite the fact that hearings normally involve participants from the pre- and post-established market level.[113]

Commission decisions taken on the basis of Article 9 of Regulation 1/2003 have only declaratory legal effects, as opposed to the constitutive effects of the former individual exemptions. Hence, they do not have binding force, whether for the Commission itself, for the courts or for the respective SROs. However, the Commission's economic intentions and legal purposes, which either are published in its written statement or become evident in the declaration of non-interference itself, will usually be given high importance.[114] This factual pressure force has been criticised on the ground that in practice it would force administration upon corporations and associations without a legal foundation for doing so, and therefore this instrument should be regarded as an empowerment to tyranny by the Commission—an idea which

110 See again the proposal of M Kleine-Cosack (2004) 105.

111 See BVerfG NJW 1996, 3067 referring to pharmacies and holding that the advertising law of learned professions with chamber organisations has to be harmonised.

112 See Art 19(1) of Reg 1/2003, providing consent of the heard parties.

113 Arts 17(1) and 18(1) of Reg 1/2003.

114 OJ L 1 [2003]; S Hossenfelder and M Lutz (2003) 118 and 122.

brings horrible scenarios to one's mind.[115] Similar criticism had been raised up for a long time in the discussion about the Commission's policy of granting negative clearances (comfort letters), and can also be found in the debate on the German CG Code and the respective declaration of accordance under §161 AktG.[116] The norm-like pressure of this instrument was challenged with the argument that it is against the rule of law. It is a kind of private self-restriction with norm-like effects: if those concerned by the decision do not stick to the commitments undertaken, they risk a fine according to Articles 23(2)(c) and 24(1)(c) of Regulation 1/2003, even if the Commission steps back from its declaration of non-interference and re-investigates a possible violation of antitrust law.[117]

For testing the validity of these objections, one must discuss the existence and reach of the rule of law in the EC Treaty. The ECJ has held that so-called 'general principles of law' are applicable if public authorities restrict the basic liberties established by the EC Treaty,[118] or if only the private sphere of citizens is touched.[119] Dogmatic theory has pointed out that these decisions, despite substantial deficits,[120] contain aspects of European basic rights.[121] Only a few authors argue for the existence of a European rule of law,[122] while many others deny it, but see the existence of a procedural protection through the guarantees offered by court control.[123]

As to the reach of the rule of law, it is evident that no parliamentary legislation is required, but regulations, which give protection through court control, are sufficient.[124] First of all, the different forms of legal acts described in Article 249 EC are relevant: regulations, directives and decisions. However, Article 249 EC is not an exhaustive list.[125] Further forms of legal acts do exist and can be adopted at the discretion of the empowered EU authorities, which are only restricted by the principles of feasibility, necessity and proportionality.[126] Even oral decisions are sometimes possible, although these can be controlled through law suits brought before the ECJ if the said principles are violated.[127]

The objections against the procedure of Article 9(2) of Regulation 1/2003

---

[115] K Schmidt (2003) 1242.

[116] See P Hommelhoff and M Schwab (2003) 60.

[117] But see K Schmidt (2003) p 1242.

[118] See Case 11/70 [1979] ECR I–1125; Case 4/73 [1974] ECR 491; especially in relation to Art 49 EC, see Case 62/90 [1992] ECR I–2575; see also D Triantafyllou (1996) 156 and 166.

[119] See Joint Cases 46/86 and 227/88 ECR I–2859; see also D Triantafyllou (1996) 168.

[120] See especially D Nickel (1980) 161.

[121] JA Frowein (1981) 195; for further references, see D Triantafyllou (1996) 165.

[122] K Bahlmann (1982) 10; D Triantafyllou (1996) 168.

[123] Nettesheim (2002) n 76.

[124] See Cases 46/87 and 227/88 *Hoechst AG* [1989] ECR I–2859; see also D Triantafyllou (1996) 169, n 972.

[125] Nettesheim (2002), no 74.

[126] Nettesheim (2002), no 78.

[127] Joined Cases 316/82 and 40/*83 Kohler/Rechnungshof* [1984] ECR I- 641; Nettesheim (2002), no 76.

seem to be groundless. The EU rule of law only exists in a weak form. Hence, it does not provide for regulations, directives or decisions of the Commission that they have to contain all essentials of legally-binding effects. It is sufficient, that the Commission is empowered formally to take a decision to close its investigation on the basis of accepting a commitment. Everything else can be left to an informal statement of the Commission, since the workability, necessity and proportionality of such a commitment is not in question.

4. Block Exemptions and General Codes of Ethics

If the Commission does not agree with what certain chambers of liberal professions—by using their discretionary powers discussed above—want to be exempted from Article 81(1) EC, it can issue a block exemption regulation establishing narrower pre-conditions. Also this instrument of antitrust policy will be used because certain accepting commitments by SROs are regarded to reach not far enough. By using the instrument of accepting such commitments, the legal differences between the branches of the learned professions would probably become more pronounced, rather than being eliminated through harmonisation. However, harmonisation is highly desirable, if not necessary, on constitutional grounds.[128] Therefore, alternatives to what has been dealt with so far have to be seen in more general instruments. The following discussion focuses on block exemptions.

The well-established instrument of block exemptions could be seen as an adequate means for antitrust clearance. The adoption of block exemptions is still possible, because they were not based on Regulation 17/1962, but on Article 81(3) EC or Article 83(2)(b) EC, which are both untouched by Regulation 1/2003. Also, the legal nature of block exemptions is very general, which would permit a Europe-wide application to all comparable liberal professions. Finally, block exemptions have 'constitutive' effects, which means that the Commission itself and courts become legally bound by them. Hence, if a block exemption were adopted, the SROs would receive what they may need: certainty about the legality of their rulings.

Nevertheless, there are serious reasons pleading against the introduction of block exemptions in this area. One especially serious objection is the fact that this form of 'legalisation' has to be seen as regulation of a traditional kind, which does not make sufficient use of competitive self-regulation. Block exemptions may leave room to act, but their borders can only be drawn by the so-called 'black' (and, under the older block exemptions, 'white') clauses. Crossing the border into the zone of the black clauses strictly results in an

[128] See M Kleine-Cosack (2004) 71, n 238.

antitrust violation. Therefore, something 'absolute' is put into effect, instead of leaving it to competition and the market to decide which set of regulations eventually prevails as the best.[129]

It is much more in the sense of competitive self-regulation to design and publish a non-binding catalogue of ethical norms. Such a Code is under preparation, as announced by the Commission at this Workshop.[130] For this purpose, a group of experts composed of Commission representatives, scientists and selected representatives of different liberal professions should be assembled, if one wants to follow the lines of PG. In a first step, drawing on experiences with CG, the scientists would be asked to develop a basic outline. This outline could later be modified and completed by the PG commission until a set of rules that fits all interests has been worked out. Adjustments would then be possible to make relatively quickly, which permits more flexibility than in the case of block exemptions.

VI. Concluding Remarks

The following concluding points can be summarised:

- The advertising rules applied by some important German SROs of the learned professions must be seen as relevant examples of violations of Article 81 EC. They go beyond the statutory prohibitions of solicitation, and cannot be exempted from antitrust law as such, nor are they justified by the rule of reason.
- However, simple antitrust prohibition decisions by the Commission would not lead to satisfactory effects in terms of consumer protection, since they might result in too far-reaching deregulatory effects. A preferable solution would be to oblige SROs to replace these rules with ones that are in compliance of EC antitrust law. Adequate incentives for compliance by the SROs can be discussed in the context of some new concepts of intra- and inter-professional competition, competitive self-regulation, responsive regulation and PG, which is based on the principles of separation of powers, transparency, reduction of interest-conflicts, and the motivation for value-oriented behaviour. While concepts of traditional trust established by SROs tend to monopolise and restrict competition, PG is more open to competition between its members, as well as between different entities of self-regulations.
- The convergence of legal forms of self-organisations in Europe can be

[129] See the written contribution of Roger van den Bergh in this volume.

[130] See the written contributions of Lowri Evans and Pamela Brumter Coret in this volume.

explained as a result of systems competition and as a trend to integrate elements of PG into the old system of chamber organisations. This is a good indication for competitive self-regulation. Other forms of PG have also been identified, which are characterised by comparable mechanisms and principles of governance.

- The new European antitrust procedural rules, having abandoned the legalisation monopoly of the Commission, are in harmony with primary EC law.
- While a general concept of discretion of enterprises and trade associations in questions of Article 81(3) EC cannot be approved of, such discretionary power should be given to chambers of liberal professions if organised on the bases of state acts, supervised by state authorities, and if competition protection essentially belongs to the tasks of the organisation. This can not yet be attested to the German chambers of liberal professions, but in the future some developments into this direction may be possible. One triggering advantage would be that certain provisions prohibiting advertisements of law attorneys could be legally exempted from the competition law prohibition.
- Regulation 1/2003 further favours compliance commitments by enterprises and enterprise associations, which can be used as instruments to trigger the development of professional governance ethics, too. Also, the new EC competition procedural law leaves open the possibility to adopt block exemption regulations for the modernisation of the law of liberal professions. However, the Commission's plan to publish a Code for liberal professions seems preferable. This Code should not only be worked out by the Commission itself, but can better be prepared by a team of experts consisting of Commission representatives as well as representatives from European associations of professionals and scientists.

A final warning seems to be appropriate: the Commission should not go too far into the material subjects of good professional ethics. PG mainly means 'steering' by procedural law nd recommendations. One should avoid—first of all—the danger of hampering competition systems through inadequate intervention by the public authorities: it is the competition of the legal; systems, and not the intervening strategy of the Commission, which will induce the convergence of the laws of professions in Europe.

V

*Frédéric Jenny**

Regulation, Competition and the Professions

In France, a variety of professional services, such as medical doctors, dentists, pharmacists, lawyers, accountants etc., are either regulated by public authorities or subject to self-regulation elaborated by the professions themselves. When such sectors are not publicly regulated or subject to some form of officially sanctioned self-regulation, the professionals involved tend to establish private collective agreements having the effect of regulating their members' behaviour. Typically these professional regulations contain provisions defining the conditions of entry into the profession, regarding the scope of activity of the professionals, and concerning the duties of the professionals *vis-à-vis* their clients and the duties of the professionals *vis-à-vis* other professionals of the same sector.

Collective anticompetitive behaviour resulting from compliance with the provisions of public regulatory professional codes benefit from a legal exemption from the French competition law (*Ordonnance no 86–1243 du 1er décembre 1986 relative à la liberté des prix et de la concurrence*). However, even in those cases, the competition authority (*Conseil de la concurrence*) may be called upon to decide whether the professionals have restricted competition above and beyond these regulations. For professional services for which there is no officially recognised public regulation, no such legal exemption exists for their 'self-regulation' or 'ethical code'. However, the *Conseil de la concurrence* may have to address the question of whether the anticompetitive conduct resulting from the provisions of the ethical code contributes to economic progress and can thus be exempted from antitrust law through an efficiency defence.

In recent years, the *Conseil de la concurrence* has examined the consequences of public regulation or private self-regulation of professions on competition in a number of professional sectors. Among the professions publicly regulated one can mention, for example, pharmacists,[1] medical

* Director of International Relations, ESSEC Business School, Paris, France, and former Vice-President of the Conseil de la Concurrence, Paris, France. This is a re-print of a written contribution presented at the Conference on *Anticompetitive Impact of Regulation* organized Prof Giuliano Amato and Dr Laraine Laudati at the Robert Schuman Centre of the European University Institute, Florence, 10–11 September 1999.

[1] See: Décision du Conseil de la concurrence en date du 4 février 1998 relative à une saisine et une demande de mesures conservatoires présentées par Mme Slamon Evrard in *Rapport Annuel du Conseil de la concurrence pour l'année 1998*, p 852; Décision no 98–D–56 du Conseil de la concurrence en date du 15 septembre 1998 relative à des pratiques relevées dans le secteur des officines de pharmaciens du Val d'Yerres dans l'Essone, *Rapport Annuel du Conseil de la*

doctors,[2] dental surgeons,[3] architects,[4] lawyers,[5] accountants[6] and surveyors.[7] Among the professions which are not publicly regulated but in which the professionals have established a private code of self-regulation are advertising agencies,[8] optometrists,[9] private detectives,[10] operators of ambulances services,[11] real estate agencies,[12] experts in construction,[13] experts in art,[14] etc.

---

concurrence pour l'année 1998, p 652; Décision no 97–D–26 du 22 avril 1997 relative à des pratiques mises en œuvre dans le secteur du portage de médicaments à domicile, *BOCCRF*, 8 July 1997; Décision no 97–D–18 du 18 mars 1997 relative à des pratiques relevées dans le secteur du portage des médicaments à domicile, *BOCCRF*, 29 April 1997; Décision no 90–D–08 du 23 janvier 1990 relative à des pratiques constatées en matière de fixation de la durée d'ouverture des pharmacies libérales, *BOCCRF*, 22 February 1990.

[2] Décision no 96–D–49 du 3 juillet 1996 relative à certaines pratiques mises en œuvre dans l'organisation des services de garde des médecins du Grand Amiens; Décision no 95–D–8 du 19 décembre 1995 relative à certaines pratiques relevées dans le secteur des prothèses articulaires, *BOCCRF*, 15 May 1996.

[3] Décision no 97–D–25 du 22 avril 1997 relative à des pratiques mises en œuvre par les syndicats de chirurgien-dentistes de l'Indre et Loire CNSD 37 et du Rhône CNSD 69, BOCCRF, 8 July 1997 ; Décision no 89–D–36 du 7 novembre 1989 relative aux pratiques relevées sur le marché des prothèses dentaires, *BOCCRF*, 1 December 1989.

[4] Décision no 96–D–18 du 26 mars 1996 relative à des pratiques mises en eouvre par le conseil régional de l'ordre des architectes d'Auvergne et des cabinets d'architecture à l'occasion d'un marché public, *BOCCRF*, 27 July 1996; Avis no 95–A–19 du 7 novembre 1995 relatif à une demande d'avis présentée par le conseil régional de l'ordre des architectes de la région Aquitaien sur les prestations de maîtrise d'œuvre effectuées par les associations Pact-Arim, *BOCCRF*, 12 February 1996; Décision no 95–D–35 du 10 mai 1995 relative à des pratiques relevées dans le secteur de la distribution pharmaceutique dans la vallée de l'Arve, *BOCCRF*, 25 July 1995.

[5] Avis no 90–A–02 du 4 janvier 1990 concernant l'avant-projet de loi relatif à l'exercice sous forme de sociétés des professions libérales soumises à un statut legislatif ou règlementaire dont le titre est protégé, *BOCCRF*, 22 février 1990.

[6] Avis 97–A–12 du 17 juin 1997 relatif à une demande d'avis présentée par l'ordre des experts comptables, les syndicats professionnels IFEC (Insititut Français des experts comptables), ECF (Federation des experts comptables de France) et l'association syndicale «Promouvoir la profession comptable», portant sur la restriction d'exercice de leur activité professionnelle dans le domaine juridique, *BOCCRF*, 18 November 1997.

[7] Décision no 98–D–28 du conseil de la concurrence en date du 21 avril 1998 relative à une saisine et à une demande de mesures conservatoires présentée par M Seguin, géomètre-expert, *Rapport annuel du Conseil de la concurrence pour l'année 1998*, p 399.

[8] Avis 87–A–12 du 18 décembre 1987 relatif au secteur de la publicité, *BOCCRF*, 26 December 1987.

[9] Avis 89–A–12 du 12 septembre 1989 relatif à un projet de préambule des statuts de la chambre syndicale des opticiens de la région Rhône Alpes, BOCCRF, 30 September 1989.

[10] Décision no 92–D–39 du 16 juin 1992 relative à des pratiques relevées dans le secteur des agents privés de recherches, *BOCCRF*, 15 August 1992.

[11] Décision no 95–D–6 du 24 octobre 1995 relative à des pratiques mises en œuvre par des entreprises de transport sanitaire avec le centre hospitalier Robert-boulin de Libourne, *BOCCRF*, 24 January 1996.

[12] Décision du 9 avril 1996 relative à des pratiques relevées dans le secteur de l'administration de bien et de l'expertise immobilière, *BOCCRF*, 3 September 1996.

[13] Décision no 97–MC–01 du 4 février 1997 relative à une demande de mesures conservatoires présentée par le ministre délégué aux finances et au commerce extérieur dans le secteur du contrôle technique des constructeurs, *BOCCRF*, 11 June 1997.

[14] Décision no 98–D–81 du Conseil de la concurrence en date du 21 décembre 1998 relative à des pratiques mises en œuvre dans le secteur de l'expertise des objets d'art et de collection, *Rapport annuel du Conseil de la concurrence pour l'année 1998*, p 829.

Because such public codes or self-regulation are typically found in the professional services sector and much more rarely in the industrial goods sector, it is worth asking whether, from an economic standpoint, there is a specificity which may explain the proliferation of such codes in the professional services sector. In other words, the question is whether these sectors are subject to specific market failures which could justify a restriction of competition among professionals.

I. The Nature of the Competitive Process

The ultimate goal of competition policy is to promote an efficient allocation of resources.[15] Standard economic analysis suggests that competition will lead to an efficient allocation of resources only if a number of conditions are met. Among those conditions is the condition of perfect information of economic agents. This condition applies both to the providers of goods and services and to the consumers of such goods and services. Goods and service providers must have perfect information on the technologies available, the costs of factors, etc. Consumers are assumed to know their preferences and the position and shape of their demand curves as well as the characteristics (or qualities) of the goods or services offered by the different suppliers.

Assuming that suppliers are profit-maximizers, they will automatically choose to provide the goods or services which maximise their profits, ie, the goods and services for which the difference between the price per unit that consumers are willing to pay (a measure of the utility that consumers attach to the units of the good or service given their tastes, the opportunities available to them and their budgetary constraints) and the cost of production of these units (a measure of the social cost of producing these units) is the largest. Competition among producers of a particular good or service will thus force them to minimise their costs of production and sales prices. The competitive market mechanism will thereby maximise the surplus of the economy. The position of the aggregate demand curves of consumers for various types of goods and services will indicate to producers what to produce and will contribute to the efficient allocation of factors in the economy.

It should be noted that in this classical and simplified explanation of how competitive markets work, no particular strategic role is assigned to intermediaries, such as retailers. The market is characterised as a direct confrontation between supply and demand without any need for intermediaries.

---

[15] On the goals of competition policy, see my written contribution on 'The Objectives of Competition Policy' in C-D Ehlermann and L Laudati, (eds), *European Competition Law Annual 1997: Objectives of Competition Policy*, (Oxford, Hart Publishing, 1998) 29–40.

It is clear that in the real world the assumption of perfect information of economic agents is never fully satisfied. Indeed, the role of assumptions in social science models is not to describe real life conditions but to provide us with a simplified (and therefore partly inaccurate) representation of reality. An assumption is justified only if it does not contradict other assumptions and if it allows us to derive results which are not contradicted by empirical analysis. One of the consequences of the assumption of perfect information on the part of consumers in market theory is that, when confronted with competing suppliers of a good or service, they will tend to switch to the supplier which offers them the best quality/price ratio. Thus, in the competitive model, poor performers (ie, those charging a higher price than their competitors for a given level of quality or those offering a lower quality for a given price) will have either to improve their performance or face the risk of being eliminated from the market.

The assumption of perfect information of economic agents seems to be roughly acceptable (ie, for making predictions which are consistent with empirical tests) if one considers common standardised industrial goods which are subject to repeated buying. Through various channels, including experience developed over time, advertising, the press, etc, consumers can indeed be considered to reward the suppliers which offer them the best quality/price ratio for such goods and there is ample empirical evidence that inefficient firms tend to lose market share over time and eventually have to improve their performances or face the risk of elimination from the market.

However, as goods become more complex and more differentiated, the assumption of perfect information of consumers as to what is available in the marketplace becomes more problematic. With imperfect information, consumers rely less on their experience and more on external advice or sources of information to find out where their demand curve for particular products or particular brands of a product lies or to assess the respective characteristics (quality) of competing branded goods. This is why retailers in the real economic world play a more pro-active role in the market mechanism than the basic economic model assumes.

Beyond playing a passive role of delivering the goods that consumers want to buy, retailers play a prescriptive role by selecting brands, displaying the products that they offer for sale, demonstrating the respective qualities of the goods they have selected and advising the consumer. To a certain extent they help consumers establish where their demand curves lie for various products. Thus, the strategy of retailers becomes a crucial factor in shaping the market equilibrium. Manufacturers of industrial branded goods recognised this phenomenon long ago and have developed cooperative mechanisms with their retailers so that they their products will be 'pushed'. It should be noted that the idea that retailers can 'push' the sales of a manufacturer's product directly contradicts the assumption that consumers, knowing their preferences, and having perfect information on the available goods, know precisely where their demand lies. More often than not, the cooperation sought by manufacturers will be obtained through a reduction in the level of competition among their retailers (for example, through selective or exclusive distribution systems), which creates a well known difficulty for competition authorities to assess the consequences of such cooperation mechanisms on intra-brand and inter-brand competition and to assess their welfare effects.

II. Professional Services and Market Failure

In the area of professional services, two distinctive features are worth mentioning when examining the limitations of applying the traditional simplified micro-economic model of competitive markets.

First, in many cases, customers, particularly when they are individual consumers, do not know what their needs are.

This situation violates one of the conditions necessary for competitive processes to lead to an efficient allocation of resources. Because consumers usually have very little means to get an independent assessment of where their demand curve lies and have to rely on the prescriptions of service suppliers, service suppliers are able to behave strategically and to manipulate consumer demand, which can no longer be considered as a constraint to which they adjust by channelling resources to their most socially efficient use.

The existence of a problem of 'moral hazard', in situations in which consumers do not know where their demand curve lies (and must rely on the providers of services to prescribe the appropriate level of service), can be illustrated for a number of professional services. For example, there is ample evidence that in countries where doctors are paid for each medical act performed, they have a tendency to prescribe many more medical acts than in countries in where their revenue is independent of the number of medical acts they have performed. But what is particularly obvious in the case of doctors' services is also true for a vast number of other services, such as lawyers' or architects' services etc.

Second, in many instances professional services are customised rather than standardised. This implies that it is extremely difficult *ex ante* to compare features of competing offers. At the same time, it may be difficult to assess *ex post* the value of the service provided. For example, when an architect is paid a proportion of the cost of a building or a house, it can be exceedingly difficult for the consumer of his services to determine whether the solutions adopted for the construction of a particular building were the most economical. Unless he really understand mechanics, it is also difficult for a car owner to judge whether the assessment of the garage to which his car has been towed has provided an accurate assessment of repairs needed. It may also be difficult for him to assess *ex post* whether all the repairs undertaken were justified.

The combination of these features (inability of consumers to know where their demand curve lies and inability of consumers to assess the quality of the services provided by different professionals) implies that, even in a competitive environment, too much or too little of a service may be provided (compared to where the demand curve of the consumer would lie if he had perfect information) or that (due to the impossibility of assessing the quality/price ratio of the offers of competing service providers) the price paid for the service may be higher than it would have been had the consumers benefited from perfect information.

III. Regulation and Self-regulation of the Professions

Corporate clients of professional services suppliers can, in certain cases, avoid at least part of the transaction costs implied by the moral hazard problem encountered in the provision of such services. For example, a corporation with a large fleet of trucks may find it in its interest to integrate vertically and repair its own trucks rather than being overcharged or having to face the cost of unnecessary repairs by independent garages.

Furthermore, for both corporate clients and individual consumers, leasing contracts (where feasible) can go a long way toward eliminating the cost of the above-mentioned moral hazard related to the repair services for complex machines such as computers or automobiles (since the owner of the equipment must repair it if it breaks down and has no incentive to overcharge himself or to undertake unnecessary repairs).

However, vertical integration is not an option (at least in most cases) for individual consumers. Also, the innovative type of contractual agreements which may alleviate the moral hazard problem raised by the provision of professional services may not be applicable to a wide range of services (such as the services of medical doctors or lawyers etc.). Furthermore, such contracts give rise to another externality because the users of the leased complex machines have no incentive to use them carefully since they do not have to support any of the costs associated with repairs. Thus, the existence of such contracts does not necessarily guarantee an optimal allocation of resources.

In addition, in a number of cases, individuals are particularly vulnerable to the strategic behaviour of suppliers of professional services because they do not have the choice of not consuming the service, whereas consumers of goods frequently (or usually) have the possibility of deferring or abandoning the purchase of a good and are thus in a better position to exert pressure on the suppliers. For example, a consumer considering the possibility of buying a television set or a computer can decide to defer his purchase to better explore the options available to him. An injured or sick patient requiring urgently the services of a medical doctor often does not have either the time or the mobility necessary to explore the market. Similarly, the owner of a damaged car often cannot avoid having his car repaired. In some cases (such as for services provided by lawyers, notaries public, etc.), legal constraints may require the consumer to find a provider for the service. For example, a defendant sued by a plaintiff may be forced to find a lawyer to defend himself, etc.

The vulnerability of consumers due to the combination of these factors is clearly evidenced by the variety of derogatory terms commonly used by the general public to describe the providers of some professional services (hack doctors, crooked lawyers, cheating automobile repairmen, etc.). The protection of unsuspecting consumers is (in the best of cases) one of the reasons why public authorities feel they have to regulate a number of professions. In professions which are not publicly regulated, attempts at self-regulation may (again in the best of cases) be motivated by the desire of the professionals to protect their collective reputation by limiting the amount of abuse that can be imposed on clients, given their inherent vulnerability.

This explains, at least in the case of France, why numerous professional regulations provide that the members of the profession must behave in ways which will not bring the profession into ill repute.

It is typically argued that limiting the number of entrants in a profession through the requirement of professional qualifications (for example, for lawyers, doctors, pharmacists, architects, surveyors, etc.) assessed by professionals in the field will ensure that unsuspecting consumers will not suffer from poor quality or inadequate service. An additional justification sometimes offered for restricting entry in the profession is that it will prevent over consumption (particularly in the case of medical doctors).

It is also argued that limitation of competition among the providers will benefit consumers by protecting them against deceptive tactics or false claims which could mislead them. As an example, the self-regulation of French 'building managers' (*gestionnaires d'immeubles*) prohibited them not only from aggressively seeking to obtain the clientele of one of their competitors but also required them to notify their competitors whenever the owner of a building had spontaneously decided to change building manager in their favour. The regulatory code of ethics of French medical doctors prohibits them from advertising and determines with great precision the information which can figure on their letterhead or on their door. They are also prohibited from practising in a building in which another medical doctor practising in the same field is already established unless the latter agrees to the opening of another practice in the same building. This provision is often justified on the grounds that it protects patients against a confusion between doctors and the risk of being treated by a doctor not familiar with their medical background. Another provision of this code requires that when a patient decides to consult a doctor who is not his regular doctor, the consulted doctor forwards his diagnosis to the regular doctor rather giving it directly to the patient (presumably to ensure that the diagnosis of the consulted doctor is accurate given the medical history of the patient).

It is often suggested that limiting price competition among professional service providers by the establishment of a concerted tariff will protect consumers from abusively high prices and will protect them against the temptation of certain suppliers to offer more competitive prices by decreasing the quality of the services offered. The self-regulation of French advertising agencies required them to charge for their services a uniform fee of 10% of the value of the advertising space bought by the client etc. Collective price recommendations are also common in a number of professional services such as architects' or lawyers' services, etc.

An excellent (although rather extreme) example of the kind of provisions found in professional self-regulation (and of their potential anticompetitive impact) is given by the self-regulations elaborated by the three main French professional organisations of art experts and appraisers (professions for which it is notoriously difficult for clients to assess the quality of the services rendered) which were examined by the *Conseil de la concurrence* in 1998.

Art appraisers intervene as advisers to potential buyers or sellers of art to assess both the authenticity of a piece of art and its potential value. They may also be called upon by courts to intervene in judicial proceedings. Art appraisers painfully aware of the suspicion in which they are held by consumers have organised themselves in professional organisations which are supposed to guarantee the professional quality of their members. Each of the three French professional organisations of art experts decided to fill the void in public regulation of their profession by establishing a private professional code of conduct 'so as to guarantee the quality of the services offered by their members'.

In one of these organisations, new members could only be admitted if they successfully passed a professional examination (administered by their competitors) or if they were co-opted by the other members of the organisation. In the other two organisations, admission could be only obtained through the recommendation of two members, one of these members being in the same field or a field closely related to the field of the applicant and if the applicant had more than eight years of practice in the field in one case or more than ten years in the other case. In all cases it was explicitly provided that the ruling councils of the professional organisations did not have to justify their decisions regarding the admission of new members. In all three organisations, experts could practice only in a limited number of fields (irrespective of their professional qualifications) and had to cooperate with other members of the same organisation if they were to assess the authenticity and the value of collections of objects falling in more than the three categories for which they were listed. The behavioural part of the codes required the experts to abstain from any 'unbecoming' pricing or commercial behaviour such as overcharging or lowering their fees in the hope of attracting clients or using commercial techniques to try to attract the clients of competitors.

In one of the organisations, whenever a member was called to intervene in the context of an auction, he had to enquire if another member of the organisation had assessed the authenticity or the value of the objects being auctioned during a period of three years preceding the time of the auction and, if that was the case, he had to share his fees with him. In the same organisation, if a member was called upon to assess the authenticity or value of an object, he was required to find out whether the owner of the object usually called on another expert and, if so, he was required to warn the other expert and either collaborate with him or compensate him. Finally, all three organisations published recommended tariffs and exchanged information on the names of members they had expelled for non-compliance with their self-regulations. Whether any of these provisions were useful to guarantee the quality of the expert work undertaken by members is very much in doubt.

IV. The Case against Regulations and Self-regulations in the Professions

Competition authorities tend to take a dim view of the provisions typically found in professional codes or self-regulations and to consider that they are often used as vehicles for unwarranted protectionism. They lobby for the deregulation of the professions whose professional codes result from a law or a regulation. They often sanction privately established professional codes of ethics or self-regulations with anticompetitive effects. The main reason for their scepticism is that it is usually doubtful that the restrictions to competition embedded in self-regulations or regulatory codes of conduct can demonstrably have the positive effects of eliminating or alleviating the moral hazard problem assumed to exist. For example, a provision limiting entry in the profession or the ability of operators to compete on price does not guarantee that each supplier will not induce consumers to over consume and may in fact result in a higher average price than would be obtained if competition prevailed. Similarly, a provision limiting the ability of doctors or architects to open a practice may result in less choice for consumers and therefore a more limited scope for competition than if entry conditions were more open.

One of the reasons why most regulatory codes for the professions or self-regulations are at best very crude instruments to alleviate the problem of information asymmetry faced by consumers of professional services is that such codes or regulations implicitly assume that economic competition will lead professionals to behave in a strategic fashion with regard to consumers. In order to woo consumers, clients or patients away from their competitors, it is alleged that they will have a tendency to deceive them through false claims, shoddy quality, overselling of services or charging abusively high prices, etc. which they would not do if they were not subject to the same intense economic constraint. What this approach disregards is the fact that, if the professionals are profit-maximisers, they will induce over consumption, overcharge or provide inadequate quality services, if they can get away with it, regardless of whether or not they are faced with competitive pressure. It can be argued that the elimination of competitive pressures will, if anything, exacerbate the tendency of suppliers of personal services to behave strategically. For example, the difficulty patients encounter (due to the provisions of the medical code of ethics in France) in getting a second (and contradictory) opinion when they are told that they need a treatment or an operation prevents them from assessing the accuracy of the diagnosis and leaves them with little recourse but to comply with the doctor's orders.

At the same time, because such codes are usually drafted by the professions themselves, either alone or with the relevant governmental authorities, they are subject to the familiar problem of regulatory capture. This is particularly obvious when one considers provisions which condition the ability of a practitioner to establish himself professionally to prior periods of traineeship without establishing a mechanism guaranteeing that such a traineeships can be obtained by all aspiring candidates or provisions conditioning the entry into a profession to the presentation of two or three recommendations by established professionals.

V. The Limits of Competition in the Sector of Professional Services

Promoting free entry or allowing competition among the providers of a particular service by removing the most blatant anticompetitive provisions of regulatory codes or self-regulations, although it will certainly contribute to promoting economic freedom, will not in itself always be sufficient to promote the kind of competition which could lead to an efficient allocation of resources.

As long as service suppliers in certain professions have an incentive to behave strategically by manipulating the information they provide to potential clients (ie, as long as consumers are not able to get independent assessments of where their demand curves lie and independent assessments of the qualities of the services provided by the competing suppliers), competitive market mechanisms will not fully guarantee that the information disseminated or the diversity of available contractual arrangements will always (or even in a substantial number of cases) allow consumers to make the kind of informed decisions which would be consistent with economic efficiency. Just like restricting competition constitutes an inadequate tool to solve the moral hazard problem which lies at the heart of the market failure problem in the professions, restoring competition without addressing this problem will usually not lead to the expected positive result.

The elimination of anticompetitive practices in the professional service sector is, in certain cases, likely to increase both the dispersion of prices and of the quality of services offered on the market. While this may be considered to be a positive development allowing freer choice by consumers, if consumers remain dependent on the prescriptions of service providers and are risk averse, the increased uncertainty they have to face (regarding price and quality of the services offered) may partially offset the benefits from enhanced competition. This factor could explain the scepticism or even outright hostility which consumer organisations have shown in France towards decisions sanctioning certain professions (such as lawyers or architects) which have engaged in price fixing.

VI. A Necessary Complement to Competition in the Professions

In the case of the professions, the key to promoting efficiency is to alleviate the information problem faced by consumers to determine where their demand curves lie and knowing what options are open to them.

In some professions in France, a new form of activity is emerging: the auditing of the prescriptions or the services furnished by service providers. To a certain extent this is the role played by independent experts working for insurance companies who assess the « real » damage to a car damaged in an accident and the 'true' cost of repairs (although there may be a concern about the independence of the experts from the insurance companies for which they work). In other sectors, in particular in advertising, over the last ten years we have witnessed (in France) the emergence of firms which specialise in auditing advertising agencies' proposals for their clients. It is precisely because there was a suspicion that advertising agencies (which in France traditionally receive fees based on the amount of advertising space bought by their clients) may behave in a strategic way, either by prescribing the purchase of too much advertising space or by overcharging for the advertising space they buy on behalf of their clients, that there is a demand for the services of such auditors.

Along similar lines, a recently established firm audits the budgets of advertising films for clients who have decided to have such films made to promote their products or their company. Again, it was because most commercial firms wanting to use film advertisement know very little about the film industry and because they felt that the producers of such films could behave strategically and overcharge them (in the name of artistic freedom) that 'advertising film auditors' emerged. It would seem that the same type of solution could be applied to architectural, medical or legal services.

Promoting independent auditing of the service providers prescriptions (either through commercial firms or through 'free clinics') may not be a perfect solution (since the quality of the service rendered by the auditors and their independence may also be difficult to assess) but at least it has the potential of making it more difficult for members of the professions to strategically use the fact that they provide their clients both with a prescription and with the services prescribed. Such auditing seems a necessary complement to the elimination of the most blatantly anticompetitive provisions of regulatory codes and self-regulations used by the professions.

VI

*Frank H Stephen**

The Market Failure Justification for the Regulation of Professional Service Markets and the Characteristics of Consumers

I. Introduction

The views of economists on the regulation of professional services (and indeed on regulation more generally) tend to divide between those based on a *public interest* perspective and those based on a *private interest* perspective. The public interest perspective is grounded on the concept of market failure whilst the private interest theory is grounded on the concept of regulatory capture. The market failure approach is, at least, implicit in much public policy towards professional regulation. This paper evaluates the market failure justification for regulation of professional markets on its own terms and also considers the empirical evidence on the effects of particular instruments used by regulatory bodies.

Although the term *market failure* features prominently in academic and policy discussions of professional regulation, the discussion usually quickly turns to the evaluation of particular instruments by which professional (self-)regulation is commonly exercised, with the focus very much on the profession.[1] There is usually no detailed discussion of actual markets or attention paid to the segmented nature of professional markets. The present paper adopts a different approach by emphasising that in any economy there are a number of markets in which members of a profession are the suppliers. One of the differentiating features of these markets is the nature of the 'consumer'. In many instances the consumer is not at the informational disadvantage implied by public interest perspective and consequently the case for regulation is reduced.

The next section outlines, briefly, the potential sources of market failure identified by economists in markets for professional services. This is followed by a brief review of the evidence on the impact of restrictions on competition

* Professor of Regulation, School of Law, The University of Manchester, UK.

[1] This is possibly explained, as Olsen (2002) implies, by the normative nature of the market failure approach and the positive nature of the capture theory. The empirical evidence is usually marshalled by those looking for evidence that regulation acts to the benefit of the profession and not the consumer.

in professional markets drawing on the empirical literature. The third section provides a discussion of the characteristics of consumers in such markets and the importance of these characteristics for determining whether there is market failure. The paper then concludes on the implications of the foregoing for the approach to the regulation of competition in professional service markets.

II. Market Failure in Professional Service Markets[2]

Economists who support the market failure justification generally begin from the premise that any economic activity should be free from regulation (or at least regulated only by the market) unless it can be shown that it is subject to *market failure*: left unregulated it will not generate socially efficient levels of output. The socially efficient level of output is usually taken to be that which maximises the sum of the net benefits of the activity to producers and consumers. Market failure arises when the sum of these net benefits is below the maximum attainable with the existing level of resources in the economy.

Market failure can arise from a number of sources which can be brought together under two main headings:

- structural factors;
- missing or incomplete markets.

The main structural factors leading to market failure are the existence of *market power* and *incomplete information*. 'Missing' and 'incomplete markets' are due to *externalities* or *public goods*. The types of market failure most often associated with professional service markets come under the heading of structural factors. However, it can be argued that there may be externalities from the provision of some professional services because they are of social value beyond that accruing to the professional and client. Due to an incomplete market the additional value is not taken into account by those directly involved in the market for the professional service.

The competitive process which generates efficiency requires that no single producer of a good or service (or group of co-ordinated producers) controls a sufficiently large share of that market that it can determine, by its own decision, the equilibrium combination of price and output for the market. The market power exerted by such a dominant producer (or group of producers) results in prices being higher and output lower than in a truly competitive market. A major function of competition policy in modern market economies is that of forestalling the creation of a market structure which generates market power (through mergers or collusion/restrictive practices) or where

---

[2] This section draws heavily on Stephen and Love (2002) and the literature cited therein.

the potential already exists due to historic or technological reasons (eg, economies of scale) restraining its exercise.

The second source of market failure for structural reasons is incomplete information. The competitive process will only generate an efficient outcome for a market if all actors in that market have full information as to market possibilities and alternatives. Producers require access to the same technology (and hence costs) while consumers need to have well ordered preferences over the alternatives. In particular, consumers must know what is available from different producers in the market and be in a position to make judgements about the nature of the goods or services provided including the price/quality trade-off. For some types of goods and services the latter condition is difficult to meet. Potential consumers do not have the technical or expert knowledge to make judgements about the quality of what is being offered to them or in some cases whether what they are being offered will satisfy their requirements. Indeed, in the extreme, a situation can exist where even after the service has been provided the consumer is unable to judge whether what was supplied was appropriate. The term *credence good* has been used to describe this situation.[3] Professional services are usually thought to fall into this category.

The consumer of a professional service needs the professional precisely because she/he does not have the specialist knowledge possessed by the professional. There is an information asymmetry between professional and client. This asymmetry can have two consequences: adverse selection and moral hazard.

Adverse selection affects the client's choice of professional. If clients are unable to distinguish between high quality and low quality providers before engaging one, the price they are willing to pay for the services will be lower than that which they would be willing to pay to a high quality provider if they could identify one. If the cost of providing the high quality service is greater than for low quality service, the price consumers will be willing to pay may be insufficient to keep high quality providers in the market. Consequently, high quality providers will exit the market reducing the average quality of suppliers in the market. This will lead to consumers revising downwards the price they are willing to pay, possibly generating a race to the bottom or a 'lemons market'.[4] The typical solution to this problem in professional markets has been, historically, to regulate entry to professional markets by some form of certification or licensing. In most European and North American jurisdictions this has taken the form of giving monopoly rights over some professional

---

[3] This term is due to Darby and Karni (1973). Credence goods may be contrasted with, *search goods and experience goods* (Nelson, 1970). Search goods are such that their quality can be ascertained prior to consumption, whereas experience goods need to be consumed before their quality can be ascertained.

[4] Akerlof (1970).

services to those who are members of a professional body requiring an educational qualification and a period of professional training.[5] The professional body reduces the adverse selection problem by setting and policing a minimum quality standard. However, the professional body may set the minimum quality standard above the socially desirable level.[6]

Moral hazard arises after a client has selected a supplier. As discussed above, the client is not in a position to judge whether the service being provided by the professional is necessary or adequate. Indeed, most professional services involve two separate functions.[7] First, there is the diagnosis of the problem and the identification of the services necessary to deal with it. Secondly, there is the supply of these services. In some fields these are separate activities eg, architects are employed to design buildings to satisfy a client's specified needs but they do not provide construction services. On the other hand, when a party to a dispute consults a lawyer, the latter will usually diagnose the legal problem, suggest a remedy and implement it. In such circumstances, a lawyer motivated solely in terms of financial gain may be tempted to suggest an expensive remedy in the knowledge that he/she will receive a higher fee for providing that remedy. By definition the client is not in a position to judge whether that remedy is the only one possible or even if it is likely to be successful. In the economic literature on the professions this is often described as giving rise to 'supplier-induced demand'.

In these circumstances a market for professional services is likely to generate a level of professional services which is above the optimal (or efficient) level and thus there will be market failure. This suggests that such markets for professional services require regulation to ensure that suppliers do not exploit their informational advantage. However, it can be argued that this is too sweeping a conclusion. Not all clients of professionals are necessarily at an informational disadvantage. This issue is discussed further in the next section but one.

III. Restrictions on Competition in Professional Service Markets[8]

Commentators have identified a number of instruments typically used by self-regulators of the professions that may work against the public interest:

[5] It should be noted, however, that in Finland there are no restrictions on who can provide legal advice and representation in the courts.

[6] Leland (1979).

[7] The discussion which follows is based on Quinn (1982).

[8] This section draws on Pt 7 of Stephen and Love (2002).

- restrictions on entry;
- restrictions on advertising and other means of promoting a competitive process within the profession;
- restrictions on fee competition; and
- restrictions on organisational form.

A detailed discussion of regulatory restrictions for a number of professions in EU member states is provided by Paterson, Fink and Ogus (2003).

Restrictions on entry to professional markets usually have two components: the granting of monopoly rights in a particular market to a 'profession' and the regulation of entry to that 'profession' according to educational, training or numerical criteria. Economists' empirical studies of the effects of mobility restrictions for the legal profession are largely restricted to the USA. They find, for example, that lack of reciprocity between state bar associations leads to lower numbers of practising lawyers and higher lawyer incomes. However, Lueck, Olsen and Ransom (1995) in a thorough empirical study find little support for the view that licensing restrictions affect the price of legal services. Their evidence suggests that it is what they describe as 'market forces' which are most important. Olsen (2002) in a review of the empirical literature on licensure in medical professions[9] concludes that the evidence is mixed and varies across both time and the professions covered. Button and Fleming (1992) studied the licensing of architects in the UK but found no conclusive evidence of an impact on incomes.

Love and Stephen (1996) review an extensive empirical literature which has developed on the restriction of advertising of professional services and what happens to fee levels when such restrictions are relaxed. The general thrust of the evidence from this literature is that restrictions on advertising increase the fees charged for the profession's services and that the more advertising there is the lower are fees. There are, however, a number of limitations to these studies.

The early empirical studies of advertising by members of the legal profession found that law firms which advertise, on the whole, charge lower fees than those that do not advertise. More recent studies find the stronger result that the more advertising by lawyers there is in a locality the lower are the fees charge by *all* lawyers in the locality (at least for certain transactions).[10] However, UK studies[11] have found that this result is only valid for some forms of lawyer advertising. Most studies do not distinguish between different forms of advertising.

Critics of professional advertising frequently assert that advertising will drive down the quality of services provided. Economists have examined the

---

[9] Focusing on the USA.
[10] For example Schroeter, Smith and Cox (1987).
[11] Love, *et al*, (1992) for England and Wales; and Stephen (1994) for Scotland.

relationship between advertising and quality. It has been shown formally that even if price can communicate no information directly about quality, it can do so indirectly because price serves as a positive signal of quality *when price advertising is allowed.* Price advertising is therefore welfare enhancing because it improves consumer choice. A problem arises, however, if price advertising is undertaken exclusively, or at least principally, by low-price/low-quality suppliers. In these circumstances price advertising becomes an adverse signal on quality. This is a general argument, and does not depend on price being a clear signal on quality. It is reasoned that consumers who are unable to assess quality *ex ante* (and possibly even *ex post*) and who observe a low price for a non-standardised service may assume that more knowledgeable purchasers have assessed the service as being of low quality. Professionals are keen to avoid such adverse signals on quality, and so it is concluded that price advertising will be uncommon in most professions.[12] Thus not only may advertising have an effect on quality, perceptions of quality may have an effect on the form of advertising chosen by professionals. Evidence from the USA and UK on low rates of price advertising supports this view.

The third weapon in the armoury of the self-regulating profession is the regulation of fees. Traditionally fees have been subject to control by the profession itself, by the courts or by the state through mandatory fee schedules. In some jurisdictions these mandatory scales have been transformed into recommendations. Some self-regulatory bodies, however, have retained powers to punish those who charge 'excessively' low fees for bringing the profession into disrepute. Observers of professional self-regulation are highly critical of scale fees even when they are recommended rather than mandatory.[13] It is argued that this is tantamount to cartel-like price fixing. However, economists are generally sceptical about the ability of cartels to avoid their members selling output at prices below those agreed by the cartel. One of the few studies of the impact of recommended scale fees[14] provides evidence from two jurisdictions of professionals not seeing recommended fees as being mandatory. Whilst the data rejects a 'national cartel' in both jurisdictions it is consistent in one jurisdiction with, at least, two other explanations: (1) local market competition; (2) local cartels. The study was unable to differentiate between these explanations.

Restrictions on organisational form and in particular Multi-disciplinary practice remain for a number of professions. However, there is little empirical evidence in the economics literature of their impact.

The study by Paterson, Fink and Ogus (2002) has not only extended our knowledge of the details of entry and conduct restrictions in EU professional service markets but has offered a tentative cross-country analysis. This

---

[12] This argument is due to Rizzo and Zeckhauser (1992).
[13] MMC (1970), LECG (2001) 63–65.
[14] This is reported in Shinnick and Stephen (2000).

suggests, subject to the limitations of the data, that performance is negatively correlated with the extent of regulation across professions and countries.

Overall close scrutiny of the empirical evidence in the economics literature, however, does not always support the strong rhetoric of the private interest theorists. The question to be answered is whether the typical instruments of regulation used by the professions are likely to be appropriate in dealing with the asymmetry of information between infrequent consumers of professional services and the professionals.

IV. Professionals' Clients and Information Asymmetry

Clients who are repeat purchasers of a particular professional service will gain experience of a professional's diagnostic efficiency. Such repeat purchasers may also be able to use different professionals at different times and compare their relative efficiency leading to the choice of the most efficient supplier over time.[15] Alternatively, the frequent purchaser may be in a position to generate competition between purchasers resulting in a more efficient specification of service and price. If frequency of demand by the purchaser is sufficiently high, direct employment of a professional may also be an option. Such repeat purchasers are likely to be large commercial organisations or public bodies. This suggests that there may be less need to regulate the supply of legal services to such organisations. The market can be relied on to generate the efficient level of service and cost.

On the other hand, individuals and households require some professional services less frequently. For them purchasing a house, writing a will, disputing a contract, commissioning an architect or engaging an accountant are relatively infrequent occurrences. Individual expertise and experience cannot be built up. These are the clients who suffer from an informational disadvantage with respect to the professional. Thus there is a *prima facie* case for regulation of the market for such professional services. However, the fact that individual clients lack expertise and information on quality does not mean that the market will inevitably fail. What if such information can be transferred between clients? If such experience can be easily transferred between purchasers, reputation will play a role in disciplining suppliers. In particular, if repeat purchasers can easily transfer their experience to inexperienced clients (by acting on their behalf in the selection of the professional or via a list of approved professionals) information asymmetry may be overcome.[16]

---

15 In such circumstances the professional service may be thought of as an *experience good* rather than a *credence good*.

16 This is done through legal and health expenses insurers and through organisations such as trades unions.

The foregoing suggests that there is the potential for oversupply in the professional service markets for those categories of service sought by infrequent purchasers (usually individuals) where the mechanism of reputation or the use of experienced agents do not operate. In such cases an unregulated market cannot be relied upon to generate efficient levels of output and prices.

At least two questions remain, however. Does the need for regulation of markets with infrequent purchasers justify regulation being extended to markets where purchasers are experienced? Does the justification for regulation in these areas extend to the regulatory instruments actually used by self-regulating professions?

Answering the first question requires focussing attention on the nature of the market rather than the profession. Is it reasonable to talk of market failure in the *market for legal services*, for example, given the range of different legal services that exist? Should concern not be with whether or not there is market failure in the market for a particular legal service? When someone purchases a croft[17] in the Western Isles of Scotland is he in the same market for legal services as, say, the Royal Bank of Scotland[18] seeking to sue its supplier of computers for breach of contract? The purchaser of the croft is likely to be an infrequent user of conveyance services and uses a 'high street' firm of solicitors whilst Royal Bank of Scotland is an international financial institution which is a frequent user of multifarious legal services. The solicitors competing for these two types of business will never be competing against each other in the same market. The two clients are unlikely to be competing for the services of the same law firms. In other words the 'market for legal services' is likely to be segmented into a series of different markets with different potential consumers and suppliers. Market failure due to information asymmetry is only likely to arise in those markets where consumers are infrequent purchasers.

It appears that this issue is infrequently addressed in studies of professional regulation.[19] Consequently it is difficult to judge how significant a problem it is. The report by LECG for the UK's Office of Fair Trading (OFT, 2001) discusses the issue but does not appear to take account of it in discussing individual professions—yet it indicates that the single largest source of income for solicitors is business and commercial work (paragraph 130). In fact the Law Society (2002) reports that in a sample of 585 solicitors firms 37% of gross fee income in 2001 was from private individuals and 42% from private sector and public sector organisation. Indeed for the solicitors firms in the largest size category (by number of partners) these figures were 21% and 57% respectively. On the other hand, 72% of the business of sole practitioner firms was

---

[17] A small piece of arable land together with dwelling house.

[18] The Royal Bank of Scotland has a capital value of £41bn.

[19] It does not appear to be addressed, even from a theoretical perspective in Paterson, Fink and Ogus (2003).

for private clients. Private clients accounted for 81% of the business of firms with 2 to 5 partners.

The study carried out by INDECON for the Competition Authority in Ireland (INDECON, 2003) goes further than most such studies in looking at the importance of business versus personal clients. It also investigates the frequency of use of the professions by the different types of clients. It is reported that the mean percentage of fee income from business clients for solicitors is 33%, although it is not reported whether this is a weighted or arithmetic mean. The published data does not show the data for different sizes of solicitors' firms. In the case of barristers just under half of the fee income is derived from business clients, for professional engineers the figure is 79% (with median of 90%) and for architects it is 66.7% with a median of 75%).

The INDECON report also has information on frequency of use of professional services. For personal clients this is based on a random sample of members of the public. Business clients are represented through a survey of insurance companies. In the case of solicitors 51% of the personal sample had not used one in the previous five years[20] and a further 33% not more than 5 times over that period, whereas for insurance companies the corresponding figures were 7.7% and zero. 69.2% of insurance companies had used solicitors more than 20 times in the previous year. In the case of barristers 98% of the personal sample had used a barrister less than 5 times in the previous five years, whilst 54% of the insurance companies had used a barrister more than 20 times per year.

Other professional services such as the medical professions are likely to be dominated by personal consumers. For them the information asymmetry problem remains. Nevertheless, the figures for Ireland indicate that the consumers of some types of professional services are predominately businesses or other organisations which are repeat purchasers and are unlikely to suffer from an informational disadvantage vis-à-vis producers. This suggests that public policy towards markets for professional services should become more differentiated than in the past, differentiated by profession and by consumer type within each market.

A more differentiated policy based on specific characteristics of markets is not without precedent. Both in public policy and academic discourse there has been a shift over the last twenty or so years in the attitude to public utility industries. Prior to that there had been a tendency to see such industries as natural monopolies prone to market failure. Consequently, the industry was regulated or in many cases taken into public ownership. What has changed in the last twenty years (particularly in the UK) is a clearer focus on the sectors of these industries that are the natural monopolies: the network component.

---

20 This contrast with a Law Society survey of the public in England and Wales published in 1989 which reported that only 32% of the adult population had consulted a solicitor in the previous 3 years.

The potential market failure in the electricity industry due to natural monopoly is not in electricity generation, nor is it in the supply to the final consumer but it is the transmission and distribution systems. It is the pricing of access to this system for generators and suppliers that needs to be regulated not electricity generation or supply to final consumers. A more differentiated system of regulation has developed as a consequence. In this section of the present paper it has been argued that an analogous differentiated approach needs to be taken with respect to professional services.

V. Conclusions

In markets where consumers are infrequent purchasers the focus should be on improving the information available to consumers to permit them as informed a choice as possible. The least cost way of doing this is likely to be informative advertising on the part of suppliers. Whilst this should not preclude price advertising, research evidence suggests that in many cases the incidence of price advertising will be low. A role can also be played by third parties with wider knowledge and experience of the professional service concerned in providing information that would be of assistance to infrequent consumers.[21] There is no case on consumer interest grounds for banning or restricting truthful advertising by professionals. Similarly there are no general grounds for restricting price competition within professional markets. Restrictions on price competition reduce the incentive for market entry or innovation in the provision of services which are likely to be of benefit to the consumer. These arguments point to a minimalist approach to conduct regulation which might be best enforced by requiring the professional body to justify other conduct regulation in the context of a *particular* market and on the basis of compensating for asymmetric information in the least harmful way.

Entry regulation is a somewhat more complex matter. In many professional service markets there is a case for certification based on education and some degree of practical training resulting in an identifiable level of competence, particularly where the market failure is the result of an externality eg, certain medical professions, auditing, representation in court. This process

[21] For example, solicitors in the UK who receive public funding through legal aid bodies are subject to competency an d review procedures which go beyond the professional body's requirements. Failure to meet these requirements results in the removal from the list of solicitors competent to receive such public funds. Such information may be of benefit to clients who pay for such services themselves. Similar benefits may arise from the production of approved solicitors by mortgage lenders etc.

should be protected from any control on numbers entering the profession designed to protect the economic interests of existing members.

The foregoing discussion suggests the professions should be subject to general competition law, rather than exempt from it. This would place the onus on professional bodies to justify any restrictions on competition in a particular professional service market.

VII

Roger van den Bergh

Towards Efficient Self-regulation in Markets for Professional Services

I. Introduction

A vast economic literature has shown that free markets for professional services may not produce efficient outcomes. There are three market failures that may impede a full satisfaction of consumers' wishes. A first major problem is asymmetric information. Professional services require a high level of technical knowledge that many consumers do not have. Free markets will only achieve efficient outcomes if a significant number of consumers are able to make purchase decisions on the basis of complete and undistorted price–quality judgements. Many consumers cannot judge the quality of the services offered by the professions before purchase (no search qualities). At most, some quality assessment may be possible after the services have been bought (experience qualities), but in many cases the buyers will never be able to perform a reliable quality judgement (credence qualities).[1] As a consequence, free markets for professional services will fail due to adverse selection (overall deterioration of quality) and moral hazard (supplier-induced demand).[2] Regulation of quality is a response to this problem.

A second problem is that bad performance of contracts between sellers and buyers of professional services will cause negative externalities to third parties and society at large. For example, an inaccurately drafted testament will harm the heirs of the testator and a poorly constructed bridge will jeopardise traffic safety. In a free market, these negative externalities are not internalised in the decision-making process of the suppliers.

The third market failure is known as the 'public good' problem. Professional services generate important positive externalities that are of great value for society in general. Examples include a proper administration of justice (lawyers) and increased legal certainty (notaries), as well as a high quality urban environment (architects). In a free market, suppliers of services, who do not get any reward from persons profiting from these benefits (other

[1] The distinction between search goods and experience goods was suggested by Nelson, (1970). On credence goods, see Darby and Karni (1973).

[2] It should be added, however, that in some markets consumers may be professional buyers who regularly purchase the professional services, so that markets may function efficiently.

than the contract parties) may not supply or inadequately supply public goods.

From the above arguments, it can be concluded that there is a clear need for regulation. The next questions, however, are more difficult to answer. First, what form should this regulation take? Are information remedies sufficient or is it necessary to directly regulate quality?[3] Second, who is the best regulator? Is it wise to leave this task to the professions or is state regulation preferable to self-regulation? As to the first question, legal commentators may bring the proportionality principle into play: rules should not go beyond what is necessary to achieve the desired goal of public interest. Economic commentators may suggest a benefit–cost analysis of different regulatory responses. A regulation should be imposed only if its benefits exceed its costs: when information remedies may sufficiently improve the functioning of markets, a more costly direct quality control can be avoided. As to the second question, there is again a vast literature (both economic and legal) discussing the advantages and disadvantages of self-regulation. Benefits of self-regulation include the ability to make use of the information advantage of the professions, a greater flexibility, and the internalisation of regulatory costs within the profession. Disadvantages of self-regulation are its lack of democratic legitimacy and the risk that professions may abuse their self-regulatory powers to restrict competition. Self-regulatory bodies are not accountable through normal democratic channels and third parties usually do not participate in establishing the self-regulatory regime. On top of these problems, self-regulatory rules may create entry barriers and enable the professions to achieve super-competitive profits. The problem of disproportionate regulation mentioned earlier can be seen as an example of an anti-competitive entry barrier.

This paper will not elaborate further on the need for regulation in markets of professional services, but will focus instead on the strengths and weaknesses of self-regulatory responses to market failures. It is acknowledged that self-regulation may both improve market performance and reduce competition. The basic tenet of the paper is that the state should create an institutional framework under which it becomes possible to fully profit from the advantages of self-regulation whilst at the same time minimising its disadvantages. Attention will be given to institutional issues, such as the division of regulatory powers between the state and professional bodies, the possibilities of competition between professional bodies and methods to improve the accountability of the self-regulatory bodies. In our view, a better understanding of the latter issues is crucial to achieve what is called in this paper 'efficient self-regulation'. The delegation of regulatory powers to self-

[3] A related question is whether quality should be assured by conditions governing entry into the market (*ex ante* control) or by the threat of sanctions for professionals who supply poor quality or breached public service commitments (*ex post* control). This question is not dealt with in this paper; see the contribution by Amelia Fletcher in this volume.

regulatory bodies in markets for professional services should allow them to adequately cure the existing market imperfections, without at the same time giving them scope to reduce economic welfare again by creating disproportionate distortions of competition. At the same time, the lack of democratic legitimacy should be remedied.

The paper is structured as follows: in Section II, the advantages and disadvantages of self-regulation will be reassessed. Section III then introduces two different institutional choices concerning the organisation of self-regulatory powers: co-regulation and competitive self-regulation. Both alternatives to achieve efficient self-regulation will be compared with the existing legal frameworks in the European Union and some of its Member States. Finally, conclusions and policy suggestions are formulated (Section IV).

II. Advantages and Disadvantages of Self-regulation

On the positive side, three arguments have been advanced to support the superiority of self-regulation over regulation issued by the state (Miller, 1985). First, a self-regulatory regime profits from the fact that the members of a profession have significant information advantages. Second, self-regulation is more flexible than state regulation. Finally, self-regulation generally results in the costs of regulation being borne by the profession itself. On the negative side, the counterarguments are that self-regulation enables the professions to restrict competition and that the professional associations lack democratic legitimacy to issue rules on market entry and performance. Each of these arguments merits some further discussion.

1. Information Advantages of Self-regulatory Bodies

On the one hand, it must be admitted that self-regulatory agencies typically command a greater degree of expertise and technical knowledge than the state. The professions have the best capacity to control quality and recognise low standards. Compared to the state, they have better knowledge of the ways to guarantee quality and are also better able to monitor compliance and enforce the necessary rules. A regulatory authority cannot acquire and maintain a specialised knowledge of each profession. Self-regulation minimises the information costs for the formulation and interpretation of quality standards. Thanks to the information advantages of self-regulatory agencies monitoring and enforcement costs are also reduced. This aspect is particularly important where, as with advertising, it is difficult to give a precise definition of the desired behaviour. Under such circumstances, self-regulation will not only minimise information costs but may also avoid the counterproductive results that can emanate from an adversarial relationship between the professions and public authorities (Baggott and Harrison, 1986). On a more general level, self-regulation will reduce enforcement costs since the professions will feel more committed to rules protecting the high standard of the profession enacted by themselves than to statutory regulations on quality.

On the other hand, the reduction of information costs will be achieved only if the self-regulatory bodies have sufficient incentives to control and enforce quality standards. In the past, these bodies were sometimes mostly concerned about practices harming the status and dignity of the profession, as well as 'unprofessional' behaviour in contacts with colleagues, and tended to neglect quality assurance *vis-à-vis* clients. The scepticism with respect to the efficiency of self-regulation was substantiated with evidence showing a proportionally higher number of sanctions imposed for unprofessional conduct in contacts with colleagues than for professional malpractice in relations with buyers of professional services (van den Bergh and Faure, 1991). Equally, professional bodies showed a desire to exclude competition by giving consumers the impression that the services of all professionals were equally good. For example, at the time when advertising was still largely prohibited by self-regulatory rules of the lawyer's profession and competition from neighbouring occupations (para-professions) emerged, advertisements were nevertheless made for the profession as a group. It is, of course, obvious that differences in quality do exist. Whereas competitive pressures could improve quality, professional ethics may restrict the information available to consumers and harm competition. There is thus a risk that market failures due to asymmetric information will persist.

2. Greater Flexibility

The second argument relates to the flexibility of self-regulation. It is argued that self-regulatory bodies tend to be less bureaucratic and can therefore draft and review regulations more quickly and flexibly. Flexibility is especially important in dynamic markets where consumer preferences regularly change. The argument goes that rules enacted by professional associations are more flexible and therefore less likely to stifle innovation or excessively limit consumer choice.

However, the contentions about the greater flexibility of self-regulation are also subject to the *caveat* that self-regulation should not be misused to restrict competition. If the professions can limit competition, they may be able to successfully resist competition from newcomers adopting more liberal rules. The resistance to change may be more effective when the rules are promulgated by self-regulation than when they are laid down by governmental regulation. Even if the rents have been dissipated by competition between the privileged or by newcomers, the artificial restrictions on output give rise to what Gordon Tullock has called a 'transitional gains trap' (Tullock, 1975). There is no politically acceptable way to abolish a policy that is inefficient both from the standpoint of the consumers, who pay artificially high prices, and from the standpoint of the privileged, who no longer make exceptional profits. The persons who lose will not willingly compensate the capital losses of what they consider to be immoral gainers, even though these capital losses are smaller than the overall social welfare gains from removing the output restrictions. On many occasions, only a 'revolution' will shake loose an economy's inefficient regulation. As long as the number of new entrants to a profession generates a flow of political rents from the restrictions of competition exceeding the one-time gains from eliminating them, politicians will not have an incentive to change the licensing and fees rules. At this point, it should be pointed out that the most blatant restrictions of competition have been removed thanks to courageous judgments of the European Court of Justice, which declared self-regulatory rules contrary to the freedom of establishment and freedom to provide services,[4] and the deregulation initiatives of the European Commission in the framework of the internal market programme and competition policy (For an overview, see van den Bergh, 1999). These measures have created the conditions for the 'revolution' referred to above.

3. Internalisation of the Costs of Self-regulation

The third argument in favour of self-regulation relates to its lower administrative costs. Public regulation is costly to tax payers, some of whom do not consume the product. In the case of self-regulation, costs are borne by the regulated sectors of the economy. Professional bodies can finance the costs of regulation through fees on their membership. Additionally, self-regulatory bodies have incentives to minimise costs of enforcement and compliance.

The argument that all of the costs of regulation are borne in the market in which it is imposed merits a critical assessment. If this argument holds, it remains hard to see why the distribution of the costs of regulation would be split in an efficient fashion between the sellers and the buyers. Professional bodies may pass on a substantial part of the costs to the ultimate consumers. When demand is inelastic (as is the case for urgently needed professional services) professionals may 'externalise' the great bulk of the costs.

---

[4] See in particular Case C–55/94 *Gebhard v Consiglio dell'ordine degli Avvocato e Procuratori di Milano* [1995] ECR I–4165.

4. Restrictions of Competition

As is already clear from the discussion above, the major counterargument against self-regulation is that its negative consequences of restrictions of competition outweigh any potential benefits. By charging above-competitive prices the professions would be able to earn significant economic rents and reduce overall economic welfare.

Relying on theoretical economic literature, several arguments can be advanced to support the hypothesis that associations of liberal professions may abuse their self-regulatory powers to restrict competition to the benefit of their members, enabling them to earn substantial economic rents. The professions satisfy all criteria to be qualified as powerful interest groups: they are small, well organised and able to cope with the free riding problem[5] through compulsory membership in the professional bodies. Such small groups will become effective lobbies if the financial interests are sufficiently concentrated so that the potential benefits from organising and lobbying for governmental favours will exceed the associated costs. The professional associations will often be successful in obtaining wealth transfers at the expense of the general public. Consumer interests are more diffuse and the costs of organising consumers to avoid wealth transfers are relatively high and will exceed the expected gains from doing so.

However, even though the theoretical case is strong, the empirical evidence is mixed, if it indeed exists at all. A critical survey of the empirical literature on the regulation of the legal profession has shown that the available evidence does not always support the strong theoretical predictions. For example, fixed fees are vulnerable to 'chiselling'. The ability of a cartel to enforce its rules is inversely related to the number of its members. Professional cartels have many members and will thus not always be successful in enforcing fee scales; furthermore, recommended prices will not always have the effect of raising fees. Therefore, the strong conclusions based on theoretical *a priori* reasoning by competition authorities may not have empirical support (Stephen and Love, 2000).

The recent IHS Report on Regulation of Professional Services (Paterson, Fink and Ogus, 2003) has not been entirely successful in demonstrating the welfare losses associated with self-regulation by the professions. The researchers calculated a regulation index for different EC Member States and professions. According to these indices, the intensity of regulation clearly varies across countries and professions. In the most regulated countries, there appears to be a proportionally smaller number of professionals who receive relatively higher turnover per professional. In the countries with lower degrees of

[5] On the free riding problem (ie, advantages also flow to outsiders who do not bear the costs of lobbying) see Olson (1965).

regulation, there are relatively lower revenues per professional, but a proportionally higher number of practising professionals generating a higher level of overall turnover. It thus appears from this study that excessive levels of regulation in the sector of the professions lead to lower employment and lower total wealth. The Report reached the conclusion that 'the lower regulation strategies which work in one Member State might be made to work in another, without decreasing the quality of professional services, and for the ultimate benefit of the consumer' (Paterson, Fink and Ogus, 2003, 6). Again, this conclusion may be too strong, for two reasons. First, the Report does not fully control the risk of spurious correlation. The correlation between the degree of regulation (as indicated by the regulation index) and the level of employment (or total wealth) may be caused by a third variable linked to the two others (for example: gross domestic product) that is not controlled for. Second, the Report assumes a reasonable homogeneity of quality of professional services across EC Member States. This is a very strong assumption given the heterogeneity of preferences (concerning price/quality relationships and the views on the scope of public goods to be provided by the professions) and the concomitant differences in the scope of the professional monopoly. High incomes may also reflect appropriate quality rents. As long as quality measurement does not form part of the empirical work, strong policy conclusions do not seem warranted.

In sum, the magnitude of the costs and benefits of self-regulation is ultimately an empirical issue. Before policy conclusions may be reached, both advocates of self-regulation and their critics should produce empirical evidence to sustain their positions.

5. Lack of Democratic Legitimacy

In a democracy, it is not necessarily justified that members of a profession can enact rules on market entry and conduct without any control of democratically elected Parliaments. The absence of a significant lay/consumer input into the decision making process exacerbates the problem. In some sectors there may be countervailing power on the buyers' side (for example, in the medical profession: associations of patients) but, if the latter are not well-organised, the views of consumers will not be taken sufficiently into account. To remedy this problem, consumer associations have advocated a significant consumer representation on the boards of professional bodies. A related issue, which has received attention in the current policy debate, is whether it is appropriate to combine the regulatory functions of a professional body with its representative functions.[6] In a democracy, it is perfectly legitimate that professional associations defend the interests of their members.

[6] See the *Review of the Regulatory Framework for Legal Services in England and Wales* of 2004, available at http://www.legal-services-review.org.uk/content/report/index.htm.

However, it is not immediately evident why the same associations should be empowered to regulate the profession. If a profession is entrusted with powers to pursue the general interest, democratic legitimacy seems to require that an independent public authority supervises the professional body and (dis)approves its self-regulatory rules. Alongside the concern about restrictions of competition, the desire to increase the democratic level of the current framework justifies an investigation into appropriate institutional arrangements which can cope with the possible deficiencies of self-regulation in the sector of the professions without endangering its benefits.

III. Institutional Arrangements to Achieve Efficient Self-regulation

At the outset, it should be made clear that removing all regulatory functions from the professions may not maximise economic welfare. Vesting regulatory powers in a public authority may guarantee that decisions are taken independently (provided that the public regulator is not 'captured' by the professions) and will facilitate consumer input into the decision making process. There are, however, two drawbacks. If the regulatory functions are divorced from the professions, information advantages for formulating the rules will be lost. In addition, such an approach will lessen the feeling of responsibility professionals have for the quality standards of their profession and thus increase enforcement costs.

In the 'law and economics' literature, several authors have suggested different institutional arrangements that could escape the traditional criticisms of self-regulation and keep its benefits intact. The major challenge is to design an institutional framework that makes it possible to fully benefit from the informational advantages of the professions and, at the same time, minimises the risk of anti-competitive practices and the resulting efficiency losses. Currently, the state delegates tasks conferring on the self-regulatory bodies a monopoly power to restrict supply in the relevant market. The delegation of regulatory powers to professional bodies can be analysed as a principal–agent problem. Even though self-regulation may reduce the costs of the state (in particular the legislature), there is also the risk that self-regulatory bodies will use their law-making power to benefit their members in ways that are not consistent with the public interest. If the damage to society caused by the self-regulatory restrictions are higher than they are for government regulation, the arguments asserting the cost efficiency of self-regulation may not hold.

The most important proposed solutions in the Law and Economics literature include systems of co-regulation and competitive self-regulation. The first mechanism involves co-operation between the state and self-regulatory bodies, whereas the second system is based on the concept of regulatory competition. Both co-regulation and competitive self-regulation keep regulatory functions in the hands of professional bodies, thus preserving the information benefits and the reduction of enforcement costs that would be lost if all regulatory powers were vested in a government regulator. In both systems there remains, however, a role for the state as a referee. Under co-regulation, a central regulator (possibly different regulators for each profession) approves the rules, practices and procedures of the professional bodies. Under competitive self-regulation, the role for the state is more limited. Its task is to organise competition between the different professional associations and, if necessary, to subject this competition to a set of minimum quality standards. The role of the self-regulatory bodies is then to set higher standards for their members above the statutory minimum. Under certain conditions, both co-regulation and competitive self-regulation may lead to efficient outcomes.

The next question is whether existing systems of co-regulation and competitive self-regulation in EC Member States are sufficiently well developed and well designed to achieve efficient self-regulation. In the remainder of this paper, both institutional arrangements will be further commented upon. Existing (or proposed) frameworks of co-regulation and competitive self-regulation in the Member States will be described and assessed. In addition, European law will be investigated in order to find out the extent to which the current legal framework provides sufficient incentives to develop efficient forms of self-regulation in the Member States.

1. Co-regulation

When jurisdictions adopt 'co-regulation', self-regulatory bodies enact rules but with some oversight or ratification by public authorities (Grabosky and Braithwaite, 1986). The state subjects self-regulatory rules to a public interest test and retains the last word on the contents of the rules that will govern entry into the profession and its performance. Under co-regulation, the role of the government is restricted to its function as referee. The job is to prevent self-regulation from discouraging competition within the industry, unless such restrictions of competition are deemed necessary to achieve goals of public interest and are proportionate to these objectives.

1.1 Basic Conditions for Efficient Co-regulation

Even though co-regulation reduces the scope for welfare losses, control by the state may remain ineffective for three reasons. First, the concept of 'public interest' may not be clearly defined and instruments to assess whether public interest goals are achieved may be insufficiently developed. In a first phase of the decision making, a public interest test should investigate whether rules adopted by professional bodies generate serious anticompetitive restrictions that cannot be made good by efficiency savings. To a large extent, this task can be performed by competition authorities. In a second phase, the efficiency analysis must be complemented by an examination of distributive effects (including the financial accessibility of professional services). This task may be conferred on a (specialised) public authority for liberal professions or on the competent Minister.

Second, the scope of the control by the state may be too narrow, so that not all restrictions on competition are subjected to a public interest test. The competition laws of many Member States exempt conduct of professional bodies complying with statutory provisions from the scope of the cartel prohibition.[7] The control by competition authorities will then be restricted to self-regulatory rules for professional services that are not governed by public regulation. An exclusion from the scope of the competition laws carries with it the disadvantage that restrictions on competition and their countervailing efficiency benefits cannot be judged by a specialised authority. Consequently, comparative benefits of competition authorities in comparison with public regulators will be lost. For rules having a public law character, another authority (the competent Minister or a supervisory public authority for liberal professions) will have to perform a public interest test. The contents of this test can be broader than an assessment under competition law, since it may include not only efficiency concerns but also considerations about redistribution of wealth. However, if the public interest test is defective for some reason, co-regulation will not lead to efficient outcomes.

Third, the professional bodies keep their monopoly in the field of enforcement. Whenever the professional bodies apply broadly formulated standards in individual cases, there is a risk that they will use their margin of discretion in an anticompetitive way. To maximise the benefits of self-regulation whilst at the same time minimising its costs, Ayres and Braithwaite (1992) have suggested a system of enforced self-regulation. This model differs from co-regulation, since it removes the enforcement monopoly of the professional bodies. In a system of enforced self-regulation, a public agency negotiates with every individual firm rules that take account of the particular characteristics of each firm. If the firm does not cooperate, the State may impose less tailored standards. A major benefit is that this individualisation makes it impossible for firms to charge monopoly prices. Additional advantages flow from the possibility of tailoring the rules to match the firm's circumstances, to identify least–cost solutions, and to stimulate innovation. Firms will also be more committed to tailored rules than to externally imposed standards.

---

7 See for example the French Ordonnance No 86–1243 of December 1, 1986 relative à la liberté des prix et de la concurrence.

The major drawback is the huge administrative cost. Consequently, enforced self-regulation will be cost-effective only if the firm is large and efficiency requires significantly differentiated standards across firms.[8] Given these restrictions, the option of enforced self-regulation does not seem well-suited for the professions. An alternative way to minimise the risks associated with the enforcement monopoly is to establish a framework for competitive self-regulation. This option will be further elaborated upon in the second part of this section.

1.2 An Example from the Member States: Co-regulation in the Netherlands

The scope of this paper does not allow a detailed discussion of the (often very complex) institutional legal framework within which professional bodies exercise their regulatory powers in the respective Member States of the European Union. An example does, however, seem sufficient to convey the message that basic conditions concerning the scope and the contents of the public interest test must be satisfied for co-regulation to reach efficient outcomes.

In many Member States, liberal professions are regulated by professional associations, which enjoy public law status implying that they have statutory powers. Since the interests of the profession as represented by these public law bodies can conflict with public interests, the government must closely monitor the contents of the regulations. Systems of co-regulation may remain ineffective if the public interest criteria are not clearly articulated or if control can take place only *ex post*. To achieve efficient co-regulation, the assessment of self-regulatory rules should focus on whether a regulation is serving the public interest or the interests of the profession and control should take place *ex ante*.

Recent changes of the regulatory framework in the Netherlands show an increasing awareness of the problems associated with co-regulation on the part of the Dutch government. New instruments have been put in place to achieve efficient co-regulation. A solution has been sought for the lack of definition of public interests and the absence of a structured analysis of what is and what is not covered by this term. A policy study of the Dutch Ministry of Economic Affairs (van den Heuvel, Lackner and Verkerk, 2004) has classified public interests in three categories relating to quality (including the expertise and independence of the professional and satisfactory complaints handling), accessibility (physical and financial) and macro affordability. The next step is to identify the instruments to achieve these goals: the heavier the instrument, the more serious will be the restriction of competition. Only very

[8] See Ogus (2000) with further references.

significant negative externalities or the need for a general availability of essential professional services of good quality can be arguments to impose heavy restrictions, such as domain monopolies with tied consumers and tariff regulations. Also worth noting is the switch from *ex post* control to *ex ante* control. In the past, the Minister of Justice only rarely used his powers to abolish regulations in legal professions if they undermined public interests and unnecessarily restricted competition. Under the new Notaries Act (1999) and Bailiffs Act (2001), government supervision has been increased through a prior approval requirement pertaining to relevant regulations. The Minister screens the regulations for their competition, public interest and proportionality aspects.

The Dutch example may inspire other Member States wishing to revise their regulatory systems. This does not imply that in our view the Dutch approach is already optimal. A shortcoming is that it does not clearly specify the division of work between the competition authority and other public authorities (the competent Ministers) in assessing the overall welfare effects of self-regulatory rules. To increase the transparency of the decision-making process, this shortcoming should be remedied. Another drawback is that the government is also concerned about the level of collective expenditure, since macro affordability is presented as a public interest. This approach deviates from the classic division of public interests into efficiency objectives and distributive goals. Clearly, to guarantee the financial accessibility of professional services, the macro economic costs may be high. It is, however, unclear how the trade-off between these conflicting 'public interests' (redistribution of wealth *versus* macro affordability) must be made. In spite of these shortcomings, the Dutch approach can be seen as a major step in the direction of efficient co-regulation. The broad and vague public interest criterion has been rephrased into more specific categories, which facilitate control by the state. The requirement that high levels of regulatory intervention need to be justified by concomitantly serious market failures also reflects the proportionality principle and makes it amenable to policy implementation.

1.3 European Law: A Defective Framework for Co-regulation?

Given the benefits of systems of co-regulation, one could favour their adoption throughout the entire European Union. Up until now, the adoption of such systems remains a free decision of individual Member States. European law does not explicitly require Member States to subject self-regulatory rules of professional bodies to a public interest test. Recent case law of the European Court of Justice in the area of competition law has also limited the scope of co-regulation. In the *Wouters* case, a liberal profession exemption from the competition rules of the Treaty has been created. Its effect is that a full efficiency analysis of restrictions of competition is not required. In addition, in the *Arduino* case the state action defence (making anti-competitive restrictions immune from antitrust challenges) has not been subjected to a clear and unconditional requirement that Member States must justify restrictions on public interest grounds and show that the instruments chosen are not disproportionate to achieve such goals. Consequently, governmental control of self-regulatory regimes remains largely the responsibility of Member States. If public interest tests in the Member States are either too narrow or defective, the enactment of self-regulatory rules may reduce overall welfare.

Recent case law of the European Court of Justice has limited the reach of the cartel prohibition and has thus put a limitation on systems of co-regulation. In the *Wouters* case, the Court held that not every decision of a professional body restricting competition necessarily infringes Article 81(1) of the Treaty. The prohibition of inter-professional co-operation between lawyers and accountants was considered 'necessary for the proper practice of the profession, as organised in the Member State concerned' (to guarantee the lawyers' independence), despite the effects restrictive of competition that are inherent in it.[9] Obviously, an efficiency analysis requires that the anticompetitive effects of deontological rules be balanced against their possible benefits in terms of improved quality. By excluding a test based on Article 81(3) of the Treaty, the risk remains that inefficient regulations will be kept in place. Restrictions that pass the *Wouters* test do not necessarily satisfy the exemption criteria of Article 81(3) of the Treaty. The requirements that the rules are needed for the proper practice of the profession and do not go further than necessary to reach that goal are not identical to the requirements that they improve the quality of production and distribution and give a fair share of the resulting benefits to consumers. Moreover, the monopolistic professional bodies may be able to substantially limit competition, so that the cumulative conditions of Article 81(3) will not be satisfied. Hence, the assessment of the conditions for exemption is dependent on criteria that are different from the professions' rhetoric, which stresses the need for independence. Contrary to the *Wouters* test, a full efficiency assessment must consider the possibilities of both positive and negative effects on economic welfare: (1) the achievement of economies of scope (one-stop-shopping), (2) the innovation benefits brought about by a multi-disciplinary firm, (3) the costs of supplying the service by a multi-disciplinary firm, which increase with the degree of specialisation and are inversely related to the number of partners, (4) the quality of the provided service in terms of impartiality and independence, and (5) the seriousness of the principal–agent problem, that is, the risk that the client will be directed towards a professional who is not the least–cost supplier.

In systems of co-regulation, self-regulatory rules are submitted to govern-

---

[9] Case C–309/99 *Wouters v Algemene Raad van de Nederlandse Orde van Advocaten* [2002] ECR I–1577.

mental bodies for approval. The scope of the control exercised by competition authorities was discussed above. Below the focus will be on public authorities (in many cases the competent Ministers), which exercise oversight powers in the public interest (other than competition aspects and related efficiency concerns). The relevant question, then, is whether European law makes such controls necessary and sets criteria for the way in which they are exercised. The answer seems to be that Member States should not unconditionally delegate regulatory powers to private economic operators enabling them to fix anticompetitive rules; public regulators should maintain a margin of discretion in assessing whether such rules are in conformity with the public interest.

When the state approves professional rules that limit competition, the question emerges whether the state rather than the professions will bear ultimate responsibility for infringing Article 81 of the Treaty. If the public authorities define the rules with which the professions need to comply and retain the power to adopt decisions in the last resort, the professional bodies may escape being qualified as associations of undertakings, so that Article 81 no longer applies. The responsibility then shifts to the Member States. In the past, the European Court of Justice has consistently held that Articles 3(1)(g), 10(2) and 81(1) of the Treaty are infringed when a Member State requires or favours the adoption of agreements, decisions or concerted practices which violate the competition provisions of the Treaty, or reinforces their effects, or where it divests its own rules of the character of legislation by delegating to private economic operators responsibility for taking decisions affecting the economic sphere.[10] In the past, several cartel agreements facilitated by the State were considered as an infringement of the Articles 3(1)(g), 10(2), and 81–82 of the Treaty. In this way competition law has been able to prevent harmful anticompetitive practices (such as price fixing) even in cases where these were approved by State law. In the recent *Fiammiferi* judgment, the ECJ increased the effectiveness of this prohibition by deciding that national competition authorities have the duty to dis-apply such measures.[11] The consequence of this judgment is that (associations of) undertakings can no longer claim the benefit of the state compulsion defence once the decision of a national competition authority to disapply a state measure becomes definitive. However, Member States will not violate the rules of the Treaty if they exercise effective control over self-regulatory measures.

The *Arduino* judgment states that a Member State does not infringe Articles 3(1)(g), 10(2) and 81(1) of the Treaty by adopting a law or regulation which approves, on the basis of a draft produced by a professional body of Members of the Bar, a tariff fixing minimum and maximum fees for members of the profession.[12] The debate on the interpretation of this judgment

---

[10] See Report on Competition in Professional Services, as cited above, at p 21.

[11] Case C–198/01 *Consorzio Industrie Fiammiferi (CIF)* [2003] ECR I–8055, para 51.

illustrates that co-regulation does not automatically lead to efficient outcomes. Defects of the institutional framework as organised by Member States' laws may impede efficient outcomes. In the view of the Commission, 'State measures delegating regulatory powers which do not clearly define the public interest objectives to be pursued by the regulation and/or by which the State effectively waives its power to take decisions of last resort or to control implementation' can be challenged. This includes 'rubberstamp approvals' or practices that entitle the Member State only to reject or endorse the proposals of professional bodies, without being able to change the contents of the proposals or substitute its own decisions for these proposals. In addition, the Commission states that a proportionality test would seem appropriate to assess to what extent an anticompetitive professional regulation truly serves the public interest.[13] Legal commentators have questioned this interpretation and have emphasised that no rule has been established setting forth the need of State measures to pursue legitimate public interest objectives, nor is there a rule requiring the proportionality of such measures.[14] Obviously, co-regulation will only lead to efficient outcomes if the public interest control is not defective. Since the case law of the ECJ does not explicitly require a public interest assessment, including a test of proportionality, the current European legal framework seems to be imperfect in setting the conditions for efficient co-regulation.

Even though European competition law does not require Member States to abolish state measures restricting competition in the professions in ways that cannot be justified on public interest grounds, states are not totally immune from liability since such rules may be challenged on the ground that they have restrictive effects on the freedom of establishment and/or the freedom to provide services. Article 15 of the Proposal for a Services Directive[15] requires Member States to screen their legislation fixing minimum and/or maximum tariffs and quantitative or territorial restrictions in the sector of the liberal professions. The requirements must be non-discriminatory, objectively justifiable by an overriding reason relating to the general interest, and they must satisfy the principle of proportionality. In line with the *Wouters* judgment, Article 30 of the draft Directive states that Member States may maintain restrictions on multidisciplinary partnerships and adds that, where such partnerships are allowed, the State must make sure that appropriate arrangements are in place so that the independence and impartiality required for certain professional activities is guaranteed. Finally, Article 29 of the draft Directive requires Member States to remove all total prohibitions on commercial communications. In this way, the proposed Services Directive

[12] Case C–35/99 *Arduin* [2002] ECR I–1529.
[13] Communication from the Commission, p 21–22, at points 86–88.
[14] Compare the contributions of Hanns Gilliams and Mario Siragusa in this volume.
[15] COM (2004) 2.

provides incentives to develop systems of co-regulation (unfortunately with the exclusion of professional rules on multidisciplinary partnerships).

2. Competitive Self-regulation

2.1 The Concept of Competitive Self-regulation

To understand the concept of 'competitive self-regulation', it is useful to compare the current self-regulation in the sector of the professions with other systems of private ordering. At one end of the spectrum, there are spontaneous forms of self-ordering whereas, at the other end of the spectrum, there is delegation by the state of its regulatory powers; in between one finds self-regulatory standards and enforcement mechanisms to comply with behavioural rules fixed by the legislature. Rules on behaviour may emerge spontaneously: this will occur when individuals realise the benefits they will derive from behaving in accordance with others' expectations. Such rules may become standards of behaviour for groups of individuals. Self-ordering arrangements emerged in primitive societies without a well-developed legal system. In the commercial context, self-ordering to govern business relationships can also be found, as illustrated by the development of the *lex mercatoria.* Self-regulation in the markets of liberal professions is a clear example of delegation of regulatory powers by the state. Systems of self-ordering may also emerge as compliance mechanisms with state laws. An example is the advertising industry, which developed codes of conduct in cooperation with traders and the media in order to comply with the general prohibition of misleading advertising.

Traders may voluntarily take the initiative to adopt quality standards in order to make sure that buyers receive performance which meets their expectations. One may distinguish two types of traders: those who do not intend to stay in the market for long and thus are more interested in the short term benefits of exploiting consumers and those who value repeated purchases. Whereas the former collect a premium for opportunistic behaviour, the latter will be able to earn confidence premiums in the long run. In markets where the quality of products and services cannot be observed by consumers prior to purchase, the latter category of traders will provide signals of quality, such as warranties or cooling-off periods. In addition to an insurance function and an incentive function, warranties have an important information revealing function. Cooling-off periods were introduced by mail order businesses in order to signal their reliability, a long time before the EC Directives making such periods compulsory were enacted (Rekaiti and van den Bergh, 2000). Information remedies contained in self-regulation may lead to efficient outcomes if the problem of information asymmetry is not too serious.

Clearly, information remedies will not be sufficient when it is very difficult or impossible to assess quality. Under those circumstances it is in the joint interests of suppliers and consumers to maintain quality by self-regulation and to enforce the standards. Suppliers will be better off because they protect their reputation (and confidence premiums) from opportunistic behaviour by low quality suppliers. Consumers will also be better off because they will save on the high costs of quality assessment.

Self-regulation may be a device to cure asymmetric information. Self-regulation in the sector of the professions has been characterised as an institution of trust: a social contract between society and the profession that mitigates the moral hazard problem arising from information asymmetry (Dingwall and Fenn, 1987). The use of this tool only becomes problematic at the stage where the government delegates its powers to professional bodies, giving them the power to restrict supply. Here lies the crucial difference between the efficient forms of self-regulation discussed so far and self-regulation in the markets for professional services. It is precisely the monopolistic control of supply that may enable the liberal professions to charge above-competitive prices. The logical answer to this problem is to eliminate the monopolies of the self-regulatory bodies and to force them to compete with each other. This can be achieved in two ways: by creating competition between different professions offering the same professional service (inter-professional competition) and by abolishing the exclusive right to control supply within a single profession (intra-professional competition).

Competitive self-regulation is in essence no different from competition between national public regulatory regimes. Competition between legal systems generates important benefits: it makes it possible to satisfy more preferences and to profit from different experiences (competition as a learning process). Excluding competition between legal orders (harmonisation of laws) can be economically justified only when there are significant negative externalities across legal areas, substantial economies of scale and scope, or a real risk of a race to the bottom on markets for legislation.[16] Those favouring the idea of bringing the level of regulation down to the one that exists in the least regulated Member States should fully realise that there are no strong economic arguments in favour of harmonisation and that its costs may be substantial. Harmonisation for internalising significant interstate externalities does not seem warranted because markets for professional services are mostly local. Furthermore, other arguments in favour of centralised decision-making seem weak: economies of scale in formulating rules are not easy to identify and location decisions of professionals may depend more on family ties and cultural differences than on the contents of self-regulatory regimes, so that a race to the bottom does not appear to be a likely scenario.

In contrast with the limited costs of divergent rules on professional ser-

[16] See, for further elaboration of these arguments, van den Bergh (2000).

vices, the benefits may be substantial. There are clearly different views across Member States on the tasks to be performed by liberal professions. The costs of meeting the desired performance criteria also differ due to national or regional specificity. In addition, learning processes are crucial in areas of regulation characterised by great uncertainty, such as the rules relating to the performance of professional services. The empirical work on the real-life effects of deregulation is still largely of American origin and the limited European evidence does not support strong policy conclusions. If one allows the Member States to keep their own policies, different levels of regulation will result. This will create scope for competition between different regulatory regimes, which ultimately will be won by the best rule. In a couple of years, it will become possible to assess the effects of deregulation with more confidence. Overly hasty top-down deregulation initiated at the European level will make it impossible to fully profit from the 'laboratory' of Europe and to learn from different experiences.

Different regulatory regimes also leave scope for the development of different quality assessment mechanisms. Markets for professional services are characterised by serious information asymmetries. As a consequence, one should be careful in introducing competition: markets for professional services can never be totally 'free markets'. The practice of competition authorities shows that they are mostly concerned about prices. So far, competition law does not show a convincing record in guaranteeing quality. The introduction of competition rules in markets for professional services is incomplete without a concomitant development of instruments to assess quality. In the USA, some experience has been gathered in this respect in the market of health services (for example, health cards providing information on the quality of healthcare providers[17]), but in Europe this issue remains largely unresolved. More careful thought should be given to how information asymmetries must be solved when forms of competition will be introduced in markets for professional services. Given the importance of trial-and-error in the development of adequate quality controls, scope should be left for competitive regulatory approaches.

2.2 Examples from the Member States

Since the mid–1980s, deregulation programmes in several EU Member States have created scope for competition between professions. Two prominent examples can be found in England and Wales.

The first example is the abolition of the monopoly right of English solici-

[17] We do not suggest that these assessments are unproblematic; they may cause perverse effects if health care providers refuse to help seriously ill patients in order to improve their record of past performance.

tors for conveyance services (that is, transfer of property) by creating a new profession of licensed conveyancers. With respect to the effects of this liberalisation on prices, empirical research showed that the results of the deregulation were ambiguous. An early study found that solicitors reduced fees in anticipation of imminent competition with the licensed conveyancers and that conveyance fees were lower in areas where the solicitors faced competition from the new professionals (Paterson, *et al*, 1988). A subsequent survey covering the same locations, however, revealed that fees in markets where there were both solicitors and licensed conveyancers were higher than in markets where there was no competition from licensed conveyancers and that fee practices of licensed conveyancers and solicitors had become similar (Stephen, Love and Paterson, 1994). These results show that inter-professional competition will not necessarily benefit consumers. When the number of rival professions is low (duopoly: solicitors and licensed conveyancers) and a limited range of homogeneous services is provided (transfer of property), removing a monopoly does not necessarily lead to lower prices. This finding, however, does not imply that competitive self-regulation will not work in other settings. When there is a sufficiently large number of professional bodies and services are sufficiently heterogeneous, the risk of cartelisation may be contained.

The second example is the breaking of the barristers' monopoly on higher courts advocacy. The Courts and Legal Services Act (1990) gave solicitors the opportunity to acquire rights to appear in all courts. Currently, the right to represent a client in court may be carried out by a barrister in all courts, a solicitor in the lower courts (unless the solicitor has obtained a higher courts qualification) and, in certain limited cases, by legal executives and patent agents. Applications from professional bodies seeking to become authorised to grant rights of audience or rights to conduct litigation to their members must be submitted to the Secretary of State for Constitutional Affairs (formerly the Lord Chancellor). Before giving his approval, the Secretary of State will consult with the designated judges, the Legal Services Consultative Panel and the Office of Fair Trading.

In marked contrast with the measures taken to promote inter-professional competition, no steps have been taken to make intra-professional competition possible. To the contrary, a number of legislative changes have produced perverse effects in that respect. An example of intra-professional competition would be to abolish the monopolies of the Orders of Attorneys at the different Bars and to allow several Orders to compete with each other at the same Bar (compare Ogus, 1995). Competition of this kind may eliminate the rents and preserve the benefits of self-regulation. Unfortunately, so-called liberalisation of markets sometimes goes in a direction which is exactly opposite to the system changes suggested here. Perverse effects may occur if rules aiming at a relaxation of entry conditions force public professional bodies to accept professionals who have been denied registration in the past as new members.

In the Netherlands, the Order of Attorneys has been compelled to admit employed lawyers (Cohen, 1996). This reform has kept the monopoly intact and has increased the control powers of the public professional body. To stimulate competition it would have been wiser to allow competition between a large number of different licensing bodies: several Orders for self-employed lawyers (intra-professional competition) and other professional bodies for employed lawyers (inter-professional competition).

2.3 Competitive Self-regulation: The Role of European Law

A full implementation of the concept of competitive self-regulation implies both competition between different professional bodies within a single Member State and openness to divergent rules on the performance of professional services across Member States.

Given the advantages of diversity in legal rules, European law should in the first place create an institutional framework that makes competition between legislators possible in those areas where such benefits may be deemed to be important. When competition between legislators does not function properly because of market imperfections on the market for legislation, corrective measures coping with such economic distortions should be taken. Here lies a second task for European law: the institutional framework should minimise the risk of a race to the bottom and provide remedies to cope with negative externalities across jurisdictions. It should also make sure that scale economies are achieved in areas of law where these are important. Given heterogeneous preferences, full harmonisation should remain an *ultimum remedium*, confined to areas of law where competition between legal rules causes substantial costs without any compensating benefits.

In an earlier publication, an integrated Law and Economics Checklist for developing efficient systems of competitive regulation has been suggested (Van den Bergh, 2000). Starting from the insight that competition between legal systems may generate important benefits, the first set of questions inquires whether such advantages are indeed important with respect to the envisaged legislative action and can be achieved within the existing institutional framework. In areas where the argument of heterogeneous preferences is strong, but competition does not function properly, rules of European law that guarantee mobility or cure information deficiencies may contribute to an efficient market for legislation. Market failures in markets for legislation (interstate externalities or a race to the bottom) and scale economies provide arguments for centralised decision-making but, given the benefits of competition in a context of heterogeneous preferences, legislative measures leaving the largest possible scope for competition between legal rules should be preferred. If a race to the bottom is realistic, it will suffice to set minimum standards, to be seen as a floor of rights from which Member States may not deviate. By contrast, if preferences are largely homogeneous, competition may lead to a spontaneous harmonisation of laws. Centralisation may then still be justified to speed up this process in case of important scale economies and/or transaction cost savings. Finally, when harmonisation seems appropriate, attention must be paid to the risk of political distortions at the level of the central government. The enactment of inefficient rules, benefiting interest groups (or bureaucrats) to the detriment of society at large, must be avoided. By taking these insights seriously, European law can create an institutional framework making effective competition between self-regulatory regimes across Member States possible.

IV. Conclusions

The serious information asymmetries in markets for professional services, which cause a risk of adverse selection (low overall quality generating severe losses to consumers) and moral hazard (supplier induced demand), may certainly justify regulation. The more difficult questions are what form this regulation should take and in which authority regulatory powers should be vested. Over recent years, the form of regulation of professional services has moved away from pure self-regulation, initiated by the professional bodies, towards a more active involvement of governments. The major challenge is to develop an optimal institutional framework, which preserves the benefits of self-regulation and at the same time minimises the risk of competitive distortions harming the public interest.

Self-regulation may be favoured because of the information benefits on the side of the regulated professions and the reduction of enforcement costs. Both co-regulation and competitive self-regulation keep these benefits intact. However, the scope for competition under both regimes differs. A problem with co-regulation is that the monopoly power of professional bodies is maintained unbroken. This is different under systems of competitive self-regulation. The latter schemes may create scope for competition between different professions offering the same service. They may also remove compulsory membership of monopolistic professional associations and thus initiate competition within a single profession. Regulatory models in Member States of the European Union exhibit characteristics of co-regulation. Regulatory powers remain in the hands of the professional bodies, but there is central oversight over these organisations. To achieve efficient outcomes, existing methods of supervision should be improved upon. It is crucial to develop procedures for a structured analysis of whether the professional rules can be justified in the public interest and impose no restrictions of competition that go further than necessary to achieve that goal. So far, the possibilities of competitive self-regulation have not yet been sufficiently explored. In particular, this paper has pointed at a possible reform that would create scope for competition between different professional bodies in the same profession by abolishing the duty to register with a monopolistic regulator.

European law does not yet provide sufficient incentives to make sure that Member States develop efficient systems of co-regulation and competitive self-regulation. There is no explicit obligation on Member States not to enact rules governing the practice of liberal professions that jeopardise social welfare. A more effective control of the regulatory framework for the exercise of liberal professions involves a clear duty on Member States to screen rules for their conformity with public interest goals. To achieve efficient self-regulation, European law should explicitly require Member States to justify self-regulatory rules that restrict competition on public interest grounds and to provide evidence that the rules are not disproportionate to achieve such goals (proportionality principle).

PANEL TWO

LEGAL ISSUES

1

PANEL DISCUSSION

Participants:

Assimakis Komninos
Benito Arruñada
Calvin Goldman
Claus-Dieter Ehlermann
Frank Stephen
Hans Gilliams
Harry First
Ian Forrester
James Venit
John Cooke
John Fingleton
Lowri Evans
Luc Gyselen
Mario Siragusa
Mark Schechter
Pamela Brumter
Rafael Allendesalazar Corcho
Santiago Martínez Lage
William Kolasky
William Kovacic

Panel Two: Legal Issues

► HANS GILLIAMS

The focus of my written contribution for this Workshop is on the application of Articles 81 and 82 EC, and not so much on the state action doctrine. As a legal practitioner, I have been involved over the last years in the application of the competition rules to regulations issued by the liberal professions. In such cases, public interest is almost always at the centre of the debate—as confirmed in the discussion we had this morning. The arguments advanced by liberal professions to resist or even deny the application of the competition rules are always a variation of the same theme: regulation is 'for the public interest'. In my written contribution, I went through the case law of the ECJ to see how such claims are treated. In short, the case law of the ECJ establishes that Articles 81 and 82 EC do not apply to restrictions resulting from state action, be it through public regulation or regulation adopted by associations of liberal professionals. For example, when the regulatory bodies issuing the restraint are composed mostly of representatives of the public authorities, the Court finds that Articles 81 and 82 EC do not apply. In other words, the EC competition rules will not be applied when there is a presumption of state action—with some very limited exceptions which are fairly well known.

In the second part of my written contribution, I briefly looked at the case law on the application of Article 10 EC in this area. In such cases, the Court pays, in my view, some lip service to the obligation of the Member States not to disregard the EC competition rules, but with due deference to the state action doctrine. It therefore seems to me that the practical effect of this case law, in terms of broadening the scope of application of the EC competition rules, is almost nil. The Court will find that there is an infringement of Article 10 EC when a state measure simply reproduces a prohibitive agreement, or when the state measure sort of throws a protecting veil over a restriction that is otherwise clearly prohibited. Many commentators have criticised the Court's case law in this area as being non-activist, or too formalistic and conservative. As a competition law practitioner, I am inclined to agree with this criticism, but to perfectly honest, I must say that I also understand the Court's position. I would personally not mind at all if the Court were to move towards a somewhat less formalistic approach, but I can understand when a judge is hesitant to question the public interest as articulated by the public authorities. I think it is difficult for a judge to invalidate a competition-restrictive state measure only on grounds that the public interest allegedly pursued is not justified, when the Treaty provisions on free movement of goods and services do not apply.

Having said this, the flip side of the coin is as follows: the problem with this conservative case law is that it does not permit the application of the EC competition rules to restrictive measures that are not attributable to the state, or in other words, restrictions that are attributable to the liberal profession. This is why I have problems with the *Wouters* judgment.[1] In the first part of this judgment, the Court finds that the competition rules apply to the ban resulting from the Dutch MDP Regulation prohibiting members of the Dutch national bar association from engaging in (certain) multi-disciplinary partnerships because the Dutch authorities have not sufficiently articulated what was the public interest protected through the MDP Regulation (which was promulgated by the Dutch national bar association). The only guideline from the Dutch public authorities was that the bar association should 'regulate in the interest of a proper practice of the profession'. The Court found this formulation to be fairly vague, insufficient to qualify as state action. In the second part of the judgment, the Court goes on to review the legality of the mentioned ban under Article 81(1) EC, finding that the measure appreciably restricts competition and affects trade between the Member States, but still concludes that Article 81 EC does not apply, because the restrictive measure is in the public interest—it protects consumers, and contributes to the sound administration of justice.

I find it strange that the Court invents the substance of the public interest at stake in a situation where the Court itself states that the public interest has not been clearly defined by the Dutch authorities. The only point of support of this finding is the reasoning, so to speak, that the ban in question is anchored in the prevailing public perception in the Member State concerned. As legal council to Mr Wouters, I spent quite a number of hours and euros in research on the so-called 'prevailing public perception in the Member State concerned', and interestingly found—we pointed this out to the Court, but to no avail—a Report of the Dutch government on a slightly different area, namely the law of notaries, which concluded that the ban in the MDP Regulation 'should be abolished within a reasonable period of time, maybe a year or two'. So, the fact that the Court found that the ban in the MDP Regulation was 'in line with the prevailing perception' seemed to me a little audacious. I am not so much troubled by the deferential position of the Court, as by its apparent willingness to decide for itself what the public interest should be. I am not so sure that national judges would also feel empowered to determine for themselves what constitutes a public interest if the public authorities in their jurisdiction have not defined it. And drawing inspiration from 'prevailing perceptions' sounds risky to me, because, after all, what kind of perception are we talking about here? Is it the perception of the profession in general, of its individual members, or the perception of consumers? On matters that are controversial, it is very likely to have a range for different perceptions, and this is fine in a democracy—that is what a demo-

[1] Case C–309/99 *Wouters* [2002] ECR I–1577.

cracy thrives on. But it also seems to me to be democratic principle that, when faced with different, contrasting perceptions, it is for the public authorities, and not for the professions, and not even for the judiciary branch, to determine what is in the public interest. For all these reasons, I am a little less eager than my colleague Mr Ian Forrester to see the *Wouters* doctrine continued in the Court's practice.

▸ IAN FORRESTER

I will start with a bit of holiday guidance: if anyone of you is thinking of going on holidays to Sweden, especially with small children, and during the summer months, I strongly recommend travelling with every possible medicine that might be necessary, because otherwise it may take 7½ hours to get a packet of aspirin. Why is that relevant to our discussion? Because Mr Hanner, a gentleman who is assuredly tiresome and inconvenient in the eyes of an authority but who deserves a modest statute in the pantheon of heroes of European law, is challenging the Swedish pharmaceutical monopoly.[2] He says that selling anti-nicotine patches and anti-nicotine chewing gum in his shop when pharmacies are closed is a good thing, and by the way, people should better buy his anti-nicotine chewing gum rather than cigarettes. Yet cigarettes are freely sold in any shop in Sweden—and in other EC Member States, for that matter—but selling anti-nicotine chewing gum is prohibited—along with selling heroin—in Sweden, unless sold in a pharmacy which is owned and operated by the State.

When I started counselling Mr Hanner, I thought, 'this case will give me the opportunity to improve a lot on my knowledge of the learned professions—and I will have something intelligent to say at the EUI Competition Workshop on the subject since pharmacists are members of an ancient profession with special rules and duties. In the meantime, however, I discovered that this case has nothing to do with the learned professions, but just with greedy state monopolies. The *Hanner* case is a good illustration of a more general presumption, which is that, when the state regulates by prescribing the rules which seem contrary to common sense (with which I heretically believe competition law ought to be consistent). It is all in the public interest, and you all had better stay away, because the state always knows best about what the people need. And if the Swedish state says it is dangerous for an aspirin to be sold other than by an employee of the state pharmacy system, then it should be so. Sweden is unique in Europe, and it shares with only two other countries in the world, which are. . . . North Korea and Cuba the exceptional distinction of having a total prohibition on the sale of any paramedical products other than by a state employee.

---

[2] Case C–438/02 *Åklagaren v Krister Hanner*, case currently pending before the ECJ (Opinion of Advocate General Léger delivered on 25 May 2004) judgment delivered on 31 May 2005.

Having said this, it is easy to make fun of the Swedish pharmacy monopoly. And it would be wrong, however tempting, to draw the conclusion that any restrictions imposed by professional organizations are foolish and inherently suspect. I can offer—as I am sure other people around the table could offer—other examples of professional arrangements, particularly in small countries, which are, so far as one can see, rather good. One example, from my own personal experience in Scotland: Scottish solicitors have an extremely severe rule about the keeping of accounts and clients' money. In short, if a Scottish solicitor takes money from a client without justification, all other solicitors in Scotland indemnify the victim. That is really impressive, and goes beyond what a government would normally impose upon the learned professions.

Now, it is easy to say that the Scottish example is good and the Swedish pharmacy case is bad, but I am not sure where this would get us. I would submit that any rule adopted by a professional body is highly likely to restrict competition, if only in that those who have done five years of training, for example, get in, and those who have done four years of training do not. This will certainly inconvenience some. The incumbents will like it, and those not admitted will not. There is no shortage of controversies about individual problems. Some of the professional rules are stupid, and it is easy to mock them, but for others it is more difficult to see whether they are justified or not.

What is the EC rule that we suggest courts or national competition authorities should follow? From our discussion so far, it is still unclear to me what EC rule we could recommend to be followed by the European courts. Most of the participants, including Hans Gilliams, seem to regard the *Wouters* decision[3] as a regrettable error. I would point out that this decision was taken by the full bench of the ECJ, it took a long time to produce, and the Court obviously thought a lot about it. It is clear that there were difficulties in reaching this conclusion, and many improvements can be suggested, but this decision was not an accident and there is no point in hoping it did not exist. The court was telling us something. One reason is that in Europe there is huge regulatory diversity. There is a wide range—even wider since 1 May 2004—of professions, professional organizations, and professional regulations. We are not here to set up a completely new regulatory structure, or to say that henceforth all professions should be regulated in one or another manner. Now, whether we like it or not, under the existing circumstances the ECJ decided that competition-restrictive rules adopted by a private professional body are justified if adopted 'in good faith', so to speak. This is an important legal development. In my written contribution I stated that, in 10 years time, this judgment may be regarded as a platypus—ie, something fascinating, a curiosity, a one-off with no lineal descendants—or alternatively, as a *Cassis de Dijon*[4]—

[3] See above n 1.

[4] Case 120/79 *Rewe Zentrale v Bundesmonopolverwaltung für Branntwein (Cassis de Dijon)* [1979] ECR 649.

the famous ECJ judgment of 25 years ago. In terms of EC law, such a decision is equivalent to an inflection point, a moment at which history takes a different turn. I do not think that the ECJ judges took this decision just because the case is concerned with lawyers interested in entering partnerships with lawyers. I presume they attempted to establish a rule valid for all professions and *quasi*-professions.

What guidance, or criteria can we extract from *Wouters*? According to this decision, it is acceptable under EC law that Member States reach different conclusions on multi-disciplinary partnerships. In the case of *Wouters*, the ECJ found that the Dutch ban on multi-disciplinary partnerships between accountants and lawyers does not infringe EC law. Taking as a point of departure some of the reasoning in *Cassis de Dijon*, I attempted in my written contribution to offer some guidance on the application of the *Wouters* rule in the future. You may remember that, in *Cassis de Dijon,* the ECJ said something along these lines: 'what does not kill the French, cannot kill the Germans'.

As to multi-disciplinary partnerships, some Member States think they should be allowed, and some others find it justified to ban them. Is there a way to build some kind of consensus among the Member States on adopting either one position or the other? Do other Member States have the same position? Have they considered taking it? Maybe that should be relevant for a Member State in deciding whether to endorse a private sector rule or not.

Non-discrimination principles should also be a factor to consider in taking such a decision. I once sued the New York bar for not allowing me to join it—not because I might have an abominable character or I lack legal knowledge, but simply because I did not possess a Green Card. One of the grounds for rejecting my candidacy was that the state of New York has a significant number of unemployed lawyers, and there was no reason to add aliens to this pool of hungry job seekers. I challenged this decision on the basis of the 14th Amendment, which extends the equal protection clause to all persons, and I am happy to say that I prevailed. Non-discrimination could be an additional indicator of the justification for a given private sector rule. Is everyone consistently regulated, or is it that only the 'unwelcome visitors' are regulated? Another yardstick could be: does the private sector rule make any sense?

There are a number of situations in Europe where we are burdened by ridiculous regulations. The case of Mr Hanner in Sweden is one example. I commend European diversity, and I realize that it is not possible to produce EC regulation dealing adequately with every single aspect of this area. So we have to trust local regulators. But I also recognise that, in Europe, we also have a long list of ridiculous local regulations, (so does the US) and from time to time these may be overturned by the wholesome application of EC law.

To sum up, we ought to accept that the *Wouters* decision is the recognition by the ECJ of a reality, namely that it is not possible for EC law to second-guess every restrictive private sector regulation, and that sensible private sector regulation based upon a real knowledge of the industry may often be the best way of achieving adequate protection of the interests of the various parties involved. I think we should not regard *Wouters* as an embarrassment, but rather as a necessary evil, and seek to predict how it may be applied in the future.

► John Cooke

I remember that one of the very first cases I appeared in at the ECJ, many years ago, was about access to the legal profession in one Member State (*R Reyners v Belgium* [1974] ECR 639). I remember that quite a number of Member States intervened in that case, and one was supported by a strong delegation from the bar association of that country. Their argument was not about whether and to what extent Article 81(1) EC (with the different numbering back then) applied to the legal services, but whether the Treaty of Rome *as a whole* applied to the legal profession. About a year ago, as I was crossing the hall in the Court's building, and I saw a group of people that I vaguely recognised. When I checked the Court's calendar, I realised why: the Commission was bringing that same Member State to Court for failing to implement the Professional Services Directive. And there it was, the same delegation, invoking I suppose much the same arguments. . . .

In the written contribution for this Workshop I expressed my doubts as to whether it is any longer useful to talk about 'liberal professions' in the context of competition law enforcement. The truth of the matter is that almost every self-respecting service provider nowadays believes that he is providing a professional service. As I noticed over the years, when new services emerge, the first thing the service providers want to do is to proclaim themselves as a new professional category. I remember that, many years ago in Ireland, architects were not regulated as a profession, but the Royal Institute of Architects had a long history, and anybody who obtained an university degree as an architect became a member of this Institute. The way in which this service evolved through the years is similar to the way in which the category of solicitors emerged in Ireland and the UK: in the early 19th Century, a demand for paralegal services emerged, and solicitors became a separate service provider, and eventually a learned profession. In Ireland, technical draftsmen were initially employed in architects' offices but as they came to be engaged directly by building contractors to prepare drawings when planning regulation was introduced, they came to have aspirations towards forming a profession of their own. They adopted a statute, and as the upper chamber in the parliament has a panel for the professions, they managed to persuade it to recognise them as an electing body—in other words, as entitled to nominate people for election to the upper chamber. And of course, all hell broke when the Royal Institute realised that a sort of para-architect profession had emerged and was seeking to obtain official recognition.

One of the interesting things about the so-called 'liberal professions' is that they are, in a sense, in a constant state of evolution and flux. Not only are entirely new services evolving as the market and technology developments demand, which then constitute themselves as 'liberal professions', but at the same time there is a tendency for the traditional professions to become diluted. I do not know if there is statistical proof of these tendencies. However, if you think of a learned profession as 'a group of service providers characterized by the need for detailed or extensive or advanced study of an art or science and characterized by extensive regulation',[5] then in a sense the medical profession, for example, seems to be losing part of the rationale for being qualified as such. As mentioned earlier, nowadays the services of the medical profession are not any longer provided exclusively by self-employed practitioners. By the same token, the state is the ultimate provider of many of the legal services nowadays.

In my view, possibly there is only one real issue regarding the application of competition rules to the liberal professions, and that is, can service providers justify a special treatment under competition rules by reference to public interest? It is not enough to argue that liberal professions are distinct because they are characterised by specialised knowledge and the existence of detailed regulation in that area. Throughout the evolution of the learned professions, starting from the medieval guilds, one of the main characteristics of the classic learned profession is that its members are almost exclusively self-employed and adhere to a certain code of conduct, including the obligation of integrity and disinterest. It was always recognised that the advanced knowledge acquired and membership of the profession (in other words, what we call nowadays 'information asymmetry') imposed upon the professionals a duty to act in accordance with certain standards and limitations, in the public interest. In those early times there was no public regulation; the professions were exclusively self-regulated. The rationale for self-regulation was that, what we call nowadays 'information asymmetry' between the members of the profession and the public required acceptance of a duty to act in accordance with certain standards, which were themselves established not on the basis of the direct commercial interest of the professionals, but on the public interest.

These seem to me to have been the essential characteristics of what we used to call 'the learned professions'. Nowadays these settings are eroded and being replaced by the ever-increasing involvement of governments, mainly through control, in all sorts of services—the 'health and safety' obsession of modern life. In this sense, the need for the public to rely upon the assumption of voluntary self-restraint by the members of a profession has been, to a large extent, replaced by public regulation. I was very interested in Prof Arruñada's

[5] See Commission Report on competition in the professional services, COM (2004) 83 final, available at www.europa.eu.int/comm/competition/liberal_professions/final_comm_en.pdf.

comments this morning on the current reduced demand for notary services and the contrast between solicitors and notaries in conveyancing services. That is a good example of the way in which the functions of the learned professions have evolved. Until the state began to intervene in guaranteeing the validity of title to land, the only guarantee that a purchaser of land had (certainly in England and Ireland and, I think, in many continental European countries as well) was the trust he placed in the validity, accuracy and quality of the conveyancer's service. Once land registries, as public services, came into play, that need to rely on trust disappeared. I suspect this is why it became possible in the UK to open up conveyancing services to competition, by abolishing the monopoly of solicitors on conveyancing. This might not have been possible if the state's interest in assuring the accuracy of title to land had not become a public interest issue. I think that the same phenomenon occurred in the 20th Century in other services.

I will conclude by adding another quotation, besides the one made earlier to Boccaccio and his *Decameron*. Erasmus remarked that, already in his time, '[. . .] the rage for possession has got to such a pitch that there is nothing in the realm of nature, whether sacred or profane, out of which profit cannot be squeezed.'

► Assimakis Komninos

A brief comment on *Wouters*.[6] I was struck by the manner in which this judgment was received by competition lawyers: *Wouters* is now treated in some basic competition law textbooks as an exception, some commentators speak about an EC rule of reason, while others think that EC competition law should embrace this ruling, etc. I personally think that *Wouters* is a normal case, but it does not belong to the area of competition law—it should not be in competition law textbooks, but in EC law textbooks. This is a constitutional law case, solving a specific conflict between the competition rules and other norms. Now, if we see *Wouters* as a kind of exception, then there is a danger that other policy considerations may be imported into the competition law analysis, be it in the context of Article 81(1) EC or Article 81(3) EC, and as a result, the 'purity' of EC competition law analysis may be endangered. *Wouters* balances EC competition law and Article 81 EC as a whole with an extraneous norm, and this is why it is very much like the free movement cases, which the Court has been deciding for decades. It is a pure balance case. In my written contribution for the Workshop, I relied on a specific theory of German constitutional law specialists, which is called 'the theory of practical concordance'. This means that, basically, first you try to reconcile two conflicting norms, and if this is not possible, then you proceed to the resolution of the conflict. That is what I believe the Court tried to do in *Wouters*.

[6] See above n 1.

This also explains the peculiar language used for reasoning the judgment—the 'yes, but' and so on. The Commission has also been doing this—trying to reconcile conflicting norms—in other cases. And I believe that the Commission's approach in the *Guidelines on the application of Article 81(3) EC*,[7] which almost completely ignores *Wouters*, except for a specific footnote on an unrelated subject, is correct.

▸ Harry First

In my paper I attempted a sort of a comparative analysis between EC law and US law in the area of liberal professions—meaning that, each one of you reading the paper will probably think that I got it only half right. . . . The European lawyers will figure that I only got the US side okay, and the US lawyers will figure that only the European side is probably right. So I urge you not to consult each other today about these cases. . . .

What I tried to do in this paper is to separate the doctrinal issues from the analytical ones. I did not want to get caught up in either European or US doctrine, in particular as to the *per se v rule of reason* dance we have in the US. What interested me in reading these cases and thinking about them was the analytical approach to the issues involved, and the results in both systems. I do not have a particular expertise in the area of the learned professions—actually I teach antitrust. But as it turned out while writing the paper, a good deal of the important US antitrust doctrinal cases were actually litigated in the context of professional restraints, particularly horizontal restraints.

I learned several interesting things during this exercise. One of them is that the institutional context matters, both in terms of the results and the ways to go about the analysis. Of course, courts articulate more general rules of law, which are then to be used or not. A case (or a court decision) is always what we make of it. This is the root of the disagreement we heard earlier about *Wouters*.

Having said this, I wanted to talk first about the basic analytical questions that I think courts have to ask in cases involving the learned professions. I'll expose the main conclusions that I arrived at from this comparative law exercise, and then I will lay out some questions for further discussion. It seems to me that, on both sides of the Atlantic, there are basically two types of questions being asked in competition cases involving the learned professions. One is: what are the competitive effects of the restraint in question? As an antitrust lawyer, whenever I deal with this question I think about markets. The first set of issues revolves around the market concerned. The second set of questions revolves around government involvement: how do we deal with the fact that governments are involved in professional restraints?

---

[7] OJ C 101 of 27 April 2004.

Going back to the 'competitive effects' analysis, the first question to ask is whether competition law applies to the area or liberal profession concerned. Second, what are the anticompetitive effects, and how do we analyse those? Third, what are the justifications for the restraint? On government involvement, the basic question is to what extent the action of the private actors concerned becomes a governmental action. Is there a delegation of power from the government to the private actors? Is the government reviewing in any way the actions undertaken by the private actors? These issues are tackled in both the EU and the US enforcement systems.

There are some similarities between the EU and US jurisdictions in terms of analysing the effects on competition. Both sides agree that professionals are covered by competition law, as a starter. This is no mean achievement: in the state of New York, for example, professionals are not covered by the state competition law. So, the fact that both the EU and the US agree on this is something notable. Past that, the competition analysis in each of the two systems is quite different, particularly on the question of public interest justification. In the US, as you may already know, the public interest defence is simply not considered in antitrust cases, whereas in the EU this is the main defence invoked in cases involving the professions. (A little caveat on the US side: although the courts do not consider the public interest defence, it must be said that they are actually somewhat uncomfortable with this in cases involving the professions, in ways that I will explain later.) Finally, although the two systems perform different analyses and apply different approaches once past the coverage of competition rules issue, in the end, cases come out quite in the same way. Going through the ECJ cases I was a bit surprised at the Court's willingness to take bar association regulation sort of completely outside the scope of competition law. I found that to be a surprising result of the competition analysis, and maybe part of it flowed from a woeful analysis of the effects on competition. This is not to say that it is easy to analyse the effects on competition, but I think that in this case the Court did not even get close to starting a real competition analysis. In terms of the government involvement issues, I confess that I did not understand very well the *Fiammiferi* judgment.[8] So my understanding, based on the three ECJ cases discussed here (*Wouters*, *Fiammiferi* and *Arduino*[9]), is that regulation from lawyers in the Netherlands is outside the scope of EC competition law, but that from match makers in Italy is not. . . . I hope someone around this table will explain to me if and why that is so.

Turning to the US side: *California Dental*[10]—a case already mentioned several times in this debate—and other relevant cases quoted by US participants at this Workshop in their written contributions show that the US courts are

[8] Case C–198/01 *Consorzio Industrie Fiammiferi* [2003] ECR I–8055.

[9] Case C–35/99 *Arduino* [2002] ECR I–1529.

[10] *California Dental Assn v FTC,* 128 F3d 720, vacated and remanded, 526 US 756 (1999).

readily accepting the information asymmetry theory. When I read *California Dental*—which is close to an incoherent decision as well—I asked myself: where do we see this theory applied in the Court's analysis? The decision has more to do with analysing whether dentists qualify as a profession, but the Court latches on to this economic concept of information asymmetry as a way to give more latitude to professional self-regulation. One of the interesting things I noticed in reading *California Dental* is the use of the word 'professional': you find it throughout Justice Souter's opinion, but it does not appear anywhere in Justice Breyer's dissent. For Justice Breyer, dentistry is like plumbing, and he says it is hard to see why it should be bad for a dentist to advertise his services if for a plumber it is not.

In *Hoover v Ronwin*,[11] however, the Court's reasoning is basically on the governmental action side. In this decision, the US Supreme Court establishes basically that, if a state 'blesses' professional regulation, there is no need to check whether that regulation is justified. The case concerned a rule adopted by the Arizona bar association, which capped the passing rates at the bar examination on a quantitative basis, so as to keep down the number of lawyers practicing in Arizona. The Court established that this was not an antitrust issue, as long as the state of Arizona had approved the bar examiners. So, not only are the professions treated more gingerly in the US than in Europe, but also, lawyers are treated even better. . . . A sceptic might think: who decides these cases? Well, I did not write this in the paper, but Justice Powell, who wrote this opinion, was a former president of the American Bar Association. Some may think this is regulatory capture. . . . Justice Stevens, on the other hand, wrote on this case a dissenting opinion going back to bread-baking guilds in the 14th Century, arguing that the professions have been up to these kinds of limitations forever, and it is about time to be more realistic about their motivations.

In relation to *Wouters*, as far as I can tell, there is only one US antitrust case challenging the bar association's role in limiting multidisciplinary practice. In the case in question, the complainants wanted to provide less expensive legal services to poor people, and not more expensive services to richer corporations. The 7th Circuit had no trouble dismissing the action . . . without any kind of antitrust analysis. So, in a certain sense, there may actually be more in terms of antitrust analysis in *Wouters* than in the US case law.

One of the questions that arise is: can we ignore the courts' instinct to treat the professions as different from other businesses? Antitrust specialists are sceptical about assertions that the professions are different from other markets, but the courts are reacting differently, so how do you deal with this? There is also, admittedly, a justified reason for the courts to have this instinct: not all professional regulation is self-interested; sometimes the objectives are

---

11 466 US 558 (1984).

mixed. Take the *Indiana Federation of Dentists* case,[12] where the arguments put forward by the dentists to justify not handing x-rays to clients to be shown to their insurance companies were that the insurance companies did not have specialised staff to read these x-rays, and they had no interest in the good health of the patients. I agree with the court's decision—this was an antitrust violation—but the situation is a little more ambiguous than we might consider at first sight.

Another issue is that, both in Europe and the US, antitrust enforcement in the area of the professions may in practice be limited to price fixing (and I would hope that, after *California Dental,* the judges will go back to a stronger approach to advertising limitations), and not a whole lot more than that. Actually, this may be enough for antitrust enforcers to work on, but there may also be real limits to what antitrust can do.

Last, a question that has emerged several times in our discussion, and which may not be strictly an antitrust issue, but rather a more general public policy problem: beyond antitrust enforcement, what other mechanisms can be used for examining the justifications for professional regulation and narrowing it down to what is really needed? In the EU, this issue might be tackled on the basis of the proportionality principle.

► William Kolasky

I agree with about 90% of what Prof Harry First has said. The one aspect on which I disagree is his description of the attitude of the US courts and antitrust enforcement agencies toward the learned professions. I accept that there are cases like *Hoover,*[13] but if you look at the Supreme Court's case law since *Goldfarb,*[14] cases like *Hoover* are really outliers. In fact, as I showed in my written contribution, there are something like eight or nine other US Supreme Court cases since *Goldfarb* that played an important role in shaping the analytical framework for dealing with horizontal restraints in general. In each and every one of these cases, the Supreme Court treated direct horizontal restraints among professionals as to price and output very harshly, just as harshly as it would have treated the same restraints if established by plumbers or homebuilders.

Where you actually find a difference is in the area of the so-called 'second order restraints', or professional advertising—and I want to talk briefly about these, because they are quite interesting. In *Goldfarb,* the Supreme Court suggested that the fact that a restraint operates upon a profession rather than a business should make a difference. Recently I re-read this decision, and I was reminded of a meeting with our Securities and Exchange Commissioner during the review of the *Price Waterhouse/Coopers & Lybrand* merger by the

[12] *FTC v Indiana Federation of Dentists*, 476 US 447 (1986).

[13] See above n 11.

[14] *Goldfarb v Virginia State Bar*, 421 US 773 (1975).

US Department of Justice, where a senior executive from Price Waterhouse made the mistake of referring to accounting as an 'industry'—the regulator immediately jumped to correct him. I would add that this merger was reviewed both in the US and the EU,[15] and neither agency mentioned in their decisions that accounting is a profession—it was simply irrelevant to the merger analysis. Accounting is a profession that back then had five companies worldwide, each having 3 or 4 billion dollars annually in revenue, so I wonder if that is not a business. . . .

I believe that *Trinko*[16] reflects more accurately the current US approach, whereby antitrust analysis should take into account the structure and circumstances of each industry at stake. Part of that is an awareness of the significance of regulation. This is true for telecommunications, and it played a very important role in the Court's decision in this case, but it is equally true of professional services. In this regard, there is nothing different about professional services. However, I agree with Prof Frank Stephen when he points out that this is not enough, because the antitrust enforcer should look at the individual markets, and not 'the industry'.

After this prelude, allow me to turn to what I think are the five key issues in this area, and discuss the experience in the US over the last 30 years with these issues. The first is the so-called 'public service element' of professional services. Someone referred earlier to the fact that, in the liberal professions, quality, accessibility, and affordability are particularly important. My question is: why are these attributes more important in the case of legal services, for example, than in the case of telecommunications services, where there is regulation designed to ensure universal service at affordable rates? And this leads to another question: what exactly do we mean by 'learned professions'? I do not think that economists have any less education than lawyers, and yet, perhaps because they understand the value of markets, economists have managed to avoid regulation, and are not termed as a liberal profession. What is the difference between an economist selling consulting services and a lawyer? I referred this morning to my home-building experience: well, as part of that, we discovered that we also had termites, and when I wanted to deal with this problem, the first thing I was told by my general contractor was: 'We need an etymologist to examine the problem.' Meaning, someone clearly as learned as any lawyer, and certainly solving a problem that for me was every bit as important as having counsel from a lawyer. So, where do we draw the dividing line between professions and other services? It is true that, to some extent, some professional services are vested with a serious public service element. That is particularly true of auditing, where we expect certified public accountants in auditing companies to basically watch out for the interests of the investing public. Ironically, though, that leads to a very interesting

[15] For the Commission's decision, see Case M1016, OJ C 376 of 11 December 1997.

[16] *Verizon Communication Law Offices of Curtis v Trinko*, 124 US 872 (2004).

principal–agent problem, because, who selects the auditors? It is the firm being audited, and not the investors. And we have seen what happens when companies do not hire auditors who do a good job, or let their auditors not do a good job: the company's reputation, and sometimes its future, is in jeopardy. A non-professional category which frequently claims to be vested with the public interest—believe it or not—are the liquor dealers. One of the justifications for state regulation of liquor sales is that over-consumption of alcohol is bad, and in fact we need to limit the supply of alcohol and raise prices to protect ourselves from drinking too much. So, claims of serving a public service are not limited to well-educated professionals.

Second comes the issue of market failures. As we discussed earlier, claims of market failure are nearly ubiquitous, and it really is just a question of their degree. There is no doubt that in many industries the potential for market failure may justify regulation, but it is equally important to recognize—as somebody said this morning—that regulation is often inefficient, especially private regulation or regulation by agencies who are captured by the regulated, which happens all too often. And sometimes regulation is simply useless. A wonderful recent example is a consent decree by the Antitrust Division of the US Department of Justice against major brokers charged with fixing prices on the market for securities. Part of this consent decree was to require that each of them hire an antitrust compliance officer. One of my tasks over the last several years has been to train some of these compliance officers. What I found out was that they were almost invariably the newest hires, usually the ones with the poorest educational background, who the company does not trust to buy and sell stocks, and their turnover was of about every 12 months—which for me was quite lucrative, of course, because I got to teach the course every year. . . . But clearly, what value was there to having those compliance officers on site? So, I think we need to be sceptical of market failure arguments, and we need to look at them on a market-specific basis. We should also apply the kind of proportionality test that the EU is proposing, where, if you are going to regulate, then regulation has to be reasonably tailored to achieve the public interest objectives and be the least restrictive means to achieve the objective.

This brings me to the next issue, which is: who regulates? Should it be done by the industry itself, or by the state? There are actually some values to self-regulation. It is sometimes more efficient, because the people in the industry understand their markets better than public officials do. But the fact of the matter is, in the US we have adopted a set of rules whereby, if you do have self-regulation, then in order to avoid the application of antitrust law you need to satisfy the state action doctrine, which requires a clearly articulated state policy and active state supervision. I think the question in *Hoover* was whether or not those requirements were met. If you do not have state action, and you deal with self-regulation by the industry, the public interest defence falls out of the equation—the analysis will only be about the effects of the restraints on competition, and not whether the restraints serve a public interest. The interesting thing is that the US Constitution actually becomes antitrust law with respect with state regulation—and this notion comprises regulation by private entities that qualifies as state action—at least with respect to advertising. The 1st Amendment has been used to strike down regulation on grounds that it restricts, for example, price advertising by professionals, on grounds that it is over-paternalistic. So, we have a sort of upside-down situation, where restraints that are imposed or endorsed by the state are quite free of scrutiny, whereas second-order restraints actually receive a fairly close scrutiny under the 1st Amendment.

Next point: it is very important to look for less restrictive alternatives of regulation, and possibly allow the market to solve some of the issues. The first and most effective *ex post* way of intervening is, as mentioned by Amelia Fletcher, through tort law. Any of us in the private law practice knows the extent to which fear of malpractice claims reduce the risk of malpractice. The second is the reputation effect. Mistakes made by professional service firms do have serious reputation repercussions. The third way was mentioned by William Kovacic: the demand for information could be met by third-party sources. He gave us the example of a review of law schools, but I think all of us have at hand another close example, that of the growing number of guides to the legal practitioners in different areas issued by various chambers.

Finally, on the potential for market responses: there has been a lot of talk about the restrictions on entry into the professions, and there is no question that this is the most frequently used vehicle for keeping prices high. (By the way, this is not limited to the professions—the city of New York strictly restricts the availability of taxi licences.) However, when the profession overdoes it with entry restrictions, the market responds. The best example is Japan, where, as far as I understand, the passing rate for examinations for admission to the bar is of about 2%–3%. The result of this is not necessarily much higher fees for practicing lawyers in Japan, but that most legal work in this country is done by lawyers who have failed the admission exam but work for private law firms. So, the strategy of limiting entry can sometimes be self-defeating.

One last comment related to the point made by Prof Arruñada, namely that markets are dynamic by nature and that they are constantly changing in terms of technology, organisation and demand. I have worked on the review of the *Price Waterhouse/Coopers & Lybrand* merger, which took us from 6 big accountancy firms down to 5. The reason for that merger was competition with Arthur Anderson, which was the largest accountancy firm at the time and had a thriving information technology consulting business. I remember that we received letters of concern from the French bar association, objecting to the merger because they were concerned that 'the big 5' accountancy firms were going to take over the market for legal services. What eventually happened was that Arthur Anderson split. Then, concerns about independence of auditors were raised, especially on the background of the Enron affair, and now most of 'the big 5' have divested their consulting practices, and Arthur Anderson has gone out of business. This is interesting, because it shows there is a risk when the antitrust enforcer (in this case it was the European Commission to adopt this position) finds there is no problem with a merger reducing the number of market players from 6 to 5, whereas there would be a problem with a 5–to–4 merger. In fact, we eventually ended up with only 4 firms, because one of the remaining big 5 went out of business. When reviewing mergers, the antitrust authorities have to ensure that enough firms are left operating on the market, in case there are unforeseen further developments. Moreover, as William Kovacic suggested, we should also look at the effects of the mergers retrospectively. This has actually been done in the case of the auditing industry. I remember a very good econometric study on the last round of mergers, back in 1990, which found that they had actually helped reduce fees. However, if the study were to be repeated today, we would find that the auditing fees are much higher than in 1997, before the *Price Waterhouse/Coopers & Lybrand* merger. Is this the result of this merger and the closure of Arthur Anderson? Not necessarily. More likely, it is the result of the fact that, after Enron and other accounting scandals, investors are demanding much more thorough and expensive auditing than they used to.

► CALVIN GOLDMAN

I will try to summarise some relevant aspects from Canada's experience in this area. Canada has traditionally played the role of in-between Europe and the US, and the area of interface between antitrust law and the regulation of the liberal professions is no exception in this sense. Like the US, we are a common law system, and like the US we make extensive use of the courts. Unlike the US, we do not have anything near to the vast amount of private litigation, so, most of these cases are determined through proceedings brought by our federal Competition Bureau. In Canada, the professions are generally regulated at the level of the provinces, through specific statutes. Canada is, of course, quite diverse, and the provinces take great pride in their legislative autonomy. Court decisions in this area of law taken over the last 50 years have often been contested. In a nutshell, similar to what occurred in the US, cartel-like activities were generally prohibited by courts upon an action brought by the federal Competition Bureau whenever the statutory scheme under which the professions operated did not specifically require or authorise price-fixing.

An interesting example is the case brought by the federal Competition Bureau against restrictions imposed by the bar associations on the purchase of professional insurance by lawyers. Restricting the possibility for the lawyers to purchase such insurance only from bar structures was qualified by the Competition Bureau as an act of monopolisation. The Bureau lost this case—the High Court found that this was an area within the scope of state law, so federal law was not applicable. A whole range of professions were challenged in court in Canada, including notaries and pharmacists, of course, but also land surveyors, optometrists and health care professionals other than medical doctors (the latter being governed by state statutes). The most contested cases involved lawyers. From my experience at the Competition Bureau, I can tell you that these were exceptionally hard-fought battles, among many reasons, because lawyers have former colleagues on the bench. The Competition Bureau decided to bring a case against both lawyers and real estate agents, on account of the excessive fees charged for real estate transactions. (I do not need to mention the relevance of such purchases in the consumers' lives.) The Competition Bureau relied in its argumentation on previous US cases like *Goldfarb*, and respectively, the existent proof that the US bar had not fallen apart because competition was allowed following such cases. The arguments invoked in defence by the real estate boards, that they could not do a proper job of selling homes unless charging 4.5% to 5% of the transaction value (which is often above 1 million dollars), were ridiculous.

The Competition Bureau obtained more favourable publicity through this case than, I dare say, in any other case brought to this date. The public recognised the benefit of antitrust law enforcement, and this had a spin-off effect in other cases, where the Competition Bureau had faced difficulties in previous years. The courts became more aware of the pro-competitive activities of the Competition Bureau. In cases such as *Garland*[17] (a recent decision adopted by the Supreme Court of Canada) or *Mortimer*,[18] our courts narrowed down the scope of the public interest defence. The courts established that federal antitrust law applies in this area *except* in cases where the professional statute specifically requires or approves the anticompetitive conduct in question. This means that, in the 'grey area' where the law entitles the professions to regulate without giving specific directions about the scope of such regulation, the courts will apply antitrust principles. This is a very important development, because it goes in the direction of expanding the reach of antitrust law enforcement in the area of professional regulation.

Finally, on a point that was brought up earlier by William Kolasky, namely, issues of merger control in the debate on the interface between antitrust law and the regulation of the professions: I wanted to mention that, while at the Canadian Competition Bureau, I was also involved in the review of the famous *Price Waterhouse/Coopers & Lybrand* merger, as well as that of the subsequent one, with Arthur Anderson. William Kolasky is right: in the review of these mergers, accountancy was treated like any other industry. Part of the reason for this—at least in Canada—is that there was nothing on mergers in the statute covering accountancy licensing—other than provisions

---

17 *Garland v Consumers' Gas Co* [2004] SCC 25.

18 *Mortimer v Corp of Land Surveyors (British Columbia)* (1989) 35 BCLR (2d) 394 (SC) (QL).

on licensing, standards for approval, etc. Think of examples where a statute governing certain telecoms industries, or specific high-tech industries, or electricity generators being privatised, where, in addition to licensing, a statutory body needs to approve the merger. The Canadian Competition Bureau reviews some of these mergers—in telecoms, energy, etc—from the standpoint of their effects on competition. We recently had a case of this kind—which eventually got settled before the court hearing—where there was a real contest as to which statute should prevail: federal antitrust law, the sectoral statute, or the state statute governing aspects of the licensing.

To conclude, there are lots of issues still to be clarified in this area. A couple of years ago, the Canadian Competition Bureau issued a bulletin that attempted to clarify some of these issues. Some of us believe, respectfully, that the purpose of the bulletin was not achieved, but this is also partly due to the fact that this is a constantly-evolving and difficult area of law enforcement.

► LUC GYSELEN

In my written contribution for this Workshop I focused on the standards for assessing the legality of anticompetitive state measures on both sides of the Atlantic. In this oral intervention, I would like to cover three main issues relevant to this comparative analysis.

First, the constitutional environment for this kind of assessment is profoundly different in the EU as compared to the US. This difference initially led to diametrically-opposed state action doctrines. The origins of the state action doctrines are to be found, on the EU side, in the *GB-INNO-BM* decision,[19] and on the US side, in *Parker vs. Brown*.[20] In the latter decision, the notion of state liability refers in principle to state immunity.

My second point is about state action doctrines in the EU and in the US nowadays. Having reviewed the case law on both sides, I believe that the two standards have evolved towards convergence, or at least that the EU doctrine has moved closer towards the US standards, as refined in *Midcal*[21] and *Ticor*[22]-*Arduino*[23] stands as proof for this affirmation.

Third, there is certainly room for further clarification and refinement of the current EU standard. A couple of issues in this respect: first, we should not forget that the constitutional environment is quite different in the EU and the US—and I think that Mark Schechter brought out this aspect very well during the discussion we had this morning. The EC Treaty contains a number of explicit prohibition provisions directed at state measures that impede market integration, free movement of goods or services, etc. As we do have all these

---

19 Case 13/77, [1977] ECR 2115.

20 317 US 341(1943).

21 *California Liquor dealers v Midcal Aluminium* 445 US 87 (1980).

22 *FTC v Ticor Title Insurance Co* 504 US 621 (1992).

23 See above n 5.

prohibition provisions against restrictive state measures in the Treaty, the logical consequence is that regulatory measures restricting competition should also be prohibited. The problem is that we do not have an explicit constitutional limitation to these measures. However, Articles 3(1)(g) and 10 EC contain the principles that can fill this lacuna. Back in the 1970s, the ECJ established that there were constitutional negative implications on any state interference in the competitive process—a sweeping statement, and perhaps also a sign of judicial activism, but that is another topic. The US constitutional environment is, of course, profoundly different. It contains no provisions prohibiting state measures that interfere with market integration. There is the commerce clause, but this is no more than an affirmative grant of power to the federal congress to regulate interstate commerce, including the setting of such limitations. The US Supreme Court established in *Parker v Brown* that, if there is genuine state action, it should be immune from the application of the Sherman Act.

As I already mentioned, having reviewed the case law on both sides of the ocean, I believe I have found a more marked move on the European side towards the US legality standard. It is certainly true that, until *Arduino,* and even *Fiammiferi*,[24] the Court still paid lip service to what I call the two-prong legality standard, as restated in *van Eycke.*[25] In *Arduino* you can clearly see that, if a state measure which restricts competition is the expression of a clearly-articulated state policy toward competition, and it is actually state-supervised as well, then it is immune from the application of EC competition rules. I am not going to discuss here whether the Court applied that doctrine (the clear articulation, plus the 'active supervision' test) well in *Arduino*, but it certainly is addressed in the decision. I also think that there is a difference between *Arduino* and *Fiammiferi*, where there was much less state involvement in many respects.

One issue that I think the Court should still clarify and refine, is as follows: the case law seems to indicate that, at present, the main criterion for deciding cases in this area has become determining whether the state assumes full responsibility for the restriction of competition, by clearly articulating its policy and actively supervising its implementation. It would be helpful if the Court laid down this criterion directly, rather than referring to *van Eycke*. As I already mentioned, this is a two-prong test, whose second part, the 'active supervision' test, clearly needs further refinement. According to this test, when the state deprives its own legislation of its official character by delegating it to private bodies, responsibility for taking anticompetitive decisions will run afoul of Articles 81 and 3(1)(g) EC. As I explained in my written contribution, at present the two limbs of the test contradict one another. So, the first

24 See above n 4.

25 Case 267/86 *van Eycke v ASPA* [1988] ECR 4769.

thing to do is to eliminate this ambiguity and state very clearly that we have basically imported the US doctrine.

A second issue that remains to be clarified is the constitutional underpinning of the current doctrine. We have to acknowledge the fact that there is no express Treaty provision prohibiting all anticompetitive state measures altogether. There are prohibition provisions applicable to other state measures interfering with market integration, but there is nothing specifically directed at anticompetitive state measures. So, we cannot read in the Treaty such a general ban. Now, what is the (more limited) interpretation to be given to Articles 3(1)(g) and 10(2) EC, it is difficult to determine. In my own view, when the state only lends some sort of 'deferential' support to a private anticompetitive arrangement, it has not carefully reflected on whether the act is in the public interest or not. So, another point to be clarified is whether the *GB-INNO-BM* theory still stands in place, and if so, how should it be interpreted? I think this doctrine should be revisited in light of recent developments in *Arduino*.

Third, the Court should make it very clear that if, and only if, the anticompetitive state measure in question is clearly articulated and actively supervised, there should be no further stage of assessment on the substantive merits of the policy in question. If, by contrast, the state measure consists of delegating the decision-making power to private bodies, the issue of justification becomes relevant. However, the analysis would not focus on public interest, as in *Wouters*, but on justifications under Article 81(3) EC, as in the case of private restrictions on competition.

Having said that, the current situation should not be considered dramatic, because a good deal of the state measures restricting competition may very well run afoul of an explicit prohibition provision in the Treaty. As we discussed this morning, some anticompetitive state measures restrict the free circulation of services—as in the case of the Scandinavian pharmacy monopoly.[26] In all cases where a Treaty prohibition provision is infringed, the analysis will have to take into account the justification issue.

To conclude, I argued that the test currently applicable in this area could be refined on several counts: first, we need a more clear articulation of the 'active supervision' test. In my written contribution I examined this issue in more detail, and I just wanted to add that I find this point difficult to tackle. We tend to presume that the test for 'a clearly articulated and actively supervised policy' is satisfied only if the state is actively involved in the regulatory and decision-making process, as well as in the monitoring of implementation. This approach may eventually lead to an over-burdening of the regulatory process. Moreover, is it up to Commission to tell the Member States how to regulate? Some Member States have a tradition of deregulation; others are far more hands-on in terms of regulation.

---

[26] See above n 2.

My last point relates to Prof Harry First's earlier intervention: I also believe that, in most of the cases decided in this area so far, the Court has skipped addressing two preliminary issues. One is: where does the restriction of competition occur? In *Wouters*, the Court did not address this issue. The second is that of effects on interstate commerce. The Commission has explained in a Notice that it will not presume effects on intra-Community trade in cases where the main anticompetitive effects are felt in one Member State, and therefore such effects will have to be proven.[27] However, in none of the state action cases decided so far did I find any reference to well-developed tests for assessing effects on intra-Community trade.

► SANTIAGO MARTÍNEZ LAGE

The written contribution for this Workshop that I prepared together with Rafael Allendesalazar Corcho focuses on the Spanish experience in relation to the interface between competition law and professional regulation. In our view, Spain has quite an exceptional enforcement record in this area. First of all, the existence of professional associations is, so to speak, enshrined in Article 36 of our Constitution—accidentally, two articles before freedom of competition, which is covered in Article 38. Currently, there are more than 50 professional associations operating in our country. The Spanish Act regulating professional associations, dating from 1974 (before the adoption of our Constitution), is quite restrictive. At the same time, the Spanish Competition Act includes exemption provisions with a very wide scope of application, allowing professional associations to escape from the application of our competition rules. Nevertheless, after what we call in our paper 'a long and winding road', nowadays Spain may not be the most liberalised country in so far as the professions are concerned, but it is certainly not any longer among the most restrictive countries in this respect. This state of affairs is basically the consequence of the fact that the Spanish national competition authority has, since 1992, dealt with more than two dozen cases involving professional regulation for surgeons, architects, stockbrokers, lawyers, notaries, etc. (By the way, as you may imagine, I continue to disagree with Prof Arruñada's reply to my earlier observation, but I will not continue this debate now.) Since my colleague Rafael Allendesalazar Corcho has personally acted as counsel on many of these cases, I will pass him the floor.

► RAFAEL ALLENDESALAZAR CORCHO

As Santiago Martínez Lage just mentioned, the Spanish enforcement practice in this area saw notable changes after 1992. This was not due to amendments of the law, but rather to the fact that the Spanish government requested our

[27] European Commission (2004): Guidance on the effect on trade concept contained in Articles 81 and 82 of the Treaty, OJ C 101, 27 April 2004.

competition authority to report on the changes required in order to modernise the Spanish economy and prepare our entry into the European Monetary Union. The first report prepared by our competition authority in response to this request concerned the professions. It is worth noting that this report preceded the Commission's liberalisation endeavours in the area of the professions—it was published at a time when EU policy was mainly focusing on free movement of services, and not (yet) on the competition law enforcement aspects related to professional regulation. The mentioned report examined in particular barriers to entry, pricing and non-pricing restrictions. On barriers to entry, the conclusion of the report was that, given that in Spain professionals are very numerous, there was no perceived need for fostering external competition, but rather, it was necessary to eliminate regulatory elements that foreclosed competition among the Spanish professionals. Thus, although the report acknowledged the existence of a demand to eliminate obligatory membership of professional bodies, the conclusion was that it was not indispensable to eliminate this obligation. The report defined non-pricing restrictions as those restrictions imposed on both the professional and the client, and suggested that all geographical and business structure restrictions should be removed. In addition, the report suggested eliminating restrictions on advertising, as they impeded young professionals from penetrating the market. Finally, the report argued for eliminating price restrictions in any form whatsoever—at the time, Spanish law allowed professional associations to establish minimum and maximum fee ceilings.

Soon after the publication of this report, the Spanish government submitted to the Spanish Parliament for approval the draft of a law transposing its recommendations. It just so happened that the Parliament was dissolved soon after the submission of this draft, so the legislative framework for the professions remained unchanged for another four years. In the meantime, however, the Spanish Competition Tribunal started to apply the provisions of our national competition law to the area of the professions. Professional associations sought to deny the applicability of competition law provisions to their acts, arguing that their status was equivalent to that of public administrative bodies, and therefore not subject to the decisions of another administrative body such as the Competition Tribunal. The Competition Tribunal rejected these arguments and gave a very strict interpretation to exceptions from the scope of application of national competition law. In 1996, an amendment of the law on the professions enshrined the principle of application of competition law to the professions.

I find it important to note that, even though there is a clear and explicit call from both from the Competition Tribunal and the Spanish government to apply competition law to the professions, our courts have been a bit reluctant to do so, even after the 1996 amendment of the competition law. In particular, the Spanish courts have been quite willing to consider several 'particularities' of the professions in order to justify restrictions of competition. For example, the courts established that restrictions on advertisement by lawyers and the prohibition of contingency fees are compatible with our competition rules. So, I think that there is a difference of perception: on the one hand, the efforts of the competition authorities to liberalise professional sectors, and on the other the restraint of the courts to apply competition rules to the same.

► JAMES VENIT

I find it difficult to accept that lawyers, for example, are not like other economic actors, and therefore are not subject to the competition rules as other economic actors. The idea that the legal profession should be treated differently because lawyers need to get a degree is rather peculiar and strange, besides being distasteful to advocate by a lawyer. I think we should set an example, rather than try to flout the examples that we set for others. It is interesting that the relevant jurisprudence does not focus on the notion of economic actors and entities, as it often appears in the jurisprudence involving state actors engaging in economic activities, and where the Court spends a lot of time agonising over whether or not they are economic entities, etc.

Having cleared this, the rest becomes pretty easy. Enforcement becomes tricky again once there is state involvement. I found Luc Gyselen's written contribution excellent in elucidating the issues at stake in this area, but I would not know how quickly they are going to be resolved by the Court. I think this is an area where just by reading the jurisprudence one may get hopelessly lost, as the doctrine has moved and shifted from case to case. There is a tremendous need for consolidation. And I also believe that the constitutional setting in the EU is particularly complex: there is clearly a scope for regulation, but it is also clear that the state is very often the most anti-competitive actor on the scene.

I would conclude with a sort of a plea for deregulation: in Brussels, the practice of competition law actually grew up in a completely non-regulated environment. The Belgian bar did not begin to regulate foreign lawyers until about 10 years ago. During the 60s, 70s and 80s there was a huge influx of foreign law firms practicing EC law, and mostly competition law, which were clearly responding to a demand that could not be satisfied by the domestic market. I believe that this was a rather positive experiment, arguing very strongly for the absence of a need for regulation. The Belgian bar has been rather gentle in its approach to subsequent regulation, and more welcoming than bars in other European countries—like France, for example, where, if you are not fluent in French, you will never be admitted to the bar.

► CLAUS-DIETER EHLERMANN

One point that struck me in the discussion on *Wouters*:[28] I think we should make a distinction between, one the one hand, cases started by the

[28] See above n 1.

Commission, and where there will be a full examination not only of the law, but also of the facts (especially since the reinforcement of the role of the Court of First Instance), and on the other hand, cases in which a national court requests a preliminary ruling, where by definition the Court's examination is largely limited to questions of law. Of course, in the latter case, some of the facts will also have to be examined in order to give a meaningful interpretation to the law. But the two procedures remain fundamentally different. *Wouters* was a request for preliminary ruling.

Now, Luc Gyselen certainly knows the current situation better, but in the past, at least as long as I was at the Commission, I think that the Commission had never tried its hand at applying the EC competition rules (which were primarily designed to discipline private undertakings) against Member States violating them. In other words, the European jurisprudence was back then the fruit of cases brought as requests for preliminary rulings and initiatives taken at the national level. This is why it is important to understand certain differences in the Court's procedures and decision-making outcomes.

► MARIO SIRAGUSA

First of all, I do not agree with the idea that *Wouters* is an exception, or an accident. *Wouters* and *Arduino*[29] were decided by the Court in full composition. To the contrary, I think that the Court has found a very well-balanced equilibrium, and purposefully defined the borderline of those issues for many years to come.

I think that *Wouters* and *Arduino* should be interpreted together. In *Wouters*, the Court considered regulation by independent national bodies or associations. As Ian Forrester pointed out, in this case the Court gives a margin of discretion to the national professional bodies and associations, recognising that certain matters have to be regulated at the local level, and that there are differences between the Member States. This does not necessarily imply that, if something is done differently in one Member State, another Member State should follow it. Nor does it imply that the more restrictive solutions practiced in some Member States are necessarily bad. In *Wouters*, the Court contrasted the position of the Dutch bar association with that of bar associations in other Member States, which are less restrictive, but also recognised that the Dutch bar association exercised discretion in a proper way. I think this is very much in line with the decentralisation and modernisation objectives of the Commission's recent reform with respect to the application of Article 81 EC: the Court considered that, in matters like this, probably the local authorities are best placed to apply Article 81 EC—as we have seen was done in Spain. This does not imply unfettered discretion given to the national bar associations, because the Court's decision does indicate

---

[29] See above n 5.

that the bar associations have to follow some principles in exercising this discretion—they have to look at whether there are less restrictive alternatives. But this proportionality test has to be done at the local level, and with a certain degree of discretion.

On *Arduino*, I agree with Luc Gyselen's analysis. In this case, the Court recognised that, if there is state action (as indeed was the case), then Article 81 EC does not apply. I agree, the state action doctrine has been simplified and brought closer to its US equivalent. In this case, I also think that the Court wanted to set some balance between self-regulation and state regulation. If the Court had not recognised a degree of discretion to the national bar associations, having taken the position that it took in *Arduino*, the effect would have been that all national bar associations lobby for state regulation, because the only way to keep professional regulation outside the scope of Article 81 EC would have been to have state intervention of the *Arduino* type. I think that the Court was well aware of this possibility, so it took a step backwards and gave to the national bodies and associations the degree of discretion necessary in order to avoid a rush towards state regulation. I think this is a well thought-out and balanced system.

Finally, I found interesting James Venit's description of the Brussels legal scene in the 60s and 70s. However, as you may remember, legal advice, in contrast to litigation, was also 'not regulated' in several other Member States. Moreover, in Brussels we were not allowed to appear before national courts for many years. So it was only the ECJ and the Commission being liberal and allowing us to plead cases. Regulation, on the other hand, is not always negative—it can also be positive and important.

► Benito Arruñada

I am afraid that in our discussion we continue to frame issues in terms of the professions themselves. This was relevant for the 19th Century, but is no longer so nowadays. In our times, most professional services are provided by professional firms, and not by individual professionals. This substantially changes the paradigm: certain problems that were typical for individual professionals, such as information asymmetries, are different when we deal with firms, while new problems appear, such as that of agency between firms and employees. And the presence of firms modifies the context for the regulators themselves. Let me just point out one of the aspects making the regulation of professions—understood as industries with professional firms—very complex and difficult. I will use an example: firm A provides a service to client B. To motivate and control its professionals, the firm promises full satisfaction or reimbursement to the clients. After being served, customer B claims to be unsatisfied, but firm A argues that client B is abusing the guarantee and acting opportunistically. If the court is open to these kinds of claims, and rules for client B, this will hinder the development of 'the private legal orders', whereby firms improve their acting through mechanisms of reputation and competition. From this perspective, the main issue becomes: to what degree should firms be allowed to act as judges of their relational contracting, and how to allow competition among such firms, who in fact act as control frameworks. We have been talking about self-regulation and the possibility of having competition between self-regulation structures. This is precisely what professional firms do: develop a self-regulating structure for their members. If we do not allow such structures to develop, we would be hindering the most promising solution for the 21st Century.

► JOHN COOKE

I largely agree with Mario Siragusa: unquestionably, there is significance to the *Wouters* judgment, although it is not immediately clear how far this significance goes. My own view is that it is significant in a relatively confined area. On the one hand, it could be argued that the relevance of this judgment is not necessarily limited to legal services, or even to the professions, and it may well apply more generally, wherever a Member State can make a genuine and legitimate justification for having some inherent restraint in order to guarantee the achievement or attainment of some greater public interest. Contrary to what I understood that James Venit was saying, I do not think that anybody would seriously suggest nowadays that a professional service as such could fall outside the scope of Articles 81 and 82 EC. The real issue is to what extent particular facets, or structures, or rules relating to a particular service issued on the basis that it is a professional service, can be said to fall outside the scope of Article 81 EC based on some overriding public interest. It seems to me that one way of reading *Wouters* is as a recognition by the ECJ of the existence of divergent public interests and of the limits to the public interest in competition rules. Articles 81 and 82 EC protect the EC public interest in an efficient functioning of the market. *Wouters* seems to limit the prevalence of the EC public interest by recognising that there are circumstances, such as the need to secure sound administration of justice, in which a divergent public interest has also to be taken into account. This has always been inherent in the approaches that different Member States have taken to the regulation of different professional services, even if it has not been specifically formulated as such. Furthermore, even within the application of a single set of rules, there may be divergent public interests to take into account. About 10 years ago, Ireland decided to solve the problem by opening up legal services to competition and abolishing bans on advertising by solicitors. Contrary to the prevailing view at the time, namely that solicitors would be difficult to persuade to take to an open and competitive market, actually they took to it with such enthusiasm, that in short even the public buses were covered with legal advertising. The effect was that the cost of insurance shot up, as a result of the increased litigation, and recently Ireland had to re-introduce restraints on advertising by solicitors. So, it seems to me that *Wouters* goes no further than recognising the limits of any public interest consideration in this regard.

► Lowri Evans

These comments are very encouraging for the Commission. We perceive *Wouters* as a progressive judgment which, in a sense, underpinned the policy approach subsequently taken by the Commission in this area. The Commission and the competition authorities of the Member States saw *Wouters* as a signal encouraging us to embark on an analysis of the public interest justifications for, and factual circumstances of, different types of professional regulation in the Member States. Indeed, the Court ruled on this case based on the factual aspects relevant to the Dutch context, specifying that the solution might have been different under German conditions.

Another interesting—but less commented on so far—aspect of *Wouters* is that it clearly underlines that professional regulation in one Member State may affect intra-Community trade. This is a very obvious principle, but it is nonetheless useful to have it clearly spelled out, thus closing previous debates on the subject. I am also glad that Judge Cooke finds that these are principles that apply more generally. Indeed, the Commission already applied them in a case regarding sport rules, where we used the arguments of the *Wouters* judgment to reject the complaint brought against the UEFA rule on ownership of football clubs.

► Ian Forrester

Although generally I am quite sceptical and unenthusiastic about the subsidiarity principle, perhaps this discussion shows the usefulness of this principle. I do not think that the Commission could produce a regulation imposing, for example, that architects and quality surveyors can or cannot form partnerships in the EU, or that doctors no longer have the monopoly on giving injections. But the idea of the Commission advocating for best practices, and actual enforcement being done at national level, with economists and other wise persons (sometimes lawyers) pointing out the foolishness of national regulation—that could work.

► Hans Gilliams

Ian Forrester and Mario Siragusa seem to argue that, in essence, the Court told us in *Wouters* that we will have to rely on the good faith of a profession regulating itself, and we should not nose around with competition law arguments when regulation is done in good faith. There are two things that bother me about this test. The first one is obvious: this test is fairly vague. It not only gives discretion to the profession, but also to the judges. As such, it is probably a fantastic recipe for lots of litigation and lawyers making a lot of money, but I am not convinced that this is the right test. The second reason is more fundamental. *Wouters* was about a very specific circumstance, where the Court found that there was no articulation of public policy and the rule at issue considerably restricted competition. Under such circumstances, to go on and decide that these rules nevertheless fall outside of EC competition rules if the professional body regulates in good faith, that of course has the effect of excluding consumer empowerment, because the professional rules by definition are being made by professional bodies of practitioners who sit together and decide what is good for the profession, and there is no guarantee whatsoever that a consumer point of view is actually taken into account. In the *Wouters* case, there were various reports and surveys indicating that, especially among corporate customers, there was significant demand for multidisciplinary partnerships. So the effect of the Court's good faith test in this case is equivalent to saying: we do not care about what consumers want. I think that, for an orthodox competition lawyer, this is fairly troubling. Mario Siragusa argued that, if the Court had not taken *Wouters* out of the reach of EC competition law, maybe this would have led to a rush towards state regulation so as to satisfy the *Arduino* test. My response to that would be: so, let that happen. Let national authorities think about professional rules case by case, and perhaps, after having balanced all interests at stake, maybe they would find them justified. If not, at least that would have had the merit of enabling a forum where a supposedly neutral assessor takes into account all of the interests at stake, including consumer interests.

► William Kovacic

On *Wouters*: some years ago, we had in the US a similar debate about multidisciplinary practices. Beyond actual court litigation, there was a serious effort to get the American Bar Association amend its rules so as to permit multi-disciplinary practices. I was a part of a Task Force established by the Antitrust Section of the American Bar Association to produce a report on those rules. It was very clear that the ban on multi-disciplinary practices was anticompetitive. Moreover, the consumers of legal services wanted the ban to be eliminated, and arguments against this simply did not carry water. One of the strong arguments for eliminating the ban is that one can be a member of the bar and work for a corporate client, and therefore it would be hard to justify allowing a member of the bar to work for a corporation while not allowing him to work for a multi-disciplinary organization. The only argument against the elimination of the ban that may have had some force was that there may be a conflict between the duties of auditing firms and lawyers, because auditors are supposed to be independent, whereas lawyers owe a duty of loyalty to their clients. But this may be a potential justification for a rule prohibiting auditors and lawyers to work in the same law firm, as opposed to prohibiting multi-disciplinary practices.

Very briefly, on Prof Arruñada's comments: I also think it is important to understand that we need to stop using a 19th Century paradigm when talking about professional services markets, and instead move to the 21st Century. Nowadays, most professional services are provided by very large firms. There is a great deal of knowledge about the behaviour of firms, and we need to apply it in this area, taking it into account when we define markets, for example. One of the things that struck me as being particularly archaic in the approach to market definition in the review of the accounting merger cases mentioned before was that the Commission viewed the geographic market as national in scope, because the auditors in these firms were licensed at the national level. But there was no consideration given to the fact that, when those accounting firms competed for attracting customers, they were competing in at least a European-wide market, or a global market. It is important to look at this issue from the perspective of the customers as well, and not just from the perspective of a given regulatory structure.

► MARK SCHECHTER

I would disagree with Mario Siragusa if he implies going along a path whereby the EC Member States can identify some public interest so as to put aside the application of EC competition rules. This way, Europe would be walking into the same morass in which we find ourselves in the US with the state action doctrine, whereby any state that decides, for its own reasons, whatever those reasons might be, to displace competition with regulation, it can choose to do so, with all the adverse effects that this choice may have. This situation flows from our federal constitutional system, and there is not much we can do about it. William Kovacic and I will talk tomorrow in more detail about whether something can be done about it. I would suggest for Europe to take a middle path, perhaps establishing that competition rules are overridden only if a well-defined public interest is identified, and moreover, only if it compensates for the negative effects derived from the competition restriction. I think that it is all too easy for states, under tremendous lobbying pressure from various economic interests, to very loosely define public interest, thus protecting in reality narrow parochial interests that are adverse to overall consumer welfare. Do you really think it is reasonable to require that only doctors administer shots? With all due respect, this is just a red herring—one can define a public health interest less narrowly, for example by requiring that shots be given only by qualified and capable people. The problem with regulation is that, if the public interest rationale is not carefully scrutinised, it just becomes a pretence for protecting tremendous inefficiencies.

► CLAUS-DIETER EHLERMANN

We may discuss this problem in more detail tomorrow, because, as it has been said, the proportionality principle applies clearly to state-imposed restrictions on fundamental freedoms, like the free movement goods, services and capital. But, as we read in some of the written contributions for this Workshop, the ECJ seems hesitant to apply this principle in the context of the state action doctrine. We will see whether holding to this position is sustainable, or instead in the future we should introduce a sort of generic 'exception for non-economic public interest reasons' in the application of Article 81 EC so as to avoid abuses.

► FRANK STEPHEN

It seems to me that, in the discussion of this morning and this afternoon, there was recognition that information asymmetry characteristics do exist in most services. At the same time, in the course of our discussion this afternoon we seem to have come back to re-drawing a dividing line between professional restrictions and restraints on competition. This reminds me of some research done some years ago on the deregulation of legal advertising in Scotland. At that time, the Law Society of Scotland allowed Scottish solicitors to advertise their firms in amateur dramatic society programmes, for example, but the first case where the Law Society of Scotland took action against a firm for advertising was because they had sponsored a football team, and this was interpreted as 'bringing the profession into disrepute'. . . . The argument was something like: this sponsorship amounted to advertising for the criminal parts of the population who went to watch football matches, as opposed to the people who went to support their local amateur dramatic society.

Once again, I underline that it is important to define professional services as markets. I keep coming back to this issue of markets, but in my understanding, one of the main reasons why the Irish government changed position on legal advertising and supported the re-introduction of a restriction, is because such advertising had an impact on the government's budget—the government was the defendant in a good part of the cases stimulated by this advertising. So there are interests to defend when it comes to governments as well. I think we have to be careful about generalising starting from particular cases. There is actually a good deal of research showing that advertising, and in particular lower price advertising by professionals, does not really come about—this is because the advertising of lower prices by a professional is taken by the uninformed consumer as an adverse signal on quality. A final point on this: I was most surprised to discover that, in spite of their conservative reputation, Scottish solicitors are much more prone to advertise than American attorneys.

► JOHN FINGLETON

Not being a lawyer, the only thing I can say about *Wouters* is that probably it will help increase the revenues of the bar, if only from having to explain its implications. . . . *Arduino* seems inconsistent to me, at least in the following sense: it seems to imply that, if the state allows price-fixing, this is acceptable, but if the state chooses a different instrument, for example, regulating entry in a way that is considered 'disproportionate', this is not acceptable. This would introduce a sort of distortion in the choice of instruments by the state, to the extent that it will induce professional bodies to go to the state authorities in order to introduce various restrictions in competition. Suppose that an association of pharmacists, for example, intends to introduce a restriction on entry. The association will go to the state, which has the choice to either limit entry or fix prices for this service. *Arduino* seems to encourage the states to take the second route, rather than the first, and this effect seems to me to be problematic.

John Maynard Keynes once said that, in his times, to argue government intervention to the city of London was like arguing Darwin's origin of species to a bishop—the first reaction would be moral, not intellectual, and the more compelling the arguments, the more indignant and angry the response. Nowadays, things seem to be exactly the opposite: when the Irish competition authority talks to Irish professional bodies about competition issues, the reaction is almost a sort moral indignation. I am wondering if this reaction is not, at least in part, due to *Arduino*. For example, the Irish Pharmaceutical Union argued that allowing more entry into the market would result in pharmacies closing. It is completely illogical, but they see it almost as a moral point. Quite often, people appeal to moral principles instead of actually engaging in debate on the real issues.

And finally, one question: it is not clear to me whether these cases are considered under Article 81(3) EC. In other words, does this provision allow a fully-fledged test on the public interest at stake? I thought that Article 81(3) EC can capture quite a lot of circumstances, but I gather from this discussion that things are not so clear. And what about adding Articles 10 and 86 EC to the picture? Does the Commission have a 'strategy' in this respect? Is the Commission thinking of reviewing some of these professional rules under Article 81(3) EC, and asking the national competition authorities to join in this exercise? For instance, the national competition authorities could encourage professional bodies to self-assess their own rules under Article 81(3) EC. If the assessment would be done under other Articles 10 or 86 EC, the test is quite different.

▸ CLAUS-DIETER EHLERMANN

I read this interpretation for the first time in Assimakis Komninos' paper. Surprisingly, there seems to be quite a large consensus in this room on the notion that it would be dangerous to bring such 'non-economic' public interests into the application of Article 81(3) EC, because this would also allow the industrial policy, or 'national champion' ideas, to creep back into the application of this provision, and this is something that competition specialists do not welcome. So it is to a certain extent protecting the purity of Article 81(3) EC, if I understand this reasoning correctly.

▸ JOHN FINGLETON

What I am wondering is: if the Dutch court had come to examine those issues after 1 May 2004 [the date of coming into force of Regulation 1/2003], would we ever have had a *Wouters* judgment?

▸ CLAUS-DIETER EHLERMANN

This is a point you have also raised in your written contribution, namely whether *Wouters* is to a certain extent a 'contextual' decision. I personally do not think this case was decided as it was just because it was close to the coming into force of Regulation 1/2003—there is something more to it. The purpose, as I said before, is to preserve the 'virginity' of Article 81(3) EC. I remember having read a superb paper authored by Ian Forrester listing the different objectives that have been pursued in time by different Commissions under Article 81(3) EC.

I think that the state action theory, being outside Article 81(3) EC, has still to be harmonised to a certain extent with the limits resulting from this provision—for instance, in the sense of not creating dominant positions. At the moment, these limits are not considered in the state action doctrine. I believe we would have to bring in something similar to the proportionality principle. This would be a big step, going along the lines suggested earlier by Profs Arruñada and Stephen and by William Kolasky: if we accept something like a privilege for the so-called 'liberal professions', this privilege should be narrowed down to where it is really needed. Also, the occasional purchasers of professional services have different needs from regular purchasers, like municipalities or companies, and we would have to introduce these distinctions, which can very well be made in the context of the fundamental freedoms, but not under a global approach *à la Wouters*. In other words, *Wouters* needs to be refined and targeted on market failures, on true, rather than false public interests.

▸ MARIO SIRAGUSA

I must insist, but I really do not see any contradiction between *Wouters* and *Arduino*. *Wouters* is concerned with regulation set up by an association of enterprises, to which, there is no doubt, Article 81 EC applies. *Arduino* is concerned instead with regulation established through state action. These are two completely different situations, right?

In *Wouters*, the interesting aspect is that this judgment gives regulatory discretion to the local professional bodies, but at the same time, I think, it also provides a test to determine whether such regulation is over-restrictive. I quote from the judgment: 'A regulation such as the one at stake could therefore reasonably be considered to be necessary in order to ensure the proper practice of the legal profession as it is organized in the Member State concerned.' I think this allows, for example, consumer associations to ask the local authorities to check whether the regulation at issue is or is not necessary in order to ensure the proper practice of the legal profession as it is organised in that Member State. Maybe this test is not very sophisticated, but it can be further elaborated. But is this test really different from the one applied in 'historical' Article 81 EC cases such as *Pronuptia*,[30] or judgments finding justified restrictions related to location clauses in franchise agreements designed to protect information confidentiality? This is a reasoning that is not at all new in our very rich jurisprudence in the application of Article 81 EC. So I think the Court is simply saying that in these matters we should leave some discretion to the local professional bodies, subject to local controls and the proportionality test otherwise common to Article 81 EC cases.

Arduino is totally different—it is a case concerned with a state action situation. I found very interesting the position taken by the Court in this case, because it looks like a very radical switch towards the total immunity approach practised in the US. In fact, the Commission's attempt in the report on professional services[31] to construe from *Arduino* a proportionality test for the public interest is wishful thinking, because there is no such thing in the Court's judgment. Claus-Dieter Ehlermann has put the finger on the real issue here: there is no such test in *Arduino*. Now, of course, Luc Gyselen is right to point out that there are other Treaty provisions on which to rely in this respect. But this means only that state action falling outside the scope of EC competition rules could still be reviewed under other Treaty provisions. The question is: should the Court elaborate a proportionality test applicable to state action?

Once again, I do not see any contradiction between *Wouters* and *Arduino*, and I do not think that self-regulation is *per se* a bad thing. Self-regulation is also a symptom of democracy, and I do not think it is a good idea to encourage professional associations to seek always to be regulated by acts of parliament. I think we should leave some freedom to independent organisations, subject to compliance with the Treaty principles.

► RAFAEL ALLENDESALAZAR CORCHO

A brief reply to Prof Arruñada, in relation to his comments on professional services in the 21st Century: it is true that nowadays professional services are provided mainly by firms, but the clients are very often individuals. This does not reduce asymmetry—to the contrary, it might even increase it. We should acknowledge that many professional rules are intended to protect the final consumer, which is very often an individual. I am not saying that I am against competition among the professionals—especially since I come from Madrid,

[30] Case 161/84 *Pronuptia* [1986] ECR 353.

[31] Commission Report on competition in the professional services, COM (2004) 83 final, available at www.europa.eu.int/comm/competition/liberal_professions/final_comm_en.pdf.

where there are 2.9 lawyers for every taxi driver, and I assure you that there is intense competition among these lawyers. I believe in competition, but I also think we must take into account the interests of the final consumers. Firm clients can look for their own interests much better than individual clients. Remember the example I mentioned before, related to prices of plumbing? What do people finally do in order to circumvent these problems? They go through insurance companies, so that they do not have to worry over the cost of repairing their houses. As an individual consumer, I am not at all convinced that I am better off with an insurance company only because I do not know how much a lawyer, a doctor, a plumber, and a car repairman is going to charge me.

► WILLIAM KOLASKY

One question that surfaces in the debate on the current state of the law in different jurisdictions is: how much do broader interest considerations make their way into the deciding of cases? My intuition is that, regardless of what the legal nominal standard is—that is, whether they are declared to be 'in' or 'out'—in reality, such considerations are always taken into account. This background is always there, no matter how the court has been formally instructed to decide the case. As a consequence, competition authorities always have to take such considerations into account in formulating its enforcement policy. This means identifying exactly the interests at stake and the assumptions incorporated into the public interest standard. Let me mention a couple of examples of such assumptions, and how I think they might be addressed.

One such assumption is that competition will produce adverse distributional effects. US antitrust enforcers tend to think very seriously about distributional effects, even when not planning to argue them in court. I will give you an example of a case currently on the role of the FTC: it involves state regulation requiring that, every time a dental hygienist went to a public school to provide fluoride treatments in order to prevent oral cavities, a dentist would have to be present in order to supervise each and every procedure. This regulation obviously had the effect of diminishing the supply of the service in question. It eventually became clear that it made sense for the oral hygienists to provide the treatment unattended by a dentist, and that the treatment reduced dramatically the likelihood of getting oral cavities, even if the dental hygienist did not do a perfect job in each and every case. To construct our case, we brought into the debate the interests of poorer individuals from public schools who would have been the beneficiaries of the treatment, mainly Afro-American students. Our point was that, essentially, what the dentist association wanted to secure was a high-quality level of the service or none, whereas poorer clients might have been better off with a lower level of the service than if getting nothing. It is like when someone wants to buy a car—not everybody can buy a Mercedes. We did not explicitly argue the adverse distributional effects of the regulation in question, but the facts were there for the court to look at.

The second assumption is related to professional advertising: sometimes we tend to assume that any advertising is inherently deceptive at some level—in other words, any advertising going beyond the publication of the name and address of the service provider is inherently deceptive. We did (and sponsored) a lot of research on how consumers perceive information coming through advertising. The results were that many consumers, including those in the more vulnerable groups, have a striking ability to sort out claims. Let me give you an example: our experiments have shown that customers are able to distinguish between two types of advertisement for food products, one claiming that scientific evidence shows absolutely and conclusively that by consuming a certain food product consumers do not get heart diseases, and the other stating that scientific research is still not conclusive, but evidence so far suggests that consuming a certain food product will produce a certain effect on health. Consumers know the difference between a guarantee and a non-conclusive promise. This is an important avenue of research that competition agencies will have to be willing to undertake if taking up against the implicit assumption that advertising is always deceptive.

Finally, in relation to John Cooke's point about increased private litigation as a result of legal advertising in Ireland, it would be interesting to know if the increased number of private claims were valid. If the claims were vindicating legitimate rights, I would think that the outcome of advertising was positive—if, to the contrary, one wants to keep private litigation under control irrespective of whether the claims are valid or not, this is just an exercise in civic hypocrisy.

► CLAUS-DIETER EHLERMANN

I think there is an extremely important implicit point in what you said: of course, lawyers tend to reason differently from the economists, that is, less in terms of results and more in terms of procedures. However, if you have a difficult substantive issue to decide, it is a great merit to find the appropriate and more transparent procedure for doing so. This is similar to another important point made this morning, about facilitating the flow of information.

► HARRY FIRST

First, I agree with William Kolasky: it is true that even if we take public interest nominally out of antitrust enforcement, it will still creep back in. If we look at the US case law at least, it does pop out in different ways. Since today in the US we cannot really talk openly about it, it comes back in the form of economic theory—like in *California Dental*[32]—or an excessive state action doctrine.

[32] See above n 6.

William Kolasky's remarks also remind us that the effort to develop a factual record, and to try to understand these restrictive practices in the context of their institutional settings, is very important. One of the problems with the EU case law (and I am not sure if it is possible to remedy this) is that the factual basis behind the Court's judgments is not clearly examined, and examined from an economic perspective.

The discussion on *Wouters* reminded me of what happened in the US post–*Trinko*,[33] where some said this judgment did not mean much, and others thought it would have notable effects on future enforcement. This sort of debate opens up a doctrinal pit in competition policy. In the US, there is a long history of public interest functioning as a sinkhole for competition enforcement when it comes to state regulation, although it tends to be shadowed in the larger debate on the balance between non-economic and economic considerations in antitrust enforcement. At the same time, I think it is safer to place public interest considerations in the context of economic analysis, and in this sense, it is unfortunate that *Wouters* pulls this issue out of the reach of competition rules.

On government involvement, it seems to me that this issue appears both in *Wouters* and in *Arduino*. The regulation of the Dutch bar, as far is I understand, was actually subject to a state action insofar as it was published under the implicit authorization of the government. The difference is that, in *Arduino,* the Italian Minister of Justice approved the rates. In the US, we had the *Ticor* case,[34] where the Court established that an implicit or 'negative option' approval by the state is not sufficient to qualify as state action or 'active supervision' by the state. In this sense, the US and EU systems may be moving sort of in the same direction.

► Luc Gyselen

Overall, I agree with Mario Siragusa, with three qualifications. First, I believe that, conceptually speaking—I am not talking about the concrete application to the case at hand—the approach in *Wouters* is similar to that adopted in cases involving ancillary restraints. As a matter of fact, the Opinion delivered by Advocate-General Léger in *Wouters* quotes *DGL*,[36] the Danish cooperative case, which is an ancillary restraints case.

Second, on the public interest grounds taking professional regulation out of the scope of Article 81(1) EC: in the same judgment, the Court stated that the regulation at stake should be treated as a decision by an association of undertakings within the meaning of Article 81(1) EC, and that, because the

---

[33] See above n 12.

[34] *Federal Trade Comm'n v Ticor Title Ins* 504 US 621 (1992).

[35] See above n 4.

[36] Case C–250/92 *DLG* [1994] ECR I–5641.

legislator had not given the Dutch bar a mandate to take into account public interest, it does not fall within the scope of the same provision. So either there is a blatant contradiction in this, or there is something else—and I believe it is something else.

Third, in my view, this reasoning is not even novel, because the Commission itself had applied it back in 1999 for clearing a ban on deceptive advertising under Article 81(1) EC.[37]

► CLAUS-DIETER EHLERMANN

On the Danish cooperative case, I think there is more to it than the ancillary restraint aspect. There is also the principle of solidarity within a cooperative, which is a bit like the exception from Article 81 EC applicable to health insurances.

► SANTIAGO MARTÍNEZ LAGE

In my opinion, *Wouters* is more in line with the American approach after *Bates v State Bar of Arizona*[38] than *Arduino.* If I understood *Wouters* correctly, it is an application of the rule of reason, which in EC competition law is possible only outside of price competition. On the other hand, *Arduino* is clearly a case of price competition, and there I see a conflict with the US tradition after *Goldfarb*. In other words, there is a difference between the US approach and *Arduino* that may find its reasons in the state action exception, but it needs to be stressed that a comparison with the current US practice would not lead us further on in this direction.

► CALVIN GOLDMAN

Following up on William Kovacic's remarks on information and advertising, I would point out what may be obvious to some, and that is the real difficulties in getting the adequate kind of professional advertising. For example, in Canada and the US, at least, the advertising of new drugs must contain information about side-effects. But if you ever heard any of those drug advertisements, you will remember they go so fast, that the info on possible side-effects is almost subliminal, and therefore of little assistance to the public. Drug companies claim that more clearly spelled out information about primary and secondary effects would scare everyone off the drug. So quite often it is difficult to ensure that professional advertising is balanced and sufficiently informative for the public.

---

[37] *IMA*, Commission Decision of 7 April 1999, OJ L 106 of 23 April 1999, upheld by the CFI in *MA v Commission*, Case T–144/99 [2001] ECR II–1087.

[38] 433 US 350 (1977).

PANEL TWO

LEGAL ISSUES

2

WORKING PAPERS

I

*Pamela Brumter Coret**

Freedom of Establishment and Freedom to Provide Services for Regulated Professions in the Internal Market: New Initiatives by the Commission

The Lisbon European Council in March 2000 adopted an economic reform programme aiming to make the EU the most competitive and dynamic knowledge-based economy in the world by the year 2010. In the field of the 'liberal' (regulated) professions, steps towards these goals have been taken by the Commission through initiatives based on competition policy, on the one hand, and on internal market policy, on the other hand.

I. The Internal Market Initiatives of the Commission to Increase Competitiveness in the Field of 'Liberal' (Regulated) Professions

As a step towards achieving the Lisbon Agenda objective of making the EU the most competitive economy in the world by 2010, the Commission has recently adopted different measures aiming at increasing competitiveness in the field of 'liberal' (regulated) professions. They concern the application of EC competition rules in this field, and the implementation of two fundamental freedoms of the EU Treaty, ie, the freedom of establishment and the freedom to provide services. With the aim of achieving a real internal market for services, the Commission, in particular, adopted two proposals concerning the regulated professions: the draft *Directive on the recognition of professional qualifications*,[1]

* Head of the Regulated Professions Unit, Internal Market Directorate General, European Commission, Brussels.

[1] See European Commission (2002): Proposal for a Directive of the European parliament and of the Council on the recognition of professional qualifications, COM (2002) 119(01) of 7 March 2002. See also Amended Proposal for a Directive of the European Parliament and of the Council on the recognition of professional qualifications (presented by the Commission pursuant to Article 250(2) of the EC Treaty), COM (2004) 317 of 20 April 2004; updates on the state of the debate concerning the adoption of the proposal available at http://europa.eu.int/comm/internal_market/qualifications/future_en.htm#20050511.

and the draft *Services Directive*,[2] which establishes a horizontal legal framework facilitating conditions for establishment and cross-border service provision. The Services Directive complements the Directive on the recognition of professional qualifications, given that it deals with questions other than professional qualifications such as professional indemnity insurance, commercial communications and multi-disciplinary activities.

The close relationship between the Treaty provisions on competition and those on freedom to provide services and freedom of establishment has been acknowledged by the European Court of Justice in the recent *Wouters* judgment.[3] In this case, the Court concluded that EC competition rules, on the one hand, and the Treaty rules on freedom to provide services and establishment, on the other hand, had not been infringed.[4]

The steps taken by the Commission in order to enhance competition in the field of liberal professions are discussed in detail by other contributors to this publication. As explained in the *Report on Competition in the Professional Services*, adopted by the Commission in February 2004,[5] the Commission identified five main categories of potential restrictions in professional regulation:

- Price-fixing;
- recommended prices;
- advertising regulations;
- entry requirements; and
- reserved rights and regulations governing business structure and multi-disciplinary practices.

The Report invites regulatory authorities and professional bodies in the Member States to review the existing rules in this area, and in particular to check whether they are justified (ie, pursue a legitimate public interest objective), necessary in order to achieve that objective, and whether the scope of the restrictions imposed is proportionate to the objectives pursued. The report concentrates on six professions: lawyers, notaries, accountants, architects, engineers and pharmacists.

A few remarks on the steps taken by the Commission in the field of freedom to provide services and freedom to establish: on 13 January 2004, the Commission adopted the proposal for a *Directive on Services in the Internal*

---

[2] European Commission (2004): *Proposal for a Directive of the European Parliament and of the Council on Services in the Internal Market*, COM (2004) 2 final of 5 March 2004. Updates on the state of the debate concerning the adoption of this proposal are available at http://europa.eu.int/comm/internal_market/services/services-dir/index_en.htm.

[3] Case C–309/99, [2002] ECR I–1577.

[4] See for example Point 122. The Court concluded that it was not contrary to Arts 81, 43 and 49 of the Treaty for a national regulation to prohibit any multi-disciplinary partnerships between members of the Bar and accountants, since that regulation could reasonably be considered to be necessary for the proper practice of the legal profession, as organised in the country concerned.

[5] COM(2004) 83 final of 9 February 2004.

Market,[6] which aims at facilitating conditions for establishment and cross-border service provision. This would benefit a large variety of different services which are currently affected by a broad range of internal market obstacles of a legal or administrative nature.[7]

These obstacles occur in particular in two types of situation:

- when a service provider from one Member State wishes to provide a service from his/her Member State of origin in another Member State, particularly by moving to the other Member State on a temporary basis. For example, he/she may be subject to a legal obligation to establish himself/herself in the other Member State or he/she may need to obtain an authorisation there or be subject to the application of rules on the conditions for the exercise of the activity; and
- when a service provider from another Member State wishes to establish himself/herself in another Member State in order to provide his services. For example, he/she may be subject to over-burdensome authorisation schemes, excessive red tape, discriminatory requirements, economic tests, etc.

Accordingly, the aim of the draft Services Directive is to establish a legal framework to eliminate certain legal obstacles to the achievement of a genuine internal market in services, and to guarantee service providers and recipients the legal certainty they need in order to exercise these two fundamental freedoms enshrined in the Treaty in practice. The Directive envisages a mix of mutual recognition, administrative cooperation, harmonisation where necessary, and self-regulation. However, the Commission has not adopted a 'one-size-fits-all' approach. It is certainly aware of the specific nature of the regulated professions, which the draft Services Directive fully takes into account. Those provisions of the proposal which concern regulated professions specifically acknowledge that applicable rules and regulations (including self-regulatory measures) shall reflect the specific nature of each profession.

The most relevant provisions for the liberal professions are the following:

- Article 14 of the draft Directive contains a list of 'prohibited' requirements concerning freedom of establishment that, on the basis of existing jurisprudence of the European Court of Justice, are clearly unjustifiable (such as discriminatory requirements based directly or indirectly on nationality) and which should be eliminated by the Members States from their legal systems.

---

[6] See above n 2.

[7] European Commission (2002): Report from the Commission to the Council and to the European Parliament on the State of the Internal Market for Services, COM (2002) 441 final of 30 July 2002.

- Article 15 of the draft Directive, instead, requires the Member States to examine requirements that have restrictive effects on freedom of establishment and/or the freedom to provide services but may nevertheless be justified. among the listed requirements, which need to be evaluated, are fixed minimum and/or maximum tariffs and quantitative or territorial restrictions.[8] Member States will have to conduct a 'screening' of their legislation and evaluate these restrictions in the light of the conditions established in the jurisprudence of the European Court of Justice, as reflected in the Directive: the requirements must be non-discriminatory, objectively justifiable by an overriding reason relating to the general interest as recognised in the jurisprudence of the European Court of Justice, and satisfying the principle of proportionality. Overriding reasons of general interest which, according to jurisprudence, can justify such restrictions are, for example, public health or consumer protection, provided the restrictions are 'proportionate'. The Directive provides that the Member States will have to draw up reports, which will be available to the other Member States and interested parties for consultation. Finally, on the basis of a large-scale consultation, the Commission will then prepare a synthesis report accompanied, if necessary, by proposals for further initiatives.
- Similarly, Article 30 of the draft Directive, in line with the *Wouters* judgment,[9] provides that with respect to regulated professions Member States may maintain restrictions on multi-disciplinary partnerships, if justified in order to guarantee compliance with the rules governing professional ethics and conduct, which vary according to the specific nature of each profession. Those Member States which do allow multi-disciplinary partnerships will have to ensure that conflicts of interest and incompatibilities between certain activities are avoided, that the independence and impartiality required for certain activities is secured, and that the rules governing professional ethics and conduct for different activities are compatible with one another, especially as regards matters of professional secrecy. Furthermore, the Member States will have to draw up reports on the restrictions related to multi-disciplinary activities which they consider justified to maintain. For example, in *Wouters* the Court established that

[8] This includes quantitative or territorial restrictions in the form of limits fixed according to population or a minimum geographical distance between service providers (Art 15(2)a), requirements other than those concerning professional qualifications which reserve access to the service activity in question to particular providers by virtue of the specific nature of the activity (Art 15(2)d), and the ban on having more than one establishment in the territory of the same State (Art 15(2)e).

Some case law already exists in this field: for example, the Court established in *Bouchoucha* (Case C–61/89, ECR I–3551) that 'in the absence of harmonization at Community level regarding activities which fall solely within the scope of the practice of medicine, Article 52 of the EEC Treaty does not preclude a Member State from restricting an activity ancillary to medicine such as in particular, osteopathy exclusively to persons holding the qualification of doctor of medicine'.

[9] See above n 3.

multi-disciplinary partnerships between members of the Bar and accountants could lawfully be prohibited in the Netherlands, since rules of professional ethics governing the two professions (in particular, professional secrecy) are contradictory and could result in conflicts of interest.

- Article 29 of the draft Directive establishes rules on commercial communication. It provides that the Member States shall remove prohibitions on commercial communications (advertising, sponsorship, etc) by the regulated professions, while ensuring at the same time that they comply with professional rules which relate to the independence, dignity and integrity of the profession as well as to professional secrecy, according to the specific nature of each profession.
- Finally, Article 39 of the draft Directive invites the Member States and the Commission to encourage the drawing up of Codes of Conduct and other quality-enhancing measures, such as quality charters, by the professional Associations at Community level in order to establish common rules for commercial communications, professional ethics and conduct appropriate to each profession.

The above-mentioned draft Directive is complemented by the proposal addressing the obstacles arising in the recognition of professional qualifications, which hinder access to professional activities in another Member State. This latter proposal is a re-cast and modernisation of already-existing law applicable with respect to professional qualifications of the regulated professions.

Indeed, a quality policy is also essential to enhance competitiveness by protecting consumers in an area where the asymmetry of information is high. Internal market rules are a means to meet this concern and contribute to the second goal of the Lisbon agenda which is to make the EU the most dynamic knowledge-based economy in the world by 2010. Qualifications are at the core of a knowledge-based economy.

II. The Internal Market Policy also Aims at Safeguarding Quality in the Field of Regulated Professions

The European Parliament adopted on 16 December 2003 a resolution on market regulations and competition rules for the liberal professions, underlining

> the importance of rules which are necessary, in the specific context of each profession, to ensure the impartiality, *competence*, integrity and responsibility of the members of that profession so as to guarantee the *quality* of their services, to the benefit of their clients and society in general and to guarantee the public interest. (emphasis added)

The European Parliament also notes 'the *high qualifications* required for the liberal professions, the need to protect those qualifications that distinguish the liberal professions for the benefit of European citizens and the need to establish a specific relationship based on trust between the liberal professions and their clients' (emphasis added).

Similarly, in its *Report on Competition in the Professional Services*,[10] the Commission points out that

> a defining feature of professional services is that they require practitioners to display a high level of technical knowledge. Consumers may not have this knowledge and therefore find it difficult to judge the quality of the services they purchase. Professional services are 'credence goods' the quality of which cannot easily be judged either by prior observation or, in some markets, by consumption or use.

Under Articles 149 and 150 of the EC Treaty, each Member State is responsible for its own educational content and organization. It is up to the Member States to choose whether or not and how to regulate professional activities on their territories. In accordance with Articles 39, 43 and 49 of the EC Treaty, Community law facilitates movement of professionals between the Member States through mechanisms by which migrants can see their qualifications recognised in the Member State where they wish to work, provide services or establish themselves—and which is not their Member State of qualification.

The principle of mutual recognition developed in the field of free movement of goods since the famous *Cassis de Dijon* judgment[11] is well-known. Member States are obliged to accept on their territory products which are legally produced and marketed in another Member State. The Member States may only challenge the application of the principle in cases where, in particular, public safety, public health, the protection of consumers or of the environment are at stake. Similarly, Member States cannot prevent fully-qualified migrants from working on their territory.

However, at present EC law allows the host Member States to ensure *a priori* that the qualifications of migrants willing to work on their territory match national requirements for the same activity.[12] The host Member States can prohibit entry on their markets of people who are 'under qualified' according to their standards, provided these standards have not been harmonised at European level or after having compared the migrants' qualifications with their standards.

The *acquis* in this field includes 15 Directives: 3 'general system' ones Directives, and 12 'sectoral' ones, dealing with seven individual professions

---

[10] See above n 5, at point 25.

[11] Case 120/79 *Rewe Zentrale v Bundesmonopolverwaltung für Branntwein (Cassis de Dijon)* [1979] ECR 649.

[12] This is all the more important considering that the scope of activities for a profession with the same name can vary widely from one Member State to another. For example, 'engineers' are classified differently in the Member States according to their fields of activity and/or their level of qualification.

(architects, dentists, doctors, midwives, nurses, pharmacists and veterinary surgeons, lawyers).[13] Some of these texts entered into force more than

---

[13] The three 'general system' Directives are as follows:

Council Directive 89/48/EEC of 21 December 1988 on a general system for the recognition of higher-education diplomas awarded on completion of professional education and training of at least three years' duration;

Council Directive 92/51/EEC of 18 June 1992 on a second general system for the recognition of professional education and training to supplement Directive 89/48/EEC;

Directive 1999/42/EC of the European Parliament and of the Council of 7 June 1999 establishing a mechanism for the recognition of qualifications in respect of the professional activities covered by the Directives on liberalisation and transitional measures and supplementing the general systems for the recognition of qualifications.

The twelve 'sectoral' Directives are as follows:

Council Directive 93/16/EEC of 5 April 1993 to facilitate the free movement of doctors and the mutual recognition of their diplomas, certificates and other evidence of formal qualifications;

Council Directive 78/687/EEC of 25 July 1978 concerning the coordination of provisions laid down by Law, Regulation or Administrative Action in respect of the activities of dental practitioners;

Council Directive 78/686/EEC of 25 July 1978 concerning the mutual recognition of diplomas, certificates and other evidence of the formal qualifications of practitioners of dentistry, including measures to facilitate the effective exercise of the right of establishment and freedom to provide services;

Council Directive 85/432/EEC of 16 September 1985 concerning the coordination of provisions laid down by Law, Regulation or Administrative Action in respect of certain activities in the field of pharmacy;

Council Directive 85/433/EEC of 16 September 1985 concerning the mutual recognition of diplomas, certificates and other evidence of formal qualifications in pharmacy, including measures to facilitate the effective exercise of the right of establishment relating to certain activities in the field of pharmacy;

Council Directive 77/453/EEC of 27 June 1977 concerning the coordination of provisions laid down by Law, Regulation or Administrative Action in respect of the activities of nurses responsible for general care;

Council Directive 77/452/EEC of 27 June 1977 concerning the mutual recognition of diplomas, certificates and other evidence of the formal qualifications of nurses responsible for general care, including measures to facilitate the effective exercise of this right of establishment and freedom to provide services;

Council Directive 80/155/EEC of 21 January 1980 concerning the coordination of provisions laid down by Law, Regulation or Administrative Action relating to the taking up and pursuit of the activities of midwives;

Council Directive 80/154/EEC of 21 January 1980 concerning the mutual recognition of diplomas, certificates and other evidence of formal qualifications in midwifery and including measures to facilitate the effective exercise of the right of establishment and freedom to provide services;

Council Directive 78/1027/EEC of 18 December 1978 concerning the coordination of provisions laid down by Law, Regulation or Administrative Action in respect of the activities of veterinary surgeons;

Council Directive 78/1026/EEC of 18 December 1978 concerning the mutual recognition of diplomas, certificates and other evidence of formal qualifications in veterinary medicine, including measures to facilitate the effective exercise of the right of establishment and freedom to provide services;

Council Directive 85/384/EEC of 10 June 1985 on the mutual recognition of diplomas, certificates and other evidence of formal qualifications in architecture, including measures to

20 years ago, in the late 70s or in the early 80s. In March 2002, a proposal for a *Directive on the Recognition of Professional Qualifications* was adopted by the Commission in order to consolidate and modernise the existing rules.[14]

For the seven individual professions listed above, the right to become established as a self-employed person or employee in an EU Member State is acquired on the basis of automatic recognition of diplomas awarded by a Member State that fulfil minimum training conditions. Therefore, for these professions, quality and free circulation are ensured by the harmonisation, at EU level, of training conditions.

However, harmonisation of training conditions, which could not be extended to other professions, remains the exception. For the other professions falling under the so-called 'general system' (ie, activities where no such harmonisation took place), other mechanisms were put into place in order to facilitate the free movement of professionals, while ensuring that these facilitating measures would not undermine the quality of the services provided in a given Member State. Where the comparative examination of qualifications acquired in another Member State substantially differ from those required by national rules, the host Member State may impose on migrants a period of adjustment or an aptitude test in order to demonstrate having acquired the necessary knowledge and skills.

Additionally, the host Member States are allowed to check *a priori* the 'good character' of migrants, and to demand proof that they are not and have not previously been declared bankrupt, and have not previously been the subject of professional or administrative disciplinary measures. Of course, these prior checks also have to comply with the fundamental freedoms guaranteed by the Treaty.[15] The Directives, therefore, limit the discretionary powers of Member States. They also provide that reasoned decisions must be taken

facilitate the effective exercise of the right of establishment and freedom to provide services;

Council Directive 77/249/EEC of 22 March 1977 to facilitate the effective exercise by lawyers of freedom to provide services; Directive 98/5/EC of the European Parliament and of the Council of 16 February 1998 to facilitate practice of the profession of lawyer on a permanent basis in a Member State other than that in which the qualification was obtained.

The texts of the above-mentioned Directives, together with successive amendments etc, are all available on http://www.aic.lv/ace/tools/dir_en/default.htm.

[14] See *above* n 2.

[15] In Case C–55/94 *Gebhard* [1995] ECR I–4165, the Court recalled that even if

> where the taking-up or the pursuit of a specific activity is subject to certain conditions in the host Member State, a national of another Member State intending to pursue that activity must in principle comply with them, . . . national measures liable to hinder or make less attractive the exercise of fundamental freedoms guaranteed by the Treaty must fulfil four conditions: they must be applied in a non-discriminatory manner; they must be justified by imperative requirements in the general interest; they must be suitable for securing the attainment of the objective which they pursue; and they must not go beyond what is necessary in order to attain it.

See also Case C–3/95 *Reisebüro Broede* [1996] ECR I–6511.

within a given deadline and that migrants should have the right to appeal them before a jurisdiction.

These prior checks are, however, still perceived to be essential by Member States, in particular for health care professions; the Member States made it clear at the discussions held in May 2004, during which political agreement was reached on the proposal for a *Directive on the Recognition of Professional Qualifications*,[16] that it was not sufficient for consumers to be informed about the qualifications of a professional supplying a service in their country but that, for certain professions with health and safety implications, the competent national authorities should be given the means to check, his/her qualifications *a priori*. The original proposal of the Commission, which was based on the principle of the state of origin for the provision of services, in consistency with the draft Services Directive, has not been endorsed by the Council. As a result of the political agreement:

- The host Member State will be entitled to apply its disciplinary provisions for all professions to a migrant legally established in another Member State, but only as far as these provisions relate to professional qualifications (for example, the use of professional title).
- The host Member State may also require the migrant when he/she first moves to its territory, to provide a prior declaration with accompanying documents.[17] Automatic *pro forma* registration in the host Member State will be possible, using the prior declaration.
- Prior checks which may suspend the right to move to another Member State have been limited to professions with health and safety implications, for which Member States can demonstrate that an *a posteriori* check would take place too late to be genuinely effective (ie, the proportionality test).

This agreement, reached on 18 May 2004, will be confirmed by the Council in the common position to be adopted in the following months, and will be the subject of a second reading by the European Parliament later this year.[18]

To briefly comment on this process, it appeared from the negotiations that had taken place so far that the Member States were not ready to rely on coop-

---

[16] See above n 2.

[17] For the first provision of services, Member States may require that the declaration is also accompanied by the following documents:
- proof of the nationality of the service provider;
- certification in the sense that the holder is legally established in a Member State for the purpose of practising the activities concerned;
- evidence of professional qualifications;
- proof (by any means) that the service provider has practised the activity at issue for at least two years during the previous ten years.

[18] Se Common position adopted by the Council with a view to the adoption of a Directive of the European parliament and of the Council on the recognition of professional qualifications, of 21 December 2004, available at http://europa.eu.int/comm/internal_market/qualifications/future_en.htm#20050511. The draft Directive was approved by the European Parliament on 11 May 2005—see Press Release on the above-mentioned website.

eration between competent authorities and information provided by the migrant to consumers, or to accept that a professional authorized to practice in one Member State and fully-qualified under the standards of this Member State should be entitled to provide a service in another Member State without the latter being informed and in a position to check the migrant's qualifications in case of doubt. This situation should, however, be reviewed in the light of the development of administrative cooperation, as stated in a new Recital introduced in the draft Regulation.

This outcome will have to be taken into account in the framework of the draft Services Directive, as the two Directives will apply jointly to the services provided by regulated professions. The aspects covered by the Directive on professional qualifications shall not be overruled by the Services Directive. In particular, an exemption to the rule of the state of origin, as inserted in Article 16 of the Services Directives, will have to be inserted for the purpose of provision of services by qualified professionals.

To conclude this brief review of the Commission's internal market services' initiatives, and to link them with EC competition policy, it appears that these initiatives are complementary: individual competition decisions *v* a legislative instrument creating a European legal framework and including a mutual evaluation procedure and harmonisation of some essential requirements at Community level. They will be implemented at a different pace. Competition decisions can be adopted straight away, whereas the draft Directives will enter into force at the end of the legislative process and after the transposition period. Despite this different timing, the different initiatives, to some extent address similar types of restrictions which create restrictions of competition and, at the same time, hamper the freedom of establishment and the freedom to provide services. In the long run, the combined effect of these different measures should lead to a better functioning of the internal market for services and higher quality provided by professional practitioners, as well as to an increase of competition across national borders throughout the Union.

II

John D Cooke[1]

Vocation as Commodity

For those of us who live at some distance from the cutting edge of contemporary social trends, the Commission's draft report on competition in the professional services[2] contains one startling gem of cultural intelligence: according to the Commission, the modern European 'liberal professions' include the oral hygienists of Finland. (paragraph 5, footnote 5). Unfortunately, for those interested in keeping abreast of important social changes, this pronouncement comes without any explanation. We are not told precisely why oral hygienists constitute a liberal profession or, more importantly, why such professionals are in this case confined to Finland. No doubt the men and women following this vocation in Helsinki have devoted many hours to the study of this discipline and have acquired a high degree of skill in the techniques of dental cleansing, but it would be useful to know what particular characteristics they possess which distinguish them from the oral hygienists in other European centres of dental excellence. Are the Finnish hygienists the descendants of some medieval guild? Are they the inheritors of a deontological code handed down from generation to generation like some Nordic saga? Has Finland started a trend? Can the liberal profession of oral hygienist be expected in future years to spread throughout all the other 24 Member States of the European Union? If so, what should our reaction be?

Of course, the question is probably as old as the guilds: it all depends on what you mean by 'liberal profession'. Indeed one might query whether the 'liberal professions' exist any longer. The Commission's definition: 'liberal professions are occupations requiring special training in the liberal arts or sciences, for example lawyers, notaries, engineers, architects, doctors and accountants' (*ibid*, paragraph 5) is of little use: every service provider thinks his/her occupation involves a special skill.

If the Commission's job in applying Articles 81 and 82 EC is to regulate competition amongst undertakings, then any self-employed person who holds himself out as providing a service in return for reward is an 'undertaking' who falls within the scope of those articles. From the purely mercenary perspective of competition law enforcement, it does not matter whether a service provider thinks he is a member of a liberal profession or not.

---

[1] Judge: European Court of First Instance. Such views as are expressed are personal.

[2] See *Commission Report on competition in the professional services*, COM (2004) 83 final, available at www.europa.eu.int/comm/competition/liberal_professions/final_comm_en.pdf.

There is today no estate agent, public relations executive or snake oil salesman who does not believe that he is the member of a profession. No practitioner of any of these arts would have a moment's hesitation in insisting that he is providing a 'professional service'. Indeed, it is one of the phenomena of our age that ever more diverse and exotic groups of service providers come together with the deliberate aim of establishing themselves as 'professions'. The Commission's draft report refers to the commonly understood characterisation of a liberal profession as having a 'high level of regulation either imposed by national governments or self-regulation by the professional bodies'. Thus, ironically, the according of special privileges or exemption from competition rules to some service providers because they are regarded as members of a profession, operates as an incentive to all service providers to mimic the trappings of professional institutes in the hope of attracting equivalent standing and treatment.

There is no doubt, of course, that the concept of a 'liberal profession' has been evolving over the last century or so. On the one hand, service providers who would hitherto have been content to come together to form a trade association or craft guild, insist upon achieving the higher status of a 'profession'. On the other, there has undoubtedly been a dilution of what might have been previously regarded as the essential characteristics of membership of the long-established and learned professions. In the 19th Century the status of a professional would surely have been confined to the traditional areas of the church, the law, medicine and education. Quite apart from the need for an extensive period of apprenticeship and advanced education in the art or science concerned, membership of those professions involved acceptance of obligations of independence, integrity, impartiality and personal disinterest which were considered to be entirely distinct from, and superior to, the values and characteristics attributed to the pursuit of a mere trade. Thus, the English or Irish barrister or the French *avocat* was regarded as having accepted a personal professional duty to remain at all times at arm's length from his client's interest; never to act when to do so would involve him in a conflict of interest and at all times to advise his client honestly and objectively, irrespective of the commercial consequences of such advice for himself.

(If you look closely at the back of the gown of a junior barrister, you can still see today a small black flap in the approximate area of the shoulder blade. Much as the useless fin of a marine mammal may be the vestigial foot of some prehistoric ancestor, the flap is all that remains of the small pouch which the medieval member of the Outer Bar wore over his shoulder so that a grateful client might drop a coin into it behind his back, to save him the embarrassment of being seen to receive cash up front. Even today, however, the barrister has no legal entitlement to recover payment of fees even when agreed; such is the legal status of his obligation of professional disinterest.)

It was also, I think, a distinguishing characteristic of membership of a profession that the practitioner was regarded as having a personal responsibility for the integrity and validity of the advice or service which he provided. Thus, members of a profession were expected to practise primarily as sole practitioners, the only form of combination permitted being that of an unincorporated partnership where all members of the firm took joint and several responsibility for one another. Practising behind the shield of incorporation with limited liability was regarded as fundamentally inconsistent with the status of professional practitioner.

This feature of personal responsibility for the integrity of a professional service and the rules of conduct which enforced compliance with it, had their rationale in what we must nowadays call 'asymmetry of information'. Only practitioners admitted to the practice of the craft understood its mysteries so that the patient or client had no way of knowing whether the service was safe or the advice honest. Adherence to a code of conduct on pain of expulsion with loss of livelihood was the profession's assurance to the public that its interest was safe-guarded.

From this point of view, a great deal has changed for members of even the traditional professions, particularly since the expansion of the welfare state after the Second World War. In most Member States of the Union, the membership of the medical profession is now predominantly employed, and employed in the public service. The concept of direct personal responsibility for the judgment and quality of service has been transferred, for all practical purposes, to the employer, hospital or health board. Similar social and economic trends have also affected the legal profession in that a majority of practitioners in most Member States are employed either by other lawyers, by commercial undertakings or by government agencies. Where professional services are concerned, the State has become the dominant consumer and ultimate emptor.

While the basic concepts which underpinned the status of a member of the traditional professions has been eroded in this way, the public perception of professional status is simultaneously altered by the apparent willingness to accept that professional status can be created or acquired for any given activity. Occupations which would once have been content to combine as a trade association for the protection of the commercial interest of their members, feel compelled to improve their social status by assuming what they conceive to be the trappings of a profession. They devise training courses and confer upon themselves professional diplomas which carry the entitlement to add impressive letters to the surname. Professional and social standing can thus be enhanced by advancing through the masonic steps of the craft from associate to member to fellow.

An elected council promulgates a code of conduct which has, of course, the sole purpose of promoting the highest standards of professional service in the interests of the public. Invariably, these para-professions commence by endeavouring to be as representative of the activity as possible and existing unregulated practitioners are encouraged to join. Once the association becomes identified with the occupation, access to membership becomes more difficult (in the interest, of course, of promoting higher standards) and in the final stage the ultimate badge of professional standing is the installation of a monopoly by persuading government that the particular service should, by law, be available *only* from members of the professional association in question. In the common law countries incorporation by charter, especially royal charter, is especially advantageous.

I. The *RECI* Case

Some years ago there was an interesting example of this phenomenon which led to litigation in Ireland. The Electricity Supply Board, ('ESB') the sole national utility in the electricity sector at the time, sought, in the interests of rationalisation, to divest itself of various activities, including that of maintaining an inspectorate whose job it was to approve new electrical installations in houses and businesses for connection to the grid. It approached the two main trade associations of electrical contractors and proposed that they join together to establish a register of electrical contractors for Ireland (RECI). This opportunity received, understandably, an enthusiastic response, and the two associations overcame their traditional rivalry to establish RECI, a body whose function it would be to establish standards of qualification and competence for providing services as an electrical contractor and register qualifying electricians as members. In return, the ESB undertook that henceforth no connection to the national grid would be made unless certified by a member of RECI. Membership would not be compulsory but an unregistered contractor would have to pay a fee to have his work approved by a RECI member before a connection would be made.

This body then set about laying down the rules for admission to the register, including rules covering training and qualification, minimum years' experience as an electrician, financial standing, necessary investment in equipment and premises and so forth. These rules, while posing no problem for the main electrical contracting companies, caused consternation amongst large numbers of self-employed electricians or small family firms outside the major towns and cities.

In time-honoured Irish tradition, these in turn formed a rival organisation and brought proceedings against both RECI and the ESB. They complained that the rules establishing the register amounted to an agreement between undertakings which violated the domestic equivalent of Article 81 EC, and, as against the ESB, they alleged abuse of a dominant position by making access to the national grid dependent upon the approval of an association of undertakings with whom the ESB had done a deal in order to divest itself of the commercial burden of its certification function. Section 4 of the Irish Competition Act of 1990 corresponds exactly with Article 81 EC, and the defendants responded by notifying the arrangements made by the ESB to establish RECI to the Irish Competition Authority for exemption.

This resulted in the rules being amended to remove the stipulations which were clearly designed to favour the large and medium sized contractors to the exclusion of smaller firms and individual undertakings. The Irish courts found that although the ESB had introduced its arrangements in good faith and with a view to improving safety standards in the public interest, the arrangements had an anti-competitive effect in that non-registered contractors were compelled to pay a RECI member who might well be a local competitor to certify his work, thereby making it difficult to compete on price. They also held that the advertising campaign conducted by RECI to encourage the public to deal only with RECI contractors, created among the public the impression that non-registered contractors were less reliable. (*Donovan v ESB* (1994) II IR 305) The case illustrates well the alacrity with which any group of skilled operators will readily use an opportunity for self-regulation and an excuse to serve the public interest as a means of promoting self-interest.

The Irish electrical contractors were, of course, following in a very ancient tradition in having the declared objective of protecting the public interest by ensuring high standards of safety, while at the same time believing that this could best be achieved by assuring that there was no 'unfair competition' from operators with lower costs and overheads. The medieval guilds, from which several of the modern professions derive their origins, had the same dual function. Membership of a guild of bakers or butchers was an assurance to the public that the bread or sausages contained no more than the permitted levels of sand or sawdust. This was quite clearly in the public interest. But the guilds also regarded it as a part of their essential function to set the terms and conditions of apprenticeships and to fix trading hours and even prices. To the modern customer of a department store it may seem somewhat bizarre that the law requires sales in many continental European countries to take place only at fixed times, twice a year. Why should a shop-keeper not decide for himself the most opportune time to sell off end-of-line stock? This legislative approach to opening hours, holiday periods and other trading conditions has its origins in the rules of the medieval guilds and their ability as powerful social organisations of the time to procure that their concepts of fair trade became the rule of law. If the majority of bakers in a town agreed that Wednesday should be a half closing day, it would be 'unfair competition' on the part of any dissenter to poach customers by remaining open while they are closed.

So if it is relevant or possible to treat certain forms of commercial activity as distinct because they can be qualified as having 'professional' characteristics for the purpose of applying competition rules, the only real issue is that of deciding whether and to what extent the terms and conditions upon which the provision of a given service is organised can justify derogating from the basic rules of competition policy in deference to some distinct public interest or value other than that of maintaining the equilibrium of commercial competition in those services.

We are often inclined, however, to take at face value the celebrated assertion from Shaw's play 'The Doctor's Dilemma' that 'all professions are conspiracies against the laity' and to take it for granted that all restrictive practices in professional services are the result of the pursuit by the profession itself of its own commercial interests. Not infrequently, however, it is the ambition of the legislator to control or manipulate professional services that brings about restraint and distortion. Some ten years ago, or thereabouts, politicians and the media in Ireland became convinced that legal services were becoming too costly and the burden on the civil legal aid system was becoming too great. The answer, according to the politicians, was to open those services to increased competition by outlawing the profession's self-restraint on advertising and by removing obsolete stipulations against 'no foal, no fee' agreements. Far from being hide-bound conservatives in this area, however, Irish lawyers took to the new regime with such enthusiasm that within a short period of time, American-style advertising ('first consultation free') began to appear on public hoardings and the sides of buses. As a result, within a matter of a few years accident litigation rapidly increased, damages awards mounted and, as a consequence, employer and motor insurance became so hugely expensive as to be unavailable to small and medium-sized employers and younger drivers.

Once it became apparent that the difficulty of access to justice for accident victims was greatly outweighed in electoral terms by the outrage of industry and the plaintiff reproaches of uninsurable 18-year olds, political backtracking and reappraisal was inevitable. Last year new legislation reintroduced restraints upon lawyers advertising. Thus the public interest works both ways. The public as a consumer and purchaser of professional services may have an interest in ensuring that any given professional service is provided on the most efficient and economic terms possible through active competition amongst the practitioners or undertakings concerned. On the other hand, the public and, particularly, public authorities, may have a legitimate interest in permitting the adoption of self-restraint practices by a profession or in intervening to impose them, in order to prevent prejudice being caused to some related or opposing public interest.

II. The *Wouters* case

The judgment of the Court of Justice of 19 February 2002 in the *Wouters* case[3] is of obvious importance as the first instance in which the European Court has attempted to provide a legal basis for resolving this dilemma. Indeed, it may be of increasing importance in future years because of the manner in which the new enforcement regime of Regulation 1/2003 puts the application of Article 81 EC in its entirety into the hands of the national competition authorities and national courts. It raises the intriguing possibility that there exists a margin of appreciation or assessment not only in respect of the fulfilment of the conditions for application of Article 81(3) EC but also for the non-application of Article 81(1) EC by reference to hitherto unspecified criteria of higher public interest. If restrictions on the forms of practice and association amongst lawyers can be justified by reference to exigencies of the sound administration of justice, it is by no means inconceivable that there exist equivalent values which could legitimately justify restraints amongst medical practitioners, accountants or even, perhaps, oral hygienists.

The judgment of the Court in the *Wouters* case is, of course, remarkable as many observers have pointed out, in the manner in which it succeeds in disapplying Article 81(1) EC to the regulation adopted by the Netherlands Bar in 1993 prohibiting joint practice by lawyers and accountants, without recourse to the exemption provisions of Article 81(3) EC. It accepts the proposition rejected by Advocate General Léger namely, that it is permissible to introduce into the provisions of paragraph 1 considerations which are linked to the pursuit of a public interest objective. Faced with an argument which invited the Court to introduce a form of 'rule of reason' into Article 81 EC, the Advocate General pointed out that the European Court had hitherto admitted only very limited use of the 'rule of reason' approach and then only in the form of establishing a competitive balance sheet as to the effects of the agreement as pro or anti competition. He acknowledged that existing case law recognised that if an agreement taken as a whole encouraged competition on the market and its restrictive clauses were essential to the performance of the agreement, it could escape the prohibition. Such a 'legitimate goal' could only be accepted however, in terms of promoting competition. Nobody in the case claimed that the effect of the regulation was to encourage competition on the market in legal services, although the Luxembourg government appears to have suggested that it could have such positive effects. The Court, however, held that even where an agreement, such as the 1993 Regulation, has anticompetitive effects, it is nevertheless permissible to look at the overall context

[3] Case C–309/99 *Wouters* [2002] ECR I–1577.

in which those effects are produced in order to decide whether the consequential restrictions on competition are inherent in the pursuit of a public interest objective such as that of ensuring that the consumers of legal services and the sound administration of justice are provided with the necessary guarantees in relation to integrity and experience (see paragraph 97 of the judgment). It thus reached the conclusion that a national regulation of that type when adopted by a bar acting as an association of undertakings rather than a public regulatory authority, does not infringe Article 81(1) EC because it could reasonably have considered that the regulation, despite the effects restrictive of competition that are inherent in it, was necessary for the proper practice of the legal profession as organised in that Member State. (Paragraph 110).

On the face of it, the implications of the judgment are not confined to the legal profession or, indeed, to the professions as such but could conceivably extend to arrangements by trade associations in other areas of activity where recourse to some higher objective of a public interest could be invoked. If the legal profession can rely upon the need to ensure the independence of its practitioners and the sound administration of justice, presumably the medical profession could invoke the need to protect public health and electricians the need to ensure public safety.

But it is also interesting to speculate as to whether the effects of this judgment will last. Perhaps it is merely a one-off aberration in the evolution of the Community competition rules. If it had fallen to be decided after 1 May 2004 and the commencement of Regulation 1/2003, would the result have been the same?

The *Wouters* case arose out of litigation before the Dutch national courts between the practitioners concerned and the Netherlands Bar. The 1993 Regulation had apparently been notified by the Bar to the Commission for exemption under Article 81(3) EC but no decision had been taken, so that proof of compliance with the conditions of Paragraph 3 was not available either to the Bar or the European Court as an escape route from this dilemma. Today it would presumably be open to the Bar to counterclaim on the basis of Article 2 of Regulation 1/2003, seeking a declaration that the conditions for exemption were fulfilled and thus open to the Dutch Court and, by way of reference under Article 234 EC, to the European Court to apply Article 81(3) EC.

On balance, however, it seems highly unlikely that Article 81(3) EC could have availed the Netherlands Bar in the circumstances of the case. The criteria of paragraph (3) remained the criteria of competition while the European Court of Justice dis-applied paragraph (1) by reference to the totally distinct criterion of a public interest objective.

In effect, the Netherlands Bar and the professions generally may have reaped a temporary benefit from the fortuitous timing of the litigation and the new regulation. Had the courts concerned been fully empowered as they are now to employ Article 81(3) EC it may well have been more difficult to embark on so radical a departure from existing jurisprudence.

The judgment can, however, be read as a recognition of the legitimacy of the values that historically underpinned the traditional professions namely, the acceptance by practitioners that the privilege derived from possession of special skills and knowledge which are of inherent value to the community, brought with it the duty to practise the profession on terms that subjected personal gain and interest to the higher interests of the common good.

Whether the same can be said of estate agents and public relations executives is questionable. It is now not just inevitable, but established law that the rules of commercial competition apply to services including both those traditionally recognised as professional services and those entirely new services whose providers aspire to the same status. To many it may seem regrettable that this should be so, because it is the necessary consequence of the application of competition rules to services that the professional service ceases to be valued as a vocation and is evaluated only as a commodity. The judgment in *Wouters* may at least have postponed briefly the day when professional services are assessed exclusively by reference to their commercial value.

Erasmus, another Dutchman, who, of course, lived at a time when much of every day life was ordered by the rules of the guilds, observed: 'Nowadays the rage for possession has got to such a pitch that there is nothing in the realm of nature, whether sacred or profane, out of which profit cannot be squeezed.'

Mr Wouters' objective may have been to make legal practice more efficient and profitable by entering the embrace of Arthur Andersen. In the result, his case has, at least for the moment, given the profession a basis for declining the attractions of inter-professional intimacy.

III

*Harry First**

Liberal or Learned?

European and US Antitrust Approaches to the Professions

I. Introduction

The recent European interest in bringing antitrust enforcement to the professions mirrors a recent (as well as long-standing) antitrust enforcement interest in the US.[1] Although the legal issues in both systems are, in some sense, similar, the legal analyses used by the courts in Europe and in the US are different. Whatever the differences in legal analyses, however, the judicial results in the two systems actually end up being distressingly similar and, from my point of view, distressingly wrong.

This essay focuses on three recent cases decided by the European Court of Justice that involve the legal issues raised in enforcing antitrust law against the professions—*Wouters*, *Arduino*, and *Fiammiferi*—and a comparison of those cases with similar cases in the US. The essay begins with some general observations about applying antitrust to the professions. The next part of the essay discusses the three European Court of Justice cases. The essay then explores how the legal issues decided in those cases have been handled by the US Supreme Court. The essay concludes with some comparison of the two systems, arguing that both have given too much deference to professional regulation.

II. A Walk Down Chestnut Street

I recently had the pleasure of visiting Philadelphia, the city in which I grew up. I say a pleasure because I visited as a tourist, rather than as a resident, and

* New York University School of Law.

[1] For the key documents detailing the European Commission's initiatives in reviewing competition policy and the professions, see http://europa.eu.int/comm/competition/liberalization/conference/libprofconference.html. For a review of recent US FTC enforcement, see TJ Zywicki, 'Competition Policy and Regulatory Reforms: Means and Ends' (2003) 7–8, available at http://www.ftc.gov/speeches/other/031120zywickijapanspeech.pdf.

so was able to do the things that tourists do but residents rarely do, that is, visiting places of historical interest.

And so I found myself walking down Chestnut Street, in the older, Colonial part of the city. This part of Philadelphia features the beautiful and historically important buildings from the time when the United States was still a Colonial outpost of England. Standing in front of the impressive Carpenters' Hall, where the First Continental Congress met in 1774 to list the grievances of the Colonies against England, I looked at the explanatory plaque posted by the National Parks Service. What caught my eye was this description of the Carpenters Company, which erected and owned the hall. The plaque explained that the Carpenters Company was a group of Philadelphia master builders. They banded together 'to establish architectural standards, to set prices for work, and to aid members' families in times of need.'

Price-fixing in Colonial America? Another example of a professional association with the mixed goals of standard setting, improving their craft, and helping their members? Yes to all of it. Indeed, further inquiry reveals that the Carpenters Company was neither a company (that is, an enterprise) nor, indeed, did its members engage only in carpentry.[2] Although many were craftsmen, 'their unique talent lay in drawing plans for a building, hiring bricklayers, glaziers and carpenters, then supervising construction and engineering.'[3] Their Rule Book, written by a committee of 'reputable carpenters,' considered 'the several parts of carpentry, and set a price on every particular part, according to the mode of finishing, either by the square, yard, or foot.'[4]

The Carpenters Company thus serves as a useful reminder of some important aspects of professional associations. First, these associations have deep historical and cultural roots. The idea of the Carpenters Company was itself brought from England by its early members who were well acquainted with London's Worshipful Company of Carpenters, whose own traditions arose out of medieval guilds.[5] Second, the concept of what is a profession is elastic.

---

[2] See CG Karsch, *Historical Tour of Carpenters Hall*, available at http://www.ushistory.org/carpentershall/history/tour/800.htm.

[3] See above.

[4] Introduction, Articles of the Carpenters Company of Philadelphia: And their Rules for Measuring and Valuing House-Carpenters Work p vi (1786), reproduced in CE Peterson, (ed), *The Rules of Work of the Carpenters Company, of the City and County of Philadelphia* (1971). Competing price books were issued from time to time by different societies, see Introduction, *The Rules of Work,* above, pp xv–xvii. One of these competing societies was absorbed into the Carpenters Company, following which the Company issued its 1786 price book which set out higher prices than before ('to expect work now . . . for the same price by the square that the workmen had then [thirty years ago], can hardly be deemed equitable or just', Articles of the Carpenters Company, above, at vi). The Articles also provided that members would not undertake work begun by another member unless the other member had been paid, had a provision for arbitration of disputes among the members, and included a procedure for providing assistance to members, widows, or minor children of members, 'being by accident or sickness reduced to want.' See Articles of the Carpenters Company, above, pp x–xi (Articles VII, VIII, IX).

[5] See Karsch, above n 2. It is not clear whether there were any British price books devoted solely to carpentry, however, see Introduction, *The Rules of Work,* above n 4, 5, p x.

Carpenters, or builders, in Colonial days likely did the work that professional engineers do today.[6] We can recognize them as professionals, but we easily recognize a host of other fields as professional and license them accordingly. Whether we consider beauticians, morticians, opticians, or social workers to be learned professions or not is beside the point; legislatures have been convinced to license and regulate them all.[7] Third, professional associations may very well have mixed aspirations. Clinical social workers, recently licensed in New York, for example, are legitimately concerned about consumers being harmed by receiving psychotherapy from the untrained, but they are also concerned about their ability to compete against other mental health professionals.[8]

None of these three factors has stopped antitrust litigation against professional organizations, of course. To take just one example, lawyers, too, fixed rates in Colonial times, a fact mentioned in the debates over the passage of the Sherman Act,[9] but this did not prevent the Supreme Court from finding that lawyers' price fixing is subject to the Sherman Act.[10] Nevertheless, these three factors—deep historical roots, the connection between professions and state regulation, and potential public interest objectives—have had their effect on the effort to apply antitrust to the professions. Antitrust analysis, whether under EU law or US law, must evaluate the competitive effects of professional restraints. That evaluation seems inevitably to be affected (or infected) by the first and third of these factors. Similarly, state involvement in licensure or regulation of a particular profession may give rise to an immunity from antitrust liability, whether under European or US law. The ubiquity of such regulation means that too deferential a view of state regulation could put many of these restraints beyond the scope of antitrust control.

---

[6] See *National Soc of Professional Engineers v United States* 435 US 679, 681 (1978) ('Engineering is an important and learned profession') discussed below text accompanying nn 70–75.

[7] For an earlier review, see RD Blair and S Rubin, *Regulating the Professions* (Lexington MA, Lexington Books, 1980) (noting 1975 survey finding more than 100 professions and occupations licensed by various states).

[8] See M Wineburgh, 'Are Clinical Social Workers An Endangered Species?' (2004) 35 *The Clinician* 1, calling for higher training standards for clinical social workers to enable them to compete better against other mental health practitioners: 'Any reduction in standards for clinical social work training is particularly heinous at a time when 25,000–50,000 mental health practitioners are about to become newly licensed and entitled to compete for social work jobs.'

[9] See 21 *Cong Rec* 2726 (1890) (remarks of Senator Morgan).

[10] See *Goldfarb v Virginia State Bar* 421 US 773 (1975), discussed in below text accompanying nn 77–82.

III. The Approach of the European Court of Justice

1. Competitive Effects

1.1 Wouters

Of the three recent Court of Justice cases, the one that speaks most directly to competitive effects analysis is *Wouters,*[11] a case which involved the regulation of lawyers in the Netherlands. In 1994 Wouters, a lawyer in Amsterdam and a partner in the accounting firm of Arthur Andersen, sought to practice law in Rotterdam under the name of Arthur Andersen. The Supervisory Board of the Rotterdam Bar informed him that such practice would violate regulations adopted in 1993 by the College of Delegates of the Bar of the Netherlands. Those regulations forbad lawyers from maintaining professional partnerships with non-lawyers, unless given specific authorization. The regulations also specifically stated, however, that partnerships with accountants would not be authorized. Wouters (and another lawyer who sought to become a partner in Price Waterhouse) appealed this decision to the courts; the Netherlands Council of State eventually referred to the Court of Justice a number of questions for preliminary ruling relating to the interpretation and application of the EC Treaty.

In the words of the Advocate General, the case raised 'the difficult question of the application of Community competition law to the professions.'[12] My concern, however, is not so much with the doctrinal ins-and-outs of the EC Treaty, although they are obviously critical for giving a legal answer to the questions presented in the case. Rather, I want to focus on the major analytical questions, so as to better understand and critique the Court's conclusion.

1.2 Is Law a Business?

Perhaps one might think that lawyers, as members of a 'liberal' profession, are not involved in business in the same way as steel makers or automobile sellers.[13] The suggestion seems barely to survive its articulation, however. Whatever their training or professional standards, lawyers sell a product and their behaviour affects the allocation of economic resources in society. If

---

[11] Case C–309/99 *Wouters* [2002] ECR I–1577.

[12] Opinion of Mr Advocate General Léger, para 1.

[13] The Commission defines liberal professions as occupations requiring special training in the liberal arts or sciences. European Commission, *Report on Competition in Professional Services* (2004) para 1, available at http://europa.eu.int/comm/competition/antitrust/legislation/#liberal.

lawyers restrain competition in a market for legal services, their conduct should be covered by competition law.

The Court of Justice had little trouble in deciding that lawyers are covered by Article 81 EC.[14] Lawyers are undertakings under Article 81(1) EC because they are 'engaged in economic activity, offering goods and services on an economic market.'[15]

Wouters didn't bring suit against individual lawyers, however. The target of his suit was the Bar of the Netherlands, the body of lawyers that adopted the allegedly anticompetitive regulation. The Bar itself is not directly engaged in economic activity in the sense that it does not sell a service in a market. Should the Bar be considered an 'undertaking'?

The Court had little trouble reaching the Bar's activity under Article 81(1) EC, finding that the Bar was simply an association of undertakings. Putting aside for the moment the discussion in the Court's opinion relating to the Bar's public duties, the Court appeared willing to view the Bar as an aggregate of lawyers, acting as the regulatory body of a profession, the practice of which constitutes an economic activity.[16]

Deciding that the Bar is an association of undertakings seems perfectly plausible as a matter of the formal language of Article 81(1) EC. The real issue, though, is whether the interpretation of the concept of 'undertaking' might be used to block the courts from evaluating conduct engaged in by (private) parties that has adverse economic effects, that is, conduct that affects the creation and allocation of economic resources in society. By articulating the test in terms of whether the party before the court 'offers goods or services on a market,' the Court has subtly directed the question to what a defendant's business activity is, rather than to what might be the economic effects of a defendant's conduct. The question becomes 'what does the defendant do' rather than 'what's the harm'.

The difference may be subtle (and, perhaps, even required by the language of the Treaty), but it does have legal effect, as shown when the Court gets to the question whether the Bar is covered by Article 82 EC. In this part of its opinion the Court decides that the Bar is not an undertaking under Article 82 EC because it 'does not carry on any economic activity' and is not 'a group of undertakings' because the lawyers who are members of the Bar 'are not sufficiently linked to each other to adopt the same conduct on the market with the result that competition between them is eliminated.'[17]

---

[14] The decision was taken prior to the renumbering of the Articles of the Treaty, but all discussions in this essay will use the current numbering.

[15] *Wouters*, paras 46, 47. Indeed, the point was not contested before the Court, see Opinion of Advocate General at para 47, and is consistent with earlier decisions rejecting arguments based on the status of 'liberal professional' carrying out intellectual activities, see Case C–35/96 *Commission v Italy* [1998] ECR I–3851, paras 34–38 (customs agents).

[16] *Wouters*, para 58.

[17] See above, paras 112, 113.

It is difficult to understand why the Bar's conduct would be covered by Article 81 EC and not Article 82 EC. Functionally, the Bar is the device for coordinating (indeed, compelling) the behaviour of all registered lawyers in the Netherlands (the Bar is an integrated bar in which all lawyers are members[18]). Its ability to restrict competition or, if its market position is sufficiently dominant, to abuse its position, is not dependent on whether the Bar itself sells services. Had the question of coverage been viewed as one related to the economic effect of the organization's conduct, rather than to the business in which the organization engages, a more sensible result might have followed. That is, the Bar would have been subject to Articles 81 and 82 EC and then the proper analytical questions could then have been posed under both provisions.[19]

1.3 What Are the Anticompetitive Effects of the Bar's Restraint?

Once the Bar is covered under competition law, the analytical question becomes what are the anticompetitive effects of a regulation which prohibits partnerships with non-lawyers? A first cut at this question produces the answer that the restraint is obviously anticompetitive. Some lawyers and accountants, to take this particular application of the regulation, believe that they would be more effective competitors if they were able to offer these complementary products in a single firm. Why else do they want to form such partnerships? And why else might the Bar oppose them? Indeed, the pro-competitive argument is intuitively plausible. Transactions costs can be reduced when economic transactions are handled within a single firm; perhaps the new firm's organization will also lead to the offering of new services to clients that might not otherwise have occurred. The regulation, however, prohibits this form of more effective competition, to the ultimate potential harm of consumers of legal services.

This is the approach that the Court takes, at least initially, stating that the Regulation has an adverse effect on competition.[20] But how do we know that

---

18 See above, para 5(1).

19 The Court further clouded the analysis by treating the 'collective' question as one involving the issue whether the Bar exercises collective dominance, compare *Wouters*, para 114 with Opinion of the Advocate General, para 150 (collective dominance requires oligopolistic position in the market), which would appear to call for an economic analysis of the markets involved. The Court found that the legal profession 'is not concentrated' and that members of the bar 'account for only 60% of turnover in the legal services sector in the Netherlands' (*Wouters*, para 114). This would appear to be a rather superficial approach to the question of market definition and power, one that is particularly puzzling in light of the Advocate General's view that the he could not take a position on the question of collective dominance because the file did not contain the 'matters of law and fact necessary to that end' (Opinion, para 153).

20 *Wouters*, para 86. See also *ibid*, para 87 (one-stop shopping), para 89 (scale economies might reduce costs to consumers). The Advocate General also found 'persuasive' the arguments that the Regulation restricts competition. *See* Opinion of the Advocate General, paras 116–21.

this is the case? The Regulation, after all, does not forbid lawyers from hiring accountants and offering joint services (or *vice versa*), nor does it prohibit law firms and accounting firms from jointly bidding for clients. The regulation does not set fees for services, nor does it forbid accountants from becoming lawyers (or *vice versa*). And what, exactly, are the markets in which the disappointed lawyers would like to compete? What product do these lawyers sell? What do we know about the geographic scope of the markets (are they national? international?). What do we know about the power of the Bar of the Netherlands to effect competition in such markets?

From the Court's opinion, we know nothing of the answers to these questions. For all we can tell, lawyers' services are completely undifferentiated, the consumers of those services are completely homogeneous, and the choices consumers face for providers of legal services are limited to law firms in the Netherlands. Of course, one might guess that Mr Wouters' desire to be a partner in Arthur Anderson indicates that the facts are otherwise; but the Court does not inquire.

1.4 What Are the Justifications for the Restraint?

It might seem that the Court's superficial approach to competitive effects would lead directly to a finding of a violation of Article 81(1) EC. As a policy matter, this would not appear to be a bad result. The arguments about the potential inefficiencies of the Regulation are certainly plausible. In any event, if joint lawyer-accounting firms do not provide better (or cheaper) services to clients, the market will soon enough end the experiment, or lead to some other evolution in firm structure which we cannot now predict. This is the advantage of markets over regulation.

The problem is that the Court's superficial approach did not lead to a finding of a violation of Article 81(1) EC. Instead it led to a superficial decision that the regulation did not violate Article 81(1) EC after all. The reason for so finding was the Court's willingness to accept as a justification the Bar's purpose in regulating the legal profession, specifically, its power to make rules relating to 'organization, qualifications, professional ethics, supervision and liability' which insure that consumers of legal services and the 'sound administration of justice' are served by being guaranteed 'integrity and experience.'[21] After all, lawyers are bound by rules of secrecy; accountants are not. The rule forbidding joint partnerships is therefore necessary 'to ensure the proper practice of the legal profession' and the rule does not go beyond what is 'necessary' to carry out that objective.[22] Thus, the Bar's Regulation does not infringe Article 81(1) EC 'since that body could reasonably have considered that that

[21] See *Wouters*, para 97.
[22] *Ibid,* paras 107, 108.

regulation, despite the effects restrictive of competition that are inherent in it, is necessary for the proper practice of the legal profession, as organized in the Member State concerned.'[23]

This is a disappointing outcome in many ways.[24] First, the Court takes an uncritical approach to the public interest objectives of professional regulation (or, at least, to professional regulation of lawyers by lawyers). One need not be a complete cynic to acknowledge that professional self-regulation is not likely to be solely an exercise in public regarding behaviour. The Court's approach, however, virtually puts any anticompetitive motivation and effect aside, simply relying on the Bar's 'reasonable judgment' that the restraint is necessary. Second, the Court takes an uncritical approach to the proportionality of the restraint to the problem involved. The Court focuses on what is 'necessary to ensure the proper practice of the legal profession', surely an extraordinarily broad goal, and does not explain why the ban could not be narrower.[25] Third, the Court provides little by way of limiting principles for when a public interest justification will take conduct outside the scope of Article 81 EC, either with regard to the types of professions involved or the types of professional restraints.

At bottom, however, the analytical problems with the decision result from the failure to acknowledge the messiness inherent in judging the anticompetitive effects of, and justifications for, restraints by professional groups. Some professional restraints might be easy to judge, for example, those that directly restrict price competition. Most, however, are more complicated, institutionally and economically. Indeed, the Court was as disserved by the too-ready acceptance of the regulation's anticompetitive effect as it was by the too-ready acceptance of the Bar's purported justifications. A much deeper examination of the pro- and anti-competitive effects of the restraint needed to be done before reaching a conclusion on whether the restraint violated Article 81 EC.

2. Government Involvement

How should competition law take account of governmental involvement in the regulation of the professions? Each of the three recent Court of Justice

---

[23] See *Wouters*, para 110.

[24] I put to the side the doctrinal question whether the justifications should more appropriately be considered under Art 81(3) EC, compare Opinion of Advocate General, para 113. It may be that with the adoption of the Modernization Regulation, and the demise of the notification system, the courts will be more willing to include conduct under 81(1) and then consider whether the conduct qualifies for a defence under Art 81(3) EC.

[25] Compare Opinion of Advocate General, paras 189–96 (exploring less restrictive alternatives, but concluding that there is insufficient evidence to settle the question of proportionality).

decisions deals with this question (although one arises outside the context of professional regulation). Given the ubiquity of such involvement, this is a question that cannot be avoided when attempting to apply competition law to professional restraints.

2.1 Arduino: *What Governments Can Do*

Mr Arduino, a careless Italian driver, lost a damages suit brought by the owner of the vehicle with which he collided. The Italian magistrate, when determining costs to be borne by Mr Arduino, refused to apply the fee for the plaintiff's lawyer as fixed by the bar association, even though the fee schedule was established pursuant to a statutory scheme dating back to 1933. The Magistrate believed that the fee fixing violated Article 81(1) EC. The question referred to the Court of Justice was whether Articles 10 and 81 EC preclude a Member State from adopting the statutory scheme in question.

The Court's decision turned on the process that Italy had chosen for setting lawyers' fees. Fees are set initially by the National Council of the Bar (Consiglio Nazionale Forense, or CNF), a committee of bar association members elected by the bar membership. These fees are set every two years; by statute, they depend on the value of the amount in dispute and are to be set as minima and maxima for each procedural step in the proceeding (the awarding court has discretion to depart from either bound, but it must give its reasons for the departure).[26] The fee schedule determined by the CNF must be approved by the Minister of Justice, after obtaining the opinion of the Interministerial Committee on Prices and consulting the Council of State. The fees that the Magistrate refused to award were the result of some apparent negotiation between the Minister and the CNF related to the amount of an increase in fees, as a result of which half the increase became effective on 1 October 1994, with the other half effective on 1 April 1995.

The Court focused on the responsibility of Italy, rather than the bar association, noting that although Article 81 applies only to undertakings, and not to laws of Member States, nevertheless, Article 10 and Article 81 together indicate that a Member State cannot enact legislation or regulations that render competition rules 'ineffective'.[27] This might be the case, for example, if the state divests itself of legislative authority by delegating responsibility for economic decisions to 'private economic operators', who then, presumably, act in their self-interest to restrain competition.[28]

The Court then pointed out that even with delegation, the resulting decision could still be one of state legislation or regulation. For example, the

[26] See *Arduino*, paras 5–7, 9.
[27] *Arduino*, para 34.
[28] *Arduino*, para 35.

decision could be delegated to members of the professional organization who were independent of the economic interests being regulated and who were required to take account of the public interest, including the interests of consumers, under defined criteria.[29]

Curiously, perhaps, this example did not describe Italy's process in this case, a fact acknowledged by the Court.[30] Rather, all that was involved in terms of public oversight of the fee schedule was its review and approval by the Minister of Justice, in consultation with two other ministries, plus the Minister's ability to get the CNF to amend its proposal (apparently the case here). Indeed, there is no indication of the criteria used by the Minister for granting or withholding approval, or even whether there are any statutory criteria at all.[31] Yet, this procedure was enough for the Court. State law reserved to the state the power to approve, 'on the basis of a draft produced by a professional body . . . a tariff fixing minimum and maximum fees for members of the profession.'[32] Italy did not violate Articles 10 and 81 EC.

2.2 Wouters: *What Governments Can't Do*

Wouters involved a regulation of the Bar of the Netherlands forbidding partnerships with non-lawyers. Pursuant to the Netherlands' statute, such regulations are adopted by the Bar's College of Delegates, made up of bar association members elected by the membership (the regulation could have been proposed by the Bar's General Council or by at least five delegates). Regulations are to be adopted in the interests of the proper practice of the profession and the College is given authority to adopt regulations which are necessary for the administration and organization of the bar. Adopted regulations are communicated to the Ministry of Justice and published in the Official Gazette.[33] An adopted decision can be suspended or annulled by royal decree within 6 months of its adoption if it is 'contrary to law or to the public interest'; if a suspended provision is not annulled within a year, it comes back into force.[34]

The Court decided that the Bar's adoption of the regulation in *Wouters* was subject to Article 81(1) EC, as we have seen. But why wasn't this regulation considered an action of the state, rather than one attributable to this 'association of undertakings'? The Court pointed out that the Council and the Bar's governing bodies are composed 'exclusively of members of the Bar elected

[29] Arduino, paras 37, 38.
[30] See *Arduino*, paras 38, 39.
[31] The reason for delaying the full increase was apparently the concern over inflation in the Italian economy, as expressed by the Interministerial Committee on Prices, see *ibid*, para 10.
[32] *Arduino*, para 44.
[33] *Wouters*, para 9.
[34] *Wouters*, para 12.

solely by members of the profession' and that the Bar is not required to adopt regulations based on 'specified public interest criteria.'[35] If the state wants professional association regulation to be 'State measures', then it must 'define the public-interest criteria and the essential principles' with which the association's rules must comply and it must 'retain [. . .] its power to adopt decisions in the last resort'.[36]

But the price fixing done by the Italian bar in *Arduino* was not subject to public interest criteria nor was it done by an independent group. The only difference between the price fixing done by the Italian bar and the regulation done by the Netherlands bar was that the Italian Minister of Justice was required to approve the regulation before it would enter into force, whereas the Netherlands regulation went into force unless annulled by government decree. The Court in *Wouters* did not focus on this difference (or, indeed, even mention it), so it is difficult to say why this difference should be critical. One might speculate that the Netherlands' 'negative option' system is more prone to being a rubber-stamp for the Bar, but that is not necessarily so. For all we know, Ministers of Justice in Italy are generally inclined to approve bar association fee fixing while bar regulation in the Netherlands is closely reviewed and sometimes annulled.

Taking *Wouters* together with *Arduino* thus yields an unsatisfying articulation of the principles for deciding when professional association regulation will be attributable to the association rather than being viewed as a 'State measure'. The factual distinction between the two cases indicates that it might take very little to make such rules into government action. Although *Wouters* drew attention to the composition of the Bar association and the lack of articulated public interest criteria to guide its decision, *Arduino* held these were not critical. Considering that the two cases were decided on the same day, it is difficult to conclude that more is required than simply an affirmative government review prior to implementation.

2.3 Fiammiferi*: A Further Limitation on Government Regulation?*

The third case, *Fiammiferi*, involves Italy's regulation of its match industry, rather than its legal services industry. Under laws dating back to 1923 Italy has been regulating the prices and output of Italian match makers. It established a consortium of Italian match companies, the Consorzio Industrie Fiammiferi (CIF), with the exclusive right to manufacture and distribute matches in Italy. Under an agreement between the CIF and the government, the Ministry of Finance sets the price of matches and a 'quota allocation committee' sets and allocates match production quotas.[37] The committee

[35] See *Wouters*, paras 61, 62.

[36] *Wouters*, para 68.

[37] See CIF, paras 6, 7.

consists of an official of the State Monopolies Board and four members of the industry; its quota decisions must be approved by the State Monopolies Board. Quota transfers (which apparently occur with some frequency[38]) must be approved by the Ministry of Finance.[39] The agreement had provided that Membership in CIF is compulsory, but it is no longer so.[40]

A complaint by a German match manufacturer about its inability to enter the Italian market led the Italian Competition Authority to open an investigation, which subsequently expanded to include an agreement between CIF and Swedish Match whereby CIF purchased a quantity of matches in return for Swedish Match's agreement not to enter the Italian market. The Authority decided to disapply Italy's legislative framework, as contrary to the EC Treaty including Article 81(1) EC, and to find that CIF's quota allocation agreements violated Article 81(1) EC. These decisions led ultimately to a referral to the Court of Justice.

The first question referred to the Court was whether the Authority was correct in disapplying Italian law. The Court said not only that the Authority was correct in so doing, but that it had a duty to disapply the law. Member states cannot, through legislation or regulation, 'render ineffective the competition rules that apply to undertakings'.[41] Where anticompetitive conduct 'is required or facilitated by national legislation . . ., specifically with regard to price-fixing or market-sharing arrangements', a national competition authority must disapply the national legislation and may impose penalties for all future conduct and for prior conduct which had only been 'encouraged' but not required.[42]

This led to the second question referred to the Court. Could the CIF be held liable for its quota allocation decisions taken before the legislation was disapplied? Although the Court decided that the Italian referring court would have the responsibility for answering this question, it suggested a two-part framework for analyzing the question. First, does the legislation preclude an undertaking from engaging in 'autonomous conduct' which might then restrain competition? Second, if there can be autonomous conduct, are the undertakings to be blamed or is the conduct 'actually attributable to the Member State concerned'?[43] Applying this framework, the Court suggested, first, that there was substantial room for making private decisions with regard to the quotas, decisions that might be anticompetitive (for example, in quota transfers),[44] and, second, indicated that the statutory procedures for determining and reviewing the quotas are not sufficient for them to be viewed as

[38] See CIF, para 72.
[39] *Ibid,* para 7.
[40] *Ibid,* paras 11, 15.
[41] *Ibid,* para 45.
[42] *Ibid,* para 58.
[43] *Ibid,* para 66.
[44] *Ibid,* paras 68–74.

having been 'taken by a public authority', thereby taking them outside the scope of Article 81(1) EC.[45]

It is somewhat difficult to square this decision with the Court's approach to the regulation of lawyers in *Arduino*. First, the Court in *Arduino* did not indicate that Italy's regulation of lawyers' fees would be disapplied in the future. But if state regulation that requires or facilitates anticompetitive price-fixing of matches must be disapplied, then why should Italy still be free to require or facilitate price fixing of legal services? Does *Fiammiferi* call into question Italy's (and every Member State's) regulation of the fees set by professional associations (and all other competitive aspects of professional regulation)? Presumably all these regulatory regimes at least facilitate professional agreements that may adversely affect competition. Will they be disapplied in the future?

Second, the Court in *Arduino* found that the price fixing was the result of the state's action rather than the action of the bar association. Critical in *Arduino* was the fact that public ministries reviewed and approved the fee schedule. In *Fiammiferi* quota allocations and transfers were approved by public ministries as well, but the Court said that 'public authorities do not have an effective means of controlling decisions taken by the quota-allocation committee'.[46] But why was such approval considered effective in *Arduino* and not in *Fiammiferi*? Further, the Court in *Fiammiferi* also pointed out that four of the five members of the quota allocation committee were from the industry (the fifth was a public official), with the result that the decisions could be made exclusively in pursuit of private interests.[47] But the same was true for the bar association's fee schedule, a fact which did not matter to the Court in *Arduino*.

Presumably, future Court decisions will provide answers to these puzzles. *Fiammiferi* indicates that the Court may now be more inclined to place anticompetitive private conduct within the control of competition law even though that conduct is subject to some degree of state regulatory control. Whether this will make state involvement in professional regulation legally irrelevant seems unlikely, however. Perhaps what will emerge is an approach to government involvement which looks at the 'autonomous conduct' of the professionals and their association and at the extent to which the government retains effective control.

3. Conclusion: Competition and the Liberal Professions

The three Court of Justice decisions do not articulate a careful framework for applying European competition law to the liberal professions. State

45 *Ibid*, paras 76–79.
46 *Ibid*, para 78.
47 *Ibid*, para 77.

involvement may easily exempt such conduct from coverage (or maybe not, depending on the development of *Fiammiferi*), but that might not matter anyway in light of the Court's approach to the question whether the regulation comes within the prohibition of Article 81(1) EC. For the moment, the Court shows a ready willingness to accept public interest justifications for professional regulation without either a close evaluation of the anticompetitive effects of such regulation or an effort to assess how strong those justifications are in relation to the anticompetitive effects. Without further development, the result may be to allow the liberal professions great latitude to engage in self-regulation that furthers the private economic interests of the profession itself.

IV. The US Approach to Applying Antitrust Law to the Learned Professions

1. Competitive Effects

1.1 California Dental Association v Federal Trade Commission

Perhaps to a surprising degree, antitrust analysis of horizontal restraints in the United States has been shaped in the context of the professions. *California Dental Association v FTC*[48] is the most recent Supreme Court case applying antitrust to a restraint by a professional organization, but it is only the most recent in a long line of cases involving the professions, including doctors, dentists, lawyers, and engineers.[49] Uniformly, these cases have had a significant impact on the development of general antitrust doctrine. Closer examination reveals how important it is that these cases were set in the context of a profession.

California Dental involved a restriction on advertising by the members of the California Dental Association (CDA), a voluntary non-profit association of local dental societies in California to which some 19,000 California dentists belonged (about ¾ of the dentists practicing in that state). The CDA had adopted a Code of Ethics forbidding advertisements that are 'false or misleading in any material respect'; CDA members agreed to abide by that Code. The CDA and its local societies enforced this Code in a way that required so

---

[48] 526 US 756 (1999).

[49] See, *eg*, *FTC v Superior Court Trial Lawyers Ass'n* 493 US 411 (1990) (application of *per se* rule to boycotts) (lawyers); *FTC v Indiana Federation of Dentists* 476 US 447 (1986) (application of rule of reason to joint withholding of information from buyers) (dentists); *Arizona v Maricopa County Med Soc* 457 US 332 (1982) (application of *per se* rule to maximum price fixing) (doctors).

much disclosure of fee information that it was extremely difficult for dentists to advertise discounts and special rates; CDA regulation also prohibited claims about the quality of dental services. The Federal Trade Commission found that the CDA's conduct violated Section 5 of the Federal Trade Commission Act (the functional equivalent of finding a violation of Section 1 of the Sherman Act) and the case eventually reached the Supreme Court.

Although the Court in *California Dental* did not view the case as a vehicle for discussing the application of the antitrust laws to the professions, it serves that inquiry well. As with my earlier discussion of the European cases, I am less concerned with the ins-and-outs of antitrust doctrine (specifically, the meaning and application of the rule of reason and *per se* rule) than I am with the light the case sheds on the questions relevant to applying antitrust to the professions. Thus, the same analytical questions can be asked of *California Dental* as were asked of *Wouters*.

1.2 Is Dentistry a Business?

The question whether dentistry should be considered a 'business' was not even raised before the Court, at least not in those direct terms. This is because the question had already been decided nearly 25 years before in a case involving lawyers, *Goldfarb v Virginia State Bar*,[50] where the Supreme Court had been pressed to decide that the 'learned professions' do not involve 'trade or commerce' within the meaning of Section 1 of the Sherman Act. The Court rejected the argument. The exchange of a service for money, even a legal service, is commerce, said the Court. 'It is no disparagement of the practice of law as a profession to acknowledge that it has this business aspect.'[51]

The ready finding that professions are business, however, does not fully suppress the more subtle point that professions may not be quite like other businesses, and associations of professionals perhaps are not quite like other associations. In fact, the issue was raised in a way in *California Dental*. The CDA is a non-profit professional association; the Federal Trade Commission Act gives the FTC jurisdiction only over an organization 'organized to carry on business for its own profit or that of its members'.[52] The Court had little trouble finding the CDA was covered (the Association was clearly concerned about bringing economic benefit to its 'profit-seeking professionals'[53]), but it also left open the possibility that some organizations of profit-making entities might lie outside the jurisdictional reach of the FTC, for example, organizations 'devoted solely to professional education'.[54]

---

[50] 421 US 773 (1975).
[51] *Ibid*, p 788.
[52] See 15 USC 44, 45(a)(2).
[53] See, p 767.
[54] *Ibid*, p 766.

Putting aside the technical statutory question, US courts have on occasion put certain restraints outside the Sherman Act as not 'trade or commerce' because of some level of discomfort with the notion that antitrust rules should apply to the activities in question. An old example is baseball, viewed famously as an 'exhibition' rather than as 'commerce' by Justice Holmes;[55] a more recent one is college accreditation.[56] These cases may today be viewed as discredited, or naive, because we can see that baseball teams and colleges are both concerned with pecuniary benefit, with selling a service, and so should not be allowed to engage in anticompetitive behaviour to advance their economic interests.[57] Making such organizations subject to competition law should rest on the effect the restraints have on the creation and allocation of economic resources, the main focus of antitrust; but, just as in Europe, the courts tend to focus on whether the defendant is concerned with economic profit.

Should antitrust be uncomfortable with equating a profession to any other business?[58] The Supreme Court, in a well-known footnote in *Goldfarb,* left this door open:

---

[55] *Federal Baseball Club v National League* 259 US 200, 209 (1922) ('the exhibition, although made for money, would not be called trade or commerce in the commonly accepted use of those words. As it is put by defendant, personal effort, not related to production, is not a subject of commerce.'). Interestingly, Holmes gave lawyers as an example to support his argument. In response to the argument made by the plaintiff that 'trade or commerce' was shown by the fact that the defendants travelled across state lines to play their games, Holmes wrote: 'That which in its consummation is not commerce does not become commerce among the States because the transportation that we have mentioned takes place. To repeat the illustrations given by the Court below, a firm of lawyers sending out a member to argue a case . . . does not engage in such commerce because the lawyer or lecturer goes to another State.' *Ibid.*

[56] See *Marjorie Webster Junior College, Inc v Middle States Ass'n*, 432 F 2d 650 (DC Cir), cert denied, 400 US 965 (1970) (Sherman Act does not apply to school accreditation activities done with a non-commercial purpose).

[57] For a review of the application of antitrust law to law school accreditation, see M Lao, 'Discrediting Accreditation? Antitrust and Legal Education' (2002) 79 *Washington University Law Quarterly* 1035. See also H First, 'Competition in the Legal Education Industry (II): An Antitrust Analysis' (1979) 54 *New York University L Rev* 1049, 1089–99 (arguments for applying antitrust law to legal education industry).

[58] Note that the professions remain outside the coverage of New York state antitrust law, see *People v Roth* 52 NY2d 440; 420 NE2d 929; 438 NYS2d 737 (1981) (professions not covered by state's Donnelly Act, rejecting application of *Goldfarb* to New York state law) (indictment of physicians for group boycott); In re *Estate of Freeman*, 34 NY2d 1; 311 NE2d 480; 355 NYS2d 336 (1974) (lawyers' minimum fee schedule not subject to Donnelly Act because legal profession is not a 'business or trade' within the meaning of the Act). 'A profession is not a business. It is distinguished by the requirements of extensive formal training and learning, admission to practice by a qualifying licensure, a code of ethics imposing standards qualitatively and extensively beyond those that prevail or are tolerated in the marketplace, a system for discipline of its members for violation of the code of ethics, a duty to subordinate financial reward to social responsibility, and, notably, an obligation on its members, even in non-professional matters, to conduct themselves as members of a learned, disciplined, and honorable occupation. . . . Interwoven with professional standards, of course, is pursuit of the ideal and that the profession not be debased by lesser commercial standards (see Drinker, *Legal Ethics*, pp. 210–273)'.

> The fact that a restraint operates upon a profession as distinguished from a business is, of course, relevant in determining whether that particular restraint violates the Sherman Act. It would be unrealistic to view the practice of professions as interchangeable with other business activities, and automatically to apply to the professions antitrust concepts which originated in other areas. The public service aspect, and other features of the professions, may require that a particular practice, which could properly be viewed as a violation of the Sherman Act in another context, be treated differently. We intimate no view on any other situation than the one with which we are confronted today.[59]

1.3 What Are the Anticompetitive Effects of the Restraint?

According to the Federal Trade Commission, the CDA's enforcement of its code of ethics precluded its members from advertising many types of claims about price. For example, statements that a dentist's fees were low, reasonable, affordable, or inexpensive could not be made. General discounts to seniors could not be advertised. Coupons offering a general percentage discount to new patients were prohibited. Guarantees could not be advertised. Dentists could not say things such as 'latest in cosmetic dentistry' or 'gentle dentistry in a caring environment.' In fact, the FTC found that all claims about quality were precluded.[60]

A first cut at analyzing the anticompetitive effects of the CDA's code of ethics is that the restrictions have an obvious negative impact on the ability of dentists to compete. The regulations reduce the amount of easily conveyed information available to consumers in the marketplace. This harms a consumer's ability to consider price and quality when choosing a dentist and diminishes the ability of dentists to compete against each other on the basis of price and quality.

Such adverse effects would appear to be at the core of what competition law forbids. Indeed, so thought four Justices of the Supreme Court in the case. Justice Breyer, writing for the four, said: '[W]hy should I have to spell out the obvious? To restrain truthful advertising about lower prices is likely to restrict competition in respect to price—the central nervous system of the economy.'[61] If consumers do not know about price, there will be no pressure on dentists to reduce their fees; if consumers are uninformed about quality, dentists' incentives to compete on quality are reduced. 'That, at any rate, is the theory of the Sherman Act', wrote Justice Breyer. 'And it is rather late in the day for anyone to deny the significant anticompetitive tendencies of an agreement that restricts competition in any legitimate respect, let alone

59 421 US 788 n 17.

60 See 526 US 781, 783–84 (Breyer, J, concurring and dissenting).

61 *Ibid*, p 784–85.

one that inhibits customers from learning about the quality of a dentist's service.'[62]

The majority of the Court, however, did not see the anticompetitive effects as 'obvious'. For the majority, the 'threshold' question was whether 'professional price and quality advertising' should come within the general antitrust rule that would apply to other types of advertising.[63] The reason why the answer to this question was not obvious is the nature of professional services markets where information is asymmetric between knowledgeable professionals and poorly informed lay patients ('striking disparities between the information available to the professional and the patient'[64]).

> In a market for professional services, in which advertising is relatively rare and the comparability of service packages not easily established, the difficulty for customers or potential competitors to get and verify information about the price and availability of services magnifies the dangers to competition associated with misleading advertising. What is more, the quality of professional services tends to resist either calibration or monitoring by individual patients or clients, partly because of the specialized knowledge required to evaluate the services, and partly because of the difficulty in determining whether, and the degree to which, an outcome is attributable to the quality of services (like a poor job of tooth-filling) or to something else (like a very tough walnut).[65]

Thus, said the Court, the restraints might 'possibly [have had] no effect at all on competition' or even 'might plausibly be thought to have a net procompetitive effect' by 'reducing the occurrence of unverifiable and misleading across-the-board discount advertising.'[66]

Although subsequent commentary about *California Dental* has mostly been concerned about the effect of the decision on *per se* and rule of reason analysis, what is more interesting for purposes of this essay is the importance of the professional services setting to the Court's analysis.[67] Justice Souter's majority opinion constantly refers to the fact that a profession is involved. '[R]estrictions on professional advertising could have different effects from those normally found in the commercial world,' the Court reminds us. By contrast, the dissenting opinion never uses the word 'profession' in its analysis. Standard price theory is all that is necessary to make the prediction of adverse competitive effect.

---

62 See 526 US p 785 (internal citations omitted).

63 See 526 US 771.

64 *Ibid.*

65 *Ibid*, p 772.

66 *Ibid*, pp 771, 773.

67 For further discussion of the professional services context of the decision, see S Calkins, '*California Dental Association:* Not A Quick Look But Not The Full Monty' (2000) 67 *Antitrust Law Journal* 495, 510–19 (discussing the Supreme Court's 'discomfort' with professional advertising).

It is difficult to say whether the Court will be as willing to accept information asymmetries in other markets as a reason for doubting normal predictions of anticompetitive effect arising out of price and quality advertising restrictions.[68] What is striking, however, is the lack of critical application of this economic observation to the restraints involved. If information asymmetry is a problem in professional markets, how does a rule that keeps information from consumers solve the problem? If the rarity of price advertising makes it more difficult for consumers to verify truthfulness, how will this be solved by keeping information rare? If a dentist isn't 'gentle', will a consumer be hurt more because the consumer expected otherwise? What's wrong with having markets deal with these information asymmetries rather than relying on agreements among competitors whose interests are in maintaining these asymmetries, not in remedying them?

Had the Court approached these restraints with the scepticism it would normally show when competitors restrain price and quality advertising, the Court would at least have shifted the burden to the defendants to show that their restraints promoted competition. But the Court pointedly did not do so.[69] This makes it hard to avoid the conclusion that the Court's approach was more affected by the 'professional' aspect of the case than it was by some economic theory of information asymmetries. Indeed, one might conclude that the Court seized on a clever economic observation to justify its desire to give greater deference to agreements among professionals than it would have given to agreements among steel makers. Professionals may be subject to the antitrust laws, but the Court may still think that a profession (or at least the legal profession) is still not fully 'commerce'.

1.4 What Are the Justifications for the Restraint?

When the Court in *California Dental* seized on the economic theory of information asymmetry to question the anticompetitive effect of the advertising restrictions imposed by the CDA, it cited to the footnote in *Goldfarb* for the proposition that professions might not be 'interchangeable with other business activities'. Nevertheless, the Court did not take up *Goldfarb*'s invitation to consider the 'public service aspect of the profession'. Rather, the Court only discussed how the economics of a market for professional services might differ from the economics of a market for other goods or services.

The Court's decision to discuss economic theory, rather than 'public service', reflects the subsequent history of the *Goldfarb* footnote. In *National Society of Profession Engineers v United States*[70] the Supreme Court

---

[68] Professor Calkins doubts that the Court will accept similar arguments in other markets where 'information disparities loom large'. See *ibid*, p 518.

[69] See 526 US 775 n 12.

[70] 435 US 679 (1978).

reviewed an ethical rule that forbade engineers from providing a fee proposal or bid until after the prospective client had chosen the engineer. One of the Society's defences was that the ethical rule was reasonable 'because competition among professional engineers was contrary to the public interest.'[71] Engineers might submit deceptively low bids (deceptive because cheap engineering might actually result in more expensive buildings); low bids might also mean poor-quality engineering services and potentially unsafe buildings.

The Supreme Court in *Engineers* rejected the Society's public interest justification. In the Court's view, the Sherman Act reflects a judgment that markets produce the best goods and services at the lowest prices. Preventing unsafe products is not adequate justification for setting aside that judgment; many industries produce products that can cause harm. Nor is the prevention of 'unethical' deception a justification; ethical norms can be justified under the Sherman Act only if they promote competition. The Court concluded: '[T]he cautionary footnote in *Goldfarb* cannot be read as fashioning a broad exemption . . . for learned professions'.[72]

Justice Blackmun wrote an interesting concurring opinion, in which he was joined by Justice Rehnquist. Although willing to strike down the Society's rule as overbroad, Justice Blackmun felt it was unnecessary to decide that the antitrust laws, as applied to professions 'long consigned to self regulation', could never 'take account of benefits other than increased competition'.[73] He warned about shaping the Sherman Act to 'such a narrow last' that it would reach ethical rules 'which have a more than *de minimis* anticompetitive effect and yet are important in a profession's proper ordering'.[74] For example, medical associations might have minimum standards of competence, which have the effect of limiting entrants; or lawyers might prescribe certain forms of price advertising, which could reduce competition. Care must be taken, Justice Blackmun wrote, to leave 'enough elbowroom for realistic application of the Sherman Act to professional services'.[75]

California Dental shows that Justice Blackmun need not have worried. Although a 'public interest' justification (like the one asserted in *Wouters*, for example) might not be considered by US antitrust courts, a reframing of that justification to fit into an economic theory will be considered. So, for example, *Engineers* today might be recast on the basis of information asymmetries (professional engineers know far better than clients what the results of cheap engineering might be) rather than relying on the need to protect the public

---

71 435 US 679 (1978), p 684.
72 *Ibid*, p 696.
73 *Ibid*, p 699.
74 *Ibid*, p 700.
75 *Ibid*, p 701.

from the effects of competitive markets.[76] Similarly, bar associations might seek to reframe rules against multidisciplinary practice as an efficient way to insure that consumers will get the conflict-free and confidential legal services that they expect lawyers to provide and which is a necessary product characteristic of legal services. If the courts show themselves willing to entertain such broad efficiency claims, with little scepticism about their validity, the application of the antitrust laws to professional association activities could be substantially undermined.

2. Government Involvement

The first case to raise the issue of government involvement in professional regulation as a defence to antitrust liability was *Goldfarb v Virginia State Bar*, decided by the Supreme Court in 1975.[77] The fixed fee schedule that the Goldfarbs encountered, when they sought a lawyer to examine the title on the house they wanted to buy, was set by the local bar association in the Goldfarbs' community. The local bar association did not enforce the fee schedule; that was done by the State Bar Association, which had issued ethical opinions indicating that fee schedules cannot be ignored and that habitual undercharging 'raises a presumption' of misconduct. Membership in the State Bar Association was required to practice law in Virginia. By statute in Virginia, the State Bar Association was an 'administrative agency' of the Virginia Supreme Court, to be used by the Court to investigate and report violations of the rules adopted by the Supreme Court to regulate the practice of law in Virginia.[78] The Virginia Supreme Court had also adopted ethical rules for lawyers which stated that bar association fee schedules provide guidance on what fees are 'reasonable'.[79]

The Bar Association's defence rested on an earlier Supreme Court case, *Parker v Brown*, in which the Court held that the Sherman Act covered only 'business combinations', not 'state action'.[80] The Supreme Court in *Goldfarb*,

[76] But see *FTC v Indiana Fed. of Dentists* 476 US 447 (1986) 462–63, rejecting 'quality of care' justification for dentists' concerted effort to withhold dental x-rays from insurance companies; argument that easy use of x-rays by insurance companies will lead to rejection of insurance claims for dentistry that patients need is 'flawed both legally and factually'; 'The argument is in essence, that an unrestrained market in which consumers are given access to the information they believe to be relevant to their choices will lead them to make unwise and even dangerous choices. Such an argument amounts to nothing less than a frontal assault on the basic policy of the Sherman Act'. National Society of Professional Engineers, cited above, at 695. Moreover, there is no particular reason to believe that the provision of information will be more harmful to consumers in the market for dental services than in other markets.'

[77] 421 US 773 (1975).

[78] See *Goldfarb*, 421 US 776–77 and n 2.

[79] *Ibid*, p 789 n19.

[80] See 317 US 341 (1943) 351.

however, had little trouble deciding that the conduct involved was not 'state action' because it could not 'fairly be said that the State of Virginia through its Supreme Court Rules required the anticompetitive activities of either respondent'.[81] State law left regulation to the Supreme Court; that Court mentioned fee schedules, but did not require the Bar Association to set them or to adopt the sort of price floor that the Goldfarbs encountered. It may be that the fee schedules 'complemented' state regulation; it may even be that they were prompted by it; but adherence to minimum fee schedules was not 'compelled by direction of the State acting as a sovereign'.[82]

The extent to which 'state action' in the professional context depends on a compulsory directive of the state was tested two years later in *Bates v State Bar of Arizona*.[83] *Bates* involved a disciplinary action brought by the State Bar against two lawyers for violating its disciplinary rule against advertising. The State Bar is an integrated bar (to which all licensed attorneys in Arizona must belong). The disciplinary rule was adopted by the Supreme Court of Arizona pursuant to the Court's rule that the 'duties and obligations of members [of the bar] shall be as prescribed by the Code of Professional Responsibility of the American Bar Association . . . as amended by this Court.'[84] The disciplinary rule was identical to the ABA and the State Bar rule banning all lawyer advertising, subject to certain limited exceptions.[85]

Although one might have thought that the State Bar was not exactly compelled to adopt the rule which was subsequently adopted by the State Supreme Court (just as no state organization compelled the Virginia Bar to adopt minimum fee schedules), the Supreme Court in *Bates* had no trouble deciding that the Bar was immune under the state action doctrine. '[T]he challenged restraint is the affirmative command of the Arizona Supreme Court . . . [which] is the ultimate body wielding the State's power over the practice of law . . . and, thus, the restraint is "compelled by direction of the State acting as a sovereign".'[86]

Much state regulation, however, is adopted by a state agency (often a sectoral regulatory agency) after being proposed by the very parties being regulated; the regulated party must then comply until the regulation is changed. If such conduct is to be considered an immune 'compulsory directive', much state regulation would fall outside the scope of the antitrust laws. The Court was aware of this problem (indeed, having denied an immunity in such a case decided the previous year involving a tariff for light bulbs[87]), so the Court made clear why the argument for immunity was particularly compelling in

81 See above, at 790.
82 *Ibid*, p 791.
83 433 US 350 (1977).
84 *Ibid*, p 360 n 12.
85 *Ibid*, p 355 and n 5.
86 *Ibid*, p 359–60 (internal citations omitted).
87 See *Cantor v Detroit Edison* 428 US 579 (1976), discussed in *Bates*, 433 US 360–62.

this case. This case was not about light bulbs; it was about regulating lawyers: '[T]he regulation of the activities of the bar is at the core of the State's power to protect the public.'[88] The Court added:

> We note, moreover, that the Court's opinion in Goldfarb concluded with the observation that '[i]n holding that certain anticompetitive conduct by lawyers is within the reach of the Sherman Act we intend no diminution of the authority of the State to regulate its professions.' Allowing the instant Sherman Act challenge to the disciplinary rule would have precisely that undesired effect.[89]

The Court concluded its discussion of the state action defence, however, with language that presaged a somewhat different approach to the defence: [90]

> The disciplinary rules reflect a clear articulation of the State's policy with regard to professional behavior. Moreover, as the instant case shows, the rules are subject to pointed re-examination by the policy maker—the Arizona Supreme Court—in enforcement proceedings. Our concern that federal policy is being unnecessarily and inappropriately subordinated to state policy is reduced in such a situation; we deem it significant that the state policy is so clearly and affirmatively expressed and that the State's supervision is so active.

The two threads at the end of the Court's opinion in *Bates*—clear expression of state policy and active supervision—emerged three years later in *California Retail Liquor Dealers Ass'n v Midcal Aluminum, Inc.*[91] as the Supreme Court's statement of the test for the state action defence, a test to which the Court continues to adhere. *Midcal* arose the context of California's regulation of resale prices of wine, prices which were established by wine producers and distributors pursuant to a state statute which required wholesalers and retailers to sell wine at the resale price established on the schedule posted by the producer or distributor. The Court had little trouble rejecting an immunity defence. Although the statutory scheme qualified for the defence under the first part of the test (the policy of resale price maintenance was 'clearly articulated and affirmatively expressed as state policy'[92]), it failed the second part of the test. The scheme was not '"actively supervised" by the State itself'.[93] California did not establish price, or review the reasonableness of the price schedules, and there was no 'pointed re-examination' of the program. National policy favouring competition 'cannot be thwarted by casting such a gauzy cloak of state involvement over what is essentially a private price-fixing arrangement'.[94]

88 *Ibid*, p 361.
89 *Ibid*, p 360 n 11.
90 *Ibid*, p 362.
91 445 US 97 (1980).
92 *Ibid*, p 105.
93 *Ibid.*
94 *Ibid*, p 106.

The Supreme Court has since applied the *Midcal* test in a number of cases, but two are particularly important for our discussion. The first is *Hoover v Ronwin*, decided four years after *Midcal* but also the most recent Supreme Court decision to apply the state action defence in the context of the professions.[95] Ronwin had taken the Arizona bar examination and was given a failing grade by the bar examiners. The bar examiners (the seven members of the Arizona Supreme Court's 'Committee on Examinations and Admissions') were chosen by the Arizona Supreme Court from a list of nominees prepared by the Arizona State Bar Association's Board of Governors. Under Arizona Supreme Court rules they were given authority to examine applicants, grade and score the applicants 'as the Committee deems appropriate in its discretion', and recommend for admission to the bar those applicants who have the requisite qualifications.[96] Ronwin subsequently sued the bar examiners for conspiring to restrain trade, in violation of Section 1 of the Sherman Act, alleging that the bar examiners set the passing grade on the examination with reference to the number of new attorneys they thought desirable, rather than with reference to competence. The case having been decided on the pleadings, the Court was required to take Ronwin's factual allegation as true (even if it might turn out to be otherwise).

The Supreme Court, by a 4 to 3 vote, held that the examiners were immune under the state action defence. One might have expected the majority opinion, written by Justice Powell, to apply *Midcal's* two-part test, particularly given the fact that Justice Powell had authored *Midcal*. But the Court barely referred to *Midcal*. Instead, it returned to *Bates* and chose to emphasize the theme of sovereign action. *Bates* was viewed as a case where the State Supreme Court had acted in exercise of the state's 'sovereign' legislative power, with the Bar being viewed only as an agent of the Court.[97] Exercise of legislative power alone made the bar examiners' conduct in this case into 'state action'. *Midcal* was distinguished as a case where the challenged conduct was not that of the State 'acting as sovereign,' therefore requiring further inquiry into whether there was a 'clearly articulated and affirmatively expressed policy' to displace competition with regulation.[98] Ignored was *Midcal's* willingness both to review the legislative purpose of the California statute and the fact that the Court found that the legislative policy to displace competition was 'forthrightly stated and clear'. (Ignored, too, was *Bates'* reference to the fact that the State's decision to restrain trade was 'clearly and affirmatively expressed'.) If there were a policy in Arizona to use the bar examination to limit competition among lawyers, that policy was neither

---

[95] 466 US 558 (1984).

[96] *Ibid*, p 562.

[97] *Ibid*, p 568: 'A state supreme Court, when acting in a legislative capacity, occupies the same position as that of a state legislature. Therefore, a decision of a state supreme court, acting legislatively rather than judicially, is exempt from Sherman Act liability as state action.'

[98] *Ibid*, p 579 n 33.

stated nor clear,[99] and it certainly was not implicit in the delegation to the bar examiners (lawyers, after all) to grade applicants and recommend candidates for admission to the bar based on those grades. But the Court turned unwilling to examine closely the state's actions. 'The reason that state action is immune from Sherman Act liability is not that the State has chosen to act in an anticompetitive fashion, but that the State itself has chosen to act.'[100]

The second case is *FTC v Ticor Title Insurance Co*,[101] the Supreme Court's most recent articulation of the state action doctrine. In *Ticor* the Federal Trade Commission alleged that six title insurance companies had fixed the fees for title searches and examinations. Title insurance companies are regulated by state insurance agencies and the fees for these searches had been approved by those agencies. Some of the states, however, approved the fees using a 'negative option' rule; that is, the insurance companies filed the rates and the rates became effective unless they were rejected within some set time period. Whatever the potential for active review in such a setting, the Administrative Law Judge before whom the cases were tried found that 'at most' the filings were checked for mathematical accuracy and some were not checked at all.[102] The Court held that this did not constitute 'active supervision', rejecting the Court of Appeals' approach which would have found active supervision so long as there was a staffed and funded regulatory program in place.[103] The Court did not hold that an immunity could never arise in a negative option system (there were, after all, 'detailed findings' in the case indicating weak supervision[104]), nor did the Court set out 'some particular form' of state regulation that would always be required.[105] But where there was 'no finding of substantial state participation', where private actors were involved 'throughout', and where price fixing was involved, the Court could not accept 'a vague imprimatur [of approval] in form and agency inaction in fact'.[106] The insurance companies' conduct was thus subject to antitrust control.

Although *Ticor* can technically be distinguished from *Hoover*,[107] nevertheless, its approach to the state action doctrine is fundamentally different. Critical to the Court's articulation in *Ticor* of the reason for the doctrine is

[99] A point made several times in the dissenting opinion, see, *eg*, *ibid*, p 594 (Stevens, J, dissenting).

[100] *Ibid*, p 574.

[101] 504 US 621 (1992).

[102] *Ibid*, p 638.

[103] *Ibid*, p 637.

[104] *Ibid*.

[105] *Ibid*, p 639.

[106] See above.

[107] *Hoover* purported not to apply the *Midcal* test because it found the bar examiners to be agents of the Supreme Court, acting as legislative sovereign. Even if the Court in *Hoover* had used the *Midcal* test, it would have focused on the first prong ('clearly articulated state policy') which was not at issue in *Ticor*. Indeed, the Court in *Ticor* does not even mention *Hoover*.

that the doctrine provides an opportunity to the states to displace competition and 'subject discrete parts of the economy to additional regulations and controls'.[108] Citing *Midcal*, the Court explained that a state may displace competition with regulation only 'if the displacement is . . . intended'.[109] To paraphrase *Hoover*, the reason for state action immunity is not that the state has acted, but that the state has acted intentionally to restrict competition. 'Neither federalism nor political responsibility is well served by a rule that essential national policies are displaced by state regulations intended to achieve more limited ends.'[110]

Of course, there is another way to distinguish *Ticor*'s close examination of the state's regulatory policy from *Hoover*'s too-ready willingness to remove the bar examiners from antitrust scrutiny. *Ticor* did not involve the professions. *Hoover* involved not only the professions generally, but lawyers specifically. Indeed, both points were emphasized by Justice Stevens in his dissent in *Hoover*.[111] With regard to restraints by and for lawyers, Stevens wrote:

> The Court also no doubt believes that lawyers—or at least those leaders of the bar who are asked to serve as bar examiners—will always be faithful to their fiduciary responsibilities. Though I would agree that the presumption is indeed a strong one, nothing in the sweeping language of the Sherman Act justifies carving out rules for lawyers inapplicable to any other profession.[112]

It may be, however, that this is precisely the effect of the Court's interpretation of the state action doctrine.

3. Conclusion: Competition and the Learned Professions

The Supreme Court's antitrust jurisprudence with regard to the learned professions purports, on the one hand, to articulate and apply general antitrust principles to the specific cases involved. On the other hand, the results in those cases, and, perhaps, even the way in which the Court articulates its general principles, have been deeply affected by the professional setting in which the cases arise. The Court's analysis of competitive effects has tried to set aside non-economic 'public interest' principles, but various Justices have remained uncomfortable with this approach and the Court has always been concerned that its broad application of antitrust principles might sweep aside long-standing norms of professional regulation and their enforcement. The result has been that different doctrines end up doing some of the work of the public

108 *Ibid*, p 632.
109 *Ibid*, p 633.
110 *Ibid*, p 636.
111 See, *eg*, 466 US 582–84, 598–99.
112 *Ibid*, p 598.

interest rationale. The Court thus stresses that an important characteristic of the market for professional services is information asymmetry; these asymmetries may transmute otherwise bad restraints into good. The Court also gives somewhat broader leeway to the states to allow professional associations to engage in regulation without incurring antitrust liability. Both aspects of the Court's jurisprudence make it more difficult to apply antitrust law to the learned professions, more difficult than it ought to be.

V. Liberal or Learned: Does It Make a Difference?

1. Protecting the Professions

The review of the three recent decisions of the European Court of Justice involving the professions, and the review of the US Supreme Court's longer decisional trail applying antitrust to the professions, bring us to roughly the same spot. Courts in both systems have applied competition law to the professions with less strength than it has been applied to other economic enterprises. Further, when it comes to the professions, courts in both systems have shown a particular willingness to treat lawyers well. Observers prone to favour capture theories of regulation would not be surprised at this outcome, particularly with regard to lawyers. Even articulating capture theory in more neutral terms, it might be that lawyers turned judges know something about bar association self-regulatory efforts and so might feel more inclined to see professional regulation in a public interest light (and particularly lawyer regulation).[113]

Even if the two systems appear to end up in the same spot, however, there are interesting similarities and differences between them. Putting aside differences in statutory language, and doctrines specific to either system, the two systems examine competitive effects differently and articulate a 'state action' defence somewhat differently. There are aspects of the US approach that I would hope the European Court would adopt; there are aspects of the US approach that I wish the US would lose. It is to both that the essay now turns.

2. Competitive Effects

The European Court of Justice's analysis in *Wouters* of the competitive effects on the ban on multidisciplinary practice basically leaves the issue

[113] Note that Justice Powell, author of both *Midcal* and *Hoover v Ronwin*, was President of the American Bar Association from 1964–65.

unexplored. An economic analysis of the effects of a restraint on competition is at the heart of antitrust, however, and should not be glossed over, particularly when the restraint's competitive effects are not obvious on their face. A ban on multidisciplinary practice is one of those restraints that raise particularly difficult issues for economic analysis. Taking the issue outside of antitrust through a broad 'public interest' defence, as the Court did, seems particularly misguided. This means that the assessment of the restraint's ultimate impact will be left to the legal profession itself, whose members may have at least some self-interest in the matter.

The United States, on the other hand, now appears willing to explore too much, at least with regard to the professions (and, perhaps, more generally). *California Dental* has made it easy for a defendant to raise an economic justification. This justification may be enough to place a heavy burden of proof on the plaintiff, even if a closer examination of the justification would show that the justification is wanting or is overly broad. There are efforts now to find ways to narrow *California Dental*, particularly by increasing the burden of proof on the defendant with regard to the purported justification and by carefully considering the existence of less restrictive alternatives.[114] The success of these efforts is uncertain, of course, and the possibility exists that *California Dental* will subsequently be narrowed by viewing it as a case particularly concerned with professional restraints. This would be good for antitrust generally, but less good for antitrust as applied to the professions.

Antitrust's basic insight is that professional self-regulation is necessarily self-regarding, at least in part if not in whole. The insight rests on the lessons of history and on basic economic theory that gives great weight to economic incentives in determining behaviour. As Justice Stevens wrote in his dissenting opinion in *Hoover v Ronwin*, '[f]or centuries the common law of restraint of trade has been concerned with restrictions on entry into particular professions and occupations.'[115] We may have historically shown a concern for protecting the public from 'purveyors of inferior goods and services',[116] but we have also found that '[e]xperience in the administration of the Sherman Act has demonstrated that there is a real risk that private associations that purport merely to regulate professional standards may in fact use their powers to restrain competition which threatens their members.'[117] Competition analysis which shields professional association behaviour from testing for economic effect is thus likely to harm consumers and the public interest.

---

[114] See, *eg*, In the Matter of *Polygram Holding, Inc*, Docket No 9298 (Federal Trade Comm'n, 2003), http://www.ftc.gov/os/2003/07/polygramopinion.pdf (where restraints are 'inherently suspect' defendant has burden to come forward with 'cognizable and plausible justifications'), aff'd, 416 F3d 29 (DC Cir 2005).

[115] 466 US 582, 583.

[116] *Ibid*, p 584.

[117] *Ibid*, p 600.

3. Government Action

Parts of the Court of Justice's approach to government action, and parts of the US approach to this issue, are closer than might at first appear. Both systems are concerned about unsupervised delegation of authority to professional groups to restrain trade. Both systems agree that competition law should not apply to state restraints. In neither system is 'negative option' regulation sufficient, at least negative option regulation that amounts to no review at all.

Indeed, it may be that one can tease out of *Fiammiferi* a concern for some of the same issues that have concerned US courts. *Fiammiferi* looks first at the extent to which anticompetitive conduct is compelled by the state, an issue of concern in cases like *Goldfarb* and, in some respect, *Midcal*. Compulsion is important not only because it removes discretion from a party with respect to its conduct, making liability for that conduct unfair, but also because compulsion demonstrates clearly a state policy to displace competition with regulation. *Fiammiferi* also looks at whether discretionary conduct ('autonomous conduct') can be blamed on the party or is attributable to the state. This concern is similar to the concern expressed in *Midcal* and *Ticor* for whether the state actively supervises the conduct, or whether the state's action can more accurately be viewed as a 'gauzy cloak' thrown over an otherwise private agreement.

When we compare cases like *Bates* and *Hoover* with *Fiammiferi*'s disapplication approach, however, real differences emerge. *Fiammiferi* indicates that the European Court may be less willing to give Member States the power to set up systems of private regulation than US courts are.[118] On the face of it, this is a peculiar result. States in the US federal system are presumably subordinate political units, part of a single federal system. Member States in the European Union, however, retain greater sovereignty, bound together by treaty to form the European Union. One might think, then, that European countries would have more flexibility to override competition with regulation, while US states should have less.

One way to explain the possible difference between the two systems is to consider the purposes that lie behind the articulation of a state action defence in the two systems. The United States, as a centralized government, may need to emphasize principles of federalism and state autonomy so as to counteract the centralizing tendency of US political institutions. Europe, on the other hand, needs a principle of integration to counteract the decentralizing tendency of what is still a union of sovereign countries. This might lead the

[118] See EM Fox, 'State Action in Comparative Context: What If *Parker v Brown* Were Italian?' in Barry Hawk, ed., *Fordham corporate Law: International Antitrust Law and Policy* (New York, NY, Juris Publ, 2004) 463.

US to be more solicitous of federalism and Europe to be more solicitous of integration and uniformity. Although in neither case can the central courts allow the states unfettered ability to set economic policy, or forbid the states from having any say in economic policy, the two systems may need slightly different approaches to a state action defence so as to keep each system in appropriate balance.

When we look at the current state of the law with regard to professions, however, it is difficult to say today which system is more in danger of giving undue deference to state involvement in professional regulation. On the European side it is unclear what facts matter most to the Court of Justice, whether it is the make-up of the professional body that establishes the rule or the extent of the review given by state officials. On the US side it is not clear exactly how much oversight of the professions a state government must provide to qualify those professions for the defence. When it comes to lawyers, it is unclear whether lawyers now have an absolute immunity to engage in self-regulation by virtue of the fact that state courts turn bar-written ethical codes into court rules. Interestingly enough, the one reported US antitrust case attacking bar association ethical rules banning multi-disciplinary law partnerships was cursorily dismissed on the basis of the state action defence, citing *Hoover v Ronwin* and *Bates*, with neither the district court nor the court of appeals needing to make any effort to assess the competitive effects of the regulation.[119] Comparing this result to the Court of Justice decision in *Wouters*, it turns out that deference to lawyer regulation resulted in a weaker antitrust review in the United States than in Europe.

4. Applying Competition Law to the Professions

Threaded through all of the doctrine, in both systems, is the question whether it is appropriate to treat the professions 'just like' any other business. Both systems clearly place the professions, whether liberal or learned, within the scope of competition law. But both systems also struggle with how different the analysis of professional restraints should be.

Should competition law just accept the idea that professions will be subject to different competition rules? Should cases like *Wouters* be treated as an 'exception' to EC law carved out only for the professions?[120] The case for

[119] See *Lawline v American Bar Ass'n*, 956 F2d 1378, 1383(7th Cir, 1992) (unincorporated association of lawyers, paralegals and laypersons whose goal was to provide legal referral services at low cost), cert denied, 510 US 992 (1993). For a review of the multidisciplinary practice debate, including the American Bar Association's views, see American Antitrust Institute, 'Converging Professional Services: Lawyers Against the Multidisciplinary Tide' (2000), available at http://www.antitrustinstitute.org/books/multidisc.cfm.

[120] See European Commission, *Report on Competition in Professional Services*, COM (2004) 3 final, at para 5.1.5 (discussing the '*Wouters* exception').

doing so would be to cabin what may be an inevitable distortion of doctrine created by the pretence that professions are being treated 'the same'. The case against doing so is that other industries might successfully make similar claims of acting in the public interest and that courts are not the right forum for recognizing such claims in one industry but not another.

In the United States antitrust courts have often resisted suggestions for individualized approaches to antitrust, under a statute which has no such distinctions. The courts have often stated that such distinctions are more legislative than judicial, a task more for Congress than the courts.[121] Taking this approach is no assurance of the best policy result; legislation is not always wise.[122] But at least it means that the result will reflect a more democratic decision than any the courts can make.

VI. Conclusion

This essay has reviewed three recent cases decided by the European Court of Justice relating to the application of competition law to the professions. These cases show the effort made by that Court to assess the competitive effects of these regulations and to consider whether the regulations are immune from liability because they are actions of a Member State rather than the private parties. The essay has also reviewed a group of cases decided by the US Supreme Court which consider similar issues.

From the Carpenters' Company to the National Society of Professional Engineers, from the 14th century bread baking guilds in England discussed by Justice Stevens in *Hoover* to the bar associations that today seek to keep law firms from having accountants as partners, professional regulation has featured efforts to avoid competition *and* efforts to protect the public. The

121 See, *eg, Arizona v Maricopa County Med Soc* 457 US 332, 354–55 (1982) ('By articulating the rules of law with some clarity and by adhering to rules that are justified in their general application, however, we enhance the legislative prerogative to amend the law. The respondents' arguments against application of the *per se* rule in this case therefore are better directed to the Legislature. Congress may consider the exception that we are not free to read into the statute.')

122 For a recent example, see 15 USC 37b (giving antitrust exemption for participating in a 'graduate medical education residency matching program' and applying exemption to then-pending litigation). With regard to this provision's legislative history, see 150 Cong. Rec. S3968 (daily ed 8 April 2004). 'Unfortunately, the conferees were not as fair or reasoned in their judgment when they decided to include an antitrust exemption for graduate medical resident matching program in this conference report. This antitrust exemption was not reviewed or debated by either the Senate or the House, much less voted upon. The exemption will end many of the claims in an ongoing lawsuit brought by a number of medical students and residents that has already survived efforts to have it dismissed. . . . We should have had the opportunity to debate this issue and determine whether there was any merit to the exemption, rather than see the exemption mysteriously appear on an unrelated bill. It appears that this provision, enacted in this way, is nothing more than a giveaway to one particular special interest.' (remarks of Sen Kohl).

widespread enactment of competition laws has meant that the competitive effects of these professional efforts can be tested in many courts. The review of the cases in this essay, however, whether decided in Europe or in the United States, indicates that professional regulation is today given too much deference by the courts and that antitrust (or competition law) challenges have been made more difficult than they should be. Apparently courts yet need to be convinced that professional regulation can harm consumers in much the same way as competitive restraints can in other industries. The burden to make that case rests now with the enforcement agencies to develop the enforcement proceedings, and the factual support, to change judges' minds.

IV

Ian S Forrester, QC[1]

Where Law Meets Competition: Is *Wouters* Like a *Cassis de Dijon* or a Platypus?

I. Introduction: From Pharmacists to Lawyers

When I heard that this year's meeting would consider the application of the competition rules to the liberal professions, I volunteered to discuss the situation of the pharmacists, since I was involved in the currently-pending case of *Krister Hanner*.[2] That case does indeed involve the application of the competition rules to the operations of pharmacists in Sweden. However, having looked more closely, the general relevance of the case for a discussion of how the competition rules must be adapted to the challenge of highly-regulated professions seems doubtful. If the case is of general relevance, it is as an example of the justification of unnecessarily severe restrictions by the invocation of dubious and imprecise concerns of public policy and public health. I shall therefore begin this paper with a review of the *Hanner* case, and then pass on to some broader reflections about the more challenging judgments of *Wouters*[3] and *Arduino,*[4] after which I will attempt to propose a rational structure within which future controversies about competition and the professions may be addressed in a continent of great cultural, historical and regulatory diversity. In short, I contend that the *Wouters* case may be an exotic curiosity without lineal descendants, like the platypus.[5] Or that the *Wouters* case may turn out to be what is called in the computer industry an inflection point, a moment at which a fresh slope of history begins. European lawyers with a taste for history can see in *Cassis de Dijon*[6] the beginning of a new era in the

---

[1] Queen's Counsel, Visiting Professor, University of Glasgow; White & Case, Brussels. Warm thanks are expressed to my colleague Assimakis Komninos of the Athens Bar, and to Sandra Keegan of the Louisiana Bar, for contributions to this paper. The opinions expressed are wholly personal

[2] Case C–438/02 *Åklagaren v Krister Hanner*, currently pending.

[3] Case C–309/99 *JCJ Wouters v Algemene Raad van de Nederlandse Orde van Advocaten* [2002] ECR I–1577.

[4] Case C–35/99 *Arduino* [2002] ECR I–1529.

[5] A small, aquatic, egg-laying mammal, *Ornithorhynchus anatinus*, with webbed feet, a tail like a beaver's, a poisonous spur claw on one foot and a horny beak resembling the bill of a duck: in full, 'duckbill platypus'. It inhabits rivers and their banks in Eastern Australia and Tasmania. It has no evolutionary descendants.

[6] Case 120/79 *Rewe Zentrale v Bundesmonopolverwaltung für Branntwein (Cassis de Dijon)* [1979] ECR 649.

application of the rules on free movement of goods; in that case, the European Court concluded that if blackcurrant liqueur were freely sold in France without poisoning the population, German fears of inducing widespread alcoholism were an implausible basis for preventing its sale in that country, and that the existence of prohibition was not therefore *a priori* a justification for forbidding the sale of the product in Germany. When the *Cassis de Dijon* judgment was adopted, it was more easily understood than *Wouters*. Perhaps the Court will need a second *Wouters* to clear its mind.

II. The *Apoteket* and Mr Hanner

Mr Hanner forms part of the tradition of individual citizens whose taking of points of principle have contributed to the development of Community law, an heir to Ms. Watson, the *au pair* threatened with deportation from Italy; Mr Bulloch, the Scottish licensed grocer who had a disagreement with Johnnie Walker; Judge Donner (charges on imports of books); and Ms Defrenne, the Sabena stewardess who had to take earlier retirement than a man.

Mr Hanner ran a health goods shop in Stockholm in which he wished to sell a range of products contributing to well-being and a healthy lifestyle. Among those products are patches and chewing gum for those endeavouring to give up smoking. There is no doubt that these products are a significant advantage to some of the population of former smokers, and they are indeed freely sold in a variety of retail outlets in a number of countries, including Denmark, whose experience ought to be of some relevance to Sweden. However, they form part of the universe of products falling within the Swedish pharmaceutical monopoly.

35 years ago, Sweden decided to bring pharmaceuticals and pharmacies within the then fashionable policy of nationalisation. All pharmacists would in future work for a state-owned enterprise, the Apoteket, and only the Apoteket could lawfully supply a wide range of prescription and over-the-counter (OTC) medicines at retail level. Swedish legislation is exceptionally severe in the comprehensiveness of its prohibition of private enterprise in the entire sector. Mr Hanner argued that only three countries on earth, Sweden, North Korea and Cuba, make it a crime for someone not employed by the state to sell prescription and non-prescription or OTC medicines. Perhaps his truculent opposition explained his prosecution for breaking the law. The Swedish Apoteket system is certainly unique in Europe. A number of credible studies assert that the profession of pharmacist in Sweden is the most restricted in Europe.[7]

---

[7] In a survey prepared by IHS Wien for the Commission, pharmacists in Sweden scored a maximum 12 points indicating that they were the most regulated liberal profession surveyed. See http://europa.eu.int/comm/competition/publications/prof_services/executive_en.pdf.

To make things more difficult for independent retailers, the legislation adopts a wide definition of what constitutes a pharmaceutical product. The monopoly covers a wide range of products that can be sold freely (or over-the-counter in certain classes of shops) in other EU Member States, such as anti-smoking products, aspirin pills for headaches, nasal decongestants for colds, anti-travel-sickness pills, children's cough medicines, or treatments for the symptoms of minor ailments like diarrhoea, indigestion, flatulence, sore throats and itchy eyes. Most Apoteket stores open from 9am to 5pm on weekdays and close on Saturdays and Sundays. Sweden, a country whose population is geographically very dispersed, has considerably fewer pharmacies per head of population than other EU countries[8] (Apoteket has only 900 outlets for the whole country; there are a further 1,000 agents in rural areas who stock a few products and who have no qualified pharmacist), and sells fewer competing brands of common over-the-counter products. According to Mr Hanner, this means less choice, less inter-brand competition and, for non-prescription products, no price competition. It is also difficult for new products to enter the market, as the Apoteket, the sole gatekeeper, must agree to stock them in the shops which it owns. And, predictably, the profession of pharmacist is less esteemed in Sweden than in other Member States.

Nevertheless, the Swedish state decided in the 1970s that the best means of delivering medicines, whether potent or mild, is by a state-owned monopoly where all pharmacists effectively work for a state entity. How is that choice to be examined in Community law? Successive reports have doubted the appropriateness of the Apoteket system.[9] The Swedish government is no doubt speculating that the outcome of the Hanner case might afford an opportunity for reform and privatisation. Of course, even if Mr Hanner were to prevail, there is a range of commercial and regulatory models within which Sweden could arrange for the effective distribution of medicines, without the continued existence of a monopoly. The Advocate General's recent Opinion[10] takes the view that the national pharmacies system is incompatible with Articles 31 and 86(2) of the Treaty.

As noted above, Hanner, after closer inspection, is not a liberal professions case. It pertains more to a state monopoly range of cases. However, the

[8] Sweden has one pharmacy per 11,095 inhabitants while other EU countries have one pharmacy between 1200–3600 inhabitants. See Konkurrensverket, 'Konkurrens vid försäljning av läkemedel' (1999) 4 *Rapport* 70.

[9] The most recent government study in 1998 suggested that the business of *Apoteket* should be exposed to competition and that sales of non-prescription medicinal products in regular stores should be considered. See SOU, *Läkemedel i vård och handel: om en säker, flexibel och samordnad läkemedelsförörjning (betänkande)* (SOU, 1998): 28, Fritzes offentliga publikationer, Stockholm, pp 17, 254 *et seq.* Similar conclusions were reached by the Swedish Competition Authority in 1999, which proposed abolishing *Apoteket*'s monopoly on non-prescription medicinal products—see Konkurrensverket (1999), above n 8.

[10] Advocate General Léger's Opinion was rendered on 25 May 2004.

process of arguing the case has allowed me to reflect on the broader question of regulation of the various professions and its legality under European law.

III. Private Regulation and Public Regulation

Barriers to entry to liberal professions are evidently in the public interest to the extent that they involve mechanisms to ensure that sufficiently skilled persons write our wills, remove our appendices, and design our buildings, or involve procedures to enhance quality or accessibility for persons who might not otherwise be able to obtain a necessary service. I submit that it is impossible to contemplate unregulated practice of a liberal profession. There may be social or political or economic difficulties associated with some of these rules: having a structure which required candidates entering the profession to survive without compensation during two or three years (as used to be the tradition at the Scots Bar) yielded talented young bar members selected by a Darwinian process of survival. Alternative mechanisms have now been established to address the social implications of limiting access to the profession to those with the financial means of surviving. Likewise, controlling how members of the profession describe themselves to potential clients may enhance competition by making the marketplace better informed. On the other hand, it may have the effect of reducing competition by prohibiting, on the grounds of aesthetics and taste, professionals from making their merits known to potential clients. I make three propositions. First, it is almost unimaginable that such rules can be eliminated. Second, states have long experience in encouraging, directly or indirectly, respect for such rules. Third, there is much diversity in Europe in professional structure governance and working practices.

European Community law has regularly been confronted by such rules. The Court of Justice's approach in cases like *Meng*,[11] *Reiff*[12] and *Ohra*[13] has

[11] In Case C–2/91 *Criminal Proceedings against Wolf W Meng* [1993] ECR I–5751, the supervisory bodies of the German insurance industry adopted rules forbidding insurance brokers to provide rebates to customers. These discounts corresponded to the commission that the brokers receive from underwriters on issuance of a policy. Meng, who was prosecuted for infringing these rules, claimed they were incompatible with the EC Treaty. The ECJ rejected Meng's arguments.

[12] Case C–185/91 *Bundesanstalt für den Güterfernverkehr v Gebrüder Reiff GmbH & Co KG* [1993] ECR I–5801, involved the setting of road freight tariffs by boards composed of experts selected by the German Federal Ministry of Transport from a list of nominees recommended by industry members and trade associations. The relevant law provided that the members of the board would serve in an honorary capacity and would not be bound by their respective employers.

[13] Case C–245/91 *Criminal Proceedings against Ohra Schadeverzekeringen NV* [1993] ECR I–5851, concerned a prosecution for infringement of a Dutch law prohibiting insurance companies from granting rebates to those whom they insured. The Court held that since the Dutch rules neither imposed nor encouraged an illegal understanding between those in the insurance industry, they did not reinforce any anti-competitive understanding and had not been preceded by any private sector agreement or understanding.

been non-activist.[14] These three cases were something of a surprise during a period of judicial activism and pro-competitive reform. Where members of the guild met round the table to discuss the conditions by which their operations would be commercially governed, and where the conclusion of that discussion was made legally obligatory by state authority, the horizontal cooperation did not render the state rule which succeeded it unlawful. Thus, Member States could look at the result rather than at the route for achieving the result, even if this entailed some elimination of competition. A certain degree of price-fixing has also been accepted by the Commission, if the aim and result of such price-fixing is to ensure quality control.[15] Therefore, there were certainly grounds for believing that constraining horizontal competitive activity within a professional structure could be treated with a certain amount of tolerance.

IV. Regulation of Liberal Professions: The Problem of Lawyers

The liberal professions justify regulation of their activities by invoking quality control, promoting high standards of access, ensuring effective and transparent competition, and the like. The legal profession is particularly closely regulated on the grounds that such regulations, by contributing to the good administration of justice, uphold the rule of law. The lawyer is granted a number of important privileges, which include rights to represent parties in disputes, initiate litigation, prosecute claims against the state, public bodies and other third parties, defend those accused of crimes, hold client funds, prepare and, on occasion, execute legally-binding documents, administer estates, prepare and supervise the execution of testamentary documents, and buy and sell immovable property.[16] The counterpart of these privileges is that the legal profession is strictly regulated. Lawyers must respect, in letter and in spirit, detailed standards which are commonly codified in professional regulations. Breach of these rules may result in exclusion from the profession.

---

[14] See D Tzouganatos, 'State-Imposed Competition Restrictions and Community Legal Order' (1996) 2 *Dikaio Epicheiriseon kai Etairion* 344, (in Greek), pp. 351–52, who suggests that the Court's prudent line was influenced by the Commission's reluctance to support a more radical approach.

[15] See eg, Commission Decision 87/408/EEC of 13 July 1987 *Baltic International Freight Futures Exchange Ltd*, OJ L 222/24 [1987]. Reference is also made to the tribulations over German-language-book price-fixing (Cases COMP/C–2/34.657 *Sammelrevers*; COMP/C–2/37.906 *Internetbuchhandel*; COMP/C–2/38.019 *Proxis/KNO*). The Commission reached a settlement in these cases in 2002—see Press Release IP/02/461, 22 March 2002; European Commission (2002): *32nd Report on Competition Policy*, pp 203–4.

[16] See Advocate General's Opinion in Case C–309/99 *Wouters* [2002] ECR I–1577, para 174.

Although the legal profession is strictly regulated in every EU Member State, it operates differently in each. The rules on civil legal aid, the notarial function, criminal defence, patterns of partnership, administrative law, qualification for and admission to the profession, the confidential status of correspondence between bar members, even dress and deportment, all vary from jurisdiction to jurisdiction.

The *Wouters* case concerned the legality of bar prohibitions on partnerships between accountants and lawyers. Whether lawyers may enter into partnership with accountants, architects or other professions has been debated for at least 25 years in a number of countries. There has certainly been reticence in the EU of 15 about allowing lawyers' participation in such structures. The position of the Council of Bars and Law Societies of the European Union (CCBE) on multi-disciplinary partnerships (MDPs) has been cautious. In 1999 the CCBE stated:

> The legal profession is a crucial and indispensable element in the administration of justice and in the protection available to citizens under the law . . . . CCBE consequently advises that there are over-riding reasons for not permitting forms of integrated co-operation between lawyers and non-lawyers with relevantly different professional duties and correspondingly different rules of conduct. In those countries where such forms of co-operation are nevertheless permitted, lawyer independence, client confidentiality and disciplinary supervision of conflicts-of-interests rules must be safeguarded.[17]

The treatment of MDPs varies. In France, due in large part to the strong position of the 'Big Five' accountancy firms,[18] the position of MDPs was hotly debated. A decision of 14 March 1998 by the French National Bar Council officially allowed *avocats* to form associations and partnerships with members of other regulated professions, including accountants and auditors, subject to strict restrictions and obligations.[19] Under German federal law, integrated MDPs between lawyers, accountants, tax advisers and notaries are authorised.[20] An integrated MDP may take the form of shared offices, or a partnership, or a limited-liability partnership, or a limited-liability professional corporation. In Austria MDPs are not allowed.[21] In Spain, MDPs were recently allowed, subject to certain conditions.[22] In Sweden, the title of *Advokat* is protected, but the scope of professional activity reserved to an *Advokat* is limited. A person who has a law degree but has not qualified as an

---

[17] Position of CCBE on integrated forms of cooperation between lawyers and persons outside the legal profession, available at: http://www.ccbe.org/UK/uk.htm (emphasis added).

[18] PWC, Ernst & Young, Deloitte & Touche, KPMG and Arthur Andersen. Today it would be more correct to speak of the 'Big Four'.

[19] Art 16 of the Règlement Harmonisé des Barreaux de France.

[20] S 59(a) of the *Bundesrechtsantwaltsverordnung*, adopted on 1 August 1959, last amended on 9 March 2000.

[21] S 21(c) of the *Bundesrechtsantwaltordnung*.

[22] Art 29 of the Estatuto general de la Abogacía Española.

Advokat may find employment as a legal professional. Thus, the establishment of an MDP is theoretically feasible in Sweden. However, the Swedish Bar—*Sveriges advokatsamfund*—has to a certain extent been able to resist the participation of *Advokats* in MDPs. Thus, '[i]f the activities of an advocate are carried on in the form of a corporation or partnership, only advocates may be part owners or shareholders unless the board of the Bar Association grants a waiver.'[23] In Switzerland, MDPs between lawyers and non-lawyers are only allowed in the canton of Zurich. In other cantons, registered lawyers may not enter MDPs. It is very likely that the canton of Zurich will have to align its rules with the rules of other cantons.

It is common for the leaders of a liberal profession to be on the defensive side, and for those recommending change to accuse the regulators of either inflexibility or of protecting their own self-interest. From the foregoing anecdotal survey, I think it is fair to conclude that MDPs between lawyers and accountants are considered to present difficult issues, and that opinion on whether to permit such partnerships is divided. Some regulatory bodies of the legal profession have accepted them, and some have not. There is no consensus. There are solid deontological and practical reasons to be advanced against them. There are also respectable reasons for liberal toleration of economic innovation in their favour.

V. *Wouters*: The European Court of Justice Speaks

The *Wouters* judgment demonstrates the difficulty of addressing regulatory restrictions of competition.[24] Two Dutch lawyers, Messrs. Wouters and Savelbergh, who were members of the Amsterdam and Rotterdam Bars respectively, separately applied to the *Nederlandse Orde van Advocaten* (NOVA) for authorisation to enter into partnership with the Dutch practices of the then Price Waterhouse and Arthur Andersen. Both applications were refused by NOVA on the basis of its 1993 Regulation on Joint Professional Activity concerning partnerships with other professions. This regulation does not impose an absolute ban on partnerships with non-lawyers. It allows partnerships between lawyers and certain other professions such as notaries and patent agents, subject to the overriding principle that a NOVA member must not enter into any arrangement that might jeopardise the independence of

[23] Ch 8, S 4 of the *Rattegangsbalken* (the Swedish Code of Judicial Procedure). See also para 38 of the *Stadgar for Sveriges Advokatsamfund* (Regulations of the Law Society of Sweden).

[24] The *Wouters* judgment (see above n 3) was rendered on 19 February 2002, at the same time as the Enron events in the US leading to the demise of large public companies due to accounting controversies, and where accountants were believed to have behaved improperly. This point has not been missed by some of the commentators of that judgment. See eg, L Idot, '*Avocats et droit de la concurrence: la rencontre a eu lieu . . .*' (2002) 5 *Europe* 5.

members of the Bar. NOVA prohibits lawyers from entering MDPs with accountants on the grounds that this is necessary to protect the lawyer/client confidential relationship. After various appeals were rejected by NOVA, Wouters and Savelbergh initiated proceedings before the Dutch courts. Both cases ultimately came before the *Raad van State* (Dutch Council of State) which referred to the ECJ for a preliminary ruling under Article 234 of the EC Treaty a number of questions relating to the application of EC competition law to the professions.

The key question was whether the rules of NOVA were caught by Article 81 EC. As would be expected, NOVA argued that its rules were not caught by the basic prohibition of Article 81(1) EC. However, the Court found that when NOVA adopted a regulation such as the 1993 Regulation, it was neither fulfilling a social function, nor exercising the powers typical of those of a public authority; it was acting as a regulatory body. On the basis of these considerations, the Court found that NOVA must be regarded as an association of undertakings within the meaning of Article 81(1) EC.

The Court went on to examine whether the Regulation appeared to have an adverse effect on competition and, if so, whether, despite the effects restrictive of competition, it might fall outside the prohibition in Article 81(1) EC.[25] In considering possible adverse effects on competition, the ECJ found that the areas of expertise of NOVA members and of accountants might be complementary. Since legal services more and more frequently require financial advice, an MDP between members of NOVA and accountants would make it possible to offer a wider range of services. The Court said at paragraph 87: '. . . [C]lients would thus be able to turn to a single structure for a large part of the services necessary for the organisation, management and operation of their business (the 'one-stop-shop' advantage).'

The Court also felt (rather optimistically, perhaps) that the advent of large partnerships might lead to a fall in legal fees: 'Nor, finally, is it inconceivable that the economies of scale resulting from such multi-disciplinary partnerships might have positive effects on the cost of services.'

Thus, the Court held that the Dutch ban on MDPs was liable to limit production and technical development within the meaning of Article 81(1)(b) EC.

The ECJ then considered the possible pro-competitive effects of the ban. The Luxembourg government, intervening, argued that the ban on MDPs might be pro-competitive, as there was a risk that MDPs might bring the market for legal services into the highly structured arena of the accountancy profession and thus reduce the number of law firms. However, the Court held that conflict of interest rules applicable to lawyers presented a structural limit and would prevent the extensive concentration of law firms. This would obvi-

[25] The MDP regulation was notified by the Dutch Bar to the Commission under Art 81(3) EC after the disciplinary proceedings against Messrs Wouters and Savelbergh had been commenced.

ously reduce the number of opportunities for MDPs with highly concentrated professions such as accountancy. The ECJ also held that competition in legal services could be guaranteed by a less restrictive measure than a complete ban on accountant/lawyer MDPs. In light of all these factors, the ECJ found that the 1993 Regulation was liable to have an adverse effect on competition. It also held that NOVA's ban on MDPs was likely to affect trade between EC Member States, because it applied to foreign lawyers and accountancy firms seeking to form partnerships with practitioners in several EC Member States. The ECJ closely examined, and rejected, the arguments advanced by NOVA in support of the proposition that the rules were not caught by the prohibition of Article 81(1) EC, either because of the way in which the rules were adopted or because of their potential economic impact on consumers. The anxious reader of the judgment would by now have concluded that NOVA was going to lose. However, this was not the end of the matter. The Court then considered whether, notwithstanding the ban's impact upon competition, Article 81 did in fact apply to NOVA's rules on MDPs.

The Court held that for the purposes of application of Article 81(1), account had to be taken of the overall aims of NOVA's rules, and whether the consequential restrictive effects of competition were inherent in the pursuit of those objectives. The Court held at paragraph 97:

> . . . [n]ot every agreement between undertakings or any decision of an association of undertakings which resists the freedom of action of the parties . . . necessarily falls within the prohibition laid down in Article [81(1)] of the Treaty. For the purposes of application of that provision to a particular case, account must first be taken of the overall context in which the decision of the association of undertakings was taken or produces its effects. More particularly, account must be taken of its objectives, which are here connected with the need to make rules relating to organization, qualifications, professional ethics, supervision and liability, in order to ensure that the ultimate consumers of legal services and the sound administration of justice are provided with the necessary guarantees in relation to integrity and experience.

NOVA argued that its rules were necessary to promote the independent giving of legal advice and avoid conflicts of interest. The ECJ echoed its observation in *Klopp*[26] and stated that in the absence of specific Community rules in the field, each Member State is in principle free to regulate the exercise of the legal profession in its territory. For that reason, the rules applicable to that profession may differ greatly from one Member State to another. Since *Klopp*, a number of judgments of the ECJ have upheld the

---

[26] Case 107/83 *Ordre des avocats au Barreau de Paris v Onno Klopp* [1984] ECR 2971, para 17. This judgment dealt with a German lawyer, who had been refused access to the Paris Bar on the sole ground that he kept an office in another Member State. The Court held that although Member States may regulate the exercise of the legal profession in their own territory, they could not require a lawyer to have only one place of establishment within the then EEC.

right of a Member State to establish rules governing the exercise of a professional activity in its territory.[27]

According to the ECJ, even if some Member States allowed MDPs between lawyers and accountants, the Dutch Bar was nevertheless entitled to consider that the objectives pursued by the 1993 Regulation could not be attained by less restrictive means than a ban on MDPs. The fact that one Member State imposes stricter rules than another Member State does not mean that the former's rules are disproportionate and, thus, incompatible with EC law. The ECJ found it acceptable for some Member States to authorise MDPs between lawyers and accountants, while others did not.

The ECJ did not say that legislating to permit MDPs would be unlawful. It did say that the Dutch rule prohibiting MDPs was not unlawful.

The Court then noted that the Dutch rules on professional conduct require the members of NOVA to remain independent from public authorities, other operators and third parties, by whom they must never be influenced. By contrast, the profession of accountant is not subject in the Netherlands to comparable requirements of professional conduct. Conflicts of interest might often arise within MDPs between lawyers and accountants: for example, where an MDP was responsible for producing the financial accounts of a company in respect of whose sale its legal services were also required.[28]

The Court agreed that NOVA was entitled to consider that its members might no longer be in a position to represent their clients independently and in the observance of strict professional secrecy, if they were to belong to an organisation which was also responsible for producing an account of the financial results of the transactions in respect of which their services were called upon, and for certifying those accounts.

The ECJ attributed notable weight to the freedom of the bar to regulate its own affairs, and, in so doing, to restrict the freedom of its members to engage in certain activities. As a result of this analysis, and despite the fact that the rule in the 1993 Regulation restricted competition, the Court found that it was not caught by the prohibition of Article 81(1) EC. The test used by the Court was whether NOVA had grounds for concluding that the needs of the profession called for a ban.

In sum, the ECJ held that the anti-competitive restrictions resulting from the 1993 Regulation did not go beyond what was necessary to ensure the

---

[27] In Case C–96/85 *Commission v France* [1986] ECR 1475, the Court stated that nationals of a Member State who pursue their occupation in another Member State are obliged to comply with the rules that govern the pursuit of the occupation in question in that Member State. In Case C–55/94 *Gebhard v Consiglio dell'Ordine degli Avvocati e Procuratori di Milano* [1995] ECR I–4165, the Court held that the taking-up and pursuit of certain self-employed activities may be conditional on complying with certain provisions laid down by law, regulation or administrative action justified by the general good, such as rules relating to organisation, qualifications, professional ethics, supervision and liability.

[28] See *Wouters*, above n 3, paras 102–3.

proper practice of the legal profession. Accordingly, EC competition rules did not prohibit NOVA from taking a carefully considered measure to ban MDPs between lawyers and accountants in the Netherlands.

Advocate General Léger took a different line but reached the same destination. The main difference between the two routes lies in the evaluation of Article 81(1) EC. Mr Léger rejected NOVA's argument that because its rules could be justified as necessary to ensure the maintenance of professional standards, the restrictions resulting from such rules fell outside Article 81(1) EC. NOVA had invited the Court to adopt a form of 'rule of reason'[29] enabling all professional rules which are intended to ensure observance of the ethical rules particular to the legal profession to evade the prohibition laid down by Article 81(1) EC. The Advocate General stated:

> In Community competition law, the 'rule of reason' may carry several meanings. . . . [T]he Court has made limited application of the 'rule of reason' in some judgments. . . . [I]t follows from those judgments that, irrespective of any terminological dispute, the 'rule of reason' in Community competition law is strictly confined to a purely competitive balance-sheet of the effects of the agreement. Where, taken as a whole, the agreement is capable of encouraging competition on the market, the clauses essential to its performance may escape the prohibition laid down in Article [81(1)] of the Treaty. The only legitimate goal, which may be pursued in accordance with that provision, is therefore exclusively competitive in nature. [T]he argument put forward by the interveners and the Commission goes far beyond the scope of the competition balance-sheet allowed by the Court's case-law.[30]

This analysis seems to view competition as a phenomenon separate from the professional activity in question. The Advocate General held that only rules necessary to promote competition itself may be taken into account for determining whether Article 81 applies. Public interest concerns not rooted in competition law doctrine do not remove an activity from the scope of Article 81(1) EC. He, thus, concluded that NOVA's rules prohibiting MDPs were caught by Article 81(1) EC. The Advocate General's line of reasoning to a certain extent echoed the recent *Métropole Télévision* case, where the Court of First

---

[29] Both the CFI and the ECJ have flirted with more relaxed approaches to a 'rule of reason', where the pro-competitive benefits of an arrangement would be balanced against its restrictions when considering the applicability of Art 81(1) EC, rather than when considering its eligibility for an exemption under Art 81(3) EC. The ECJ in *Wouters* seems to go beyond a 'rule of reason' approach by stating that certain rules adopted in pursuit of public interest considerations are valid even if they restrict competitive freedom.

[30] Advocate General's Opinion, paras 102–5. According to the Advocate General, the Commission argued for a four-stage test. First, establish whether the relevant professional rule restricts competition; second, examine the objective of the legal rule; third, review whether the professional rule is necessary if the objective it pursues is to be obtained; and fourth, the professional rule should be applied objectively and without discrimination.

Instance held that 'the existence of a rule of reason in Community competition law is doubtful.'[31]

However, while the Court found that the key to answering the Dutch Council of State's questions lay in Article 81(1) EC itself, the Advocate General found the key to answering them in Article 86 EC. Having held that the prohibition on MDPs did fall within Article 81(1) EC, he went on to consider the impact of the limited derogation from the competition rules under Article 86(2) EC.[32] since the Advocate General had held that NOVA was not an undertaking for the purposes of Article 82 EC, he thought that Article 86(2) EC did not apply to it. Nevertheless, Dutch lawyers might perhaps collectively and individually satisfy the elements of Article 86(2) EC. Clearly, those lawyers were independent undertakings. Given the essential role of legal advisers in a state governed by the rule of law, they performed services of general economic interest exhibiting special characteristics. Furthermore, Dutch law gave lawyers the right of audience before all national courts. Accordingly, they were entrusted with particular tasks by the Dutch authorities.

Independence, respect for professional secrecy and the need to avoid conflicts of interest are indispensable for the discharge of those public service tasks, which form the very core of the legal profession. The Advocate General argued that MDPs would pose a threat to the independence of lawyers. Since accountants were required by law to impart to the competent authorities information regarding their client's activities, if an accountant's duty bound a lawyer, this would hinder the lawyer's observance of the rules of professional secrecy.

There is indeed a significant difference between the role of the lawyer and the accountant when it comes to giving tax advice. The lawyer may say 'This is rather bold, and might be challenged, but if challenged you would argue as follows . . .'. The accountant preparer of the tax declaration who will certify the propriety of the accounts may feel compelled to insist that the client taxpayer adopt a cautious approach failing which the accountant will not represent the client. It is not difficult to imagine circumstances where full partnerships between lawyers and architects or lawyers and accountants might contribute to the client's problems, although in other cases the multidisciplinary services available might be convenient. Accordingly, said the

---

[31] Case T–112/99 *Métropole Télévision (M6) v Commission* [2001] ECR II–2459. The difference in approach between the CFI in *Métropole* and that of the ECJ in *Wouters* has been the subject of review in the legal press. In the former case the CFI limited its analysis to competition grounds under Art 81(3) EC, while in the latter the ECJ balanced the restrictive effect on competition against the integrity of the legal profession under Art 81(1) EC. See eg, V Korah, 'Rule of Reason: Apparent Inconsistency in the Case Law Under Article 81' (2002) 1 *Competition Law Insight* 24; P Manzini, 'The European Rule of Reason—Crossing the Sea of Doubt' (2002) 23 *European Competition L Rev* 392.

[32] Neither the Advocate General nor the ECJ considered whether NOVA's ban on MDPs might be eligible for an exemption under Art 81(3) EC, since the Dutch Council of State did not raise this matter and such exemptions at the time could be issued only by the Commission.

Advocate General, the restriction on competition was necessary to uphold the very essence of the legal profession's functions. The ban on MDPs did not prevent lawyers or accountants from offering their services separately to clients in the Netherlands or, indeed, elsewhere.

Finally, the Advocate General considered what was necessary to allow NOVA members to carry out their public service tasks. Firstly, NOVA only banned the closest forms of partnership between accountants and lawyers. The Advocate General dismissed the argument by supporters of MDPs that 'Chinese walls' (preventing the transfer of information between accountants and lawyers), contractual undertakings and other mechanisms were sufficient to comply with the rules of professional conduct of the legal profession. He felt that these suggested solutions did not provide adequate safeguards. He seems to have considered that the ban was not disproportionate, although he suggested that the Dutch courts should decide the relevant factual matters.

Accordingly, provided that the ban on MDPs was reasonably necessary in order to safeguard the integrity of the legal profession, the Advocate General held that it would benefit from the derogation from the application of the competition rules available in Article 86(2) EC to public service entities.

VI. *Wouters* and *Arduino* Read Together

The remarkable readiness of the ECJ to limit the scope of application to the legal profession of the EC competition rules was further demonstrated in the judgment in *Arduino*, rendered on the same day as *Wouters*. *Arduino* concerned the legality of a scale setting the minimum and maximum fees chargeable by lawyers for their services in Italy. The Italian Ministry of Justice adopted this fee scale on the basis of a draft prepared by the governing body of the Italian bar, the *Consiglio Nazionale Forense* (CNF). Before approving a fee-scale, the Ministry must, under a statutory procedure, consult the Italian Council of State and the Inter-ministerial Committee on Prices. The ECJ was asked by a lower Italian court to rule on whether Articles 10 and 81 EC precluded Member States from adopting, in accordance with statutory procedures, a measure approving a tariff fixing minimum and maximum fees for members of the legal profession, this question having arisen between Mr Arduino and a lawyer in Pinerolo, during the legal proceedings following a car accident there, one element thereof being the fixing of legal costs.

In its judgment, the ECJ held that although EC competition rules focus mainly on the conduct of undertakings, Article 81 (read in conjunction with Article 10) EC also prohibits EC Member States from adopting rules which would render the application of EC competition law ineffective. Articles 10 and 81 EC are infringed:

> [. . .] where a Member State requires or favours the adoption of agreements, decisions or concerted practices contrary to Article 81 or reinforces their effects, or where it divests its own rules of the character of legislation by delegating to private economic operators responsibility for taking decisions affecting the economic sphere.[33]

The Court continued: 'In that regard, the fact that a Member State requires a professional organisation to produce a draft tariff for services does not automatically divest the tariff finally adopted of the character of legislation.'[34]

The ECJ first examined whether the Italian state had divested its own rules of the character of legislation when it obliged the CNF to present a draft tariff for fees payable to members of the Italian bar. The Court noted that the CNF was not required to take public interest criteria into account when preparing this draft. Moreover, the draft required Ministerial approval before it could enter into force. Finally, the Italian courts could depart from the maximum and minimum fees fixed by the Italian legislation.

The ECJ therefore held that the Italian state could not be said to have delegated to private economic operators responsibility for decisions affecting the economic sphere, which would have meant that the measures were not legislation. Moreover, for the reasons outlined in the preceding paragraph, the Italian state had not favoured the adoption of anti-competitive arrangements, nor reinforced their effects. Thus, according to the Court, Italy was entitled to adopt a fee scale when this was done pursuant to a procedure laid down in domestic legislation.

Advocate General Léger's Opinion in *Arduino* also deserves study. As in *Wouters*, he chose a different path from that ultimately taken by the Court.[35] The Advocate General recommended a two-stage test. It should first be considered whether the state measure appreciably affects competition within the meaning of Article 81 EC. If so, this does not necessarily mean that the state measure is in breach of Articles 10 and 81 EC: a Member State may have legitimate reasons for reinforcing the effects of the agreement in question. In that case the Member State may seek to justify the measure on the basis of Article 10 EC, provided that three separate elements are satisfied. These are: that the public authorities exercise effective control over the impugned conduct; that the State measure pursues a legitimate aim; and that the state measure is proportionate to the aim pursued.

Furthermore, Articles 10 and 81 EC do not apply to rules where the public authorities reserve to themselves the power to fix the essential terms of an economic decision. Advocate General Léger concluded that the Italian authorities maintained sufficient control over the fee scale. Moreover, the Italian legislation was primarily intended to guarantee a high level of quality

[33] See *Arduino*, above n 3, para 35.
[34] See above, para 36.
[35] Advocate General's Opinion, para 97.

in respect of the services supplied by members of the profession; this undoubtedly constituted a legitimate objective in the public interest.

Thus the Advocate General held in *Arduino* that a state measure which affects competition may nonetheless be in conformity with the state's duty under the EC Treaty not to hinder competition; and insofar as it is a binding state measure, the behaviour of those who obey it is not prohibited as an anti-competitive practice.

Like *Wouters*, *Arduino* signaled the possibility of limiting the application of the EC competition rules when allegedly anti-competitive conduct pursues, or is linked to, the regulation of the legal profession.

VII. The Implications of *Wouters* as a Competition Law Case: First in a Dynasty or an Evolutionary End of the Road?

Wouters may represent an important judicial milestone for the competition lawyer. For at least 20 years, lawyers have been encouraging the Commission to adopt a less expansive approach to the application of the competition rules. It has been suggested that the Commission should re-calibrate the reach of Article 81(1) EC and as a result rely less on Article 81(3) EC; this approach would dispose of more arrangements on the grounds that they presented no problem under Article 81(1) EC than on the grounds that they were eligible for an exemption under Article 81(3) EC. There have been many academic articles on the subject.[36] There have also been some interesting judgments from the two European courts in such cases as *European Night Services*,[37] but nothing quite so striking as *Wouters*. This judgment may portend even more radical changes for the interpretation and application of Article 81 EC. In *Wouters*, the ECJ held that not every agreement or decision which restricts the freedom of action of one or more undertakings necessarily falls within the prohibition laid down in Article 81(1) EC. To decide whether the Article 81(1) EC prohibition applies, the Commission, national courts, and national

---

[36] There are dozens, going back at least 20 years. See I Forrester and C Norall, 'The Laicization of Community Law: Self-Help and the Rule of Reason: How Competition Law Is and Could be Applied' (1984) 21 *Common Market L Rev* 11; I Forrester, 'Competition Structures for the 21st Century' in B Hawk, (ed), *International Antitrust Law and Policy 1994*, *Annual Proceedings of the Fordham Corporate Law Institute* (Juris Publ, New York, NY, 1995); I Forrester, 'The Reform of the Implementation of Arts 81 and 82 Following Publication of the Draft Regulation' (2001) 28 *Legal Issues of Economic Integration* 173. See also S Kon, 'Article 85, Paragraph 3: A Case for Application by National Courts' (1982) 19 *Common Market L Rev* 541; J Venit, 'Brave New World: The Modernization and Decentralization of Enforcement under Articles 81 and 82 of the EC Treaty' (2003) 40 *Common Market L Rev* 545.

[37] Joined Cases T–374/94, T–375/94, T–384/94 and T–388/94 *European Night Services Ltd v Commission* [1998] ECR II–3141.

competition authorities should consider whether public interest issues are at stake. Provided the effect on competition results from the pursuit of those objectives, then despite the restriction of certain parties' freedom of action, the Article 81 EC prohibition may not apply.

To put it another way, the competition rules of the Treaty are not governed exclusively by competition law concerns. Other legitimate considerations may also have to be respected. If the measures concerned are necessary for a worthwhile purpose (such as safeguarding the integrity of the legal profession), they may be objectively justified and hence fall outside the EC competition rules.[38]

VIII. *Wouters* as the Beginning

I now offer the proposition that *Wouters* may be the first step in a new experimental approach to the application of the competition rules. I remind us that the scope and meaning of Articles 30 to 36 of the EEC Treaty (now Articles 28 to 30 EC) engendered immense difficulty and controversy from the late 1960s.[39] It was originally believed that the prohibition on obstacles to imports and exports of goods between Member States was directed at intentionally discriminatory ones, not 'indistinctly applicable' measures which happened coincidentally to hinder imports.[40] However, in *Dassonville*, the Court adopted a bold and simple test:

---

[38] The ECJ's approach in *Wouters* may be compared to the approach of the US Supreme Court in *Californian Dental Association (CDA) v Federal Trade Commission (FTC)*, 119 S Ct 1604 (1999) (CDA). In this case, the FTC maintained that the CDA's advertising ban on process and quality was anti-competitive. The court held, however, that such a ban could be lawful as it prevented bogus claims regarding quality of service to patients that distorted the market. Thus, the highest courts in both sides of the Atlantic have upheld that restrictive regulation by professional bodies may be pro-competitive.

[39] On the parallelism between the Treaty rules on competition and on free movement there is abundant literature. See eg, J Stuyck, 'Libre circulation et concurrence: les deux piliers du marché commun' in M Dony and A de Walsche, (eds), *Mélanges en hommage à Michel Waelbroeck*, vol II, (Bruylant, Brussels, 1999) 1477 *et seq*; K Mortelmans, 'Towards Convergence in the Application of the Rules on Free Movement and on Competition?' (2001) 38 *Common Market L Rev* 613; J Baquero Cruz, *Between Competition and Free Movement: The Economic Constitutional Law of the European Community* (Oxford, Hart Publishing, 2002) 153.

[40] Commission Directive 70/50/EEC of 22 December 1969 based on the provisions of Article 33(7), on the abolition of measures which have an effect equivalent to quantitative restrictions on imports and are not covered by other provisions adopted in pursuance of the EEC Treaty, OJ L 13/29 [1970]; for an example of a discriminatory measure, see the *French blanket* controversy, where in 1968 France forbade by Ministerial Decree the sale of blankets having dimensions other than those prescribed by the state, which were indeed those used by the French industry. See P Oliver, *Free Movement of Goods in the European Community*, 3rd edn, (London, Sweet & Maxwell, 1996) 89.

> 5. All trading rules enacted by Member States which are capable of hindering, directly or indirectly, actually or potentially, intra-community trade are to be considered as measures having an effect equivalent to quantitative restrictions.[41]

This, however, did not solve all the questions. Where the law was not harmonised as between Member States, what should be done where the product was lawfully (and traditionally) made in France, then unlawfully sold in Germany? It could rarely be shown conclusively that Member State legislation was motivated by bad-faith protectionism, although it could often be observed that a Member State regulation corresponded to the industrial and dietary traditions of that state. The European Court was confronted with a string of arguments concerning the composition of foodstuffs, including the ingredients of blood sausages, the level of cocoa butter in chocolate and many other delicacies. Then came the case about blackcurrant liqueur made near Dijon and commonly used as an ingredient of Kir, the preferred tipple of a celebrated cleric who enjoyed mixing crème de cassis with white *Bourgogne aligoté* wine. German law allowed the sale of weaker alcohols (like wine at 12°) or stronger alcohols (like schnapps at 40°), but not alcohols of intermediate (20°) strength. After years of delicately balancing Member State sensitivities, the European Court brusquely declined to pursue that path any longer. It stated:

> Obstacles to movement within the Community resulting from disparities between the national laws relating to the marketing of . . . products . . . must be accepted in so far as those provisions may be recognized as being necessary in order to satisfy mandatory requirements relating in particular to the effectiveness of fiscal supervision, the protection of public health, the fairness of commercial transactions and the defence of the consumer.[42]

It went on to say: 'There is therefore no valid reason why, provided that they have been lawfully produced and marketed in one of the Member States, alcoholic beverages should not be introduced into any other Member State . . .'.[43]

This meant that even if a Member State in good faith and without discriminatory intent has prohibited the domestic production and sale of a product, it loses the capacity to forbid the sale of the imported product. Thus once the product has been lawfully put on sale in one Member State, it benefits from free movement principles even in a country where it could not lawfully have been marketed. In other words, the basic rule should be full faith and credit. If the product was successfully and uncontroversially sold in one Member State, then *a priori* it should be capable of being sold in every Member State. Restrictions by Member States upon the free movement of goods could be justified by certain 'mandatory requirements' pertaining to the public

---

[41] Case 8/74 *Procureur du Roi v Dassonville* [1974] ECR 837, 852.

[42] *Cassis de Dijon*, above n 6, para 8.

[43] *Ibid*, para 14.

interest, such as the protection of consumers or of the environment, and if the principles of non-discrimination and proportionality apply. In other words, the Court was prepared to adopt a trust-based approach with regard to Member State regulatory measures, tempered by commonsense.

For most of the 1970s and 1980s the Court, at a time of political paralysis, proved activist in using Article 28 EC as a federalising enzyme,[44] in order to attain the integration of the national markets into a common market. This process was not without controversies. At the same time the Court was promoting a principle of full faith and credit in the European legal order. The Court's *credo* was that if no harm was incurred by the marketing of a product in one Member State, no harm should be expected in another Member State whose measures restricted free movement. To this principle the Court recognised exceptions, justified by the social, moral and cultural diversity between the Member States and by their reasonable concerns based thereupon. National measures relating Sunday trading[45] or to the organization of a national monopoly on the retail of alcoholic beverages[46] were mostly considered under this category.

As to services and the professions, Articles 45, 46 and 55 permit exceptions from the freedom to provide services if the activity in question relates to the exercise of official authority or to public policy, public security and public health. There have been judicially-created exceptions that are justified on the basis of imperative requirements of public interest. Certain national measures restrictive of the free movement of services have been considered lawful, if they are not directly or indirectly discriminatory and if they comply with the principle of proportionality.[47] Thus, rules inspired by the moral and social values dominant in a particular Member State have been found lawful

---

[44] See eg, D Kommers and M Waelbroeck, 'Legal Integration and the Free Movement of Goods: The American and European Experience' in M Cappelletti, M Seccombe and J Weiler, (eds), *Integration Through Law*, vol I: *Methods, Tools and Institutions*, Book 2: *Forces and Potential for a European Identity*, (Walter de Gruyter, Berlin, 1986) 197 *et seq*.

[45] Eg, Cases C–145/88 *Torfaen Borough Council v B and Q plc* [1989] ECR 3581; C–169/91 *Council of the City of Stoke on Trent and Norwich City Council v B and Q plc* [1992] ECR I–6635. (There was a judicial U-turn because the original test was too sophisticated.)

[46] Case C–189/95 *Criminal Proceedings against Harry Franzén* [1997] ECR I–5909, commented by P-J Slot in (1998) 35 *Common Market L Rev* 1183, an interesting contrast with the *Hanner* case. The Swedish alcohol monopoly was deliberately designed to make the sale of alcohol rather difficult by limiting severely the numbers of outlets and excluding private retail initiatives. It survived judicial scrutiny, though some practices had to be modified. The pharmaceutical monopoly also limits the consumption of medicines, especially over-the-counter medicines available without a doctor's prescription, by opening its shops for only a limited number of hours on weekdays. Its defenders assert that the *Apoteket* is doing its best with limited resources. Its critics say that a competitive environment would stimulate demand and improve the range and availability of services available, and that it is very aware of its public service obligations (similar controversies have occurred about post offices).

[47] See eg, S O'Leary and JM Fernández-Martín, 'Judicially-Created Exceptions to the Free Provision of Services' in M Andenas and W-H Roth, (eds), *Services and Free Movement in EU Law*, (Oxford, OUP, 2002) 163 *et seq*.

under Community law. This is the case for rules on gambling services and products.[48]

In all these cases the Court of Justice seems to apply a sort of 'majoritarian rule', even though this is never expressly stated in the text of its judgments: is the national measure compatible with common sense? Is it to be found in various forms in other Member States? If the answer to both questions is affirmative and the rule in question does not look too strange, the Court may well consider it in conformity with Community law.

Let us consider how this approach would fit with what was said by the Court in *Wouters*. *Wouters* clearly had to deal with a highly regulated profession. There may have been accusations that the Bars were protecting their members' interests, but they were not echoed in either the judgment or the Opinion. The Court seemed ready to accept the good faith of the regulators in promoting the public interest in the protection of clients of a member of the Bar providing legal assistance. Account was taken of the regulator's good faith and well-intentioned-ness, as well as the reasonableness of the restriction of competition. This the Court states expressly in paragraph 110 of its judgment: '[the Bar of the Netherlands] could reasonably have considered that [the] regulation . . . despite the effects restrictive of competition that are inherent in it, is necessary for the proper practice of the legal profession, as organised in the Member State concerned.' (emphasis added)

It remains to be seen whether this judgment represents a *sui generis* importation of free movement methodology into the field of competition law or the route forward for the future. *Wouters* may be a 'one-off', a special exception for the unique status of lawyers and the unique problems of regulating them, a legal platypus, fascinating but unique. Alternatively, it may be the beginning of a series of further legal developments governing the status of arrangements which fall between government regulation and private sector organisation.

We might see industries which have traditionally been influenced by guild traditions trying to build exceptions for private sector self-regulation, when the regulators can plausibly claim to be acting in good faith. It will be difficult for the ECJ not to make further concessions if it adheres to the logic of *Wouters* and *Arduino*. The potential category of exceptions would be very large, especially as the setting of fee tariffs was approved in *Arduino*. If a professional association of lawyers may suggest minimum charges, and the state may accept them, without seriously infringing the interests of consumers (who may well be unable to differentiate between the quality of services provided by different members of the profession), why not architects, quantity surveyors and others?

[48] Cases C–275/92 *HM Customs and Excise v Gerhard and Jörg Schindler* [1994] ECR I–1039 (lottery tickets); C–124/97 *Markku Juhani Läärä v Khlakunnansyyttäjä (Jyväskylä) and Finland* [1999] ECR I–6067 (gaming equipment).

I am astonished by the contrast with long-standing competition law orthodoxy. These two cases establish new principles that contradict long-believed dogmas. In the old *Dutch cement cartel* case of 1972,[49] the Applicant argued that the price-fixing at issue was beneficial for the public interest. The Court rejected this argument firmly. Maybe we will see more such exotic arguments. Fashions change, as do dogmas.

IX. A Test for the Future

In the following paragraphs I propose some criteria that might be considered in order for regulatory measures applicable to the liberal professions to be accepted as lawful under EC competition law.

1. Reasonableness

The Court of Justice in *Wouters* placed emphasis on the reasonableness of the restriction of competition. While it would not be appropriate to introduce a fully-fledged 'rule of reason' approach, the measure involved should appear to be a genuine attempt to deal with certain regulatory risks in a reasonable manner.

2. Non-Discrimination and Nationality

I venture to assert that nationality could no longer be seriously advanced as a ground for rejecting an otherwise qualified candidate for the profession. *Van Binsbergen*[50] was one case about obstacles to foreign qualified lawyers: the perhaps doubtful patriotism of the foreign lawyer was not accepted as a ground to exclude a candidate for bar membership in the US Supreme Court case of *In re Griffiths*.[51] In my own case, a ground offered by the bar authorities for declining to admit to the New York Bar foreign citizens not in possession of permanent resident status was the level of unemployment of US citizens who were members of the New York Bar: that decision was over-

[49] Case 8/72 *Vereeniging van Cementhandelaren v Commission* [1972] ECR 977.
[50] Case 33/74 *Johannes Henricus Maria van Binsbergen v Bestuur van de Bedrijfsvereniging voor de Metaalnijverheid* [1974] ECR 1279.
[51] *In re Griffiths*, 413 US 717 (1973).

turned after an appeal based upon the Fourteenth Amendment to the Constitution which extends the equal protection of the laws to citizens and non-citizens alike. It will be interesting to see whether access to the notarial profession (a public function in, for example, Belgium) could be made to depend on nationality.

3. The Majoritarian Rule, or, the Absence of Folly

While some degree of deference to local eccentricities and moral/social values is called for, it will certainly be significant if the rationale behind the restrictive measure is shared in some other Member States,[52] thus not representing a national 'folly'.[53] This would entail some comparative effort among the EU Member States with reference to objectives and outcomes.

4. Proportionality

Any restriction imposed upon competition with a view to regulating in a reasonable way a profession must be compatible with the principle of proportionality.[54] Therefore, an equilibrium between aim and effect should be attained, possibly taking into account experiences in other EU Member States too (this would be a parallel enquiry to the prior 'majoritarian' question). The proportionality test is inherent not only to the free movement rules

[52] See in this direction M Poiares Maduro, 'Striking the Elusive Balance Between Economic Freedom and Social Rights In the EU' in P Alston, (ed), *The EU and Human Rights* (Oxford, OUP, 1999) 451; S Weatherill, 'Recent Case Law Concerning the Free Movement of Goods: Mapping the Frontiers of Market Deregulation' (1999) 36 *Common Market L Rev* 51, 69, with reference to the free movement case law.

[53] This does not mean to exclude, however, a genuine distinctiveness within particular Member States, especially if there are strong moral or social values. Compare the *Irish abortion* case, where the underlying question was the severe Irish constitutional rule against abortions: Case C–159/90 *The Society for the Protection of Unborn Children Ireland Ltd v Stephen Grogan* [1991] ECR I–4685; and *Van Duyn* (Case 41/74 *Yvonne van Duyn v Home Office* [1974] ECR 1337), where the Court upheld the United Kingdom's refusal to grant Mrs van Duyn leave to enter the UK to take up employment as a secretary with the 'Church of Scientology'. The Court held that a Member State in imposing restrictions justified on grounds of public policy, was entitled to take into account the fact that the individual concerned is associated, with some body or organisation, whose activities it considers socially harmful. On the other hand, in the case of 'barmaids' suspected of prostitution, the ECJ was more tolerant. It said that public order could not be invoked to justify deporting French ladies sitting in windows in the red-light district of Liège unless Belgian ladies were likewise subject to repressive or other measures intended to combat the same conduct (Joined Cases 15 and 116/81 *Adoui v Belgium and City of Liège; Cornuaille v Belgium ('Belgian Barmaids')* [1982] ECR 1665).

[54] *Wouters*, para 109.

but also to the EC competition rules, both under Article 81(1) EC[55] and under Article 81(3) EC.

5. Efficiency

The market for services is not as homogeneous as that for goods. The ways in which the liberal professions are regulated vary greatly. Just taking lawyers, we can observe that in the UK and in Ireland the profession is split between general practitioners who may operate in partnerships, and specialised pleaders who are individual sole practitioners. In several countries a small number of pleaders enjoy rights of audience in the cour de cassation or equivalent. In the 1970s, Commission officials would sometimes describe a rich stew of divergent regimes and then say 'il faut le régulariser'. Europe is not as homogeneous in regulatory or legal terms as the United States. This diversity should be occasion not for embarrassment but rather for pride. Nevertheless, there is a non-chauvinist reason for resisting the proposition that greater efforts to achieve regulatory approximation are necessary: the burden of pursuing consistency is quite likely to exceed the advantages of consistency. The challenge for competition law enforcers will be to distinguish the desirable from the undesirable. One thoroughly undesirable outcome would be if there were to be an inevitable honouring of the deplorable, a local foolishness which does no good to anyone except the protected incumbents. I think of the Port of Genoa cases.[56] The question should be whether removing a particular measure which evidently affects competition will yield a better or worse environment. If restrictions exist they should be enforced consistently; and if they are never enforced against the locals they ought not to be enforced against the incomers. The rules should, however, be efficient and be applied in such a manner that the result aimed at can be attained. They should not represent inefficient remnants of the past, neither should they constitute a way to extract money from the users of the services concerned.

---

[55] Under the ancillary restraints doctrine for example. Interestingly enough, Whish in the 5th edn of his well-known competition law book, categorises *Wouters* as a *sui generis* case of 'regulatory ancillarity'—see R Whish, *Competition Law*, 5th edn, (London, Sweet and Maxwell, 2003) 120 *et seq.*

[56] Compare Case C–179/90 *Merci convenzionali porto di Genova SpA v Siderurgica Gabrielli SpA* [1991] ECR I–5889.

X. Conclusion

The *Wouters* and *Arduino* judgments were a surprise for many, probably most, observers. The Court seems to have had difficulty in reaching its conclusion, but it seems unlikely to change its mind in the near future. It is perhaps more likely to produce a refinement or a clarification when the next case arises. It would appear very difficult for the Court not to apply a like degree of tolerance to other professions. Judges know their own profession best, but they could not plausibly conclude that their profession was uniquely in need of protection from the consequences of the competition rules. It therefore seems likely that *Wouters* and *Arduino* will have descendants.

There is no *a priori* reason why publicly-imposed regulations should automatically be entitled to deference while privately-imposed ones are entitled to suspicion. Indeed, the best regulations are those which are based on a thorough understanding of the industry, and industry members are the best source of that knowledge. I am not convinced that the state is always the best regulator, nor that state regulations are consistently wise or proportionate. New rules have emerged in abundance over the last five years on the subject of financial services in Europe, the UK, the USA and other countries. Consumers of financial services in the UK are copiously warned and reminded about uncertainties, and offerors of financial services are subject to a correspondingly heavy burden of supervision, reporting, complaints procedures and the like. In the UK there are thousands of complaints which are slowly being examined by an independent body. I am doubtful if there has been a commensurate improvement in the quality of the financial services being offered. It is reported that regulations imposed hastily in Wall Street have unintended, even foolish, consequences, such as requiring a legally-qualified 'chaperon' to be present whenever certain sensitive matters are discussed. Well-informed and practically-useful regulations are more likely to emerge from the private sector than the public sector. Protectionist and unreasonably restrictive regulations can also emerge from the private sector, but I am not convinced that for that reason *Wouters* was wrongly decided.
In 2004, competition is very fashionable. There will soon be 100 nations with a competition statute and an enforcement agency. In 1974 enthusiasm for competition was something of an eccentricity on the part of regulators, public and private. There has been a huge transformation in 30 years. I would submit that we should give importance to the result as much as to the process when considering how to examine the regulation of the liberal professions under the competition rules. Competition is a goal, but it is not the only goal, and competition can be achieved by more than one route. Other goals, like efficiency, humanity and (even) cultural richness are valid pre-occupations. We have to accept that the competition rules can make a wholesome

transformation to how society functions. Perhaps the impact of the Autorità Garante in Italy is the most striking of several possible candidate examples. For the (doubtless numerous) situations where national regulation of the professions may contain excessive derogations from competition and commonsense, the ECJ may have to decide whether to expand or limit what it said in *Wouters*. The goal of competition law is to promote competition. Articles 81 *et seq* EC are not the only or the exclusive means to reach that result.

V

Hans Gilliams[1]

Competition Law and Public Interest: Do We Need to Change the Law for the (Liberal) Professions?

I. Introduction

In an essay published in 1993 in the *Revue du Marché Commun*,[2] Prof Claus-Dieter Ehlermann—at that time serving as Director General of the Commission's Directorate-General for Competition—announced that his administration would be looking into a more active enforcement of the Treaty competition rules *vis-à-vis* the liberal professions.[3] Ehlermann's initiative produced some results, and plenty of controversy.

The Commission in subsequent years did in fact conduct a few proceedings in relation to (restrictive arrangements adopted by) liberal professions. Not surprisingly, action was first taken against hard core restrictions, namely in *CNSD*[4] (relating to price fixing by the Italian national council for customs

[1] Eubelius, Brussels. The reader should be informed that I acted as counsel to Mr JCJ Wouters, the applicant in the *Wouters* case discussed in this paper. However, all opinions expressed herein are purely personal. This paper is dedicated to the memory of my father, Stefan Gilliams, who passed away during the writing hereof.

[2] CD Ehlermann, "Concurrence et professions libérales: antagonisme ou compatibilité?' (1993) 36 *Revue du marché commun et de l'Union européenne* 136.

[3] The analysis presented in this paper does not require a definition of what constitutes a 'liberal profession' since the application of the competition rules to a given profession (or activity) does not hinge on whether or not that profession/activity is to be considered as 'liberal'. I concur with the Commission (see the Professional Services Report cited at below n 9) that liberal professions may be best described as occupations requiring a special training in (liberal) arts or sciences, involving the provision of services that incorporate a high level of technical knowledge, and usually characterised by a high degree of regulation. The Commission says that it 'concentrates' on the professions with which it has had experience and cites lawyers, notaries, accountants, architects, engineers and pharmacists. The Commission's practice also has dealt with patent agents and customs agents, and the ECJ has considered rules adopted by a professional association of physicians. And obviously there are many other professions and occupations, such as tax consultants, land surveyors, real estate agents, IT consultants, business consultants, that also would seem to be entitled to the 'liberal' qualification.

[4] Commission Decision 93/438/EEC of 30 June 1993, Case IV/33.407 *CNSD* OJ L 203 [1993], p 27. An application for annulment of this decision was dismissed by the Court of First Instance ('CFI') in a judgment of 30 March 2000, Case T–513/93 *CNSD/Commission* [2000] ECR II–1807. The CFI had suspended its judgment on the matter until the Court of Justice ('ECJ') ruled on an application from the Commission for a declaration that Italy had infringed Art 10 EC on account of the legislation that empowered the CNSD to set binding tariffs. See Case 35/96 *Commission v Italy* [1998] ECR I–3851.

agents) and in *COAPI*[5] (relating to price fixing by the Spanish national association of industrial property agents). A few years later, the Commission issued a Statement of Objections against certain aspects of a code of conduct of an association of patent agents; subsequent to the amendment of the code, an exemption was granted *EPI*,[6] relating to the Code of Conduct of the Institute of Professional Representatives before the European Patent Office). More controversial matters were addressed by the ECJ in the context of references for a preliminary ruling, both decided on 19 February 2002: *Arduino*[7] (a compulsory fee schedule for lawyers, prepared by a professional association and approved by Ministerial Decree) and *Wouters*[8] (a ban on fee sharing between bar members and accountants). Further to these judgments, DG Competition engaged in what Commissioner Monti referred to as a 'stock-taking exercise' with respect to the application of the competition rules to liberal professions. That exercise eventually resulted in a 2004 Commission Communication, the 'Report on Competition in Professional Services'.[9] The Professional Services Report identifies a number of regulatory restrictions (price fixing, recommended prices, advertising regulation, entry requirements and reserved rights, and regulations governing business structure, including restrictions on multi-disciplinary partnerships) which in the Commission's view have the biggest potential to harm competition and accordingly should be scrutinised closely for their compatibility with the competition rules. The Ninth EU Competition Law and Policy Workshop (in the context of which this paper is submitted) offers an apt opportunity to consider the present state of the law—which in essence has been shaped by the ECJ.

The issue of the application of the competition rules to liberal professions almost always arises as a result of restrictive regulations that have been adopted by (or upon a proposal of) an association representing the interests of the practitioners of the relevant profession (a 'professional association'). Professional associations typically argue against an 'orthodox' application of the competition rules, stating that the restrictive regulation (often implemented by the profession itself by way of 'self regulation') pursues the public interest and on that basis is not subject to the constraints of national and Community competition rules. This paper will address the question of whether and when the 'public interest', as (purportedly) expressed in a restrictive regulation, is relevant to the applicability and interpretation of Articles 81 and 82 EC.

---

[5] Commission Decision 95/188/EEC of 30 January 1995 in Case IV/33.686 *COAPI* OJ L 122 [1995], p 37.

[6] Commission Decision 99/267/EC of 7 April 1999, Case IV/36.147 *EPI Code of Conduct* OJ L 106 [1999], p 14.

[7] Case C–35/99 Criminal Proceedings against Manuele Arduino [2002] ECR I–1529.

[8] Case C–309/99 *Wouters* [2002] ECR I–1577.

[9] *Commission Report on competition in the professional services*, COM (2004) 83 final, available at www.europa.eu.int/comm/competition/liberal professions/final comm en.pdf, hereinafter referred to as 'the Professional Services Report'.

In particular, this paper aims at ascertaining whether action by the public authorities[10] is required (and, if so, what degree of action) in order to allow restrictive professional rules to escape the applicability of the competition rules. The relevance of State regulation for the applicability of the competition rules is of course not an issue that only arises with respect to liberal professions. But there has always existed a special relationship between liberal professions and the public authorities. Many liberal professions have enjoyed or continue to enjoy special or exclusive rights with respect to the exercise of certain activities (often in return for certain obligations being imposed on practitioners by the public authorities[11]), and many liberal professions have been granted some form of rule-making authority by the public authorities.

I will address the relevance of the public interest for the applicability of the competition rules to liberal professions on the basis of the case law of the ECJ and the CFI relating to three different—but interrelated—subjects:

- cases clarifying when and to what extent the public regulation of a given activity has the effect of excluding the applicability of the competition rules altogether (below, part II);
- cases clarifying the circumstances in which a restrictive regulation is attributable to the State (rather than to practitioners of the profession or their associations), thereby falling outside of the scope of the competition rules (below, part III); and
- the so-called '*Wouters*' exception to the applicability of the competition rules (below, part IV).

By way of conclusion, I will consider the coherence of the current state of the law (below, part V).

---

[10] The expression 'public authorities' as used in this paper has a generic meaning and refers to any bodies (whether national, international, federal, regional or local) that are vested with public authority and the actions of which are in the public interest. It does not, however, refer to professional associations that under national law have public status and that are *required* to further the public interest (unless the substance of the latter expression has been sufficiently articulated by public authorities of a superior level).

[11] In this paper I will not discuss whether and under what circumstances practitioners of liberal professions can aspire to the qualification of undertakings 'entrusted with the operation of services of general economic interest' within the meaning of Art 86 EC To be sure, I do not *a priori* exclude that public regulation applicable to liberal professions has the effect of requiring the practitioners of a given profession to provide a universally available service at price and other conditions approved by the public authorities and with a guarantee of continuity, which would cause the relevant profession to qualify under Art 86 EC For example in certain Member States, process servers (in Belgium: '*gerechtsdeurwaarders/huissiers de justice*') may so qualify. However, this will be the exception rather than the rule; for example, I do not agree with the position taken by Advocate General Léger in *Wouters* (see paras 135–54) to the effect that bar members in the Netherlands may be so qualified, given the absence of sufficiently detailed public regulation that imposed requirements of the aforementioned type on the liberal profession. In any event, I believe that the most controversial issues are likely to arise with respect to Arts 81 and 10 EC, and not with respect to Art 86 EC.

II. (Public) Regulation of 'Economic Activities' and the Concept of 'Undertaking'

This section discusses the case law confirming that the public authorities may impose regulation that eliminates all potential for competition, thereby excluding the applicability of the Treaty's competition rules.

In order for the Treaty's competition rules to apply, the regulation at issue must qualify as an agreement, a concerted practice or an abuse of dominant position that is attributable to one or more 'undertakings' or to a decision by an 'association of undertakings'.

It is settled case law that the concept of undertaking covers 'any entity engaged in economic activity, regardless of the legal status of the entity or the way in which it is financed'.[12] In other words, (government) regulation of the profession at issue will not remove that profession from the applicability of the competition rules. The wording employed by the ECJ leaves little doubt that practitioners of (liberal) professions will only in exceptional cases *not* be considered as 'undertakings' within the meaning of Articles 81 and 82 EC. The ECJ in *Höfner*[13] even held that the *Bundesanstalt für Arbeit* (the German Federal Office for Employment), an agency that is part of the German Federal Republic and that offers employment procurement services free of charge is an undertaking since, in the words of the Court, 'employment procurement is an economic activity'[14] and 'employment procurement has not always been, and is not necessarily, carried out by public entities'.[15]

It may be different where the regulatory framework imposed by the public authorities on a certain activity does not leave the 'undertakings' carrying out such an activity any scope for competition. In such a case, the applicable regulation may have the effect of preventing the profession from being considered as carrying out an 'economic activity'. In the case law of the Court, the latter expression refers to 'any activity consisting in offering goods and services on a given market'.[16] Even if it seems difficult to deny that providing insurance against (inability to work on account of) sickness and maternity is an economic activity, the ECJ in *Poucet* nevertheless held that organisations that by virtue of public regulation are charged with the management of social security schemes that cover such risks do not qualify as 'under-takings'. Underlying that conclusion was the finding that the activity of such 'organisations' was subject to regulation that did not leave them any scope to compete (contribu-

---

[12] See, eg, *Wouters*, at para 46, and Joined Cases C–180/98 to 184/98 *Pavlov* [2000] ECR I–6451, para 74 in each case with references to earlier case law.

[13] 23 April 1991, Case C–41/90 *Höfner* [1991] ECR I–1979.

[14] Para 21 of the judgment.

[15] Para 22 of the judgment.

[16] See, eg, *Wouters*, at paras 47–48 (lawyers) and *Pavlov*, at paras 75–76 (medical specialists).

tions and levels of benefits were all defined by the State), and that the applicable regulation was inspired by the principles of solidarity and not-for-profit.[17]

In *Wouters* the Court added that the competition rules also will not apply to 'activity [that is] connected with the exercise of the powers of a public authority', and that consequently an entity that exercises 'powers which are typically those of a public authority' will not qualify as an 'undertaking' (immediately adding that the exercise, by a professional association of bar members, of regulatory authority delegated to it by the State, does *not* qualify as the exercise of public authority).[18] However, it would seem that this rule is a subset of the *Poucet* rule: whether or not an activity is connected with the exercise of public authority will depend on the applicable regulatory framework. Indeed, it would seem difficult to consider any activity as 'inherently' or 'typically' being that of a public authority. Conceptions relating to the role of the State differ to a considerable extent from Member State to Member State and it may be that an activity (for example surveillance of a port) in one Member State as a result of public regulation is entirely withdrawn from competition whereas in another Member State the organisation of the surveillance is left to private initiative (the port authority contracts with a security company to obtain surveillance services).[19]

The Court's judgment in *FFSA*[20] makes clear that *Poucet* is to be construed narrowly: where the affiliation with the insurance scheme is optional (instead of compulsory) and where the applicable rules leave the (not for profit) oper-

---

[17] Joined Cases C–159/91 and C–160/91 *Poucet and Pistre* [1991] ECR I–637, para 18. See also the judgment of 16 March 2004, Joined Cases C–264/01, C–306/01, C–354/01 and C–355/01, AOK Bundesverband a.o, not yet reported. The reference to the goal of the applicable regulation (solidarity and not for profit) seems a rather tenuous basis to distinguish *Höfner*. Presumably the (German) regulation that was before the Court in *Höfner* also required the governmental entity (the Bundesanstalt für Arbeit) to offer services on a not for profit basis; what is more, the issue in *Höfner* related precisely to a rule that barred anyone else (ie, 'for profit' companies) other than the Bundesanstalt to offer such services. It is difficult to imagine that where, as was the case in *Poucet*, the applicable regulation excludes a given activity entirely from competition, the sole (and government controlled) provider can still be qualified as an 'undertaking'. Of course, *Höfner* related to the interpretation of Art 82 EC (the issue was whether the sole provider, by being manifestly unable to provide part of the services that had been reserved to it, had 'abused' its dominant position), and I am not sure that the ECJ would be ready to apply the same rule in an Art 81 EC context.

[18] *Wouters*, paras 57–58. The Court referred to its earlier judgments in Case C–364/92 *SAT Fluggesellschaft* [1994] ECR I–43, para 30, concerning the control and supervision of air space, and in Case C–343/95 *Diego Calì & Figli* [1997] ECR I–1547, paras 22 and 23, concerning anti-pollution surveillance of the maritime environment.

[19] Comparable qualification issues arise in connection with the Treaty provisions on the free movement of persons—Art 39(4) EC provides that the prohibition on discrimination as regards the free movement of workers between Member States does not apply to employment in the public service. The ECJ has come to define the concept of 'public service' as relating to 'posts which involve direct or indirect participation in the exercise of powers conferred by public law and duties designed to safeguard the general interests of the State or of other public authorities and thus presume on the part of those occupying them the existence of a special relationship of allegiance to the State and reciprocity of rights and duties which form the foundation of the bond of nationality'. See Case C–405/01 *Colegio de Oficiales de la Marina Mercante Española v Administración del Estado* [2003] ECR I-10391, para 39.

[20] Case C–244/94, [1995] ECR I–4013.

ator of an insurance scheme some room to compete (eg, by leaving some form of choice in terms of the level of benefits that are paid out), the operator will be qualified as an undertaking. Of course, and as discussed in the subsequent parts of this paper, the applicable regulation may have far-reaching effects with respect to the operation of the competition rules.

The Court's case law discussed above was developed around the concept of an 'undertaking', but focuses on the regulation of a given activity. Accordingly, it is not excluded that a business entity that is engaged in various activities with respect to one activity does not, and with respect to another activity does, qualify as an 'undertaking'.

In summary, *public* regulation that with respect to a certain professional activity excludes all scope for competition will have the effect of removing that activity from the application of the competition rules. The ECJ does not require proof that the applicable regulation serves the public interest. To be sure, it cites the goal of 'solidarity' underlying the regulation, but it does so only to explain that such a goal is not compatible with competition on the market. The case law confirms that the Treaty (and in particular Article 3(g) EC) does not preclude the Member States from opting for an entirely regulated market that does not leave any room for competition and thus excludes the application of the competition rules.

III. Public Involvement In the Rule Making Process and the Concept of 'Associations of Undertakings'

This section discusses the case law that recognises that restrictive rules and agreements may escape the applicability of the competition rules if they may be attributed to the public authorities.

1. Overview of the Case Law

If practitioners of liberal professions are undertakings then it would seem rather obvious that their professional associations (often known under lofty denominations such as 'councils', 'societies', or 'institutes') are to be considered as 'associations of undertakings' within the meaning of Article 81 EC. However, the regulatory framework applicable to liberal professions is often of a mixed private/public nature, and it may be that professional associations—and their actions—become intertwined with the public authorities to such a point that there really would seem to be a shared responsibility for the restrictive practice or rule. The main situations that have been reviewed by the

ECJ have been where:

- the professional association has been set up pursuant to legislation, or under national law is to be regarded as a 'public body' (which could imply, for example, that its decisions are to be challenged before administrative courts);
- the relevant rules have been adopted by a 'semi public' body that is composed in part of public officials and in part of 'representatives' of the profession;
- the professional association has been granted regulatory powers by the public authorities;
- certain basic principles regarding the regulation of the profession have been set by the public authorities and these principles have been complemented by the professional association;
- the public authorities have adopted rules upon a proposal (or pursuant to lobbying) by the professional association.

The state of the (case) law relative to each of these hypotheses is discussed below. These factual situations are by no means mutually exclusive categories. The Court's case law was developed on the basis of the specific national regulatory framework in the matter at hand. Of course, the regulatory framework differs significantly from Member State to Member State, and even within the same Member State. Professions are often regulated in a highly diverse fashion. However, these case positions have in common that the Court in each case has had to grapple with the question of (a) who—the professional association or the public authorities—is in fact responsible for the regulation that brings about the restriction of competition and (b) if the responsibility lies with the professional association, whether that association is to be considered (in general or with respect to the adoption of the restrictive rule at issue) either as an association of 'undertakings' or as a part of the public authorities. These are crucial questions for the applicability of the competition rules, since it is settled case law that 'Article [81 EC] . . . relates only to the conduct of undertakings and does not cover measures adopted by Member States by legislation or regulations'.[21]

1.1 The Professional Association that Adopted the Regulation Is a 'Public Law Body'

The law relating to this hypothesis is clear. It is well-settled case law that the applicability of the competition rules is not affected by the fact that the relevant association has been incorporated by the public authorities, is gov-

[21] See, eg, Case C–2/91 *Meng* [1993] ECR I–5751, para 14. *Meng* related to German legislation precluding insurance brokers from passing on to their clients the commissions paid to them by the insurance companies.

erned by public law,[22] or that it has been entrusted with 'tasks in the public interest'.[23] However, that case law is based on the hypothesis that the decision making process within the relevant association is not controlled by the public authorities.

1.2 The Body or Committee Adopting the Regulation Is Composed In Whole or in Part of 'Representatives of the Public Authorities'

According to the current state of the case law, regard must be had to the composition of the 'associations'—or rather of the body of such associations that adopts the rules from which the relevant restrictions result. The case law[24] is to the effect that the qualification 'association of undertakings' may be avoided where a majority of the members of the relevant body are 'representatives of public authorities'[25] (as opposed to representatives of private operators[26]). If such a 'State majority' exists, the relevant body (at least for purposes of determining whether the restrictive regulation is subject to the competition rules) will not be an association of undertakings but instead will be considered as an emanation of the public authorities.

1.3 The Regulation Is Adopted on the Basis of Regulatory Authority Delegated by the State

This hypothesis involves the public authorities granting regulatory competence to the professional association so as to enable that association to adopt rules of professional conduct. Until *Wouter,* there remained some measure of uncertainty as to whether the qualification of 'association of undertaking' could also apply in the case of associations to whom the public authorities have granted regulatory and/or disciplinary powers. Typically, such regulatory powers are granted in order to enable the profession to ensure the

---

[22] See, *eg, Wouters* at paras 65–66. This case law originates with the Court's judgment in Case 123/83 *BNIC* [1983] ECR 391 (relating to a body instituted by the public authorities, composed of representatives appointed by the public authorities and enjoying regulatory powers to take action in the public interest).

[23] See the Opinion of Advocate General Léger in *Wouters*, at paras 79–81.

[24] See, eg, Case C–153/93 *Delta Schiffahrts* [1994] ECR I–2517, at paras 16–18 and 23, confirmed in *Arduino* (cited in above n 7) at para 37.

[25] Note that it does not suffice that the relevant individuals are *appointed* by the public authorities: they must be *representatives* of the public authorities, ie, it must be demonstrable that in participating in the decisional process, they represent the position of the public authorities. See, *eg, CNSD*, cited in above n 4, at para 41, where the Court notes that nothing in the applicable national legislation prevents the body from acting in the exclusive interest of the relevant profession. See also the Opinion of Advocate General Léger in *Wouters*, at para 83.

[26] Case C–96/94 *Spediporto* [1995] ECR I–2883, paras 23 and 25.

'proper exercise' or the 'dignity' thereof, and in many legal systems it is expressly or implicitly understood that such regulatory powers are to be used in the 'public interest'.

Wouters related to a delegation, by the Dutch legislator to the Dutch National Bar Association, of the power to adopt regulations to ensure 'the proper practice of the profession'.[27] The Court held that the Bar in exercising those powers could not claim an exemption from the competition rules, and said that it would be different only where

> [the] Member State, when it grants regulatory powers to a professional association, is careful to define the public-interest criteria and the essential principles with which its rules must comply and also retains its power to adopt decisions in the last resort. In that case the rules adopted by the professional association remain State measures and are not covered by the Treaty rules applicable to undertakings.[28]

Wouters makes clear that this exception is a fairly narrow one: the Court considered and rejected the argument that a law society that has been vested by the public authorities with the power to adopt regulations that are in the interest of 'the proper practice of the profession' is not an association of undertakings.[29]

It may be that a delegation of rule-making power by the public authorities to a professional association constitutes an infringement, *by the delegating Member State*, of Article 10 EC. However, that does not exclude action from being taken on the basis of Articles 81 or 82 EC against the beneficiary of the delegation as well. For example, the Court in *CNSD* first noted that the CNSD had been conferred, by the Italian authorities, regulatory powers, and subsequently analysed the regulation that had been adopted by the CNSD pursuant to those powers, finding that the CNSD in adopting that regulation

---

[27] The '*rules relating to organisation, qualifications, professional ethics, supervision and liability*' of bar members in the Netherlands are adopted on the basis of regulatory powers that have been conferred on the Bar by law and that enable the Bar to adopt regulations that are required to ensure 'the proper practice of the profession'. The substantive content of the latter rule has not been set by the Dutch public authorities.

[28] *Wouters*, at para 68, cited in the Professional Services Report at point 71. A similar approach is reflected in *Arduino* (cited in above n 7), where the Court noted that a tariff proposal prepared by the interested profession could not qualify as 'legislation' since the public authorities had not articulated public interest criteria that the profession was required to take into account. Thus, the Court concluded, it could not be said that the applicable legislation ensured that the body making the proposal 'conducts itself like an arm of the State working in the public interest' (paras 38–39 of the judgment).

[29] *Wouters*, at paras 62 and 65–69. Neither will it be sufficient that the public authorities have the possibility to apply for annulment, *a posteriori* (Bredael S, Misson L B, de Bandt P, 2004): '*droit* de la concurrence et exercice de pouvoirs réglementaires par les ordres professionnels: quelques réflexions et une tentative de synthèse au vu de l'arrêt de la Cour de Cassation du 25 septembre 2003 et de la jurisprudence récente de la Cour de Justice', *Tijdschrift Belgisch Handelsrecht/Revue de droit commercial* 22 (hereafter 'de Bandt, *et al*'), at para 35, with reference to the Opinion of Advocate General Léger in *Wouters*, para 74.

had infringed Article 81(1) EC.[30] Thus, the Court did not consider that the grant to the CNSD of regulatory powers (which grant was qualified by the Court as being contrary to Article 10 EC) had the effect of exempting it from the competition rules.

1.4 The Regulation Adopted by the Professional Association 'Bears Out' Principles That Have Been Set by the Public Authorities

It may be that the public authorities adopt a number of basic rules (possibly general principles, such as the requirement for practitioners to preserve their 'independence' or to give priority to the interest of the customer/client), which rules are then 'elaborated' by the professional association. Do the latter rules escape the applicability of the Treaty's competition provisions?

The case law on this hypothesis is not entirely clear. It is settled case law that participants to an arrangement that runs afoul of Article 81 EC will not be able to escape the application of the competition rules on account of the public authorities having *favored or encouraged* the conclusion of that arrangement. It is only if (and to the extent) certain behaviour (including regulation) is *imposed* by the public authorities that the behaviour will fall outside the scope of Article 81 EC: State compulsion excludes that the restriction flowing from such compulsion is attributable to the behaviour of undertakings. However, the latter exception is narrow in scope; for example, the Court of First Instance has held that if the allegedly 'imposed' agreement *precedes* the action by the public authorities, Article 81 EC will apply: '[. . .] if a State measure encompasses the elements of an agreement concluded between traders [. . .] or is adopted after consulting the traders concerned and with their agreement, those traders cannot rely on the binding nature of the rules in order to escape the application of Article [81 EC]'.[31]

In spite of the apparent strictness of the conditions developed in the Court's case law (which was developed in connection with arrangements that seemingly entailed serious infringements of Article 81 EC, such as market sharing), it would seem that, *to the extent* a professional regulation does no more than

---

[30] *CNSD*, cited in above n 4 in particular paras 45–51 of the judgment. See also the Commission's decision in *EPI* (cited in above n 6), where it was held that even if national or international public authorities delegate to a professional association the power to adopt rules which lead to practices which restrict competition, the exercise of that power is still subject to Art 81 EC.

[31] Case T–387/94 *Asia Motor France* [1996] ECR 961, paras 60–61. A parallel can be drawn with the case law of the United States Supreme Court, which in *Goldfarb v Virginia State Bar* 421 US 773 (1975), invalidated minimum tariffs which had been adopted by the bar of the State of Virginia and the bar of the district of Fairfax County. The Court held that the bar of Virginia, which had been given regulatory authority by the public authorities, was not obliged by the public authorities to impose the minimum tariffs, so that they remained subject to the competition rules ('it is not enough that [. . .] anti competitive conduct is "prompted" by state action; rather anti competitive activities must be compelled by direction of the State acting as sovereign').

implement a mandatory rule that (already) has been adopted by the public authorities, and provided the public authorities have reserved to themselves the power to adopt decisions in the last resort, then the professional regulation should not be subject to the competition rules.[32] Indeed, in such a case and on the basis of the *Wouters* test discussed in the previous subsection, it is difficult to deny that the restriction flows from the rule as adopted by the public authority, and not from action by (an association of) undertakings.

However, *Wouters* leaves little doubt that vague standards such as the 'duty to secure the dignity' of the profession will not shield professional associations, in developing a regulatory framework for the profession, from the application of Article 81 EC. Nor will it suffice that the professional association at issue has been entrusted by the public authorities with certain 'public interest' requirements, or is required to take account of the public interest in developing its rules. Under *Wouters*, in order to escape the qualification as 'association of undertakings', it will be necessary that the public authorities both define with sufficient clarity the public-interest criteria that the relevant entity needs to comply with, and retain the power to adopt decisions in the last resort.[33]

1.5 The Regulation Is Adopted by the Public Authorities Pursuant to a Proposal From or Lobbying by the Profession

It is sometimes alleged that public authorities 'assist' a profession adopt restrictive regulation by adopting public rules pursuant to lobbying by the profession, or by 'rubber stamping' regulation of which the substance has been prepared by the profession.

The case law relating to this hypothesis has been correctly qualified as formalistic.[34] By and large the Court refuses to look beyond the author of the rule and ascertain whether the public authorities in adopting the regulation at issue have independently considered the merits of that regulation as being in the 'public interest'. For example, in *Meng*[35] the regulation that the public authorities had imposed was preceded by a (presumably illicit) agreement between undertakings, and the Commission had pointed out to the ECJ that the public regulation in essence had reproduced the substance of that

---

[32] See, eg, Case C–38/97 *Autotrasporti Librandi* [1998] ECR I–5955: a commission that is *not* composed of a majority of government representatives nevertheless falls outside the scope of the competition rules because in adopting its recommendations it is required to take into account specific public interest criteria.

[33] See also Case C–198/01 *Consorzio Industrie Fiammiferi* [2003] ECR I–8055, para 67, where the Court makes it clear that the smallest manoeuvring margin suffices to confirm that there is a decision by an association of undertakings and not by the public authorities.

[34] N Reich, 'The November Revolution of the European Court of Justice: *Keck, Meng* and *Audi* Revisited' (1994) 31 *Common Market Law Review* 459.

[35] Cited in above n 21 above.

agreement. The Court nevertheless refused to confirm the applicability of Article 81 EC to the regulation.[36]

The case law exceptionally admits that Article 81 EC applies to measures that formally seem to have been adopted by the State, where it appears that the public authorities have not reserved to themselves the final say with respect to the regulation at issue and have merely conferred to the restrictive regulation the 'cloak' of public authority. That was the case in *CNSD*.[37] The CNSD was a professional association of customs agents[38] that under Italian law had the power to issue binding rules on tariffs. The tariffs set by the CNSD were *subsequently* rendered generally binding by a Decree of the Minister for Finance. The ECJ held that the State had 'wholly relinquished to private economic operators the powers of the public authorities as regards the setting of tariffs'[39] and that the Ministerial Decree 'assisted' the CNSD in imposing an illicit rule by conferring on the tariff an 'official character [. . .] such as to deter customers who might wish to contest the prices demanded by customs agents'.[40]

By contrast, in *Arduino*,[41] the ECJ was asked to rule on a compulsory fee schedule for lawyers. That schedule was adopted by the professional association but could not enter into force unless it had been approved by Ministerial Decree. There was little doubt that the decree was a rubber stamp: the public authorities had not laid down public interest criteria that the professional association had to take into account in adopting the tariff, and accordingly the Court acknowledged that

> the national legislation at issue in the main proceedings does not contain either procedural arrangements or substantive requirements capable of ensuring, with reasonable probability, that, when producing the draft tariff, the [Consiglio nazionale forense—the National Council of the Bar] conducts itself like an arm of the State working in the public interest.[42]

Nevertheless, the Court in its judgment[43] simply restated the *Meng* rule: 'Article [81 EC] of the Treaty is, in itself, concerned solely with the conduct of undertakings and not with laws or regulations emanating from Member States'. This conclusion seems to be based on the circumstance that (unlike in *CNSD*) the tariff could not enter into force without the approval of the

---

[36] *Meng* recalls the earlier judgment in Case 229/83 *Leclerc/Au Blé Vert* [1985] ECR 1 (known as '*Leclerc petrol*'), which related to the imposition by the French authorities of minimum retail prices for the sale petrol. Even though there was little doubt as to the purpose of the rule at issue, the Court simply noted that Art 10 EC does not prohibit Member States from setting minimum retail prices.

[37] Cited in n 4 above.

[38] Customs agents under Italian law are considered to be a liberal profession.

[39] Para 57 of the judgment.

[40] Para 59 of the judgment.

[41] Cited in n 7 above.

[42] Para 39 of the judgment.

[43] Para 34.

public authorities and that the Minister, before approving the tariff, had consulted with an intergovernmental committee. In other words, the public authorities had maintained the power to adopt decisions in the last resort even though it was far from certain that in adopting these decisions they adequately considered the public interest.

Meng and *Arduino* would seem to create a safe haven for lobbying: as long as the regulation is formally adopted by the State,[44] it is not governed by the competition rules, and it does not seem to matter in this respect that the public authorities have done nothing more than rubber stamp a proposal the substance of which has been entirely determined by the profession. That does not mean that a State measure adopted pursuant to lobbying is immune from challenge under Article 10 EC (see below, part III–3.) or under the Treaty provisions relating to the free movement of goods and persons and the freedom to provide services, but it does mean that the Treaty's *competition rules* can not be applied to the professional regulation or, stated differently, that the professional association for purposes of that regulation at issue is not to be considered as an 'association of undertakings'.[45]

2. General Observations

Essentially, the Court's case law in each of the scenarios discussed above attempts to ascertain who bears (primary) responsibility for the (substance) of the regulation at issue.

As to regulations adopted by the public authorities on the basis of a proposal by the interested profession, the Court—see hypothesis 5—applies a simple but formalistic approach: it refuses to 'look beyond' the formal author of the regulation and to determine who has actual responsibility for the substance of that regulation. Thus, Article 81 EC will not apply to 'legislation' (eg, a rule imposing fixed sales prices) that makes the conclusion of a prohibited

[44] And as long as the regulation remains in force. Indeed, it may be the case that the relevant State measure is invalidated (or disapplied) on the basis of Art 10 EC (see Section III3). The ECJ has held that the 'State compulsion' defence ceases to apply as from the time that the relevant State measures is declared contrary to Art 10 EC See *Fiammiferi*, cited in above n 33, para 55.

[45] Could the competition rules apply to the (members of) the professional association in as far as they engage in collective lobbying (i.e., abstraction being made of the intended result of the lobbying effort)? The answer might be to the affirmative if and to the extent the collective efforts have an anticompetitive purpose, such as inciting the public authorities to adopt a regulation that restricts competition to the benefit of the lobbying parties. In the United States, even a proposal to introduce certain standards may be incompatible with antitrust law where the proposal, before its adoption, is already being applied by competitors in the market. Compare American Antitrust Institute, 'Converging Professional Services: Lawyers against the Multidisciplinary Tide', to be found at www.antitrustinstitute.org, analysing the compatibility with antitrust laws of the proposal made by the American Bar Association's Commission on Multidisciplinary Practices to allow MDPs only in very limited circumstances.

agreement superfluous when that legislation (although with a clear anti-competitive purpose) has been 'proposed' by undertakings, but adopted by the public authorities themselves. It will be different only where the public authorities, further to the conclusion of a restrictive agreement between some undertakings, simply require other undertakings to join or comply with that arrangement or when the public authorities require all market participants to comply with a restrictive arrangement set by certain market participants—such requirements will not take the restrictive arrangement out of Article 81 EC.[46]

As to regulations adopted by professional associations, the Court's approach is *not* formalistic and accepts that such regulations under certain conditions can be attributed to the public authorities, thus taking them out of the scope of the competition rules. The standard that pervades the case law discussed above (hypotheses 3 and 4) would seem to be that a regulation or action of a professional association may still *escape* the application or Article 81 EC where it appears that the Member State has assumed responsibility for the substance of that rule or decision and has maintained control over its final adoption.[47] In such a case, the Court accepts that the regulation or action at issue does not originate with (an association of) undertakings but rather with the public authorities.[48]

---

[46] See Case 229/83 *Édouard Leclerc* [1985] ECR 1 ('*Leclerc books*'). The Court in that case examined French legislation imposing on book publishers and importers a statutory obligation to fix retail prices unilaterally. The restriction resulting from that legislation made it unnecessary for the publishers and importers to conclude resale price fixing agreements with wholesalers of the books. The Court thus considered whether legislation 'which renders corporate behaviour of the type prohibited by article [81 EC] superfluous [. . .] detracts from the effectiveness of Article [81 EC] and is therefore contrary to [Art 10 EC] of the Treaty' (para 15 of the judgment). The French legislation at issue in the end was left alone, since the Commission in the Court's view had not yet clearly developed its policy as to the (im)permissibility of resale price fixing of books and thus the substantive content of Art 10 EC on this issue was not 'specific enough' to support an objection against the legislation at issue (paras 18–20). The same approach is reflected in Joined Cases 209–13/84 *Asjes* [1986] ECR 1425, where in an *obiter dictum* the Court pointed out that the public homologation of tariffs set on the basis of prohibited price fixing is contrary to Art 10 EC; presumably in addition to the non-enforceability of the publicly endorsed tariffs, action also could be taken against the undertakings that set such tariffs.

[47] Compare the judgment of the United States Supreme Court in the case *Midcal* (*California Liquor Dealers v Midcal Aluminium* 445 US 97 (1990)) in which the test for so-called 'state action immunity' (exemption from the competition rules for certain matters attributed to the public authorities) was clarified as follows: the behaviour or the decision with regard to which the request for non-applicability of the competition rules is made, must be *clearly articulated* by the public authorities and *expressly imposed* as a matter of public policy, and furthermore the implementation of that policy must be *actively supervised* by the state itself.

[48] Although the Court's case law is not clear on this issue, it suggests that a professional association can escape the qualification of 'association of undertakings' with respect to *individual* matters—ie, it is possible that the association with respect to some matters is to be considered an association of undertakings that is subject to Art 81, whilst with respect to other matters it is not so considered, on account of the public authorities having assumed responsibility for the latter. See also van de JW Gronden and KJM Mortelmans, '*Wouters*: is het beroep van advocaat een aparte tak van sport' (2002) *Ars Aequi* 441, para 11. This (as also pointed out by Advovate General Léger in his opinion in *Wouters*, para 81 *et seq*) is rather confusing, but would seem to

Sometimes the 'attribution' to the public authorities will be confirmed with respect to the (conduct of the) professional association as such. The two examples identified in the case law are where the governing body of the professional association is composed of a majority of 'representatives of the public authorities' (hypothesis 2) or where the delegated regulatory authority can be exercised only to implement carefully defined public-interest criteria (hypothesis 3). In such cases, the professional association *as such* will not qualify as an association of undertakings and all of its actions will fall outside the scope of the competition rules. Taking a professional association out of the scope of the competition rules is a rather drastic step; the test should therefore ensure that the association's actions cannot reasonably be attributed to anyone else other than the State.

The Professional Services Report takes the position that in order to escape the qualification of 'association of undertakings', a body must comply with *both* of the aforementioned conditions, ie, it must be composed of a majority of representatives of the public authorities *and* it must be bound to observe public interest criteria.[49] That position may seem stricter than the case law discussed above (case position 2),[50] but it is difficult to imagine that representatives of the public authorities, when participating in the decisional process, are not (also) bound to implement pre-defined public-interest criteria; if they are not, then it would seem difficult to qualify them as 'representatives' of the public authorities.

A trickier question—and this is essentially scenario 4—arises when the professional association *as such* qualifies as an association of undertakings, but adopts a regulation (or takes an action) that (also) may be attributed to the State. In such a case, the applicability of the competition rules will need to be ascertained on a case by case basis. The question is then whether the professional association *with respect to the regulation at issue* may be regarded as an association of undertakings (or, stated differently, whether the regulation at issue may be considered as originating with an association of undertakings or rather with the public authorities). There may be easy cases, where a professional regulation does no more than implement a mandatory rule that (previously) has been adopted by the public authorities.

However, the reality will often be less straightforward, in particular where the public authorities have limited themselves to promulgating basic 'principles' that may allow for a narrow or a broad interpretation. For example,

be inherent in the Court's approach (as articulated in *Wouters*), which consists in determining who has the responsibility for any given matter. See also AJ Vossestein, Annotation on *Wouters* and *Arduino* (2002) 39 *Common Market Law Review* 841 and 853.

49 Professional Services Report, at point 71.

50 In fact, the Commission would seem to refer to a '*Reiff*' type of situation (see below, n 50 and accompanying text), where the majority of the body's members are not representatives of the public authorities but rather 'independent experts' that are required to take into account all relevant interests (including the public interest and the interest of consumers).

take the factual situation that was before the ECJ in *Wouters*: a bar association was required by the public authorities to ensure, by the adoption of binding rules, the independence of all bar members. In the case before the Court, the bar association had 'interpreted' the requirement that bar members preserve their independence by prohibiting partnerships between bar members and accountants, whilst allowing bar members to work as salaried lawyers for large firms, or to engage in partnerships with professions such as notaries and tax consultants. In such cases, the question will be[51] whether the 'interpretation' of the basic rule is correct, whether the 'derived' rules are in fact necessary to ensure (compliance with) the basic rule and whether the public authorities have maintained the power to adopt the final decision.

It may well be that a situation falls in more than one of the aforementioned hypotheses. In such a case the court, on the basis of a combination of factors, will have to assess whether the regulation at issue, *on balance*, can be said to be attributable to (an association of) undertakings. *Reiff*[52] is a case in point. The ECJ in that judgment examined compulsory transportation rates set by a tariff board made up of 'tariff experts' appointed by the public authorities on a proposal by the interested private operators. The Court noted that the tariff experts could *not* be regarded as representatives of the interested private operators (without expressly saying, however, that they had to be regarded as representatives of the public authorities; see hypothesis 2) and that the experts in adopting the rates were *also* required to take into account the interests of others besides the interested private operators (without saying, however, that the rates had to be in accordance with principles set by the public authorities; see hypothesis 3). On the basis of those two findings, the Court held that the decisions adopted by the tariff board were not decisions of associations of undertakings.[53] *Reiff* demonstrates that a regulation that does not completely satisfy any of the conditions developed by the Court to attribute such a regulation to the public authorities, is nevertheless taken out of the applicability of the competition rules on the basis of the *cumulative* effect of the public regulation that applies to the association or its decisions.[54]

At the end of the day, in order to be able to deal with the wide variety of regulation that applies to the professions and to their decision-making process, the ECJ (and courts in general) must make a case-specific assessment of all relevant factors of the matter at hand. On the basis of the case law discussed above, these factors would appear to be

[51] Of course, this question arises differently after the ECJ created the '*Wouters*' exception—see below, Section IV.

[52] Case 185/91 *Reiff* [1993] ECR I–5801.

[53] Paras 16–19 of the judgment. This part of *Reiff* was rehearsed in *Arduino* (cited above in n 7), at paras 16–17.

[54] See also de Bandt, *et al*, above n 65, at para 31.

- whether and to what extent the public authorities have influenced or controlled the decision-making process of the association;
- whether and to what extent the regulation at issue implements sufficiently clearly articulated public-interest criteria; and
- whether and to what extent the public authorities have the actual power to reverse or amend the substance of the rule that has been adopted.

The public interest concept becomes relevant where a restrictive regulation has been adopted by a professional body (ie, where there is no governmental compulsion and where the body is not composed of a majority of government representatives). Such a regulation nevertheless can escape the applicability of the competition rules where it pursues public interest goals that have been articulated by the public authorities. The case law illustrates that the required degree of articulation may vary according to the 'involvement' of the public authorities with the author of the regulation. For example, where (as in *Wouters*) (all of) the members of the body are clearly representatives of the practitioners and not public authorities, the public authorities will need to carefully define the public interest criteria and principles for the body to escape the qualification of association of undertakings. If, by contrast, (as in *Meng*) the members of the body are appointed by the public authorities and if there is an expectation that these individuals, although not formally representing the public authorities, in adopting the relevant rules will primarily further public-interest goals, then the Court may be less demanding in terms of the articulation, by the public authorities, of the public interest criteria to be observed or implemented by the body.

3. State Liability for Imposing Arrangements That Otherwise Would Be Prohibited by the Competition Rules

3.1 Article 10 EC: The Issue

The Court's formalistic approach—regulations adopted by the public authorities in any event do not fall within the scope of the competition rules—raises the question of whether Community law entails any restrictions on the ability of the public authorities to adopt—presumably further to lobbying by the relevant profession—rules that restrict competition in the relevant professional services.

That question has been addressed by the ECJ on the basis of Article 10 EC.[55] That provision requires the Member States to 'abstain from any

[55] Art 10 EC is a provision that is directed at the Member States, not at undertakings. Art 10 EC, when read in conjunction with Art 81 EC, may be considered as an unconditional and sufficiently precise rule, thus satisfying the requirements for direct effect. That—in conjunction

measure which could jeopardise the attainment of the objectives of the Treaty'. Article 10 EC—read in combination with Articles 3(g) and 81 EC—has given rise to the so called 'State action' line of case law. That case law is based on the routinely repeated principle that the Member States may not introduce or maintain in force measures, even of a legislative or regulatory nature, which may render ineffective the competition rules applicable to undertakings.[56] According to the Court, such is the case where a Member State either (a) requires or favours the adoption of agreements, decisions or concerted practices contrary to Article 81 EC or reinforces their effects or (b) deprives its own legislation of its official character by delegating to private traders responsibility for taking economic decisions affecting the economic sphere.

The 'State action' case law has been developed in large part in the context of regulated activities, including the activities of liberal professions. I will consider below whether and to what extent that case law has the effect of 'expanding' the reach of the Treaty's competition rules discussed above. The case law on Article 10 EC will only create such 'expansion' if it has the effect of prohibiting restrictive regulation that—on the basis of the case law discussed in Sections II and III—is not caught by Articles 81 or 82 EC.[57]

A closer look at the Court's case law makes clear that Article 10 only in very limited circumstances precludes 'anticompetitive' State measures.

---

with the primacy of Community law—implies that the validity of a state measure can be challenged if it infringes Art 10 EC read in conjunction with Art 81 EC See *Fiammiferi* (cited above in n 33), where the Court confirms that the duty to disapply national legislation that contravenes Art 10 EC also rests on national competition authorities (paras 49 and 50 of the judgment).

[56] The most insightful analyses of the ECJ's case law on this issue were authored several years ago by Gyselen. See L Gyselen, 'State Action and the Effectiveness of the EEC Treaty's Competition Provisions' (1989) 26 *Common Market L Rev* 33; L Gyselen, 'Anti-competitive State Measures under the EC Treaty: Towards a Substantive Legality Standard' (1994) 19 *European L Rev* 55. Note that Mr Gyselen in his paper submitted for this Workshop, partly changes his views as to the implications of Art 10 EC for State measures that are restrictive of competition. See Sections III3.4. and *v* of his contribution in this volume.

[57] To clarify, it may be the case that a given regulation *at the same time* gives rise to the applicability of Art 81 EC (since it entails action by an undertaking or an association of undertakings) and of Art 10 EC (since a Member State has been involved with the restrictive regulation at issue). In such cases, however, the practical relevance of Art 10 may be limited, since the regulation at issue may be prohibited on the basis of Arts 81 or 82 already. For example in *BNIC*, (Case 123/83 *BNIC v Clair* [1995] ECR 403), the '*Bureau National Interprofessionnel du Cognac*', an organisation that had been created pursuant to a French statute, had set fixed minimum purchase prices for potable spirits. These minimum prices were made generally binding by Ministerial order. The Court confirmed that the Ministerial order did not preclude Art 81 EC from applying to the minimum purchase price arrangement. The State measure at issue did no more than reinforce the effects of an anticompetitive rule and thus almost certainly violated Art 10 EC However, the Court (which, to be sure, was dealing with a request for a preliminary ruling that had not referred to Art 10 EC) simply stated that Art 81 EC could be applied directly to the restrictive rule at issue. Thus, the State action case law will extend the application of Art 81 EC only in situations where the competition rules do not (as such) apply *ratione personae*—on account of the restrictive measure being adopted (or compelled) by the public authorities.

3.2 *The Prohibition on Requiring or Favouring Prohibited Agreements, or Reinforcing the Effects Thereof*

As mentioned already, Article 10 EC has been interpreted by the ECJ as prohibiting Member States from *requiring or favouring the adoption of agreements prohibited by Article 81, or reinforcing their effects*. Article 10 EC will expand the prohibition of Article 81 EC only to the extent that Article 10 EC precludes State measures that 'require' undertakings to engage in behaviour that, *absent* such compulsion by the State, would be caught by Article 81 EC. The ECJ case law only in exceptional circumstances qualifies State measures as fitting that description. For example, in *Meng,*[58] as mentioned already, the regulation that the public authorities had imposed was preceded by a (presumably illicit) agreement between undertakings. The Commission had pointed out to the Court that the public regulation in essence had reproduced the substance of that agreement. The ECJ—following Advocate General Tesauro's opinion—nevertheless refused to confirm the applicability of Article 81 EC in rather terse terms:

> Rules applicable to a particular branch of insurance cannot be regarded as reinforcing the effects of a pre-existing agreement, decision or concerted practice unless they simply reproduce the elements of an agreement, decision or concerted practice between economic agents in that sector (paragraph 19 of the judgment).[59]

Against the background of this rather strict test, it is not surprising that there exist little or no precedents of public rules 'simply reproducing' the elements of an otherwise prohibited agreement. It may of course be the case that public rules of this nature exist, but that their 'link' to the prohibited agreement remains unknown, or unproven. Indeed, as the ECJ pointed out

> [s]ince the prohibition on participating in anti-competitive agreements and the penalties which offenders may incur are well known, it is normal for the activities which those practices and those agreements entail to take place in a clandestine fashion, for meetings to be held in secret, most frequently in a non-member country, and for the associated documentation to be reduced to a minimum.[60]

That observation undoubtedly also applies to the 'reproduction' of prohibited arrangements in the form of mandatory public rules.[61]

---

[58] Cited in above n 21.

[59] The 'simply reproduce' test would seem to go back to Case 311/85 *Vereniging van Vlaamse Reisbureaus* [1987] ECR 3801.

[60] Joined Cases C–204/00 P, C–205/00 P, C–211/00 P, C–213/00 P, C–217/00 P and C–219/00 P *Aalborg Portland A/S ao* [2004] ECR I–0000, at para 55.

[61] A case in point is the *Asia Motor* litigation, relating to a market-sharing arrangement allegedly concluded at the direction of the French authorities, who, it was claimed, have obtained from certain importers of Japanese cars an undertaking to limit imports to 3% of the total market in return for increasing the obstacles to importing in France other Japanese brands. In response to requests for information sent out by the Commission, the French authorities apparently instructed the importers not to reply to certain questions. See Case T–7/92 *Asia Motor France* [1993] ECR II–669.

3.3. The Prohibition On the Delegation of Regulatory Powers

Article 10 EC also entails a prohibition on 'depriving legislation of its official character by delegating to private traders responsibility for taking economic decisions affecting the economic sphere'. The 'delegation' prohibition should come to apply in the case of regulations that, on the basis of a delegation of rule-making authority, are adopted by a body (or committee) (i) the majority of the members of which have been appointed or proposed by interested economic operators instead of by the State),[62] and/or (ii) which does *not* adopt the regulations pursuant to public interest criteria that have been sufficiently articulated by the public authorities.

In practice, there are very few cases in which the Court finds that the delegation prohibition has been infringed. *CNSD*[63] is one of these rare cases. The Court declared incompatible with Article 10 EC an Italian law requiring the national association of customs agents to adopt compulsory tariffs for services to be rendered by customs agents. The compulsory tariffs were not determined by reference to any public interest criteria, and the association was not subject to any government supervision.[64] However, *Arduino* demonstrates that it suffices that the public authorities formally adopt a restrictive rule, even if there are serious indications that they have done little more than to rubber stamp the relevant measures.

The 'delegation' prohibition seems to have suffered a further blow in *Wouters* where the ECJ, at least implicitly, held that the delegation prohibition *cannot* apply in the event the (substantive content of) the regulations do (does) not contravene Article 81 EC. As Gyselen[65] has observed, this may be difficult to reconcile with *Leclerc books*[66] (public regulation may make the conclusion by private undertakings of a prohibited agreement *superfluous*). In my view, delegation of rule-making power that enables the beneficiary of the delegation to set the parameters of competition should be prohibited *per se except* if (and I would think that this is what the Court in *Wouters* referred to) the *subject matter* of the rule/decision adopted on the basis of the delegated

---

[62] This first condition appears in the Court's earlier case law (see for example the aforementioned judgments *Reiff*, above n 52, and *Delta Schiffahrts*, above n 24), to be linked with the question of whether there is an undertaking or an association of undertakings (see above, Section IIIA, case position 2).

[63] Cited at n 4 above.

[64] Note, however, that *CNSD* does not extend the substantive scope of Art 81: the CNSD itself had also been charged by the Commission with an infringement of Art 81 (see the Commission decision cited in n 4 above), and the ECJ ruling was given pursuant to an application by the Commission for a declaration that the Member State in question, too, had infringed Art 10 EC (read in combination with Art 81 EC).

[65] L Gyselen, 'De Vlaamse balies, multidisciplinaire samenwerking en EG-Mededingingsrecht: Prelude tot het arrest van het Hof van Cassatie' in *Liber Amicorum Jean-Pierre de Bandt* (Brussels, Bruylant, 2004).

[66] Cited in above n 46.

power, pursuant to the *Wouters* exception (see below, part IV), falls outside the scope of Article 81 EC. Indeed, the ECJ in earlier case law struck down a public rule that authorised a dominant undertaking to draw up the specifications for the products that could legally be sold on the market, to monitor the application thereof, and to grant (or refuse) type-approval for the relevant products.[67] Such legislation, the Court observed, is tantamount to conferring upon the dominant undertaking the power to determine at will which products may be sold on the market, thereby placing that undertaking at an obvious advantage over its competitors and making it impossible to maintain effective competition on the market.[68] That case law would also seem to preclude delegation of regulatory authority to a professional association, in particular where (as was the case in *Wouters*) that authority permitted the adoption of rules that also affect the position of competitors (accountants wanting to share fees with bar members). However, the ECJ in *Wouters* decided that the rule adopted on the basis of the delegated authority did not, on account of its substance, fall within Article 81 (see below, part IV) and went on to state that in such a case, there was no need to consider the compatibility of the delegated authority with Article 10 read in conjunction with Articles 3(g) and 81 EC.

3.4. Does Article 10 EC Have Any Added Value Vis-À-Vis Articles 81 and 82 EC?

After *Meng* and *Arduino*, the 'added value' of Article 10 EC as compared to Articles 81 and 82 EC seems extremely limited. Except where the public measure simply reproduces a prohibited agreement (*Meng*), or unnecessarily covers a prohibited agreement with the cloak of public authority (*CNSD*), or entirely delegates to a private body the power to set binding parameters for competition on the market (*CNSD*), Article 10 EC does not preclude restrictive arrangements that are not already caught by Articles 81 and 82 EC. The ECJ's attitude certainly comes across as formalistic (see above part III–2). But I believe (as much as I am tempted by the idea of a court striking down State measures that impose restrictions that cannot reasonably be justified in the public interest) that the Court's approach is defensible. Public authorities may have a variety of public interest reasons for introducing regulation that has a restrictive effect on competition, and Article 3(g) EC does not call for such regulation to be prohibited. That is also confirmed by the case law discussed in part II of this paper. In sum, it seems difficult to argue that State measures that are compatible with the 'four freedoms' may still be prohibited by Article 10 of the Treaty solely on account of their restrictive impact on competition.

---

[67] Case C–18/88 *Régie des télégraphes et téléphones v GB-Inno-BM* [1991] ECR I–5941.

[68] Paras 25–26 of the judgment.

IV. *Wouters*—a 'Liberal Profession' Exception to Article 81 EC?

The foregoing sections led to the conclusion that (restrictive) measures that either are attributable to the public authorities or that implement clearly articulated public interest considerations will escape the applicability of Articles 81 and 82 EC and, except in quite rare circumstances, will not be prohibited by Article 10 EC either. This section will deal with the hypothesis of a restrictive arrangement that cannot be attributed to the public authorities and does not implement clearly articulated public interest considerations. In *Wouters,* the Court was confronted with an arrangement that was found by the Court to be restrictive of competition and to have the potential to affect trade between Member States. Nevertheless, the ECJ in *Wouters* held that the arrangement was *not* caught by Article 81, without it being necessary to review whether that regulation satisfied the conditions of the third paragraph of Article 81 EC.

1. The Judgment . . .

In *Wouters*, the Court ruled on a regulation (the 'MDP Regulation') of a professional association (the Dutch National Bar Association) which prohibited Dutch bar members from engaging in (certain) multi-disciplinary partnerships (or 'MDPs'). The proceedings before the ECJ arose from disciplinary proceedings that the Dutch Bar, on account of an alleged transgression of the MDP Regulation, had taken against two bar members (Messrs. Wouters and Savelbergh) who were deemed to have engaged in unauthorised professional cooperation with accountants belonging to Arthur Andersen and PWC member firms.[69]

The judgment as to the applicability of Article 81 EC contains two parts that in tone and argument are strikingly different. The first part of the judgment contains two findings. First, the Court holds[70] that the Bar in adopting the MDP Regulation was to be considered as an association of undertakings, since the Bar's governing bodies are composed only of bar members (and not of government representatives), and since the Dutch State failed to require

[69] The defendants, two bar members, had joined tax partnerships of Arthur Andersen and PWC, respectively. The MDP Regulation did not prohibit partnerships between bar members and tax consultants. However, the Dutch Bar authorities considered that the internal arrangements between the various Arthur Andersen and PWC member firms had the effect of tax consultants (and thus also the bar members associated with such tax consultants) sharing fees with accountants, one of the few professions that were 'non eligible' for sharing fees with bar members.

[70] Paras 56–71 of the judgment.

the Bar, in adopting the MDP regulation, to implement specified public-interest criteria (as discussed already, the Bar was empowered to adopt regulations so as to ensure the 'proper practice of the profession'[71]). Second, the ECJ finds that the MDP Regulation appreciably restricts competition and affects trade between Member States.[72]

The Court, in spite of those two findings, does *not* conclude that the MDP Regulation falls within the scope of Article 81 EC. Instead, the judgment in a second part rather abruptly changes course. The ECJ (paragraphs 97–110) holds that the regulation, in spite of its restrictive effects, does not fall within Article 81(1) EC. The Court bases that finding on the consideration that the MDP Regulation's

> objectives [are] connected with the need to make rules relating to organisation, qualifications, professional ethics, supervision and liability, in order to ensure that the ultimate consumers of legal services and the sound administration of justice are provided with the necessary guarantees in relation to integrity and experience.[73]

The Court then goes on to conclude that the Dutch Bar 'could reasonably have considered that [the MDP Regulation] despite the effects restrictive of competition that are inherent in it, is necessary for the proper practice of the legal profession, as organised in the Member State concerned'.[74] The Court's approach in the second part of the judgment mirrors the approach taken by the Commission in *EPI*.[75]

---

71 See the discussion in Section III, Point 1.3 above.

72 Paras 86–96 of the judgment.

73 Paras 97 of the judgment.

74 Para 110 of the judgment.

75 Cited in above n 6. In that Decision, the Commission, too, considered as not falling within Art 81 EC 'genuine' rules of professional conduct (a prohibition on misleading advertising) in spite of the inherent restrictive effect of such rules, since such rules were said to be necessary to prevent confusion of consumers. By contrast, a prohibition on comparative advertising and on soliciting clients of other professionals was not considered as necessary (see recital 43); the Commission, nevertheless and rather remarkably, exempted the latter bans as a transitional measure:

> [. . .] a changeover from a system of virtually total prohibition on advertising and on the supply of unsolicited services, as currently exists, to one of total freedom, involves a significant transformation of the framework within which professional Representatives operate. If this changeover is made suddenly, there is a potential risk of confusion in the mind of the public such as might damage the image that professional Representatives give to institutions participating in the administration of justice. (recital 46)

The CFI *Institute of Professional Representatives Before the European Patent Office*, (Case T–144/99, [2001] ECR II–1087) ruled on an application that had been brought against the Commission's decision that the prohibition on comparative advertising and client solicitation ran afoul of Art 81 EC The CFI accepted that the Commission could consider an across the board ban on comparative advertising as restrictive of competition (paras 72–75 of the judgment). It rejected the applicant's argument 'that the prohibition of comparative advertising was based on the discretion, dignity and necessary courtesy that must prevail within a profession' with the rather ambiguous observation that 'where it is not shown that the absolute prohibition of comparative advertising is objectively necessary in order to preserve the dignity and rules of conduct of the profession concerned, the applicant's argument is not capable of affecting the lawfulness of the Decision' (paras 76–77 of the judgment).

Wouters is a remarkable judgment in that the reason given by the Court in the judgment's first part to confirm that the MDP regulation was adopted by an association of undertakings and thus is subject to Article 81 EC (the 'proper practice of the profession can not be regarded as a sufficiently clearly articulated a public interest purpose') appears to be thrown overboard in the second part (the competition rules do not apply to restrictive effects that are inherent in rules that have been adopted to ensure the proper practice of the profession). The contrast between the two parts of the judgment caused Van de Gronden and Mortelmans[76] to observe that the first part of the judgment reads like a dissenting opinion. In fact, the inclusion in the judgment of the first part has the effect of *emphasising* the weight of the statements to be found in the second part:

2. . . . Does Not Easily Fit Into Existing Competition Law Categories . . .

Much has been written about how *Wouters* fits in with existing case law. I do not think that the judgment is based on the 'ancillary restraints' doctrine—it does not identify a non-restrictive subject matter of the regulation at issue that itself is pro-competitive and that would require 'ancillary restrictions' in the form of a ban on MDP's. The regulation in *Wouters* is qualified by the Court as pursuing compliance with professional conduct rules; such rules in essence impose *restrictions* on practitioners so as to ensure that the profession is carried out in accordance with certain principles (which invariably are qualified by the authors of the rules as being in the 'public interest'). It is true that the Court in *Wouters* points out that the restrictive effects of the MDP Regulation are 'inherent' in the pursuit of the proper practice of the legal profession,[77] but that does not make such pursuit pro-competitive.

Nor can it be said that paragraphs 97–110 of *Wouters* introduce a 'rule of reason' in Community competition law. A 'rule of reason' approach may be compared to the application of the third paragraph of Article 81 EC: the restrictive effects of an arrangement are balanced against efficiency benefits that may be expected to result from the arrangement. The Court in *Wouters* does not engage in such a balancing exercise—it does not attempt to identify any efficiencies within the MDP Regulation.[78]

What the Court seems to be doing in *Wouters* is to create a limited 'subject matter' exception to Article 81(1) EC to the benefit of certain professional conduct rules. Provided such rules aim at securing compliance with certain

---

76 Article cited in above n 48, at para 14. See also the critical observations of E Deards, 'Closed shop versus one-stop shop: the battle goes on' (2002) 27 *European L Rev* 618, 622–23.

77 See paras 97 and 110 of the judgment.

78 See further the discussion of National Society of Professional Engineers.

'fundamental principles' of the profession (independence and professional secrecy) that reflect the 'prevailing conceptions' on the professions in the Member State at issue, and provided the restrictive effects inherent in such rules do not go beyond what is necessary to ensure compliance with the profession's principles, then the professional conduct rules will escape the application of Article 81 EC altogether.

3. . . . And Is to Be Understood In the Context of Its Intended Result

An intriguing question is *why* the Court in *Wouters* introduced an 'escape route' from Article 81. After finding that the regulation had restrictive effects on competition and affected trade between Member States, it could have confirmed that the regulation at issue came within the scope of the first paragraph of Article 81, and have left it to the Commission to ascertain whether the regulation qualified for an exemption under the third paragraph of Article 81 EC (the regulation had been notified by the Dutch Bar to the Commission for an exemption). I believe that there are two reasons why the Court, instead of taking such a seemingly orthodox approach, chose to provide a rationale so as to exclude the MDP Regulation from the applicability of Article 81 EC altogether.

The first reason relates to the procedural consequences that would have resulted from a judgment confirming that the MDP Regulation, on account of its restrictive effects, fell within Article 81(1) EC. The Dutch Council of State had referred questions on the first paragraph of Article 81 EC only. The reason for not raising the interpretation of Article 81(3) EC was that the MDP Regulation had been notified by the Dutch Bar to the Commission only *after* the commencement of the disciplinary proceedings—implying, pursuant to the then applicable Regulation No 17/62, that any exemption granted by the Commission could not operate retroactively so as to salvage the disciplinary measures taken *vis-à-vis* both bar members. Thus, a finding by the Court that the MDP Regulation fell within the scope of Article 81(1) EC would effectively have resolved the national proceedings against the Dutch Bar and 'for' Arthur Andersen and PWC. The judgment creates the impression that the Court wanted to decide the—highly politicised—matter itself, and in favour of the Dutch Bar, which left it no choice but to hold that the MDP Regulation was compatible with the first paragraph Article 81 EC.

Would the Court have been faced with the same dilemma if the matter had arisen after the entry into force of Regulation 1/2003—ie, now that an exemption under the third paragraph of Article 81 EC no longer requires a (timely) notification to the EC Commission? Could the Court then have based the second part of its judgment on Article 81(3) EC—confirming that (or leaving it for the Commission to ascertain whether) the MDP Regulation qualifies for an exemption on that basis? That is far from certain—and that, I believe, is the second reason for the Court in *Wouters* to clear the MDP Regulation on the basis of Article 81(1) EC.

The Court, in paragraph 100 of the judgment, notes that the 'essential rules' adopted by the Dutch Bar on the basis of its regulatory power to ensure the 'proper practice of the profession' were rules relating to 'the duty to act for clients in complete independence and in their sole interest, the duty [. . .] to avoid all risk of conflict of interest and the duty to observe strict professional secrecy'. This makes clear that the MDP Regulation does not produce efficiency gains. The restrictive effects (discussed in the first part of the *Wouters* judgment) are not required to achieve a more efficient practice but rather a 'proper' practice of the profession. Indeed, the essential submission of the Dutch Bar was that the MDP Regulation pursued the public interest—by precluding 'unfair' competition from large accounting firms—and therefore should not be prohibited by the competition rules of the Treaty.

Therefore, it does not seem likely that the MDP Regulation, if the Court had confirmed that it fell within Article 81 EC, would have qualified for an exemption under the third paragraph of Article 81 EC. This is apparent from the Commission's 'Guidelines on the application of Article 81(3) of the Treaty'—which were issued in connection with the entry into force of Regulation 1/2003. The Guidelines state that, in order to benefit from an exemption under the third paragraph of Article 81, the restrictive arrangement must produce efficiency gains: it should '. . . contribute to improving the production or distribution of goods or to promoting technical or economic progress'.[79] The Guidelines in that respect emphasise:

> Any claim that restrictive agreements are justified because they aim at ensuring fair conditions of fair competition on the market is by nature unfounded and must be discarded [. . .]. The purpose of Article 81 is to protect effective competition by ensuring that markets remain open and competitive. The protection of fair competition is a task for the legislator in compliance with Community law obligations [. . .] and not for undertakings to regulate themselves.[80]

The Court in *Wouters* may well have understood that Article 81(3) EC can not provide a basis for exempting this type of arrangement, and that accordingly the MDP Regulation could be cleared only by holding that it falls outside of Article 81 altogether.

---

[79] Para 48.

[80] Para 47 of the Guidelines, with reference to Case T–29/92 *Vereniging van Samenwerkende Prijsregelende Organisaties in de Bouwnijverheid (SPO)* [1995] ECR II–289.

4. Is *Wouters* a Variation on Albany?

In *Albany,*[81] the Court held that collective labour agreements that pursue social policy objectives fall outside Article 81(1) EC by virtue of their nature and purpose. In particular, the Court observed that

> [i]t is beyond question that certain restrictions of competition are inherent in collective agreements between organisations representing employers and workers. However, the social policy objectives pursued by such agreements would be seriously undermined if management and labour were subject to Article [81(1)] of the Treaty in seeking jointly to adopt measures to improve conditions of work and employment.[82]

The Court's approach in *Wouters* bears resemblance to *Albany*. Indeed, the Court in *Wouters* held that restrictive effects that are 'inherent' in rules of professional conduct that seek to ensure the proper practice of the profession do not trigger the application of Article 81 EC. In both cases, restrictions that are 'inherent' in arrangements that pursue certain (non-efficiency related) objectives are held to fall outside of Article 81 EC.

It is open to debate whether the 'proper practice of the legal profession' can be regarded as a 'social policy' objective. But *Wouters* and *Albany* would seem to be based on the same rationale: to the extent arrangements pursue *public interest objectives*, their 'inherent' effects, even if they are restrictive of competition, are not prohibited by the Treaty's competition rules.

There is an important difference between *Wouters* and *Albany*, however. In *Albany*, immunity was granted to agreements that pursue social policy objectives, and there is little doubt that the Court understood this expression as referring to objectives set by the public authorities.[83] This is also apparent from *Pavlov*[84] in which the ECJ held that the *Albany* exclusion did not apply to a supplementary pension scheme that had been introduced by a professional association and that provided for compulsory participation by all members of the profession. The Court conceded that the case was close to *Albany* because the pension scheme, by guaranteeing a certain level of retirement benefits, was intended to improve working conditions. However, the Court refused the *Albany* exemption from the competition rules, observing

---

[81] Joined Case C–67/96 *Albany International,* C–115/97 to C–117/97 *Brentjens' Handelsonderneming* and C–219/97 *Maatschappij Drijvende Bokken* [1999] ECR I– 6121.

[82] Points 46–47 of the judgment.

[83] See, for example, para 87 of the judgment, where the Court acknowledges the restrictive effects of the rule at issue ('Doubtless, some undertakings in the sector might wish to provide their workers with a pension scheme superior to the one offered by the Fund'). The Court then finds that these restrictive effects have clearly been intended by the public authorities: 'However, the fact that such undertakings are unable to entrust the management of such a pension scheme to a single insurer and the resulting restriction of competition derive directly from the exclusive right conferred on the sectoral pension fund'.

[84] Cited in n 12 above.

that the pension scheme had not been introduced on the basis of a collective bargaining agreement, and that there was no possibility for 'such agreements [to] be made compulsory by the public authorities, for all the members of the profession'.[85] That makes it possible to reconcile the *Albany* rule with the case law discussed above, according to which the competition rules will not apply to an agreement to the extent it does no more than pursue public interest goals set by the public authorities.[86]

Wouters, of course, was a different case. As mentioned already, the Court in *Wouters* found that the MDP Regulation did *not* pursue any clearly articulated public interest goals: the Dutch public authorities had not defined the essential principles of what constitutes the 'proper practice of the profession' and precisely for that reason the Court had concluded that the MDP Regulation was a decision adopted by an 'association of undertakings' within the meaning of Article 81 EC. That is why *Wouters* can not properly be associated with *Albany*. As stated above (part IV–2), *Wouters* is a *subject matter* exception to the competition rules: the MDP regulation at issue in *Wouters* did not escape the application of the competition rules on account of its author, or on account of any action taken by the public authorities, but instead on account of the subject matter of that regulation and the goals pursued by that regulation.

In spite of the difficulty to reconcile *Wouters* with the Court's pre-existing case law, there is little doubt that the judgment is to be considered as one of principle. From its inception, the case was generally regarded by the various bar associations as a matter of principle—the Dutch Bar association maintained that the case really was about the need to safeguard the 'independence of the profession', whilst Arthur Andersen and PWC stated that the MDP Regulation was inspired by the resolve to keep (large) 'accounting' firms out of the legal market. The case attracted much attention (especially in the legal world), and no less than nine governments as well as the CCBE intervened in the proceedings before the Court, all in support of the submissions of the Dutch Bar. The case was heard by the full Court, and the Court after the oral hearing considered the matter for more than 14 months before issuing its judgment. It is therefore necessary to carefully consider the implications of the judgment for competition law.

One question that is immediately begged by the judgment is whether the 'Wouters' defence is available only to the legal profession, or only to 'liberal' professions (which would raise the further question how to distinguish 'liberal' from other professions). The judgment is silent on this point, but it is obvious that the Court intended to salvage restrictive self regulation by the legal profession from an orthodox application of the competition rules. That suggests that the Court will not extend the rule beyond the legal profession or

[85] Points 67–69 of the judgment.
[86] Compare Section III1.4 above.

beyond (certain?) liberal professions. That will raise delicate issues of equality of treatment—it does not seem easy to justify a different application of the competition rules for liberal professions on the one hand and 'ordinary' economic activities on the other hand.[87] In the remainder of this paper, I will assume that the '*Wouters* defence' is available to liberal professions only. I will discuss two further issues raised by the judgment: what will be the role of the public interest for the application of the competition rules in situations such as the one that was before the Court in *Wouters* (sections E and F below), and whether courts and competition authorities in applying the '*Wouters* defence' should recognise a margin of discretion to the benefit of the relevant profession (section G below).

5. Does *Wouters* 'Privatise' the Public Interest?

Wouters is likely to be invoked by numerous professional associations to claim antitrust immunity for rules that *in the view of those associations* serve the public interest. It would presumably be claimed that *Wouters* confirms that the professions themselves are best placed to decide how best to protect the consumers of the relevant services. For example, the paper written by Mario Siragusa for this volume[88] states that the 'defining feature' of *Wouters* is the Court of Justice's 'recognition of a margin of discretion of bar associations in deciding what they deem appropriate and necessary to protect the proper practice of the profession in their respective Member States'.[89] It is fair to expect that such a 'margin of discretion' will also be invoked by other liberal professions. Consider, for example, the claim of an association of engineers that 'excessive price competition' between professionals should be excluded because it may create safety risks. That claim has in fact been made and rejected.

More than 25 years ago, the US Supreme Court considered an antitrust challenge against the canon of ethics of a liberal profession (the National Association of Professional Engineers) that prohibited competitive bidding[90] by the association's members.[91] The association alleged that the canon was justified under the Sherman Act, because it was adopted for the purpose of

[87] It is likely that the authors of restrictive practices will attempt to rely on *Wouters* by arguing that such practices serve the public interest. For example, an association of manufacturers of building products could attempt to justify a requirement that all of its members comply with certain quality standards (set by the association) on the basis of the assertion that the association's standards are 'justified by the need to protect public safety'. The likely result is that the Court in its future case law will impose limits on the availability of the *Wouters* defence.

[88] 'Critical Remarks on the Commission's Legal Analysis in its Report on Competition in Professional Services'.

[89] See his contribution in this volume.

[90] The canon was to the effect that the engineer had to be selected by the client without any negotiation or discussion on the fees to be applied by the engineer.

[91] *National Society of Professional Engineers v United States* 435 US 679 (1978).

minimising the risk that competition among professional engineers would lead to 'deceptively low bids, and would therefore tempt individual engineers to do inferior work with consequent risk to public safety and health'. The Supreme Court (per Justice Stevens) stated that

> the asserted defence rests on a fundamental misunderstanding of the Rule of Reason [. . .] We are faced with a contention that a total ban on competitive bidding is necessary because otherwise engineers will be tempted to submit deceptively low bids. Certainly, the problem of professional deception is a proper subject of an ethical canon. But [. . .] the equation of competition with deception, like the similar equation with safety hazards, is simply too broad; we may assume that competition is not entirely conducive to ethical behaviour, but that is not a reason, cognizable under the Sherman Act, for doing away with competition.

This would seem to square precisely with the warning in the Guidelines on Article 81(3) EC:[92] the protection of fair competition is a task for the legislator and not for undertakings to regulate themselves.

Does *Wouters* in fact create a discrepancy between EC and US competition law on such a fundamental matter? On a closer reading, I believe that the ECJ's judgment, while undoubtedly significant, needs to be nuanced in several respects.

Wouters admittedly creates a paradox. The Court states that where professional conduct rules cannot be said to pursue goals that have been sufficiently clearly articulated by the public authorities, such professional conduct rules, in spite of their restrictive effects, nevertheless can escape the application of the competition rules if it appears that they pursue public-interest goals. That of course begs the question as to *who* will decide whether the rules of conduct set by the profession do in fact further public interest goals. The ECJ clearly did not intend to issue a blank check to the profession. Indeed, the Court in *Wouters* does its best to stress the 'public interest' content of the MDP regulation at issue. It observes that the regulation's

> objectives [are] connected with the need to make rules relating to organisation, qualifications, professional ethics, supervision and liability, in order to ensure that the ultimate consumers of legal services and the sound administration of justice are provided with the necessary guarantees in relation to integrity and experience.[93]

The Court also stresses that the MDP Regulation aims to ensure that 'in the Member State concerned, the rules of professional conduct for members of the Bar are complied with, having regard to the prevailing perceptions of the profession in that State'.[94]

---

[92] See above.

[93] Para 97 of the judgment.

[94] Para 105 of the judgment. The (authentic) Dutch language version of the judgment (*'gelet op de in die lidstaat heersende opvattingen over dit beroep'*) makes clear that the ECJ does not refer to the perceptions as held by the Dutch National Bar Association, but instead to the prevailing perceptions in the Netherlands *with respect to* the legal profession (see also the French version of the judgment: *'compte tenu des conceptions de cette profession qui y prévalent'*).

This can only mean that, in the event of a challenge on the basis of the competition rules against a rule of professional conduct, it will be for the court hearing the case to decide whether or not the rule of professional conduct at issue does in fact pursue the public interest. In other words, it will be for the court[95] to define, *in the absence* of (sufficient) guidance by the public authorities, what constitutes the public interest having regard to the 'prevailing perceptions' in the relevant Member State. Thus, *Wouters* does not create a 'safe harbour' for (the restrictive effects inherent in) professional self regulation, nor does the judgment state that it is up to the professions to decide on the type and degree of self regulation that is aimed at ensuring public interest goals. What *Wouters* does say is that restrictive self regulation may escape the prohibition of Article 81, even if it does not implement sufficiently clearly articulated public-interest goals,[96] provided a court confirms that such regulation does in fact pursue the public interest in the light of the prevailing perceptions in the relevant Member State.

The same conclusion results from a recent judgment[97] of the Belgian Supreme Court that considered the compatibility with the competition rules of a regulation that had been adopted by the Flemish Bar Association and that contained an across the board ban for bar members to engage in multidisciplinary partnerships. The Court, precisely on the basis of the *Wouters* judgment, invalidated the MDP ban promulgated by the Flemish regional bar because it considered that there was no demonstrable rationale for an *indiscriminate* ban. Thus, the Belgian Supreme Court was willing to ascertain which *level* of regulation is in fact required to secure the values referred to in *Wouters* (independence of bar members and prohibition on representing conflicting interests, so as to ensure the sound administration of justice and the protection of consumers of legal services). In other words, it is ultimately the competent court (and not the professional association that is the author of the restrictive regulation) that will determine what the 'public interest' entails and the restrictions that can be considered as justified in the light of the public interest as defined by the court.

---

[95] The same conclusion will apply where the matter is being dealt with by a competition authority. In such a case, it will be for the competent authority to determine the conformity with the public interest of the restrictive arrangement that is at issue.

[96] On the margin of discretion that the Court seems to recognise for the author of the rules at issue, see Section IV, Point 7 below.

[97] Hof van Cassatie, 25 September 2003, *Orde van Vlaamse Balies*, Case No C03.0139.N, discussed by L Gyselen (see above n 65) and J-P de Bandt (see above n 28).

6. Should the Public Interest be defined by Courts Where the Public Authorities Have Abstained from Doing So?

Wouters remains troubling to the extent it suggests that it is ultimate for courts or national competition authorities, on the basis of 'prevailing perceptions' (and it is unclear how the Courts are to identify such perceptions in the absence of a sufficiently clearly articulated public policy), to define what constitutes the public interest, and whether rules adopted by a professional association do in fact pursue that interest. It is open to debate whether national courts will consider themselves sufficiently empowered to make such an assessment in a situation where the public authorities have *abstained* from doing so.[98]

Most observers may believe that *Wouters* was an 'easy' case, since it is unlikely to be disputed that the independence of the legal profession and the prohibition on conflicts of interest is in the public interest (ie, on the ground that it protects consumers of legal services). However, the Court did not (expressly) limit the availability of the '*Wouters* defence' to the legal profession, or indeed to liberal professions. And even if only liberal professions could invoke the defence, not all cases are easy. Consider the claim by an association of pharmacists that a pharmacy should not be operated in large-surface outlets because such outlets compromise the quality of the service to consumers, or the claim of an association of physiotherapists that certain treatments, in order to protect public health, should not be dispensed other than by medical specialists with a specific degree. Such assessments are likely to give rise to disputes: competition authorities and consumer groups might disagree on whether such rules are required to protect consumers. It is hardly surprising that opinions as to what is in the public interest differ. That is why

---

[98] To be sure, courts in applying the EC Treaty rules on the free movement of persons and goods are required to assess whether measures that may restrict such movement are justified on public interest grounds—but the relevant public interest grounds are articulated by the Treaty (eg, the protection of public health) or in the case law of the ECJ (eg, the protection of the environment). Moreover, courts in applying these rules of the Treaty are dealing with State measures, which may be presumed to further the public interest. See, eg, Case 294/00 *Deutsche Paracelsus Schulen/Gräbner* [2002] ECR 6515, where national legislation restricting medical training to certain institutions and prohibiting advertising for such training held to comply with the freedom of establishment because each Member State is at liberty to set in accordance with its understanding of the protection of public health, the appropriate level of protection. Especially the latter principle can hardly be transposed to the competition rules (*inter alia* because the determination of the appropriate level of protection also entails a consideration of the interests of consumers). Conversely, I believe that the Treaty rules on the 'four freedoms' cannot as such be applied to measures that are *not* attributable to the State (ie, to measures that do not and were not supposed to implement a clearly articulated public interest purpose). The Court in *Wouters* does review the compatibility of the MDP Regulation with the freedom to provide services but in doing so appears to make a much more deferential review than it would normally make in connection with State measures.

in a democratic system the public authorities, who are supposed to balance all individual interests in an equal fashion, are to define what constitutes public interest. Leaving such issues to be decided on a case by case basis by a court or by a competition authority is likely to create results that are unpredictable and that may even be considered arbitrary.

The latter point is illustrated by the aforementioned judgment of the Belgian Supreme Court. The Belgian Supreme Court interpreted *Wouters* as enabling a professional association to adopt professional conduct rules provided the restrictions inherent in such rules are proportionate with the purpose they pursue *and which has been imposed by the public authorities*. The reference to *Wouters* as requiring that professional conduct rules pursue a purpose that has been imposed by the public authorities is remarkable since *Wouters* relates precisely to a situation where the public interest has *not* been sufficiently articulated by the public authorities.[99] The Professional Services Report of February 2004 in explaining *Wouters* also refers to a 'specific public interest purpose' (which expression would seem to substitute the reference in the judgment to 'the sound administration of justice').[100]

The problem may be less serious than it seems. First, it should be recalled that the *Wouters* rule will come to apply only in the case of professional conduct rules that pursue public interest goals that have *not* been sufficiently clearly articulated by the public authorities. Thus, there is no reason to apply the *Wouters* rule if and to the extent the public authorities have defined, with sufficient clarity, the essential requirements for access to and exercise of the profession. Second, the burden of proof will rest on the party that asserts the lawfulness of the restrictive regulation; that party will need to demonstrate to the satisfaction of the competent court that the regulation at issue does in fact pursue the public interest in the light of prevailing national conceptions.

---

[99] See above. It is also interesting to recall that the German *Bundesverfassungsgericht* (ruling of 14 July 1987, 1 BvR 537/81, 195/87, BVerfG, vol 76, pp 171 *et seq*) invalidated professional conduct rules prohibiting inter-professional cooperation between bar members, notaries and accountants because it considered that rules adopted by the German bar association must only have 'internal' effects (*ie,* these effects must not go beyond the limits of the profession and must not interfere with fundamental rights, including the freedom to exercise a profession). It is, *inter alia,* on the basis of this judgment that the German legislator has promulgated statutory rules authorising inter-professional co-operation (see §59a of the Bundesrechtsanwaltsordnung, which authorises co-operative relationships between bar members and several other professions, including accountants). Furthermore in a judgment dated 8 April 1998 (1 BvR 1773/96), the *BundesVerfassungsGericht* declared unconstitutional the prohibition of partnerships between bar members who are also notaries and accountants. Such a prohibition cannot, the BverfG stated, be inferred from an interpretation of the applicable professional rules but only from clear (statutory) rules adopted by the public authorities. The German Constitutional Court confirmed the so called 'essential policy reservation' ('Wesentlichkeitsvorbehalt') principle: with respect to the exercise of a profession, the legislator must personally establish the essential policy direction; establishing this direction cannot be left to others (such as, for example, a bar association).

[100] Compare para 75, 1st indent, of the Professional Services Report, with para 97 of *Wouters*.

At the end of the day, *Wouters* may be understood as encouraging public authorities to articulate public interest goals themselves.[101] The Commission's Professional Services Report echoes evolving conceptions as to the benefits that are likely to result from competition in liberal professions, or as to the level of regulation that actually is necessary in respect of certain liberal professions. Such evolving conceptions may in time become 'prevailing conceptions' within the meaning of *Wouters*—and also may lead to the public authorities articulating public interest goals more clearly with respect to any given profession. That would seem to be a solution that is preferable to courts or national competition authorities making such assessments on a case by case basis.

7. Does *Wouters* Create a 'Margin of Discretion' for Liberal Professions In Devising Regulations that Are Said to Serve the 'Public Interest'?

Whilst *Wouters* requires the public interest claims of a profession to be validated by a court (or a competition authority), the judgment would seem to apply a rather deferential test in considering whether the inherent effects of the MDP ban go beyond what is necessary to ensure compliance with the rules of professional conduct.[102] Indeed, the Court observes that the regulation banning MDP's does not fall within Article 81 since 'the Bar of the Netherlands [. . .] could reasonably have considered that that regulation, despite the effects restrictive of competition that are inherent in it, is necessary for the proper practice of the legal profession, as organised in the Member State concerned'.[103] The rationale for this deferential attitude presumably is the Court's intention to leave the bar sufficient room to develop professional conduct rules without being subject to strict judicial scrutiny. Unfortunately, however, the test as expressed in the judgment would seem to be based on circular reasoning. As mentioned already, the *Dutch Bar* had, without the involvement of the public authorities, determined what constitutes the 'proper practice of the legal profession, as organised in the Member State concerned'. Thus, it seemingly did not serve any purpose for the Court to

[101] By way of comparison in (most states of) the United States, rules of professional conduct for lawyers are adopted by the court system, not by the profession itself—the American Bar Association does propose 'model' rules and the state bar associations, on the basis of those rules, make 'recommendations' to the court system. But the power to finally adopt the relevant rules remains with the court system (for example in New York, the Appellate Division of the New York Supreme Court performs this function).

[102] This has also been pointed out in the contributions of Ian Forrester and Mario Siragusa to this volume; see also L Gyselen in *Liber Amicorum Jean-Pierre de Bandt* (cited in above n 65), at p 21.

[103] Para 107 of the judgment.

review whether the Bar's MDP Regulation was more restrictive than necessary to achieve the goals that were set by the Bar itself.

If the *Wouters* test actually is circular, that would mean that the scope for judicial review is non-existent. It is difficult to imagine that such a result was intended by the Court. This issue is likely to resurface in the future since it is central to the *Wouters* doctrine: the exemption from the competition rules is granted precisely to allow for self regulation. Here, too, in the case of a dispute it will be up to the competent court (or competition authority) to define the margin that it believes is necessary for the profession to develop and enforce professional conduct rules. I expect that the width of such a margin will largely depend on the Court's views as to the 'weight' and 'purity' of the professional conduct rules at issue. Rules that are not perceived as genuinely critical to preserving the profession's core values, or that are suspected of (also) pursuing interest of the practitioners (rather than of consumers) are not likely to be treated with great deference.

The *Wouters* judgment, incidentally, does not exempt the Dutch Bar's MDP rule in an unconditional manner. Indeed, the Court points out that the MDP Regulation seeks to ensure that bar members are at all times in a position to advise and represent their clients independently and in the observance of strict professional secrecy, and that those rules of professional conduct would be impaired where bar members 'belonged to an organisation which is also responsible for producing an account of the financial results of the transactions in respect of which their services were called upon and for certifying those accounts'.[104] This paragraph of the judgment indicates that an MDP ban would *not* be justified *vis-à-vis* MDPs that separate 'legal' and 'audit' functions (ie, that do not perform audit functions for clients that are represented by the firm's bar members).[105] Thus, in *Wouters* the Court itself seems to have defined what level of (MDP) regulation is necessary to secure compliance with the principles of independence and professional secrecy. Incidentally, this also demonstrates that *Wouters* has a considerably narrower scope than some liberal professions would like to believe.

Some participants in this Workshop have argued that under *Wouters,* a profession should enjoy sufficient discretion in devising rules of conduct, and that the competition rules do not preclude 'good faith' rules, regardless of the

---

[104] Point 105 of the judgment. The Court's statement is to the effect that in an MDP between bar members and accountants the bar members may need to litigate or counsel on balance sheet items that have been previously been certified by the accountant—and in doing so, they may contradict the accountant's assessment. In other words, the Court suggests that the problem is for the *accountant* and not for the bar member. That raises doubts concerning the Court's reasoning, since it sought to salvage a prohibition imposed by the Dutch National Bar Association—whilst the Dutch accountants' professional association had expressly stated that they did *not* oppose MDPs with bar members.

[105] It would have been interesting to see how the referring court applied the Court's ruling, but the two bar members at issue withdrew their applications before the Dutch Council of State could decide the matter based on the ECJ's guidance.

restrictive effects thereof. I do not share that view. First of all, it would result in all sorts of restrictive practices escaping the competition rules altogether without the consumer interest being taken into account. As reported in some of the other papers submitted to the workshop, economic research suggests that professions tend to impose quality standards that are unnecessarily high.[106] Allowing such standards to be imposed on all professionals may result in consumers having less choice between service providers and paying unnecessarily high prices. In the second place, in the event of a dispute, the burden of proof rests on the profession to demonstrate that the restrictive rules do in fact pursue the public interest, and are necessary to achieve the stated public interest goal. To be sure, *Wouters* suggests that a court may be satisfied if it finds that the profession made a good faith appreciation of the necessity of the rule. But the assessment of the matter by an independent judge (or competition authority) would seem to be crucial in order to ensure that the restrictive rule is in fact required to achieve the public interest. Lest we forget, the public interest consists in the protection of consumers, not of the profession.

Nor do I agree with the proposition that a margin of discretion is necessary to avoid a situation in which liberal professions would be required to constantly apply to the public authorities for approval of their rules of professional conduct, or be continuously subject to litigation in connection with such rules. Once again, the competition rules apply only where professional rules and arrangements entail an appreciable restriction of competition, and even rules and arrangements that create an appreciable restriction will escape the competition rules where they pursue a clearly articulated public interest purpose. Scrutinising professional conduct rules on the basis of the competition rules would not seem to be undesirable where such rules create an appreciable restriction *and* can *not* be said to pursue a public interest purpose that has been clearly articulated by the public authorities. Indeed, in such a case, there would seem to be little reason for an overly deferential attitude by courts and competition authorities—on the contrary, in such a case, claims that restrictive rules are 'necessary in the public interest' probably should be reviewed with some measure of scepticism.

V. Le Nouveau Droit de la Concurrence, Est-Il Arrivé?

The case law discussed in Sections II to IV of this paper makes clear that restrictive rules governing the activities of liberal professions in many instances may escape the applicability of the Treaty's competition rules as a result of action by the public authorities. Public regulation of the profession

---

[106] See, eg, the evidence discussed in the contributions of Frank Stephen and Benito Arruñada for this volume.

at issue may exclude all scope for competition on price and output, which will have the effect of removing that profession entirely from the applicability of the competition rules (*Poucet*). In cases where public regulation leaves some scope for competition, it still remains the case that the competition rules '. . . relate [. . .] only to the conduct of undertakings and do [. . .] not cover measures adopted by Member States by legislation or regulations' (*Meng*). The Court's test to determine whether a measure has been adopted by the public authorities is a formalistic one. In particular, it does not matter that the restrictive public measures have been adopted further to lobbying by a profession, and nor does it matter that the substance of the regulations suggests that the public authorities have yielded to considerations of partiality (*Meng, Arduino*). Except where the public authorities have simply reproduced the elements of a prohibited agreement), the ECJ's case law on Articles 81 and 82 EC simply presumes that public regulation furthers the public interest.

The case law also makes it clear that Article 10 EC does not provide significant 'added value' to Articles 81 and 82 EC. Article 10 EC as interpreted by the Court does not broaden the substantive scope of the competition rules or, stated differently, Article 10 EC does not require State measures to comply with the substance of the competition rules. By and large, Article 10 read in conjunction with Article 81 EC only (a) precludes the Member States from imposing ('simply reproducing') an agreement (and not just its substance) that is prohibited by Article 81 EC (*Meng*) or making such an agreement superfluous by conferring on certain parties the right to 'impose' the restrictions on other market participants (*Leclerc Books*) and (b) prohibits the Member States from delegating to an (association of) undertaking(s) regulatory authority that allows the beneficiary of such delegation to set the parameters of competition (*CNSD/Arduino*). Outside of these limited hypotheses, the ECJ refuses to assess the substantive compatibility of public regulation with the competition rules. Article 10 EC does not prohibit the Member States from adopting measures that are restrictive of competition.[107]

The ECJ has been criticised by more than one learned author[108] for taking a too prudent approach with respect to the applicability of the competition rules to measures that (formally) have been adopted by the public authorities. In my view, the Court's approach is defensible: it is delicate for a court to set aside measures by (or that may properly be ascribed to) the public authorities on the basis that such State measures defeat the useful effect of the competition rules—the idea being that State measures must be presumed to bear out the public interest and that Article 10 EC (by contrast to the Treaty rules on the 'four freedoms') does not provide courts with a mandate to second guess

---

[107] To clarify: I am assuming that the public measures at issue are compatible with the Treaty rules on the 'four freedoms'.

[108] See, eg, N Reich, as cited in above n 34, and B van der Esch, 'Loyauté fédérale et subsidiarité à propos des arrêts du 17 novembre 1993 dans les affaires *Meng*, *Ohra* et *Reiff*', *Cahiers de Droit Europeen* 523 (1994), at p 538.

the State's reasons for imposing measures that have an anti-competitive effect and perhaps even an anti-competitive purpose.

The reverse side of the Court's rather formalistic approach would seem to be that measures that may *not* be attributed to the State must be fully subject to the competition rules, *regardless* of the public interest purpose that they allegedly pursue. And indeed the pre–*Wouters* case law was to the effect that restrictive regulations that have been *adopted by a profession* will be caught by Article 81 EC unless it is demonstrated that such regulations implement (or comply with) sufficiently clearly articulated public policy and where the public authorities have maintained the power to adopt decisions in the last resort. That case law is reproduced in 'part I' of *Wouters* (see above, part IV–1).

Wouters (or at least 'part II' of the judgment) marks an important shift in the law. The ECJ accepted that the restrictive effects inherent in regulations that have been adopted by (associations of) undertakings that may *not* be attributed to the public authorities and that relate to matters for which the public authorities have *not* set a sufficiently clearly articulated public policy, nevertheless may entirely escape the application of the competition rules when such rules are found to pursue the 'public interest'. The *Wouters* exception requires the defendant of the restrictive regulation to demonstrate, to the satisfaction of the competent court or authority, that

- having regard to the 'prevailing perceptions' in the relevant Member State, the regulation aims at securing compliance with the public interest;
- the regulation is (reasonably?) necessary for the attainment of the public interest; and
- the restrictions are 'inherent' in such a regulation.

Wouters stands in a sharp contrast with *National Society of Professional Engineers*: whilst the US Supreme Court firmly rejected the 'public interest' defence invoked by a professional association of engineers as being based on a 'fundamental misunderstanding' of the law, the ECJ upholds such a defence invoked by a professional association of bar members. Nevertheless, *Wouters* in practice does not 'privatise' the public interest concept to the benefit of the professions. Instead, the ECJ shifts the burden to the courts (and the competition authorities) to ascertain whether, 'in the light of prevailing national perceptions', restrictive measures adopted by a profession may be said to pursue (and to be necessary for the attainment of) public interest purposes. It is open to question whether courts and competition authorities will consider themselves sufficiently empowered to engage in such determinations. Just as the ECJ has felt uncomfortable in second-guessing State measures as being inspired by anticompetitive purposes, courts may feel uncomfortable in confirming that non-State measures pursue the public interest in areas where the public interest has *not* been articulated by the public authorities. And even if courts do venture to make such determinations, it seems odd that the public interest should be defined on a case by case basis by individual judges.

The Bar in the *Wouters* case found a rather sympathetic ear with the ECJ. Many judges are former members of the bar, and judges by nature are sensitive to claims that restrictions are necessary to ensure 'the sound administration of justice'. In addition, there may well have existed more than just a temporal coincidence between the Court's consideration of the *Wouters* case and the demise of Arthur Andersen in the wake of the Enron debacle. Is that enough to discount *Wouters* as an example of the old chestnut that 'hard cases make bad law'? Probably not. *Wouters* is clearly perceived by liberal professions (and intended by the ECJ) as a trend-setting judgment. Therefore, it will be necessary to consider its implications outside of the legal profession, and even outside of the liberal professions. Both the Commission and national competition authorities should expect the 'public interest' defence to be raised on a regular basis—and not just by (associations of) liberal professions. Accordingly, sooner or later the ECJ will have to clarify the implications of *Wouters:* whether (and if so, why) only 'liberal' professions can invoke the public interest defence, whether courts and competition authorities as a matter of Community law are under a duty to review public interest defences even in the absence of a definition by the competent national authorities of what constitutes the public interest, and how 'prevailing national perceptions' are to be ascertained with respect to matters where the public authorities have abstained from articulating a clear public policy.

Mr Forrester[109] believes that *Wouters* may well represent an important judicial milestone for the competition lawyer—and I take it that 'milestone' is being used in the sense of a 'signpost'. Mr Forrester suggests that, after *Wouters*, the lawfulness of restrictive measures may henceforth need to be considered on the basis of criteria such as 'reasonableness', 'absence of folly', 'proportionality' and 'efficiency'. If that is the direction we are heading towards, why then has the Commission turned out such a large number of notices that aim at clarifying competition law for judges and practitioners? And what will be the consequences of such an approach in the 'decentralised' system that has now been created by Regulation 1/2003 and that entrusts primary responsibility for the application of the EC competition rules to the courts and competition authorities of the 25 Member States. Are we slated for a '*gouvernement des juges*'? Perhaps it is prudent to hold off on canonising *Wouters* as the new cornerstone of EC competition law until we have had the time to fully consider the ramifications for the law of a consistent application of the judgment. In the meantime, I suggest that we heed the warning of Mr Justice Stevens in National Association of Professional Engineers[110] that 'we may assume that competition is not entirely conducive to ethical behaviour, but that is not a reason [. . .] for doing away with competition'.

---

[109] See his contribution to this volume, in particular Sections VII–IX.

[110] See above.

VI

*Calvin S Goldman, QC and Benjamin R Little**

The Regulated Conduct Defence in Canada

I. Introduction

In a speech at the opening session of the Seoul Competition Forum this past April, Dr Ulf Böge observed that the actions of governments in certain regulatory circumstances may be more detrimental to competition than those of private companies.[1] Dr Böge stated that it is often the case that 'governments themselves [. . .] cause damage to consumers and reduce overall welfare due to distortions and restraints of competition resulting from their laws, regulations or concrete administrative practices.'[2] Dr Böge's comments are of course of central interest to the focus of this conference on the proper relationship between competition law and the liberal professions. His comments also have particular resonance in the Canadian context.

Canada's *Competition Act*[3] (the 'Act') is a (federal) law of general application that hovers over all sectors of the economy. Governments, however, at the federal and provincial level, can pass laws that carve out sectors and shield them from the application of the Act. In so doing, as Dr Böge's comments indicate, those governments have elected, in the exercise of their public interest mandate, to prioritise public interest objectives other than those promoted by competition laws (more efficient markets, lower prices, wider product choice and greater innovation). The central challenge, therefore, in Canada (as elsewhere), with respect to regulation of the liberal professions, is to appropriately balance the public interests protected by competition law against the public interest objectives achieved through regulation. This challenge necessitates establishing the line between the circumstances in which competition law should operate and those circumstances in which it is necessary to carve-out protection for a profession, risking the sort of damage to consumers and overall welfare described in Dr Böge's remarks.

---

* Calvin S Goldman is a partner at Blake, Cassels & Graydon, LLP, Toronto. He is a former Commissioner of the Canadian Competition Bureau and a former Vice-Chair of the OECD Competition Law and Policy Committee. Benjamin R Little [BA (Queen's University), MPhil (Oxford), JD (University of Toronto)] is an associate at Blake, Cassels & Graydon, LLP, Toronto.

[1] See Dr Ulf Böge (2004), speech delivered on the occasion of the Opening Session of *the Seoul Competition Forum 2004*, Seoul, Korea, 20 April 2004. Dr Böge is President of the Bundeskartellamt in Bonn, Germany.

[2] *Ibid*, p 2.

[3] *Competition Act*, RSC 1985, c C–34.

Before proceeding to the focus of this paper—Canada's regulated conduct defence (the 'RCD')—it is useful to describe one excellent Canadian example of a situation where Dr Böge's comments are particularly pertinent. In the late 1980s, as a result of inquiries initiated by the Competition Bureau (the 'Bureau'), then headed by Calvin Goldman, an Order of Prohibition was issued on consent against the Canadian Real Estate Association and nine real estate boards. The subject matter of the inquiry was a range of anti-competitive practices by real estate agents in Canada including the commission fees that Canadians were paying for their homes. The Order specifically prohibited the respondents from engaging in such anti-competitive activities as fixing or controlling commission rates and listing service fees, prohibited restrictions on advertising and incentives, and restricted real estate boards from refusing memberships and listing service access. Given that purchasing a home is the single most important financial event in the lives of most Canadians, the Bureau pressed hard to prioritise competition law over the protection of a particular sector or licensed service. The Order obtained in this case is widely regarded as one of the most comprehensive Orders of Prohibition ever issued by the Canadian courts in a competition law case. If real estate agents had been able to shield themselves in Canada from the application of competition law through a specific carve-out provided by state legislation, then the reduction in consumer welfare discussed by Dr Böge would have persisted unchecked.

II. Overview

This paper provides a brief overview of Canada's RCD.[4] It is intended as a Canadian comparative contribution to the EUI Workshop on competition law and the 'liberal professions'.[5] Canada's experience with the RCD is highly

---

[4] This paper has used the language 'regulated conduct defence' for the primary reason that this is the term most commonly used to describe the principle. It has also been referred to as the 'regulated conduct exemption', the 'regulated conduct doctrine', the 'regulated industries exemption', the 'regulated industries defence', and the 'regulated industries doctrine'. The use of the word 'defence', however, suggests that the RCD is only available as a defence to a charge under the Competition Act, as is discussed further down in this paper it is not clear that this is a correct interpretation of the relevant jurisprudence; rather, it is more of a jurisdictional exception to cases otherwise subject to enforcement under the Act.

[5] The US equivalent of the RCD is the 'state action doctrine'. In *Parker v Brown* 317 US 341 (1943) ('*Parker*'), the US Supreme Court held that the *Sherman Act*, which prohibits combinations or conspiracies in restraint of trade, does not prohibit the States from restricting competition. The Court held that while the federal Sherman Act intended to protect competition, it was not intended to limit the sovereign regulatory power of the States. Since *Parker*, the US Supreme Court has developed the doctrine to apply to situations where States have delegated authority, for example to a municipality or regulatory board. The current two-part test requires that the

germane to the focus of this Workshop. Not only is the RCD the main legal mechanism for resolving conflicts between the activities of regulated 'liberal' professions and Canadian competition law, but some of the key cases on the RCD in Canada have involved the self-governing legal profession. For example, the legal profession, which is regulated in most respects by our provinces, has challenged the authority of the Bureau to apply its law in relation to such areas as advertising (in the *Jabour*[6] case) and professional insurance (in *Re Law Society of Upper Canada and Attorney General of Canada, et al.*[7] (the '*Law Society*' case)). Further, the Bureau has proceeded against county bar associations for cartel-like activities in *Waterloo Law Association v Attorney General of Canada*[8] ('*Waterloo*') and *R v Kent County Law Association, et al.*[9] In addition to the legal profession, there are numerous other examples of the application of the *Act* against professions, including notaries,[10] land

State (1) must clearly articulate and affirmatively express intent to displace federal antitrust scrutiny and (2) must actively supervise the conduct (*California Retail Liquor Dealers Ass'n v Midcal Aluminum Inc* 445 US 97 (1980)) ('*Midcal*'). The States Action doctrine has been applied in many cases involving the liberal professions, including law, accounting, and medicine. In one prominent example, *Goldfarb v State of Virginia* 421 US 773 (1975) ('*Goldfarb*'), the US Supreme Court decided that a fee schedule published by a voluntary County Bar Association constituted unlawful price fixing. The fee schedule contained a list of recommended minimum prices for certain legal services enforced through the threat of disciplinary action by the State Bar. The court noted that, although the ethical codes established by the State mentioned advisory fee schedules, they did not direct the association to supply them or require the type of price floor that arose from the respondents' activities. *Goldfarb* also disallowed the immunity on the basis that the challenged action was not compelled by the State. However, it should be noted that more recent decisions have held that compulsion by the State is not required to invoke the doctrine (*Midcal Town of Hallie v City of Eau Claire* 471 US 34 (1985); and *Southern Motor Carriers Rate Conference Inc v United States* 471 US 34 (1985).

While Canada's RCD and the US States Action doctrine have been developed by the courts in the UK, the comparable law is statutory. The *Competition Act* (UK), 1998, c 41 (the 'UK Act') allows for exemptions for violations of certain offences of the act. Designated professional rules are one such exemption. Part I of Sch 4 (the 'Schedule') to the UK Act stipulates that any regulation, codes of practice or statements of principle fall within the professional rules exemption. In order to qualify for this exemption, professional rules must be designated by the Secretary of State and must fall within a prescribed list of professional services set out in the Schedule. It should be noted that the Office of Fair Trading is presently calling for reform or deletion of this section of the UK Act. Further, the Law Society and the Royal Institute of British Architects are voluntarily revising their professional codes of conduct to bring them into line with the UK Act's objectives.

[6] *Attorney General of Canada v Law Society of British Columbia* [1982] 2 SCR 307.

[7] [1996] 67 CPR (3rd) 48 (Ont Ct Gen Div).

[8] [1986] 58 OR (2nd) 275 (Ont SC).

[9] [1988] 7 LW 738–021 (Ont SC).

[10] The Notaries Association of Rivière-du-Loup pleaded guilty to a charge of price fixing, resulting in a fine of $25,000 and the issue of a prohibition order to prevent the commission of similar new offences (Competition Bureau, News Release, 'Notaries' Association Pleads Guilty to Price Fixing', 26 April 2000).

surveyors,[11] pharmacists,[12] optometrists[13] and, as described above, real estate agents.[14]

The paper continues with three parts. Part III situates the RCD within the relevant Canadian legal framework, and provides a general description of the content of the defence and the foundational cases. Part IV makes the point that despite a lengthy history of relevant jurisprudence, considerable uncertainty remains regarding the scope of the doctrine. This uncertainty has been compounded by a recent Information Bulletin on the Regulated Conduct Defence (the 'Bulletin') released by the Bureau that appears to be inconsistent in certain respects with the case law on the RCD. Part V provides some concluding observations.

III. The Need for and Legal Framework of the RCD

As indicated above, Canada's *Competition Act* is a law of general application. With a limited number of express exceptions,[15] the Act applies to the conduct of all business activity in Canada.[16] These exceptions do not include regulated industries or conduct (including professional associations), in respect of which the Act is virtually silent.[17] The statutory authority of regulators often

[11] The Fédération des arpenteurs-géomètres du Québec (Land Surveyors) pleaded guilty to one count of price maintenance (Competition Bureau, News Release, 'Fédération des arpenteurs-géomètres du Québec fined $50,000 for maintaining fees', 10 March 1997).

[12] The British Columbia Professional Pharmacists Society was convicted of conspiring to fix prices (*Regina v British Columbia Professional Pharmacist's Society and Pharmaceutical Association of the Province of British Columbia* [1970] 64 CPR 129 (BCSC) (QL).

[13] Regulations of the British Columbia Optometric Association prohibiting the location of an optometrist's office in certain locations were upheld by the British Columbia Court of Appeal, reversing a decision of the lower British Columbia Supreme Court. The lower Court found the regulations to be *ultra vires* the statutory authority granted to the Board of Examiners to regulate the profession, as being unreasonable in the restraint of trade, discriminatory and depriving a selected group of practitioners of long-possessed property rights of goodwill. The lower Court held that restrictions regarding non-affiliation with others engaged in selling optical services were unobjectionable as they were directed at the unprofessional practice of steering. The Court of Appeal held that the regulation was within the power of the defendant to enact as it was 'concerning the practice of optometry'. In the absence of evidence that it was passed capriciously or in bad faith, the test that the Court had to apply was not whether the regulation was reasonable, but whether it was unreasonable. While the regulation, as all regulations, was in restraint of trade and discriminatory, *it did not fail on those accounts as there was not the additional ingredient of unreasonableness* (Columbia, 1984) 57 BCLR 153 (SC) (WL), rev'd [1985] BCJ No 1672 (CA) (QL)).

[14] See the discussion of this matter in the introduction of this paper. See also, Consumer and Corporate Affairs Canada, News Release, NR–10164, 'Real Estate inquiry resolved by Order of Prohibition', 20 December 1988.

[15] For example, amateur sport, collective bargaining and securities underwriting.

[16] The Act contains both criminal and civil ('reviewable matters') offences.

[17] Reference to regulated industries or conduct in the Act is limited to Ss 125 and 126 which permit the Commissioner of Competition to appear before a regulatory board or tribunal to make representations in respect of competition.

includes powers that may significantly alter the normal forces of competition (for example, setting prices, fees, charges, and output for the regulated product or service). It is therefore not surprising that courts have been called on to address situations where conduct generally prohibited by the Act is mandated or authorized by a regulatory body. The RCD provides a mechanism to resolve these conflicts.

The RCD is a common law doctrine that provides the basis for an exemption from or defence to the application of the Act where the impugned conduct is required or, arguably, authorized pursuant to valid legislation or regulation. In the *Jabour* case, the Supreme Court of Canada identified the principles underlying the application of the RCD: 'When a federal statute can be properly interpreted so as not to interfere with a provincial statute, such an interpretation is to be applied in preference to another applicable construction which would bring about a conflict between the two statutes.'[18]

The Supreme Court very recently cited and endorsed this principle in *Garland v Consumers' Gas Co.*[19] ('*Garland*').

The framework of the RCD was developed in relation to the criminal law sections of the Act's predecessor legislation (the *Combines Investigations Act*). The key cases in this framework are the 'trilogy' of *Reference Re: The Farm Products Marketing Act*[20] ('*Farm Products*'), *R v Can. Breweries Ltd*[21] ('*Canadian Breweries*') and *Jabour*. It seems likely that the Supreme Court's decision in *Garland* will join their ranks.

In *Farm Products*, the Supreme Court considered whether the price-fixing activities of a marketing agency, constituted under valid provincial Ontario legislation, contravened the criminal provisions of the *Combines Investigation Act* (the predecessor to the present *Competition Act*) by unduly restricting competition. The Court found that the activities in question did not contravene that Act and established the following principles:

- Any scheme that is within the authority of the provincial legislature cannot be against the public interest when the legislature is seized of the power and obligation to take care of that interest in the province.[22]
- The Act only prevented voluntary agreements made against the public interest; where there is a legislated obligation to act, as opposed to an element of voluntariness, the doctrine applied and there would be no grounds for a criminal prosecution.

[18] Above n 6 at para 91.
[19] [2004] SCC 25.
[20] [1957] 1 SCR 198.
[21] [1960] OR 601.
[22] This is often referred to as the 'public interest' argument and stands for the proposition that the regulated conduct defence will apply where the regulation under review has been validly enacted.

- Competition legislation does not *prima facie* apply to marketing schemes that the legislature has exempted from the scope of anti-monopoly legislation. This means that an activity specifically regulated by valid legislation will fall outside the provisions of competition legislation and potentially benefit from protection under the regulated conduct defence.

The *Canadian Breweries* case has often been cited as the leading elaboration of the basic nature of the RCD. *Canadian Breweries* involved a prosecution under the *Combines Investigation Act* against Canadian Breweries *Ltd* for having been a party to a 'combine' by participating in a series of mergers in the brewing industry. The Crown alleged that the merger operated to the detriment of the public interest by lessening price competition.[23] The defendants successfully claimed that provincial regulation of the sale of beer had displaced price competition. The case stands for the proposition that where provincial legislation has conferred on a commission or board the power to regulate an industry and fix prices, and that power has been exercised by the authorized body, the Court must assume that the power is exercised in the public interest. *Canadian Breweries* also established that the RCD only applies to activities specifically subject to regulation and does not apply to activities falling outside the regulatory scheme.[24]

The third case in the 'trilogy', *Jabour*, represents the first application of the RCD to the legal profession, and therefore is of central interest to this paper. *Jabour* resulted from a Law Society of British Columbia (which governs lawyers in the Province of BC) challenge to an inquiry by the Director of Investigation and Research (the 'Director', now the 'Commissioner') into the Society's disciplinary proceedings against a lawyer who had advertised his fee schedule in contravention of the Code of Professional Conduct promulgated by the Benchers of the Law Society. In a unanimous decision, the Supreme Court held that the Law Society of British Columbia's general mandate to set standards of proper conduct gave it sufficient authority to prohibit BC lawyers from advertising their services. The Court reasoned that the conspiracy provisions of the *Combines Investigation Act* were directed at conduct that unduly lessened competition, and that compliance with valid provincial legislation (which must be presumed to be in the public interest) cannot be

---

[23] Note that this was a criminal prosecution; mergers now are governed by the civil (reviewable practices provisions of the Act).

[24] This principle was reinforced in *Industrial Milk Producers Association v BC Milk Board* [1988] 47 DLR (4th) 710 where Reed J of the Federal Court of Canada stated at p 726:

> It is not the various industries as a whole which are exempt from the application of the *Competition Act*, but merely activities which are required or authorized by the federal or provincial legislation as the case may be. If individuals involved in the regulation of a market situation use their statutory authority as a springboard (or disguise) to engage in anti-competitive practices beyond what is authorized by the relevant statutes, than such individuals will be in breach of the *Competition Act*.

said to be 'undue' and therefore illegal.[25] The Court also reasoned that the conspiracy offence contemplated voluntary agreements or combinations, and that the Law Society could not be said to be voluntarily agreeing when discharging responsibilities assigned to them by statute.

The most recent addition to the RCD jurisprudence is the Supreme Court's decision in *Garland.* Although the full implications of this decision are still being considered, the decision appears to narrow the availability of the RCD.

In *Garland*, the respondent gas utility had imposed a late payment penalty that was found to violate the usury provisions of the *Criminal Code.*[26] The Court held that the RCD did not shield a provincially regulated gas utility from criminal liability. The Court further held that in order for the RCD to be available, Parliament must indicate, either expressly or by necessary implication, that the usury provisions of the *Criminal Code* 'granted leeway' to those acting pursuant to a valid provincial regulatory scheme. The Court stated that Parliament must 'unequivocally express' its intention to shield regulated conduct from a criminal provision. More specifically, the Court observed that 'in the previous cases involving the regulated industries defence, the language of "public interest" and "unduly" limiting competition has always been present', and the absence of such recognition of the 'public interest' in the usury provision of the *Criminal Code* 'precludes the application of' the RCD.

Essentially, the decision appears to stand for the proposition that the RCD does not apply unless the criminal provision specifically contemplates that the party may use the RCD. Given that previous RCD cases deemed validly enacted provincial legislation to be in the public interest and therefore sufficient to invoke the defence, the holding in Garland appears to represent a shift in Canadian law. The Supreme Court in *Garland* specifically rejected the argument that an act authorized by a valid provincial regulatory scheme cannot be contrary to the public interest.

From a practical perspective, in terms of the liberal professions, the vast majority of cases have involved the conspiracy provisions of the Act (or its predecessor legislation) which involve an 'undueness/public interest' test that *Garland* indicates is sufficient to demonstrate Parliament's intention to allow the RCD.[27]

The cases discussed above provide some idea of the legal underpinnings of the RCD in Canada. There are some excellent, more detailed, discussions of

---

25 The word 'unduly' remains in the conspiracy provisions in S 45 of the modern Act.

26 *Criminal Code*, RSC 1985, c C–34.

27 One issue that the *Garland* decision appears to raise is whether the RCD would be unavailable to those accused under the *per se* offence criminal provisions of the Act (for example, price maintenance), or any of the other provisions of the Act, which do not contain express language evidencing such an intention. Further, there is a current proposed amendment to the Act that would split the conspiracy offence into a *per se* offence for 'egregious' hard-core conspiracy behaviour and a lesser offence that would likely include the public interest/undue wording. If this amendment proceeds, the *Garland* decision appears to indicate that the RCD may not be available to parties accused of the *per se* offence.

the case law on the RCD available for interested readers.[28] For the purposes of this brief paper, however, a key point to note is that the jurisprudence remains unsettled on many of the key aspects of the RCD. The following section identifies some of these unresolved issues, and critically assesses the Competition Bureau's recent attempt (pre-*Garland*) to clarify the content and scope of the RCD.

IV. Unresolved Questions

A partial list of some of the key unsettled questions regarding the content and scope of application of the RCD includes:

- What extent of regulation is required to trigger the application of the RCD?
- Given that the legal framework of the RCD was developed in relation to criminal matters, does the RCD apply to the civil (reviewable matters) provisions of the Act?
- Does the RCD apply differently to 'regulators' and 'regulated'?
- How does the RCD apply to self-governing regulators of the sort often found in the liberal professions?
- Is the RCD a defence to a charge already brought or an exemption from the application of the Act to be considered at the outset of any proceeding under the Act?

In an effort to clarify some of these issues, on 17 December 2002, the Competition Bureau released an 'Information Bulletin on the Regulated Conduct Defence' (the 'Bulletin'). The stated purpose of the Bulletin is to 'outline and clarify the Bureau's position with regard to the jurisprudence on [the] regulated conduct defence.' Unfortunately, the Bulletin falls short of its purpose.[29] Perplexingly, the Bulletin does not even refer to the 'jurisprudence' that it purports to clarify.[30] Further, as described below, the Bureau adopts a

[28] For a more fulsome discussion, see CS Goldman and J Bodrug, *Competition Law of Canada* (New York, NY, Juris Publishing, 2004) at ch 11.

[29] There was no opportunity for public comment on the Bulletin (as has been the Bureau's general approach in recent years on similar matters).

[30] As the National Competition Law Section of the Canadian Bar Association put it in its October 2003 Submission to the Competition Bureau Information Bulletin on the Regulated Conduct Defence:

> [. . .] the RCD Bulletin does not cite a single case or attempt to reconcile the Bureau's enforcement approach with the case law establishing the RCD In this sense, the RCD Bulletin not only fails to state the law. If effectively ignores the body of cases that form the very basis of the RCD This is of considerable concern, since practical opportunities to obtain judicial clarification on the scope and content of the RCD (or judicial vindication of a broader view of the doctrine) are relatively rare.

very narrow view of the application of the RCD that, according to some commentators, is 'not well supported by the jurisprudence.'[31]

> First, the Bulletin asserts that the RCD only applies to a regulated firm in situations where the regulateds' conduct is *mandated or required* by the regulator and that conduct is contrary to the *Act*.

It is doubtful that this is an accurate summary of the jurisprudence on the extent or nature of regulation required to trigger the application of the RCD. As discussed above, in *Jabour*, the Supreme Court held that the Law Society of British Columbia's broad regulatory mandate to set standards of proper conduct gave it sufficient authority to prohibit advertising without attracting liability under the *Act*. This decision appeared to contrast with the decisions in *Farm Products* and *Canadian Breweries*, which exempted activities that had been *specifically authorized* under provincial legislation (ie, the fixing of prices and/or reducing output). According to some interpretations, *Jabour* extended the scope of the RCD to activities broadly or generally authorized, as opposed to specifically authorized.

However, it remains unclear how far *Jabour* has actually extended the doctrine. Some observers point to the unique facts of that case, which were detailed at some length in the Court's decision.[32] Further, subsequent cases appear to have narrowly applied the decision in *Jabour*. In *Industrial Milk Producers Association, et al v Milk Board et. al.*[33] ('*Industrial Milk*') for example, the Federal Court implied that absent *explicit authority* for a provincial marketing board to fix quotas, the RCD would not apply. The decision in *Jabour* might also be distinguished from cases involving conduct arising from a voluntary agreement among members of a regulated industry. *Waterloo*, another landmark liberal profession decision in the RCD jurisprudence, best illustrates this distinction.

Waterloo involved an application by the members of a county law association whose fee-setting activities were being investigated under the conspiracy provisions of the Act for a declaration that the provisions of the Act did not apply to their activities because they were governed by the Law Society of Upper Canada.[34] In dismissing the application, the Ontario Supreme Court

---

[31] See B Zalmanowitz, 'Competition Bureau Releases Information Bulletin on the Regulated Conduct Defence' (2003) 21 *Canadian Competition Record* 39.

[32] These unique facts include the nature of legal services, the fiduciary position of solicitors, the status of members of the bar as officers of the courts, and the responsibility to protect the general public placed on the Benchers by the provincial legislature.

[33] [1988] 47 DLR (4th) 710 (FCTD).

[34] In *Waterloo*, it was admitted that the Executive of the Association had met to discuss a proposed fee schedule and sanctions that could be used against members to enforce it. After the new schedule was adopted, the Executive indicated to members that non-adherence to the schedule would be regarded as a breach of accepted ethical and professional standards. At a subsequent Association meeting, a great majority of lawyers practising real estate law in the area unanimously ratified the schedule. The Ontario Supreme Court issued an order of prohibition against

distinguished the case from *Jabour* on the basis that the Law Society in *Jabour* was a provincially authorized regulatory body discharging its responsibilities pursuant to its constitutive statute as opposed to a voluntary body with no regulatory authority in *Waterloo*. In the Court's view, the county law association was simply a group of individual lawyers who were members of a Law Society but acted together through an association. The Court also pointed to the fact that the BC *Law Society Act* empowers the Benchers to broadly define conduct unbecoming a member as conduct which it deems to be contrary to the best interest of the public or of the legal profession—the Ontario *Law Society Act* contains no similar provision. Finally, the Court seemed to narrow the highly deferential approach to the necessary extent of authorization in *Jabour* by recognizing that it may be sufficient if impugned activities are 'merely authorized, and not actually required.'[35]

A similar approach to *Waterloo* was adopted in *R v Independent Order of Foresters.*[36] In that case, Mr Justice Grange, speaking for the Ontario Court of Appeal, cited *Waterloo* favourably, and clearly expressed the view that a direction or at least an authorization to perform the prohibited act was necessary to invoke the RCD. Most recently, in the *Law Society* case, the Ontario Court (General Division) stated that 'the regulated conduct defence will apply to individuals and companies which are subject to regulation, and to regulatory agencies themselves, provided the impugned conduct is *mandated, required or authorized* by validly enacted legislation'[37] (emphasis added).

The case of *Mortimer v Corp. of Land Surveyors (British Columbia)*[38] ('*Mortimer*') is another important decision relevant to the question of the required extent or nature of regulation. *Mortimer* indicates that the courts may narrowly construe the scope of regulatory statutes in order to give greater recognition to competition policy objectives, even in regard to professions regulated to protect the public interest. This case involved an appeal by a land surveyor who had been found by the Board of Management of the Corporation to have failed to observe the tariff of fees for professional services then in effect. While the *Land Surveyors Act* empowered the Corporation to pass bylaws, 'not inconsistent with the Act, with regard to the tariff of fees for professional services',[39] the by-law in question required mem-

---

the Waterloo Law Association (and another against the Kent County Law Association, which had proceeded in a similar manner) under s 30(2) of the Act [now s 34(2)] prohibiting the Association, amongst other things, from continuing to fix fees in connection with legal services and from promulgating any schedule of fees for legal services for a period of ten years. The Association admitted on the record of the proceedings that the tariffs were designed to prevent widespread discounting by some members. The record also indicated that there would be disciplinary sanctions against members who charged lower fees than those stipulated in the schedule.

[35] *Waterloo*, above n 8, p 282.

[36] [1989] 26 CPR 229 (Ont CA).

[37] Above n 7, p 54.

[38] [1989] 35 BCLR (2nd) 394 (SC) (QL).

[39] *Ibid*, para 6.

bers to observe the standards set out in a booklet containing tariffs or fees for professional services. In allowing the appeal, and quashing the conviction, the Court held that the *Land Surveyors Act* was insufficiently clear to allow the imposition of a mandatory minimum tariff of fees, which was the practical effect of the by-law. As the Court commented:

> There is much to be gained in giving professional bodies the power to regulate themselves. I do wonder, though, if the common good is served by providing to a professional body (monopolistic in nature) through legislative authority and without limitations, the power to engage in activities which would be illegal if carried out by anyone else. Surely in these circumstances, a strict construction of the legislation is a reasonable approach.[40]

The Court held that in order to set a minimum fee tariff the legislation would have had to make specific provision for a 'minimum fee tariff'.

In *Mortimer*, the Court dismissed the notion that set minimum fees are required to regulate the profession and protect the public from poor quality work. The court stated that: 'One can reasonably expect professionals persons, having legislative approval to govern themselves, when discharging their professional duties to act professionally. This must include, almost by definition, a refusal to do cut-rate work for cut-rate prices'.[41] The court further elaborated that the concept of a single rate for all professionals in a member body is 'is simply not reasonable'[42] given that the work is so varied not only as to its complexity, but also as to the time required to complete it.

It seems clear, therefore, that the courts have sought to narrow the expansive approach in *Jabour* regarding the extent of regulatory oversight required to trigger the RCD. However, it is similarly apparent that the Bulletin's limitation of the application of the RCD to conduct 'mandated or required' is an excessively narrow approach unsupported by the jurisprudence which, at a minimum, supports the extension of the RCD to 'authorized' conduct. The proper debate, it is suggested, is over the *extent* of authorization required.[43]

---

[40] *Ibid*, para 20.
[41] *Ibid*, para 24.
[42] *Ibid*, para 22.
[43] The US Supreme Court has also considered the extent of authorization required to demonstrate the intent to limit competition in regulated conduct type cases. Generally the US approach is broader than the Canadian approach. The general principle is that 'the federal antitrust laws do not forbid the States to adopt policies that permit, but do not compel, anti-competitive conduct' (*Southern Motor Carriers Rate Conference Inc v United States* 471 US 34 (1985) 64). On the other hand, the court has also held that a very general grant of power is not sufficient (*Communications Co v City of Boulder* 455 US 40 (1982)). In terms of the extent of supervision required, US case law indicates that this decision hinges on whether the relevant entity is public or private. In one leading case the US Supreme Court held that action by a municipality did not require state supervision of its activity because the public nature of the entity resulted in a minimal danger that the municipality was not acting pursuant to a clearly articulated state policy (*Town of Hallie v City of Eau Claire* 471 US 34, (1985) 40). In cases where state supervision is required it has been held that to meet the supervision requirement the State must exercise 'independent judgement and control' over the activity in question. (*FTC v Ticor Title Ins Co* 504 US 621 (1992) 634).

> Second, it is the Bureau's position that the regulated conduct defence applies only where there is a *clear operational conflict* between the regulatory regime in question and the *Act*, meaning that obedience to the regulatory regime requires contravention of the *Act*.

Commentators have noted, however, that nowhere in the jurisprudence on the RCD has the judiciary ever required an operational conflict between the Act (or its predecessors) and the regulatory legislation as a condition for application of the RCD.[44] Rather, as described above, the RCD is a principle of statutory interpretation pursuant to which the Act is read down so that it does not apply to conduct that is the subject of provincial regulation in order to *avoid* conflicts. Further, in other recent Bureau statements on the scope of the RCD, there has been no reference to the need for a prior 'operational conflict' before the application of the RCD. For example, in 1996, the Director of Investigation and Research described the RCD in the following way:

> A determination in any specific case of whether the regulated conduct defence might be available involves consideration of a number of factors, including the following: (i) whether the relevant legislation is validly enacted; (ii) whether the activity in question falls within the scope of the relevant legislation and has been specifically authorized; (iii) whether the authority of the public body has been exercised; and (iv) whether the activity or conduct in question has frustrated the exercise of regulatory authority by the public body.[45]

It is important to note that the Bulletin expressly states that it supersedes any and all prior statements by the Bureau respecting the scope of the RCD. This would, of course, include the above summary.

> Third, according to the Bulletin, the regulated conduct defence applies not only to the criminal provisions of the *Competition Act*, but also to the reviewable practices and merger provisions.[46]

---

[44] T Kennish and J Bolton, 'The Regulated Conduct Defence: Time for Legislative Action' (2003) 21 *Canadian Competition Record* 52.

[45] Submission of the Director of Investigation and Research, Competition Bureau, to Canada Post Corporation Mandate Review Committee (15 February 1996), p 59.

[46] Arguments were made recently regarding the applicability of the regulated conduct defence to mergers in the recent Astral acquisition of certain radio assets from Telemedia in 2002. The transaction was subject to regulatory approval by the industry regulator, and was approved, by the Canadian Radio and Telecommunications Commission ("CRTC"), in accordance with its enabling legislation. The Commissioner filed an application to block the merger under the merger provisions of the Act. The parties to the merger argued in Federal Court that the CRTC had exclusive jurisdiction to rule on the transaction and relied, in part, on the RCD, arguing that since the CRTC approved the merger, the conduct had been 'required or authorized' by statute or by a statutory body validly exercising its authority. The Bureau took a narrow view of the defence before the Court. Unfortunately (in terms of developing the RCD jurisprudence) the issue was resolved between the parties before the Court had an opportunity to render a decision and a consent agreement was registered. For an analysis of the Astral/Telemedia case, see DJ Brown, 'The Competition Bureau's Information Bulletin on the Regulated Conduct Defence: Observations from the *Astral/Telemedia* Case' (2003) 21 *Canadian Competition Record* 43.

The issue of the application of the RCD to the civil provisions of the Act has long been debated, and the Bureau's clear statement on this may be viewed as a welcome development. However, the Bureau's position raises as many questions as it resolves.

Most importantly, it is unclear whether the jurisprudence on the RCD supports the Bureau's position. This doubt stems from the fact that the bulk of the jurisprudence on the RCD has developed in the context of criminal cases, and, as indicated above, early application of the doctrine turned on the criminal nature of the alleged offences.[47] By contrast, the *Law Society* case is widely cited in support of the proposition that the regulated conduct defence is available where the conduct at issue is a reviewable practice. In that case, the Law Society of Upper Canada successfully invoked the RCD in seeking a declaration that the Act did not apply to the Law Society in the operation of its mandatory insurance scheme. The complaint against the Law Society alleged that the insurance scheme contravened three 'civil' provisions in the Act: abuse of dominant position, tied selling and exclusive dealing. It should be noted, however, that in the *Law Society* case the Director conceded for the purposes of that proceeding that the RCD exempts a regulator from the application of the civil provisions of the Act (where the conduct at issue was authorized by valid provincial legislation) and, as a consequence, the Court did not examine the scope of the defence or the case history in any great detail. Further, in subsequent remarks, the Director stated '. . . there is no jurisprudence whatsoever on whether the defence applies to the civil provisions [. . . and . . .] the full application of the defence to these provisions remains to be determined.'[48]

While there is limited case law supporting the proposition that the RCD extends to reviewable practices, there are strong arguments supporting this interpretation. First, although the individual civil provisions of the Act do not contain any 'public interest' requirements, the same public interest concerns underlie the Act's civil and criminal provisions. Indeed, as some observers have noted, the premise underlying the Act is that the public

---

[47] In *Farm Products*, for example, as described above, the Supreme Court ruled that any scheme which is otherwise within the authority of the provincial legislature cannot be against the public interest when the legislature is seized of the power and the obligation to take care of that interest. One component of the criminal offence had been that such actions be contrary to the public interest; accordingly, acting pursuant to the provincial statute could not have resulted in a contravention of the relevant competition laws. Following another line of reasoning, Justice Rand concluded that price-fixing activities undertaken by a marketing board could not be criminal offences because the *Combines Investigation Act* prohibited only voluntary combinations or agreements against the public interest. Absent any voluntariness, there was no basis for prosecution under the *Combines Investigations Act*.

[48] See 'Notes for a presentation on behalf of the Director of Investigation and Research to the Manitoba Public Utilities Board re: Review of Natural Gas Supply Procurement, Transportation and Storage Functions of Centra Gas Manitoba Inc. and Review of Guidelines for Acceptable Conduct Between Centra Gas Manitoba Inc. and Affiliated Companies' (9 July 1996) 4.

interest is best served when markets are competitive.[49] Second, certain conduct that was criminal under the Act (or its predecessor) is now civilly reviewable or, in some, cases, 'dual-track' (meaning that the Commissioner can elect to pursue the matter under either criminal or civil provisions—for example, in the area of misleading advertising). Third, from a practical perspective, it has been observed that:

> [i]f the conduct is authorized or endorsed by the state then one would think that the Canadian equivalent of the state action doctrine would protect the person obeying the state sanctioned action from any civil suit. Indeed it would be a brave lawyer who would advise a client to obey a provincial or federal regulator if the result was to the contrary[50]

—that is, if the 'result' still lead to a civil suit. Finally, the fact that both the Competition Law Section of the Canadian Bar Association ('CBA') and the Bureau now support this position indicates that there is now a broad consensus on this question.[51]

However, despite the concession made by the Bureau on the theoretical applicability of the RCD to civil matters, some commentators (including the CBA) have expressed concern over the circumstances in which parties could actually successfully invoke the RCD in the civil context. This concern relates to the Bureau's assertion in the Bulletin that the RCD only applies to situations where there is a 'clear operational conflict' between regulatory legislation and the Act and where conduct is mandated or required (and not simply authorized, as had been contemplated by previous case law). The difficulties with such limits are obvious since, for example, it is difficult to conceive of a 'mandated or required' merger case with a 'clear operational conflict'—such a scenario would require that a regulator mandate or compel a merger otherwise prohibited under the Act. On the other hand, there may be more applicability to abuse of dominance cases as there was in the *Law Society* case, again, especially in relation to state-authorized activities by a dominant entity otherwise regulated by state law.

---

[49] See the Preamble Section 1.1 of the Act; *Director of Investment and Research v Laidlaw Waste Systems Ltd* [1992] 40 CPR (3rd) 282 (Comp Trib) 332; *Alex Couture Inc v Attorney-General of Canada* [1991] 38 CPR (3rd) 292 (Que CA) and House of Commons Debates, First Session, Thirty-Third Parliament, Volume VIII, at 11927–11929.

[50] W Grover and D Kidd, 'Regulated Conduct/State Action', paper presented at the Canadian Bar Association 1995 Annual Competition Law Conference, Toronto, September 1995 (2005).

[51] The National Competition Law Section of the Canadian Bar Association endorsed the position in its October 2003 'Submissions on the Competition Bureau Information Bulletin on the Regulated Conduct Defence'. In those same submissions, the CBA Section stated that it, in fact, considered the issue to have been settled ever since the *Law Society* case despite the fact that that case contains no explicit statement to that effect.

> Fourth, the Bureau draws a distinction between self-governing regulators (for example, many of the liberal professions) and regulators of public institutions (such as marketing boards). In the Bureau's view, 'the activities of self-regulators may be subject to greater scrutiny as to whether the agency is acting within its scope of authority due to the [. . .] concern that they may be regulating in their own interest.'

The Bureau's distinction is novel. It is also difficult to reconcile with the Supreme Court's decision in *Jabour* where the Court exercised considerable deference to the Law Society of British Columbia (although, as described above, the Supreme Court in *Jabour* went to great lengths to identify unique aspects of that case). According to some observers:

> the Supreme Court's message in *Jabour* was clearly that the Commissioner has no authority to question a legislature's determination that self-regulation is the most appropriate means to serve the public interest, and indeed no jurisdiction to enforce the Act in the context of conduct mandated, required or authorized by the self-regulatory body.[52]

The same conclusions can be readily derived from the *Law Society* case, above.

> Fifth, the Bulletin suggests that the scope of the RCD is more limited for regulateds (persons subject to the regulatory regime) than regulators (persons charged with implementing the regulatory regime).

The Commissioner's view, expressed in the Bulletin and in the Commissioner's submissions in *Astral/Telemedia,*[53] is that, for regulateds, the RCD operates only as a defence to a criminal charge in respect of conduct that is compelled (but not authorized). Again, the issue is of fundamental importance—if the RCD operates as a defence, it can only be raised after a charge; however, if it operates to exempt conduct from the Act, the Commissioner's jurisdiction to proceed may be challenged at the outset. One observer has noted:

> While it is arguably true that the treatment of regulators in the jurisprudence has been more favourable than that of regulateds, this would seem to owe more to the origin of the RCD in cases dealing with regulators and the paucity of case law dealing with regulateds. No RCD case to date has expressly recognized such a distinction, including *Jabour* from which the modern conception of the RCD as applying to conduct that is required or authorized derives.[54]

Apart from the cases referred to in the discussion under the 'Fourth' issue above, the jurisprudence provides little support for any further distinction in

---

[52] National Competition Law Section of the Canadian Bar Association, 'Submissions on the Competition Bureau Information Bulletin on the Regulated Conduct Defence' October 2003, at 8–9.

[53] Refer to above n 45.

[54] J Brown, 'The Competition Bureau's Information Bulletin on the Regulated Conduct Defence: Observations from the Astral/Telemedia Case' (2003) 21 *Canadian Competition Record* 43, 47.

the treatment of regulators and regulateds. Recent cases also cast considerable doubt on the proposition that the RCD only applies as a defence to a criminal charge. For example, in *Waterloo*, the Court recognized that while

> the 'regulated industries' exemption to the combines legislation has been traditionally dealt with as a 'defence' to a charge [. . .] that is not to say that a case might not be clear enough in its factual context to justify a decision on a constitutional basis that a person sought to be made subject to the federal combines jurisdiction is not constitutionally subject to that jurisdiction.

In other words, in a 'clear case' a charge may not be jurisdictionally supportable and therefore challenged well ahead of trial.

The *Law Society* case, discussed above, is also a key case on the issue of whether the RCD operates as a defence or exemption. In that case, the Law Society, upon hearing from the Department of Justice that the Director intended to proceed with his (already extensive) inquiry and seek a court order to compel the production of information, filed an application seeking a declaration that the Act did not apply to it or its Benchers in the operation of its mandatory insurance program. The Director argued that the application was premature. The Law Society argued that where the issue is whether the Director has jurisdiction to continue his inquiry, an application to contest his jurisdiction can never be premature. More specifically, the Law Society argued that once the Director had made preliminary inquiries to satisfy himself that the Law Society was acting pursuant to validly enacted legislation, the inquiry should be terminated. The Court agreed with the Law Society.[55]

In *Director of Investigation and Research v Tele-Direct (Publications) Inc,*[56] ('*Teledirect*') a similar jurisdictional issue arose before the Competition Tribunal. The key point from that matter for the purposes of this discussion is the Tribunal's statement that:

> . . . this is not a case where the alleged lack of jurisdiction can be said to be readily apparent. Rather it is one where connected and overlapping jurisdictions are alleged to exist and where dividing lines will ultimately have to be drawn by reference to Parliament's intent in enacting the competing statutes, and the relevant facts. Whether this should be done in the context of a preliminary hearing is not for me to decide.[57]

Commentators have observed that ask a matter of practice the decision in *Teledirect* indicates that the RCD may provide an exemption to a charge under the Act:

---

[55] If it is determined that the Act does not apply to a party, then, obviously, RCD arguments are not necessary. It is only where it is determined that the Act does apply that RCD issues will arise.

[56] [1995] 59 CPR (3rd) 398 (Comp Trib).

[57] *Ibid,* p 400.

> It may be that the characterization of the regulated conduct doctrine as an exemption or defence is largely theoretical and that the real issue is whether there are material facts in dispute which require a full hearing before the court or tribunal will be in a position to determine whether the regulated conduct doctrine is applicable.[58]

It is therefore clear that the Bureau's distinction between the proper deference to be accorded regulateds (vs regulators), as well as the unqualified statement that the RCD operates only as a defence, are both without sufficient support in the relevant jurisprudence.

V. Conclusion

As the discussion in this paper illustrates, Canada has had a long history of cases involving the proper relationship between competition law and various professions. Remarkably, however, there still remain significant unresolved questions in the jurisprudence regarding the scope and applicability of the RCD. This, it is suggested, reflects the difficulty involved in balancing the public interests promoted and protected by competition law against the public interest objectives achieved through regulation. As the theme of this Workshop demonstrates, these important issues are now being examined in fora such as this one. Through the exchange of doctrinal and case experiences in various jurisdictions, we may all benefit in meeting the enforcement challenges in this particular area of competition policy.

[58] Above n 27, at 11–31.

VII

*Luc Gyselen**

Anti-competitive State Action in the Area of Liberal Professions: An EU/US Comparative Law Perspective

I. Introduction

Originally, the term 'liberal' was an epithet of those arts or sciences that were 'worthy of a free man'.[1] In this original meaning, it fully applies to the liberal professions. However, the term 'liberal' also means 'free from restraint'. In that sense, the epithet is a bit of a misnomer when applied to the liberal professions. These professions are often regulated, either by the members of the professional groups themselves (self-regulation), by the state authorities (public regulation) or by a mix of self-regulation and public regulation. One way or another, regulation means: managed competition. This is where competition law kicks in.

In 2002, the European Commission ordered a study into the regulations applicable to liberal professions and made no secret about its expectations:

> ideally, the results of the study would help the Commission to benchmark Member States according to the 'quality' of their regulations in this area, and provide sufficient economic evidence to at least suggest that some liberalisation, yet to be determined, would be beneficial to the whole European economy and in particular to consumers.[2]

In 2003, the study was published.[3]

In its 2004 Communication on Competition in the Professional Services, the Commission reported that the study had met its expectations. The conclusion of the Report was that 'more freedom in the professions would allow

---

* The author wrote a first draft of this contribution while being Head of Unit at the European Commission's Directorate General for Competition (DG COMP). On 1 July 2004 he left DG COMP to become a partner at the Brussels office of Arnold & Porter LLP He is indebted to his former colleagues Philippo Amato, Sandra De Waele and Ruth Paserman for providing him with relevant background material, and to Robert Weiner from Arnold & Porter's DC office, for drawing his attention to some recent US case law on the so-called 'dormant commerce clause'. The final text of this contribution was completed on 21 August, 2004.

[1] See the Shorter Oxford English Dictionary on historic principles, 3rd edn, (Oxford, Clarendon Press, 1988).

[2] See European Commission, *32nd Annual Report on Competition Policy* (2002), para 206.

[3] See 'Economic impact of regulation in the field of liberal professions in different Member States', report available at http://europa.eu.int/comm/competition/publications/prof_services/executive_en.pdf.

more overall wealth creation' and that 'a significant body of empirical research shows the negative effects that excessive regulation may have for consumers'.[4] The Commission announced that it would therefore 'like to see [the regulatory] restrictions reviewed and, where they are not objectively justified, removed or replaced by less restrictive rules' (emphasis added).[5] On balance, the Commission's policy line is a moderate one: total de-regulation may not be required to enhance consumer welfare; some form of less restrictive re-regulation may suffice.

In its 2004 Report, the Commission also remains soft-spoken with regard to law enforcement. It 'believes that the best way to achieve overall change would be voluntary action of those responsible for setting the existing restrictions' and it invites the regulatory authorities of the Member States and the relevant professional bodies to 'consider whether the existing restrictions pursue a clearly articulated and legitimate public interest objective, whether they are necessary to achieve that objective and whether there are no less restrictive means to achieve this'.[6] Strict enforcement of EC competition law whereby these regulatory authorities and professional bodies would find themselves on the receiving end, does not appear to be a priority. As far as self-regulation is concerned, the Commission will only carry out case work 'where appropriate' and give the lead to national competition authorities and courts whenever the restrictions have—as is often the case—their 'centre of gravity in a Member State'.[7] In the case of public regulation, the Commission's law enforcement will also be low-key: only 'at a later stage, if necessary, the Commission does not exclude infringement procedures'.[8]

The present contribution will focus on the liability of Member State authorities under EU competition law when they enact and enforce anti-competitive public regulations concerning liberal professions (state liability). Building on existing case law outside the area of liberal professions, the European Court of Justice (hereafter the Court) has addressed this state liability issue only twice so far. In *Commission v Italy* (hereafter *CNSD*), it confirms the Commission's view that the Italian regulatory authorities are liable for their role in a price fixing agreement among customs agents.[9] In the

---

[4] COM (2004) 83 final in particular paras 16 and 23. See also Commissioner Monti's speech on 'Competition in professional services: new light and new challenges', given before the *Bundesanwaltskammer* in Berlin, March 2003: 'In countries with low degrees of regulation, there are relatively lower revenues per professional but a proportionately higher number of practising professionals generating a relatively higher overall turnover' and 'this would suggest that low regulation is not a hindrance but rather a spur to overall wealth creation'.

[5] *Ibid*, para 90.

[6] *Ibid*, paras 92–94. See also Commissioner Monti's speech 'Proactive competition policy and the role of the consumer' for the European Competition day in Dublin on 29 April 2004.

[7] *Ibid*, para 100.

[8] *Ibid*, para 102.

[9] Case C–3596 *Commission v Italy* [1998] ECR I–3851. For reference purposes, hereafter *CNSD* (the acronym of the association whose price fixing arrangement was subject of a prohibition Decision pursuant to Art 81 EC (see *below* n 11).

preliminary ruling case *Arduino*,[10] the Court concludes that these state authorities are not liable for their role in collusive price fixing amongst attorneys.

References to the Court's case law concerning the liability of private undertakings (especially *Wouters*)[11] or concerning the impact of state regulations on the liability of private undertakings (*Ladbroke–Fiammiferi*)[12] will be made only in so far as that case law can enlighten our analysis of the state liability issue.

In the present contribution, references will be made to the US 'state action' doctrine. In our view, this comparative law perspective will provide useful guidance for a clarification of the EU case law.

We will first provide the constitutional context for the comparison between EU and US law. This will tell us something about the model of federalism on either side of the ocean. In the US, one is—on balance—more relaxed about state sovereignty than in the EU (below part II). We will then run through the EU state action cases, including those concerning the liberal professions, (below part III) and—in considerably less detail—through the leading US cases (below part IV). Finally, we will explain that some convergence between the two bodies of case law is beginning to emerge, subject to some further clarification of the EU case law (below part V). We will end with a summary of the main 'theses' advanced in the present contribution.

---

[10] Case C–35/99 *Arduino* [2002] ECR I–1529. A follow-up case is currently pending before the Court (see Case C–94/04 *Cipolla v Fazari*, request for preliminary ruling, pending at the time of writing).

[11] In its preliminary ruling of 19 February 2002, (Case C–309/99 *Wouters, Savelbergh, Price Waterhouse Belastingsadviseurs NV and Algemene Raad van de Nederlandse Orde van Advocaten* [2002] ECR I–1577), the Court concluded that Art 81(1) EC did not apply to a ban on multidisciplinary partnerships between attorneys and accountants active in the Netherlands. It does therefore not have to address the issue whether the Dutch public authorities are liable for their involvement (see para 118).

The remaining case law concerning the liability of private undertakings stems essentially from three Commission decisions: a) Decision of 30 January 1993, *CNSD* (Italian customs agents), OJ L 203 [1993] (prohibition of price fixing, upheld by the Court of First Instance in Case T–513/93 *CNSD v Commission* [2000] ECR II–1807) Decision of 30 January 1995, *COAPI* (patent agents in Spain) OJ L 122 [1995] (also prohibition of price fixing, not challenged) and c) Decision of 7 April 1999, *IMA* (international patent agents) OJ L 106 [1999] (negative clearance for a ban on misleading advertising and short exemption for a disproportionate ban on comparative advertising, upheld by the Court of First Instance in *IMA v Commission*, Case T–144/99 [2001] ECR II–1087).

On 24 June 2004, the Commission adopted a fourth decision prohibiting a price fixing arrangement among Belgian architects (not yet reported, see press release IP/04/800).

[12] See Joined Cases C–359/95 P and C–379/95 *P Commission v Ladbroke Racing Ltd* [1997] ECR I–6265 (in particular para 33) and Case C–198/01 *Consorzio Industrie Fiammiferi (CIF) v Autorità Garante della Concurrenza e del Mercato* [2004] ECR I–8055 (in particular paras 47–51).

II. The Origin of the EU and US State Action Doctrines

1. State Liability in the EU

In the preliminary ruling case *GB-INNO-BM*, the Court established the principle that Member States can, in principle, be liable for anti-competitive measures that run against the spirit of Article 81/Article 82 EC.[13]

At stake was a Belgian state measure which put in place a resale price maintenance (RPM) scheme for cigarettes produced in or imported into Belgium. The end price to consumers had to correspond exactly to the amount appearing on the tax labels affixed to the cigarette packages and bought in advance by the manufacturer or importer. The prohibition of a higher price aimed at preventing manufacturers and importers from undervaluing their products at the time of paying the taxes whereas the prohibition of a lower price aimed at preventing the retail selling structure from becoming too concentrated to the disadvantage of small retailers.[14]

The national court had two questions for the Court. First, it wondered whether the state measure was lawful in light of two provisions featuring in the EC Treaty's chapter on 'Principles'. It referred to Article 3(1)(g) EC, according to which the main activities of the Community include 'a system ensuring that competition in the internal market is not distorted' (emphasis added) and to Article 10(2) EC, pursuant to which Member States 'shall abstain from any measure which could jeopardise the attainment of the objectives of the Treaty' (emphasis added). Did a state measure violate these Treaty provisions, read in combination with Article 82 EC, if it was of such a nature as to encourage private undertakings (*in casu*, the tobacco manufacturers and importers) to abuse their dominant position? Second, the national court asked whether any abusive company behaviour remained unlawful under Article 82 EC even if it was encouraged by such a state measure.[15]

The Court answers the second question in the affirmative.[16] As to the first question, it is more cautious. It invites the national court to examine whether the state measure is 'likely to affect trade between the Member States'.

---

[13] *Case 13(77 GB-INNO-BM v ATAB* [1997] ECR 2115. Throughout the present contribution we will refer to the relevant EC Treaty articles by using the current numbering, not the numbering valid prior to the adoption of a consolidated version of the EC Treaty in 2001.

[14] *Ibid*, paras 17–18.

[15] In its second question, the national court even assumed that the state measure itself could not be prohibited by Art 3(1)(g) EC and Art 10(2) EC.

[16] Cited above, n 13, at para 34: 'At all events, [Art 82 EC] prohibits any abuse by one or more undertakings of a dominant position, even if such abuse is encouraged by a national legislative provision'.

However, the Court's judgment contains an observation that sows the seeds of a state action liability doctrine: 'while it is true that [Article 82] is directed at undertakings, nonetheless it is also true that the Treaty imposes a duty on Member States not to adopt or maintain in force any measure which could deprive that provision of its effectiveness' (emphasis added).[17] In the same breath, the Court states in more general terms that 'Member States may not enact measures enabling private undertakings to escape from the constraints imposed by [Article 81 to Article 89] of the Treaty' (emphasis added).[18]

What is the constitutional basis for this emerging state liability doctrine? The Court's reasoning goes roughly like this. In its opening statement, the Court observes that 'the single market system which the Treaty seeks to create, excludes any national system of regulation hindering directly or indirectly, actually or potentially, trade within the Community' (emphasis added).[19] It then recalls 'the general objective set out in Article 3(1)(g) EC' which is to preserve a system of undistorted competition. This objective 'is made specific in several Treaty provisions concerning the rules on competition, including [Article 82 EC]'.[20] The Court finally quotes Article 10(2) EC, according to which Member States must not adopt measures 'which could jeopardise the attainment of the objectives of the Treaty' (emphasis added).[21] Hence, Member States must refrain from enacting measures which 'could deprive [Article 82 EC] of its effectiveness'.[22]

The Court's reasoning is concise. However, since the starting point of its reasoning is the 'single market system', the Court appears to rely essentially on the complementarity between the EC Treaty's 'market integration' and 'undistorted competition' objectives. More specifically, it sees the Treaty's provisions pertaining to 'competition' as levers for market integration. Hence, it views anti-competitive state measures as—in principle—unlawful obstacles to such integration.

Everyone who is even remotely familiar with EU law knows that this is not the first time that the Court has established a link between 'undistorted competition' and 'market integration'. It suffices to recall its case law on vertical territorial restraints under Article 81 EC ever since *Grundig Consten*.[23] Nor is it the last time, as is illustrated by its case law from the early nineties which revitalised Article 86 EC (after thirty years of almost dormant existence) as a basis for de-monopolising regulated sectors such as telecommunications and

---

17 *Ibid*, para 31.
18 *Ibid*, para 33.
19 *Ibid*, para 28.
20 *Ibid*, para 29.
21 *Ibid*, para 30.
22 *Ibid*, para 31. The Court then also draws an analogy with Art 86(1) EC, which prohibits state measures 'contrary *inter alia* to the rules provided in Art 81 to 89 EC (see para 32).
23 Joined Cases 56 and 58/64 *Consten v Commission* [1966] ECR 449.

energy.[24] However, in *GB-INNO-BM* the Court makes an unprecedented leap. Whereas there are explicit Treaty provisions in the chapter on 'competition' that prevent companies from agreeing on territorial restraints (Article 81(1)(c) EC) and prevent state authorities from creating monopolies (Article 86 EC), there is no provision banning anti-competitive state measures other than state aids.[25]

The unprecedented nature of *GB-INNO-BM* is further illustrated by a comparison between the constitutional status of these anti-competitive state measures and that of state measures which restrict the free movement of goods, persons, services or capital within the Community (the so-called 'four freedoms'). Let us take the latter measures first. Article 3(1)(c) EC provides that the activities of the Community shall include 'an internal market characterised by the abolition, as between Member States, of obstacles to the free movement of goods, persons, services and capital' (emphasis added). This provision is implemented in a series of specific Treaty provisions which explicitly prohibit the Member States from impeding the free flow of goods, persons, services or capital within the Community. These provisions (Article 28, Article 39 and 43, Article 49, Article 56 EC) are known as 'negative integration' instruments because they seek to achieve market integration by prohibiting the state measures that impede this integration.[26] Anti-competitive state measures have a different status. Article 3(1)(g) EC merely provides that the activities of the Community shall also include 'a system ensuring that competition in the internal market is not distorted'. It does not provide for the abolition of all anti-competitive state measures, even if they jeopardise 'the single market system', to use the *GB-INNO-BM* formula. Nor are there any 'negative integration' provisions in the EC Treaty that explicitly prohibit such measures across the board.

Given the prominent reference to 'the single market system' in its judgment and the presence of EC Treaty provisions explicitly prohibiting state measures which interfere with market integration, either directly (free movement: Article 28, Article 39 and 43, Article 49, Article 56 EC) or indirectly (competition: Article 86), the *GB-INNO-BM* Court seems to have had a constitutional lacuna in mind. It must have taken the view that state measures which

---

[24] Case C–202/88 *France v Commission* [1991] ECR I–1259 and Case C–18/88 *RTT v GB-INNO-BM* [1991] ECR I–5941. It will be recalled that Art 86 EC (at the time Art 90 EEC) was initially—ie in the draft EEC Treaty—part of Art 31 EC (at the time Art 37 EEC) which deals with state import/export monopolies and belongs to the Chapter of provisions prohibiting restrictions of the free movement of goods.

[25] Admittedly, we are stretching it a little bit. Back in the mid-sixties, the Court did have to settle the controversy about the applicability of Art 81 EC to vertical restraints. Nor was it clear from the text of Art 86(1) EC (at that time Art 90(1) EEC) that it banned state measures granting exclusive rights.

[26] Separate 'positive integration' provisions (Arts 94 and 95 EC) provide a legal basis enabling the Community legislator to achieve market integration by 'approximating' such measures, ie, by substituting a harmonised regulatory regime for them.

interfere with the system of undistorted competition within the meaning of Article 3(1)(g) EC can be just as pernicious for the single market system and—hence—that there must be a basis in the EC Treaty for challenging these measures. According to the Court, Article 3(1)(g) EC, read in combination with Article 10(2) EC, provides this basis.[27]

In essence, according to the Court, there is an implied constitutional limitation on anti-competitive state measures that supplements the EC Treaty's 'negative integration' provisions which impose express constitutional limitations on state measures restricting the free movement of goods, persons, services and capital or which create specific distortions of competition (eg, legal monopolies). States are therefore—in principle—liable for adopting anti-competitive measures.

2. State Immunity in the US

The picture concerning the US is different. In contrast with the EC Treaty, the US Constitution does not contain any 'negative integration' provisions. Nor does it contain provisions specifically pertaining to competition (let alone provisions concerning competition that could be compared with 'negative integration' provisions). In our view, this explains to a large extent the basic premise underpinning the US Supreme Court's 'state action' doctrine, ie, that anti-competitive state measures are—in principle—immune from the application of the federal antitrust laws, even if they frustrate the latter's objectives (or—to use the European Court's jargon—even if they deprive these laws of their effectiveness).

In *Parker v Brown*, the Court explains: 'We find nothing in the language of the Sherman Act or in its history which suggests that its purpose was to restrain a state or its officers or agents from activities directed by its legislature' (emphasis added). That being so, 'in a dual system of government in which, under the Constitution, the states are sovereign, save only as Congress may constitutionally subtract from their authority, an unexpressed purpose

[27] It is true that the Court does not see much of a lacuna in the case at hand. Thus it observes that '*in any case*, a national measure which has the effect of facilitating the abuse of a dominant position capable of affecting trade between Member States will generally be incompatible with Articles [28 to 31] which prohibit quantitative restrictions on imports and exports and all measures having equivalent effect' (see para 35; emphasis added). It also invites the national court to check whether the state measure at stake '*as such* is capable of affecting trade between the Member States' within the meaning of Art 82 EC (para 38; emphasis added) and whether it is '*in itself* likely to hinder (. . .) imports between Member States' within the meaning of Art 28 EC (para 56; emphasis added). In other words, the Court is not convinced that the state measure falls under either chapter of Community law at all. However, it is not unusual for the Court to introduce legal concepts with potentially sweeping consequences in cases where these concepts do not have an impact on the outcome.

to nullify a state's control over its officers and agents is not lightly to be attributed to Congress' (emphasis added).[28]

The Court makes two points. First, it is congressional intent that matters ('purpose'). Second, without an express intent of Congress to prohibit states from enacting anti-competitive measures, these measures are outside the reach of the federal antitrust laws ('unexpressed purpose').

For a proper understanding of these statements in their constitutional context, one must start with the so-called 'Commerce Clause' set out in Article I, Section 8 of the US Constitution. This clause grants Congress the power to 'regulate commerce (. . .) among the several states (. . .)'. It only contains an affirmative grant to Congress of (federal) power to regulate interstate commerce.[29] In EU jargon, the Commerce Clause is a 'positive integration' provision. It does not impose explicit limitations upon the individual states' power to regulate interstate commerce. Nor does any other provision in the US Constitution contain such a limitation. In EU jargon: the US Constitution contains no 'negative integration' provisions that explicitly prohibit states from interfering with market integration within the United States. This does not mean that the individual states face no limitations of their power to regulate interstate commerce. Such limitations can arise in two specific situations.

First, state action that conflicts with valid federal legislation is pre-empted. In other words, when Congress makes use of its federal power to regulate interstate commerce and a state enacts a measure that conflicts with the federal measure, the state measure will be set aside. This follows from the Supremacy Clause set forth in Article VI of the US Constitution according to which 'This Constitution, and the Laws of the United States which shall be made in Pursuance thereof, (. . .) shall be the supreme Law of the Land'.

In *Parker v Brown*, the Supreme Court found no federal pre-emption in the case at hand because it found no trace in the language or in the history of the Sherman Act that Congress has intended to restrain the states from controlling its officers and agents, even if the latter's action restricted competition. Quite to the contrary, the Supreme Court pointed out that the California state law was indeed in line with federal policy.[30]

Second, in the absence of federal legislation, state measures may violate the so-called 'dormant' or 'negative' Commerce Clause. This is the Supreme Court's judicial creation. Typically, state measures which discriminate against out-of-state goods or services and thereby impose burdens upon inter-

---

[28] *Parker v Brown* 317 US 341(1943).

[29] The broad boundaries of the federal power to regulate commerce are set out in the Tenth Amendment to the US Constitution: 'the powers not delegated to the United States by the Constitution, nor prohibited by it to the States, are reserved to the States respectively, or to the people'.

[30] In particular, Congress had authorised the Secretary of Agriculture to establish or fund similar state-directed stabilisation programs for a series of agricultural commodities.

state commerce that are incommensurate with putative local state gains will be held unconstitutional.[31]

It follows that there is a major difference between the US Constitution and the EC Treaty. The Commerce Clause in the US Constitution is geared towards 'positive integration' since it contains an affirmative grant to the federal Congress of the power to regulate interstate commerce. It has nothing in common with the set of 'negative integration' provisions in the EC Treaty which explicitly prohibit—in principle—all state measures that interfere with the four freedoms and thereby impede market integration. The US Supreme Court has to some extent closed the gap by introducing and developing the 'dormant' Commerce Clause doctrine. However, in contrast with the abundant EU case law on free movement of goods, persons, services and capital, this 'sister' doctrine has no basis in the text of the US Constitution and its application often gives rise to intense debate among the Supreme Court's Justices.[32]

In our view, the specific 'positive integration' rationale behind the Commerce Clause and the absence of 'negative integration' provisions in the US Constitution explain why anti-competitive state action in the US enjoys—in principle—immunity from the application of the federal antitrust laws.

III. EU State Action Doctrine

1. The Two-Pronged Liability Standard as Restated in *van Eycke*: an In-Built Inconsistency

11 years after GB-INNO-BM, the Court retained a two-pronged liability standard for anti-competitive state action in *van Eycke*: a Member State would deprive Article 81 EC of its effectiveness if it were 'to require or favour the adoption of agreements, decisions or concerted practices contrary to Article 81 or to reinforce their effects, or to deprive its own legislation of its official character by delegating to private traders responsibility for taking decisions affecting the economic sphere'.[33]

The second limb of this liability standard ('delegate to private traders the responsibility for taking decisions affecting the economic sphere') finds its

[31] See the US Supreme Court's judgment in *Camps Newfound/Owatonna v Town of Harrison* 520 US 564 (1998) concerning a state property tax law containing an exemption for property owned by charitable institutions but excluding from this exemption organisations operated principally for the benefit of non-residents.

[32] See, eg, Justices Scalia and Thomas' dissenting opinions in the case mentioned in the note above.

[33] Case 267/86 *Van Eycke v ASPA* [1988] ECR 4769, para 16.

origin in the early (vertical) resale price maintenance cases *GB-INNO-BM* (1977), *van de Haar* (1984), *Leclerc/Au Blé Vert* (1985) and *Cullet/Leclerc* (1985) where there was no evidence of an agreement, decision or concerted practice falling within the scope of Article 81(1) EC. The first limb ('require or favour the adoption of agreements . . . contrary to Article 81 or to reinforce the effects thereof') originated in the subsequent (horizontal) price-fixing cases *Asjes* (1986), VVR (1987) and *BNIC/Aubert* (1987) which clearly involve an anti-competitive agreement or decision within the meaning of Article 81(1) EC.[34]

In our view, the recent case law, in particular the judgments concerning the liberal professions (*CNSD* and *Arduino*), has evolved towards a single liability standard that focuses on the 'delegation' limb of the van Eycke standard. However, for a proper understanding of *CNSD* and *Arduino* (as we read it), it is useful to revisit the cases up to, and including, *van Eycke*.

1.1 State Deprives Its Own Legislation of Its Official Character by Delegating to Private Traders Responsibility for Taking Decisions Affecting the Economic Sphere

The resale price maintenance (RPM) cases all have in common that one formal condition for the application of Article 81(1) EC is not fulfilled: there is no agreement between the retailers and the suppliers of cigarettes (*GB-INNO-BM* and *van de Haar*), books (*Leclerc*) or fuel (*Cullet*). In each case, the state measure imposes upon the retailers the obligation to charge an end price to consumers unilaterally fixed by the suppliers. In *van Eycke* terms, these suppliers are 'private traders' to which the state authorities have delegated the 'responsibility for taking decisions affecting the economic sphere'.

In *GB-INNO-BM*, the Court observes that states 'may not enact measures enabling private undertakings to escape from the constraints imposed by [Article 81 to 89] EC' (emphasis added). This suggests that the issue is the circumvention of the EC Treaty's competition provisions. The facts in *GB-INNO-BM* seem to confirm this. The Belgian legislator had adopted the decree imposing RPM for cigarettes following a proposal from a member of the House of Representatives who was secretary of the national wholesalers' federation. For many years, this federation and the manufacturers' organisation (Fedetab) had endeavoured to make all retailers enter into RPM agreements. The decree now saved them the trouble of having to enter into such agreements. As a consequence, they could 'escape from the constraints

[34] See above n 13. See also Joined Cases 177–178/82 *van de Haa* [1984] ECR 1797; Case 229/83 *Leclerc v Au Blé Vert* [1985] ECR 1; judgment of 29 January 1985, Case 231/83 *Cullet v Leclerc* ECR 305; Joined Cases 209 to 213/84 *Asjes ('Nouvelles Frontières')* [1986] ECR 1425; Case 311/85 *Vereniging van Vlaamse Reisbureaus (VVR) v Sociale Dienst* [1987] ECR 3801; Case 136/86 *Bureau National Interprofessionnel du Cognac (BNIC) v Aubert* [1987] ECR 4789.

imposed' by Article 81 EC.[35] Surprisingly, the national court only refers to Article 82 EC in its request for a preliminary ruling.

The facts in *van de Haar* are identical to those in *GB-INNO-BM*. This time the Dutch court does raise the Article 81 EC issue and the Court peddles back from its *GB-INNO-BM* statement:

> whilst it is true that Member States may not enact measures enabling private undertakings to escape from the constraints imposed by Article [81] EC, the provisions of that Article belong to the rules on competition 'applying to undertakings' and are thus intended to govern the conduct of private undertakings in the common market (and) are therefore not relevant to the question whether legislation such as that involved in the cases before the national court is compatible with Community law.[36]

Less than a year later, however, the Court brings back to the forefront the circumvention issue as identified in *GB-INNO-BM*. Acknowledging that the French decree imposing RPM for books does not require the conclusion of agreements within the meaning of Article 81(1) EC, the Court asks itself in *Leclerc*

> whether national legislation which renders corporate behaviour of the type prohibited by Article [81(1)] superfluous, by making the book publisher or importer responsible for freely fixing binding retail prices, detracts from the effectiveness of Article [81] and is therefore contrary to the second para. of Article [10(2)] of the Treaty (emphasis added).[37]

The Court does not take it any further. It refers to the Commission's lack of substantive policy guidance in this field to conclude that—until further notice—Member States can enact legislation that eliminates retail price competition for books.[38]

A few weeks later, in *Cullet*, the Court discards the applicability of Article 10(2) and Article 81 EC in favour of another French decree imposing RPM for fuel because the state authorities have themselves fixed the end price: 'rules such as those concerned in this case are not intended to compel suppliers and retailers to conclude agreements or to take any other action of the kind referred to in article [81(1)] EC' but rather 'entrust responsibility for fixing prices to the public authorities'.[39]

In *van Eycke*, the Court comes to a similar conclusion with regard to a Belgian decree that grants holders of certain saving accounts an exemption from revenue tax, provided their banks comply with a maximum credit

---

35 Cited above, n 13, pp 2120–21.

36 Cited above, n 34, para 24. This is almost the reverse formulation of the statement in *GB-INNO-BM* quoted above, para 12 ('while it is true that [Art 82 EC] is directed at undertakings, nonetheless it is also true that the Treaty imposes a duty on Member States not to adopt or maintain in force any measure which could deprive that provision of its effectiveness').

37 Above n 34, para 15.

38 *Ibid*, paras 18–20.

39 *Ibid*, paras 26–27.

interest rate (comprising a basic rate and a fidelity premium) set by the Minister of Finance. According to the Court, it is indeed 'apparent from the legislation in question that the authorities reserved for themselves the power to fix the maximum rates of interest on savings deposits and did not delegate that responsibility to any private trader'.[40]

What is ultimately the rationale behind this 'responsibility' limb of the liability standard as summarised in *van Eycke*?

The wording in *GB-INNO-BM* ('measures enabling private undertakings to escape from the constraints imposed by [Article 81 to 89 EC]') and even more so in *Leclerc* ('legislation which renders corporate behaviour of the type prohibited by Article [81(1) EC] superfluous') suggests that the Court objects to anti-competitive state measures when they enable private undertakings to circumvent the scope of Article 81(1) EC.

However, *Cullet* and *van Eycke* prove that this is not the decisive criterion for distinguishing lawful from unlawful state measures. Indeed, if the state authority assumes full responsibility for the restriction of competition, the sweeping *GB-INNO-BM* statements about the need to preserve 'the single market system', including 'a system ensuring that competition in the internal market is not distorted' (Article 3(1) g EC), and about the Member States' duty to 'abstain from any measure which could jeopardise the attainment of the objectives of the Treaty' (Article 10(2) EC) become entirely irrelevant. It follows that Member States can lawfully place private undertakings outside the reach of Article 81 EC, provided they do not associate these undertakings in the legislative or regulatory process.

One final comment at this stage. The Court uses a very crude tool for checking whether or not the state assumes full responsibility. If the state itself puts in place the restriction of competition, its measure is ipso facto safe (*Cullet* and *van Eycke*), even if the state does not monitor compliance.[41] In contrast, if the state delegates to the undertakings the power to put in place the restriction, it cannot be excluded that it deprives Article 81 of its effectiveness (*Leclerc*), even if it monitors compliance with the restriction. Without further refinement, the delegation criterion for distinguishing lawful from unlawful state measures is arbitrary: the nature of the product in one sector (eg, gasoline) may give the state authorities an option (eg, to set the price themselves) which they do not have for other products (eg, books).[42]

---

[40] Above n 33, para 19.

[41] We do not suggest that the public authorities did not monitor compliance with the price restrictions at stake. We only point out that the Court did not specify that monitoring *ex post* was a relevant factor for assessing whether or not the government assumed full responsibility. Perhaps the Court took such monitoring for granted.

[42] See L Gyselen, 'State Action and the Effectiveness of the EEC Treaty's Competition Provisions' (1989) 26 *Common Market L Rev* 33, 44.

1.2 State Requires or Favours the Adoption of Agreements, Decisions or Concerted Practices Contrary to Article 81 or Reinforces Their Effects

The horizontal price fixing cases preceding *van Eycke* differ from the vertical RPM cases because the presence of an agreement or decision within the meaning of Article 81(1) EC was undisputed. The tariffs bilaterally agreed upon between airlines in *Asjes*, the ban on discounts featuring in the ethical code of travel agents in VVR as well as the production quota agreed among cognac producers and retailers in BNIC were all held to infringe Article 81(1) EC (in spite of the state intervention to which we now turn).[43]

In each of these cases, the state intervention was held to infringe Article 3(1)(g) EC, read in combination with Article 10(2) and Article 81 EC, because it reinforced the effects of the agreement or decision held to be unlawful under Article 81 EC. In *van Eycke*, the Court concluded—subject to the national court's review—that the Minister of Finance did not reinforce the effects of a pre-existing price cartel among banks when he set maximum levels for the basic interest rate and the fidelity premium. The Court distinguishes the case from VVR. Yes, banks had agreed on a maximum fidelity premium shortly before the Minister fixed a maximum for that premium as well as for the basic rate. However, a state reinforces the effects of a pre-existing agreement 'only if it incorporates either wholly or in part the terms of [these] agreements'.[44] In the case at hand, it was not apparent that the Minister had 'merely confirmed the method of restricting the yield on deposits and the level of maximum interest rates adopted under pre-existing agreements'.[45]

How do state measures which reinforce the effects of restrictive agreements deprive Article 81 EC of its 'effectiveness' (to use the *GB-INNO-BM* term of art)?

Perhaps the Court takes the view that such measures send the wrong signal to the participants in these agreements by giving them the impression that their behaviour is lawful. This impression in turn may make them less aware of the constraints imposed upon them by Article 81 EC. If a state authority rubber-stamps a tariff agreement between airlines (*Asjes*), codifies the travel agents' ban on discounts (*VVR*) or extends a quota agreement between producers and retailers to the entire sector (*BNIC*), it indeed seems to blur the perception of the undertakings involved as to what is objectively lawful and what is not under Article 81 EC. The fact that Article 81 EC itself continues

---

[43] In *GB-INNO-BM* terms, the state measures did not enable these undertakings to 'escape from the constraints' imposed by Art 81 EC Incidentally, the Court had already condemned the BNIC arrangement in a separate case: see Case 123/83 *BNIC v Clair* [1985] ECR 391, paras 20 and 23.

[44] Above n 33, para 18.

[45] *Ibid.*

to apply and—hence—that the undertakings will—in the end—not escape from the constraints imposed by it, does not matter.

If the above explanation is correct, one could argue that there is some sort of complementarity between the two limbs of the liability standard as restated in *van Eycke*: state authorities are liable, on the one hand, when they delegate to private undertakings the power to restrict competition in such a way that they escape from the constraints of Article 81 EC (objective element) and, on the other hand, when they codify restrictive agreements between such undertakings and thereby cast doubt in their minds as to whether they escape from these constraints (subjective element).

However, this attempt to find internal consistency in the liability standard is not convincing. In fact, the two limbs of this standard contradict each other: state measures which require the adoption of restrictive agreements or reinforce the effects thereof (first limb) fall within the reach of the EC competition provisions even if the public authorities do not deprive their measure of its official character because they retain full responsibility for the restriction of competition (second limb). Consider, for instance, the public authorities' decision in *VVR* to codify—and thereby reinforce the effects of—the travel agents' pre-existing ban on discounts in a Royal Decree.[46] There is little doubt that through this codification, the public authorities assumed full responsibility for the restriction of competition at stake. In *van Eycke*, the first case in which the Court cumulatively applies the two limbs of the liability standard, the contradiction would have surfaced had the Court not concluded that the facts were distinguishable from those in VVR (see paragraph 43 above). This distinction enabled it to conclude that the effects of the pre-existing price cartel among banks had not been reinforced by the Minister's measure.

2. The Two-Pronged Liability Standard as Applied Since *van Eycke*: Towards a Single Standard

After *van Eycke*, the Court initially continued to cumulatively apply the two limbs of the liability standard. In *Meng*[47] and *OHRA*,[48] the inconsistency between the two limbs does not surface—as in *van Eycke*, but for a different reason: there was no evidence of any agreements within the meaning of Article 81 EC. In *Reiff*,[49] the Court eventually comes to the same conclusion.

In the two subsequent 'liberal profession' cases, *CNSD* and *Arduino*, the existence of agreements within the meaning of Article 81 EC was undisputed

[46] For a development of this argument, see my contribution cited above, n 42, pp 47–48.
[47] Case C–2/91 *Meng* [1993] ECR I–5751.
[48] Case C–245/91 *OHRA Schadeverzekeringen* [1993] ECR I–5851.
[49] Case C–185/91 *Reiff* [1993] ECR I–5801.

in light Asjes.[50] In our view, the Court here clearly stated that what ultimately matters is whether or not the state authorities assume full responsibility for the restriction of competition.

2.1 The Two Prongs of the Liability Standard Cumulatively Applied in Meng, OHRA *and* Reiff

The two insurance cases, *Meng* and *OHRA*, are only worth a brief mention. In both cases, the state measures prohibit the grant of discounts or other special advantages to clients. According to the Court, the prohibitions are 'self-contained' (*Meng*) or 'self-sufficient' (*OHRA*), as they are unrelated to any agreement involving the undertakings and do not involve any delegation of regulatory power to them. Under either limb of the liability standard, it is therefore clear that the state authorities assumed full responsibility for the restriction of competition. Article 3(1)(g) EC, read in combination with Article 10(2) and Article 81 EC, is therefore inapplicable.

The *Reiff* case is more interesting. The Court has a more careful look at the facts before concluding that—here too—the state authorities assumed full responsibility for the restriction of competition.

In Germany, carriers of goods by road have a statutory duty to charge minimum tariffs for their services. A board of experts must submit tariff proposals to the Minister of Transport for his approval. In formulating these proposals, the board must take into account a variety of conflicting interests, namely those of farmers, small and medium sized undertakings, and regions which are economically weak or have inadequate transport facilities. The board must also consult a committee representing clients. The board members discharge their duties in an honorary capacity; they receive no instructions from the road transport companies that have suggested their names to the Minister. The Minister of Transport himself or his representative can attend the board meetings. The Minister either approves the board's tariff proposals or fixes the tariffs himself if the public interest so requires. In both cases, he must act in agreement with the Minister of Economic Affairs. A federal office for long-distance carriage of goods by road monitors compliance with the approved tariffs.

One immediately senses from this brief summary of facts that the state authorities were pursuing a clear public policy of restricting price competition in this sector, that they were actively involved in the tariff setting process and that they monitored compliance with the policy. Whatever restriction of competition was put in place state authorities assumed full responsibility.

In our view, this is exactly what the Court concludes. However, tied to the two-pronged liability standard, it artificially assesses one set of facts in light

---

[50] Cases cited above, nn 9, 10 and 34 respectively.

of the first prong (ie, 'require or favour the adoption of agreements . . . contrary to Article 81 EC or reinforce the effects thereof') and another set of facts in light of the second prong ('delegate to private traders responsibility for taking decisions affecting the economic sphere').

Under the first prong, the Court concludes that the tariff proposals do not qualify as a decision of an association of undertakings within the meaning of Article 81(1) EC because the experts were honorary board members who received no instructions from the transport sector and had to take into account a variety of economic interests. They were therefore not the representatives of the road transport sector.[51]

Under the second prong, the Court notes that the Minister of Transport remained in charge of the process at all relevant moments: he decided on the composition of the board of experts, he (or his representative) would attend its meetings and, if the Minister of Economic affairs agreed, he either approved the tariffs submitted by the board or fixed these tariffs himself if the public interest so required.[52] These facts were sufficient for the Court to conclude that 'the public authorities have not delegated their powers regarding the fixing of tariffs to private economic agents'.[53] Apparently, this conclusion does not—in the Court's view—hinge on the question as to whether the Minister (or his representative) actually attended the board meetings and/or whether he ever effectively interfered in the tariff-setting itself or rather just rubber-stamped the board's proposals.

As pointed out above (see paragraph 48 above), in *Reiff* the contradiction between the two limbs of the liability standard does not surface because the Court concludes that the tariff board's proposals do not amount to a decision of an association of undertakings within the meaning of Article 81(1) EC. Literally all facts—although their assessment is artificially split under the first limb and the second limb—confirm that this is a case where the public authorities assume full responsibility for the restriction of competition.

2.2 *The Emergence of a Single Liability Standard in the Liberal Profession Cases* CNSD *and* Arduino

In the two liberal profession cases, *CNSD* and *Arduino*, the Court breaks new ground. While noting in both cases that the public authorities require private undertakings to conclude price-fixing arrangements and reinforce the effects of thereof, the Court does not stop its analysis there. It examines whether, in doing so, the public authorities remain fully responsible for the restriction of competition thus put in place. In *CNSD*, the answer is negative (and the state

51 Cases cited above, nn 9, 10 and 34 respectively, paras 17–19.
52 *Ibid*, para 22.
53 *Ibid*, para 23.

measure is unlawful) whereas in *Arduino*, the answer is positive (and the state measure is lawful).

a. CNSD

The Italian National Council of Customs Agents (CNSD) has a statutory duty to set minimum and maximum tariffs for the services provided by customs agents. The basic Law does not prevent the *CNSD*—when setting these tariffs—from acting in the exclusive interest of the profession. The *CNSD* members are elected by a series of departmental councils and they elect a president amongst themselves. The basic Law which empowers the *CNSD* to set these tariffs does not confer upon the Minister the power to approve the tariffs. However, the Minister has approved the litigious tariffs by a decree and published the tariffs in the Official Journal. Pursuant to the basic Law, the tariffs are compulsory. Agents who contravene them face disciplinary sanctions and may lose their job in case of recidivism.[54]

According to the Court, it was clear that the state authorities had required the conclusion of an agreement contrary to Article 81 EC and had assisted the customs agents in ensuring compliance with that agreement.[55] The Court thus distinguishes the case from *Reiff*. In fact, there is little 'air' between the facts in *CNSD* and those present in *Asjes*, *VVR* and BNIC, where the Court declared the state measures to be unlawful on the basis of the formalistic first prong of the *van Eycke* liability standard ('require or favour the adoption of agreements . . . contrary to Article 81 or reinforce the effects thereof'). In *CNSD*, however, the Court goes on to assess the state measure under the second prong of the *van Eycke* standard. More specifically, it examines whether the Italian authorities had delegated to the association of customs agents the responsibility for restricting competition. The Court decides that there had indeed been such a delegation and declares the state measure to be unlawful.

In other words, the decisive reason for holding the state authorities liable under Article 3(1)(g) EC, read in combination with Article 10(2) and Article 81 EC, is that these authorities did not assume full responsibility for the restriction of competition: they 'declined to influence [the] terms' of that agreement,[56] they in fact 'wholly relinquished to private economic operators the powers of the public authorities as regards the setting of tariffs'[57] and 'although no provision laid down by law or regulation confers on the Minister for Finance the power to approve the tariff, it remains the case that the Decree of the Minister for Finance (. . .) bestowed upon it the appearance of a public regulation'.[58]

---

[54] These facts can be distilled from paras 2 to 9, 41 and 59 of the judgment.

[55] See para 55.

[56] *Ibid.*

[57] See para 57.

[58] See para 59.

The conceptual point we wish to make here is that the Court focuses for the first time its attention entirely on the question as to who assumes responsibility for the restriction: the association of private undertakings or the public authority? In the Court's view, the former does. Hence, the latter's decision infringes Article 3(1)(g) EC, read in combination with Article 10(2) and Article 81 EC.

One can of course always dispute the factual validity of this conclusion. After all, the National Council of Customs Agents is under a statutory duty to adopt the tariffs, the competent Minister takes the decision to endorse the Council's proposal (although the basic Law does not explicitly confer such power upon him) and the publication of the tariffs in the Official Journal enhances compliance. All these elements of fact suggest that the public authorities assumed a good deal of responsibility by putting in place and enforcing the restriction of competition. It is a matter of degree, and in *CNSD*, the Court concludes that the involvement of the public authorities was not substantial enough to discard the applicability of the Treaty's competition provisions.

b. *Arduino*

The Italian Council of the Bar (CNF), like the *CNSD*, also has a statutory duty to set minimum and maximum tariffs for the services provided by its members in the course of civil or criminal proceedings. The basic Law spells out which criteria the CNF must take into account when setting the minimum and maximum tariffs but these criteria (eg, the monetary value of disputes, the level of the court seized or, in criminal proceedings, the duration of the proceedings) are not 'public-interest criteria, properly so called'.[59] CNF members are elected by fellow attorneys. While empowering the CNF to set these tariffs, the basic Law provides that the Minister must approve them after consulting two public bodies: an inter-ministerial committee on prices (CIP) and the Council of State. The Minister and the CIP take their job seriously. Taking into account the CIP's concern about the rise in inflation, the Minister opted for a staggered implementation of the CNF's proposal to increase the fees. Pursuant to the basic Law, the court dealing with the civil or criminal proceedings at hand must determine the exact level of the payable tariff in line with the tariff scale adopted by the CNF and approved by the Minister. The Supreme Court of Cassation has jurisdiction to hear appeals in case of dispute.[60]

The Court drastically re-formulates the referring national court's questions. The *Pretore* had inquired whether the CNF's tariff decision, approved

---

[59] Cited above, n 10, para 38.

[60] As a matter of fact, the *Arduino* case was triggered by a ruling of a national court (the *Pretore di Pinerolo*) which—according to the Court of Cassation—had not complied with the approved tariff scale. For a full survey of the facts, see paras 5 to 12 of the judgment.

by the Minister, fell within the scope of Article 81(1) EC and, if so, whether it fulfilled the conditions to benefit from Article 81(3) EC. The Court ignores these questions and observed that 'the national court seeks essentially to ascertain whether [Article 10(2) EC] and [Article 81 EC] preclude a Member State from adopting a law or regulation which approves [the tariff decision in question]'. In other words, the Court decides to address the state liability issue.

As will be shown below, the Court follows its CNSD line by focusing on the second prong of the *van Eycke* standard: who has assumed final responsibility for the restriction of competition? The association of private undertakings or the public authority? In contrast with CNSD, the Court concludes that the public authority has. Hence, the state measure is lawful. The fact that the public authority required the CNF to adopt a decision contrary to Article 81 and reinforced the effects thereof (as in *Asjes*, *VVR* and *BNIC*), appears to be irrelevant. The first prong of the *van Eycke* standard thus sinks into oblivion.

The Court's opening statement sets the tone: 'The fact that a Member State requires a professional organisation to produce a draft tariff for services does not automatically divest the tariff finally adopted of the character of legislation'.[61] In other words, from the outset, the Court takes the view that the second prong of the *van Eycke* standard ('delegate to private traders the responsibility for taking decisions affecting the economic sphere') is the decisive one.

It then concedes that 'the national legislation at issue in the main proceedings does not contain either procedural arrangements or substantive requirements capable of ensuring, with reasonable probability, that, when producing the draft tariff, the CNF conducts itself like an arm of the State working in the public interest'.[62] In this respect, it distinguishes *Arduino* from *Reiff*: the CNF is composed exclusively of members of the Bar elected by their fellow members and, when setting the tariffs, it does not have to take into account 'public-interest criteria, properly so-called'.[63]

'That said', the Court continues, 'it does not appear that the Italian State has waived its power to make decisions of last resort or to review implementation of the tariff'.[64] The Court identifies three factual elements that support this conclusion. First, without ministerial approval, the CNF's decision does not enter into force. Second, the Minister (with his consultative public bodies) plays an active role in reviewing the CNF's decision. Third, implementation is in the hands of the courts (with a monitoring role for the Supreme Court of Cassation).[65]

---

61 See para 36.
62 See para 39.
63 See paras 37–38.
64 See para 40.
65 See paras 40–42.

The Court concludes:

> In those circumstances, the Italian State cannot be said to have delegated to private economic operators responsibility for taking decisions affecting the economic sphere, which would have the effect of depriving the provisions at issue in the main proceedings of the character of legislation. Nor (. . .) is the Italian State open to the criticism that it requires or encourages the adoption of agreements, decisions or concerted practices contrary to Article [81] of the Treaty or reinforces their effects.[66]

The Court can hardly be more outspoken. As in CNSD, the sole relevant issue is whether the state authorities assume full responsibility for the restriction of competition. The Court perceives no need to qualify the CNF's decision as one that falls inside or outside the scope of Article 81(1) EC. All the Court says is: even if such a decision falls within the scope of Article 81(1) EC, even if the basic Law requires the adoption of such a decision and even if the Minister's approval reinforces the effects of such a decision (ie, even if the state measure falls squarely within the first prong of the *van Eycke* liability standard), the Member State concerned is not 'open to criticism' as long as it assumes full responsibility for its action by actively supervising the CNF's decision-making and monitoring compliance with the approved CNF decision.

In *CNSD*, the outcome under the first and second prong of the *van Eycke* standard was identical. Here in *Arduino*, the outcome is different and it is unambiguously clear that the analysis under the second prong prevails.

As in *CNSD*, one can always question the factual validity of the Court's assessment in *Arduino*. However, the least one can say is that the state measure in *Arduino* implies a greater deal of involvement on the side of the public authorities. The basic Law spells out the calculation criteria, requires that the Minister approve the proposed tariffs, provides for an active review of the Bar Council's proposals by the Minister and by two other public bodies and—last but not least—confers the power to implement the tariff decision to the courts under the judicial review of the Supreme Court of Cassation.

An interesting issue—not definitively settled in our view—is whether, in the Court's view, the public authorities only assume full responsibility for the restriction of competition when they make effective use of their power to supervise the decision-making and to monitor compliance with the decision once adopted. In *Arduino*, there was evidence of such active supervision. In contrast, in *Reiff* there was not, yet the state measure in the latter case was also found to be lawful. The answer may be that active supervision is required where the decision-making bodies elected by the sector concerned solely represent the interests of that sector (*Arduino*) whereas a more relaxed legality

[66] See para 43.

standard can apply to bodies which look more like 'the arm of the state working in the public interest' (*Reiff*). As will be seen, this interpretation is in line with US case law.

For the sake of completeness, we briefly refer to *Cipolla*,[67] a 'follow-up' case to *Arduino* in which the national court queries whether a state decree prohibiting derogations from, *inter alia*, the minimum fees laid down for the services of lawyers is compatible with Article 3(1)(g) EC, read in combination with Article 10 and Article 81 EC. The answer seems to be straightforward: this state measure does not reinforce the effects of a pre-existing price cartel, since the scale of minimum fees at stake has been qualified in *Arduino* as resulting from a state measure. Again, the Italian state assumes full responsibility for this supplementary restriction of competition.

3. Recent Cases involving State Action but not Focusing on the State Liability Issue

In the last few years, there have been three more cases in which anti-competitive public regulation has occurred but in which the Court has essentially dealt with the question as to whether the private undertakings or entities involved were liable under Article 81 EC. The Court's judgments do little to clarify the conditions under which public regulation runs a foul of Article 3(1)(g) EC, read in combination with Articles 10 and 81 EC. We shall nevertheless mention these judgments because they raise some interesting points. In fact, one of them (*Fiammiferi*) indirectly addresses the state liability issue and—in light of *CNSD* and *Arduino*—does so in a somewhat puzzling way.

a. Wouters[68]

In *Wouters*, in contrast with *Arduino*, the Court focuses on the applicability of Article 81(1) EC to the self-regulation at issue. The Court finds that the National Dutch Bar Association (NOVA) had valid reasons for banning multidisciplinary partnerships between attorneys and accountants. While it qualifies NOVA's decision as one of an association of undertakings which restricts competition and affects interstate trade, it nevertheless rejects the applicability of Article 81(1) EC to this decision. In the *volte face* recital 97 of its judgment, the Court observes that

> (. . .) account must be taken of [the decision's] objectives, which are here connected with the need to make rules relating to organisation, qualifications, professional ethics, supervision and liability, in order to ensure that the ultimate consumers of

[67] Cited above, n 10.
[68] Cited above, n 11.

> legal services and the sound administration of justice are provided with the necessary guarantees in relation to integrity and experience

and that 'it has then to be considered whether the consequential effects restrictive of competition are inherent in the pursuit of those objectives'. The Court concludes that NOVA's decision does not go beyond what is necessary in order to ensure the proper practice of the legal profession.[69]

Elsewhere, we have 'de-dramatised' recital 97 by observing that i) the Court's reasoning amounts to a variant of the ancillary restraints doctrine under Article 81(1) EC (as the Court's own reference to *Gøttrup-Klim* in recital 109 seems to confirm) and ii) the Commission itself cleared a ban on deceptive advertising in IMA under Article 81(1) EC on similar grounds (by accepting that the ban was necessary for the independence and integrity of patent agents).[70] While one can also read some sort of 'public interest' exception into recital 97, we have further argued that this would contradict recital 62, where the Court observes that NOVA 'is not required to [adopt deontological measures] by reference to specified public-interest criteria' (emphasis added). This observation leads the Court to conclude that NOVA is an association of undertakings within the meaning of Article 81(1) EC.[71] This does not mean that the Court's ancillary restraints approach in recital 97 might not suffer from a series of shortcomings.[72]

Since NOVA's decision to restrict competition falls outside the scope of Article 81(1) EC, the state liability question becomes entirely academic for the Court.[73] For the same reason, the Court sees no grounds for applying the Treaty provisions on the freedom of persons and services (Article 43 and Article 49 EC) to NOVA's decision.[74]

b. *Fiammiferi*

In *Fiammiferi*,[75] a German match manufacturer complained to the Italian antitrust authority, that due to a series of anti-competitive arrangements entered into by the consortium of domestic match manufacturers (CIF), it was experiencing difficulties in distributing its products on the Italian market. The CIF contended that a complex regulatory framework governing the

---

69 See para 109.

70 See L Gyselen, 'De Vlaamse balies, multidisciplinaire samenwerking en EG-mededingingsrecht: prelude tot het arrest van het Hof van Cassatie' in *Liber Amicorum Jean-Pierre de Bandt* (Bruxelles, Bruylant, 2004) 95, 113–14.

71 *Ibid*, pp 114–15. For the reference to *IMA*, see above n 11.

72 For an identification of these shortcomings, see the contribution cited above, n 70, pp 115–16.

73 See para 118. In the contribution cited in n 70, we argue that the Dutch legislation delegated substantial regulatory powers to NOVA although it also provided for a surveillance mechanism somewhat similar to the one at stake in *Reiff*.

74 See para 122.

75 Cited above, n 12.

production, distribution and sale of matches required it to conclude these arrangements and, as a consequence, precluded its members from engaging in autonomous conduct. The CIF cited *Ladbroke*, according to which Article 81 and. 82 do not apply 'if anti-competitive conduct is required of undertakings by national legislation or if the latter creates a legal framework which itself eliminates any possibility of competitive activity on their part' because 'in such a situation, the restriction of competition is not attributable, as [Article 81 and Article 82] implicitly require, to the autonomous conduct of the undertakings'.[76]

The central anti-competitive arrangement was a production quota system pursuant to which the match manufacturers belonging to the CIF membership were entitled to production volumes which corresponded to their existing market share.[77] Although the regulatory framework provided for a quota system, it did not spell out the criteria to be used for the allocation of such quotas.[78] A 'quota-allocation' committee comprising one representative of the CIF, three representatives of the manufacturers and a government official from the State Monopolies Board acting as chairman had—by a simple majority vote—linked each manufacturer's production quota to its existing market share. The State Monopolies Board approved this committee's decision. The quota system left room for some derogations, although these are not required by the regulatory framework. Some (eg, the transfer or exchange of quotas among the members) had to be approved by the Ministry of Finance. Others (eg, the reservation of a 15% quota for imports) are unrelated to the regulatory framework.[79] A 'quota-compliance' committee, solely comprising representatives of the manufacturers, is in charge of implementing the system and of monitoring compliance with it.[80]

The CIF also entered into some agreements with third parties which were not foreseen by the regulatory framework. Thus, it entered into an exclusive dealing arrangement with the Conaedi, a body representing virtually all warehouses in charge of the wholesale distribution of monopoly goods in Italy. It also agreed to purchase a quantity of matches from one foreign manufacturer (Swedish Match) corresponding to a pre-determined percentage of Italy's consumption.[81]

In *Fiammiferi*, the Court essentially refines its Ladbroke case law about the impact of state legislative or regulatory action on the liability of private undertakings under Article 81 EC. However, in doing so, the Court also deals

---

[76] See *Ladbroke*, cited above, n 12, para 33.

[77] It is true that the legislation also eliminates price competition between the match manufacturers but this restriction of competition does not seem to have been a cause of concern for the complainant (see para 36).

[78] See paras 6–7 and 70.

[79] For these details about the quota allocation system, see paras 7 and 72–73.

[80] See paras 8, 13 and 79.

[81] See paras 17–18, 28 and 74.

with the legal status of the state action itself in light of Article 3(1)(g) EC, read in combination with Article 10(2) and Article 81 EC.

In the first part of its judgment, the Court warns that national legislation precluding undertakings from engaging in autonomous conduct does not shield these undertakings forever against the constraints of Article 81 or Article 82 EC. After a quote of the *van Eycke* legality standard, the Court unfolds the following reasoning: i) a Member State that requires or favours the adoption of anti-competitive agreements, infringes Article 10 and Article 81 EC and moreover disregards its duty—pursuant to Article 4 EC and Article 98 EC—to conduct its economic policy in accordance with the principle of an open market economy;[82] ii) 'the primacy of Community law requires any provision of national law which contravenes a Community rule to be disapplied', not only by the national courts but also by the National Competition Authority (NCA);[83] iii) while the NCA may not impose penalties upon the undertakings concerned in respect of past conduct required by national legislation, these undertakings may face penalties for conduct 'subsequent to the decision to disapply the national legislation, once the decision has become definitive in their regard' (emphasis added).[84]

In the second part of the judgment, the Court examines whether the relevant national legislation really precluded the match manufacturers from engaging in autonomous conduct in the *Ladbroke* sense. The Court in fact doubts that this was the case.

First, although the national legislation provided for a quota system, it did not impose calculation criteria on the quota allocation committee, nor did it provide for transfers of quotas, exchanges of quotas or reservations of import quotas.[85] Second, the quota allocation committee was in a position to exclusively serve the private interests of its member undertakings. Four of its five members were 'representatives of the manufacturers, whom nothing in the relevant national legislation prevents from acting exclusively in their own interests' and 'the committee, which takes decision by simple majority, may adopt resolutions even if its chairman, the only person with public-interest duties, votes against them, and the committee can therefore act in accordance with the requirements of the member undertakings'.[86] Third, 'the public authorities do not have an effective means of controlling decisions taken by

[82] See paras 46–47.

[83] See paras 48–50.

[84] See paras 58 and 52–55. The Court also deals with the situation in which the national legislation merely 'encourages' or 'facilitates' anti-competitive conduct. Apart from extending the NCA's 'duty to disapply' to this type of legislation, the Court repeats existing case law according to which such legislation never shields the undertakings from the application of Arts 81 or 82 EC although it can be a mitigating factor when it comes to setting the level of the penalty (see paras 56–58).

[85] See paras 70–73.

[86] See para 77.

the quota allocation committee'.[87] In other words, when these authorities approved the committee's decisions, they merely rubber-stamped them. Fourth, the public authorities had no say at all in the quota-compliance committee, 'which was composed solely of CIF members on the basis of agreements drawn up by the member undertakings'.[88]

Although the Court leaves the final word to the national court, it is thus inclined to conclude that the national legislation did not preclude the match manufacturers from engaging in autonomous conduct within the meaning of Ladbroke and—hence—that these manufacturers were liable under Article 81 EC.

By the same token, the Court suggests that the Italian public authorities did not assume full responsibility for the restriction of competition stemming from the production quota system. To impose a duty upon the NCA to disapply this regulatory framework—as the Court does in the first part of its judgment—therefore seems in line with *Arduino* where the 'full responsibility' standard is decisive.

However, the question as to whether *Fiammiferi* is consistent with *Arduino* is more complex than that. It raises in fact two separate questions.

The first one is purely factual: is there enough difference between the facts in the two cases to conclude that the public authorities are fully responsible for the restriction of competition in *Arduino*, but not in *Fiammiferi*? As in *CNSD* and *Arduino*, one can always dispute the factual validity of the Court's assessment. However, in our view, the answer is affirmative. Apart from the fact that the match manufacturers were under a statutory duty to set up a production quota system, they largely had their hands free. They decided on the allocation criterion (ie, existing market shares) and the actual allocation and compliance decisions were also autonomous acts. In short, whatever the public authorities approved, their approval was a mere rubber-stamping (see paragraph 86 above).

The second question is conceptual, hence more fundamental: does the Court hold the public authorities liable in *Fiammiferi* because they fail to assume full responsibility for the restrictive production quota system? The answer seems to be negative.

The Court addresses the responsibility issue (in the second part of its judgment) in order to determine whether the private undertakings can invoke Ladbroke to escape from the scope of Article 81 EC. At this stage, the Court has already concluded (in the first part of its judgment) that the national legislation must be disapplied when it requires or facilitates the adoption of anti-competitive agreements within the meaning of Article 81 EC. The second prong of the *van Eycke* liability standard ('delegate to private traders

[87] See para 78.
[88] See para 79.

responsibility for taking decisions affecting the economic sphere') does not enter the equation. This seems to be a puzzling return to the 'old' approach followed in *Asjes*, *VVR* and *BNIC*.

c. *AOK*

In this case—also known as the German *Krankenkassen* case[89]—the main question was whether associations of sickness funds were acting as associations of undertakings (and, if so, whether they restricted competition) within the meaning of Article 81(1) EC when performing their statutory duty under paragraph 35 of the Code of Social law to agree on maximum reimbursement amounts for medicines. If Article 81(1) EC applied, the next question was whether the associations of sickness funds could justify their action on public service grounds pursuant to Article 86(2) EC.

The Court takes the view that the associations of sickness funds 'merely perform an obligation which is imposed upon them by paragraph 35 of the Code of Social Law in order to ensure continuance of operation of the German social security system'.[90] The Court acknowledges that the Code leaves it to the associations to set the exact reimbursement amounts but it observes that, in any event, this is an area in which the sickness funds 'do not compete'[91] because they are 'compelled by law to offer to their members essentially identical obligatory benefits (. . .)'.[92] The Court concludes that, by agreeing on maximum reimbursement amounts, the associations of sickness funds do not engage in economic activity falling within the scope of Article 81 EC. Therefore, the Court does not have to address the justification issue under Article 86(2) EC.

This case is only of marginal interest for the state liability issue. However, Advocate General Jacobs briefly addresses this issue in his opinion. Taking the view that Article 81(1) EC might very well apply to the price-fixing activities of the associations of sickness funds but without ruling out that these associations could invoke Ladbroke to escape from the constraints of Article 81–1 EC, he turns to the state measure itself and adds: 'it should be remembered that the applicable provisions of German law might themselves be open to challenge on the ground that they violated the obligation imposed upon Member States by virtue of Articles 3(1)(g), 10 and 81 EC (. . .)'.[93]

---

[89] Joined Cases C–264/01, C–306/0, C–354/01 and C–355/01 *AOK Bundesverband, Bundesverband der Betriebskrankenkassen v Ichtyol-Gesellschaft Cordes, Hermani & Co* [2004] ECR I–2493.

[90] See para 61, and also para 63: '. . . the (. . .) associations perform an obligation which is integrally connected with the activity of the sickness funds within the framework of the German statutory health insurance scheme'.

[91] See para 62.

[92] See para 52.

[93] See para 85 of Advocate General Jacobs' Opinion, delivered on 22 May 2003.

AG Jacobs does not develop this point further, understandably so, since this point was not raised by the national court. However, we tend to view this case as one in which the public authorities have assumed full responsibility for the restriction of competition resulting from these price-fixing activities. Hence, *Arduino* would seem to apply. Of course, the public authorities have delegated to the associations of sickness funds the power to regulate an important parameter of competition. However, the Code of Social Law has clearly articulated the reasons for this delegation of powers. Moreover, it provides for a series of procedural modalities and substantive criteria which the associations must follow when engaging in their price-fixing activities. Finally, if the associations do not succeed in determining the maximum reimbursement amounts, the decision is taken at ministerial level. It would therefore seem that the public authorities actively supervise these price-fixing activities.

IV. US State Action Doctrine

1. The Main Supreme Court Judgments

Building on the *Parker v Brown* wisdom that the Sherman Act—enacted pursuant to the Constitution's Commerce Clause—contains no language suggesting that its purpose is to restrain a state from (anti-competitive) activities directed by its legislature, the Supreme Court develops an immunity standard for anti-competitive state measures in *Midcal*.[94]

1.1 The Immunity Standard in Midcal

In *Midcal*, the Supreme Court observes that state action will enjoy immunity from the application of the federal antitrust laws if it meets two requirements. First, the restriction of competition must be 'one clearly articulated and affirmatively expressed by the state itself'. Second, where conduct of private undertakings is involved in the implementation of the state policy, this conduct must be 'actively supervised by the state itself'.

Like the liability standard in the EC, this immunity standard is two-pronged. However, the two prongs of the *Midcal* standard are—by their very nature—not only consistent with one another; they complement each other. The 'active supervision' requirement 'serves essentially an evidentiary function: it is one way of ensuring that the [private] actor is engaging in the

[94] *California Liquor Dealers v Midcal Aluminium* 445 US 97 (1980).

challenged conduct pursuant to state policy'.[95] Together the two requirements mandate the courts to check whether the state regulators have assumed full responsibility for restricting competition. If they have, the state measures are outside the reach of the federal antitrust laws.

1.2 Parker v Brown

Parker v Brown[96] concerned a California production quota system for raisins grown in that state but largely destined for export to other states. A state regulation authorised the establishment of such a system, a state authority instituted it and state officials supervised it. A raisin producer sued these officials for breach of Section 1 of the Sherman Act (the US equivalent of Article 81 EC). However, the Supreme Court rejected the complaint, noting that 'it was the State which has created the machinery for establishing the (quota) program' and that such a programme 'was never intended to operate by force of individual agreement or combination' within the meaning of Section 1 but 'derived its authority and its efficacy from the legislative command'.[97]

Thus—and for the constitutional reasons already set out above (see paragraphs 20–25 and 97)—the Supreme Court established the rule that states are not liable under federal antitrust law if they retain full responsibility for setting up and operating the anti-competitive production quota system. In comparison, the European Court of Justice finds state liability in *BNIC* and *Fiammiferi*, which also concern production quota systems, without examining the degree of active state involvement in these systems (see paragraphs 43–45 and 91–92).

1.3 Midcal *and other Relevant Cases Before and After*

In *Midcal*, the facts are essentially similar to those in the European RPM cases (*GB-INNO-BM*, *van de Haar* and *Leclerc*): a California decree requires wine producers to publish resale price schedules and dealers to sell at these prices. One dealer successfully sues the state officials who administer this RPM scheme for violation of Section 1 of the Sherman Act. According to the Court, although the decree reflects a clearly articulated state policy to restrict competition, there is no 'extensive official oversight'[98] of the restriction put in place as the state officials never reviewed the reasonableness of the retail prices set by the producers or otherwise monitored market conditions. The

---

[95] *Town of Hallie v City of Eau Claire* 471 US 34 (1985) 46.

[96] Cited above, n 28.

[97] *Ibid*, at pp 352 and 350. For the Court, it was immaterial that the Californian farmers had lobbied for the quota system and that they had approved the programme instituted by the state authority.

[98] See p 104.

Court concludes that the federal antitrust policy cannot be 'thwarted by casting a gauzy cloak of state involvement over what is essentially a private price fixing arrangement'.[99] Incidentally, the Court finds state liability although the price-fixing arrangement itself does not fall within the scope of Section 1 in the absence of any collusion.[100]

Obviously, in *Midcal* the Supreme Court's position is diametrically opposed to that of the European Court of Justice in *van de Haar*. It is also more outspoken than the position of the Court in *Leclerc*, according to which state liability could not be ruled out when the legislator renders collusive behaviour prohibited by Article 81 EC superfluous (see paragraph 35 above).

a. *The 'Clear Articulation' Requirement*

Two pre–*Midcal* cases concerning liberal professions are often referred to as having inspired Midcal. In *Goldfarb*,[101] the Supreme Court held that the adoption and enforcement of minimum fee schedules for lawyers in Virginia was not immune from antitrust challenge because the state decree had merely granted a general mandate to the state supreme court to regulate the practice of law and because the court had further delegated this regulatory power to the state bar association, which used it to engage in a price-fixing arrangement. In the Court's view, this is essentially a 'private anti-competitive activity'. In contrast, in Bates[102] the Supreme Court found immunity for a rule prohibiting attorneys from advertising their services. The rule has been enacted and enforced directly by the Arizona state supreme court.

One post–*Midcal* case sheds further light on the 'clear articulation' requirement. In *Southern Motor Carriers*,[103] the US government sued a number of private transport companies for a violation of Section 1 on the ground that they conspired to fix rates for the intra-state transport of goods. The state decree provided that the transport companies could choose either to submit a joint rate proposal to a regulated rate bureau or to propose their own individual rates to that bureau for approval. While the decree did not therefore compel price collusion, it was at least an option permitted by the decree. The Supreme Court accepts that mere authorization of a specific restriction of price competition in a state statutory scheme can reflect a 'clearly articulated' policy to restrict such competition even if the state does not micro-manage the rate bureaus' decision-making.[104]

---

[99] See p 105.

[100] A couple of years later in a similar case, the Supreme Court did away with this issue by observing that 'the regulatory scheme may be attacked under S 1 as a *hybrid* restraint where private actors are granted a degree of private regulatory power' (*Liquor Corp v Duffy* 479 US 667 (1987)).

[101] *Goldfarb v Virginia State Bar* 421 US 773 (1975).

[102] *Bates v State Bar of Arizona* 433 US 350 (1977).

[103] *Southern Motor Carriers Rate Conference v United States* 471 US 48 (1985).

[104] *Ibid*, at 63–64.

b. The 'Active Supervision' Requirement

In two post–*Midcal* cases, the Supreme Court sharpened the 'active supervision' requirement.

In the liberal professions case *Patrick*,[105] a physician who was disciplined by a peer review board of a public hospital successfully argued that the state-authorised peer review system violated Section 1. Although this system granted supervisory powers to a public agency, the Supreme Court observes that these powers did not enable the agency to screen the substantive merits of decisions adopted by the peer review board. The Court concludes that the system failed to meet the 'active supervision' test which 'requires that state officials have and exercise power to review particular anti-competitive acts of private parties and disapprove those that fail to accord with state policy' (emphasis added).[106]

In *Ticor*,[107] the Supreme Court confirmed the point made in *Patrick*. In this case, companies performing title searches of real property and selling title insurance jointly proposed rates to rate bureaus and they did so pursuant to state law (*cf Southern Motor Carriers*). The state's scheme provided that the proposed rates would automatically become effective after a certain period of time, unless the regulatory agency overseeing the rate bureaus objected to them. In fact, this agency did a poor job in supervising the rate proposals. The Supreme Court concludes that the scheme failed to meet the 'active supervision' test. The Court notes:

> where prices or rates are set as an initial matter by private parties, subject only to a veto if the state chooses to exercise it, the party claiming the immunity must show that state officials have undertaken the necessary steps to determine the specifics of the price fixing or rate-setting scheme. The mere potential for state supervision is not an adequate substitute for a decision by the State.[108]

The *Ticor* facts (as those in *Southern Motor Carriers*) bear some resemblance to those in *Asjes*, where the state authorities merely rubber-stamped tariff proposals submitted by airlines. However, the Court found state liability in *Asjes* on the basis of a formalistic reasoning which has nothing in common with the one mandated by the two-pronged *Midcal* standard (see paragraph 43–45). It is very well possible that the Member States would have failed to meet the 'active supervision' test in *Asjes* but the point is that such a test was not relevant for the Court.

We had to wait for the European Court's judgments in *CNSD* and *Arduino* to see the emergence of a liability standard ('full responsibility') which conceptually comes close to the US Supreme Court's two-pronged immunity

---

105 *Patrick v Burget* 486 US 94 (1988).

106 See p 101.

107 *Federal Trade Commission v Ticor Title Insurance Co* 504 US 621 (1992).

108 *Ibid*, at 638.

standard. Whether the two Courts apply their standard with the same strictness, is a separate issue. At first sight, the facts in *CNSD* and *Goldfarb* (the pre–*Midcal* case clarifying the 'clear articulation' test) are similar, and in both cases the state authorities are held liable. It is harder to compare *Arduino* with *Patrick* (the pre–*Ticor* case clarifying the 'active supervision' test), *inter alia* because the type of restriction at stake is different. It is unclear whether the Italian authorities in *Arduino* meet the 'active supervision' test. On the one hand, they do not screen the substantive merits of the CNF's tariff proposals, as *Patrick* seems to require. On the other hand, these proposals only concern minimum and maximum tariffs and their implementation (once approved by the Minister) is in the hands of the courts who must determine the precise level of the tariffs due in the particular litigation pending before them.

2. The Federal Trade Commission's 2003 Report

Recently, the Federal Trade Commission (FTC) called upon the lower federal courts not to erode the 'clear articulation' and 'active supervision' requirements of the *Midcal* standard.[109] It also voiced a more fundamental concern about the impact of the state action doctrine—even if applied rigorously—on interstate commerce and, more generally, on the 'sink or swim' together model of federalism.

2.1 Concern about Relaxation of the Midcal *Standard in the Lower Courts*

As to the first prong, the FTC is worried that courts read too quickly into state regulations, which grant private undertakings or their associations broadly termed powers to regulate their business, a clearly articulated policy specifically aimed at displacing competition. The FTC points out that 'once conduct is authorised, anti-competitive forms of that conduct arguably are foreseeable in the sense that they could occur'. The FTC argues that something more is needed when the goal is to ensure that the anti-competitive conduct flows from a 'deliberate and intended state policy'.[110]

The FTC refers to a liberal professions case as a bad example. In *Earles*,[111] a Louisiana statute merely authorised a state board of certified public accountants to 'adopt and enforce all . . . rules of professional conduct . . . as the board may deem necessary and proper to regulate the practice of public

[109] Office of Policy Planning, Report of the State Action Task Force, September 2003.
[110] See p 26.
[111] *Earles v State Board of Certified Public Accountants* 139 F 3d 1033 (Acco, 1998).

accounting in the state of Louisiana'. This state board had used its broad mandate to prohibit accountants from *inter alia*, from participating in other businesses or occupations that impair their independence or objectivity. The Court of Appeals found in this statute a 'clear articulation' of a policy which 'rejected pure competition among accountants.[112]

This brings to mind *Wouters*, where the Dutch legislator also confined itself to giving a broad mandate to the National Bar Association to regulate the activities of attorneys (see footnote 73) but where the Court neatly avoids addressing the state liability issue. In light of *Goldfarb* (see paragraph 104 above), the FTC would probably argue that one cannot read into the Dutch legislator's mandate a clear articulation of a policy favouring a ban on multi-disciplinary partnerships between attorneys and accountants (as adopted by the Bar Association).

With regard to the second prong, the FTC notes that the Supreme Court has not given concrete guidance, although leading cases like *Ticor* indicate that some degree of substantive review of the anti-competitive activity is in order.[113] The FTC also expresses a specific concern with regard to the entities which should be subject to the 'active supervision' test. In its view, the lower courts unduly 'stress that the public nature of a group's activities obviates concerns about anti-competitive conduct'. The FTC refers once more to *Earles*[114] and to another liberal professions case, *Hass*.[115] Relying on *Goldfarb*, the FTC questions 'whether public visibility of the activities of professional entities such as bar organizations or accountancy boards is sufficient protection against self-serving conduct'.[116]

---

[112] See p 35.

[113] The FTC notes at p 37: 'the cases require the reviewing official to engage in a "pointed re-examination" of a state-authorized price-setting program (*Midcal*), review of the "reasonableness" of prices and contractual terms and contractual terms (*Midcal*), reach the "substantive merits" of peer review decisions (*Patrick*), determine whether the private action "accorded with state regulatory policy" (*Patrick*) and exercise "sufficient independent judgement and control" to ensure that "the details of the rates or prices have been established as a product of deliberate state intervention" (*Ticor*).'

[114] See p 38. In *Earles* (cited above, n 111), the Court of Appeals observes (at 1041): 'Despite the fact that the Board is composed entirely of certified public accountants who compete in the profession they regulate, the public nature of the Board's actions means that there is little danger of a cosy arrangement to restrict competition'.

[115] *Ibid.* In *Hass v Oregon State Bar* 883 F 2d 1453 (9th Cir, 1989), a case in which the state bar association required its members to purchase malpractice insurance from it, the Court of Appeals also refers to the fact that the records of the Bar are open for public inspection and that its meetings are open to the public.

[116] See p 39.

2.2 Concern About Interstate Spill-Overs

The FTC also voices a much more fundamental concern which remains relevant even if the two-pronged immunity standard of *Midcal* is applied strictly: 'the state action doctrine fails to take account of the efficiency losses and the breakdowns in the political process posed by interstate spill-overs'.[117] It refers to *Parker v Brown* as an obvious illustration of the 'spill over' problem. California's production quota system for raisins led to a price increase and thus to higher revenues in California but the cost of this price increase 'spilled overwhelmingly into other states' because between 90% and 95% of the raisins were shipped out of state.

In fact, the FTC is pointing at a paradox here. On the one hand, the state action doctrine is rooted in a federalist model according to which state sovereignty is the rule. On the other hand, 'when anti-competitive state regulations tend to produce in-state benefits but out-of-state harms, states have incentives to over-regulate in ways that reduce welfare for the nation as a whole'.[118] And the FTC concludes: 'It is a strange sort of federalism that pays homage to the political role of citizens of states that benefit from a regulation but disregards the concerns of citizens of states that are directly harmed'.[119]

The FTC recommends to 'introduce sensitivity to such spill-overs into the case law, either through its adjudicatory/litigation positions or through selective amicus filings'.[120]

V. Emerging Convergence Between EU and US State Action Doctrines

In our view, today's leading EU cases concerning state action are *CNSD* and *Arduino*. Taking *Arduino* as reflecting best the current case law on this side of the ocean,[121] we can compare the EU and US case law on state action with reference to three issues. First, which anti-competitive state measures fall within the scope of Article 3(1)(g) EC, read in combination with Article 10(2) and Article 81 EC? Second, can those measures that do nevertheless be saved

[117] See p 40.

[118] See p 41.

[119] See p 42. The FTC recognizes, however, that none of the recent state action cases 'involved fact-patterns that would have brought interstate spill-over concerns to the forefront' (see n 192 at p 44).

[120] See p 56.

[121] As explained above (paras 60–62), the Court already introduced the 'full responsibility' standard in *CNSD* but this is less visible because the outcome (ie, state liability) is identical under the first and second prongs of the *van Eycke* standard.

on objective justification grounds and, if so, on which grounds? Third, how must one assess the impact of anti-competitive state measures on interstate commerce?

1. State Measures Falling Within the Scope of Article 3(1)(g) EC, Read in Combination with Article 10(2) and Article 81 EC

1.1 The Court's Case Law

It will be recalled (see paragraph 64) that the state measure in *Arduino* provided a regulatory framework for the CNF's tariff decision 'upstream' (by imposing on the CNF a statutory duty to adopt such a decision, by setting calculation criteria, by stipulating that the tariff proposal had to be approved by the Minister before it could enter into force and by requiring ministerial scrutiny of the tariff proposal prior to the approval) as well as 'downstream' (by conferring upon the courts the power to implement the tariff decision—once adopted and approved—and by mandating the Supreme Court of Cassation to monitor the courts' implementation of that decision).

In the Court's view, this regulatory framework does not trigger state liability. Let us recall its 'cascade' of reasoning. To begin with, 'it does not appear that the Italian State has waived its power to make decisions of last resort or to review implementation of the tariff' (ergo: the state has retained full responsibility). It follows that 'the Italian State cannot be said to have delegated to private economic operators responsibility for taking decisions affecting the economic sphere, which would have the effect of depriving the provisions at issue in the main proceedings of the character of legislation (ergo: the state measure is lawful under the second prong of the *van Eycke* standard). Finally, 'nor (. . .) is the Italian State open to the criticism that it requires or encourages the adoption of agreements, decisions or concerted practices contrary to Article [81] of the Treaty or reinforces their effects' (*ergo*: it is irrelevant that the state measure would be unlawful under the first prong of the *van Eycke* standard).

In our view, when a state authority retains full responsibility for the restriction of competition at stake, it is bound to meet the US Supreme Court's two-pronged *Midcal* test.

Whether or not the Italian authorities did indeed retain full responsibility for the restriction of competition in *Arduino* is another matter. It concerns the factual robustness of the Court's assessment. Probably, the restriction is 'one clearly articulated and affirmatively expressed by the state itself' in the basic Law. It is less clear whether the restriction is also 'actively supervised by the state itself'.

In *Fiammiferi*, the Court is more ambiguous (see paragraphs 89–92 above). According to the Court, an NCA has the duty to disapply state measures which either require or facilitate (and thereby legitimise or reinforce) conduct contrary to Article 81(1) EC. The Court clearly relies on the first prong of the *van Eycke* standard. The degree to which the state has delegated to the match manufacturers the responsibility for this conduct does not seem to matter for the lawfulness of the state measure. Later in its judgment, the Court suggests that there is actually a good deal of delegation and, as a consequence, that the state measure has no Ladbroke–type of impact on the manufacturers' conduct. One could add that the state measure would therefore also be unlawful under the second prong of the *van Eycke* standard. Although the Court does not make the latter point, it is perhaps a reason for not reading into *Fiammiferi* a conscious return to the 'old' approach followed in *Asjes*, *VVR* and *BNIC* and reflected in the first prong of the *van Eycke* standard.

1.2 The Commission's 2004 Communication

In this Communication, the Commission relies on *Arduino* to take the view that

> State measures delegating regulatory powers which do not clearly define the public interest objectives to be pursued by the regulation and/or by which the State effectively waives its power to take the decisions of last resort or to control implementation can (. . .) be challenged under [Article 3(1)(g) EC, read in combination with Article 10(2) and Article 81 EC] (emphasis added).[122]

We recognise in this language the 'clear articulation' and 'active supervision' requirements. The Commission seems to confirm this by giving two examples of unlawful state measures: 'rubber-stamp approvals' and 'practices whereby the authorities of a Member State are only entitled to reject or endorse the proposals of professional bodies without being able to alter their content or substitute their own decisions for these proposals'.[123] In neither of these two cases do the public authorities assume full responsibility for the restriction of competition.

However, the next passage in the 2004 Communication is more equivocal. In the Commission's view, 'a proportionality test would seem appropriate to assess to what extent an anti-competitive professional regulation truly serves the public interest' (emphasis added).[124] Seen through lawyers' glasses, this passage implies that Article 3(1)(g) EC, read in combination with Article

---

[122] Cited above, n 4, para 86.
[123] *Ibid*, para 87.
[124] *Ibid*, para 88.

10(2) and Article 81(1) EC, applies to all anti-competitive professional regulations, whatever the degree of responsibility assumed by the public authorities, and—as a consequence—that these regulations are only lawful if they constitute a proportionate means to achieve a (legitimate) public interest objective.

In our view, this would not be in line with *Arduino*. However, the passage may have to be read differently. It may reflect the Commission's more modest policy ambition to invite the national regulatory authorities to examine themselves *ex ante* whether their proposed anti-competitive policy meets the proportionality test.

Moving away from 'the policy' and returning to the law, we conclude as follows. If our reading of the case law, and in particular of *CNSD* and *Arduino*, is correct, the Court should abandon the confusing two-pronged liability standard as restated in *van Eycke* (with its internal inconsistency: see paragraphs 46–47 above) and replace it by a *Midcal*-type of standard. However, clarification would be welcome, all the more so after *Fiammiferi* where the Court went back—perhaps unintentionally—to the first prong of the *van Eycke* standard.

Would the introduction of a *Midcal*–type of standard ignore the fundamental constitutional differences between the EC Treaty and the US Constitution (see part I above)? In light of *CNSD* and *Arduino*, we believe not. In *GB-INNO-BM*, the Court read into Article 3(1)(g) and Article 10(2) EC an implied constitutional limitation upon any possible state interference with the system of undistorted competition in the common market. However, to turn all anti-competitive state measures into potentially unlawful acts—on the sole basis of these provisions and in the absence of an express EC Treaty provision specifically prohibiting such measures—would ignore the fact that all other state measures impeding market integration are only unlawful under Article 3(1)(c) and Article 10(2) EC in combination with an express EC Treaty provision which specifically prohibits such measures (eg, Article 28 EC, etc.).

For the rest, a strict application of the 'clear articulation' and 'active supervision' requirements would be in order (as the FTC's recommendations show). In our view, the Court has already set the example in *CNSD* (state liability) and in *Reiff* and *Arduino* (no state liability) but there is certainly room for a stricter application of both requirements (see paragraphs 110 and 123 above). Under the 'clear articulation' test, public authorities could be required to undertake a genuine cost/benefit analysis of their proposed anti-competitive regulation and to communicate its results before enacting the regulation. Under the 'active supervision' test, they could be required to undertake regular substantive reviews of their policy (or have such review undertaken by an independent body).

In this context, one could add that in *Arduino*—as indeed in most other state action cases—hard core restrictions of competition (eg, RPM, price-fixing, quotas) are at stake. In our view, this certainly calls for particular vigilance when applying the *Midcal* standard. One must examine whether the state really supports these hard core restrictions. However, once the state is found to be fully behind them, neither the Commission nor the Court should review the substantive policy justifications for the restriction. This brings us to the next section.

2. Objective Justifications

2.1 The Court's Case Law

In *Arduino*, the Court does not examine the substantive policy merits of the state measure in question. This would seem quite normal. If the state measure does not fall within the scope of Article 3(1)(g) EC, read in combination with Article 10(2) and Article 81(1) EC, because it amounts to a genuine state measure, that must be the end of the analysis. If the state authorities play an active role in the adoption and enforcement of the restriction of competition, the presence of public interest grounds is a given and it is not for the Commission or the Court to vet the merits of these grounds when assessing the state measure under EC competition law.

One could counter this argument by developing the following reasoning. State measures impeding the free movement of goods, persons, services or capital are prohibited pursuant to the relevant EC Treaty provisions (Article 28, Article 39 and 43, Article 49, Article 56 EC) unless they can be shown to pursue legitimate objectives and to do so in a proportionate manner (ie, no equally efficient, less restrictive alternative). This substantive legality test is either spelled out in the EC Treaty itself (Article 30, Article 39(3), Article 46(1), Article 55 and Article 58(1)(b) EC mentioning objective justifications such as public policy or public security) or has been developed by the Court (eg, the *Cassis de Dijon* mandatory requirements[125]). If anti-competitive state measures for which the Member States assume full responsibility, are not subject to a similar substantive legality test, the lacuna that the Court tried to fill in *GB-INNO-BM* remains in place. These state measures can indeed also undermine the 'single market system' to which the Court refers so prominently in *GB-INNO-BM*. If all 'negative integration' Treaty provisions are

[125] Case C–33/76 *Rewe-Zentral v Bundesmonopolverwaltung für Branntwein* [1979] ECR 649 in particular para 8:

> obstacles to movement within the Community resulting from disparities between the national laws relating to the marketing of the products in question must be accepted in so far as those provisions may be recognised as being necessary in order to satisfy mandatory requirements relating to the effectiveness of fiscal supervision, the protection of public health, the fairness of commercial transactions and the defence of the consumer.

meant to form a 'seamless web' of instruments designed to establish the common market within the meaning of Article 2 EC, such a lacuna is hard to explain or justify.[126] Today, one could even strengthen the above reasoning by observing that Article I–3(2) of the draft Treaty establishing a European Constitution brings 'market integration' and 'competition' together on the same footing.[127]

In light of *CNSD* and *Arduino*, the Court's answer to this counter-argument seems to be as follows. While the 'negative integration' measures do indeed form a seamless web,[128] the point is that there is no express 'negative integration' Treaty provision prohibiting all anti-competitive state measures similar to the prohibition provisions directed against the state measures that impede the free movement of goods, persons, services and capital (see also above).

As a consequence, the only scenario in which anti-competitive state measurers could be subject to a substantive assessment of their merits would be one where these measures restrict not only competition but also the free movement of goods, persons, services or capital. This scenario is by no means unrealistic. In many state action cases, the applicability of the Treaty provisions concerning the free movement of goods or services has also been raised.[129]

The question remains whether anti-competitive state measures which do fall within the scope of Article 3(1)(g) EC, read in combination with Article 10(2) and Article 81(1) EC, can be 'saved' on the basis of substantive objective justifications. In our view, the answer is affirmative. However, this answer has nothing to do with the 'seamless web' idea. The reasoning is as follows. Since these state measures involve a good deal of delegation, they necessarily fail to reflect a 'clearly articulated' and 'actively supervised' public policy. Hence, neither the state authorities nor the undertakings concerned

---

[126] Building on the 'seamless web' idea, we argued some time ago that anti-competitive state measures should be assessed on the basis of the same substantive criteria as those traditionally used to assess state measures which infringed 'the four freedoms' (see L Gyselen, 'Anti-competitive State Measures under the EC Treaty: Towards a Substantive Legality Standard' (2003) *European Law Review* special issue on 'Competition Law Checklist 1993' 55).

[127] Article I–3 deals with the Union's objectives. Its second para reads as follows: 'The Union shall offer its citizens an area of freedom, security and justice without internal frontiers, and an internal market where competition is free and undistorted'.

[128] In judgments such as *Bosman* or *Wouters*, the Court has actually recognised the need for consistency in the analysis of impediments on free movement and restrictions of competition. In *Bosman*, the Court concluded that the football transfer system was not justified under Art 39(3) EC and *hence* was not justified under Art 81(3) EC either. Conversely in *Wouters*, the Court concluded that the ban on multidisciplinary partnerships between attorneys and accountants was justified under Art 46(1) EC (right of establishment) or Art 55 EC (freedom to supply services) for the reasons set out in its assessment of that ban under Art 81(1) EC, ie, because the ban 'could reasonably be considered to be necessary for the proper practice of the legal profession, as organised in the country concerned'.

[129] See, eg, the early *RPM* cases, *GB-INNO-BM*, *van de Haar*, *Cullet and Leclerc*, but also *VVR*, *van Eycke* and *Wouters*.

can successfully invoke (in favour of the restriction of competition) public interest grounds similar to those found in Article 30 EC and the other Treaty provisions concerning state measures limiting the four freedoms. The only available objective justifications are therefore those which can be invoked under Article 81(3) EC. As the Commission explains in its recent notice, this provision provides a basis for clearing agreements that restrict competition but which 'may at the same time have pro-competitive effects by way of efficiency gains'.[130] In other words, it provides for an efficiency defence.[131] There is thus no room for non-economic, public interest justifications.

2.2 The Commission's 2004 Communication

In its 2004 Communication, the Commission takes a different stand with regard to objective justifications. It is in part more generous, in part more severe.

The Commission's 'more generous' attitude applies to the 'rubber-stamp approvals' or 'practices whereby the authorities of a Member State are only entitled to reject or endorse the proposals of professional bodies without being able to alter their content or substitute their own decisions for these proposals' which fall within the scope of Article 3(1)(g) EC, read in combination with Article 10(2) and Article 81(1) EC.[132] Addressing the issue of objective justification, the Commission observes that 'a proportionality test would seem appropriate to assess to what extent an anti-competitive professional regulation truly serves the public interest' and that 'for this purpose, it would be useful that each rule had an explicitly stated objective and an explanation how the chosen regulatory measure is the least restrictive mechanism to effectively attain the state objective' (emphasis added).[133]

In our view, an anti-competitive state measure either unambiguously reflects a 'clearly articulated' and 'actively supervised' public policy or it does not. It would seem to us that rubber-stamp approvals or the other decisions referred to by the Commission cannot, by their very nature, reflect such a policy. If this is correct, we cannot see how a Member State could save these measures *ex post* on public interest grounds by relying on some 'explicitly stated objective' as a justification for them and on some 'explanation' about their proportionate character.

The more severe part of the Commission's attitude has already been commented upon (see above). The Commission envisages the application of a proportionality test for all anti-competitive regulations, whatever the degree of responsibility assumed by the public authorities. From a strictly legal point

---

[130] See Commission Guidelines on the application of Art 81(3) EC OJ C 101 [2004], para 33.
[131] A distinction is made between cost efficiencies and qualitative efficiencies (see paras 59–72).
[132] See para 87 of the Guidelines quoted above.
[133] See para 88 of the Guidelines quoted above.

of view, this statement is at odds with *Arduino*. However, the Commission's sole intention may have been to invite the national regulatory authorities to apply self-restraint on a voluntary basis (see above).

3. Impact on Interstate Commerce

Leaving aside the early RPM cases and *Asjes*, the state action cases, including those concerning liberal professions, raise purely intra-state competition problems. However, the Court has consistently held that a restriction of competition (whether resulting from a state measure, from an agreement or from a combination of both) which extends to the whole territory of a Member State affects interstate trade within the meaning of Article 81(1) EC because it 'has, by its very nature, the effect of reinforcing the compartmentalisation of markets on a national basis, thereby holding up the economic interpenetration which the Treaty is designed to bring about'.[134]

It follows from this broad formula that intra-state restrictions of competition can affect interstate trade even if they do not hinder such trade or—to put it in familiar antitrust language—even if they do not foreclose interstate competition. As the Court puts it in *van de Haar*, 'Article [28] of the Treaty, which seeks to eliminate national measures capable of hindering trade between Member states, pursues an aim different from that of Article [81], which seeks to maintain effective competition between undertakings'.[135]

However, in its recent guidelines on the 'effect on trade' concept contained in Article 81(1) and Article 82 EC, the Commission explains that cartels covering a single Member State are capable of reinforcing the 'compartmentalisation of markets' because their participants 'normally need to take action to exclude competitors from other Member States'.[136] In other words, in the Commission's eyes, these state-wide restrictions will affect interstate trade because of their foreclosure potential. This view surely applies mutatis mutandis to anti-competitive state measures.

---

[134] See *CNSD,* cited above, n 9, para 48 referred to in *Arduino*, cited above, n 10 (para 33) and copied in *Wouters*, cited above, n 11 (para 95). The Court might add some plus-factors (as it did in *CNSD* and *Wouters*) but even without such factors, an effect on interstate trade will be found (see *Arduino*).

[135] Cited above, n 34, para 14.

[136] See *Commission Guidelines on the effect on trade concept contained in Arts 81 and 82 of the Treaty* OJ C 101 [2004], para 79. The Commission adds that 'it is not decisive whether such action against competitors from other Member States is in fact adopted at any given point in time' (para 80). For instance, 'if the cartel price is similar to the price prevailing in other Member States, there may be no immediate need for the members of the cartel to take action against competitors from other Member States. What matters is whether or not they are likely to do so, if market conditions change' (*ibid*).

In addition, in line with the—often forgotten—qualification in *Béguelin* and *La Hesbignonne*[137] that the restriction must affect interstate commerce to an appreciable extent, the Commission announces in its recent guidelines that it will deem agreements to fall outside the scope of Article 81(1) or Article 82 EC where there is no appreciable affectation of trade ('NAAT').[138] This NAAT rule is no doubt also valid for anti-competitive state measures.

As a consequence, anti-competitive state measures that do not—actually or potentially—create appreciable foreclosure effects would seem to fall outside the scope of Article 3(1)(g) EC, read in combination with Article 10(2) and Article 81(1) or Article 82 EC. In any event, this conclusion would be consistent with the Commission's recent guidelines on the concept of interstate trade. Perhaps one can add an a fortiori argument. Article 3(1)(g) and Article 10(2) EC only contain an implied constitutional limitation upon anti-competitive state measures. In contrast, state measures that restrict the free movement of goods (or mutatis mutandis persons, services or capital) are subject to express constitutional limitations that are set forth in Article 28 EC (or the other applicable prohibition provisions). Even in this area, the Court has narrowed the scope for challenging the relevant state measures.[139]

As we have seen, the FTC's warning concerning interstate commerce goes in the opposite direction (see paragraphs 116–18 above). Without—of course—calling into question the principle of state action immunity in view of the US constitutional context, the FTC refers to the facts in Parker *v* Brown and warns that state action may have substantial negative spill over effects upon interstate commerce. The FTC admits that few state action cases show 'fact-patterns that would have brought interstate spill-over concerns to the forefront' (see footnote 119). Nevertheless, the FTC notes that 'when anti-competitive state regulations tend to produce in-state benefits but out-of-state harms, states have incentives to over-regulate in ways that reduce welfare for the nation as a whole' and that 'if such a state regulatory regime is allowed to override a national policy in favour of competition, efficiency goals will be frustrated'.[140] The FTC offers no operational proposals but notes that

[137] Case 22/71 *Béguelin Import v GL Import-Export* [1971] ECR 949; and Case 27/87 *Louis Erauw-Jacquery v La Hesbignonne* [1988] ECR 1919, para 17.

[138] Cited above, n 136, paras 50–57. The NAAT rule gives rise to a refutable presumption in this respect.

[139] Joined Cases C–267 and 268/91 *Keck and Mithouard* [1993] ECR I–6097, para 16:

> Contrary to what has been decided, the application to products from other Member states of national provisions restricting or prohibiting certain selling arrangements is not [caught by Art 28 EC], provided that those provisions apply to all affected traders operating within the national territory and provided that they affect in the same manner in law and in fact, the marketing of domestic products and of those from other Member States.

[140] See its Report, cited above, n 109, at p 41.

'greater recognition of the nation's competition policies in settings involving significant interstate spill-overs could provide substantial benefit'.[141]

In short, there is a two-fold contrast between the US and the EU perspective on interstate trade.

First, the Commission's guidance on the concept of interstate trade suggests that the state action liability doctrine should be kept 'in the box', ie, should be reserved for cases where the Community's jurisdiction is beyond doubt. In contrast, the FTC warns that the current US state action immunity doctrine does not adequately address the negative impact of anti-competitive state measures on interstate trade.

Second, the spill over effect which the FTC has in mind is similar to the negative impact on interstate commerce in BNIC: a production quota system set up in one state causes harm to out-of-state citizens because they pay more for the product than in the absence of such a system. This 'spill over' concept focuses on harm to out-of-state consumers, whereas (with the exception of BNIC) the EU case law focuses on harm for out-of-state competitors in the form of foreclosure. No surprise—some will say—to find once more the emphasis on consumer welfare in the US as opposed to the EU, where the focus is on the competitive process.

VI. Conclusion

We conclude the present contribution with a summary of six 'theses'.

First, there is growing convergence between the US and EU case law on state action. The US Supreme Court's two-pronged *Midcal* test leaves no room for challenging 'clearly articulated' and 'actively supervised' anti-competitive state measures. The substantive merits of these measures are not screened under this test. In *CNSD* and *Arduino*, the European Court advances a similar legality test: state measures whereby the public authorities retain full responsibility for the restriction of competition fall outside the scope of Article 3(1)(g) EC, read in combination with Article 10(2) and Article 81 EC. These measures too are lawful, whatever their substantive merits. However, in light of the ambiguity in *Fiammiferi*, confirmation from the Court would be welcome.

[141] See its Report, cited above, n 109, at p 44. In n 180, at p 42, the FTC observes that 'one answer might be that this is a problem better addressed by the Constitution's negative commerce clause' but that 'this avenue provides challenges of its own'. As we have mentioned before (see para 27 above), the negative or dormant commerce clause case law (for which there is no textual basis in the US Constitution) is far less well-established than the EC case law banning state measures that raise obstacles to the free movement of goods, services, etc. (on the basis of explicit prohibition provisions in the EC Treaty).

Second, if *CNSD* and *Arduino* indeed stand for a scaled-down state action doctrine along the lines of *Midcal,* clarification would also be welcome about the precise modalities for the application of this doctrine. More specifically, when can it be concluded that an anti-competitive state measure is sufficiently 'clearly articulated' and 'actively supervised' to pass muster?

Third, state measures by which the public authorities have delegated to private undertakings the responsibility for restricting competition fall within the scope of Article 3(1)(g) EC, read in combination with Article 10(2) and Article 81(1) EC, and must be assessed anti-competitive agreements within the meaning of Article 81(1) EC. If these measures restrict competition to an appreciable extent and produce an appreciable effect upon interstate trade, the state authorities can argue that their measures generate efficiency gains within the meaning of Article 81(3) EC. These gains must be distinguished from public interest grounds, which have no place in Article 81(3) EC (see paragraph 136 above). Here too, clarification would be welcome since none of the cases has so far led to an assessment of possible objective justifications for the anti-competitive measures concerned.

Fourth, 'clearly articulated' and 'actively supervised' anti-competitive public regulations can be challenged if they also restrict the free movement of goods, persons, services or capital within the meaning of the relevant EC Treaty provisions, as interpreted by the Court. Public interest objectives can, however, save such state measures, provided these measures constitute a proportionate means to achieve these objectives.

Fifth, in its guidelines on the concept of interstate trade, the Commission has announced that it will examine more carefully whether or not agreements restricting competition also have an effect on interstate trade. For consistency reasons, the foreclosure rationale as well as the 'NAAT' rule must also apply to anti-competitive state measures.

Sixth, the narrow margin left by *CNSD* and *Arduino* to challenge anti-competitive state measures under the EC Treaty's antitrust provisions combined with its own interpretation of the interstate trade concept (based on the case law) may have inspired the Commission to play up its 'competition advocacy' role and to play down its 'law enforcement' role in its 2004 Communication regarding competition in professional services.

VIII

*William Kolasky**

Antitrust and the Liberal Professions: The US Experience

In 2005 we celebrated the 30th anniversary of the Supreme Court's decision in *Goldfarb v Virginia State Bar*[1] holding that the antitrust laws apply to what we in the United States used to call the 'learned professions.' In the 30 years since that decision, the Supreme Court has decided eight antitrust cases involving the application of the antitrust laws to these professions. In this paper, I examine these decisions and the framework they have created for applying the antitrust laws to professional services.

As this review will show, the cases involving the application of the antitrust laws to the learned professions that have reached the Supreme Court have often involved direct restraints on price and output agreed among competing providers of professional services. The Court has consistently, and correctly, treated these as naked price-fixing agreements that are just as unlawful when adopted by lawyers and doctors as when adopted by trash haulers or road pavers. Another string of cases that has reached the Supreme Court has involved restrictions on the advertising of professional services, often in the name of preventing false or misleading advertising. Here, the Court has taken a more nuanced approach, condemning those advertising restrictions that deny consumers truthful information about the prices at which services are available, while showing more tolerance for restrictions that might serve a procompetitive objective by protecting consumers from false or misleading claims.

With that prelude, let us review the decisions. We will then close with a brief coda on whether the liberal professions should be entitled to special treatment under the antitrust laws. We conclude that they should not.

I. *Goldfarb v Virginia State Bar*

Lewis Goldfarb and his wife contracted to buy a home in Fairfax County, Virginia. The finance company demanded title insurance, which required a title examination that only a member of the Virginia State Bar could legally

* Wilmer Cutler Pickering Hale and Dorr LLP.

[1] *Goldfarb v Virginia State Bar* 421 US 773 (1975).

perform. When they contacted a lawyer, he quoted them a fee of 1% of the value of the property, which was the fee specified in a minimum-fee schedule published by the Fairfax County Bar Association. Trying to find a lawyer who would charge a lower fee, Mr Goldfarb wrote to 36 other Fairfax County lawyers, all of whom quoted the exact same fee. Goldfarb paid the fee, then filed a class action against both the State Bar and the County Bar alleging that the minimum fee schedule constituted price fixing in violation of Section 1 of the Sherman Act.

In defending their actions, the State and County Bars argued, first, that 'learned professions' such as law are not covered by the antitrust laws because they do not constitute 'trade or commerce.' The Supreme Court squarely rejected this argument. It held that the language of Section 1 contains no exception for professional services and that there is no other basis for exempting individuals who sell their services for money from the Sherman Act. The Court observed, however, that '[t]he fact that a restraint operates upon a profession as distinguished from a business is, of course, relevant in determining whether that particular restraint violates the Sherman Act.'[2]

The Bars argued, second, that the state action doctrine protected their minimum fee schedule. The state action doctrine derives from a Supreme Court decision, *Parker v Brown*,[3] in which the Court held that the antitrust laws did not apply to a state-sanctioned California program that restricted competition among growers for the express purpose of restricting output and maintaining prices in the market for raisins. In *Goldfarb*, the Court held that the state action doctrine did not shield the defendant's minimum fee schedule because there was no Virginia statute authorizing the State or County Bar to promulgate minimum fees. While Virginia law authorized the State Supreme Court to regulate the legal profession, the Court's rules did not authorize the State or County Bar to set minimum fees. Therefore, even though the State Bar might be a state agency for some limited purposes, such as issuing ethical opinions, that status did not, the Court held, 'create an antitrust shield that allows it to foster anticompetitive practices for the benefit of its members.'[4]

II. *Virginia State Board of Pharmacy v Virginia Citizens Consumer Council*[5]

While not an antitrust case, *Virginia State Board*, decided just one year after *Goldfarb*, merits examination because it involves the closely related issue of to

[2] *Goldfarb v Virginia State Bar* 421 US 773 (1975), pp 788–89, no 17.
[3] 317 US 341 (1943).
[4] *Goldfarb*, pp 791–92.
[5] 425 US 748 (1976).

what extent the First Amendment limits the ability of the states themselves to regulate professional advertising. The First Amendment to the US Constitution is a key provision of our Bill of Rights. It provides that Congress and, by virtue of the Fourteenth Amendment, the states, 'shall make no law . . . abridging the freedom of speech.'

In *Virginia State Board*, the Supreme Court considered the validity under the First Amendment of a Virginia statute barring pharmacists from advertising the prices for prescription drugs. In holding the statute unconstitutional, the Court held for the first time that the First Amendment protects commercial, as well as political, speech. In reaching this conclusion, the Court cited the consumer welfare benefits of such speech, observing that 'commercial speech serves to inform the public of the availability, nature, and prices of products and services, and thus performs an indispensable role in the allocation of resources in a free enterprise system,' citing *FTC v Procter & Gamble (Clorox)*,[6] an antitrust case. The Court held, however, that the First Amendment would not protect affirmatively false or misleading commercial speech and that there might be other circumstances in which the state might be able to justify restrictions of commercial speech that would not be permitted in the case of purely political speech.

The Court proceeded to examine the justifications proffered by Virginia for prohibiting pharmacists from advertising prescription drug prices. Central to these were claims that the ban was essential to the maintenance of professionalism among licensed pharmacists. The state argued, among other things, that advertising would create price competition that might cause the pharmacist to economize at the customer's expense and would reduce the image of the pharmacist as a skilled and specialized craftsman, necessary to attract talent to the profession. The Court rejected these proffered justifications, noting the presence of a potent alternative to this highly paternalistic approach:

> That alternative is to assume that this information is not in itself harmful, that people will perceive their own best interest if only they are well enough informed, and that the best means to that end is to open the channels of communication rather than to close them.[7]

III. *Bates v State Bar of Arizona*[8]

The next case, *Bates v State Bar*, decided one year later, brings together strands of *Goldfarb* and *Virginia State Board*. In it, the Court held that restrictions on

[6] 386 US 568 (1967).
[7] *Virginia State Board Of Pharmacy* 425 US, 748 (1976) at 770.
[8] 433 US 350 (1977).

attorney advertising imposed by the Supreme Court of Arizona constituted state action not subject to attack under the Sherman Act, but that the restrictions violated the First Amendment insofar as they prohibited publication of a truthful advertisement concerning the availability and terms of routine legal services.

On state action, the critical difference between *Bates* and *Goldfarb* was that the advertising restrictions in *Bates* were contained in a disciplinary rule promulgated by the Arizona Supreme Court itself. The rules, therefore, satisfied both elements of what has since become the standard two-part test for state action: (1) they reflected 'a clear articulation of the State's policy with regard to professional behavior' and (2) they were subject to 'active state supervision.'[9]

The disciplinary rule at issue in *Bates* broadly prohibited lawyers from publicizing their services through advertisements of any kind. The advertisement at issue contained a simple listing of routine legal services, such as uncontested divorces and name changes, offered by the firm placing the advertisement and the fees the firm charged for those services. Following its decision in *Goldfarb*, the Court held that just as the First Amendment does not allow a state to prevent pharmacists from advertising prices for prescription drugs, so, too, does it bar a state from prohibiting lawyers advertising the availability and terms of routine legal services.

In so holding, the Court considered and rejected six possible justifications for the restrictions proffered by the state: the adverse effect on professionalism, the inherently misleading nature of attorney advertising, the adverse effect on the administration of justice, the undesirable economic effects of advertising, the adverse effect of advertising on the quality of service, and the difficulties of enforcement of more targeted restrictions. The Court was careful, however, to limit its ruling to the facts before it, noting in particular that it was not addressing 'the peculiar problems associated with advertising claims relating to the quality of legal services,' which 'under some circumstances, might well be deceptive or misleading to the public, or even false.'[10] The Court thus left the door open for regulation of professional advertising, both by the state and even, as we shall see, by private professional associations.

IV. *National Society of Professional Engineers v United States*[11]

The National Society of Professional Engineers is a professional association representing the more than 12,000 consulting engineers who perform services

[9] 433 US 350 (1977), p 362.
[10] *Ibid*, p 366.
[11] 435 US 679 (1978).

in connection with the study, design, and construction of buildings and other structures. The Justice Department sought to enjoin the Society from enforcing a canon of ethics that prohibited competitive bidding by its members.

The Court accepted at the outset that engineering is 'an important and learned profession.'[12] The Society argued that the canon was a reasonable restraint of trade because 'competitive pressure to offer engineering services at the lowest possible price would adversely affect the quality of engineering' and thereby endanger public health and safety.[13] Construing this as an argument that 'competition among professional engineers was contrary to the public interest,' the Court rejected the argument out of hand. It held that '[t]he Sherman Act reflects a legislative judgment that ultimately competition will not only produce lower prices, but also better goods and services,' and that this 'statutory policy precludes inquiry into the question whether competition is good or bad.'[14]

As in *Goldfarb*, the Court again acknowledged that 'by their nature, professional services may differ significantly from other business services,' and that ethical norms designed 'to regulate and promote competition' for professional services might, therefore, survive scrutiny under the antitrust laws.[15] But the Court held that this could not save a total ban on competitive bidding. Responding to an argument that the ban was needed because otherwise professional engineers might be tempted to submit deceptively low bids, the Court agreed that 'the problem of professional deception is a proper subject of an ethical canon,' but held that a canon barring competitive bidding altogether was an overbroad means of pursuing that objective.

V. *Arizona v Maricopa County Medical Society*[16]

The Maricopa County Medical Society represented some 1,750 physicians, or about 70% of the practitioners in Maricopa County. The Society formed the Maricopa Foundation to perform three primary activities. The first was to establish a schedule of maximum fees that participating doctors agreed to accept as payment in full for medical services performed for patients insured under plans approved by the foundation. The second was to review the medical necessity and appropriateness of the treatment provided by its members to these patients. The third was to draw checks on insurance company accounts to pay doctors for services for covered patients. In performing these

[12] *Ibid*, p 679.
[13] *Ibid*, p 684.
[14] *Ibid*, p 695.
[15] *Ibid*.
[16] 457 US 332 (1982).

functions, the foundation was considered an 'insurance administrator' by the Director of the Arizona Department of Insurance.

The Arizona state attorney general brought an action alleging that the agreement among participating physicians as to the maximum fees they would accept was a *per se* violation of Section 1 of the Sherman Act. By a 4–3 vote, the Supreme Court agreed.

In reaching this result, the Court rejected arguments by defendants that the *per se* rule should not apply because the agreements at issue were among members of a profession, were in an industry with which the judiciary had little antitrust experience, and were alleged to serve procompetitive purposes. The Court's discussion of the first two arguments could best be discussed as peremptory. Citing *Goldfarb*, the Court again acknowledged that the public service aspect and other features of professions might permit some practices that might otherwise be unlawful under the antitrust laws, but reiterated that a price-fixing agreement could not be justified on either public service or ethical grounds. The Court also rejected the argument that it should not apply the *per se* rule because the judiciary had little experience in the health care industry, observing that requiring the *per se* rule to be 'rejustified for every industry that has not been subject to significant antitrust litigation' would undermine the rationale for having *per se* rules in the first place.[17]

Turning to the defendants' proffered procompetitive justifications, the Court held that while there might well be some benefit to knowing in advance what fees doctors would charge for their services, 'it is not necessary for the doctors to do the price fixing' and that insurance companies were capable of setting the maximum fees they would be willing to pay and obtaining binding agreements to those fees from individual physicians.[18] The court was careful to note, however, that the situation might be different if, for example, a clinic offered complete medical coverage for a flat fee because that would involve 'the type of partnership arrangement in which a price-fixing agreement among the doctors would be perfectly proper.'[19]

VI. *FTC v Indiana Federation of Dentists*[20]

Indiana Federation arose from efforts by insurers to require dentists to submit dental x-rays along with their insurance claims. In the early 1970s, the Indiana Dental Association, representing some 85% of the dentists in

---

[17] 457 US 332 (1982), p 349.
[18] *Ibid*, p 352.
[19] *Ibid*, p 357.
[20] 476 US 447(1986).

Indiana, enlisted member dentists not to submit x-rays. After the Association consented to an FTC order requiring it to cease and desist from this effort, a group of dentists formed the Indiana Federation of Dentists to carry on the fight. The federation's membership was very small—fewer than 100 dentists—but it succeeded in enlisting 100% of the dentists in one mid-sized city and 67% of the dentists in another to refuse to supply x-rays to insurers.

The Court began its analysis by noting that this policy resembled a 'group boycott' of the kind that is sometimes said to be *per se* illegal under the antitrust laws, but the Court declined to invoke the *per se* rule for two reasons. First, according to the Court, 'the *per se* approach has generally been limited to cases in which firms with market power boycott suppliers or customers in order to discourage them from doing business with a competitor,' a situation not present in this case.[21] Second, the Court observed that, 'we have been slow to condemn rules adopted by professional associations as unreasonable *per se*,' citing *Professional Engineers,* a somewhat questionable assertion after *Maricopa.*

The Court proceeded nevertheless to find the agreement by members of the Federation not to supply x-rays to insurers unlawful under a truncated rule of reason analysis. First, the Court found that such a refusal limits consumer choice and is, therefore, unlawful '[a]bsent some countervailing procompetitive virtue—such as, for example, the creation of efficiencies in the operation of a market or provision of services.'[22] Second, the Court held that the Commission's failure to make detailed findings as to market definition was not fatal both because the dentists involved 'constituted heavy majorities of the practicing dentists in their communities and because "proof of actual detrimental effects, such as reduction of output, can obviate the need for an inquiry into market power, which is but a surrogate for detrimental effects."'[23]

Third, the Court held that it was not necessary for the Commission to prove that the refusal to supply x-rays made dental service more costly because a refusal to supply such information was 'likely enough to disrupt the proper functioning of the price-setting mechanism of the market that it may be condemned even absent proof that it resulted in higher prices.'[24] Fourth, and finally, the court rejected the Federation's argument that x-rays, standing alone, are not adequate bases for diagnoses of dental problems. In the Court's view, arguing that giving customers access to information they believe to be relevant to their choices will lead them to make unwise and even dangerous choices, was 'nothing less than a frontal assault on the basic policy of the Sherman Act.'[25]

---

[21] *Ibid,* p 458.
[22] *Ibid,* p 459.
[23] *Ibid,* p 460.
[24] *Ibid,* p 461.
[25] *Ibid,* p 463.

VII. *FTC v Superior Court Trial Lawyers Association*[26]

Superior Court Trial Lawyers arose when a group of lawyers in Washington, DC conducted a highly publicized boycott, refusing to continue to represent indigent criminal defendants in the DC Superior Court until the District government increased the fees paid for such representation. (The fees at the time were capped at $30 an hour, less than 10% of what a lawyer in private practice might charge.) The case attracted particular interest because of the argument that the boycott was protected political activity, designed to encourage legislative reform.

The Supreme Court took a different view. The Court held that since the agreement among the lawyers was designed to obtain higher prices for their services, it was a *per se* unlawful naked restraint on price and output. In reaching this conclusion, the Court accepted that the boycott may well have served a worthwhile cause and that increased fees might well improve the quality of representation indigent defendants received, but held that '[t]he social justifications proffered for defendants' restraint of trade . . . do not make it any less unlawful.'[27]

VIII. *California Dental Association v FTC*[28]

The most recent, and in many ways most interesting, Supreme Court decision applying the antitrust laws to professional services is *California Dental Association.* Whereas the intervening decisions had all involved direct restraints on price and output competition, *California Dental* returned the Court to the subject of its two earliest forays into this area—professional advertising.

The California Dental Association ('CDA') is a voluntary non-profit association of local dental societies to which some 19,000 dentists belong, representing about 3/4 of the dentists practicing in California. The Association's code of ethics provided that while dentists may advertise, 'no dentist shall advertise . . . in a manner that is false or misleading in any material respect.'[29] Advisory opinions implementing this canon allowed dentists to advertise price discounts, but required that those advertisements disclose the non-

---

[26] 493 US 411(1990).
[27] *Ibid,* p 424.
[28] 526 US 756(1999).
[29] *Ibid,* p 760.

discounted price and the size and other terms of the discount. The advisory opinions also stated that claims as to quality of service were likely to be false or misleading because such claims 'are not susceptible to measurement or verification.'[30]

The FTC found both restrictions unlawful under the antitrust laws. The Commission treated the restrictions on discount advertising as *per se* unlawful price fixing. In the alternative, it held that the restrictions on both price and quality claims were unlawful using a highly truncated rule of reason analysis. The ninth Circuit Court of Appeals reversed the Commission with respect to its classification of the restrictions on discount advertising as *per se* unlawful, but otherwise affirmed the Commission's decision.

The Supreme Court reversed. The Court held that both the Commission and the Ninth Circuit had erred in truncating their rule of reason analysis in a manner that did not require the Commission to offer empirical evidence that CDA's advertising restrictions had an anticompetitive effect. The Court pointed out that the decisions in which it had found restraints unlawful through a similarly abbreviated analysis were all cases like *Professional Engineers* and *Indiana Federal* involving direct restraints on price or output. By contrast, the restrictions on advertising imposed by CDA did not 'present a situation in which the likelihood of anticompetitive effect is comparably obvious.'[31] As the Court explained, the restrictions adopted by CDA were, 'at least on their face, designed to avoid false or misleading advertising in a market characterized by striking disparities between the information available to the professional and the patient.'[32] *California Dental*, therefore, involved exactly the issue the Court had left open in its earliest decisions applying the antitrust laws to the liberal professions—namely, to what extent do the special characteristics of markets for professional services justify ethical restrictions on potentially false or misleading advertising.

This is an issue with which the Court had grappled repeatedly in the quarter century since *Goldfarb* and *Bates* in a series of cases involving the constitutionality under the First Amendment of state-imposed restrictions on professional advertising. These cases are catalogued and discussed in an article by outgoing FTC Chairman Tim Muris in an article published in 2000.[33] (Footnote 17 is the portion of the Court's opinion in *Goldfarb* in which the Court reserved the possibility that the special characteristics of the professions might justify ethical restraints not permitted in more prosaic industries, such as plumbing.)

As Chairman Muris' article shows, there were four cases between *Bates* and *Cal Dental* in which the Court applied the First Amendment to state-imposed

---

30 *Ibid,* p 761.

31 *Ibid,* p 771.

32 Ibid.

33 T Muris, '*California Dental Association v Federal Trade Commission*: The Revenge of Footnote 17' (2000) 8 *Supreme Court Economic Review* 265.

restrictions on professional advertising. In three of these the Court struck down state bans on professional advertising. In *Shapero v Kentucky Bar Association*,[34] the Court held that a ban preventing lawyers 'from soliciting legal business for pecuniary gain by sending truthful and nondeceptive to clients known to face particular legal problems' violated the First Amendment. In *Peel v Attorney Registration and Disciplinary Commission*,[35] the Court held that the state had breached the First Amendment by censoring an attorney for violating an Illinois bar rule against advertising oneself as a specialist because he truthfully advertised on his stationary that he was certified in civil trial advocacy by the National Board of Trial Advocacy. And in *Edenfield v Fane*,[36] the Court struck down a Florida ban on certified public accountants soliciting business with letters to potential clients. In the fourth and most recent of these cases, *Florida Bar v Went For It, Inc*,[37] the Court reached the opposite result, upholding a Florida rule barring a lawyer from contacting or writing for 30 days to anyone who had been injured, or to relatives of those who had been injured or killed, in accidents.

It is apparent from these decisions that by the time it heard *California Dental*, the Court had substantial experience weighing the costs and benefits of professional advertising. This experience plainly informed the Court's decision in *California Dental*. The Court's opinion includes a thorough review of the economic literature dealing with professional advertising. As the court observed, that literature shows that the markets for professional services are 'characterized by striking disparities between the information available to the professional and the patient.'[38] In these markets, the resulting 'difficulty for customers or potential competitors to get and verify information about the price and availability of services magnifies the dangers to competition associated with misleading advertising.'[39] This problem is compounded because

> the quality of professional services tends to resist either calibration or monitoring by individual patients or clients, partly because of the specialized knowledge required to evaluate the services, and partly because of the difficulty in determining whether, and the degree to which, an outcome is attributable to the quality of services (like a poor job of tooth filling) or to something else (like a tough walnut).[40]

Personal relationships further complicate the picture. As antitrust officials and lawyers who often marvel at the poor choices clients make in picking lawyers to represent them before the agencies, we know whereof the Court was speaking.

---

34 486 US 466 (1988).
35 496 US 91 (1990).
36 507 US 761 (1993).
37 515 US 618 (1995).
38 *California Dental*, p 771.
39 *Ibid*, p 772.
40 *Ibid*.

Based on this reading of the economic literature, the Court concluded that

> The existence of such significant challenges to informed decisionmaking by the customer for professional services immediately suggests that advertising restrictions arguably protecting patients from misleading or irrelevant advertising call for more than cursory treatment as obviously comparable to classic horizontal agreements to limit output or price competition.[41]

The Court held, therefore, that the FTC and Ninth Circuit should not have presumed, without empirical evidence, that CDA's efforts to regulate false or misleading advertising were anticompetitive, but should instead have engaged in a more detailed 'enquiry meet for the case,'[42] taking into account 'the countervailing, and at least equally plausible, suggestion that restricting difficult-to-verify claims about quality or patient comfort would have a procompetitive effect by preventing misleading or false claims that distort the market.'[43]

What is somewhat surprising is the vigor with which defenders of the FTC have criticized what appears on its face to be an eminently sensible decision by the Court to require that the agency be put to its proof. The Court's decision in *California Dental* is fully consistent with the general trend in antitrust jurisprudence, both in the United States and, more recently, in Europe, to challenge unproven theories and to demand more empirical evidence to support claims of anticompetitive harms.[44]

IX. Coda

In the 30 years since *Goldfarb*, we have moved from an industrial, largely domestic, economy to a truly global information economy. As part of this transformation, professional services of all kinds have come to play an increasingly central role, and the size of professional service organizations has grown accordingly. First accounting and now law firms have become truly global in scale, with several generating annual revenues in excess of $1 billion. In addition, many other kinds of services now require education equivalent to what was formerly required only of the 'liberal' or 'learned' professions. Business consultants, investment managers and bankers, real estate brokers, and many others now have as many or more years of education as lawyers or accountants. And many of these other service industries are at least as highly

---

[41] *Ibid*, p 773.

[42] *Ibid*, p 781.

[43] *Ibid*, p 778.

[44] See W Kolasky, '*California Dental Association v FTC*: The New Antitrust Empiricism' (1999) 14 *Antitrust* 68.

regulated as lawyers, doctors, dentists, and accountants. And it is at least an open question which of these professions is more deeply imbued with a sense of public service and public responsibility.

With all of these changes, there is something almost quaint, if not entirely archaic, in speaking of the liberal professions, or in suggesting that the antitrust rules that apply to these professions should be any different from those that apply to any other industry. In applying antitrust and competition laws to any industry, it is incumbent on the agencies and courts to take into account the particular characteristics of the markets involved, including any regulatory overlay to which that industry may be subject. As our Supreme Court wrote just this term in *Verizon Communications v Law Offices of Curtis v Trinko*,[45] 'Antitrust analysis must always be attuned to the particular structure and circumstances of the industry at issue. Part of that attention to economic context is an awareness of the significance of regulation.'[46] That this is true of the liberal professions does not, in any way, differentiate them from any other industry.

In practice, the US antitrust agencies fully understand this. They have, therefore, endeavored to apply the antitrust laws to the learned professions in the same manner as they do to other industries, taking into account the special characteristics of the markets in which they operate. To quote our greatest President, Abraham Lincoln, 'it is altogether fitting and proper' that they should do so.

---

[45] 124 SCt 872 (2004).

[46] *Ibid*, p 880.

IX

*Santiago Martínez Lage and Rafael Allendesalazar Corcho**

Professions and Competition in Spain: A Long and Winding Road

I. Professions and Professional Associations in Spain

Two simple facts reveal the importance in Spain of both the professions regulated by professional associations and the professional associations themselves: (i) the large number and great variety of professional associations; and (ii) the profusion of regulations governing their activity.[1]

1. Professional Categories

There are approximately 50 professions in Spain organised into professional associations, from the most traditional (lawyers, architects, doctors, etc) to the most unusual (weapons engineers or civil band conductors).

These professions can be categorised according to various criteria.

Based on the requirements to practise, one usually distinguishes between:

Unregulated professions: which can be practised without any academic or administrative qualification accrediting the knowledge of the practice (and registration in the relevant professional association is not compulsory);

Regulated professions: for which a prior administrative qualification is required;

Qualified professions: for which a university degree is required;

Membership professions: for which, in addition to holding an academic qualification, it is obligatory to be a member of the appropriate professional association.

Depending on the type of activity, a further distinction is usually made between the *liberal professions*, which are strictly private, and *public service professions* which, despite being private activities, provide a significant public service.[2]

---

* Partners at Martinez Lage & Asociados.

[1] As stated by the Competition Court (*Tribunal de Defensa de la Competencia*, hereinafter 'TDC') in its Report on the Free Exercise of the Professions of June 1992 (hereinafter 'the 1992 Report'), 'within the service sector the professional services subsector is, without doubt, the most highly regulated in the Spanish economy if one disregards those subject to statutory monopolies, and that which is the least subject to external competition' (p 9).

[2] The most typical examples are notaries public and land and companies registrars.

We will focus in this report essentially on the liberal membership professions, since we believe that these may raise the greatest doubts from the point of view of competition law. If only because they require compulsory membership, these professions are subject to a greater extent to the regulations which, as we shall see below, the professional associations can adopt to govern their activity.[3] We shall examine how the Spanish competition authorities, the legislator and courts have addressed the problems related to the application of competition rules to these professions from different perspectives and with different outcomes.

2. Regulations Governing Professional Activity

The various professional associations are subject to a series of regulations governing their activity, which include practically every tier of the regulatory pyramid.

The existence of professional associations is enshrined in Article 36 of the *1978 Spanish Constitution* itself (hereinafter, 'SC'): the SC devotes Article 36 to professional associations: 'The law shall regulate the specific features of the legal provisions governing professional associations and the practice of the qualified professions. The internal structure and operation of the associations shall be democratic'.

Article 36 SC falls under the chapter on 'Rights and Freedoms'. If it is assumed that the structure of the Constitution reflects the paramount importance which the constituent Parliament attached to the various principles governed by the Constitution, one need do no more than note that this article on the professional associations precedes Article 38 SC, which establishes 'freedom of enterprise in the context of the market economy' which, in turn, is directly linked to the protection of competition.[4]

Yet even before the 1978 Constitution, the professional associations had been the object of specific general regulations contained in *Ley 2/1974 de Colegios Profesionales* (Law on Professional Associations)[5] (hereinafter, 'LCP').

---

[3] As the TDC states in its 1992 Report, these membership professions 'have the huge backing of State power (. . .) as a result of compulsory membership' (p 11).

We should not think, however, that the associations of unregulated professions are unable to make decisions capable of affecting competition. By way of illustration, if you want to know how much a qualified archaeologist might charge you for giving a lecture, you would only need to go to the website of the General Council of the *Colegios Oficiales de Doctores y Licenciados en Filosofía y Letras y en Ciencias de España* (official associations of Spanish doctors and bachelors in humanities and sciences) to find out that the recommended rate is 210.87.

[4] Recitals to *Ley 16/1989 de Defensa de la Competencia* (Competition Law), hereinafter LDC.

[5] Ley 2/1974 de Colegios Profesionales of 13 February 1974 (BOE [Official State Gazette] no 40 of 15 February 1974).

We would like to draw attention to the following aspects of this statute:

> It is a pre-constitutional law, passed in the latter years of a political system which described itself as an 'organic democracy', since citizen participation in government was not channelled through directly-elected representatives but through State organs.[6] These organs included the professional associations, which were regarded as 'an organic channel for participation by the Spanish people in representative public functions and other tasks in the public interest'.[7]

The LCP is a short law, containing only nine articles, since its sole purpose is to set out the basic legal principles common to the various professional associations, ensuring 'the autonomy of the associations, their legal personality and full capacity to perform their professional as well as administrative duties relating to regulation of the professions in observance of the general law'.[8] Each professional association, in turn, is governed by its statute and by its internal rules, subject to any laws regulating the profession concerned.[9]

The LCP classifies the professional associations as 'public law corporations, protected by law and recognised by the State, with legal personality and full capacity to perform their duties'.[10] Together with this public function, the courts have ruled that the professional associations perform private duties in the interests of the profession.[11] Spanish professional associations can

---

[6] Accordingly in the recitals to the LCP it was stated: 'The principle of organic representation enshrined by the Spanish constitutional system is implemented by means of participation by the people in legislative tasks and the other general interest functions, which takes place via the family, municipality, trade union and any other organically represented entities recognised for this purpose by statute (. . .). The entities referred to include the professional associations (. . .)'.

[7] Recitals to the LCP In the same vein, the old Art 1.4 stated that 'the Professional Associations are the organic channel for participation by professionals in representative public functions and other general interest tasks, on the terms laid down in statute'. Furthermore Art 5.1a) defined as the primary purpose of the professional associations the role of 'acting as a channel for organic participation in tasks in the general interest in accordance with the law'.

[8] Recitals to the LCP.

[9] Art 6.1 LCP.

[10] Art 1.1 LCP.

[11] For example, Judgment of the Castilla y León High Court (Tribunal Superior de Justicia) no 46/2002 of 15 of March 2002 referred to this dual nature of the associations as follows:

> First, as regards the public nature of the duty, although it is true that, as stated by the judgment in question, professional bodies to a large extent and essentially serve private ends, basically those protecting the interests of the profession, this does not, however, mean that one can deny the public aspect which the State itself has seen fit to attribute to them. One cannot deny the dual nature of these corporations, referred to in legal writing and by the Constitutional Court itself (for example judgments of 5 August 1983, 15 July 1987 of 18 February 1988, and those corporations, whilst having a core of private purposes which explains their existence in the first place, nevertheless adopt public legal forms, are created by statute and, above all, perform both functions which involve compulsory collaboration with public authorities and quite clearly public functions delegated by those authorities, whether intended also for the immediate protection of their interests, or directly to protect the public interest, functions whose performance by a purely private law entity would not be acceptable, (. . .). Consequently, whether the immediate purpose is the protection of the profession or whether it is in certain cases, directly the public interest, there is no doubt that the professional associations perform functions which could only be performed by a public

therefore be regarded as dual—public and private—bodies. As we will see below, this issue has a decisive effect on whether or not actions by the associations are subject to the LDC.

Despite the fact that the LCP is pre-constitutional, there have been few amendments to it.

In 1978, a number of articles of the LCP were amended and certain sections removed in order to adapt the basic regulation of the associations to the change in political system which was about to end with the approval of the Constitution. It is worth noting that the 74/1978 Law, which amended the LCP, was passed by the Parliament on 26 December 1978, the eve of the approval of the Constitution (27 December 1978).

It is also worth pointing out that all the other amendments to the LCP have been specifically aimed at stipulating and consolidating the fact that professional associations have to comply with competition law. We shall see in greater detail the various stages in which this increasing subordination has gradually gelled.

The LCP recognises the self-regulatory powers of associations. In this regard, Article 6.1 LCP stipulates that 'professional associations, without detriment to the laws governing the profession in question, are governed by their statutes and internal regulations'.

The *General Statutes* comprise the basic rules applicable to all associations within the same profession. These provisions are drawn up by the General Councils (for those professions which have different territorial associations) or by the national associations, and must be approved by the Government.[12] Each association, for its part, draws up its *individual Statute* which must comply with the General Statutes, and is approved by the Council.[13]

In order to 'regulate the professional activity of its members, within the limits of its competence, ensuring ethical standards and the requirements of professional dignity',[14] the associations have the power to adopt *internal rules, provisions and decisions.*[15] They must exercise this power subject to all other provisions of the law—and, as we shall see below, specifically the LDC—and in accordance with the principles of necessity and proportionality.[16]

---

authority, under, moreover, monopoly conditions. . . . And, as regards the purpose, the State will in any event have taken into account that although the immediate purpose may be private, there is a public interest in the regulating it in a certain way, since it would otherwise have kept the legal forms available to associations strictly to the realm of private associations and would not have given them public tasks.

12 Art 6.2 LCP.

13 Art 6.4 LCP.

14 Art 5.i) LCP.

15 Art 5.t) LCP.

16 In this regard, the *Tribunal Supremo* (Supreme Court) stated in its judgment of 29 February:

it is the current *Ley de Colegios Professionales* (law on professional associations) itself which, mindful of the great diversity in the world of the professions and of the eminently ethics-related nature of this type of professional obligation or duty, for the purposes of the specific

This brief description of the regulatory framework would not be complete if we did not point out that, in Spain, in addition to national provisions, the regional governments (*Comunidades Autónomas*) can also issue regulations relating to professional associations.[17] One should likewise take into account that in a number of professions, as well as a National Council which embodies all the associations in Spain, there are regional councils consisting of the associations in that autonomous region.[18]

As we will see below, potential conflicts between the associations' regulations and competition have arisen not only at this lower level of association regulations, but also in relation to in the General Statutes notwithstanding the fact that they have to be approved by the Government.

II. Professional Associations as Bodies Subject to the LDC

Until the early 1990s, the debate in Spain was whether acts by professional associations were subject to the prohibitions in Articles 1 and 6 LDC, equivalent to Articles 81 and 82 EC. Although the Government since 1996 has expressly confirmed that the associations fall under the LCD, we shall see that even before then the TDC decided that it could review their decisions and even penalise them.

There were essentially two arguments which the associations, prior to the 1996 legislative reform, used to refute that they were accountable to the LDC: (i) the first, in turn, contains two closely-related facets: on the one hand, the legal nature of the associations and, on the other, the nature of their acts; and (ii) the second relates to the legal basis for their actions under the LCP. One should note that these are purely legal arguments, very different from the more economic ones which have been considered in other jurisdictions (asymmetry of knowledge by professionals and clients, quality of service, the

approach to be taken to them refers back to the self regulatory powers of each corporately-organised profession provided the mandatory requirements of compliance with the general law are adhered to and they are shown to be necessary and reasonably sufficient to ensure compliance with the fundamental duties of every member (behaviour which is compliant with ethics, dignity, respect for the rights of individuals, good faith in the course of professional activity, etc).

[17] Accordingly, one should cite the following Laws governing professional associations: Catalan Law 13/1982; Canary Islands Law 10/1990; Andalusia Laws 6/1995 and 10/2003; Castilla y León Law 8/1997; Madrid Law 19/1997; Basque Region Law 18/1997; Valencia Law 6/1997; Aragon Law 2/1998; Navarre Law 3/1998; Balearic Islands Law 10/1998; La Rioja Law 4/1999; Castilla-La Mancha Law 10/1999; Murcia Law 6/1999; Cantabria Law 1/2001; Galicia Law 11/2001; Extremadura Law 11/2002.

[18] For example, the Council of Bar Associations of the Community of Madrid comprises the Bar associations of Madrid and of Alcalá de Henares.

public service nature of the profession, etc) in seeking to justify a nuanced application of competition rules to the professions.

1. Professional Associations as Corporations under Public law

Under Article 1 LCP, professional associations are 'public law corporations, protected by law and recognised by the State (. . .) with full capacity to perform their duties'. Furthermore, Article 8 states that 'acts deriving from the bodies of the associations and from the General Councils, whenever subject to administrative law shall, once internal remedies have been exhausted, be subject to appeal directly to the contentious-administrative courts'.

In short, the associations invoked the fact that they were 'public authorities' whose actions were 'administrative acts'. They were therefore not, they asserted, accountable to the TDC (which, despite its name, is an administrative body)[19] and their actions could be reviewed by the contentious-administrative courts, but not by any other administrative body.

In response to the contention that the associations were a public authority, the TDC responded as early as 1992 that 'professional associations clearly have a strictly private basis and fundamentals, although public power is delegated to them for specific purposes'.[20] It again addressed the issue a few months later, giving a much longer and more fully reasoned reply:

> A second objection, related to the first, is the claim that the professional association should not be treated as an economic agent and therefore is not subject to the *Ley de Defensa de la Competencia* [Competition Law—emphasis added]. On the contrary, its activity as an economic agent is perfectly consistent with the work of protecting the private interests of its members. Indeed, as stated by the Constitutional Court (STC 20/1988 of 18 February FJ4), professional associations are 'sector corporations which are set up to protect primarily the private interests of their members, but which also serve the public interests. Because of this, they are legally constituted as public bodies or public law corporations'. In protecting private interests they act in the same way as any business association, and are therefore economic agents equivalent to those associations. Accordingly, for example, when an association claims fees on behalf of a member it is acting as an economic agent providing a service to a member (a fee collection service) as if it were a specialised firm. This service is the antithesis of what may be described as an administrative act, since the action in question is regarded as a service provided by the

[19] In Spain, the TDC is the only competent body to establish the existence of practices prohibited by the LDC, subject to the fact that its decisions are reviewable by the contentious-administrative courts. The TDC can apply Arts 81 and 82 EC, although in this case jurisdiction is shared with the *Juzgados de lo Mercantil* (Commercial Courts) set up by *Ley Orgánica para la reforma concursal* (organic law on insolvency reform) *8/2003 of 9 July*, and which will take effect on 1 September 2004.

[20] Decision of 20 November 1992, Proceedings 313/92, *Colegio de Arquitectos Vasco-Navarro*.

professional association to the member, a purely commercial or non-commercial service as indicated by many judgments of the *Tribunal Supremo* [Supreme Court—emphasis added]. (. . .)

The economic agents treated as businesses for the purposes of Community competition law, which is similar in all respects to Spanish law, are all those bodies which perform economic activities, irrespective of their legal status (Judgment of the ECJ of 12 December 1974, *Walgave v UCI* and of 23 April 1991, *Höfner and Elser v Macroton*). At the same time, any activity, including non-profit activities which form part of economic exchanges, is an economic activity (judgment of the ECJ of 20 March 1985, Case 41/83 *Republic of Italy v Commission*).

Accordingly, this TDC ratifies its view that the professional association, so often referred to as an economic agent and as a business for the purposes of competition law, should be treated as any other professional or business association when it protects the private interests of its members.[21]

Reading the Decisions in which the anti-competitive nature of acts by associations was questioned for the first time clearly reveals the way in which, in response to the associations' straightforward objection to their actions being reviewed by the competition authorities, the TDC replied with an equally extreme position, minimising the public nature of the associations and emphasising their profile as economic agents which seek essentially to protect the private interests of their members. It should be noted however that, once the legislature and the associations themselves have acknowledged that associations' acts which have an economic impact are subject to the LDC, the TDC has shown itself more inclined to acknowledge the dual (public and private) nature of the associations and their actions:

The question has also been raised as to the nature of the decisions in dispute and whether this is administrative activity on the part of the associations or activity liable to fall within the scope of competition provisions. It is true that professional associations, as public corporations, form part of what is known as institutional government and have a dual nature—that of public authorities and of professional guilds—and it will therefore be necessary to examine in each case the function they are performing. Whilst that is so, it is no less true that the TDC has a long history of applying competition provisions to decisions by professional associations of an economic content. This trend has been consolidated with the statutory reform of professional associations by *Real Decreto-Ley* (Royal Decree-Law—emphasis added) of 7 June 1996 and its subsequent conversion into a Law of 14 April 1997 after due parliamentary procedure. From the time of that statutory amendment there has been no room for further discussion of something which the TDC has been stating for a long while: the LDC applies to decisions by professional bodies which have economic significance.[22]

The TDC therefore regards the professional associations as economic agents to which not only Article 1 LDC but also the prohibition on the abuse of

---

21 Decision of 30 December 1993, Proceedings 333/92, *Placonsa*.

22 Decision of 4 March 1999, Proceedings R335/98 *Colegios Notariales*.

dominant position under Article 6 LDC applies, at least in the case of professions where membership is compulsory and with respect to practices of the associations limiting the provision of services by their members. It has also found that, in the event of infringement, the relevant fine can be imposed on an association:

> Similarly, case law has continually distinguished between the acts of the professional associations within delegated administrative powers and their acts as private professional associations. Where an association does not act with delegated administrative power but defends the interests of its members or performs an economic activity, it is behaving in exactly the same way as a business association, and can be liable to a fine for infringing competition regulations.[23]

In conclusion, the TDC has never allowed the fact that the LCP confers the status of public law corporations on professional associations to be an insurmountable obstacle to their being fully subject to the prohibitions and sanctions under the LDC, which should come as no surprise since the TDC has even gone so far as to fine a municipality for unfair competition.[24]

2. Acts by Professional Associations

Closely related to their status as public corporations under the LCP is the fact that the LCP itself states that the acts of the associations, 'wherever they are subject to an administrative law . . . will be subject to direct appeal to the contentious-administrative courts.'

From the outset, the associations sought to find in this provision grounds for contending that their acts were administrative acts which could not be subject to review by another administrative body such as the TDC. In the Decision on the Vasco-Navarro architects' association cited above, the TDC rejected this argument outright:

> Professional associations quite clearly have a strictly private basis and fundamentals although public power is delegated to them for specific purposes. For those purposes alone their actions are subject to review by the contentious-administrative courts, not because they are administrative acts, but because these courts have a better understanding than the ordinary courts of matters involving particular forms of authority, even though they may be simply granted or delegated by the State because they are more accustomed to addressing matters and issues which deal with questions of authority or manifestations of power, whether or not they take the form of administrative acts. (. . .) Allocation of the case to such a court, however,

---

[23] Decision of 28 July 1994, Proceedings 339/93 *COAM.* Certification is a power expressly referred to in Art 5.q) LCP and is typical of the associations covering construction professionals such as architects or civil engineers. Certification is configured as a mandatory decision by which the association confirms that a project complies with the law.

[24] Decision of 7 April 2003, Proceedings 535/02 *Eléctrica Eriste.*

in no way implies that their acts are administrative. They remain acts of private persons; they are based and founded on the exercise of delegated power by a member of civil society, not by a public authority, and as acts by private persons they are of course fully subject to the rules on free competition laid down by the LDC.

With this argument, as one can see, the TDC asserts that acts of the associations are subject to the LDC by questioning whether they are true administrative acts and regards them solely as administrative acts for the purposes of their review by the administrative courts.

A few months later, in its Decision of 28 July 1994, the TDC would again rule on the possibility of reviewing the acts of associations. In that case, the TDC changed its approach slightly since, rather than denying that an act was administrative, it seemed inclined to find that it had jurisdiction to review any act of an association which affects competition and does not have sufficient legal exemption. Accordingly, the TDC began by acknowledging that 'it does not have jurisdiction to review the administrative acts of a professional association vis-à-vis its members, for which there is an administrative and contentious course of action . . .', but then went on to specify:

. . . but it must examine whether a particular practice restricts competition and infringes the provisions of Competition Law with which all players, their associations and corporate bodies must comply. It has jurisdiction—it is the only body which has it at first instance—to examine whether an act by a professional association or by any other institution with delegated public functions constitutes a genuine administrative act outside the realm of business and which cannot be examined under the provisions of Competition Law.[25]

Since then, the TDC has taken the view that, when an association acts as an economic agent, making decisions which impact on the activity of third parties, we are no longer dealing with decisions 'of a purely administrative nature' but with practices which are subject to the LDC:

---

[25] Decision of 28 July 1994, Proceedings 339/93 *COAM*. This view was not, however, undisputed, since one of the members of the TDC delivered a highly-argued dissenting opinion in which it was stated, amongst other things:

My view is that Article 1 does exclude administrative activity.

I believe that the argument deriving from a systematic consideration of the LDC in the context of the law is sufficient. An administrative act enjoys a presumption of lawfulness which can be refuted but in order to ensure legal certainty in compliance with the rules which establish by whom, before whom and on what grounds this can be done (rules established in the present case, by Article 8 of the 1974 *Ley de Colegios Profesionales* [Law on Professional Associations—emphasis added]). Giving the Service or the Court power to review administrative activity with no other condition than a preliminary value judgement about a vague concept—that it 'might' affect competition—would mean giving it power which would run parallel to the system established for reviewing administrative acts and which would cover practically all administrative involvement in economic life—with the exception of state aid—irrespective of the reasons for that involvement, because all involvement is restrictive).

> In this case, COAVN is acting as an economic agent and does not make purely administrative decisions outside the course of business but its conduct has an effect on the economic activity of third parties with separate legal personality and must be examined by the TDC for its impact on free competition according to LDC.[26]

As we will see below, this debate as to whether acts by associations are subject to the LDC was also laid to rest by the legislature with the reform of the LDC and the LCP undertaken in 1996.

Nor is it any less striking that here too, once the reform legally confirmed the TDC's position, it seemed more open to acknowledging that acts regulating the profession, and which do not 'strictly have economic content', are part of their activity as an 'institutional authority' and fall outside the scope of the LDC.[27]

3. Statutory Exemption under Article 2.1 LDC

A third argument had traditionally been invoked seeking to exempt the acts of professional associations from the prohibitions of the LDC, or at least of

---

[26] Decision of 29 October 1999, Proceedings 444/98 *Colegio de Arquitectos Vasco-Navarro.*

[27] Accordingly in its Decision of 3 July 2003, Proceedings 545/02, *Colegio Notarial de Granada*, the TDC, contrary to the suggestion of the *Servicio de Defensa de la Competencia* (Competition Service), held that the bringing of penalty proceedings against a notary public for, amongst other practices, sending out a blanket mail shot announcing an intention to give discounts, was not contrary to Art 1 LDC The TDC held that the association's practice was not 'strictly economic in content' but that it had acted in exercise of its sovereignty (*'ius imperi'*) as a public corporation regulating the profession, that is, as an institutional authority:

> Professional associations are entities which have a dual public and private nature, since they are, on the one hand, public corporations forming part of what is known as the institutional authority and are charged, amongst other things, with regulating their respective professions and ensuring professional ethics within those professions and are also, on the other hand, professional guilds whose decisions are subject in the same way as those of any economic operator, to the Competition Law where they have an economic impact on the market. This has been the jurisprudence of this Court for a long time, subsequently consolidated in statute with the statutory reform of the professional associations under Royal Decree-Law of 7 June 1996 and its subsequent conversion into a Law of 14 June 1997 pursuant to due parliamentary procedure. As from that statutory amendment, there has no longer been any scope for discussion as to whether decisions by professional associations which have economic impact are subject to the LDC, but this has not implied any modification of the hybrid nature of the aforementioned professional associations, with the effect that when a professional association acts in its role as a public corporation regulating the profession in exercise of sovereignty, its decisions will remain subject to challenge before the contentious-administrative courts, whilst when it acts as an economic operator, its actions are amenable to proceedings before the administrative competition bodies, the Service and the Court.
>
> In the present case, having regard for, on the one hand, all the acts by the defendant notary public and, on the other, the grounds used by the Notarial College of Granada in order to bring the aforementioned disciplinary proceedings against that person, the Court takes the view that the acts of the association cannot be classified as acts of strictly economic content, but that the association in question acted as an institutional authority . . .

Article 1 LDC,[28] based on the statutory exemption foreseen in Article 2.1 LDC. In its original wording the aforementioned article stated that:

1. The prohibitions under Article 1 shall not apply to agreements, decisions, recommendations and practices arising from the application of a law or of any statutory provisions which may be issued in implementation of a law.
2. The Competition TDC shall have power to issue a reasoned proposal to the Government, via the Minister of Finance for the amendment or elimination of the restrictive practices set out the statutes.[29]

Accordingly, when an association was charged with any restrictive practice, it would immediately link its action to one of the functions attributed to associations in Article 5 LCP. If the conduct could not be directly linked to any specific function referred to in that article (such as 'regulating the minimum fees of the professions. . . .' (Article 5ñ LCP) it would be included under the heading of the generic self-regulation function (Article 5i LCP[30]) or the residual category (Article 5u LCP[31]).

Additionally, the associations argued that, since the TDC has power, under Article 2.2 LDC, to propose to the Government any statutory amendments it considers necessary to remove the statutory protection in question, in the event of doubt as to whether a particular practice was exempt or not, the TDC should not proceed with sanctions but should apply to the Government to clarify the situation.

In the few first years after the approval of the LDC in 1989, the TDC frequently applied Article 2 to exempt a number of decisions made by associations, which were anti-competitive[32] under Article 1 of the LDC.

However, immediately after it published its 1992 Report on Liberal Professions, the TDC was much more reluctant to entertain the statutory exemption. Thus, in a Decision of 10 November 1992 (Proceedings A 30/92, *Real Estate Association—Asociación de expertos inmobiliarios*) it stated that Article 2.1 LDC could not be given a 'broad interpretation' to the point of refusing to exempt a practice covered by a decree and not by law:

[28] The legal exemption provided in Art 2 LDC only refers to prohibitions contained in Art 1 LDC Prohibition of abuse also applies when the dominant undertakings' position on the market was established by a legal provision (Art 6.3 LDC).

[29] The statutory exemption only applies to the Art 1 LDC prohibitions (restrictive agreements) but not to those under Art 6 LDC (abuse of dominant position). Art 6.3 LDC in fact provides that 'the prohibition should also apply to cases where the dominant position in the market of one or more undertakings has been established by statutory provision'.

[30] 'Within the scope of its competence, to regulate the professional activity of members, ensuring ethical conduct and professional dignity and due respect for the rights of individuals and exercising disciplinary powers in professional and membership matters'.

[31] 'Such other functions as operate in the professional interests of members'.

[32] Accordingly in 1990 the TDC made three orders dismissing a further three claims against various medical colleges for setting minimum fees on the grounds that it found those agreements to be protected by the LCP: Decisions of 10 October 1990, (Proceedings A3/90, *Colegio de enfermería de Barcelona),* 16 October 1990, (Proceedings A4/90), *Colegio de Médicos de Sevilla),* 12 November 1990 (Proceedings A7/90), *Colegio de Médicos de Valencia).*

> First, the general question of deciding which administrative provisions can turn the practices prohibited by Article 1 into authorised practices, in accordance with the exemption under Article 2.1. The TDC takes the view that under Law 16/1989, all the practices described in Article 1 of that law must be considered prohibited, and must only authorise those which, as stated in Article 2.1, arise from application of a law or from any regulatory provisions issued in implementation of a law. Consequently, the TDC takes the view that the practices described in Article 1 are prohibited, even where they have a basis in administrative provisions, unless those provisions comply with the requirements set out in Article 2.1. The TDC takes the view that it cannot accept a broad interpretation, in which the practices would move from prohibited to authorised by having a basis in any form of provision. They have to be norms which are directly related to the conduct under consideration.
>
> Secondly, the specific question of whether the provision providing the basis for the practice in this case—Decree 3248/1969 of 4 December—is or is not a 'regulation implementing the Law' arises. (. . .) This Decree can only prevent action being taken against acts which appear to be anticompetitive if it was made in implementation of a law (. . .).
>
> However, without denying the validity of a provision and therefore preventing its application to other matters, the TDC can rule that, since Decree 3248/1969 is not 'prima facie' a regulatory provision applying a law, it cannot be grounds for an exception to the application of Article 1 of Law 16/1989, since it is not a regulatory provision issued in implementing a law.

Such an extreme view was robustly disputed by one TDC member in a dissenting vote in which, amongst other considerations, he stated:

> In my view it is clear that the Competition TDC cannot pursue practices, even though they are clearly anti-competitive, if they have a basis in regulatory provisions.
>
> It is for the contentious-administrative courts alone to decide on a regulation. Whilst a regulation is in force the administrative bodies have a duty to comply with it and are not entitled to omit, disregard or refuse to apply it. When they find that a regulation is unlawful, they resort to the legal processes that are available. (. . .) Since in this case there is a Decree (3248/1969 of 4 December), this TDC, which is an administrative body with no personality distinct from that of the Central Government, should have submitted to and complied with it in its Decision, without prejudice to the right to avail itself of the mechanism established in Article 2.2 of the Competition Law.

This very interpretation of Article 2.1 LDC is confirmed in Article 2.2 LDC itself. It is not without reason that the latter provision comes under the very same statutory heading as the former, 'practices authorised by law', thereby reducing the scope of the authority of the TDC when it finds itself judging anti-competitive practices authorised by an administrative provision. This is precisely the reason for the aforementioned power to make proposals to the Government, which the law gives to very few, exceptional, administrative bodies.

> To find otherwise would, in my opinion, place the party subject to regulation in an impossible dilemma: it either has to adapt its conduct to the provisions of the

> Regulation, in which case it could be penalised by this TDC, or it has to infringe the provisions of the Regulation, in which case, by definition, it infringes that regulatory provision.

From a reading of all the TDC rulings on professional associations one can deduce that, until the 1996 reform, the TDC took the view that General Statutes did provide a legal basis for conduct which would otherwise be contrary to Article 1 LDC, but on the other hand denied that the lower-ranking rules of associations had regulatory force.

Accordingly, for example, in 1994 it upheld the dismissal of a claim brought by Mr Pablo Casado Coca[33] against restrictions on advertising by lawyers contained in the General Statutes of the lawyers' profession (Estatuto General de la Abogacía), stating that:

> The existing restriction on advertising has its basis in the General Statutes of the lawyers' profession issued under LCP.
>
> It is plain that there is a statutory prohibition to treat a situation such as that described by the appellant as an anticompetitive practice, since there is a clear, legal banner which, whilst it remains in force, shelters the provisions of Article 31 of the *Estatuto General de la Abogacía* [emphasis added].
>
> It is for the legislature, therefore, to make the appropriate changes to the law if it sees fit.
>
> What is more, it should be noted that the TDC is not the body responsible for removing provisions by annulling them if they violate a higher-ranking one. That is the exclusive task of the contentious-administrative courts. . . .
>
> Quite a different matter is the scope which can be attributed to certain statutory and regulatory restrictions where they are amenable to interpretation, for which the TDC has established the principle of interpretation in favour of freedom, seeking at all times to bring competition to the market on the terms laid down by the Competition Law 16/1989.[34]

We will see later on that, after the 1996 reform, in the view of the TDC not even the practices directly founded in the General Statutes (which, it is worth remembering, are drawn up by the associations or their Councils but must be approved by the Government[35]) remain covered by the statutory exemption under Article 2.1 LDC.

As regards lower-ranking provisions adopted by the associations in the exercise of their self-regulatory powers of the profession under the LCP, the TDC has systematically refused to recognize that these are regulatory provisions giving rise to a statutory exemption. Thus, in relation to an abstention order issued by the Architects' Association under the Regulation on Competitive Tendering (*Reglamento de Concursos*), the TDC stated:

---

[33] Mr Casado Coca was also at the source of the famous judgment of 25 January 1994 of the European Court of Human Rights ruling on whether advertising by lawyers complied with the Human Rights Convention.

[34] Decision of 2 November 1994, Proceedings 83/94 *Publicidad Abogados*.

[35] Art 6.2 LCP.

It should be added that, furthermore, the 'abstention order' has no basis in any regulation or in the slightest provision whatsoever. On the contrary, its sole basis is a so-called 'Regulation on Competitive Tendering' which, despite the misnomer, is not a Regulation at all. It is merely an internal decision issued by the Ordinary Plenary Meeting of the *Consejo Superior de Colegios de Arquitectos* [Superior Council of Architects' Associations—emphasis added] laying down rules which are totally contradictory to the right to freedom of competition since they provide for collective agreements which prevent competition, in this case throughout the national market.

(. . .) Where Law 16/1989 reads that the authority of a regulation can, where applicable, justify restrictions on competition, it is of course referring to the authority of regulations in the strict sense. That is, to a written provision issued by the Government authorities in exercise of a power conferred by statute on a government body especially empowered to do so. It does not refer, in any way whatsoever, to any decision adopted by a collective or group, however significant it may be, in exercise of a domestic self-regulatory power, which quite clearly has no effect *vis-à-vis* third parties—since such collectives and their authorized bodies have absolutely no power to bind anyone beyond the confines of the organization, and when they adopt a decision or resolution within the organization itself, this must always be in full compliance with the general requirements of lawfulness, in our case the Competition Law.

Admittedly, any decision made internally within an organization can have repercussions on third parties, that is, as legal writers put it, it can give rise to a specific advantage or constraint for a person subject to the law other than the person in respect of whom the internal rule is issued. In competition law, however, for such a corporate rule, issued internally but projected outside the organization, to justify a restrictive practice which would have to be tolerated by that third party (the authority issuing the call for tenders) and accepted by the TDC, it must be a genuinely regulatory provision. If it is not, the TDC can and must disregard the pseudo-administrative protection claimed and go straight to the heart of the matter, judging the act in question in the context of competition law, and in turn in the framework of the law in general.[36]

It remains striking that the TDC, instead of seeking to argue on technical legal grounds that internal rules approved by the associations under Article 5.t) LCP should not, of themselves, be sufficient to justify restrictions on competition, took a much more radical stance (and probably one lacking in respect for the LCP) when it stated that those rules did not amount to 'the slightest provision whatsoever'. This debate is in any event now sterile in the light of the amendments made by the legislature to both the LCP and to the LDC confirming that decisions by associations are subject to the LDC.

In short, the early 1990s saw open confrontation between the TDC and the professional associations. The former regarded the latter as a permanent source of restrictions on competition and a direct cause of the high rates of

---

[36] Decision of 20 November 1992, Proceedings 313/92, *Colegio de Arquitectos Vasco-Navarro.*

inflation in Spain at the time. The associations, for their part, flatly denied the TDC any standing to monitor their actions. As we will see below, the outcome of this confrontation has clearly been in favour of the TDC, which managed to persuade the Government of the need to remove any statutory loophole behind which the associations could take cover to avoid being subject to LDC.

III. The Current Provisions under which the Associations are Subject to the LDC

Since 1996, the Government has instigated several partial reforms of the LDC and of the LCP designed to make the activity of professional associations increasingly subject to competition rules. Before setting out these changes and their effects, however, it is necessary to consider their background, in particular the Report written by the TDC in 1992 with its 'Proposals to bring the rules on the membership professions into line with the provisions on free competition in force in Spain'.

1. The 1992 Report on the Free Exercise of the Professions

In May of 1992, the Congress of Deputies approved the Europe Convergence Plan (*Plan de Convergencia con Europa*), intended to prepare Spain for incorporation into the future European Economic and Monetary Union. In connection with this Plan, the Government commissioned the TDC to prepare a number of reports analysing how to improve the competitiveness of the Spanish economy. The first to be drawn up by the TDC was, in fact, that relating to exercise of the membership professions.

Before giving a brief description of the Report and its recommendations, it seems fair to acknowledge the early concern of the Spanish competition authorities with issues relating to the professions. Indeed, although the OECD had already published its 1985 Report on 'Competition Policy and the Professions', the EEC on the other hand had at that time done little or nothing 'to free this sector of the economy since its interest in the sector has focused not so much on ending internal monopoly situations but on enabling other EEC nationals to take advantage of the situation on the same terms as Spanish nationals'.[37] In fact, the famous article by Prof Claus-Dieter

[37] 1992 Report, p 7.

Ehlermann, then Director General for Competition, introducing the debate[38] would not be published until a year later.

The 1992 Report refers only to the membership professions and excludes those in the public service professions. In effect, although the TDC takes the view that their activity is in certain respects suspect from the point of view of competition, it nonetheless acknowledges that 'the approach for reform of these professions needs to be different from that adopted for the professions studied in this report'.

The TDC groups the restrictions on competition analysed by it into three categories: (i) barriers to entry; (ii) restrictions on competition not directly related to prices; and (iii) price-related restrictions.

Under the barriers to entry heading, the TDC examined the qualification requirement, compulsory membership of an association, the requirements for membership and the prohibition on creating new associations. In this regard, the TDC found that in Spain the number of members in the majority of the qualified professions was sufficient for it not to be necessary to introduce competition from outside the associations, but that it was enough, for the purposes of achieving the social benefits of competition, to ensure that the members could compete with each other. To that end, it recommended keeping the system of barriers to entry to the profession but to remove the restrictions on its exercise.

The restrictions on competition not directly related to prices are those which 'are not imposed on both parties, the professional and the client, but on the professionals themselves'. In this regard, the TDC recommended removing the geographical restrictions on the work of professionals and the restrictions on the structure of the business.

In terms of restrictions on advertising, and after referring with praise to the situation in the United States (the Supreme Court had not yet handed down its famous ruling in *California Dental Association*[39]) the TDC recommended removing such restrictions, since they acted to the detriment in particular of entry by young professionals. In this respect, the TDC found that advertising by professionals should be subject only, in the same way as all other sectors of the economy, to the limits laid down in the Advertising Law (*Ley General de Publicidad*) and in the Unfair Competition Law (*Ley de Competencia Desleal*).[40]

Naturally, the TDC was also radically in favour of removing all price-related restrictions. It even expressed its opposition to guideline tariffs, which

---

[38] C-D Ehlermann, 'Concurrence et professions libérales: antagonisme ou compatibilité?' (1993) 36 *Revue du Marché Commun et de l'Union Europeéne* 136.

[39] *California Dental Association v FTC* 526 US 756 (1999).

[40] Ley 3/1991 de Competencia Desleal (hereinafter, LCD).

it branded as a 'consciously parallel practice',[41] and was especially against percentage-based tariffs, which it deemed 'particularly harmful to the national economy'. The TDC also favoured making the collection of payment via the associations voluntary rather than compulsory, and limiting the certification of projects to technical aspects and excluding economic aspects.

As a separate issue, the TDC referred to codes of ethics. Although overall it assessed them positively,[42] it stated that the associations had been misusing them in attempting to regulate the internal conduct of members of the profession in relation to each other. The TDC therefore concluded that they should be kept but only 'provided any hint of corporate protection is expunged from them'.

The 1992 Report ends with an interesting section in which the TDC anticipates the criticisms it predicted would be made of its liberalising recommendations, with a 'Q&A' sequence which addresses eleven possible arguments such as the special nature of the professions or prejudice to the quality of service.

We do not want to omit reference to the fact that the TDC justified the need for reform on the grounds of the statutory protection which the LCP, in its view, afforded to the majority of the restrictions examined. In this regard, the TDC concluded that 'until there is a change in the law it is impossible effectively to pursue conduct which, if it were carried on by other Spaniards, would be severely penalised'. So, what is clear is that, despite the fact that the Government eventually submitted to the *Parliament* a 'Draft Law amending the LCP, to bring the exercise of the membership professions into line with competition legislation', containing essentially the TDC's recommendations, the fact is that it did not meet with success because the Parliament was dissolved. To compensate for this situation, the TDC was then obliged to assert in its decisions openly belligerent arguments against the associations and to restrict (probably to an excessive degree), the scope of the statutory exemption under Article 2.1 LDC. Accordingly, the TDC has been able to apply the

[41] Art 1 LDC bars in addition to agreements, collective decisions or recommendations and concerted practices, the so-called 'consciously parallel practices'. These practices consist of 'coordinated behaviour by several operators in the market, which is not the result of an express or implicit agreement, but of their carrying on their respective actions with the purpose of preventing disharmony'. Decision of 12 February 2001, Proceedings R437/00 *Laboratorios Farmacéuticos.* This provision has been of very limited practical use, and has been criticised for the difficulty in separating this restriction on competition from the intelligent adaptation which competitors have to make in some highly competitive markets.

[42] P 40:

> Society can benefit from the fact that the membership professions have codes of ethics which summarise the ethical rules which must prevail in exercise of their functions and performance of their work by members of the professions. These rules single out the practice of each profession by governing the proper behaviour or each member and therefore create in the mind of the public the resulting expectations for the conduct of that professional. This means that, from this point of view, the codes can be a valuable factor in ensuring for the consumer or user that the member of the profession will comply with standardised and expected patterns of professional conduct.

LDC to the professional associations since as early as 1992 without waiting for the reform of that statute and of the LCP, which would take a further 4 years to crystallise.

2. The 1993 and 1995 Reports

Subsequent to the Report on the liberal professions, the TDC prepared two other reports ['Political remedies which could foster free competition in services and halt the harm caused by monopolies' (1993) and 'Competition in Spain: current position and new proposals' (1995)] which also touch, although tangentially, on the regulation of the professions.

In the 1993, Report the TDC responded to those who criticised the fact that in 1992 it had not recommended abolishing compulsory membership of an association, stating that the increase in competition resulting from any liberalisation of membership would be slight, whilst the benefits from the specific liberalising measures proposed would be very significant. The TDC concluded by stating that 'a moderate approach, of making the minimum changes, has successfully contributed to making it easier for the Government and society to take up the recommendations of that report'.

In the 1995 Report, the TDC looked at a number of activities directly related to professional services (commercial brokers, pharmacies, port practices, etc). Additionally, and since the recommendations for reform contained in its 1992 Report had not yet been approved, the TDC proposed a specific change consisting of passing a 'Discount Law' (*Ley del Descuento*), which would allow all providers of goods and services (ie, not only those in membership professions) who have to adhere to a fixed price, to give a discount of up to 20% off the set price.

3. The 1996 Reforms of the LCP and LDC

A few days after coming into office, the new *Partido Popular* Government, under urgency procedures, passed a package of provisions designed to revitalise the Spanish economy by adopting of series of liberalising measures. These measures were laid down in five Royal Decrees-Law, of which two are relevant for the purposes of our study:

> Royal Decree-Law 5/1996 on liberalisation measures relating to land and professional associations (Real Decreto-Ley de Medidas liberalizadoras en materia de suelo y de Colegios Profesionales) of 7 June, which made significant changes to the LCP. This Royal Decree, following due parliamentary procedure, became Law 7/1997 on liberalization measures relating to land and professional associations

(Ley de Medidas liberalizadoras en materia de suelo y de Colegios Profesionales), with terms very similar to those of Royal Decree-Law 5/1996.

Royal Decree-Law 7/1996 on urgent tax measures to promote and liberalise economic activity (Real Decreto-Ley de Medidas urgentes de carácter fiscal y de fomento y liberalización de la actividad económica) of 7 June, which amended various aspects of the LDC, although the change which interests us in this study is that affecting the statutory exemption under Article 2 LDC.

In accordance with the Preamble to Law 7/1997, the amendment of the LCP was intended to modify 'certain aspects of the regulation of the activity of professions which restrict competition, creating inflexibilities which are difficult to justify in a developed economy'. To that end, the following changes were made to the LCP:

It enshrined the general principle that the membership professions are subject to competition rules. For that purpose, Article 2.1. LCP was reworded:

The State and the Autonomous Communities shall, in their respective spheres of competence, ensure exercise of the membership professions in compliance with the provisions of legislation.

The membership professions shall be practised on terms of free competition and shall be subject, as regards the supply of services and the setting of remuneration therefore, to the LDC and to the Unfair Competition Law. Exercise of the professions shall in all other respects remain governed by general and specific legislation on the applicable substantive provisions relating to each profession.

A new Article 2.4 LCP was also inserted:

Agreements, decisions and recommendations of the associations which have economic significance shall comply with the limits set in Article 1 LDC, without prejudice to the right of the associations to apply for the individual authorisation under Article 3 of that Law.

Any voluntary agreements which may be reached by the professional medical associations on behalf of their members with representatives of unregulated health-care insurance companies to set the fees applicable to the provision of certain services are excepted from the foregoing and, therefore, shall not require the individual authorisation referred to above.[43]

A number of commentators have criticised the distinction made in the second paragraph of Article 2.1 LCP between aspects relating to the supply of services and the setting of remuneration (which would be subject to the LDC and the LCD) and others relating to exercise of the professions (subject to their own specific regulations) arguing that, in practice, it would not always be easy to separate the two situations. For the same reason, the inclusion of reference

[43] The second paragraph of this new section was inserted during the passage through Parliament, since it did not appear in Royal Decree-Law 5/1996. In order to understand this exception, we must recall that the three complaints relating to fee levels dismissed by the TDC in 1990 related precisely to proceedings brought by the insurance industry association against acts by medical associations. See n 32.

to the requirement for acts to have 'economic significance' in order to be subject to Article 1 LDC[44] has also been criticised. In this regard we feel that those objections are probably overstated, since we are persuaded that, in response to any specific situation, the competition authorities would give a broad interpretation to the applicability of the LDC.

It has also been pointed out that this general principle was redundant, in that the TDC was already applying the LDC to the associations. Here it should be noted that inclusion of this principle in the LCP has a role in clarifying the issue, but is in any event merely declarative and does not create any new law. The fact is that there is an alternative possible explanation: between 1992 and 1996, the TDC applied competition rules *avant la lettre* to the professional associations, forcibly imposing an interpretation of the LDC and the LCP which would only comply with the letter of those statutes once they had been amended.

The principle of compulsory membership remained in place, but multiple membership was replaced by a single membership. Accordingly, the new Article 3.2 LCP states:

> In order to practise the membership professions there is a strict requirement to register with the relevant association. Where a profession is organised into geographical associations, membership of one of those associations alone, which shall be that in the place of the sole or principal professional address, shall be sufficient in order to practise throughout the State.
>
> Where the associations are organised on a geographical basis to meet an unavoidable need for a residence requirement in order to provide the services, membership shall only confer entitlement to practise in the relevant geographical area.[45]

A new Article 3.3 was inserted in the LCP under which, where a professional wished to practise occasionally in an area other than that of registration, that person could be required to notify the other associations of 'the work to be carried out in their areas, in order to be subject, on such economic terms as may be determined in each case, to the authorities responsible for governance, certification, ethical monitoring and discipline.'

This section was however repealed by a subsequent amendment to the LCP under Royal Decree-Law 5/2000.

> As regards the directly economic aspects of professional activity, (i) the associations' power to set maximum fees was abolished and replaced by the ability to set scales 'which would serve merely as guidance'; (ii) the compulsory payment via the association existing in some professions was abolished in favour of an unrestricted system for occasions where it was 'freely and expressly requested by the member', and in such cases the client would have to be given a quotation or confirmation of

[44] D Vázquez Albert, *Derecho de la Competencia y Ejercicio de las Profesiones* (Madrid, Thomson Aranzadi, 2002) 116.

[45] This paragraph was added in Law 7/1997 and affects court attorneys in particular, who are required to reside in the court district in which they intend to practise.

instructions; and (iii) certification of work (visado) was retained but excluded 'fees [and] other contractual terms which would be set by free agreement between the parties'. Conversely, the rules on the fees payable to public service professions, that is, those of notaries public, commercial brokers and land and companies registrars, remained expressly in force.[46]

All these changes are essentially in line with the proposals made by the TDC in its 1992 Report. However, Law 7/1997 omitted two of its main specific recommendations: removal of the restrictions on advertising by professionals and on professional firms. This silence has not, however, prevented the TDC, applying the general principle contained in the new Article 2 LCP, from holding that the associations cannot now impose restrictions on advertising.[47]

The 1996 reform of the LCP was completed with a change to the statutory exemption under Article 2.1 LDC, approved simultaneously by Royal Decree-Law 7/1996. The scope of the statutory exemption was reduced with the addition of the following paragraph to Article 2.1 LDC: 'Conversely, [the Article 1 LDC prohibitions] shall apply to situations where competition is restricted as the result of the exercise of other administrative powers or arising from the acts of public authorities, public entities or public undertakings not enjoying that statutory protection.'

This change laid to rest once and for all the debate as to whether or not the associations are public bodies because they are excluded from application of the LDC.

4. Changes Subsequent to 1996

Subsequent to approval of the 1996 package of liberalising provisions, a further series of specific measures has strengthened the application of competition rules to the membership professions. The following are the most significant:

The system of single membership established by Law 7/1997 was amended by Decree-Law 6/2000 on urgent measures to intensify competition in markets for goods and services (*Decreto Ley 6/2000 de Medidas Urgentes de Intensificación de la Competencia en Mercados de Bienes y Servicios*), seeking 'to advance liberalisation of exercise of the membership professions, removing any barriers which may restrict the benefits of single membership'.[48] Article 3.3 LCP was therefore abolished and Article 3.2 LCP was redrafted, specifying the associations in whose geographic area the professional is not based cannot require 'payment of economic consideration other than that which they habitually charge their members for the

[46] Provision repealing Law 7/1997.

[47] We will refer below to the Decisions penalising the General Council of lawyers associations and the Madrid Lawyers' Association on these grounds.

[48] Preamble to Decree-Law 6/2000.

provision of any services received by them and which is not covered by the membership fee'; an obligation can be imposed to notify associations other than those where the member is registered of activities in their area, but no authorisation will now need to be granted.

A number of public service professions, which had been excluded from the earlier reform, have had the provisions governing their activity substantially modified.

Royal Decree-Law 6/1999 on urgent measures to liberalise and increase competition (*Real Decreto-Ley 6/1999 de Medidas Urgentes de Liberalización e Incremento de la Competencia*) established an obligation to adapt the rules of the associations of notaries public, commercial brokers and registrars to the same provisions as laid down for the other associations under the LCP, including the LDC, although only 'to the extent that they do not contradict the particular requirements of the public function performed by their members'.[49]

It also changed the fee charged by commercial brokers from a fixed fee to a maximum fee, which for the first time introduced price competition into the official certification of commercial documents. This change led to a paradoxical situation: for the same official certification services, commercial brokers could give discounts on their fees whilst notaries public remained subject to their fixed charge.

A few months later, Law 55/1999 on tax, administrative and welfare measures (*Ley 55/1999 de Medidas fiscales, administrativas y del orden social*) merged the body of notaries public with that of commercial brokers 'in the general interest and to increase free competition, with the aim of modernising and increasing the efficiency of the system of official certification, improving the service to citizens'. There are currently under these arrangements some 3000 notaries public in Spain.

Lastly, Royal Decree-Law 6/2000 introduced the option for notaries public to give a 10% discount on their fee for any kind of deed[50] and, where the transaction to which the deed relates exceeds 6 million Euros, freely to set their fees above those corresponding to that amount.

All these measures have brought about a degree of price competition between official certifying agents, although the fixed fee arrangements remain in place for land and companies registrars.

Royal Decree-Law 4/2000 on urgent liberalisation measures in the property and transport sectors (*Real Decreto-Ley 4/2000 de Medidas Urgentes de Liberalización en el Sector Inmobiliario y Transportes*) abolished the requirements for qualification and membership in order to practise as a real property agent.

Finally, we would refer to Law 5/1999, which again amended Article 2.1 LCD to restrict the scope of the statutory exemption even further.[51] The most significant

---

49 New Additional Provision Two LCP.

50 This was thus a return to a notion which appeared in the Discount Law proposed by the TDC in its 1995 Report and which was never passed.

51 Art 2.1 LDC was re-worded as follows:

> Without prejudice to any application of Community competition provisions, the prohibitions under Art 1 shall not apply to agreements, decisions, recommendations and practices resulting from application of a law.
>
> They shall, conversely, apply to situations where competition is restricted as the result of the exercise of other administrative powers or arising from the acts of public authorities, public entities or public undertakings not enjoying that statutory protection.

change was the removal of the reference to the fact that the provisions of regulations could exempt practices from the provisions of Article 1 LDC.

These changes have not dispelled our doubts as to how an individual or an undertaking should react if a provision ranking lower than a formal law requires a practice which could be restrictive of competition. There is quite clearly nothing new about this problem. As we stated in relation to the restrictive interpretation of Article 2.1 LDC which the TDC was already proposing in 1992, the dissenting opinion of a member of the TDC pointed out at that time that such an interpretation, now enshrined in statute, has the effect of

> placing the party subject to regulation in an impossible dilemma: either it has to accommodate its conduct to the provisions of the Regulation, in which case it could be penalised by this Court, or it has to infringe the provisions of the Regulation, in which case by definition it infringes that regulatory provision.[52]

In short, all the changes made in recent years to the LDC and the LCP reveal that the Government enthusiastically welcomed the TDC's proposals that the activity of professionals and of their associations should be made subject to competition rules in much the same way as all other economic operators. It is also the case, however, that even before those changes took place, the TDC forcibly imposed a broad interpretation of the LDC which enabled it to review much of the activity of the professional associations.

IV. Application of Competition Provisions to the Professional Associations by the Courts

After referring to the TDC's eagerness since 1992 to subject the professional associations to competition rules and the Government's support for that stance with the successive reforms of the LDC and LCP, we may now examine the position by the judicial courts. Contentious-administrative courts, even after those statutory reforms, have shown themselves more inclined to entertain the features specific to professional activity and to allow the associations a margin of manoeuvre in regulating certain aspects of the profession.

The effects of this differing sensitivity, which we will explore below by looking at a number of specific cases in which the same practice has been assessed differently by the competition authorities and by the courts, may become more apparent in the coming years. Indeed, if the courts come to perform the 'vital role in application of Community competition rules'[53] which they have been assigned in the process of modernising Community competition law,

[52] Dissenting opinion to the Decision of 10 November 1992, Proceedings A 30/92 *Agentes de la propiedad inmobiliaria*.

[53] Para 7 of the Preamble to Reg 1/2003.

that task is very unlikely to be relegated to Community rules alone, and will surely ultimately transcend Community competition law.

1. Review of the Economic Terms of Architectural Projects

One of the issues which has been raised most frequently before the competition authorities is how far the architects' associations, when they have to certify (*visar*) a project, can review its economic terms and take steps if they find that the project budget is not in line with its execution cost.

In order to understand the financial reasons underpinning this conflict, one has to bear in mind that the amount of the project budget is the basis for calculation of the various costs of the work. Until the 1996 amendments to the LCP, the budget enabled the architect's fees to be calculated by direct application of the fee scale in Royal Decree 2512/1977[54] and to calculate the Association's costs in certifying the project. It currently dictates the level of safety measures to be implemented by the developer during the work and the amount of the 10–year liability insurance it must procure. Finally, and most significantly, it is the basis for calculation of the municipal tax payable by the developer in respect of the work.[55] In consequence, although there is a statutory obligation for the budget to reflect the true cost of executing the work, there is a not infrequent ruse of submitting a project for review with a budget artificially lower than the real price, in order thereby to reduce all the above-referred costs which are pegged to the budget.

As stated above, one of the TDC's proposals in its 1992 Report was that certification by the Associations should be limited to the technical aspects of the project and should not cover the financial aspects. Further, when it was decided in 1996 to reform the LCP and the LDC to bring the activity of the associations under the LDC, one of the amendments to the LCP was to state that 'the certification shall not include fees or other contractual terms which would be set by free agreement between the parties'.[56]

The associations, for their part, have been extraordinarily reluctant to certify projects where they find that the budget submitted does not reflect the true execution costs of the proposed work.

---

[54] This Decree was repealed in these respects by Law 7/1997.

[55] Law 39/1988 Local Treasury (*Ley 39/1988 de Haciendas Locales*) establishes a presumption that, where the project has been certified by an Association, the budget will be the basis for calculation of the tax and that only if it has not been certified can the municipality calculate the estimated cost. There is also case law to the effect that, where the project has been certified, the municipality cannot set a different figure.

[56] This amendment to Art 5.q LCP did not appear in Royal Decree-Law 6/1996 and was inserted during its passage through Parliament which culminated in Law 7/1997.

Initially, the associations would not certify if the budget was less than that shown in tables approved by the association itself. Subsequently they gradually adopted a more flexible approach, but without totally giving up their role in reviewing the budget. Accordingly, in the most recent of the cases decided to date by the TDC,[57] the Madrid Architects' Association (*Colegio Oficial de Arquitectos de Madrid*—COAM), which had previously been penalised for making approval conditional upon the budget being in line with its own price tables, altered this practice in two ways: on the one hand, to prevent any suspicions as to the accuracy of its reference price table, COAM replaced the table with an official set of tables approved by the Autonomous Community of Madrid; on the other hand, COAM no longer made the certification conditional, confining itself to stamping the project with a warning that the budget was inconsistent with the project cost calculated on the basis of the aforementioned official set of tables.

The Association argued that its practice no longer restricted competition, since now the approval was always granted. Further, it contended that it was performing a public function, in that a number of provisions (such as the *Ley de Haciendas Locales*) conferred on certification by the Association the effect of validating the project as the basis for calculation of taxes on building work.

In response to this line of reasoning, the TDC gave an extraordinarily broad interpretation to the notion of restriction of competition, taking the view that the mere fact that the Association issued the warning in question

> is liable to create doubts in the mind of those who read it as regards the possibility that there may be an anomaly in the project being stamped and that (. . .) it gives rise to a lack of confidence on the part of the consumer. (. . .) This concern could lead the person commissioning the project to cease using the services of the architect who drew up the plans, with the effect that the COAM warning can act as a brake on the decline in budgets and, therefore, in the price of the professional services which form part of them. The warning under examination may therefore restrict and distort competition. . . .

The TDC also denied that the COAM was performing a public function, basing its argument precisely on the fact that the COAM now was not refusing approval to any project.[58]

---

[57] *COAM* Decision.

[58] It is surprising that the Association's attempt to adapt its practices to the earlier Decisions by the TDC should be used by the latter as an argument against the COAM itself:

> Secondly, if COAM's mission-obligation were to review whether the works budget conformed to market conditions, which it is not, it would not consist of the function of a purely indicative warning, rather than a straight refusal to approve the project. The fact that COAM does not opt to refuse the project reveals that, today, after publication of the aforementioned Law 7/1997 and the Decisions of this Court of 5 June 1997 (Proceedings 372/96, Arquitectos de Madrid), it is common ground that this task is not the mission of the Association.

In the light of such a vague restrictive effect, two members of the TDC issued dissenting opinions, stating that the Association was merely advising of an objective fact (that the budget was not in line with certain reference prices set by a public body) and that the restrictive effect prohibited by Article 1 LDC has to be 'at all times real, effective and possible, but in no case dependent on the subjective findings of third parties, since to do so would give rise to a degree of uncertainty inappropriate under the strict terms of penalty provisions'.

The COAM appealed the TDC's Decision to the contentious courts. Although the National High Court (*Audiencia Nacional*) had until then upheld other similar decisions of the TDC, in this case it quashed the Decision, referring expressly to the reasoning of the dissenting judgment, going on to add:

'As we already indicated in Ground in Law 1, we fully agree with the view of the dissenting judgment, and there is little to add to what was said in it. However, we do find it necessary to reiterate, in the same vein as the statement of claim, that approval by an association represents exercise of a public function which goes beyond the internal context of the relations between the association and its members, since it involves a review of exercise of the profession which the association is bound to carry out (Judgment of the Supreme Court of 27.7.2001). Exercise of this review of the profession should, plainly, benefit the members, but also individuals or consumers (Article 5i LCP as worded by Law 7/1997), as it must be recalled that under Articles 51.1 and 51.2 of the Constitution, public authorities, a sufficiently broad expression to encompass professional associations which are defined as public law corporations, shall ensure the protection of consumers and users and shall promote the provision of information to consumers. Since when it grants approval the Architects' Association, as we have seen, is manifestly performing a public function, there can be no doubt that when it acts as it did not only is it not violating the rules on free competition, but that it merely complied with duties imposed by the Constitution. At the same time, the fact that Article 5 q of the aforementioned provision expressly states that "the review shall not include fees or other contractual terms which would be set by free agreement between the parties", does not mean that the Association cannot act as it did since at no time has it refused approval or made grant of approval conditional or limited on the basis of the setting of the fees under the project, since all it has done is to offer the public objective information about the costs of the project in accordance with official scales unconnected with the Association itself, conduct which when viewed from this perspective can only be described as unimpeachable. As regards the second argument used by the appellant it only needs to be said that this is, as can be deduced from the statement of claim itself, a supplementary argument, relevant no doubt to the municipalities but not decisive in determination of this appeal since the undeniable cooperation required by law between the professional associations and the local treasury offices is not essential to determination of the matter before the court.'[59]

The reasoned analysis is particularly interesting in that the *Audiencia Nacional* had already conceded that the appeal should be upheld on the grounds set out by the TDC members who issued a dissenting opinion. From a reading of it one can deduce that, in the view of the *Audiencia Nacional*:

> The certification by the Association is a public function. And where the Association issues a certification 'it is manifestly performing a public function, [and] there can be no doubt that when it acts as it did not only is it not violating the rules on free competition, but that it merely complied with duties imposed by the Constitution'. That is, when an association performs a public function, its conduct seems not to violate competition rules, since it involves performance of a function imposed by the Constitution.
>
> The *Audiencia's* reasoning remains valid even after the legislature amended the LCP and the LDC to render the associations increasingly subject to the LDC.
>
> The statutory basis for the Association's practice and the nature of its act as public function derives from general legislation and not from the specific role assigned to certification of Architect's Association in the Local Treasury Law. Thus the same could reasonably be said about other acts of Associations

2. Advertising by Lawyers

The restrictions on advertising by lawyers imposed by their professional associations is another area in which the Spanish courts have adopted a radically different stance to that of the competition authorities.

In its 1992 Report, the TDC had showed itself to be particularly critical of the restrictions on advertising by professionals, in particular lawyers. However, none of the legislative reforms introduced since 1996 have dealt expressly with this question. Moreover, as mentioned in Section 2.3, the TDC had already had occasion to deal with this point in disciplinary proceedings in 1994, reaching the conclusion that there was an anticompetitive situation but that it was covered in the General Statutes for the Attorneys issued pursuant to the LCP. However, in 2000 and 2001 the TDC had occasion to look at the question again and came to the conclusion that, after the reforms to the LCP came into force, the legal protection for restrictions by professional associations on advertising had disappeared.

Thus, in its Decision of 18 January 2000, the TDC took the view that the Advertising Regulations approved by the General Council for the Attorneys a few months after the coming into force of Law 7/1997 which amended the LCP constituted a breach of Article 1 of the LDC and it imposed a fine of

[59] Judgment of 29 October 2003, Ground in Law Three.

€180,000 on the Council. In this context, the TDC took the view that the regulation of advertising by lawyers was clearly a matter 'with economic significance' and was therefore subject to the prohibition contained in Article 1 of the LDC. In the view of the TDC, such regulation restricts competition '[not] only where there is detriment to consumers but also where it constitutes an entry barrier for new professionals and limits the possible expansion of those lawyers who are prepared to find more active ways of making themselves known'.[60] Whilst this statement cannot be faulted from a purely theoretical point of view, it seems difficult to sustain in a market like Spain, with approximately 110,000 lawyers who are members of lawyers' associations;[61] in Madrid alone there are now more than 46,000 members of the Bar Association and more than 2000 new lawyers join each year.[62] With these figures, what entry barriers is the TDC referring to?

The following year, the TDC imposed another fine, this time of €120,000, on the Madrid's Bar Association for continuing to apply regulations which restricted advertising by lawyers after Law 7/1997 came into force. From this decision, we must highlight the analysis of the function which advertising has to perform in the professional services market:

> The Court is required to consider the important role played by advertising in the goods and services market in reducing the cost of information for consumers and users, making them aware of the existence of the different suppliers and the peculiarities of their particular offers, both in terms of price and in relation to the different characteristics of the goods and services offered. This crucial role of advertising as an information provider has a direct impact on competition, which is negatively affected where its exercise is restricted. This happens in markets for goods and services of all kinds and of course in the market for professional services provided by lawyers. To prevent or restrict the use of advertising by economic operators prevents or restricts competition between them, which has a direct effect on the public economic order of which competition is a key element in a market economy.[63]

In contrast to this reasoning which takes the view that advertising by professionals, like advertising for any other goods or services, benefits the consumer, we should remember that the US Supreme Court, in its judgment in *California Dental,*[64] reached quite the opposite conclusion when it took the view that:

The provision of professional services cannot be treated as being equivalent to the provision of other services from the point of view of the competition rules:

---

[60] Decision of 18 January 2000, Case 455/99, *Abogacía Española.*

[61] Data from the General Council of the Legal Profession for 2002. See http://www2.cgae.es/es/cgae/censo.asp.

[62] For the sake of comparison, Madrid has 16,000 licensed taxi-drivers, ie, there are 2.9 lawyers for each taxi-driver. Anyone having walked the streets of Madrid will know they will have no difficulty finding a taxi . . . let alone a lawyer.

[63] Decision of 11 October 2001, Case 504/00, *Abogados de Madrid.*

[64] Judgment of 24 May 1999, *California Dental Association v Federal Trade Commission*, 526 US 756 (1999).

The fact that a restraint operates upon a profession as distinguished from a business is, of course, relevant in determining whether that particular restraint violates the Sherman Act. It would be unrealistic to view the practice of professions as interchangeable with other business activities, and automatically to apply to the professions antitrust concepts which originated in other areas. The public service aspect, and other features of the professions, may require that a particular practice, which could properly be viewed as a violation of the Sherman Act in another context, be treated differently.

In contrast to the TDC's simplistic analysis, the Supreme Court applied the modern economic theory of markets with asymmetric knowledge[65] in order to take into consideration the impossibility of calibrating professional services and to conclude that it may be that restrictions on advertising do not have anticompetitive effects. Thus, in regard to the asymmetry of knowledge between the professional and his client, the Supreme Court states that: 'In a market for complex professional services, "inherent asymmetry of knowledge about the product" arises because "professionals supplying the good are knowledgeable whereas consumers demanding the good are uninformed".'

And in contrast to the unconditional faith in the informative value of advertising evinced by the TDC, the Supreme Court highlighted how easy it is for professional services advertising, in practice, to be misleading to the extent that the consumer lacks any comparative element that allows him to check the accuracy of the advertising messages:

In a market for professional services, in which advertising is relatively rare and the comparability of service packages not easily established, the difficulty for customers or potential competitors to get and verify information about the price and availability of services magnifies the dangers to competition associated with misleading advertising. What is more, the quality of professional services tends to resist either calibration or monitoring by individual patients or clients, partly because of the specialized knowledge required to evaluate the services, and partly because of the difficulty in determining whether, and the degree to which, an outcome is attributable to the quality of services or to something else. [. . .] The existence of such significant challenges to informed decision making by the customer for professional services immediately suggests that advertising restrictions arguably protecting patients from misleading or irrelevant advertising call for more than cursory treatment as obviously comparable to classic horizontal agreements to limit output or price competition.

The Spanish contentious-administrative courts have also proved to be reluctant to take the view that the restrictions on advertising established by professional associations constitute restrictions on competition, even after the 1996 legislative reform.

---

[65] This theory has been developed, *inter alia*, by Akerlof [see GA Akerlof, 'The Market for "Lemons": Quality Uncertainty and the Market Mechanism' (1970) 84 *Quarterly Journal of Economics* 488—cited by the Supreme Court) whose works led to him being awarded the Nobel Prize for Economics in 2001.

Thus, the judgment of the *Tribunal Superior de Justicia de Madrid* (TSJM) of 3 February 2000 begins by recalling the fact that the authority of professional associations to approve rules of professional ethics is a response to the public powers attributed to them:

> As the judgment of 21 December 1989 of the Tribunal Constitucional makes clear, the ethical rules of the profession approved by the Professional Associations are not merely treaties that set out moral duties which have no consequences in the disciplinary context. On the contrary, these rules determine mandatory obligations to be observed by the members and are a response to the public powers which the law delegates in favour of the associations. . . .

Having established the need for the professional associations to establish rules in relation to correct professional conduct, the TSJM then considers in detail whether the regulations of the Madrid Bar Association breach the provisions of the LCP in its current wording:

> The appellant also submits that there has been a breach of articles. 2.1 and 2.4 of Law 7/1997 of 14 April 1997, the *Ley de Colegios Profesionales*.
>
> [. . .] The claimant in its submissions separates two matters which it considers are independent of each other in the wording, namely the «offer of services» and the «fixing of the remuneration for them». However, if we look at the wording of the article we can see that it refers to the two things together, and not to one of them independently of the other. In other words the law deals with freedom of competition, but this freedom relates to the fixing of the remuneration in relation to the offer of services offered, hence Article 5a of the same Law provides that fee scales 'shall be for guidance purposes only'.
>
> This means that the article in question is not dealing with the possibility of offering services without more, which is logical, as the same provision refers to the *Ley de Defensa de la Competencia and to the Ley sobre Competencia Desleal*. It is enough to look at the recitals in the first of these Laws (Law 16/1989 of 17 July 1989) to see that the interpretation that we have just set out is the correct one, when it says [. . .]:
>
>> The defence of competition therefore relates not to the offer of services per se but to how the economy is affected, which means that it must relate to the prices of the services, as expressed in the aforementioned Law.
>>
>> Therefore, the *Ley de Colegios Profesionales* gives lawyers freedom when it comes to fixing the fees for the services that they offer, but that freedom cannot be extrapolated to other completely different questions such as freedom in relation to advertising the services that they provide. This is a different question and has nothing to do with the defence of competition.
>>
>> [. . .] It is correct, as the appellant says, that all resolutions, decisions and recommendations of Professional Associations are connected with professional ethics and it is also true that the defence of free competition has partially restricted the powers of such bodies, but this does not mean that a question that is not affected by the *Ley de Defensa de la Competencia*, such as advertising by lawyers, cannot continue to be regulated by them, provided that they do not

> infringe other provisions. [. . .] As the judgment under appeal adds, «this doctrine remains valid and applies in the case with which we are concerned and from the point of view of the new legislation inasmuch as advertising the fact that one is practising as a lawyer is something that goes beyond the mere economic question and is important in the sphere of professional ethics. It is therefore possible for Lawyers' Associations to regulate it without being affected by the provisions contained in Article 1 of the *Ley de Defensa de la Competencia*, since the new *Ley de Colegios Profesionales*, even though it provides that it is subject to the *Ley de Defensa de la Competencia*, when it comes to the prohibitions contained in the said Law, is referable to them only in cases of 'resolutions, decisions or recommendation with economic significance' (emphasis added).

The TSJM likewise rejects the argument that regulation by professional associations infringes Article 81 EU. In doing so it sets out the principle from the judgment of the European Court of Human Rights in the *Casado Coca* case that it should be the national legal authorities that evaluate these questions in the light of the peculiarities of each country:

> The appellant states that there was a breach of article [81 EC] (. . .)
>
> The aforementioned judgment of the European Court of Human Rights of 24 February 1994 made it clear that the practice of the legal profession is one thing and a commercial undertaking is something else when it states that:
>
>> In the Court's opinion, however, they cannot be compared to members of the Bar in independent practice, whose special status gives them a central position in the administration of justice as intermediaries between the public and the courts. Such a position explains the usual restrictions on the conduct of members of the Bar and also the monitoring and supervisory powers vested in Bar councils.
>>
>> Nevertheless, the rules governing the profession, particularly in the sphere of advertising, vary from one country to another according to cultural tradition. Moreover, in most of the Status parties to the Convention, including Spain, there has for some time been a tendency to relax the rules as a result of the changes in their respective societies and in particular the growing role of the media in them [. . .].
>
> The judgment concluded by saying that it should be the country's own legal authorities that decide what rules are most appropriate in each case, stating that:
>
>> 'Because of their direct, continuous contact with their members, the Bar authorities and the country's courts are in a better position than an international court to determine how, at a given time, the right balance can be struck between the various interests involved, namely the requirements of the proper administration of justice, the dignity of the profession, the right of everyone to receive information about legal assistance and affording members of the Bar the possibility of advertising their practices'.

As the respondent says, the current position in Spain is quite similar to the one set out in the judgment (. . .) but it is still totally possible for Lawyers' Associations to regulate advertising and to make it subject in certain circumstances to authorisation from their Governing Bodies.

The TSJM again found in favour of the rules of the Bar Associations on advertising in its judgment of 10 April 2001, placing advertising by lawyers within the professional ethics framework:

> It must be stated to begin with that the question of advertising by lawyers is a question of professional ethics, as has been unanimously recognised by both the doctrine and the various regulations that have been successively introduced on this question within the General Council of the Legal Profession and the various Lawyers' Associations. (. . .)
>
> It is therefore particularly difficult to make a finding in the abstract and without considering specific situations (. . .) the writers are in agreement that professional ethics is a particularly delicate and complex question, bearing in mind that the rules of ethics and professional dignity are on the one hand a guarantee for the citizen and the other members of the profession, but on the other hand their application may also give rise to bias and abuse against the professional due to their indeterminate nature. But in any event it is clear that the very nature of a professional activity requires that it be subject to rules that go beyond the provisions of the legal doctrine in the strict sense due to the fact that they have their origin in the principles and practices of the profession, particularly in those professions whose purpose is human relationships, of which the legal profession is the prime example. . . .

For its part, the judgment of the TSJM of 12 September 2002 concerns the provision of the Madrid Bar Association that made advertising by lawyers subject to a regime of authorisation by the Association. In this regard, the TSJM highlights the fact that the question goes beyond purely economic issues and states that the LDC must be compatible with the rest of the legislation, concluding that the regulation is justified as it allows the Association to check that the advertising corresponds to the values that the European Court of Human Rights recognised in relation to the practice of the legal profession in its judgment in *Casado Coca:*

> This doctrine remains valid and applies in the case with which we are concerned and from the point of view of the new legislation, inasmuch as advertising the fact that one is practising as a lawyer is something that goes beyond the mere economic question and is important in the sphere of professional ethics. It is therefore possible for Lawyers' Associations to regulate it, without being affected by the provisions contained in Article 1 of the Ley de Defensa de la Competencia, since the new Ley de Colegios Profesionales, even though it provides that it is subject to the Ley de Defensa de la Competencia, when it comes to the prohibitions contained in the said Law, is referable to them only in cases of 'resolutions, decisions or recommendation with economic significance.
>
> Not only that, the basis for the prohibition contained in Article 31 of the Statutes may find greater support in the purpose for which Professional Associations are acknowledged to exist, the potentiality for which is derived from Article 36 of the Constitution, by singling them out as being different from ordinary associations (. . .) Professional Associations are sectoral corporations that are responsible for the defence and promotion of the legitimate individual interests of their members. Nonetheless, historically they have been carrying out functions that clearly have a

public interest, which the Law seeks to reinforce so that they constitute an effective instrument for the satisfaction of purposes of general interest that are connected with professional practice which include, especially, the training and improvement of members, and an improvement in the quality of their professional services, which will ultimately be to the benefit of the person receiving this service. On the basis of this and in accordance with the provisions of Article 8 of the *Ley General de Publicidad* which regulates certain situations in which administrative authorisation is needed for advertising certain products, goods, activities or services, making it extend to the protection of constitutionally recognised values and rights which require such protection, it is possible to justify the prohibition on advertising to which the business of lawyers is subject. This prohibition on advertising is not absolute and it is possible to advertise by obtaining the necessary authorisation of the Governing Body, as provided in the final sub-section of Article 31.1 of the Statutes, which means that this authorisation will ensure that the Association examines the conditions on which the advertising is carried out in the interests of defending those values or principles that the European Court indicates and which ultimately only represents a properly justified interference with the right to freedom of expression. Finally, in relation to this question, we must point out, as the Recitals of the *Ley de Defensa de la Competencia* do, that even though the defence of competition is the governing principle of every market economy and has to be treated as a mandate to the public authorities that is directly linked with Article 38 of the Constitution, its protection must nonetheless be compatible with the other laws that regulate the market in accordance with other legal or economic requirements, be they matters of public policy or private questions, which leads to the conclusion that it is necessary to prohibit both the abusive exercise of economic power and those types of unilateral conduct that by unfair means are capable of significantly distorting competition. (emphasis added)

The Spanish Supreme Court has also repeatedly ruled that the regulation of advertising by professional associations is compatible with the LDC and the LCP after the 1996 reform.

Thus, the judgment of 29 May 2001 referred briefly to the fact that a rule on advertising of the Barcelona Bar Association was compatible with the reformed LCP: 'The rule of the professional association applied to subsume the conduct of the lawyer sanctioned is not changed by Royal Decree-Law 5/1996 of 7 June 1996, inasmuch as the provision on advertising established in Article 3a) is specifically aimed at the unfair capture of clients.'

The court was more explicit in its judgment of 3 March 2003, in which it took the view that the prohibition on referring to clients that have retained a lawyer's services is justified. The Supreme Court considers that it is included in the legal exemption under Article 2 of the LDC, even though it does not specify what rule would give rise to this exemption. It is also worth looking at the submissions made by the Attorney General (*Abogado del Estado*) in order to justify this restriction:

[The LDC], in prohibiting any collective resolution, decision or recommendation that is intended to produce, produces or may produce the effect of preventing, restricting or distorting competition, does not constitute an isolated provision, with absolute and unlimited value, but instead is integrated into a system that has to accept the pressure of the rest of the system, as the LDC itself specifically recognises when it states in its article two that the prohibitions contained in article one shall not apply to resolutions, decisions, recommendations and practices that result from the application of a Law or from regulations that are made under a Law.

[. . .] The Attorney General articulates his objection to the nullity of the provisions that prohibit advertising with direct or indirect reference to the lawyer's own clients on the basis that if it were to be accepted, meta-legal and meta-professional factors—identifying who is the consumer of the product—that do not necessarily classify the services from a professional point of view would become the relevant issue, so that

> as in the case of a detergent—a product that cannot be equated to the legal profession at all—the lawyer purports to be required because the person next door has requested his services; or because a particular celebrity or popular figure has done so; and even because a well-known or famous company in the sector has done so. This party does not doubt for a moment that knowing the identity and composition of the lawyer's client portfolio does not express, mention or mean qualities of the service or the person providing them.

We have produced this part of the Attorney General's response verbatim because even if we accept that it is not correct that there is a complete identity between client portfolio and quality of service, as the document so expressively sets out, we cannot however ignore the social reality that the fact that certain clients continue to receive legal services from a lawyer constitutes a powerful indication of the lawyer's professional standing.

We therefore take the view that a greater part is played when it comes to justifying this restriction by the duty of discretion and professional secrecy, which, in the terms used by the representative of the General Council, 'constitutes the cornerstone of the practice of the legal profession'.

In this context it must be noted that both the respect owed to individual clients and the lawyer's own dignity are sufficient support for the assertion that the specific restriction on advertising that is being studied here justifies us taking the view that the case comes within article two of the LDC, from the time at which the disclosure of the client means making public a services relationship which is normally conducted within the context of a discretion from which only the client could release the lawyer. Situations could therefore even arise in which an attempt is made to obtain this authorisation by a price or thing which favours those lawyers whose clients have less scruples about advertising their relationships with their lawyers, thus giving rise to certain risks of inequality or of discretion being treated as a commodity, which would not be appropriate to the dignity with which the relationship between the lawyer and client has to be conducted.

The Supreme Court has repeated this doctrine in at least two other judgments, those of 9 June 2003 and 17 December 2003.

However, not all these judicial rulings take the view that the restrictions on advertising by lawyers imposed by their professional associations are justified after the reform of the LCP and the LDC. Thus, in the judgment of 9 March 2003 which we have just cited, one of the judges gave a dissenting opinion in which he stated that after these legislative reforms the rules of the lawyers' associations are contrary to the LDC:

> I therefore take the view that as the legal profession is governed by the principle of freedom of competition and, when it comes to the offer of services, by the provisions of the LDC and the Unfair Competition Law, it is these laws, plus the Law on Advertising or the Law on personal data protection, and these laws alone that can establish the limitations on this regime of free competition and on the offer of services, which is why the mere direct or indirect reference to a lawyer's clients or the advertising of his services by the companies to which he provides them cannot be held to be contrary to the rules of professional ethics, provided that they respect professional secrecy and the provisions of the aforementioned laws.
>
> In conclusion, the rules contained in Article 25 2e) and 3 of the General Statutes of the Legal Profession are contrary to the provisions of Article 2.1 paragraph two and Article 2.4 of the LCP because they unnecessarily hinder free competition, inasmuch as their purpose is to prevent or restrict competition in the market for legal assistance, and they also encroach on the territory reserved in general terms to the Law on Advertising and to the special regulations that apply to certain advertising activities, without there being justification for this by virtue of the 'inequality or treatment of discretion as a commodity' alluded to in the judgment, which are inappropriate to the dignity with which the relationship between the lawyer and his client should be conducted, as accurate information enables a better knowledge of the professional career of the person in any environment or activity, including in the context of legal assistance, which obviously is not independent of the laws of the market, and thus the inclusion in a lawyer's «curriculum vitae» of the matters in which he has been involved is the only way of providing information to clients which, ultimately, results in a well-understood equality between practitioners.

The *Audiencia Nacional* (national appeal court) in its judgment of 9 June 2003 has also taken the view that after the reform of the LCP the restrictions on professional practice contained in the General Statutes are subject to the LDC:

> . . . all the aspects relating to the offer of services and fixing of remuneration are subject to freedom of competition and are therefore outside the regulatory scope of the Associations and Councils, as they are constituted independently of the administrative powers that they exercise. Indeed, the exposition that we have already set out of the powers exercised by the Corporate Administration show that along with public powers they exercise private powers, the first being governed by the principle of legal attribution and the second being subject to private law. From the time at which Law 7/1997 provides that the principle of freedom of competition applies in relation to the offer of the service and the remuneration for it, these aspects have been excluded from the jurisdiction of the Associations and Councils as they have to be governed by the Law applicable to such professions, and by the regulations passed pursuant to them, on the understanding that the

provisions of the regulations may never contradict the provisions of the Law due to a fundamental principle of legislative hierarchy. Therefore the regulations may not establish restrictions on the freedom of competition subsumable in Article 1 of Law 16/1989 because to do so it is necessary for a Law to provide for the exclusion of the said provision—either directly or by a legal authorisation, but in both cases expressly—or the corresponding authorisation must be obtained from the Defence of Competition Court with the requirements and circumstances provided for by law.

The claimant submits as the basis for his conduct, amongst other aspects, the arguments put forward before parliament by its members in relation to the need for a restriction on advertising by lawyers. Aside from whether such arguments are worthy of consideration from the political opportunity, the fact is, given the clear terms in which the practice of the professions is made subject to the principle of freedom of competition in Law 7/1997, there would need to be a Law laying down the restrictions which the Council is seeking to impose, as we are not dealing with a problem that involves deciding the most correct solution but rather the question is which legislative body has jurisdiction to decide it; and it is clear that it is the legislator, as it is a law that establishes the principle of freedom of competition in the exercise of the professions in terms of the provision of the service and the remuneration, and it is a law that determines the anticompetitive practices.

Having affirmed this principle, the *Audiencia Nacional* reasons that the various restrictions on advertising by lawyers that have been approved by the General Council of the Attorney restrict competition:

Having said this we have to examine whether the regulation of advertising established by the Council impacts on the aspects that are subject to freedom of competition.

First of all the approach of the decision under appeal is correct when it states that the regulation of advertising has an economic content, as advertising tends to influence the demand for products and services as a means of increasing the income of the person doing the advertising, with the advertising of goods and services being acknowledged as playing an important role in economic activity.

When it comes to the specific restrictions on advertising, we agree with the reasoning in the decision under appeal: in terms of the prohibition on carrying out advertising in relation to prices, it affects information about deregulated prices for the consumer, which define an essential aspect of the service being provided.

Photography, iconography and illustrations may, indeed, contain relevant information.

The restrictions on advertising media and the need for prior authorisation from the Governing Body in certain cases represent a restriction on the professional's freedom of initiative and the search for the most effective medium in which to advertise the service being provided.

Advertising is directly connected to the provision of the service and its remuneration inasmuch as it tends to give potential clients information on the circumstances that may lead them to opt for the service of a particular professional.

We must therefore conclude that the restriction on advertising has a direct connection with actions tending to restrict or limit freedom of competition and with the ability to do so as advertising, as has been said, affects the concurrence between supply and demand by informing potential clients of the characteristics of the service provided.

In the light of all these rulings we can conclude that the courts are by and large in favour of a regulation of advertising by lawyers through their professional associations, which in any event are moving towards increasingly less restrictive positions. The courts are making an effort to fit this exception to the LDC within the peculiar characteristics of the legal profession.

The fact is, however, that the opposite argument is more in tune with the legislative trend in Spain since 1996. This trend points unequivocally towards a deregulation of professional activity which does not recognise exceptions in principle by reference to the nature of the profession in question.

3. Contingency Fees

Another practice which is the subject of lively debate is the so-called 'pure contingency fee', in other words when the lawyer and the client agree that the lawyer's only remuneration will consist of a percentage of the proceeds of the case. The Code of Professional Ethics approved by the General Council of the Attorneys in June 2000 prohibits the pure contingency fee, although it does allow fees to be graduated by reference to the outcome of the case, 'provided that the actual payment of some sum is contemplated which at least covers the costs of providing the legal services contracted'.

The TDC, in its decision of 26 September 2002, imposed a fine of €180,000 on the General Council because it took the view that this provision was contrary to Article 1 of the LDC. One of the arguments put forward by the Council was that the contingency fee affected the independence of lawyers. In this regard, the TDC responded:

> Nor can we accept the submissions of the General Council when it contradicts the Service with the argument that the lawyer's independence would be threatened if the limitation imposed on the freedom to fix lawyers' fees by Article 16 of the Code of Professional Ethics did not exist. Indeed, even if we were to admit for the sake of argument that linking the fees of a lawyer to the outcome of the case could threaten his independence, that is not the question under consideration here, as the disputed Article 16 of the Code of Professional Ethics itself accepts that such connection is possible. The Code accepts in the said article that a lawyer may charge on the basis of results, what it does not accept is that the amount received on this basis may be less than the amount required to cover costs. Nor can we accept, as the General Council submits, that its intention was to prevent the lawyer from 'associating himself' with the client. This is expressly permitted by the disputed Article 16; what the article prohibits is that such «association» takes place on terms which mean that the lawyer is unable to cover the whole of the costs that he incurs in providing the service. In other words this is not a discussion on the legality of the contingency fee, as

> the General Council seems to suggest in its submission. Despite the decisive statement with which Article 16 of the Code begins, the contingency fee is contemplated and accepted in it, albeit only in the situation where the lawyer wins the case and not when he loses. It is merely a restriction on the freedom to fix fees that accords with what appears in Article 16.4, according to which, if the remuneration for the lawyer's professional services consists of him receiving a fixed amount, the amount has to be 'adequate, fair and decent compensation for the services provided'. This is an unjustified discrimination which significantly affects competition within the sector as it creates an entry barrier for less experienced lawyers. Certainly Article 16 of the Code of Professional Ethics of the Attorneys, in allowing the contingency fee, distorts the nature of the contract for services which was previously the form of contract that regulated the relationship between a lawyer and his client and brings it closer to the contract for works. But this distortion is the work of the General Council itself, which gave full acceptance to certain kinds of contingency fees in Article 16 of its Code of Professional Ethics.

The Decision was, however, passed with the individual vote of a member (a judge by training) who opposed the majority decision with a detailed argument. After acknowledging that, after the reform of the LCP, acts of professional associations with economic significance are subject to Article 1 of the LDC, she nevertheless took the view that the prohibition established by the Council did not restrict competition given the characteristics—rights and duties—inherent in the profession of lawyer:

> However, this does not mean either that in general terms we can say that every regulation relating to 'fees or prices' causes or may cause a distortion of competition, but rather it means that the characteristics of the market 'affected' in each case will have to be taken into account.
>
> In this case, and aside from the criticism which such regulation may merit, the fact is that under our law, as is the case in almost all European countries (in contrast to the American system) and in response to a series of long-established requirements (. . .), the lawyer forms part of the Administration of Justice (. . .) with his function being configured in a two-fold way: as a servant of the law and as a partial defender of the claims of his client, thus permitting the existence of the Professional Associations and imposing mandatory membership.
>
> In this context it is worth pointing out that a famous procedural expert has already indicated that 'the lawyer's activity must be the product of an obligation and not an interest'.
>
> A consequence of this regulation is that the relationship between the lawyer and the client is configured as a contract for the provision of services, defined by Article 1544 of the *Código Civil* [Civil Code], by which one of the parties undertakes to provide a service to the other for a stated price. In other words from the competition law perspective we can state that the lawyer offers his services in a market, which is the legal services market, in exchange for a remuneration and his function includes on the one hand the provision of legal advice (consultation, negotiation, drafting of documents) and on the other hand assistance and representation of the client in court, so that the service provided consists of the aforementioned legal services and not merely of 'winning the case'. A series of rights is derived for them from this

configuration of the lawyer's function (right to remuneration) and equally a series of duties is imposed on them (duty to inform, duty of loyalty, custody of documents, etc.), the breach of which is expressly stated to be an offence that can give rise to the exercise of its powers of sanction by the relevant Lawyers' Association.

(. . .) What the aforementioned Article 16 of the professional conduct rules does, and it is nothing more than the implementation of the provision cited which was previously contained in the General Statutes, is to enshrine the obligation—right of the lawyer 'to charge'; in other words, what it is prohibiting is the application of the 'no win no fee' maxim, trying to avoid it being agreed 'up front' on the adverse outcome of the lawyer-client relationship, the acceptance of which could give rise without doubt to an irregular capture of clients and to acts of unfair competition. Therefore I take the view that this obligation to charge is neither intended to nor has the ability to affect freedom of competition as required by Article 1 of the LDC and that instead it is merely a suitable response to the nature of the service that the lawyer provides, so that his activity is consistent and effective, trying to avoid unfair competition.

(. . .) The conclusion set out is not only obtained from more or less reasonable considerations but is also supported by the doctrine and current case law of the European Court of Justice which accept that in markets for professional services that are characterised by an asymmetrical knowledge, it may be necessary to have certain rules that ensure that the market operates under normal conditions in terms of competition, as it must be borne in mind that in these cases the consumer is rarely in a position to appreciate, '*a priori*', the quality of the services provided and it is therefore necessary to have certain rules that avoid the introduction of a logical uncertainty into the market, leading to a reduction in the general quality of the services in the long term.

Thus the European Commission itself in Decision 1999/267—the *EPI* case—in which it had to rule on rules of professional ethics of the Institute of Professional Representatives before the European Patent Office, took the view that 'some rules are necessary in view of the specific context of this profession, in order to ensure impartiality, competence, integrity and responsibility on the part of the agents to prevent conflicts of interest and to guarantee the proper functioning of the EPO'. According to the Commission these provisions 'are not liable to restrict competition if they are applied objectively and without discrimination', circumstances which are not present in this case as the rules of professional ethics that are under question today bind all the professionals practising as lawyers equally.

The *Tribunal Supremo* has also repeatedly, in its judgments of 3 March, 9 June and 17 December 2003, ruled in favour of the view that the rule of the General Council of the Legal Profession is not contrary to Article 1 of the LDC:

Like we did when dealing with advertising, we must remember here that the *Ley de Defensa de la Competencia* applicable to the fixing of lawyers' remuneration applies in full and therefore the exceptions to article one which merit the classification of 'conduct authorised by Law' and which are regulated in article two are also valid here. This means—as we have recalled in setting out our views on certain restrictions on advertising by lawyers—that if the LCP authorised them to regulate their respective professions 'looking after ethics and the respect due to the rights of individuals', any conflict of interest between the free competition that by operation of law has to govern the fixing of lawyers' remuneration and the powers to make regulations that the law grants to the professional bodies has to be decided by determining whether indeed the definition of the supposed specific rule that is regulated finds legal justification that enables it to be integrated, from the point of view of competition, within the notion of conduct authorised by Law, bearing in mind that this also includes the conduct described in 'the provisions of regulations passed pursuant to a Law.

So, by reference to these parameters, we find that within our legal system the activity of the lawyer has repeatedly and uniformly been classified as a form of contract for the provision of services, with the nuances and particularities derived from the fact that this contractual figure is developed in the highly delicate area of essential assistant to or co-operator in the Administration of Justice.

This characterisation of the services that the lawyer provides to his client in the course of proceedings by its very nature excludes in our system the idea of converting the lawyer into the holder of a contract for works or a business contract in which his role as the provider of a service that is essential to the correct operation of the State's judicial power makes him an exclusive underwriter of the risk that the decision to start proceedings always carries with it, meaning that he may thereby implicitly compromise his independent judgement when advising the client because it is not the risk assumed by the client that becomes most important but the risk assumed by the lawyer himself.

That is why, in the context of the conception of the legal profession that applies in our system, the minimal restriction on freedom of competition which is represented by the prohibition on a contingency fee agreement in the strict sense finds sufficient legal support in the fact that it is not that its acceptance is a threat to the dignity of the legal profession, but that above all it would blur the outlines of the very concept of such professional activity and would not properly respect the rights of individuals who in certain circumstances could find themselves becoming mere instruments in the lawyers' business conduct.

V. Conclusions

In this article we have attempted to explain the evolution that has taken place in Spain in relation to the application of the competition rules to professional associations. Starting from a position of virtual immunity, the TDC in the first instance and the Government in its turn have over the past decade proposed submitting such associations to the same rules as the rest of the economic sectors.

In contrast to this position, in most cases the courts have proved to be much more cautious. Even though they recognise the principle that professional activity must be governed by the competition rules, they seem to be resistant to considering professionals as mere traders who are subject to the same rules as any other economic agent. Indeed, the courts have shown an inclination to modulate the application of the competition rules to members of professional associations, taking into consideration their functions as defenders of the public interest and the special nature of certain professions.

It also seems significant to us that in the vast majority of cases analysed by the TDC or the courts, the justification for any restrictions has come via the 'rule of reason' route and not by the application of the strict criteria of individual exemption provided for in Article 81(3) EC and Article 3 of the LDC. This should not surprise us at all given the fact that the ECJ itself in its judgment in the *Wouters* case quite clearly turned to the rule of reason in order to conclude that the rule of the professional body which prohibited multi-disciplinary practices, even though it restricted competition, was not contrary to Article 81(1) EC.

Furthermore, we can also state that the vast majority of professional associations have been sensitive to the need to adapt the practice of their professions to the competition principles, eliminating many of the restrictions that traditionally existed and limiting the scope of many others. In this context we cannot ignore the fact that, in *Wouters,* the ECJ gave the Dutch Bar Association—and not the national competition authorities, not even the judge referring the case—the jurisdiction to decide whether the prohibition on multi-disciplinary practices, despite the restriction on competition that it implied, was necessary for the correct practice of the professional activity:

> a national regulation such as the 1993 Regulation adopted by a body such as the Bar of the Netherlands does not infringe Article 81(1) of the Treaty, since that body could reasonably have considered that that regulation, despite the effects restrictive of competition that are inherent in it, is necessary for the proper practice of the legal profession, as organised in the Member State concerned.

In short, it is a question of trying to find an application of the competition rules to professional activities that is, as Professor Ehlermann put it in 1993:[66]

> 'Flexible et réaliste, puisque la Commission :
>
> Ne vise pas à garantir une concurrence pure et parfaite, mais une concurrence effective et praticable—celle qui est possible dans chaque marché compte tenu de son propre contexte économique;
> Prend en compte les évolutions techniques et économiques ainsi que l'évolution concrète du Marché commun.'

[66] C-D Ehlermann, 'Concurrence et professions libérales: antagonisme ou compatibilité?' (1993) 36 *Revue du marché commun et de l'Union européenne* 136.

X

*Assimakis P Komninos**

Resolution of Conflicts in the Integrated Article 81 EC

I. Introduction

Since 1 May 2004 Europe has in place a brand new system of enforcement of competition law. Article 81 EC becomes an integrated provision that will be applied as a whole by all enforcers and courts. The innovations concerned are not only procedural in their nature but have serious repercussions for the substance of EC competition law. We attempt, firstly, to examine how competition analysis will be affected by this fundamental change and, secondly, to view in this context and try to systematise the non-competition considerations that are bound to arise. Such non-competition concerns, usually associated with the generally-defined 'public interest', underlie the whole question of the interrelationship between competition law and the liberal professions, hence the relevance of this question to the theme of this year's workshop.

Our aim is to answer the question 'what goes under Article 81(1) and what goes under Article 81(3) EC?' and to argue that this bifurcation should not be followed in the taking into account of non-competition concerns. We argue that a better approach is not to import these non-competition concerns into the substance of Article 81(3) EC, thus blurring the purity of antitrust analysis, but rather to deal with them 'at arm's length', that is, to balance them against Article 81 EC as a whole, following classical constitutional rules on the resolution of conflicts.

II. The 'New' Article 81 EC

The 'venerable' Regulation 17/1962 is now past. As a result of a long process that officially started in April 1999[1] and ended only in April 2004 with the

* White & Case, Brussels; European University Institute, Florence. I have benefited from discussions with Claus-Dieter Ehlermann, Ian Forrester, Petros Mavroidis, Julio Baquero Cruz and Ekaterina Rousseva. The usual disclaimer applies.

[1] Commission White Paper of 28 April 1999 on Modernisation of the Rules Implementing Articles 85 and 86 of the EC Treaty, COM(1999) 101 final, OJ C 132 [1999]; Commission Proposal for a Council Regulation on the Implementation of the Rules on Competition Laid Down in Articles 81 and 82 of the Treaty and Amending Regulations (EEC) No 1017/68, (EEC)

publication in the Official Journal of the 'Modernisation Package',[2] Europe has a brand new enforcement system that will be with us for long.[3] The reforms have collectively been known as the 'modernisation' of EC competition law.[4] Naturally, it is more correct to speak of modernisation of EC competition enforcement, rather than law. Indeed, it was not the direct aim of the White Paper or of Regulation 1/2003 to change substantive competition law as such. Admittedly, however, in EC competition law substance and procedure have been intermingled from the outset with the result that matters of procedure have a direct bearing on substance and vice versa.[5]

Thus, while it is true that the very broad interpretation of competition restrictions under Article 81(1) EC owes much to the ordoliberal notion of freedom of economic action,[6] it has also been common to explain this 'institutionally', based on the Commission's exemption monopoly. According to this line of thinking, the Commission's central role in EC competition enforcement, coupled with its monopoly to enforce Article 81(3) EC, and the

---

No 2988/74, (EEC) No 4056/86 and (EEC) No 3975/87 ('Regulation Implementing Articles 81 and 82 of the Treaty'), COM(2000) 582 final, OJ C 365E [2000]; Council Regulation (EC) No 1/2003 of 16 December 2002 on the Implementation of the Rules on Competition Laid down in Articles 81 and 82 of the Treaty, OJ L 1 [2003].

[2] Commission Regulation 773/2004 of 7 April 2004 Relating to the Conduct of Proceedings by the Commission Pursuant to Articles 81 and 82 of the EC Treaty, OJ L 123 [2004]; Commission Notice on Cooperation within the Network of Competition Authorities, OJ C 101 [2004]; Commission Notice on the Co-operation between the Commission and the Courts of the EU Member States in the Application of Articles 81 and 82 EC, OJ C 101 [2004]; Commission Notice on the Handling of Complaints by the Commission under Articles 81 and 82 of the EC Treaty, OJ C 101 [2004]; Commission Notice on Informal Guidance Relating to Novel Questions Concerning Articles 81 and 82 of the EC Treaty that Arise in Individual Cases (Guidance Letters), OJ C 1010 [2004]; Commission Notice—Guidelines on the Effect on Trade Concept Contained in Articles 81 and 82 of the Treaty, OJ C 101 [2004]; Communication from the Commission—Notice—Guidelines on the Application of Article 81(3) of the Treaty, OJ C 101 [2004].

[3] Compare C-D Ehlermann, 'Developments in Community Competition Law Procedures' (1994) 1 *EC Competition Policy Newsletter* 2: 'Regulation No 17 contains all the basic procedural rules for Community competition policy. *If and when it is revised, it will only be revised once for the foreseeable future*' (emphasis added).

[4] Apart from the *stricto sensu* 'procedural' modernisation, one may also speak of a broader modernisation of the EC competition rules that started in 1996 with the publication of the Green Paper on Vertical Restraints. This broader process resulted in 'new generation' block exemption Regulations of the Commission, accompanied by soft law Notices and Guidelines and based on a more economic approach, and finally in a new Merger Regulation.

[5] See, eg, DJ Gerber, *Law and Competition in Twentieth Century Europe: Protecting Prometheus* (Oxford, OUP, 1998) 334 *et seq.*

[6] In its recent Notice on Article 81(3), the Commission seems to depart from the formalistic approach it had pursued in the past, under which almost any agreement that restricted commercial freedom was considered restrictive of competition. This had meant that the substantive analysis was confined under the third paragraph of Art 81 EC Under the new Notice, assessing whether an agreement infringes Art 81(1) EC in the first place requires a substantive analysis of the market and of the economic impact of specific restrictions, while the guiding principle becomes consumer welfare.

need of uniform application of Article 81 EC in all Member States required giving a broad interpretation to the first paragraph of that provision, thus ensuring that the decision as to whether a given restriction was to be accepted, was taken in a uniform manner by the Commission.[7] This also partly explains the Commission's hesitation towards the introduction of a more economic approach or of a fully fledged 'rule of reason' in paragraph 1 of Article 81 EC (as opposed to paragraph 3), since the 'rule of reason' would have led to an indirect transfer of competencies from the Commission to national competition authorities and courts.[8] The fear was also that this might lead to a re-nationalisation of competition enforcement in Europe, since agreements benefiting from a 'rule of reason' would be granted a negative clearance under Article 81(1) EC rather than an exemption under 81(3) EC, thus inviting the application of stricter national competition law.[9]

By the same token, the abolition of the notification and prior authorisation system may also have a certain impact on the substance of EC competition law. The first signs are that the area of that impact will be the substantive relationship between the first and the third paragraph of Article 81 EC. With Article 81 EC being enforced as a unitary norm by Community and national enforcers alike, one can argue that any debate as to the bifurcation of antitrust analysis under the first and the third paragraph of Article 81 EC would only have theoretical importance. Indeed, it has been submitted that it will no longer matter if Article 81(1) EC is interpreted in such a way as to catch almost all agreements restrictive of economic freedom without any economic analysis at all, since such analysis of pro-competitive effects and, thus, the balancing against the anti-competitive effects, will immediately follow

---

[7] See, eg, JT McCullough, 'The Continuing Search for Greater Certainty: Suggestions for Improving US and EEC Antitrust Clearance Procedures' (1984) 6 *Northwestern Journal of International Law and Business* 803, 892; M Waelbroeck, 'Antitrust Analysis under Article 85(1) and Article 85(3)' B Hawk, (ed), *North American and Common Market Antitrust and Trade Laws 1987, Annual Proceedings of the Fordham Corporate Law Institute*, (New York, NY, Juris Publ, 1987) 693, 696; M Siragusa, 'Rethinking Article 85: Problems and Challenges in the Design and Enforcement of the EC Competition Rules' in B Hawk, (ed), *International Antitrust Law and Policy 1997, Annual Proceedings of the Fordham Corporate Law Institute* (New York, NY, Juris Publ, 1998) 276; M Todino, 'Le norme comunitarie di concorrenza nei poteri dell'Autorità garante della concorrenza e del mercato' (1998) 12 *Diritto del Commercio Internazionale* 751, 753; V Verouden, 'Vertical Agreements and Article 81(3) EC: The Evolving Role of Economic Analysis' (2003) 71 *Antitrust Law Journal* 525, 532 *et seq*.

[8] See eg, R Whish and B Sufrin, 'Article 85 and the Rule of Reason' (1987) 7 *Yearbook of European Law* 1, p 19; G D'Attorre, 'Una "ragionevole" concorrenza: Il ruolo della "rule of reason" dopo la riforma del diritto antitrust comunitario' (2004) 31 *Giurisprudenza Commerciale* I–80, p I–92 *et seq*.

[9] Under the previous system of enforcement, negative clearances were merely of a declaratory nature and have not been generally interpreted to constitute 'positive measures' that pre-empt the application of stricter national competition law in the *Walt Wilhelm* sense (Case 14/68, *Walt Wilhelm v Bundeskartellamt* [1969] ECR 1).

under the third paragraph of Article 81 EC, which will now be applied by the same enforcer and in the same forum.[10]

However, a first question of utmost practical importance is the burden of proof, which under Article 81(1) EC is borne by the Commission, or by national competition authorities or third parties when that provision is invoked at the national level, whereas under Article 81(3) EC it is borne by the undertakings.[11] If Article 81(1) were to be given an unqualified meaning, then the burden of proof would entirely fall upon the parties. On the other hand, if almost all balancing were to take place under the first paragraph, the Commission would be inappropriately burdened. Therefore, the current division between the two paragraphs reflects a fine balance and apportionment of the burden of proof that it would be unwise to tilt.

In addition, apart from the burden of proof, the distinction between the two paragraphs still remains significant. Firstly, as it is rightly pointed out, the Treaty itself requires a two-stage reasoning under the two paragraphs.[12] Secondly, if one gives too broad a meaning to that provision and proceeds to any economic analysis only under the third paragraph, there is a risk that the objective and the function of Article 81 EC as a whole will be compromised, since potentially idle agreements, which would otherwise have escaped the application of Article 81(1) EC, if a narrower meaning were adopted, might not satisfy the two positive and two negative cumulative conditions of Article 81(3) EC and the agreement might end up being prohibited.[13]

---

[10] See in this direction V Korah, *An Introductory Guide to EC Competition Law and Practice* (Oxford, Hart Publishing, 2000) 189, 361; C Gavalda and G Parleani, *Droit des affaires de l'Union européenne*, (Paris, Litec, 2002) 333–34, 359; A Albors-Llorens, *EC Competition Law and Policy* (Cullompton Portland, Willan Publishing, 2002) 72; V Korah and D O'Sullivan, *Distribution Agreements under the EC Competition Rules* (Oxford, Hart Publishing, 2002) 120; L Gyselen, 'The Substantive Legality Test under Article 81–3 EC Treaty—Revisited in Light of the Commission's Modernization Initiative' in A von Bogdandy, P Mavroidis and Y Mény, (eds), *European Integration and International Co-ordination, Studies in Transnational Economic Law in Honour of Claus-Dieter Ehlermann* The Hague, Kluwer International, 2002) 197; D Goyder, *EC Competition Law*, (Oxford, OUP, 2003) 94–95; J Venit, 'Brave New World: The Modernization and Decentralization of Enforcement under Articles 81 and 82 of the EC Treaty' (2003) 40 *Common Market L Rev* 545, 577. It is interesting to note that the system of legal exception in French competition law resulted in a certain attenuation of the prohibition-exemption dichotomy with the equivalent of Article 81(3) EC being rarely applied or invoked, while the French competition authority has followed a more global approach based on the rule of reason. See further L Idot, 'Le nouveau système communautaire de mise en œuvre des Articles 81 et 82 CE (Règlement 1/2003 et projets de textes d'application)' (2003) 39 *Cahiers de Droit Européen* 283, 289, at n 28.

[11] See Art 2 Reg 1/2003.

[12] See L Idot, 'A French Point of View on the Radical Decentralisation of the Implementation of Article 81(1) and (3)' in C-D Ehlermann and I Atanasiu, (eds), *European Competition Law Annual 2000: The Modernisation of EU Competition Law* (Oxford, Hart Publishing, 2001) 336.

[13] See R Wesseling, 'The Commission White Paper on Modernisation of EC Antitrust Law: Unspoken Consequences and Incomplete Treatment of Alternative Options' (1999) 20 *European Competition L Rev* 420, 423; D Tzouganatos, *Exclusive and Selective Distribution Agreements in Free and Unfair Competition Law* (Athens, 2001) text available in Greek 171–72.

Moreover, Article 81(3) EC, as applied by the Commission and by the European Courts, while corresponding to a substantial extent to the US 'rule of reason', is not a very flexible norm. It does not allow for a total welfare test, but only for a consumer surplus standard, since at least some part of the cost savings must be passed on to the consumers.[14] Furthermore, the second negative requirement for an agreement not to eliminate competition means that an agreement creating a monopoly, although socially desirable because of accruing efficiencies, will still be prohibited.[15] Therefore, it should not be excluded that certain pro-competitive agreements escape Article 81(1) EC altogether under a reasonableness test, thus being spared the more inflexible antitrust analysis of Article 81(3) EC. This leads us to the conclusion that the reform should not affect the analysis mechanism under Article 81 EC.

But which is the current standard of analysis in Article 81 EC, if there is one? The question of the relationship between the first and third paragraph of Article 81 EC and the role of economic analysis, if any, under Article 81(1) EC has always been hotly debated and it is one of the areas where the Commission's and the European Courts' approaches had not been identical in the past.[16] There is no doubt, however, that such divergence has ceased. The new economic approach of the European Commission and, at the same time, the recognition by the European Courts that a full-fledged rule of reason analysis can take place only under Article 81(3) EC has eliminated any rightly or wrongly-perceived divergence between Brussels and Luxembourg on Article 81 EC.

Thus, according to the Courts' case law, under the first paragraph of Article 81 EC, agreements have to be examined in their legal and economic context. A recent judgment of the Court of First Instance, summarises that line of cases in the following terms:

> [I]t is not necessary to hold, wholly abstractly and without drawing any distinction, that any agreement restricting the freedom of action of one or more of the parties is necessarily caught by the prohibition laid down in Article 85(1) [now 81(1)] of the Treaty. In assessing the applicability of Article 85(1) [now 81(1)] to an agreement,

---

[14] See also T Eilmansberger, 'How to Distinguish Good from Bad Competition under Article 82 EC: In Search of Clearer and More Coherent Standards for Anti-competitive Abuses' (2005) 42 *Common Market L Rev* 129, 136, who proceeds to a combined reading of Arts 81(3) and 82 EC.

[15] See, eg, K Lenaerts and D Gerard, 'Decentralisation of EC Competition Law Enforcement: Judges in the Frontline' (2004) 27 *World Competition* 313, 330, stressing that the Commission promotes 'a strict assessment of the likelihood for efficiency claims'. See further DJ Gifford and RT Kudrle, 'European Union Competition Law and Policy: How Much Latitude for Convergence with the United States?' (2003) 48 *Antitrust Bulletin* 727, 772 *et seq*.

[16] Among the older literature, see the two groundbreaking articles by IS Forrester and C Norall, 'The Laicization of Community Law: Self-help and the Rule of Reason: How Competition Law Is and could be Applied' (1984) 21 *Common Market L Rev* 11; and R Whish and C Sufrin, above n 8. On the Art 81(1) EC case law, see in general Korah and O'Sullivan, above n 10, p 80 *et seq*.

account should be taken of the actual conditions in which it functions, in particular the economic context in which the undertakings operate, the products or services covered by the agreement and the actual structure of the market concerned.[17]

This implies that a certain degree of economic analysis is called for already at the stage of that provision. Under Article 81(1) falls also the application of the ancillary restraints concept, which covers restrictions of competition that are directly related, necessary and proportionate to the implementation of a main non-restrictive transaction.[18] However, the above economic analysis should be seen more in the context of 'reasonableness' rather than as a full-fledged balancing of pro- and anti-competitive effects.[19] In *Métropole Télévision*, the CFI, though admitting that a certain degree of an economics-based approach is called for under Article 81(1) EC, took the view that the balancing of pro-competitive and anti-competitive effects, along with the full examination of the economic efficiencies accruing from an agreement, should only take place under Article 81(3) EC, which is the only provision that can accommodate a 'rule of reason' test.[20]

This case law is in full harmony with the current approach of the Commission. Such an approach can already be traced back to the White Paper and is further developed in the new Notice on Article 81(3) EC.[21] There, the Commission seems to depart from the formalistic approach it had pursued in the past, under which almost any agreement that restricted commercial freedom was considered restrictive of competition and thus violated Article 81(1) EC. Under the new Notice, assessing whether an agreement infringes Article 81(1) EC in the first place requires a substantive analysis of the market and of the economic impact of specific restrictions, while the guiding principle becomes consumer welfare.[22] Ancillary restraints are also examined under the first paragraph of Article 81 EC.[23] The Notice, on the

---

[17] Case T–112/99 *Métropole Télévision (M6) v Commission* [2001] ECR II–2459, para 76.

[18] *Métropole Télévision, ibid*, paras 107–9.

[19] See L Idot, 'Avocats et *droit* de la concurrence: La rencontre a eu lieu . . .' (2002) 5 *Europe* 5, 7; D'Attorre, above n 8, p I–99 *et seq*.

[20] *Métropole Télévision, ibid,* paras 72–77. A part of commentators had long ago argued that Art 81(1) EC could not in any case accommodate a rule of reason approach (see, eg, Whish and Sufrin, above n 8, p 23.

[21] Para 57 of the White Paper and para 11 of the Art 81(3) EC Notice. See further F Vogelaar, 'Modernisation of EC Competition Law, Economy and Horizontal Cooperation between Undertakings' (2002) 37 *Intereconomics* 19, 21.

[22] See para 13 of the Notice. See further J Bourgeois and J Bocken, 'Guidelines on the Application of Article 81(3) of the EC Treaty or How to Restrict a Restriction' (2005) 32 *Legal Issues of Economic Integration* 111, 112–13.

[23] See paras 28–31 of the Commission's Notice on Art 81(3) EC. The Commission's approach is that 'the application of the ancillary restraint concept must be distinguished from the application of the defence under Article 81(3) which relates to certain economic benefits produced by restrictive agreements and which are balanced against the restrictive effects of the agreements'. In the view of the Commission, 'the application of the ancillary restraint concept does not involve any weighing of pro-competitive and anti-competitive effects'. Such balancing should be reserved for Art 81(3) EC.

other hand, fully adopting the *Métropole Télévision* thesis, relegates all balancing between pro-competitive and anti-competitive effects of the agreement to Article 81(3) EC.

III. Non-competition Concerns and Article 81 EC

If it is now clear what kind of economic analysis takes place under paragraphs 1 and 3 of Article 81 EC, an interesting question remains as to whether that provision allows for taking into account concerns that are extraneous to competition law and to economic progress, but are expressive of other policies, such as environmental, social, or industrial policy, or of the broadly perceived 'public interest'.[24] This question becomes more relevant under the new system of enforcement because of the fear that the abolition of the Commission's monopoly of exemption may be an open invitation to national competition authorities and courts to introduce into the tests of Article 81 EC such non-competition aims or the pursuit of the parochially seen public or national interest. This was also a concern during the post–White Paper period leading to the adoption of Regulation 1/2003. The argument went that if non-competition issues were read into Article 81(3) EC, the whole thesis as to that provision's direct effect and justiciability would be weakened.[25] If things like the environment, employment policy, culture, or industrial policy had to be balanced under Article 81(3) EC, then that provision would not be sufficiently precise so as to have direct effect and to be justiciable. If, on the other hand, only competition concerns have to be examined under the four-test rule of that provision, then courts could indeed apply the latter.

Cross-section clauses in some EC Treaty Articles, such as in Articles 6 EC (environment), 127(2) EC (employment), 151(4) EC (culture), 153(2) EC (consumer protection) and 159(1) EC (economic and social cohesion), which call for the 'integrating' or 'taking into account' of the respective aims in the definition and implementation of Community policies and activities, may add to confusion. We must stress, however, that most of these cross-section clauses mean that the Community must take into account not *national* but only *Community* policies aiming at the protection of these aims. This is

---

[24] We prefer the term 'public interest' to 'public policy', which is used by some other authors. The latter term may be prone to confusion because it is used in many instances as a technical term.

[25] See R Whish, 'National Courts and the White Paper: A Commentary' in *The Modernisation of EC Competition Law: The Next Ten Years*, (2000) CELS Occasional Paper No 4, Cambridge, p 75 *et seq*; Whish and Sufrin, above n 8, p 150; U Immenga, 'Coherence: A Sacrifice of Decentralisation?' in in C-D Ehlermann and I Atanasiu, (eds), *European Competition Law Annual 2000: The Modernisation of EU Competition Law* (Oxford, Hart Publishing, 2001) 335.

explicit, for example, in Article 159(1) EC, which refers to Article 158 EC, and it is arguable that this is implicit in Articles 127(2), 151(4) and 153(2) EC. This is especially true for the two last provisions, which refer to '*other Community* policies and activities'.[26] At the same time, the Treaty itself explicitly recognises that the pursuit of certain policies must not prejudice the system of undistorted and free competition, as protected by Articles 81 EC *et seq*. Reference is made to Articles 4(1) *in fine* and (2) *in fine*, 98, 105 EC (economic and monetary union), 27(c) EC (customs union), 154(2) EC (trans-European networks) and 157(3)(b) EC (industrial policy).[27] In addition, the Court of Justice has on occasion stressed the need to also take into account the *competition rules*, while the Community formulates other policies.[28] It should also be mentioned that the protection of free competition is an aim pursued not only under Article 81 *et seq* EC and under secondary competition legislation, but also exists in other Community legislative instruments, such as in Community Directives on consumer protection.[29]

Apart from these policies that are accorded a certain primary status in the EC Treaty itself, there are also other candidate interests vying to be taken into account in the context of competition law enforcement. Culture, the 'specificity' of sport, the public interest in safeguarding the independence of the legal profession and other concerns[30] have been suggested as legitimate values that have to be balanced against or to be taken into account in the framework of the competition provisions.

We should also stress that this general question is by no means limited to Article 81 EC. It may also affect the enforcement of Article 82 EC.[31] What

---

[26] Emphasis added.

[27] See also Arts 96 and 97 EC with reference to unilateral measures of Member States adopted for environmental or social policy aims that distort the conditions of competition in the common market.

[28] See, eg, Case C–17/90 *Wieger Spedition GmbH v Bundesanstalt für den Güterfernverkehr* [1991] ECR I–5253, para 11: 'In view of the complexity of the cabotage sector, considerable difficulties still stand in the way of the achievement of freedom to provide services in that sphere. This can be done in an orderly fashion only in the context of a common transport policy which takes into consideration the economic, social and ecological problems and *ensures equality in the conditions of competition*' (emphasis added—note, however, that that case was decided before the coming into force of the Maastricht Treaty).

[29] See, eg, Council Directive 93/13/EEC of 5 April 1993 on Unfair Terms in Consumer Contracts, OJ L 95 [1993], Recital 2; European Parliament and Council Directive 97/7/EC of 20 May 1997 on the Protection of Consumers in Respect of Distance Contracts, OJ L 144 [1997], Recital 4; European Parliament and Council Directive 97/55/EC of 6 October 1997 Amending Directive 84/450/EEC Concerning Misleading Advertising so as to Include Comparative Advertising, OJ L 290 [1997], Recital 2 in fine; European Parliament and Council Directive 98/27 of 19 May 1998 on Injunctions for the Protection of Consumers' Interests, OJ L 166 [1998], Recital 4; European Parliament and Council Directive 2001/95/EC of 3 December 2001 on General Product Safety, OJ L 11 [2002], Recital 3.

[30] On the interface between competition law and the audiovisual policy see M Ariño Gutierrez, 'Competition Law and Pluralism in European Digital Broadcasting: Addressing the Gaps' (2004) 54 *Communications and Strategies* 97.

[31] For example, such non-economic concerns may be raised under an 'objective justification' defence.

makes, however, Article 81 EC more 'inviting' to the introduction of non-competition concerns, and thus more vulnerable from an antitrust point of view, is its bifurcated structure (prohibition-exception). This structure makes it tempting for some authors to argue that it must entail some inherent distinction between the substance of the first and that of the third paragraph, otherwise it would never have existed in the first place. Some of those authors would welcome the introduction of non-competition concerns in Article 81(3) EC, as this would provide for an *ex post* justification of that bifurcated structure.[32]

IV. The 'Danger' of Importing Non-competition Concerns into Article 81(3) EC

The position we adopt is that the wording of Article 81(3) EC does not appear to accommodate such non-economic aims. The advantages of a restrictive agreement that nevertheless deserves an exemption must benefit the actual consumers of the specific product and not society at large. Thus, employment or industrial policy considerations, by themselves, cannot lead to the legality of an otherwise anti-competitive agreement.[33] On the other hand, it is not excluded that such concerns may be taken into account as a *further* positive element among other economic efficiency elements of a restrictive agreement, especially if such concerns have an 'economic facet'.

Indeed, the cases where the Commission has referred to non-competition considerations in the Article 81 EC context are not rare. We can use as a paradigm the environmental benefits which have been examined by the Commission in a series of decisions under a broad economic efficiency test. To use some examples, in the *KSB/Goulds/Lowara/ITT* case, which concerned the joint research and development of a more environment-friendly pump

[32] See, eg, already van B Houtte, 'A Standard of Reason in EEC Antitrust Law: Some Comments on the Application of Parts 1 and 3 of Article 85' (1982) 4 *Northwestern Journal of International Law and Business* 497, 510 *et seq*; Siragusa, above n 7, p 285. Eleanor Fox, for her part, would have supported *de lege ferenda* a concentration of all antitrust analysis under Art 81(1) and a 'delegation' of non-competition concerns to Art 81(3) EC, with the Commission retaining its monopoly to grant such extraordinary exemptions: see E Fox, 'Intervention in Panel One Discussion: Compatibility, Efficiency, Legal Security' in C-D Ehlermann and I Atanasiu, (eds), *European Competition Law Annual 2000: The Modernisation of EU Competition Law* (Oxford, Hart Publishing, 2001) 23–24.

[33] See G Tesauro, 'Panel Discussion: EC Competition System: Proposals for Reform' in Hawk B, (ed), *International Antitrust Law and Policy 1998, Annual Proceedings of the Fordham Corporate Law Institute*, (New York, NY, Juris Publ, 1999) 223; C-D Ehlermann, 'The Modernization of EC Antitrust Policy: A Legal and Cultural Revolution' (2000) 37 *Common Market L Rev* 537, 549; J Burrichter, Intervention in Panel One Discussion: Compatibility, Efficiency, Legal Security in Ehlermann and Atanasiu, 2001, *ibid*, p 46. See also Venit, above n 10, pp 561, 578–79, according to whom the cumulative conditions elaborated in Art 81(3) EC do nothing more than establish a narrow efficiency/consumer benefit defence.

that would lead to energy savings, the Commission refered to the environmental benefits as an 'improvement in operating characteristics' and stressed the fact that the consumers would buy them at the same price as the conventional pumps. Hence the title of the relevant paragraph, 'Share of consumers in the benefit resulting from the agreements'.[34] In *Assurpol*, dealing with a co-operation agreement between insurance and re-insurance firms aiming at improving the knowledge of risks, at creating financial capacity and at developing technical expertise in insuring environmental damage risks, the whole approach of the Commission was to see all this under 'technical and economic progress' and, thus, to exempt the agreement.[35] In another case, the Commission published an Article 19(3) Notice (under the old Regulation 17) and indicated its readiness to take a favourable view of a voluntary commitment sponsored by a trade association that aimed at reducing energy consumption by televisions and video recorders in standby mode. The Commission calculated the consumer savings at ECU 480 million per year and also spoke of the 'negative externalities' involved in generating this much electricity.[36] Further, in *DSD*, the Commission exempted certain exclusivity clauses in a country-wide system for the collection and recovery of sales packaging that met the requirements of German and Community packaging and environmental legislation. While it admitted that the system in question was consistent with the objectives of German and Community environmental legislation, this did not stop it from considering the exclusivity clauses anti-competitive and from exempting them only under specific obligations. Again the exemption alluded to technical and economic progress.[37]

The most interesting of all these cases so far has been *CECED*.[38] This case is often cited by the proponents of the integration of non-competition concerns into Article 81(3) EC and criticised by those opposed to that integration. There, the Commission approved for the first time an agreement to stop production with a view to improving the environmental performance of products. The participants in the agreement, nearly all the European producers and importers of domestic washing machines, agreed to stop producing or importing into the EU the least energy-efficient machines in order to reduce the energy consumption of such appliances and thereby reduce pollutant emissions from power generation. According to the Commission, '[a]lthough participants restrict their freedom to manufacture and market certain types of washing machine, thereby restricting competition within the meaning of

---

[34] Commission Decision 91/38/EEC of 12 December 1990, *KSB/Goulds/Lowara/ITT*, OJ L 19 [1991], para 27.

[35] Commission Decision 92/96 of 14 January 1992, *Assurpol*, OJ L 37 [1992], para 38.

[36] Case No IV/C–3/36.494–*EACEM*, OJ C 12 [1998] in particular paras 11 and 12.

[37] Commission Decision 2001/837/EC of 17 September 2001, *DSD*, OJ L 319 [2001], paras 142–46.

[38] Commission Decision 2000/475/EC of 24 January 1999, *CECED*, OJ L 187 [2000].

Article 81(1) of the EC Treaty, the agreement fulfils the conditions for exemption under Article 81(3): it will bring advantages and considerable savings for consumers, in particular by reducing pollutant emissions from electricity generation'. The Commission decision to exempt the agreement takes account of this positive contribution to the EU's environmental objectives, for the benefit of present and future generations.[39]

We believe that what these cases show is that the Commission is ready to debate and to take into account concerns which are not economic in an orthodox sense, but which have economic parameters and can always be measured as such. A Commission official has recently considered the occasional Commission references to non-competition benefits of agreements as '*obiter dicta*' and has argued persuasively that it is only in appearance that some of these benefits are entirely unrelated to competition. Most of them have an economic efficiency facet or lead to some identifiable pro-competitive consumer benefit. Anything else seems to be '*ex abundantia*'.[40]

This approach is followed by the Commission in its Guidelines on horizontal agreements, where it states the following:

> The Commission takes a positive stance on the use of environmental agreements as a policy instrument to achieve the goals enshrined in Article 2 and Article 174 of the Treaty as well as in Community environmental action plans, *provided such agreements are compatible with competition rules*. Environmental agreements caught by Article 81(1) may attain *economic benefits* which, either at individual or aggregate consumer level, outweigh their negative effects on competition.[41]

In its recent Article 81(3) Notice the Commission makes this point clearer: 'Goals pursued by other Treaty provisions *can* be taken into account *to the*

[39] See 30th Report on Competition Policy–2000, paras 96–97. On *CECED*, see G van Gerven, 'The Application of Article 81 in the New Europe' in B Hawk, (ed), *Annual Proceedings of the Fordham Corporate Law Institute, International Antitrust Law and Policy 2003*, (New York, NY, Juris Publ, 2004) 429–30. For other 'environmental' cases, see the Art 19(3) Notice in Case No IV/35.742–F/2 *EUCAR*, OJ C 185 [1997], and the *ACEA* case, Reported in 28th Report on Competition Policy–1998, p 151.

[40] See Gyselen, above n 10, p 185. Similar is the approach of other (current and former) Commission officials: see E Paulis, 'Coherent Application of EC Competition Law in a System of Parallel Competencies' in Ehlermann and Atanasiu, 2001, above, p 405, who stresses that 'other objectives of the Treaty can only be taken into account if they can be subsumed under the conditions of Article 81(3)'; G Marenco, Intervention in Panel Three Discussion: Courts and Judges in Ehlermann and Atanasiu, 2001, *ibid*, p 500, describing the occasional Commission remarks going beyond competition as a forgivable weakness.

[41] *Commission Notice—Guidelines on the Applicability of Article 81 of the EC Treaty to Horizontal Cooperation Agreements*, OJ C 3 [2001], paras 192–93. Note, however, that the reference to 'aggregate consumer level' may be difficult to reconcile with the Commission's approach in the new Notice on Article 81(3), which in para 43 states that 'the condition that consumers must receive a fair share of the benefits implies in general that efficiencies generated by the restrictive agreement within a relevant market must be sufficient to outweigh the anti-competitive effects produced by the agreement within *that same relevant market*' (emphasis added).

extent that they can be *subsumed* under the four conditions of Article 81(3)'.[42] In addition, it is stated that the condition that consumers must receive a fair share of the benefits implies that the efficiencies which the restrictive agreement generates in a relevant market must be sufficient to outweigh its anti-competitive effects in *that same relevant market*.[43] The Commission, therefore, excludes taking into account non-competition concerns and benefits to other classes of consumers or to the society at large under Article 81(3) EC.

It is only in this manner that these cases and the occasional policy statements[44] of the Commission must be seen. In other words, non-competition aims cannot totally subjugate the competition and economic efficiency methodology of Article 81 EC or redeem a hopelessly anti-competitive agreement or practice. Otherwise, private parties that are engaged in anti-competitive practices would be elevated to guardians of the generally perceived public interest and the independence of competition law and policy would be jeopardised. The Commission, for its part, must only enforce the policies that have been entrusted to it. It must not, and indeed cannot, resolve conflicts of a constitutional nature, which can only be resolved in a court of law.

V. A Proposed Theory for the Resolution of Conflicts: *Wouters*

Notwithstanding the above, there are bound to be cases, where the economic facet of the non-competition concern is not evident enough, or where there are no discernible positive effects of an economic nature that can lead to an anti-competitive agreement being positively assessed under Article 81(3) EC. The interface between the general principle of free competition and other objectives of the EC Treaty or the globally-perceived public interest can be

---

42 Para 42 (emphasis added). It is noteworthy that the Commission in the equivalent para 38 of its draft Notice had included another sentence, which was, however, dropped in the final text. That sentence read: 'It is not, on the other hand, the role of Article 81 and the authorities enforcing this Treaty provision to allow undertakings to restrict competition in pursuit of general interest aims'. This change of course must certainly reflect the critical comments the Commission received with regard to this very sensitive question.

43 *Ibid*, paras 43 and 87.

44 We refer to the policy statements in Commission annual Reports on competition policy. See, eg, the statements in the 25th *Report on Competition Policy–1995*, para 85: '[The Commission] weighs up the restrictions of competition arising out of an agreement against the environmental objectives of the agreement, and applies the principle of proportionality in accordance with Article 85(3) [now 81(3)]. In particular, improving the environment is regarded as a factor which contributes to improving production or distribution or to promoting economic or technical progress'.

better examined under a more systematic analysis that lends itself to more transparency. In all these cases, we are dealing in essence with true conflicts of substantive norms, and this calls for a completely different methodology. It is more correct to balance the protection of competition and Article 81 EC (or indeed Article 82 EC), *as a whole*, against these other fundamental aims expressing the public interest, rather than to admit the latter inside the substance of Article 81 EC (in its first or its third paragraph), thus blurring the purity and independence of competition analysis.

The resolution of such conflicts at the Community law level can benefit from the theories that have been developed on conflicts between constitutional rights. According to the theory of *praktische Konkordanz* (practical concordance),[45] it should not be taken for granted that two or more substantive constitutional norms that apply to a specific set of facts are always in conflict. In every piece of legislation and in any concrete case of application a solution has to be found which allows for one principle to be applied as far as possible without violating the other. In other words, an acceptable balance is needed between two equally protected fundamental rights. The apparent conflict should not lead to a poor type of compromise, but rather to a rational balancing of contradictory values, always respecting the principle of proportionality.

This theory could well apply to the resolution of conflicts between the competition rules of the Treaty and other substantive norms, such as the protection of the environment, employment, industrial policy, etc.[46] Indeed, the Commission's approach to attempt to reconcile such non-competition values with the antitrust criteria in Article 81(3) EC through the 'economic facet' of the former can be seen as a successful application of the principle of practical concordance. In other words, the Commission, acting within the limits of its powers, tries invariably to enforce the competition rules in a manner that is friendly to these other norms. This is usually possible, if such objectives can be seen through their economic facet and if it is possible to reconcile them with competition analysis. The line of environmental cases, referred to above, if seen in this particular context, are easy to understand.

---

[45] The theory of 'practical concordance' was developed by Konrad Hesse, a German constitutional lawyer. See K Hesse, *Grundzüge des Verfassungsrechts der Bundesrepublik Deutschland* (Heidelberg, Auflage, 1999) 142. On the usefulness of this theory to the private sphere and to 'private regulation' see C Engel, 'A Constitutional Framework for Private Governance' (2003) 5 *German Law Journal* 197, 206.

[46] On the application of this principle to EC competition law, see already CU Schmid, 'Diagonal Competence Conflicts between European Competition Law and National Regulation: A Conflict of Laws Reconstruction of the Dispute on Book Price Fixing' (2000) 8 *European Review of Private Law* 155; MR Deckert, 'Some Preliminary Remarks on the Limitations of European Competition Law' (2000) 8 *European Review of Private Law* 173. We adopt that theory, albeit without necessarily adopting the views of those authors as to the result of the balancing between the conflicting norms.

The adoption of that approach may also help us to understand the recent *Wouters* ruling of the Court of Justice,[47] which has given rise to varying interpretations and which is very relevant to the theme of this year's conference. *Wouters* appears to introduce a 'rule of reason' approach importing non-competition and non-economic objectives into the first paragraph of Article 81 EC. In that sense, some commentators have spoken of a *sui generis* 'European rule of reason' or 'social political rule of reason' integrating elements of the Court's four freedoms case law.[48] Richard Whish, on his part, in his latest edition of 'Competition Law' views *Wouters* as a *sui generis* case of 'regulatory ancillarity' under Article 81(1) EC.[49]

We submit, however, that *Wouters* does not introduce a rule of reason approach, in the antitrust sense, at least as the late judge Joliet had meant it.[50] *Wouters* seems to draw inspiration from the theory of mandatory requirements that was developed in the Court's four freedoms case law.[51] The Court, thus, implicitly recognised that the non-competition concern at issue and Article 81 EC could not be reconciled and that therefore a balancing was called for. In doing so, the Court followed a constitutional law methodology, very similar to that used in four freedoms cases.

If we take a closer look at *Wouters*, we will detect a rather interesting line of reasoning:

The case concerned the decision of the Netherlands Bar Association (NBA) imposing restrictions on multi-disciplinary partnerships between lawyers and accountants and its potentially restrictive effects on competition. The Court started from the premise that lawyers are undertakings and that the NBA was

---

[47] Case C–309/99 *JCJ Wouters v Algemene Raad van de Nederlandse Orde van Advocaten* [2002] ECR I–1577.

[48] Among the many and often contradictory commentaries of this case, see VG Hatzopoulos, 'When Lawyers Ignore Competition or State and Semi-State Measures in the Light of Community Competition Rules after the *Arduino* and *Price Waterhouse* Judgments' (2002) 50 *Nomiko Vima* 863 [in Greek], 871 *et seq*; G Monti, 'Article 81 EC and Public Policy' (2002) 39 *Common Market L Rev* 1057; A Tizzano, 'Note sulla recente giurisprudenza della Corte comunitaria' (2002) 7 *Il Diritto dell'Unione Europea* 535, 546–47; J-P Keppenne, F Lagondet and S van Raepenbusch, 'Chronique de jurisprudence: Année 2002' (2003) 39 *Cahiers de Droit Européen* 433, 512–14; D'Attorre, above n 8, p I–110; G Scassellati Sforzolini and C Rizza 'La tensione fra regole di concorrenza comunitarie e regole professionali e deontologiche nazionali' (2003) 30 *Giurisprudenza Commerciale* II–8, p II–25 *et seq*; P Manzini, (2003) 'I parafernali del giudizio antitrust: Regola della ragionevolezza, restrizioni accessorie, divieto "per se"' (2003) 30 *Giurisprudenza Commerciale* II–285, p II–291 *et seq*.

[49] R Whish, *Competition Law* (London, Kluwer International, 2003) 120.

[50] R Joliet, *The Rule of Reason in Antitrust Law: American, German and Common Market Law* (The Hague, Martinus Nijhoff, 1967). See also B Vesterdorf, 'Recent Developments in the Case Law of the ECJ and the CFI in the Field of Competition Law' in Baudenbacher C, ed, *Neueste Entwicklungen im europäischen und internationalen Kartellrecht, Neuntes St Galler Internationales Kartellrechtsforum 2002* (Basel, Helbing & Lichtenhahn, 2002) 106, speaking of a 'balancing of interests other than that currently known as "rule of reason"'.

[51] See among others the analysis of J Baquero Cruz, *Between Competition and Free Movement, The Economic Constitutional Law of the European Community* (Oxford, Hart Publishing, 2002) 151–53.

in effect an association of undertakings. While NBA fulfilled a regulatory role, it was neither fulfilling a social function based on the principle of solidarity, unlike certain social security bodies, nor exercising powers which are typically those of a public authority. It acted as the regulatory body of a profession, the practice of which constitutes an economic activity. The fact that its governing bodies were composed exclusively of members of the Bar, elected solely by members of the profession, and that in adopting acts such as that regulation, it was not required to do so by reference to specified public interest criteria, supported the conclusion that such a professional organisation with regulatory powers cannot escape the application of Article 81 EC.[52]

So far so good. Then, the Court attempts to examine the Dutch regulation from an Article 81 EC angle. The Court did not have any difficulty in finding that the NBA regulation was liable to limit production and technical development within the meaning of Article 81(1)(b) EC.[53] Then, surprisingly, and while one would have expected the Court to consider the Dutch regulation invalid, since no notification had been filed with the European Commission, the Court proceeds to a U-turn and examines the countervailing benefits of that regulation. According to the Court, account had to be taken of the overall context in which the decision of the association of undertakings was taken or produced its effects, and more particularly of its objectives. The objective here was to ensure that the ultimate consumers of legal services and the sound administration of justice be provided with the necessary guarantees in relation to integrity and experience. Any consequential effects restrictive of competition were inherent in the pursuit of those objectives. Thus, the Court's conclusion was that the NBA regulation banning multi-disciplinary partnerships did not infringe Article 81(1) EC, since it could reasonably have been considered that that regulation, despite the effects restrictive of competition that are inherent in it, was necessary for the proper practice of the legal profession.[54]

Commentators of *Wouters* were quick in grasping the unconventional reasoning. While the Court had found that Article 81(1) EC was infringed, it chose to declare the prohibition inapplicable to this case, in view of the fact that the NBA regulation was justified by a specific public interest: ensuring the proper practice of the legal profession. The Court's line of reasoning seems difficult to follow, but if seen as an (unsuccessful) attempt of reconciliation of the two norms under a 'practical concordance' approach, it may become intelligible. The starting point on Article 81(1) EC can be seen as a reconciliation attempt, while when it is clear that a reconciliation is no longer possible, the Court retreats to a constitutional methodology, balancing the anti-competitive effects of the regulation at stake with the public interest. The resolution of this particular conflict results in giving precedence to the public

[52] Wouters, *ibid*, para 57 *et seq*.
[53] *Wouters*, *ibid*, paras 86–90.
[54] *Wouters*, *ibid*, paras 97–110.

interest. *Wouters*, in other words, is a typical conflict resolution case that bears many similarities with cases resolving conflicts of constitutional rights. It is true that the Court's reasoning leaves a certain 'malaise', to use the words of a commentator,[55] in bringing into competition law an approach based on free movement case law. However, since *Wouters* represents a pure conflict case as between the competition rules and non-competition objectives, it was inevitable for the Court to draw inspiration from the four freedoms line of cases, because that is an area where the Court has acquired extensive experience in dealing with the resolution of similar conflicts.

Wouters shows that pure conflicts between the Treaty competition rules and 'political' or 'public interest' or 'non-competition' concerns certainly cannot be avoided. The difficulty lies in shaping the methodology of resolving such conflicts. One possibility would be to invite these non-competition concerns into the competition law analysis, while another would be to adopt a more normative approach and deal with them as pure constitutional conflicts. Under the latter approach, which is by far more preferable, such concerns are not 'invited' into the substance of antitrust analysis. While it is neither arguable nor desirable that the principle of competition should always prevail over other genuine values, that does not mean that the purity of antitrust analysis should be sacrificed in favour of a hybrid system of competition law, where employment, the environment, public health and all different kinds of public interests are imported into Article 81(1) or 81(3) EC. That is why views as to the existence of a 'European rule of reason', though challenging, should nevertheless be rejected. The balancing between the competition rules and other values should take place neither in Article 81(1) nor in Article 81(3) EC. Rather, Article 81 EC *as a whole* may in appropriate circumstances be balanced against public interest concerns. In this sense, the non-economic norm, in *Wouters* the protection of the legal profession's independence, is not brought *into the substance of Article 81 EC* (in its first or in its third paragraph), thus blurring its purity, but is taken into account at a preceding stage, leading to an exception from the ambit of Article 81 EC as a whole, subject to a control of proportionality. Viewed in these terms, *Wouters* in reality is not an antitrust case and should find its place not in EC competition law textbooks but rather in EU constitutional ones.[56]

Following this approach would not mean that non-competition concerns would never be taken into account under Article 81 EC. According to the practical concordance method, they could be taken into account for as long

[55] Idot, above n 19, p 7.

[56] Contrast the analysis of *Wouters* by the President of the CFI, who expressed doubts as to whether that judgment would constantly be followed, particularly by the CFI (see Vesterdorf, 2002, above n 50, pp 128–29). From an institutional perspective it should come to as no surprise that the more 'orthodox' CFI, which has become the 'natural judge' in antitrust matters, may view with perplexity *Wouters* and the balancing that this judgment entails, as opposed to the ECJ, which is in essence a more 'constitutional' court with long-standing experience in the resolution of constitutional conflicts.

as the competition-economic balance remains positive. They could not, however, tilt a negative balance. This is exactly the approach that the Commission has followed in its decisions that we referred to above and, indeed, this is what Advocate General Léger had proposed in his Opinion. In paragraph 133 of his Opinion he admitted that '[a]ccording to the case-law, the wording of Article 85(3) [now 81(3)] makes it possible to take account of the particular nature of different branches of the economy, social concerns and, to a certain extent, considerations connected with the pursuit of the public interest'. But it is clear that he was ready to see such concerns only through their 'economic facet': 'Professional rules which, in the light of those criteria, *produce economic effects which are positive*, taken as a whole, should therefore be eligible for exemption under Article 85(3) [now 81(3)] of the Treaty'.[57] The fact that the Court opted to depart from this 'easy' solution and to adopt a more normative approach, notwithstanding the rather inelegant reasoning, is not a weakness, but a welcome novelty.

VI. Hierarchies

If any reconciliation between competition law and the conflicting norm cannot be attained, then we are in front of a situation of pure conflict. The resolution of a conflict of this kind inevitably poses the question of hierarchies. At this point, arises the question of the hierarchical status of the Community competition rules and their normative relationship with other Treaty objectives.

It has been argued persuasively that the four freedoms and the competition law provisions of the EC Treaty have enjoyed a certain primacy in the Court of Justice's case law and in the Commission's administrative practice.[58] Indeed, the Treaty competition provisions make up the 'economic constitution' of the European Union and their importance has been recognised by the Court of Justice on numerous occasions. Thus, with regard to Article 81 EC, the Court has stressed its primacy in the system of the Treaty, since it 'constitutes a fundamental provision which is essential for the accomplishment of the tasks entrusted to the Community and, in particular, for the functioning of the internal market'.[59]

On a number of occasions the Community Courts have indeed not shied

---

[57] Emphasis added.

[58] See, eg, E Grabitz, (1990) 'Über die Verfassung des Binnenmarktes' in J Baur, K Hopt and K Mailänder, (eds), *Festschrift für Ernst Steindorff zum 70. Geburtstag am 13 März 1990,* (Berlin, Verlag Walter de Gruyter, 1990) 1233 *et seq*; J Basedow, 'Zielkonflikte und Zielhierarchien im Vertrag über die Europäische Gemeinschaft' in O Due, M Lutter and J Schwarze, (eds), *Festschrift für Ulrich Everling*, vol I (Baden-Baden, Nomos, 1995) 54.

[59] Case C–453/99 *Courage Ltd v Bernard Crehan* [2001] ECR I–6297, para 20; Case C–126/97 *Eco Swiss China Time Ltd v Benetton International NV* [1999] ECR I–3055, para 36.

away from balancing the Treaty competition rules with other fundamental norms of Community or national provenience and usually they have granted precedence to the former. This is, in particular, the case when parties raise pleas against the competition enforcement relying upon the protection of commercial freedom or on the right to property. Advocate General Cosmas had no difficulty to summarily reject such pleas in the *Masterfoods* case that concerned the sale of ice cream and freezer exclusivity, stessing exactly the primacy of the Treaty competition rules over the right to property.[60] Similarly, the Court of Justice has rejected non-economic defences raised against the application of the competition rules on many occasions. Where the Court has seen that such arguments were unmeritorious or that simply they could not be reconciled with the core principles of EC competition law, it always came out in favour of the competition rules. To mention one example, freedom of expression and the protection of undertakings from unfair competition did not stand in the Court's way in condemning book price fixing in the *VBVB v VBBB* case. The Court held there that there was not a 'real link between the Commission's Decision and freedom of expression as guaranteed by the European Convention, even on the supposition that it might be possible to interpret it in such a way as to include guarantees regarding the possibility of publishing books in economically profitable conditions. To submit the production of and trade in books to rules whose sole purpose is to ensure freedom of trade between Member States in normal conditions of competition cannot be regarded as restricting freedom of publication which, it is not contested, remains entire at the level of both publishers and distributors'.[61]

The pre-eminence of the competition rules was tested in the context of the drafting of the new European Constitution. Initially, some had thought that such provisions had no place in a programmatic constitutional text, while others thought that the exclusion of the competition and of the free movement rules from that text might be construed as a shift away from those classical priorities of the Community and thus as a 'devaluation'. The final approach that was followed was deferential to the long-standing constitutional importance of competition law and, indeed, there are good reasons to

---

[60] Para 105 of AG's Opinion, Case C–344/98 *Masterfoods Ltd v HB Ice Cream Ltd* [2000] ECR I–11369:

'There is no doubt that Articles 85 and 86 [now 81 and 82] of the EC Treaty occupy an important position in the system of the Community legal order and serve the general interest which consists in ensuring undistorted competition. Consequently, it is perfectly comprehensible for restrictions to be placed on the right to property ownership pursuant to Articles 85 and 86 [now 81 and 82] of the EC Treaty, to the degree to which they might be necessary to protect competition. Article 222 [now 295] of the EC Treaty may in no event be used as a shield by economic operators to avoid application of Articles 85 and 86 [now 81 and 82] to their detriment.'

[61] Joined Cases 43/82 and 63/82 *Vereniging ter Bevordering van het Vlaamse Boekwezen, VBVB, and Vereniging ter Bevordering van de Belangen des Boekhandels, VBBB v Commission* [1984] ECR 19, para 34.

speak of an 'up-grading'. Thus, the new Treaty Establishing a Constitution for Europe lists competition law in the guiding principles and objectives of the Union. Article I–3(2) of the Constitution stresses that 'the Union shall offer its citizens an area of freedom, security and justice without internal frontiers, and an internal market *where competition is free and undistorted.*'[62] The listing of the principle of free competition among the paramount objectives of the Union, goes certainly further than the equivalent provision of Article 3(1)(g) of the EC Treaty. First of all, because competition law is now referred to in the primary provisions of a *constitution.* Its constitutional nature is now celebrated in the primary principles of a formal constitution.[63] Secondly, the new text constitutes progress because it refers to the principle of free competition in a positive manner ('where competition is free and undistorted'), rather than in a negative one, as is the case of the current EC Treaty ('a system ensuring that competition in the internal market is not distorted').[64] This objective constitutes a guiding principle for the interpretation of specific competition provisions and for ensuring consistency among the various policies and activities of the Union.[65] A further innovation of the Constitution of utmost significance is that competition policy has now been portrayed as the 'fifth freedom' of the chapter on the internal market.[66]

Yet it would be incorrect to adduce from the above a general rule of primacy or higher hierarchical status for the competition rules. This seems all the more so, after the Treaty of Maastricht removed from the EC Treaty the Title heading 'The Foundations of the Community', which covered all the provisions from the free movement of goods to competition law, and categorised the above as simply the Community's 'Policies'.[67] A similar categorisation is followed in the Constitution, where competition is listed as one of the Union's

---

62 Emphasis added.

63 On the principle of free competition as a constitutional principle in EU law see P-C Müller-Graff, 'L'économie de marché concurrentielle comme principe constitutionnel commun dans l'Union européenne' in *Études en l'honneur de Jean-Claude Gautron, Les dynamiques du droit européen en début de siècle* (Paris, Editions Pédone, 2004) 479 *et seq.*

64 This constitutionalisation of the competition rules has not been missed and is severely criticised by the proponents of a more 'social' Europe. See, eg, the article by Prof Antonis Manitakis under the title 'Fraudulent Constitutionalisation' in the Greek Sunday paper *To Vima*, 27 March 2005, p A39.

65 See Commissioner Mario Monti delivering his last official speech: 'A Reformed Competition Policy: Achievements and Challenges for the Future', Center for European Reform, Brussels, 28 October 2004, available at http://europa.eu.int/comm/competition/speeches.

66 *Ibid.*

67 See Basedow, above n 58, p 55. This point is also stressed by former Judge Edward, who interprets many recent cases such as *Albany* and *PreussenElektra* (Cases C–67/96, C–115/97 to C–117/97 and C–219/97, *Albany International BV v Stichting Bedrijfspensioenfonds Textielindustrie* [1999] ECR I–5751; Case C–379/98 *PreussenElektra AG v Schleswag AG* [2001] ECR I–2099) in light of these Treaty amendments. See D Edward, 'Recent Case Law of the European Court of Justice' in J Schwarze, (ed), *Europäisches Wettbewerbsrecht im Wandel* (Baden-Baden, Nomos, 2001) 51; *idem*, 'Competition and National Rule-making' in A von Bogdandy, P Mavroidis and Y Mény, (eds), *European Integration and International Co-ordination, Studies in Transnational Economic Law in Honour of Claus-Dieter Ehlermann* (The Hague, Kluwer, 2002) 136.

'Internal Policies'.

It is, therefore, not difficult to admit that the resolution of conflicts will not always lead to competition law's primacy. As in *Wouters*, in *Albany* and in a related string of cases involving social security funds, the Court did not find it difficult to resolve a similar conflict to the detriment of the Treaty competition rules. In *Albany*, it held that collective agreement between employers and employees to set up a supplementary 'second pillar' sectoral pension fund did not 'by virtue of their nature and purpose' fall under Article 81 EC.[68] In doing so, the Court balanced the competition rules against the social policy provisions of the Treaty. It placed particular emphasis on the fact that under Article 3(1) EC the activities of the Community include not only 'a system ensuring that competition in the internal market is not distorted' but also 'a policy in the social sphere'. Similarly, Article 2 EC provides that a particular task of the Community is 'to promote throughout the Community a harmonious and balanced development of economic activities' and 'a high level of employment and of social protection'. It seemed, therefore, that from an interpretation of the provisions of the Treaty as a whole which is both effective and consistent that agreements concluded in the context of collective negotiations between management and labour in pursuit of such objectives must, by virtue of their nature and purpose, be regarded as falling outside the scope of Article 85(1) [now 81(1)] of the Treaty.[69]

Irrespective of which norm prevails as a result of the balancing, our conclusion is that competition law has nothing to fear from the resolution of conflicts with other objectives of a non-economic nature, if predictable normative criteria are followed. What would be dangerous for competition law, however, would be to import into its substantive analysis extraneous theories and concerns and thus to jeopardise the purity of antitrust analysis.

VII. Epilogue: Decentralising *Wouters*

The foregoing interpretation of Article 81 EC may indeed be more appropriate under the new decentralised system of enforcement, which opens up that provision to the purview of national courts that according to some commentators are not suitable fora for the balancing of non-competition objectives.[70]

---

[68] *Albany, ibid,* para 60.

[69] *Albany, ibid,* para 54. The Court has followed the same approach in other cases affecting social policy. See, eg, Joined Cases C–115/97 to C–117/97 *Brentjens' Handelsonderneming BV v Stichting Bedrijfspensioenfonds voor de Handel in Bouwmaterialen* [1999] ECR I–6025; Case C–219/97 *Maatschappij Drijvende Bokken BV v Stichting Pensioenfonds voor de Vervoer- en Havenbedrijven* [1999] ECR I–6121; Joined Cases C–180/98 to C–184/98 *Pavel Pavlov v Stichting Pensioenfonds Medische Specialisten* [2000] ECR I–6451; Case C–222/98 *Hendrik van der Woude v Stichting Beatrixoord* [2000] ECR I–7111.

That may also explain the Commission's absolute denial in the White Paper of the possibility of any non-competition concerns being taken into account.[71] This will not mean that national courts will never touch upon non-competition concerns.[72] Nevertheless, this will be a balancing act that will be undertaken not in the context of the first or the third paragraph of Article 81 EC, but at a different level, as between the whole of Article 81 EC and the conflicting non-competition norm, always subject to the principle of proportionality.

A more specific question that arises at this point, is whether the conflicting norm itself can be applied horizontally as between individuals by a national court (horizontal direct effect). The Treaty provisions that refer to such (non-competition) policies are only addressed to the Commission and to the Community at large, therefore lacking direct effect and, in any case, they cannot be applied as between individuals horizontally. Individuals are not intended by the Treaty to be the direct enforcers or formulators of the Community environmental or employment policies. What, however, national courts will essentially do, is to take these concerns into account as *inherent limitations* to the competition rules, in the same way as a constitutional right is given effect by a court subject to inherent limitations. This methodology is very similar to the mandatory requirements limitations that have been recognised at the four freedoms area. It is only in this context that the question of justiciability must be understood. In other words, national courts will not turn themselves into the enforcers of these policies as such, but rather they will abstain from applying the competition rules—which, on their part, *are* horizontally directly effective—in a particular case.

Before concluding, a related final objection that needs to be addressed, is whether the inherent limitations to the competition rules can be relied upon by private parties. A negative answer to this would contradict the Court of Justice's existing case law. Since *Wouters* has been considered by most commentators as following a four freedoms approach and as importing into the competition field the theory of mandatory requirements, it is useful to refer to the *Bosman* case, where a similar argument had been made, according to which Member States alone were able to rely on limitations to the free movement of people principle. The Court, however, rejected this argument by stressing that 'there is nothing to preclude individuals from relying on justifications on grounds of public policy, public security or public health. Neither the scope nor the content of those grounds of justification is in any way affected by the public or private nature of the rules in question'.[73] It is

[70] See Whish and Sufrin, above n 8, p 150; Immenga, above n 25, p 357.

[71] Para 57 of the White Paper. As mentioned above, this approach is also followed by the Commission in its Art 81(3) EC Notice, which avoids any reference to a *Wouters* kind of 'exception'.

[72] See D Edward, Intervention in Panel Two Discussion: Coherence in Ehlermann and Atanasiu, 2001, above, p 296.

assumed that the same would also be true for mandatory requirements, which are not expressly mentioned by the Treaty, but which have been considered by the Court of Justice as inherent to the Treaty.

[73] Case C–415/93 *Union Royale Belge des Sociétés de Football Association ASBL v Jean-Marc Bosman, Royal Club Liégeois SA v Jean-Marc Bosman, and Union des Associations Européennes de Football (UEFA) v Jean-Marc Bosman* [1995] ECR I–4921, para 86. See also J Baquero Cruz, above n 51, p 111.

PANEL THREE

INSTITUTIONAL/POLITICAL ISSUES

1

PANEL DISCUSSION

PARTICIPANTS:

Allan Fels
Amelia Fletcher
Assimakis Komninos
Calvin Goldman
Claus-Dieter Ehlermann
David Clementi
Frédéric Jenny
Giuliano Amato
Harry First
Ian Forrester
John Cooke
John Fingleton
Lowri Evans
Mario Siragusa
Mark Schechter
Pamela Brumter
Santiago Martínez Lage
William Kovacic

Panel Three: Institutional/Political Issues

▶ GIULIANO AMATO

I would open the debate with a few remarks concerning the enforcement experience of the Italian antitrust authority the area of professional regulation. Italian professional bodies—with the help of lawyers—have spent years insisting, one case after another, that essentially the professions have nothing to do with undertakings and therefore antitrust law does not apply. To secure this end, the professional bodies practiced a sort of slalom, taking substantive decisions and then giving them official stance by having them approved or modified by some ministry. This made us (the Italian antitrust authority) waste roughly 10 years of our time—I am being very frank and brutal, and poisoned the relations between antitrust and the professions, while, after all, it would certainly make sense for all of us to sit and discuss whether these rules really make sense. Which interests do these rules protect? Having all accepted that the professions do need some sort of regulations, why not discuss what is needed and what might be outdated, etc?

It happened that Italy gave to the ECJ the opportunity to pronounce an unexpected decision in this area. In *Fiammiferi*,[1] a case concerning a sort of 18th century remainder of regulation invoked by Italian match producers, the Court established that professional regulation, be it issued by professional bodies or state authorities, did not legitimize undertakings to engage in cartel-like activities. For me personally this decision was a great satisfaction. I remember that in one of the first cases we handled when I started to chair the Italian antitrust authority consisted of disapplying Italian regulation that was not compatible with an EC directive (the case involved mobile phone companies). This approach was at that time quite unusual, somehow crossing the borders of what national competition authorities were expected to do. Thus, in a sense, *Fiammiferi* is somehow confirming our initiative back then. After *Fiammiferi*, the time has become ripe for the national competition authorities to review local professional regulation on the merits. But there are, of course, issues to be further considered, such as determining the right division of roles between the European and national authorities and keeping an adequate balance between antitrust enforcement and advocacy—or how antitrust authorities can help moulding new regulation.

▶ DAVID CLEMENTI

Shortly before the Workshop I circulated among the participants a consultation paper—published a few months ago—prepared in the context of the review that I am charged to carry out on the regulation of legal services in

[1] Case C–198/01 *Consorzio Industrie Fiammiferi (CIF) v Autoritá Garante della Concorrenza e del Mercato* [2003] ECR I–8055.

England and Wales. In my oral intervention I would like to summarise the main findings of this consultation paper. (The Final Report will be published towards the end of the year).[2]

Someone asked me before we started the Workshop how I got this job. Well, when I was summoned by our Secretary of State, I asked the same question. He replied: 'You are not a lawyer.' Since that selection criterion only excluded about 2% of our population, I thought the answer was insufficient. But eventually this turned out to be quite an exciting part of my career, and if the criteria for getting the job is knowing nothing about it, well, I discovered that there are quite a lot of things I knew nothing about. . . . As you would expect, I am picking up a completely new language in the process: I am now familiar with the term 'MDPs', I wrestled with asymmetry concepts, etc. (Sometime early in the review process I inquired about the difference between irregularity and asymmetry. I would like to share with you the answer that I got: irregularity is something uneven or non-uniform in shape or form, and *asymmetry* is . . . the place where you bury those who have died . . . ['*a cemetery*', editor's note.])

The consultation paper contains six chapters. I would like to speak in particular of two, which are relevant to our debate. One is about alternative business structures, and the other is about how to regulate them.

But before, it is worth going briefly into the characteristics of the UK legal system. First of all, we tend to talk about lawyers as a uniform single group, but certainly within the UK, and I dare say, in other jurisdictions, that is not the case. We have a large number of different types of lawyers. We have barristers, solicitors, trademark attorneys, patent agents, licensed conveyancers, immigration officials, legal executives, and, I am delighted to tell our Spanish colleagues, we also have notaries—although it is not clear to me what they exactly do in the UK context, maybe they spend most of their time notarizing documents for English people buying properties in Spain. . . .

Second, we identified that these different types of legal professions practice various restrictive practices. For example: only solicitors may be partners of solicitors' firms; only solicitors may be owners of solicitors' firms; solicitors may be employed by corporations, but give advice only to their employer, and not to third parties; barristers cannot even form partnerships with other barristers, let alone partnerships with solicitors; an US lawyer be a partner of a UK solicitors' firm, but a UK barrister may not.

In sum, one does not need to go too far with the investigation in order to find anomalies in the English legal system, and one chapter of the report is about finding ways to eliminate these restrictions. While working on this report I discovered a vast literature on multi-disciplinary practices, and very little written on what I call 'legal disciplinary practices' (LDPs). LDPs are

---

[2] The Final Report (available at *http://www.legal-services-review.org.uk/content/report/index.htm*) was published on 15 December 2005.

liberalized legal firms where lawyers and other professionals work together to provide solely legal services. In the UK, LDPs perform, for example, *pro bono* services—solicitors and barristers work together in economic units owned not by the lawyers, but generally by charities or local authorities. The question is, why is this not allowed for commercial legal services? MDPs, on the other hand, are firms where lawyers and other professionals—most notably accountants—could work together to provide legal and other professional services. One of the comments you will find in the report on the distinction between LDPs and MDPs is that 'LDPs are walking, and MDPs are running'. For the purposes of the report, I realised there was no point in discussing how to allow lawyers to work together with accountants until having worked out how to allow different kinds of lawyers to work together.

The report takes into account the differences between LDPs and MDPs, as well as whether those who manage the firm have to be the same as those who own it. In most firms there is a clear distinction between those who manage and those who own. Most regulatory systems actually go to the heart of how a firm is managed: in the area of financial services, for example, a good deal of the relevant regulation concentrates on how firms are managed, and not on who owns them. Are there any reasons why ownership should be regulated in the case of law firms? Why is it that different kinds of lawyers should not be allowed to work together? Why cannot a barrister work together with a solicitor? As I already mentioned, the main distinction between LDPs and MDPs is that, in the case of the latter, other professionals contribute to enhance the legal practice, and not to provide other professional services. But why cannot the finance director of a major international law firm be a partner?

The report also considers ownership issues, because, I think, it is important not to go to either extreme. I see no reason why certain third parties should not be allowed to own a law firm. For instance, the RAC, which is a major motoring organization within the UK, does have a sort of legal practice, because it provides legal advice to its members on motoring matters. This organization has two or three million members, and it would like to provide more general legal advice, but currently this is not permitted. Well, why not? The RAC certainly has a reputation for client service well ahead of any of the Hyde Street law firms. On the other hand, it is plain clear that we should not go to the other extreme and conclude that anybody could be the owner of a law firm. The question of who is fit to own is legitimate. Yet, how could we define the 'fitness' criteria?

Turning to MDPs, I should say that I am quite cautious. I already said that, I think, LDPs are a question of walking and MDPs are a question of running, therefore more difficult to achieve. I took note of the discussion we had yesterday afternoon, around the *Wouters* case,[3] and that there are some quite difficult ethical issues at stake when lawyers work together with accountants.

[3] Case C–309/99 *Wouters* [2002] ECR I–1577.

Each have different ethical arrangements, but they nevertheless have very similar responsibilities—including a very strong responsibility towards their clients. I think it will be hard to get to grips with MDPs until we have determined who the single regulator should be for the legal services. If we want MDPs to be regulated, we would want whoever is regulating the accounting area to consult with whoever is regulating the legal area. Since in the UK we do not have any single regulatory system—actually, we have a hodgepodge, to which I shall return in a moment—it is very difficult to see how any sort of agreement could be reached between different regulators. So, the thrust of my review is about LDPs, but I hope to do it in such a way so as not to preclude MDPs, if later on the regulator found a way to deal with them.

Turning to regulatory models, I would start with a bit of background. In the UK the regulatory system has grown over several hundred years, and its current state is often described as a maze. There is a tendency among UK lawyers to describe themselves as self-regulated, but I think that, in terms of our discussion this afternoon, the system is actually more co-regulation. There are oversight bodies—for example, in the case of barristers, rule changes are reviewed by the Department of Constitutional Affairs; trademark attorneys also have an oversight regulator, the Department of Trade and Industry; the Immigration Office is overseen by the Home Office, and the notaries are overseen by . . . the Archbishop of Canterbury! As you can see, the oversight regulators are different, have different rules, and most of them have opaque objectives. And indeed, if you look at the first chapter my report, it looks at the objectives of a regulatory system—issues such as access to justice, consumer protection, how to promote public information, how to deal at grass-root level with information asymmetries (that can be encountered even in the most straightforward type of legal transactions, such as conveyancing).

The report examines three main models of regulation. The first one consists of transferring all regulatory functions from the professional bodies to a single public regulator. It builds on the examples of the Financial Services Authority (FSA), established for the financial services in the UK. The advantage of a single regulator are: very clear objectives, one single body responsible for promoting competition, very clear lines of accountability.

At the other extreme is the second model, which is, more or less, professional regulation subject to a consistent oversight. There are advantages to this system, particularly if one gives credence to the strong roots of professional self-regulation which exist in the UK. Indeed, the UK accountancy profession was recently restructured along these lines. Nowadays we have six accountancy professional bodies, subject to the review of one single regulator, the FRC.

The third model is a variation of the second, under which there is a clear separation within the professional body between those who are responsible for regulation and representation. Actually there is quite a big debate in the

UK on this issue, and we lightly touched upon it yesterday. It is clear that the regulator must put the public interest first. In representation matters, it is perfectly legitimate to put the interests of the professional body' members first. The issue evolves around whether it is possible to combine the two. My answer is, of course it is possible, but the question is whether it is also optimal, since lawyers are very good at explaining why things which on the surface look as if they are in their own interest are indeed also public interest. There are clearly conflicts of interests here, and the issue is whether those conflicts are better dealt with inside one body, or separately.

I will conclude by saying that reform is eventually a question of political commitment. The report will put forward some suggestions of change in the regulatory model, but I am interested to see if there is a string commitment at the political level to put them into practice. It is always easy to summon another report—this is usually known as the 'long grass technique', that is, kick the ball into the long grass—instead of taking actual decisions. I am interested to see how the UK government will deal with my review, and whether there is a strong political commitment to pursue reforms.

► LOWRI EVANS

To follow up on Sir David Clementi's intervention, political commitment is exactly where the Commission got started from—effectively, by querying the Member States on their political commitment to implement the Lisbon agenda. What I wanted to talk about in this intervention is how the Commission sees the division of tasks between the European and the national level. I think that by now it should be fairly clear to everybody that the Commission is asking the Member States to do the real work. Of course, the Commission itself will seek to facilitate this work as much as possible. In February 2004 we published the report on the liberal professions, which calls on all those concerned to identify and review the regulatory restrictions existing in the area of the professions. Most of these restrictions are set up in state legislation. And it is precisely the type of review that Sir David Clementi is now undertaking on behalf of the UK government that the Commission would like to see performed on a more general level in all Member States.

The Commission has also made it clear that this exercise is not about deregulation for its own sake. I want to underline this as we recognize that a simple elimination of the existing restrictions may not introduce more competition. The reforms will have to be accompanied by what we describe as 'accompanying pro-competitive measures'. This is very important, because this is not a deregulation, but a re-regulation agenda. The other point I wanted to highlight is the political and institutional impact of the recent modernization of EC antitrust. My impression is that this impact will be even deeper than foreseen when the modernization regulation (Regulation 1 2003) was debated.

What have we been doing since the publication of the report in February 2004? Now the ball has passed to the Member States, so to speak, but we are also continuing to do some work in this area, by organising debates with the professional bodies at the European level—while we expect the Member States to discuss with the professional bodies at a national level. The focus of our dialogue with the professions is on the justification for restrictions existing in their sectors. We want to better understand their perspective. This is a free and frank exchange of views. Whenever we are not entirely convinced—and you can see more details in this respect in the report—that specific restrictive rules have a legitimate purpose, we ask for a written explanation. Second, we ask the representatives of the various professions at the European level to relay the Commission's concerns to national members. By the way, most European-level professional bodies have a European-level code of conduct. We reviewed these codes together with our colleagues from the national competition authorities. It could be said that the codes of conduct adopted at European level contain only those deontological rules on whose necessity there is consensus at the European level. So, perhaps this could be one way to look at the *Wouters* test—these are the rules generally retained as strictly necessary for the proper practice of the profession, or some sort of 'minimum standards' of what these rules should be. I think it will be interesting to compare the European-level codes of conduct with those that exist in the individual Member States.

Another part of the Commission's consultation activity relates to consumers. This is a novelty for us, because we have never discussed with consumer organizations before. It is a very interesting exercise, and I think it also makes us adopt a more prudent approach in our proposals. So far, we have realised four main things. One is that consumers do not really care whether the professionals are regulated or not. They only care about the services. They argue that simply going to a certified professional does not guarantee the quality of his–her services. Second, the consumers confirm, that there is a problem of asymmetry of information in the area of professional services. Basically, they find it is very difficult to choose among professionals. There is not enough information available to be able to make an informed choice, and advertising is only one aspect that makes such choices difficult. The third problem is that consumers find it very difficult to resolve conflicts. This is the *ex post* control aspect that we discussed about yesterday. It is very difficult for consumers to identify negligence or mistakes, or to gather proof of negligence or mistakes. Such proof often requires cooperation of other professionals, which is very difficult to get. Fourth, there is the problem of costs: consumers want *ex ante* information about costs, and currently there are few provisions regarding how to supply it better.

Since the publication of the draft report, we are extending the empirical research into the ten new Member States, which joined the EU in March 2004. Another element to consider is the coming into force of the modernization regulation (Regulation 1/2003). Now all national competition authorities are empowered to apply EC antitrust rules in their entirety, and we have also formally set up the European competition network. This reform fundamentally changed the relationship between the Commission, the national competition authorities and the Member States. There is a tangible team spirit within the European competition network, currently we are working on improving our IT systems to facilitate the exchange of information. As you all know, Regulation 1/2003 establishes mechanisms for the sharing of information between the members of the network, and I need not go into detail on this here. I just wanted to emphasize that the reform has deepened the cooperative relationship between the Commission and the national competition authorities, by putting into place clear mechanisms to identify who should do what. Now we are discussing very actively both policy and enforcement issues, and the debate takes place at case-handling level, and not just at the level of representatives, as it used to be before. I think that (ironically) we have finally achieved within Europe the same level of cooperation that we already had established between the Commission and the US antitrust agencies.

What are the implications for competition law enforcement in the area of professional services? For example, since 2002 we have been discussing with the national competition authorities, both at the political and the technical level, how to interpret and apply Article 81(1) and (3) EC in the context of the liberal professions. In this respect, the report published in February 2004 reflects the position of the national competition authorities on this subject. In terms of actual enforcement, the Commission would like to think that the national competition authorities will be doing most of the work in the future, especially since in the area of professional services the centre of gravity for enforcement is most of the time within one single Member State. Historically speaking, many of the national competition authorities already have a good enforcement record in this area, in several cases even a longer enforcement record than the one of the Commission. France, for example, has been much more active in this area than the Commission in the past, and it is quite likely that it will continue to be so in the future. The Commission will deal with such cases only when its intervention is necessary, makes sense, and if everybody agrees.

Some general points on the discussion we had so far. To pick up from what Sir David Clementi said, change in this area will be complicated, it should be approached with enormous caution and be done at the appropriate level, which is the Member State level. The Commission's contribution will be to also bring to the discussion table the impact of past deregulation, which has been mostly successful, but not always. One example is the deregulation of notary services in the Netherlands, which is not a complete success. There are tradeoffs, since one-off customers are paying more, while repeat customers usually get discounts. This means that perhaps the distributional effects of deregulation were not taken into account. So we need to study past deregulation examples and share the conclusions with people like Sir David Clementi, who are undertaking reviews at the moment.

To conclude, there are still many open issues, and the Commission does not necessarily have a suggestion as to what should be done about each. Our role is to bring these open issues on the discussion table, and to share this information with the Member States.

► PAMELA BRUMTER

Moving away from EC competition law, my intervention should bring you to the Commission's activity in implementing the EC Treaty rules on freedom to provide services and freedom of establishment. And indeed, yesterday we discussed *Wouters*,[4] a case where the Court examined the restrictions on multi-disciplinary practices also under the Treaty provisions on freedom to provide services and freedom of establishment. The Court established that, even if those measures were implemented by a professional order, they would nevertheless fall under the scope of the Treaty provisions on freedom to provide services and freedom of establishment, and examined the compatibility of the restrictions in question with these provisions.

This judgment brings nothing new, however, because it is in line with a long line of jurisprudence examining barriers to the free provision of services and to establishment. Indeed, the Commission has long been active in implementing these rules the field of liberal professions, addressing issues like professional qualifications and entry of professionals who would like to provide services or establish themselves in another Member State than the one of origin. Since the 1970s, we have been working on harmonizing professional qualifications, especially in the medical sector and for architecture. We could not pursue a very detailed harmonization in these areas, which are among the most regulated in Europe. We realised that we could not harmonize the minimum level of training required for all the hundreds of professions existent in Europe, so that in the 1980s we started to put in place a so-called 'general scheme for merchant recognition'. This system basically allows a professional to move to another Member State on the basis of the qualification acquired in the state of origin. According to this system, if the qualifications acquired in the country of origin are retained substantially different from those required within the host Member State's jurisdiction, the latter may apply compensatory measures like supplementary training or tests of aptitude. We are now in the course of modernizing this legislation, but I do not want to go much in detail on this, because this is not something new or unknown. Instead I would like to talk about a recent Commission initiative, dating from the beginning of 2004—and which also has to be seen in the context of the Lisbon

[4] See above n 3.

agenda—which consists of propose a framework directive to eliminate the main barriers to the free provision of services in the EU.[5]

The proposed directive has a wide scope of application: it does not concern only the regulated professions, but generally, all kinds of services provided by companies. However, certain provisions in this proposal address specifically the restrictions existent in the area of liberal professions. First, the directive addresses the so-called barriers to entry in a two-fold approach. On the one hand, the Member States to remove prohibitive requirements—such as nationality, residence authorizations, the prohibition to be enrolled in the professional orders of more than one jurisdiction. This kinds of measures are clearly identified as prohibitive requirements. The Member States are called to review their professional order codes in order to remove any such restrictive requirements over the transposition period. On the other hand, Article 15 of the draft regulation looks into other kinds of restrictions, which might be justified under the test resulting from the ECJ jurisprudence (general interest objective and proportionality of the measure). Article 15 of the draft regulation requires that the Member States review national legislation and regulation adopted by their professional orders under this test, and thereafter come up with reports proposing remedies. The directive proposes a 'mutual evaluation system', whereby these reports will be made available for consultation to the other Member States and to consumer organizations. On the basis of these reports and the comments received, the Commission will draft a synthesis report, proposing further action and perhaps even harmonized measures for certain sectors. This exercise implies a sort of benchmarking of the national systems, because it also enables us to compare best practices. It will also help us decide on how to define public interest, because we will be able to see how different Member States define this concept.

The proposal also contains prohibitions of specific restrictive measures, such as restrictions on multi-disciplinary practices and on commercial communication, namely advertising. Therefore, the proposal is a mixture of harmonization and prohibition measures. At the same time, the Member States are called to ensure that advertising will preserve, on the one hand, the integrity and dignity of professionals, and on the other, consumer interests. In so far as multi-disciplinary partnerships are concerned, we basically transpose *Wouters* into EC legislation. The proposed directive also encourages the Member States and professional orders to develop codes of conduct at the European level—we see such codes as a very useful instrument for diminishing the existent differences between the Member States and reducing barriers to entry. This proposal resembles a bit to what we have done in the 1980s in the field of the free circulation of goods, by using a standardization process,

[5] European Commission: Proposal for a Directive of the European Parliament and of the Council on services in the internal market, COM (2004) 2 final/3, of 5 March 2004.

which is also a voluntary instrument. We use harmonized standards in order to determine, but not to impose, harmonization, leaving room for the initiative to come from the professional orders themselves. This is harmonization by soft law, *via* voluntary instruments, of the existing standards at national level.

I will conclude by saying that the proposal also requires the Member States to ensure that the professionals inform better the consumers about the kind of services provides, but also on insurances, contractual clauses etc. The adoption of the proposed regulation will be of course a lengthy process: the scope of the proposal is enormous, so we have quite a few issues to debate, we are receiving many reactions, not only from the professionals, but also from other sectors. The prospects are that this directive will enter into force sometime in 2008.

► Giuliano Amato

Are you working together with DG Competition on this?

► Pamela Brumter

Yes, we are actually working together on this.

► Allen Fels

As you may have noticed, I started my written contribution for this Workshop with a quote from George Bernard Shaw that is highly relevant to our subject. I do not intend to go now through all the issues discussed in the written contribution, but rather concentrate on the Australian experience in this area. As some of you may know, Australia had no competition law until 1974, and until 1995, competition law was very seldom applied to the professions. At the beginning of the 1990s, the Australian competition authority produced some reports on the accountancy sector (which received a fairly clean 'bill of health' in terms of competition), on architects (again, a fairly clean bill of health), and two very large reports on the legal profession. The latter concluded that the legal profession was over-regulated and in urgent need of comprehensive reform. The legal profession was highly regulated when compared to other sectors of the economy, it was imposing substantial restrictions on the commercial conduct of lawyers and on the extent to which they were free to compete with each other, and there were adverse effects on the costs and efficiency of legal services, with a broader impact on business and consumers. We also reviewed the arguments in favour of these restrictions: was there some public benefit justification? We found that many of these regulations could not be justified on public interest grounds, and that, to the extent that there were public interest objectives to pursue in this area, they should be pursued through ethical and professional rules and disciplinary arrangements, rather than by imposing restrictions on the normal commercial and market behaviour of lawyers. My written contribution contains a short summary of the main recommendations coming out of one of these reports. These recommendations included, for example, that: competition law should apply in full in this area; statutes restricting competition should, in most cases, be repealed; there should be automatic recognition of accredited lawyers between the various states of Australia; where work was exclusively reserved for the legal profession, this should be opened up to non-lawyers to the maximum extent justified; an independent assessment system should be introduced to determine whether it was justified to restrict certain types of work to lawyers only; appropriate consumer safeguards should be introduced for services by non-lawyers; the artificial distinction between barristers and solicitors should be removed; restrictions on the ownership and organization of legal practices should be removed; and finally, that after putting into practice all previous recommendations, fee scales should also be eliminated, because they produced a cartel-like effect.

This report was fairly influential, and many, although not all, of its recommendations were eventually implemented. The Australian competition authority did not produce a similar report for the medical profession, for several reasons: we thought that simply applying competition rules to the profession was the best way of making progress with liberalization. In the 1990s the Australian competition law system was deeply reformed, and this also affected the professions—one of the amendments established that competition rules were applicable to the professions. The second relevant change was that any law, applicable to the professions or anyone else, that restricted competition, should be reviewed publicly, transparently, and independently, so as to see if the restrictions on competition were justified, and if the objectives pursued could be attained in a way less harmful for competition. Also, the amendment gave impetus to demands for swifter recognition of professional qualifications between Australia and the New Zealand.

Part of my written contribution deals with specific enforcement issues. Once the Competition Act became applicable to the professions, the Australian competition authority launched an educational exercise, organising dissemination seminars, and so on. We soon started to receive complaints about doctors engaging in collective boycotts, refusing to work in country hospitals unless receiving a pay raise, etc. We first issued a few stern warnings, and then we opened the first case against the anaesthetists. The Australian competition authority did not object in principle, but we discovered that they concluded an unlawful agreement whereby certain targeted hospitals were warned that no anaesthetist would be available without this 'on-call fee'. Fortunately, this agreement was recorded, so we took them to court. The anaesthetists regarded their profession as being above the law, and this was good news from our point of view, as it gave us an excellent opportunity to go to court. (To be frank, it was also an institutional policy choice—we decided to take the doctors to court, and not the lawyers.) The court upheld the validity of our case.

A step further was taken with the next case, involving price-fixing by the Australian Medical Association. The Medical Association, its president and executive director were all fined, and this sent out a strong warning. Another interesting case concerned gynaecologists in a little country town. They had a 'roster' agreement according to which, if any of them were absent and one of their patients needed urgent treatment, the others would look after that patient. So far, no problem with that, but the patients of one doctor who had joined in this agreement started to join a new private health insurance scheme. The other doctors became uneasy about what they perceived as an additional control of their services from the insurance company. So they decided that the patients of that doctor would be excluded from treatment under the agreement. The doctor in question had no other choice but to drop out of the roster scheme, and he wrote a letter to his patients informing them that they were excluded from the private health insurance scheme and therefore would have to pay for the services received from other doctors in his absence. We took the case to court, which imposed penalties and decided that the patients who had already paid, being excluded from the scheme, would have to be refunded. The Australian Medical Association argued that this decision would lead to a shortage doctors in this country town. The Australian government decided to inquire of whether competition law should cover doctors, and the answer to this question was eventually positive. Australian competition law makes possible for certain types of anticompetitive conduct and/or agreements to be authorized by exception from the general rules, subject to prior notification for approval by the Australian competition authority, if a substantial overriding public benefit can be demonstrated. Negative decisions of the Australian competition authority in this area can be appealed before a tribunal headed by a judge from the Federal Court.

In my written contribution I mention several other important cases in this area, but perhaps the most interesting and important is one involving restrictions on entry into the field of surgery that were imposed by the surgeons' college through their examination system, training system, and so on. To cut a long story short, we concluded that these restrictions (at least in the particular case of orthopaedic surgeons) were not aimed exclusively at preserving quality of the service, but also at keeping the number of practitioners reduced so as to be able to receive high fees. In this case we also had to deal with the question of whether the Royal Australian College of Surgeons qualified as an undertaking. Since the surgeons knew very well what had happened to the orthopaedics and the aestheticians before, the Royal Australian College of Surgeons notified these restrictive rules for approval by way of exception under the Competition Act. This started a very long investigation, which ended up with a lot of improvements being brought to the existing regulation.

For example, although the competition authority initially suggested that the issue of controlling access to the surgery profession should be left to an external, public body, it was eventually left to the college of the surgeons, but the procedures were made more transparent, and rights of appeal were introduced. I should perhaps mention that 5 years before this investigation there was another attempt to look into these restrictive practices by the Australian competition authority, and back then the government had set up a planning committee which projected the numbers of surgeons and specialists needed. 5 years later, the competition authority also looked into how these entry numbers were be determined, and found the system totally inappropriate—the number of surgeons was determined only in proportion to the population, while there are many other factors to consider. I should emphasize, however, that the largest part of restrictions on entry usually do not come from the professions, but from the governments, which believe that supply creates demand and have a strong interest in restricting entry.

I also wanted to comment briefly on the following aspect: in Australia, if a state law enables anticompetitive behaviour by a profession, such law has to explicitly stipulate that it over-rides the competition law, and its justifications have to be reviewed every two years by an independent body—this is, basically, because we did not want to leave these questions to the courts, which are reluctant to pronounce themselves on public interest objectives invoked in state legislation. This is why I found the discussion we had yesterday very interesting: in the morning we heard about what policy ought to be like, and in the afternoon we heard that the courts are rather reluctant to accept this approach. There seems to be a mismatch here. In Australia, the national government has been pushing the states to adopt liberalization policies, and it has provided strong incentives for doing so. A huge battle for control of the agenda has taken place. The competition authority tried to place the setting of policy into the hands of the central government and the parliament, while others tried to put the matter into the hands of the attorney generals. In Australia, if self-regulation restricts competition and that is not authorized by law, then it would to be authorized under the Trade Practices Act. There have been hundreds of cases so far on the role of the Australian competition authority, looking into the justification and proportionality of self-regulation. This long enforcement record gives a very mixed picture: sometimes self-regulation is done quite well, other times it is appalling. On the whole, I would agree with the suggestion made by Amelia Fletcher yesterday: perhaps the coexistence of co-regulation and self regulation is the best solution. The presence of a big stick in the background tends to make self-regulation work better. . . . Finally, I wanted to mention that the Australian competition authority also handles consumer protection issues, and we had quite a few of those in the area of the professions. In the medical area, we pressed for full informed consent in relation to medical treatments, so that patients get to know the price and risks in advance.

► William Kovacic

I intend to talk about what I think competition agencies have to do if they are to be effective in the area of the professions. My main emphasis is on institutional arrangements, and in particular, doctrine or concepts that affect the quality of their interventions and enforcement activities in the field of the professions.

One way to get started is to deal with the relevant terminology. Typically, in the US, if you ask lawyers at, say, a big antitrust conference, what they do, the US lawyers will answer: 'I am an antitrust lawyer', whereas the Europeans will answer: 'I practice competition law.' I think this makes a difference. In the US, the notion of antitrust has a 'case-centric' quality to it: it focuses on litigation, in particular on 'the big cases'. US antitrust lawyers and academics are very much like small children, they seem to be fascinated by loud explosions and vivid primary colours. They tend not to pay attention to smaller matters. The problem is that this de-emphasizes non-litigation functions. Indeed, a very popular account of US competition policy over the past four decades is what I call 'the pendulum story': antitrust is crazed in the form of intervention in the 1960s and 1970s, crazed in the form of non-intervention in the 1980s, and gets it just right from the 1990s. It is like the children's fable *Goldie Locks*: too hot, too cold, just right. The essence of the story from the 1960s through the 1980s is basically one of deranged individual enforcement officials. The images in the antitrust literature of the time depict public enforcement officials as being virtually irrational. One of Robert Pitofsky's characterizations of this period is that antitrust enforcement policy careened from one extreme to another. I associate careening with drunk driving, and this is the image of the system.

What I will depict today is a different picture, one that emphasizes major elements of continuity and institutional design, one that, indeed, promotes continuity. I find that the US record in this field has been one of continuous, progressive development, with early roots in the 1960s, and a continuing maturation and sustained effort up to the present. I will talk about the key elements of this policy development, and about the fact that investments in institutional capability are absolutely crucial to making good competition policy in this area.

I would start from the more general problem that we have been discussing for the most part of the Workshop, and which is what I would call 'the exceptionalist tradition'. I would assert that, in 115 years of US antitrust enforcement, rarely has there been an industry not to step forward at some point and argue that it should be applied antitrust rules differently, or not at all. This 'exceptionalist' impulse is extremely powerful in the US system, and no antitrust official ever made the mistake to overestimate it. The basic argument invoked across a variety of industries for being exempted or treated differently under antitrust rules has been that competition is destructive, uninhibited competition is harmful for quality, and that a variety of public interest rationales justifies suppressing competition. A closely related argument is that, even if in theory competition would be valuable, the competition authorities and courts are incompetent to make sensible judgments about the specific circumstances of the market, so that control should be entrusted to a specialized regulatory body.

This battle has been played out on two fronts. One is that of the US court system, and in this sense, the US experience is very much alike to the Australian experience, as previously described by Allen Fels. To illustrate this, I would start by mentioning *AMA*,[6] a case brought by the Federal Trade Commission in the 1970s, and concluded in the 1980s, which established the legitimacy of the federal government's efforts to control restrictions on advertising involving the medical profession. The paradox was that, the more successful the government became with this litigation, the more aggressive the industry' claims for dispensations from the antitrust rules. The consequence is that the government had to fight a two-fronts war. The lesson is that, if one focuses on litigation only, this approach would be misleading. Competition authorities need to be actively engaged in all public policy forums, and not exclusively in court litigation. In other words, competition policy has to have a multi-dimensional quality, which is why I think that the European situation is much better than the US one. Competition policy involves more than litigation—although I fully agree with Allen Fels in that without litigation the competition authorities do not have credibility. But litigation must be supplemented with competition policy advocacy, the preparation of guidelines, and the formulation of advisory opinions. An agency that only does the first is like a very poor carpenter, with a hammer only on his hands. Plus, when your only tool is a hammer, there is a tendency to see every problem as being a nail and bang it with the tool.

The key argument in my written contribution is that the knowledge base is essential for a competition authority's interventions before the courts and the legislative bodies. This is what Tim Murris, the Chairman of the FTC,[7] calls 'competition policy R&D'. Competition agencies need to model themselves just as firms do: a firm focusing only on manufacturing its existing products is destined to go out of business. Successful work in this area demands a continuing investment in new ideas and in knowledge.

How to build that? First, the competition agencies need to rely on empirical research—no court and no legislature will take only intuitions for granted, but will demand facts, or the so-called 'economic precedents'. Such 'economic precedents' are not simply cases that you pull off the shelf, but studies advancing arguments that have been empirically tested. *Ex post* assessments of how decisions have been implemented are also absolutely indispensable.

[6] *American Medical Association* 94 FTC 701 (1979) (finding liability), order enforced as modified, 638 F2d 443 (2nd Cir, 1980), affirmed by the Supreme Court 455 US 676 (1982).

[7] Tim Murris chaired of the FTC until August 2004. The chairmanship of the FTC is currently held by Deborah Platt Majoras.

Otherwise, antitrust enforcement would be very much like a hospital that performs surgery, sends the patient out the door and never talks to him/her again, taking faith that the surgery was successful. No medical professional could ever survive with that kind of practice. We have to look back at the consequences of previous efforts of reform. Comparative study is also indispensable in this area, and fortunately, there is nowadays a rich opportunity to do empirical research within individual jurisdictions and their political subdivisions, to go to hearings, seminars and workshops and learn about the state-of-the-art, to bring all of the interested parties and consult with them. In 2003, the FTC and the Department of Justice spent 25 full days hearing over 200 witnesses on a variety of health care issues, and will soon produce a report on this subject.[8] This is an example of the commitment that competition agencies have to make to the non-litigation agenda.

What do you do with this knowledge base? First, this allows to test the conceptual basis for the exceptional treatment requests. Second, this allows to check if there a good fit between the existing exceptional policies and the asserted rationales. As I suggested yesterday, very often there is a tremendous gap between the asserted justification and the actual regulatory regimes. We were talking yesterday about financial services and real estate closings. For example, in the US the competition agencies challenged rules on real estate closing that required the presence of an attorney, especially the aspect where this requirement was satisfied by the presence of the lender's attorney. This is not always good for the borrower.

The FTC discovered that there are increasingly important links between its competition policy function and consumer protection activity, and is contemplating a much deeper integration between these two functions. In this area of antitrust enforcement the relevant issues are often related to information economics, to how consumers perceive information. The FTC's dual functions are, on the one hand, to create options for consumers—and this is the competition policy side—and on the other hand, to ensure that consumers can make well-informed choices. I think that, for a long time, these two functions of the FTC converged only as a matter of historical accident, whereas nowadays we are increasingly perceiving that there is good reason to make the two of them together. And also, our cooperation with our colleagues from Europe and other international jurisdictions involve increasingly exploring these connections. This does involve accounting for institutional interdependencies. The dialogue we just had about Directorates within the European Commission working together brings to my mind the image of an archipelago where a variety of agencies have an influence on the competitive process but there is no ferry service between them. In the US, in the area of

[8] Improving Health Care: A Dose of Competition: A Report by the Federal Trade Commission and the Department of Justice (July 2004), full text available at *http://www.ftc.gov/opa/2004/07/healthcarerpt.htm*.

health care, is not just the federal and state antitrust agencies, but also our health ministry, and the Food and Drug Administration. There is a real need for a domestic competition network equivalent to one set up in the EU, which brings all of these groups together as part of a regular discussion process.

To sum up, if competition agencies want to do good work in this area, they have to make long-term capital investments in developing a base of knowledge that supports good policy-making. This requires that officials be ready accept at any one moment to make investments whose benefits may be reaped only by his/her successors. This sort of approach started to develop in the US antitrust agencies back in the 1960s. There an aphorism circulating in Washington, according to which a public official should always pick the low-hanging fruit, but if no one is planting trees, there will be no fruit to pick. And last, inter-governmental relationships are important in this area—antitrust enforcement in this domain is not a matter of looking only at what happens within the competition community. If one focuses only on a conversation with fellow competition policy regulators, only part of the problem is solved.

► MARK SCHECHTER

During our discussion yesterday, I suggested that the US experience may be of some use to Europe, not so much because it would be positive under every aspect, but to the contrary, because we had some particularly negative episodes. I would like to talk now about these problems and the institutional tools available to address them. It is well-known that in the US the prevailing view is that over-regulation, and ineffective regulation in general, impose substantial costs on consumers. So, in time, the US has become the home of deregulation, which reached airlines, trucking, railroads, natural gas pipelines, etc. There have been some notable successes, but to be clear, while it is true that these areas were deregulated, it is also true that not all regulation was eliminated. For example, airlines, which are largely deregulated, nonetheless have safety and piloting rules, some of which may still be over-restrictive. Likewise, in the wake of *Goldfarb*,[9] we sought to apply antitrust rules and deregulatory thinking to the professions. The question is, how far have we gotten exactly? In my opinion, we have been much less successful in the area of professions than in the other industries.

The problem of professional over-regulation in the US is discussed in some detail in my written contribution. The failure to make progress with deregulation, or the elimination of ineffective regulation, in the area of professions in the US is, I believe, due to three inter-related factors.

First, the members of the professions have powerful incentives to pursue rent-seeking strategies, including through use of the regulatory process. In my written contribution I mentioned by way of illustration the case of African

[9] *Goldfarb v Virginia State Bar* 421 US 773 (1975).

hair-braiders in California.[10] We can certainly discuss whether African hair-braiders are a learned profession or not, but this is an interesting example anyway, because it is very illustrative. People who intended to become African hair-braiders in California were required to take 1600 hours of cosmetology training, at a cost of $7,000.00, in order to be licensed. I think there is a very interesting contrast here by respect to the 22 hours of training to be licensed as a security guard with fire-arm, and the 110 hours for emergency medical technicians. And I should add that these 1600 hours of training did not include a single hour of hair-braiding. . . . Another example: in Louisiana, florists have to take a test in order to be licensed, and the pass rate of this test is of about 50%. If one wants to sell exclusively cut flowers, there is no need to pass this test, although if one wants to include more than one type of flowers in a cut flower bunch, he/she will be required to take the test.

This is clearly irrational and inefficient regulation, but why do the learned professions engage in such banal regulatory conduct? The answer is, because as economic actors they pursue their economic incentives. While I was still at the Department of Justice, the Antitrust Division challenged the regulation of the American Bar Association relating to the accreditation of law schools. The DOJ complaint and the accompanying competitive impact statement[11] described the ABA as acting like a guild protecting the interests of professional law school personnel—in other words, the regulation of the accreditation process aimed to protect the salaries of law professors. The notion was that the ABA had been in this case clearly captured by some of its members, in this case, the law professors. This is a recurrent problem in the regulation of professions.

The second problem is related to courts. In the US, and to me personally, somewhat distressingly, in Europe as well, we saw a development of the state action doctrine, which protects for the most part anticompetitive regulation from scrutiny under antitrust rules. Under the state action doctrine, when the state acts itself or there is some active supervision by the state of regulation enacted by private bodies, this regulation may displace competition. I think that, if Europe is heading in the same direction with the state action doctrine, it will eventually run into the same kind of problems that we face in the US in terms of allowing vast and unnecessary regulation.

The third problem is that competition authorities, to a certain extent, and courts, to a larger extent, are somewhat wary of challenging even regulatory restraints that are not protected by the state action doctrine. Assessing professional restrictions is a complex undertaking, and so, there is a tendency to avoid it. And here, I support William Kovacic's point: competition authorities do have to make investments in this area, because the aggregate negative welfare impact of restrictive professional regulation is quite substantial.

---

[10] *Cornwell v Hamilton* 80 F Supp 2d 1101, 1118 (1999).

[11] Complaint, *US v American Bar Association*, No 95–1211 (CR) (DDC), text available at http://www.usdoj.gov/atr/cases/f0200/0254.pdf (American Bar Association) 60 Fed Reg 39,421, 39,424(27 June 1995), text available at *http://usdoj.gov/atr/cases/f1000/1034.htm*.

Turning to the three basic tools that competition authorities may employ for addressing these problems, this subject was also discussed by William Kovacic, and I largely agree with what he already said. I would add that there are three main tools for addressing the mentioned problems. One is, simply, the vigorous enforcement of antitrust rules. This is important, because it alters the cost–benefit analysis for those intending to adopt parochial restraints. The US antitrust agencies are quite active in this respect: I counted 19 cases brought by the FTC since mid–2002, alleging price-fixing by doctors, and much of it was in connection with joint activities purportedly undertaken for the health and safety of consumers. State attorney generals have likewise been fairly active in enforcement.

The problem with vigorous antitrust enforcement—and this is a point that William Kovacic and Mario Siragusa addressed yesterday, the former in the correct way, and the later in the wrong way, in my view—is that, coupled with the state action doctrine, it has the effect of driving the professions into the arms of the regulating state. In the US this is a serious problem, and so, the FTC has been very active in seeking to limit the scope of the state action doctrine—which is the second intervention tool relevant in this context. A recent FTC staff report[12] described the state action doctrine as having 'become unmoored from its original objectives . . . and [being] frequently invoked to protect private commercial efforts with no relation to state policy'. I suggest that Europe should try not to arrive in the position of trying to undo something like that.

Third, competition advocacy is perhaps the approach that offers the greatest promise in dealing with regulatory restraints in the area of the professions. There is no better substitute, in terms of ways to represent consumer interests, other than to rigorously examine the justification for the restraints in question, and to ensure that any restrictions designed to address market failures are closely confined to the targeted problem, which has been well identified and defined. I would like to conclude with an example: the comments submitted by the DOJ and the FTC to several state legislatures regarding requirements that lawyers be present at real estate closings. The case of North Carolina is illustrative: the Ethics Committee of the North Carolina Bar Association adopted in 2002 two decisions stipulating that a lawyer should be present at all real estate closings in this state. The Department of Justice and the FTC wrote letters to the North Carolina legislature and the Ethics Committee of the bar association, providing some basic analytical facts: first, an estimate according to which this restriction, increased the cost to consumers by $150.00 to $400.00 for each real estate closing; second, that

[12] FTC, Office of Policy Planning, Report of the State Action Task Force: Recommendations to Clarify and Reaffirm the Original Purposes of the State Action Doctrine to Help Insure that Robust Competition Continues to Protect Consumers (2003), text available at: *http://www.ftc.gov/os/2003/09/stateactionreport.pdf*.

this measure also implied less flexibility for consumers, because non-lawyer closers were more likely to be willing to work evenings and weekends; third, there was no evidence to show that consumers would be harmed if non-lawyer assisted at the closings. These comments lead to the opening of an investigatory hearing by the North Carolina state, and ultimately, to the adoption of some major refinements to the restrictive provisions in question, which in effect allowed non-lawyers to assist at real estate closings. This is really an outstanding example of competition policy advocacy and its importance.

I would conclude with a couple of thoughts: first, the US experience indicates that aggressive antitrust enforcement should be combined with competition advocacy and efforts to limit the state action doctrine. Second point, chances are extremely good that, if the competition authorities do not step forward and aggressively represent the interests of consumers, those interests will essentially remain not represented. And last, the US antitrust community is watching with a great deal of interest how Europe deals with the issue of the professions, and we are hopeful that Europe will set for us a positive example.

► MARIO SIRAGUSA

I think the what clearly emerges from our discussion so far is that there are two ways to proceed: one is to see what can be done within the present system, by applying the current rules, and another is through intervention by the legislature and reform. Sir David Clementi offered to us the example of a country looking systematically into ways to produce legislative reforms. The Commission's proposal for a directive on professional services[13] is another example of proceeding through legislative reforms. One way to stem the problem of too much intervention by the states in the area of professional regulation is to induce governments and legislators to adopt reform. But in order to do that, we should also be clear on what needs to be done, and in parallel see what can be done within the present system. My main critique to the Commission's report on competition in the area of the professions[14] is that it creates confusion between what needs legislative intervention and what can be done under the present system. This confusion arises from a wrong interpretation of the two important cases we discussed yesterday, namely *Arduino* and *Wouters*.[15] The Commission wrongly interprets *Wouters* because it does not recognize the main rationale of this judgment, which is to grant a certain discretion to the professional associations, so as to avoid that they run to the state and get their rules imposed by it. I think that this point is sustainable after *Arduino,* where the recognizes the legitimacy of regulation adopted in

---

[13] See above n 5.

[14] *Commission Report on competition in the professional services*, COM (2004) 83 final, available at *www.europa.eu.int/comm/competition/liberal_professions/final_comm_en.pdf*.

[15] Case C–35/99 *Arduino* [2002] ECR I–1529, Case C–309/99 *Wouters* [2002] ECR I–1577.

pursuit of a public interest. So, I do not think that the adoption of an European code of conduct, which is simply a private initiative of the professional bodies, can be a tool of reference for the implementation of any public interest theory. I am not saying that I am in favour of the state action doctrine, but that is precisely what the Court has spelled out. Luc Gyselen explained this very well in his written contribution. I do not read any public interest test and proportionality test in *Arduino*, they simply are not there! So, maybe we should intervene at the legislative level, and maybe the Commission's draft directive goes a long way in that direction. Also, because of the recent decentralization of EC competition law enforcement, the Commission should be very careful in stating its positions, because those positions will be taken over by the national competition authorities, and we risk to create a mess if we are not clear as to the boundaries between legislative reform and what can be done under the present system. To conclude, on *Fiammiferi*:[16] this judgment is very important because the national authorities may have to disapply national rules that are in violation of the EC competition rules. Fine, but that does not change the test as to whether a national measure is in violation of the EC competition rules, which remains the one set in *Arduino*, and recognises state action immunity. This is the situation in Europe: I do not support it, I am simply saying that, if we want to change the system and bring effective competition in the area of the professions, we must determine first where intervention the boundaries are, and know what the antitrust authorities can do based on the current rules.

► GIULIANO AMATO

I find it very interesting that the professions tend to think, more than anybody else, that antitrust authorities and courts are incompetent to evaluate their circumstances. Historically, this has to do with the idea that the professions are something special, very different from any other business activity. It goes back to the social standings of the profession in the 19th century, I suppose. But it is a fact that they think that peer review applies to them more than to anybody else, because only they know what has to be known about their own activities. Antitrust authorities and courts usually deal with very complicated cases, often having to do with several branches of industry, and nobody challenged their competence to do so. At most, other industries might argue the analysis applied to them is wrong for some given specific reasons. But in antitrust cases involving the professions, there is almost always this preliminary objection of incompetence. And of course, when the professionals are lawyers, things are supposedly even more complicated to review. . . .

This is why I think that the Commission is on the right track in proposing the review of the justifications for restrictions resulting from professional

[16] See above n 1.

regulation. I remember an Italian antitrust case involving the association of engineers. An engineer was fined by the association for a fee that was below the minimum fee established by the association. In the motivation of this decision, the association explained which were the grounds for the fine, and added that, if they would find that the quality of the service was also lower than it should be, this would be ground for applying a second, different fine. This was an open admission that the minimum fee had nothing to do with the quality of the service.

Finally, I would like Mario Siragusa to clarify one point: in my view, the sense of *Fiammiferi* is that antitrust authorities can no go beyond the protection offered by the state action doctrine. As long as the antitrust authorities are called to disapply regulation infringing EC competition rules, this means that the state action immunity does not always apply. If one reads *Arduino* in the sense that the state action immunity remains, then the consistency between *Arduino* and *Fiammiferi* has to be found on other grounds, I suppose.

► JOHN COOKE

One point, since we are discussing institutional issues: I wonder, is it not the case that there is an asymmetry of information and expertise as between national competition authorities and other public authorities at national level? Do not national competition authorities have a duty to the public to stop governments hysterically regulating where regulation is wholly unnecessary? I was struck by one comment made by Lowri Evans, in the sense that the Commission found that the public, or the consumers, are totally uninterested in regulation or deregulation. I think that one of the lessons of the last 20 or 30 years is that national competition authorities have acquiesced too much where governments have stepped in to regulate things that do not need regulation. I was struck by a number of examples in this sense that occurred over the last few years. Take the case of a big robbery in an airport: it is discovered that it may have been an inside job, because the security firm responsible for the warehouse did not have a proper system for recruiting security guards, and some of them would turn out to be accomplished long-standing criminals. Immediately this brings about demands from politicians, the newspapers and everyone else: the security industry must be regulated. Another example: the very tragic incident some months ago in the UK, when a number of Chinese illegal immigrants drowned on a fast incoming tide close to the UK shores. Immediately the same hysteric reaction from politicians and particularly the media, saying that 'the gang masters' are responsible for this tragedy—the so-called 'gang masters' being employment agencies of an unregulated kind using unregistered immigrants to provide flexible employees for seasonal work—and that they should be regulated. As if ordinary criminal law, and ordinary law of negligence, were not enough to deal with this case. Also, I would also suspect that ordinary consumer law in

Louisiana—I am referring here to the florists case mentioned by William Kovacic—should be enough to protect gullible purchasers of bunches of flowers. So, it seems to me that national competition authorities, endowed as they are with both experience and expertise, have a greater duty to speak out against regulation when this sort of hysteria grips a Member State.

► ASSIMAKIS KOMNINOS

I would go back to Lowri Evans' remarks concerning the adoption of professional codes of conduct at the European level. I do not really see how a code of conduct agreed upon at a European level could solve the problem of whether national professional regulation is in line with EC competition rules. I think that the mere existence of a European code of conduct does not say anything about the compatibility of national professional regulation with the EC competition rules. If the idea is that the European code of conduct should be a kind of benchmark for the national codes of conduct, this would be contrary to *Wouters* and the discretion that this judgment gives to the national professional bodies. So, I really cannot see any advantage in this approach; indeed, I even see a danger in it.

► FRÉDÉRIC JENNY

I just wanted to share with you some of the impressions from this day and a half of debate. I think that there is a fairly general agreement on a number of points. One is that regulation can sometimes lead to inefficiencies, and therefore in such cases it needs to be corrected. The question is, how should it be corrected. Most of us agreed that competition law enforcement can play a useful role, but this may not be sufficient, and some kind of re-regulation could also be necessary. I think that the issue of re-regulation is crucial, and has not been sufficiently addressed in our debate. We do not have clear ideas about how to re-regulate while at the same time giving more room to competition, and what would be the safeguards to be taken to preserve the consumers' interests in the process. We heard from the Commission that the consumers do not actually care about the form of regulation, or about whether services are regulated or not, as long as they are protected and informed against bad quality of services and high prices. Now, the question is, how do ensure that? I think that economists have not thought much about how to solve the information asymmetry problems, in the area of the professions and for services in general. I was talking earlier with Lowri Evans about the baby food cases, where it has become very clear that only advertising is not going to give mothers the kind of information that they need in order to switch from one to another brand of baby milk. This is a case where competition does not work through the traditional means, consumers need something more.

Another point that we have not addressed so far is, how does one inform consumers of what a 'normal market price' is without eliminating price competition? Now, we do not like the professions to establish minimum prices, for very good reasons. But the alternative to that is not very clear. I remember that the first antitrust case we had in France in the area of professions involved a local bar that had fixed prices. The bar argued that the reason why they fixed prices was that the court has asked them to do so. The court intervenes when there is disagreement over the legal fee that one should pay, for example, and the court has no idea what the reasonable fee should be. Now, if the court does not have any idea on that, then it is clear that the consumers do not have any idea either, and they are exposed to price gouging.

In relation to a comment made yesterday both by Amelia Fletcher and Judge Cooke, I think that there is a sense among the consumers that *ex post* legal procedures are not offering them enough protection: legal procedures are long, costly, too technical, etc. So, I think that, in political economy terms, to move forward the agenda on changing the regulation of the professions, it would be very useful, rather than having against the Commission and the Member States both the professions and the consumers, arguing that deregulation and re-regulation promise an uncertain future, it would be probably best to start from the other end, and inform consumers about the analytical tools that could be used in a system where there is more competition. It is a difficult tasks, because I do not think that the economists and the antitrust authorities have really developed yet those analytical tools, but this would be the way to make consumers more interested in a reform of the professions, and render the reform swifter, at least in Europe.

► Santiago Martínez Lage

One comment, and a question for Sir David Clementi. One month ago I attended in Lisbon a seminar on the future of the legal profession. Jürgen Helmut, the Chairman of the CCBE (the Council of Bars and Law Societies of the European Communities) made a very provocative speech, in which he said—and I quote literally—that 'A relatively small number of business lawyers make millions, while an ever-growing number of lawyers earns less than the social security minimum.' He referred by way of example to the case of a large London-based law firm which has a bank loan of $150 million, and then asked whether this firm was within the same profession as an independent legal practitioner or a small law firm. He mentioned that the big law firms in London presented observations to Sir David Clementi's draft report separately from those presented by the law societies of England and Wales. In the end, he went so far as to suggest that different ethic—and I underline, ethic—rules should be applied to big law firms than those applicable to small law firms or individual lawyers.

I represent a very small law firm based in Madrid, but we are also affected by the reforms that will be introduced in the UK, because we compete with big law firms in all Europe. And I would never find it acceptable that big law firms be submitted in the UK to different ethic obligations, for instance concerning conflicts of interest, secrecy, etc. Therefore my question to Sir David Clementi is, were this proposal to be accepted, do you think there is room for big law firms to be treated differently from the regulatory point of view from individual legal practitioners or smaller law firms?

▶ JOHN FINGLETON

I wanted to address a point that Judge Cooke and Mario Siragusa have touched upon, namely the division of responsibility between the EU and national competition authorities.

I agree with Judge Cooke, it would be ideal that national competition authorities tackle this trend towards re-regulation, particularly where private interests are dressed up as public interest. But, first of all, the national competition authorities often face tremendous political pressures in this area. For example, in Ireland, the trade union movement is totally against the competition authority having any competition advocacy role at all. They think it is sort of perverse for the state to fund an agency that would attack the decisions of government, particularly when it comes to utilities—where the trade union members have strong interests. Second, the Irish competition authority at least, does not have the resources to do this work. We have seven staff members appointed to do advocacy, while our total staff is of 40. Lack of resources is a real problem. Third, there is a lot of ambiguity about our legal powers. For instance, *Fiammiferi*[17] obliges us to disapply national rules that are incompatible with EC competition rules, but we did not have yet the time and resources to examine how to put that into practice. There is also the question of the extent to which the application of Article 86 EC can be decentralized. I see it difficult that a domestic statute enable our competition authority to challenge other domestic statutes. This is why sometimes it is useful to have supranational constitutional rules at hand. I would add that the big benefits we have seen in Ireland in terms of the liberalization of air transport, telecoms, etc, are in part due to actions undertaken by the Commission and the European court, which also forced Ireland to find domestic solutions. For the other part, these results are due to action by our domestic courts. So, some external pressure is, I think, useful in this area.

Going back to Mario Siragusa's point about *Arduino*,[18] this decision does not set any proportionality test, and this is a huge problem, because one of the great benefits of EU membership is to have this proportionality test applied to domestic law. I think that ultimately matters will go in the direction that Judge Cooke wants, that is, be pushed back to the national competition authorities.

And again, I think we really need to have clarity about the decentralization

17 See above n 1.
18 See above n 15.

of Article 86 EC. The liberalization of the professions is something that the Commission will never tackle under Article 86 EC, and most national governments are afraid to tackle this area.

My point yesterday was that there is a conflict between *Fiammiferi* and *Arduino*, and at least for me, as a national enforcer, the current state of the law is very confusing.

► CALVIN GOLDMAN

To follow up on some comments made by William Kovacic and Mark Schechter, and relate them to the experience illustrated by Allen Fels, I also find that the issue of competition advocacy is critical in this area, particularly since the problems that the consumers face in the US, Canada, Australia and Europe are virtually identical. At the bottom-line, it is all a matter of conflict between price competition and the quality standards advocated by the professions. The information necessary for the consumers to make learned decisions is not readily available. In Canada we found very helpful relying on the US experience: we were able to point to post-decision facts in some of the US states, which reflected that quality had not suffered as a result of introducing price competition. And during our debate I was thinking that this is one area where this kind of discussion and exchange of international experiences can be very helpful in opening up the doors to more competition.

► AMELIA FLETCHER

I also wanted to comment briefly on the competition advocacy point. In particular, I wonder if there is scope for adopting additional legislation at the national level in order to formalize the advocacy role of the national competition authorities. I understood from Allen Fels' intervention that in Australia there may be such provisions—he mentioned that every two years state rules being in conflict with the competition regime are reviewed from the perspective of their justification and proportionality. In the UK, the recent Enterprise Act allows for competition impact considerations to be taken into account in the course of procedures for the adoption of state regulation.

First, we have the so-called 'regulatory impact assessments', which have been around for some time, but before they were focused more on environmental issues, etc. The competition impact assessments are new, and, although the government departments do them, these reports are then submitted to the OFT, which may comment itself if it does not find their content entirely convincing. The OFT does not have the authority to impose its suggestions, but this consultation process helps the flow of information, and allows the OFT to make timely competition advocacy interventions.

Second, the OFT also performs market studies, covering all sorts of aspects, including state regulation. We already performed such studies for dentists, pharmacies, taxi services, etc. At the moment we are looking into state procurement practices and subsidies not falling under the scope of EC competition rules. I wonder if the restrictions identified in all these markets would pass the proportionality test.

When the OFT formulates regulatory recommendations following up on such reports, the government has 90 days to respond, and is obliged to take our comments seriously. While we do not have the power to impose our standpoint, these provisions actually do formalize our competition advocacy role. So far we had mixed success. More precisely, we assumed that, since the government had given us the powers to submit comments on regulation, it would also be willing to take our recommendations into account, but this has proved not to be always the case. We had some positive results, however. We learned that we have to do more competition advocacy in general, including through our reports. We should not think about the pros and cons of regulation in only terms of prices for consumers, but also at the public interest justifications for imposing restrictions through regulation. Competition policy is good for the productivity of the UK economy, and alongside the Department of Trade and Industry we started to do more research into the benefits of competition in terms of productivity.

► William Kovacic

Two unrelated comments. First, in response to Sir David Clementi and Lowri Evans, on the question of separating management and ownership of professional service firms, and especially law firms. As Santiago Martínez Lage noted before, big law firms have now become global enterprises. Some of the law firms in London now have as many as 3000 lawyers, 500 partners, and operations around the world. Obviously, with this kind of scale there is a much greater need for capital than there ever has been in the past. And I know that this was an issue that the 'big five' accounting firms had faced, and one of the factors that drove Price Waterhouse Coopers and Lybrand to merge. I believe also that this is one of the factors that subsequently drove the auditing firms to spin off their IT consulting businesses—they found that those businesses required so much capital, which they were not able to provide within a partner-owned enterprise. We have seen the same thing happen with the major investment banks, which of course used to be partnerships, and are now publicly-traded companies.

The question here is, are we thinking long-term enough about the ownership structure of law firms? Should we be thinking about, for example, the possibility of allowing two classes of equity, one with voting rights, that could be held only by lawyers (partners in the firm), and a second class without voting rights, that could be held by investors? Why should we limit law firms to debt capital, and not allow them to raise equity capital? Would it not help to reduce legal fees if partners did not have to provide all of the capital out of their own pockets?

The second comment relates to Pamela Brumter's intervention. In the US we look with some jealousy to the various possibilities for intervention that the Commission has on the internal market. In the US, competition advocacy *vis a vis* the states frequently means the FTC begging the states to do the right thing, whereas you seem to have somewhat more directive authority over your Member States. Given the relative youth of the EU as compared to the US, that is really quite remarkable. In the US system, exactly because we do not have internal markets directives like you do, this vacuum has been filled through private action, through organizations like the American Bar Association or the American Law Institute, which develop, for example through law schools—where the future lawyers, judges and legislators throughout the country, a more uniform 'commercial code'. To what extent could we foresee that a pan-European Bar Association more like our American Bar Association will develop in Europe? I know that an association reuniting the Member State bars already exists, but the difference is that in the US, not only each of the state bars is a member of the American Bar Association, but also individual lawyers are members. For example, the Antitrust Section has some 8000 members, and can serve internally as a very effective competition advocate. When the American Bar Association is developing model disciplinary rules, the Antitrust Section can always remark if these rules are anticompetitive. Such an opinion might not always be listened to, but at least we get a good debate going. So I wonder, is there a need for a Pan-European bar, and can we foresee it will emerge?

► Giuliano Amato

I would like to come back to the plan of the European Commission to develop an European code of conduct for the professions. Assimakis Komninos already commented on that, and I also think the idea is very interesting, but at the same time dangerous. Yesterday I was proposing some steps for the Commission to undertake in the direction of professional governance. This idea is a kind of a step in that direction. On the other hand, we have to be aware that there is a danger in promoting self-regulation powers for the professional organizations if the European codes of conduct are made the wrong way. I think that a safe bet is for such codes to contemplate generally-accepted principles. One may conceive such codes in terms of systems competition, thus giving only an European framework for the national organizations to compete against each other, and respecting some rules while they are at it. I also agree very much to the comparison with the old codes of practice and conduct, there are historical examples to consider.

► IAN FORRESTER

I think we ought to be aware of the reality and existing constraints, and not to be too carried away by enthusiasm. Competition law is not a natural force, naturally accepted and put into place by an easy process. It requires some conflict, some resolution of challenges. In Europe we have an immense diversity of national regulations concerning what is a profession and what are the rules of that profession. These diversities are so marked that I somewhat doubt the possibility even for lawyers to achieve pan-European consistency. The classic questions that will come up are such as follows: is this truly a profession? Is the monopoly really justified? Is rule X a good rule?

There are three possible classes of actors who could be involved in remedying, or challenging, or making a better professional regulation by application of the competition principles. One is the European Commission, the second includes the national competition authorities, and the third one includes individuals—tiresome, difficult, energetic, passionate individuals like Mr Hanner and Mr Wouters, who are willing to go to court, to the press, to make trouble, and to invest time and effort and embarrassment in doing so. I submit that it is this last class of actors who to have most chance of making changes happen, even in difficult cases—Mr Hanner had an easy case in the Swedish pharmaceutical monopoly, but Mr Wouters had a more difficult case, and actually he lost.

I think that the European Commission should not get into national politics in Ireland or the UK, urging that taxi monopolies should be dismantled or that engineering diplomas are not necessary for safe engineering. And also, if John Fingleton is terrorized at the possibility of the Irish competition authority using competition law principles to change Irish professional law, then I see even less chance for Lowri Evans and the Commission to do anything useful in Ireland. So, I see the attractiveness of the idea that supranational principles coming from Brussels and Luxembourg be used, but then it would still be mainly the individuals to invoke them and put them to use. Free movement of workers is an area that has been almost entirely dependent upon private litigation, and where a huge apparatus of law has been developed by way of references for preliminary ruling from national courts to the ECJ. I am coming to the surprising conclusion that somehow this shows the limited role for the application of EC law by the European Commission, a possible role for the national competition authorities, though with difficulties, and a need for independent, tiresome, passionate individuals. It seems awfully difficult to see how change can come about without a lot of national individuals going to the trouble of making a fuss.

► GIULIANO AMATO

Yours is a very pessimistic view, according to which this is such a difficult war, that we need heroes to fight it, and when the time comes for heroes, this means that ordinary people are already defeated. I think that one of the assets that we have in Europe is the sort of habit developed by the European Commission throughout the years to negotiate with several groups of interests, reviewing and negotiate new rules. This is by now a specialty of the Commission, which sometimes works out and sometimes does not. But in this case, assuming that the professions would accept discussions on the merit, it might work.

Going back to our discussion on the proportionality test and its applicability, the Commission now has a different approach: it proposes to discuss restrictions to entry, whether they make sense, what interests are being protected. If we lead the professions towards this kind of discussion, I am sure that something will come out, and not necessarily by heroic acts. But if we keep discussing whether the proportionality test applies or not, then lawyers will be happy, because we will never get to discuss whether the existing restrictions to entry at the bar make sense.

► Frank Stephen

The question that I wanted to ask has actually been addressed by our Chairman, but I think it is worth phrasing the issue in a different way, going back to some of the issues discussed yesterday morning. My impression—as an economist—is that we tend to come back to the idea that outcomes are more important than principles. I was stimulated by Santiago Martínez Lage's point about lawyers. It seems to me, being an 'outsider' of the legal profession, that nowadays we may no longer talk about the legal profession as such—and Benito Arruñada insisted on this. We therefore need to, if not anticipate change, at least take it into account, and allow for competition to emerge. We get bogged down by continuing to talk about professions, whereas we should look at individual markets. What is a profession in Italy may not be a profession in the UK, Ireland or Finland, but the impact of regulation, be it self-regulation or state regulation, are going to be the same.

► Mario Siragusa

I agree, identifying and reviewing the existent restrictions is a very good point to start from. But once that the restrictions are identified, one has to choose the tools to attack them, so we do need principles. Is the restriction identified an agreement between undertakings in violation of Article 81 EC, or is the restriction brought about by an act of state? This is a qualification question that we cannot avoid. According to the answer to this question, the issues to be dealt with in a next step are different.

I want to answer to John Fingleton's question about the difference between *Arduino* and *Fiammiferi*.[19] For me, there is a very clear distinction between

[19] See above ftns. 15 and 1.

the two: *Arduino* is a pure case of state action, where the Court affirmed that the Italian state preserved its power to take the last resort decision. *Fiammiferi* is one of those traditional cases where a state intervention leaves room for restrictions practiced by the companies—in this case, the quota system run by the members of the cartel. The novelty in *Fiammiferi* is, the Court establishes that, once you have determined that there is a violation of the EC competition rules, the national competition authority may disregard the part related to state action. I agree that maybe it is too early to be so clear-cut on the distinction between these cases, but I think that from the theoretical standpoint it is good to start with some clarity, and maybe then the Court will develop this into further detail in the future.

I agree with Ian Forrester, individuals are very important in this battle, but then again, if you think well about all these cases, individuals are invoking principles of EC law. So, the sword that these individuals use in the battle is given by principles of law, otherwise those individuals will remain normal persons, and not become heroes.

► William Kovacic

The suggestion that I repeated for two days now is that the EU should avoid the US model with respect to the state action doctrine. While listening to the debate, and in particular to Mario Siragusa's comments, I think that there is a real possibility for the EU to require at least that some appropriate review procedures be followed when a state imposes a restraint on competition. We do not have this possibility in the US. To be more precise, transparency should become a requirement (and Allen Fels' comments were inspirational on this point), the state should perform some sort of *ex ante* cost/benefit analysis by balancing the problem against the cost of the restraint, and the state should undertake some periodic review of the actual effects of the restraint imposed. I am not saying that the Member States should be imposed these obligations through an EC directive, but maybe these could become pre-conditions for the Member States to avail themselves of the exemption for the scope of application of EC competition rules.

On the principle of proportionality, I was inspired by Judge Cooke's comment in the sense that the national competition authorities, especially after the modernization of EC antitrust, are in a very good position to carry the sword of EC competition law enforcement against restrictive professional regulation. This is likely to minimize outrageous effects of the state action doctrine such as we have in the US.

One last comment, on the report produced by the Dutch Ministry of Economic Affairs which was presented to us by Marc Hameleers. The report contains a section discussing stages and priorities for the protection of public interest in the liberal professions. I find this type of analytical exercise very useful, and if it were to be institutionalized in Europe, this would be a real step forward.

► John Cooke

William Kovacic asked if there was any likelihood of a pan-European bar emerging in the near future. I think this is not inconceivable, but I do not expect to see it happen in my lifetime. Having said that, I was a member of the CCBE for 10 years, between the mid 1970s and the mid 1980s, and I was its President in 1985 and 1986. With this inside view, I suggest you should not be misled by the fact that the CCBE promulgated a code of conduct for the European bars. It is no more than an articulation of the lowest common-denominator principles. It took a long time and a lot of effort to arrive even at that. The 1977 EC directive on legal services came as a big shock to many national bars in Europe. It implied that, as a matter of EC law, competitors from another Member State could appear in court in your jurisdiction and plead cases without having to re-qualify at the national bar, even if only on a sort of once-off passing-trade basis. It was and it remains extremely difficult to reconcile the positions on the national bars. At the end of the day, the ultimate test (not just for the legal profession, but also, to different extents, for all other professions) is to determine the set of rules that best serve the needs of a particular society. This test is not limited to economic and competition considerations, but also includes social and cultural considerations, constitutional considerations etc. The reconciliation of all of these different considerations is an exercise in which competition policy plays an important role, but this should not make us forget that competition policy is not the only factor to be taken into account.

► Giuliano Amato

Indeed, there is also a cultural problem that we need to face. In the town of Florence, for example, very old Italian rich families with noble roots going back to the Middle Ages have traditionally been assisted by family lawyers, who in their turn passed the business within the family, and so on. I remember the first time that I tried to advocate the big law firm here, I got very passionate negative reactions—they thought we wanted to destroy their secular personal loyalty relations. I had to somehow retreat, and reassure them that small family law firms will anyway survive etc.

► William Kovacic

I think that similar kinds of concerns about the ability of competition authorities to make good judgments do show up in other areas besides the professions. Every time that we probe into areas involving high technology, intellectual property, and dynamic industry settings in general, we hear a chorus of objections going in that direction. I do not know if you have the same experience in Europe, but in the US, we had to face this kind of objections from the very beginning of our antitrust enforcement system. In some ways, it is the more general concern about building agency knowledge.

A comment on Frédéric Jenny's thoughts about the search for solutions: again, this is an area where collaboration between competition authorities and consumer protection authorities can yield significant benefits. If the two are integrated within a single agency, I think there are still greater advantages in this respect, because indeed you get those two perspectives together, and that is not an automatic accomplishment by any means. The FTC's consumer protection activities have given us an enormously useful perspective on how people collect information. In the work we have done on nutrition and diet, we found that the main place in which consumers learn about these issues is not from their nutritionist, neither from their doctor, but from advertising. We did some very informative empirical work testing this finding. This offers us insight on what kinds of information people can absorb, how they absorb it, how to present it. Currently the FTC is doing a similar work on credit practices and the kind of disclosures that are mandated by our financial services regulation in relation to lending decisions and the purchase of homes. It turns out that consumers are given a dense thicket of information, only slightly shorter than the typical metropolitan phone directory. This mass of information is indigestible. So, we are working together with the financial services regulator trying to come up with forms of information that people can understand.

I think that Amelia Fletcher's point about the mixed effects of competition advocacy, and how to get information through to regulators, is very important. At the FTC we realised that, the more informative our notes are—and especially if they contain some empirical data—the more likely it is that the addressees will learn something form them. We also found out that an important audience for our education and advocacy actions are, in fact, consumer groups. Our 'do not call' campaign related to telemarketing succeeded in may respects because consumer groups fought with us to ward off efforts by the telemarketers to blunt the implementation of the rules—without them we would have failed.

Now, that is the 'Dr Jekyl' side of consumer groups. There is also a 'Mr Hyde' side to them too, that never considers a regulation that they do not like *a priori*. For example, the original draft of our pre-merger notification review mechanism required the firms to suspend their transaction until the competition agencies approved it, with no time limit. After some reflection, it became obvious that it would be better to have prior approval within a time limit, and if there was no action from the competition agencies within that time limit, the merger would be considered as approved. I remember the day we announced this change, there was a coalition of consumer groups that stood outside of our offices. Their spokesman stood before the reporters and said that this was 'the biggest sell-out since Munich'. They were convinced that this was a craven capitulation to business interests. Can you imagine what pre-merger notification would now look like without this default rule? So, one has to take with a grain of salt what consumer groups have to say.

Finally, Ian Forrester's comments about the Swedish pharmaceutical monopoly case makes me think of the value of a private right of action. In the US experience, this comes very often from the slightly-demented entrepreneur willing to push aside the fact that a thousand people are telling him he cannot win. Mr Goldfarb was an FTC attorney attempting to buy a house in Northern Virginia. When he noticed that all lawyers asked the same fee for the closing, he asked himself why that should be so, it must have been a decision of the bar. He decided to challenge the system, and this is how *Goldfarb vs. State Bar of Virginia*[20] came about.

► DAVID CLEMENTI

First, a reply to Lowri Evans, who said that consumers are not interested in regulatory issues. I think we would all agree that consumers are not interested in regulatory matters any more than they are interested in how jet engines actually work, but they are pretty interested in the outcomes, and they are certainly interested in quality and prices. I think this is a question of balance between the occasional hysteria of the consumer lobbies and the submissions of the legal profession, which are beautifully written, but nevertheless self-interested.

In response to Santiago Martínez Lage, who asked me whether my report contemplated different ethical arrangements for large and small law firms, I tend to be against such distinctions. We went through this debate when we analysed the financial markets area, where there was very little in common between some of the wholesale markets (large investment banks doing foreign exchange or IPO's) and the retail level. I think it is very hard to segment parts of profession, because they very often overlap. We could distinguish between a large and a small law firm and then spend countless days arguing where little law firms fitted. In any event, so far as the legal profession is concerned, I think there is a great deal more uniformity than in the financial services, since the concept of duty to the court and concept of duty to the client is quite uniform for large and small law firms. I lean against any suggestion of segmenting the market.

What I would favour, however, is a single regulator. Whatever the regulatory system we will put in place will, it will have to take into account the risks related to attaining its objectives. I would expect that a regulator spend a great deal more time worrying about how a small law firm dealt with its clients than how a large law firm, dealing with sophisticated clients, is actually operating.

In response to William Kovacic: he asked whether my report contemplated the ramifications of splitting management and ownership, and noted that large firms need more capital. That is certainly true. Actually I observed that

[20] See above n 9.

large law firms—and certainly the ones in London—are doing very well in that respect. However, a lot of the fresh capital needs might as well be high with smaller law firms. In any event, there is a huge debate on splitting management and ownership. William Kovacic suggested that this dilemma could be solved by introducing the concept of non-voting shares. I tend to be against splitting ownership and management issues, but this might be a way to do go forward. My observation is, however, that most regulatory systems go to the heart of who manages a firm and what system is used for doing that, rather than who owns it. I am not convinced that there is something so very precious and different about law firms so that, while legal services might be carried out by lawyers only, the firm has to be also owned by exclusively by lawyers.

▸ MARK SCHECHTER

Giuliano Amato's anecdote about Florence reminded me that any thrust at the heart of professional regulation takes on professional privilege and goes against it, so we should not be surprised if there is resistance.

One point about enforcement, which builds on what William Kovacic already commented before: picking enforcement targets is always difficult for public enforcers, and whatever target one picks, there is always the feeling that it might be impossible to achieve—if it is Microsoft, because you are too late and it is too big, or if it is the professions, because they are too diverse, and so forth. I assume that at some point, after having established the principles, the Commission will look specifically at market impact and narrow down the scope of the enforcement efforts towards the most significant cases. We will always have ridiculous regulation such as the African hair-braiding regulation in California, but no antitrust agency will succeed to eliminate all ridiculous professional regulation. So, one has to orient its enforcement efforts towards cases where the anticompetitive impact is more notable.

On the role for private action, leaving aside Mr Goldfarb, who worked for the FTC, individuals usually undertake a different cost/benefit analysis than antitrust agencies when it comes to deciding whether to act or not. Quite often we tend to think that a public enforcer needs to act so as to capture all the benefits of the intervention, but it may be that actions undertaken on an individual level also have non-negligible public spill over benefits in terms of creating a rule of law.

On the state action doctrine, I have a sort of an odd sense that the development of this doctrine on the two sides of the Atlantic may be influenced by the different constitutional settings. In the US, the problem is that the federal government is always worried not to leave enough room for localism, and by consequence the state action doctrine becomes a way of giving back something to the states. In Europe, the danger is that this doctrine will split the policy into 25 (and soon 27) different directions, so the state action doctrine may need to be stronger and more centralizing. I was always struck by the fact that US state enforcers have much more discretion in antitrust enforcement than the sovereign EU Member States, but this reflects a different constitutional nature, and this difference is important to keep in mind.

► Lowri Evans

Some comments on the European code of conduct for the professions: first of all, the content of such a code would obviously be a matter for the professions to decide. The Commission is not making any assessments about whether such codes of conduct are in line with European competition rules; rather, what the Commission would do is to examine the national codes so as to identify what public interest is being sought, where they go beyond the European codes, and all of this by recognising the existence of different national settings and different market circumstances.

Judge Cooke makes a very interesting point: of course, the national competition authorities are in a better position politically than the Commission to influence national legislature, there is no doubt about that. John Fingleton is also right, the national competition authorities are to a large extent under-resourced. However, we should remember that we have not yet reaped in full the efficiencies derived from the decentralised application of EC competition rules within the EC competition network, because this reform is very recent. So, I think that among 26 competition authorities (soon 29) we may be able to make a better fist at this in the future than it has been the case in the past. I may well imagine that we can develop common competition advocacy tools, which will bring us a huge efficiency gain. The new EC directive on professional services will oblige the Member States (if they agree on the draft directive) to review their legislation from a macro-economic perspective.

Finally, a minor but important point, from my personal perspective: I tend to think on these issues mainly from a competition law enforcer's perspective, and not from that of not a consumer protection body. Within the Commission there is also DG Health and Consumer Protection, and this Directorate did not traditionally look at consumer protection issue from our perspective either. But there is a cooperation and coordination issue here, and in this area we a working together, and we will have to do better in those terms in the future, I think.

► William Kovacic

I wanted to somewhat dissent from what Mark Schechter said about the importance of the constitutional differences between Europe and the US. This morning I read in the Herald Tribune a wonderful quote from Karl Marx, saying that those who do not remember history are condemned to repeat it, first as a tragedy, and then as a farce. I would remind Mark Schechter that one of the reasons why we have the state action doctrine in the

US is actually a case that incidentally bears his name, which was a sort of last breath of what was called 'substantive due process' in the US. The fact that judges reviewed state regulations and struck them down as unsound policy was eventually considered an error. In fact, some of our greatest jurists were the leaders of the effort to strike down the substantive due process doctrine. Oliver Wendell Holmes wrote in one of his earlier opinions that the due process clause did not respond to Herbert Spencer's theory on social dynamics.[21] Richard Posner remarked on several occasions that US competition policy is more Darwinian than European competition policy.[22] The reason for the rebellion against substantive due process was, fundamentally, that it was anti-democratic: we did not want judges to decide our policies. As Harry First has said, the reason for state action is to bring it closer to the people, to make it more democratic. The European Commission is, of course, more accountable to the people than US courts are. So, I think the constitutional differences are important, and may help explain why you could have more central direction with respect to the actions of the Member States than we have in the US.

► GIULIANO AMATO

Just a short note: the Commission does not legislate, but has a monopoly in legislative initiatives, which then have to be approved by the EU Member States. So, actually the European supremacy, if you wish to call it so, relies on EC regulations that are approved by those who have to comply with them.

► SANTIAGO MARTÍNEZ LAGE

I was very happy to hear Sir David Clementi's answer in the sense that his report does not propose different rules according to the size of the law firms. In fact, what I think was behind the President of the CCBE's suggestion was to have big law firms subject to EC competition rules, but exclude them from the code of conduct, and therefore from ethic obligations. In my opinion, this would be absurd. There is no such choice between being subjected to whether the code of conduct or the competition rules. But this does not mean that ethics is not one of the public interest that could justify a departure from the competition rules. As I understand the Court's case law, one of the public interests that may be invoked by professional associations is some special and singular obligation of that profession, that may sometimes, but not always, justify a departure from the competition rules.

---

[21] See eg, CR Sunstein, *Why Societies Need Dissent—Oliver Wendell Holmes Lectures* (Cambridge, MA, Harvard University Press, 2003).

[22] See eg, RA Posner, 'Antitrust in a Transatlantic Context', speech delivered in Brussels, Belgium, 7 June 2004.

► Claus-Dieter Ehlermann

A question for Giuliano Amato, and a reflection about the very last intervention of William Kovacic.

A few years ago Giuliano Amato organised at the EUI a seminar on the anticompetitive impact of regulation, and the book containing the proceedings of that debate[23] also proposed some action guidelines. I wonder what was the follow-up to the publication of those guidelines? I find that there is a very strong analogy between what we are discussing here with respect to the professions and the broader scope of your reflections back then.

My second reflection goes back to this intriguing discussion about the proportionality principle and the relationship between the judge and the elected parliament. If you look at the jurisprudence of the European court, the overall impression is that the proportionality principle is not so efficiently applied with respect to Community acts. This allows the European legislature a vast scope of discretion. The Court is very strict, however, with respect to national law, especially when it comes to the four fundamental freedoms. Some think that this is an unjustified double standard of review. I think the justification lies in the idea that national legislators do not care about what is going outside their own frontiers and what happens to foreigners. In other words, the Court's review brings an EU dimension into the national legislative process. The question is, would the proportionality principle ever be able to acquire, with respect not to private restrictions of competition, but to public restrictions of competition, the same role with respect to Member States laws as it already has with respect to restrictions of the four freedoms? It is very possible that we will never see the proportionality principle acquire the same role and importance as with respect to the four fundamental freedoms, because, after all, competition is not one the four fundamental freedoms. This issue is furthermore delicate it in the context of the decentralization of EC antitrust and the *Fiammiferi* ruling,[24] because I do not really see how could a national competition authority make a value judgment *vis a vis* national law under the EC proportionality principle. I remember my experience at the WTO Appellate Body in Geneva: we did not use the word 'proportionality', because—we were told—it was considered a 'dirty word' by the US Supreme Court. . . .

► John Fingleton

I think that the national competition authorities may well be the best placed to try think about whether national laws are proportionate, but I share your

---

[23] G Amato and L Laudati, (eds), *The Anticompetitive Impact of Regulation* (Oxford, Hart Publishing, 2001).

[24] See above n 1.

concern, and this goes back to my earlier comment about *Arduino*[25] and what Ian Forrester said earlier. I think that, unless there is a constitutional principle at the EU level, ultimately it is going to be the European court that gets to decide on proportionality. I do not have a problem with that, and with the fact that we—the national competition authorities—would have to be the ones to start this process, because I also think that y we are the best placed to know the facts of the matter and so forth. But until *Arduino* my biggest doubt was whether the proportionality test did apply. We had a very interesting case in Ireland where a group of professionals were collectively negotiating a price with government. The government wanted to competition authority to take up that case, because it preferred us to address it legally, than them having to tackle it politically. As soon as we had the case ready to go to court, *Arduino* appeared, and suddenly the Irish ministry in question consented to the price-fixing with this profession. I am not sure that the Irish courts, which are still relatively new to the EC competition law area, would handle as the competition authority desires a case involving Article 81 EC combined with Article 10 EC on the background of *Arduino*. But then again, the Italian antitrust authority has been much more successful in this area.

▸ GIULIANO AMATO

It is indeed a difficult issue, but the case is not entirely lost, because the proportionality principle is now entering in the European Constitution—obviously, to be applied to EU legislation, and not to national legislation, and there is also the problem of deference. But for several of our national courts the proportionality principle is anyway an ordinary instrument of interpretation of the law when it comes to fundamental rights, and it can somehow be extended. In Italy, for example, the proportionality principle is considered by the Constitutional Court incidental to the equality principle, and the equality principle applies to any field of legislation where a differentiation might be created by law between subjects A and B. If the proportionality principle is not respected, these differences might be considered a constitutional violation.

[25] See above n 15.

PANEL THREE

ECONOMIC ASPECTS
2

WORKING PAPERS

I

*Lowri Evans, Maija Laurila and Ruth Paserman**

Professional Services: Recent EU Developments and Work in Progress

On 9 February 2004 the Commission adopted a Report on competition in professional services.[1] The main purpose of this Report is to set out the Commission's thinking on the scope to reform or modernise specific professional rules. It identifies existing restrictions by profession and by Member State.

The Commission Report invites all involved to make a joint effort to reform or eliminate those rules which are unjustified. Regulatory authorities in the Member States and professional bodies are invited to review existing rules taking into consideration whether those rules pursue a clearly articulated and legitimate public interest objective, and whether there are no less restrictive means to achieve this. The Report also expressed the Commission's intention to continue to monitor consumers' opinions on the advantages and disadvantages of this type of regulation.

The Report notes that experience of past modernisation efforts in the field of professional services in some Member States shows that a simple elimination of anti-competitive mechanisms may not be enough to bring about more competition to this sector. Consequently both regulatory authorities and professional bodies should explore the need to use pro-competitive accompanying mechanisms which increase transparency and enhance consumer empowerment. Such mechanisms could include, for instance, active monitoring by consumer associations, collection and publication of survey based historical data or public announcements of the abolition of tariffs. The Commission intends to investigate the impact of different alternatives where they have been implemented and it will explore with consumer organisations at European level how to define best practice.

From an enforcement perspective it is clear that since May 2004 the national competition authorities and the national courts have a more prominent role to play in assessing the legality of rules and regulations in the professions. To the extent that competition restrictions have their centre of gravity in one Member State, administrative enforcement of the EC competition rules in the liberal professions will then mainly be the task of the relevant

* DG Competition, European Commission.

[1] European Commission '*Report on Competition in the Professional Services*' COM (2004) 83 final, available at www.europa.eu.int/comm/competition/liberal_professions/final_comm_en.pdf.

National Competition Authority. The Commission will continue to carry out casework where appropriate. A coherent application of Articles 81 and 82 EC will be guaranteed through co-ordination and cooperation within in the European Competition Network of national competition authorities.

In this paper, we summarise what the Commission has been doing in this field since the adoption of the Report, and present some ideas from the ongoing work. This is still very much work in progress. Nonetheless, it is useful to see where a more in depth debate is leading us. This will also be put in the framework of the new cooperation between the Commission and the National Competition Authorities following the modernization of EC antitrust enforcement rules. (ie, the entry into force in May 2004 of Council Regulation 1/2003[2]).

Since 1 May 2004, we are of course working in an EU of 25 Member States. There is analytical work underway covering the 10 new Member States, and we are working towards making some preliminary comparative material available in this respect in the next few months.

II. Discussions with Professional Bodies

DG Competition has invited the European level professional bodies of lawyers, notaries, accountants, tax consultants, architects and pharmacists to bilateral meetings to discuss the public interest justification of existing professional rules. The goal of these meetings is for the Commission to clarify to what extent restrictions it finds excessive in principle should be eliminated or changed. To this effect, European professional bodies are strongly encouraged to advocate change or, failing that, put forward in writing the justifications for not doing so. In particular the European professional bodies are asked to relay the Commission's concerns to the relevant national professional organisations.

There is an open door for professional organisations that want to discuss directly with the Commission services; these meetings are interesting, and undoubtedly are also leading to our developing a better understanding of the workings of the different markets for professional services.

Most European level professional bodies have issued a European level code of conduct. In some cases it serves the purpose of screening prospective member organisations; in others it is to be applied when a professional offers its services across borders. The rules identified in these codes of conduct could be argued to represent the core of the profession, those deontological values without which the profession cannot survive as such. Or, in the words of the ECJ in the *Wouters* judgment[3]: they could represent one view of what is

[2] Council Regulation (EC) No 1/2003 of 16 December 2002 on the implementation of the rules on competition laid down in Articles 81 and 82 of the Treaty, OJ L 1 [2003] 1–25.

[3] Case C–309/99 *Wouters* [2002] ECR I–1577, para 110.

'necessary for the proper practice of the profession'. Other rules, on top of the ones contained in these European-level codes—the results of weighing of different arguments put on the table by different national organisations—perhaps either do not have common support, or do not meet some sort of common general objective. It would be interesting to scrutinise the 'extra' rules that are defined at national level to identify more precisely what the different national market context that is being addressed would be.

III. Understanding Consumer Requests

In trying to understand the view and needs of consumers, the Commission has started to talk to consumer associations specifically about the liberal professions sector. We have also seen some surveys carried out by various consumer organisations across Europe. These concern: the legal profession in Scotland; lawyers in Italy and Belgium; notaries in Italy, Belgium and Spain; pharmacies in Spain, Scotland and Germany; real estate agents in Scotland and Belgium. From this small sample, the following points emerge:

1. From the point of view of the consumer, what consumers care about is the quality of the service provided by the professional. In this respect, whether a profession is regulated or not is not an issue; consumers are as concerned to get good quality and good-value services from a plumber as from a lawyer. Of course, some problems may occur more in regulated professions (for example, no possibility to negotiate the price), but others happen more for unregulated ones (for example, the unscrupulous provider). Going to a professional does not automatically guarantee quality of the service, in particular where a particular service can only be provided by professionals to whom compulsory membership applies. Overall, professional services cannot be seen as a dichotomy between those needing regulation and those that do not. It is rather a continuum, and within this continuum it could be that some professions are regulated less than what would be optimal.
2. There is indeed an asymmetry of information which makes it difficult for the consumer to choose the suitable professional: the consumer does not have the instruments to know *ex ante* the competencies, experience and professionalism of a professional. However this difficulty is increased by prohibitions or restrictions to advertising, even simply informative, by professionals.
3. A problem which particularly worries consumers is the responsibility of the professional and what happens in case of conflict. The high level of complexity of professional services implies an objective difficulty by the consumer to evaluate the correctness, usefulness and quality of the service.

This problem is exacerbated by the fact that a professional has an obligation of means, not of result. Moreover it is very difficult for a consumer to collect 'proof' of negligence, or mistakes of a professional *ex post*, proof that often requires the cooperation of other professionals who are linked to the negligent professional by a 'solidarity pact', often imposed by the deontological rules. In this area the consumer organisations believe that the role of compulsory professional insurance should be looked at from a perspective of helping protect both the professional and the consumer.

4. Consumers want some information on the costs of the professional service *ex ante*, at the moment of giving the mandate, and lament the lack of its availability. They similarly complain about bills that are seen as excessive or disproportionate to the amount of work done, and in any case independent of the result achieved. In some cases customers would like to know exactly how much they will have to pay in advance. The justification of a fixed price is often 'so that the consumer knows how much he will have to pay'. So, although Competition authorities do not accept this justification, it has to be said that some consumers would prefer to have a reference price as information. However, of course, even fixed tariffs may fail to give this certainty. For example, when customers pay an architect a percentage of the cost of the works, they have an estimate *ex ante* of the cost, but which can easily be surpassed. When customers pay a lawyer a fixed amount by act that is carried out, and not for the overall procedure, they do not know before the amount they will pay.

IV. A New Context: the European Competition Network

Applying the same substantive antitrust rules is the best basis for fostering a common culture in the application of competition policy, and this condition is met in the EU since 1 May 2004.

Also underpinning the modernized EC antitrust enforcement rules, as laid down in Council Regulation 1/2003, is the understanding that a common culture does not emerge if the different enforcers remain isolated in their respective authorities. Cooperation, mutual information and consultation between the competent authorities are therefore essential in the new system in the European Union of 25 Member States.

It was in order to further develop effective cooperation and coordination between the competition authorities that the European Competition Network, also known as the ECN, was founded. This Network operates since October 2002, and continues to develop. It is a very positive development, and its work already shows that all network members—including the Commission—are committed to cooperate and keen to develop further coordination between themselves. In particular, there is tangible team spirit, characterised by flexibility and willingness for formal and informal exchanges in this process. This is beyond what we imagined possible initially, and presumably a strong indicator as to good functioning of the new enforcement system. One example of intensive cooperation between the network members for the common good was the drafting of the *Notice on cooperation within the network.*[4]

The network can certainly be 'exploited' in many ways by its members, ranging from direct assistance in case handling to discussions on legal, economic and policy issues. The Commission is keen to set a good example in feeding material to the network in different fields, and other national competition authorities are also very proactive.

As far as case handling is concerned, of course there has always been a degree of cooperation between the Commission and the Member States' competition authorities. However, in the system of Regulation 17/62, applicable until 30 April 2004, in principle the main flow of information was from the Commission to the national competition authorities. The Commission consulted the national competition authorities on its cases, and national enforcers had the opportunity to advise—collectively—through the Advisory Committee. Regulation 1/2003 turned this consultation process into a real two-way street: the Member States' competition authorities now also inform the Commission about the cases they investigate (Article 11(3) of Regulation 1/2003) and of the decisions they envisage to adopt in order to put an end to competition infringements (Article 11(4) of Regulation 1/2003). The Regulation expressly provides for the involvement of the other national competition authorities in the overall context of close co-operation as provided for in Article 11(1) of the new Regulation. It also establishes new powers for the Member States' competition authorities that are aimed at enhancing their cooperation between each other. In particular, at the request of one network member, a case dealt with by a Member State competition authority can be put on the agenda of the Advisory Committee for a discussion. Moreover, all network members have also committed themselves to making easily accessible to all other members the information exchanged under Article 11 of regulation 1/2003. In practice this means information to the network on the important steps in a case, notably the opening of an investigation, the envisaged decisions and the closed cases. In addition, the Regulation also provides a basis for an exchange of documents to be used in evidence (Article 12) and for other mechanisms of assistance in fact-finding, including even inspections on behalf of another authority.

The ultimate structure of the ECN network will no longer in graphic terms be that of a star of two-way streets, but rather that of a multi-dimensional

---

[4] Commission Notice on cooperation within the Network of Competition Authorities OJ C 101 [2004] 43–53.

web, with the Commission and all national competition authorities involved in the overall context of close cooperation.

This probably means that formalised means of exchange like committee meetings will be the tip of the iceberg. Close cooperation will involve all layers of the respective authorities, from—the most important—bilateral to multilateral cooperation at case-handler level to the meetings of the Directors General. Discussions will range from plenary meetings on horizontal issues of common interest in effect leading to general policy orientations, to issues specific to a particular sector of the economy, for example professional services.

The new web-like structure of the ECN—and the tools devised to facilitate its exploitation including the secure electronic communication channels—allows all Network members to know what the others are doing and to get inspiration from the best of the others' initiatives. It is now set up as a real system for discussing not only who should do what, but also what should be done. The network can raise awareness of problems identified in one country (or countries) and constitutes a forum to share views as whether markets are working as well as they might be, and whether identified problems should be an enforcement priority.

V. A Coordinated Approach in Liberal Professions

In a sectoral context, and as a good general example, already in 2002 the Commission invited the Member States' and accession countries' competition authorities, the EFTA Surveillance Authority and also some regulatory authorities to informal discussions to discuss the impact of the *Arduino*[5] and *Wouters*[6] judgments in this sector. In effect, this meeting kicked off a specific sectoral component to the Network. In 2003, during and after the stocktaking exercise in the professional services sector the Commission co-operated closely with other competition authorities. Regulation of professional services was discussed in the meetings between the Directors General of National Competition Authorities on 18 June and 19 November 2003, confirming the general interest in pursuing work in this sector. A deeper discussion was then held with the sectoral experts from National Competition Authorities in November 2003 to discuss a common approach in this field. These discussions greatly contributed to the preparation of the Commission's Report, allowing the Commission to better understand the national specificities of many existing regulations. The Report therefore highlighted

[5] Case C–35/99 *Arduino* [2002] ECR I–1529.
[6] Case C–309/99 *Wouters* [2002] ECR I–1577.

the need to assess the rules in their proper context, and taking into account other regulation applying to the same economic operators, while also confirming that the guiding principles should be the same in all markets.

It is clear that the rules and regulations that most restrict competition in this sector have a national focus. They are put in place by the national regulator, legislator or other, and they apply within the boundaries of the national territory. As they generally also apply to foreign service providers and as they generally cover the whole territory of the Member State, they generally have at least a potential appreciable effect on trade between Member States. Thus Articles 81 and 82 EC are generally applicable to them.

For future cases, this means, in the ECN logic, that the competition authority of the Member State where the regulation applies is normally 'well placed' to deal with the case if one needs to be opened. The suspected infringement normally has a substantial link to its territory and the authority has ways to investigate it. Many Member States have already brought cases forward in this sector in the past, under national competition law, so this will not be new territory for most national authorities.

There may sometimes be difficulties for a national authority to bring effectively to an end the infringement, which is also one of the criteria of case allocation as stated in the Commission's Notice on the functioning of the network,[7] in particular if the public authorities endorse the restriction. This is where the discussion on the CIF[8] jurisprudence enters into play. It is discussed in other papers presented in this forum. In its recent *Consorzio Industrie Fiammiferi* (CIF) judgment the European Court of Justice decided that where undertakings engage in conduct contrary to Article 81(1) EC and where that conduct is required or facilitated by State measures which themselves infringe Articles 3(1)(g), 10(2), and 81/82 EC, a national competition authority has a duty to disapply those State measures and give effect to Article 81 EC. The ways to 'disapply' national law and their effectiveness remain to be seen in practice, and this is also something on which the ECN has already once exchanged views and can usefully do it again.

In any event, it is not excluded that the Commission takes up a case with a national focus if an important issue of competition policy is concerned, even if the national authority has the means to bring effectively to an end the infringement. This is the common understanding of the Member States and the Commission. According to the Joint Statement of the Council and the Commission on the Functioning of the Network of Competition Authorities,[9] the Commission will be particularly well placed to deal with a case if [. . .] Community interest requires the adoption of a Commission

[7] See above n 4.

[8] Case C–198/01 *Consorzio Industrie Fiammiferi* (CIF) [2003] ECR I–8055.

[9] Statement entered in the Council Minutes, 15435/02, ADD 1, available from http://register.consilium.eu.int/pdf/en/02/st15/15435–a1en2.pdf.

decision to develop Community competition policy particularly when a new competition issue arises or to ensure effective enforcement (point 19). Moreover, the Commission can take over a case which is being dealt with by one or several competition authority(-ies) which is (are) well placed to do so if [. . .] there is a need to adopt a Commission decision to develop Community competition policy in particular when a similar competition issue arises in several Member States (point 21, item d).

This means that the enforcement action can be on the part of the Commission or of the authority of the Member State where the restriction applies. If more than one authority considers a particular case as among its priorities, a discussion between them to agree on work-sharing or work allocation is in effect about the most efficient way to proceed.

In this context the recent procedure against the recommended prices for Belgian architects is worth mentioning, although this procedure was started before the coming into force of Regulation 1/2003. Even under Regulation 1/2003 the Commission would have proceeded with this case, because for various reasons the Belgian competition authority could not bring it forward. The case at hand tackled a new area and it makes sense that the Commission gives guidance in the absence of a realistic alternative. In this case, the Commission also for the first time in this sector imposed a larger-than-symbolic fine.[10]

The ECN—or its liberal professions sub-group—has not formulated any conclusions with respect to any future enforcement action in the field of professional services. At this stage, the network members have started to share views on the economic effects of different regulatory choices. The network has also started to reflect on the scope of possible intervention in case of potentially restrictive and unjustified rules. It has agreed to exchange the results of studies conducted or commissioned, the findings made public with respect to particular regulatory choices and so on.

This cooperation allows the network members to develop a coordinated stance with respect to appropriate publicity throughout the EU to important policy decisions. It seems indeed important in this sector to consider how decisions that remove restrictions taken by national enforcers could get adequate attention and contribute to the precedent value in the eyes of the market players across the EU.

---

[10] See the press release on http://europa.eu.int/rapid/pressReleasesAction.do?reference=IP/04/800&format=HTML and aged=0&language=EN and guiLanguage=en.

VI. Managing Change in this Sector

Our contacts with national competition authorities and national regulators have also brought to our attention the importance of changing the regulatory framework with due caution. There are many success stories of deregulation and re-regulation, but there is also some evidence that not all changes have produced optimal or entirely predicted results. Two examples are particularly instructive: the liberalisation in Denmark in the 1990s, and the deregulation of notaries in the Netherlands.

In Denmark, over the period 1992–97 the competition authorities removed a number of regulations that restricted competition in liberal professions, mainly recommended prices and advertising restrictions. As a consequence, liberal professions in Denmark are regulated to a lesser extent than in most of the other member states in EU.

However the result of a study from the Danish Competition Authority, reported in the authority's *Annual Report 2004*[11] is that in many liberal professions there is insufficient competition. The Authority concludes that competition problems exist where new players in the market have not challenged the existing structure of supply. In these situations there is customised practice, involving limited competition and limited development of new products. Problems also exist where consumers have difficulties in estimating or understanding the services and prices offered and therefore lack the power to provide competition pressure on suppliers. Conversely, access for new players with innovative concepts has led to greater competition, more than action on prices.

The general conclusion in the study is that the following measures will increase competition in most liberal professions without harming other public goals:

> Measures to increase information to consumers about content in the services from professionals and measures to increase consumer transparency about prices.
>
> Simplification of existing rules for contents and procedures for liberal services allowing more freedom for consumers to choose among services from different types of suppliers or to do part of the work themselves.
>
> Changes in existing regulations to make it easier for other professionals with new and alternative concepts to enter the market. An example for this concerns the real estate market. There is a Danish law which restricts the possibility to own and manage a real estate company.[12] The study shows that there is a need for new suppliers and alternative products in the real estate market in which the traditional real estate

---

[11] Konkurrenceredegørelse 2004, Konkurrencestyrelsen, available from http://www.ks.dk/publikationer/konkurrenceredegoerelsen/kr2004/.

[12] Note that some of the services offered by estate agents in Denmark are carried out by notaries in other countries.

brokers do not face much competition and in which their services are mostly based on standardised concepts. The study recommends that there should be a change in the national legislation which should make it easier for new suppliers to enter the market.

The Netherlands deregulated notaries in 1999,[13] in particular by gradually eliminating fixed fees except for some family related deeds (maximum prices were set to protect low income families) and by introducing some freedom to establishment (a notary can now be appointed at any place he or she wants to establish himself/herself, as long as the business plan has been approved) and some freedom to provide services in other districts to the one of establishment. Moreover, the rules relating to rules of conduct, professional training, duties of the notary and the notary candidate during internship have been eliminated from legislation and passed on self-regulation.

The results have been mixed. On one hand, there is much more information available on what notaries do, where to find them, even comparisons of tariffs available on the internet. According to the *Commissie Monitoring Notariaat*[14] the deregulation has mostly been a success. The quality, continuity and accessibility of notary services have not been endangered during the evaluation period. However, the fees of notary services have increased since 1999. Especially in the family practice they have increased considerably: 40% for marriage contracts (average price now €758), 27% for partnership contracts (on average now €353) and 69% for wills (€245). On average, fees in the family practice have increased by 12%. In real estate there has been a decrease of up to 50% in the notary fees in the top segment (ie, expensive houses) and a slight decrease in the middle segment, while in the low segment (houses of €133,445 until €245,000) there has been a slight increase. There appears to be a rather big difference between private consumers and professional clients such as municipalities and building corporations. The latter have been capable of demanding discounts ranging from 10 to 25%. One-off consumers do not get such discounts.

The *Commissie Monitoring Notariaat* argues that the cause for the increase in notary fees is a result of several factors: low price elasticity in this sector, too little countervailing power from the side of consumers and the fact that there is still too little competition between notaries.

This is therefore an example of trade-offs between repeat customers, and one-off customer, and also showing the different bargaining power of larger customers compared to smaller customers. It shows the importance of understanding in advance what different markets are affected by change, and how the change will affect different groups in different ways.

---

13 Wet op het notarisambt.

14 According to Art 128 of the *Wet op het notarisambt,* this Commission had the task of evaluating the effects of the new law during a transition period of three years (until 31 March 2003). The final report can be found at http://www.justitie.nl/Images/11_21107.pdf.

These two examples point to the difficulty of achieving more competition in this sector, even with regulatory change. There are also other examples of changes in regulation in other countries, some of which have been brought to our attention in the discussions with the professional bodies or the national competition authorities. The Commission will analyse in greater detail and discuss within the ECN.

VII. Issues for further Reflection

We are at the first step of a process. On one hand, as the previous section suggests, the current activity has made us wary of regulatory change for its own sake, and conscious of the need to understand the markets concerned by potential change. On the other hand, further open issues have emerged.

From our conversations with professional bodies and regulators, some general, little debated issues are emerging which need very serious further reflection. For example, it has been brought to our attention that perhaps the root of all lack of competition lies in the exclusivities. The elimination of most exclusive rights would bring competition to the market without need of action on other rules.

One radical hypothesis has been that removing compulsory membership of professional associations would solve many competition problems. The line of thought is this: professional associations with compulsory membership have a double role: they are entrusted with a public goal; however they also act as a trade union defending the interests of their members. Where membership is not compulsory, membership of a particular association is a signal, a quality label for the consumer; without compulsion, it is argued that professional associations would have to work hard to maintain their members and their clients and would therefore have an incentive to maintain high quality, more than is the case now.

More in general, some abusive practices which take advantage of the existing legislation have been brought to our attention. It is clear that the more restrictions apply to a profession (whether concerning access or behaviour) the more margin there is for behaviour to circumvent the rules or to bend them to their advantage. This is the case for every regulation, and the solution is generally to simplify the regulation, so that the margins for circumvention are reduced. This argues for a careful re-regulation around basic clear principles rather than tweaking the existing regulatory regimes.

Another issue is self regulation. Arguably, self-regulation is not adapted to the modern world. The origin of self-regulation lies in the Middle Ages. The professions were 'free' to self-regulate, and not be subject to the erratic authority of the prince. This impediment is no longer demonstrable. In a democracy, it is not necessarily justified that some groups can be 'free' of the control of democratically elected Parliaments. If a group has a role in pursuing the general interest, then such a general interest should be specified and monitored by a public authority and not by a self-regulating body. It could be imagined that such a public authority is independent, like the authorities monitoring telecommunications or financial services, or it could be imagined that more explicit 'co-regulation' models could be developed. The point here is that in a mature democracy there could be a need to separate clearly the public role from the influence of peers.

No one denies that the liberal professions have a public role to play. For example, the meeting with the European notaries professional body has alerted us to the importance of a 'preventive system of justice', ie, the existence of notaries and the certainty/authenticity of the acts can help prevent conflicts and disputes liable to lead to litigation. It is noticeable that all the former communist countries have adopted the system of a notary public. It also seems that the price fixing which occurs in this profession in most Member States does indeed represent an implicit transfer of resources, or trade-off between groups, of the kind which has become apparent after the liberalisation in the Netherlands: real estate transactions subsidise family law transactions. This may be an acceptable public goal: however, there do not appear *prima facie* reasons why it should not be made transparent. Certainly today the customer is not aware of this cross-subsidisation. It would be helpful, democratic even, if these justifications were made explicit, also because it would help to focus on whether they are truly justified and whether they are not simply a transfer of rent—extra profits—to the professional from the customer.

II

*Allan Fels**

The Australian Experience Concerning Law and the Professions

> It is not the fault of our doctors that the medical service of the community, as at present provided for, is a murderous absurdity. That any sane nation, having observed that you could provide for the supply of bread by giving bakers a pecuniary interest in baking for you, should go on to give a surgeon a pecuniary interest in cutting off your leg, is enough to make one despair of political humanity.
>
> And the more appalling the mutilation, the more the mutilator is paid. Scandalised voices murmur that operations are necessary. They may be. It may be necessary to hang a man or pull down a house. But we take good care not to make the hangman and the house breaker the judges of that. If we did, no neck would be safe and no man's house stable.
>
> George Bernard Shaw, 'The Doctors Dilemma' (1911).

I. Introduction

George Bernard Shaw has drawn attention to how the medical profession's role may differ from that of many other providers of goods and services in the economy. Are the professions different? Should they be dealt with under competition law at all? And, if so, should they be treated differently?

This paper briefly reviews the rationale for the regulation of the professions and notes the various forms which that regulation takes and how it can often have anticompetitive effects.

From a competition perspective regulation affecting the professions can be analysed from the following perspectives:

- the creation of a monopoly by the exclusive reservation of work and activity to the profession. Associated with that there may be a further division of work by the exclusive reservation of work to certain categories of that profession, eg, cosmetic surgery to be done only 'cosmetic surgeons';

* Dean, Australia and New Zealand School of Government.

- the establishment of restrictions on entry to a profession by a licensing or accreditation arrangement or by restrictions on entry by a foreigner or by a person from another region in that country;
- the imposition of restrictions on behaviour eg, regarding prices or advertising or ethics;
- there may also be particular forms of anticompetitive conduct eg, price-fixing agreements, collective boycotts etc which are in clear breach of the competition laws of the country. In some countries these forms of behaviour may be exempt from the competition law.

Against that background, the paper considers Australia's experience of the application of competition law and policy to the professions. Competition law was applied in full to the professions since 1995 and has been vigorously applied to the medical, legal and other professions, with injunctions, fines, and damages and other orders being obtained particularly in relation to price-fixing and collective boycotts. A further very important development was the Australian Competition and Consumer Commission's actions to break open the 'closed shop' arrangements of surgeons which restricted entry to their profession in an anticompetitive manner. The paper also refers in brief to the considerable, although not complete, progress in removing laws and regulations that restrict competition in the professions. It also briefly discusses a successful scheme of mutual recognition of professions between the states and territories of Australia and also between Australia and New Zealand.

II. The Regulation of the Professions

The term 'professions' embraces a wide range of services in the modern economy including: accounting, architecture, legal, medical, paramedical, engineering, perhaps estate agents and other categories which shade into skilled occupations such as electricians, plumbers, and many others.

The professions account for a significant and growing share of the production of goods and services in the modern economy. Basically professional services are provided by market means and governed by the forces of supply and demand. But in most countries they are heavily regulated with substantial direct effects on competition. Moreover, the system of regulation itself can be conducive to private anticompetitive behaviour by the professions eg, if entry to a profession is restricted, it may make cartel behaviour worthwhile.

Is there an economic rationale for regulation of the professions? There are some potentially legitimate rationales for regulating individual market transactions in the professions. The chief rationale concerns the information limitations faced by consumers (whether household or business consumers) in purchasing and using professional services. There is a high degree of imbalance between the amount of information which a professional has about his/her services and the information which the consumer has. Most services are by their nature complex and often require considerable skill to tailor to the needs of the user. It is therefore difficult for the consumer to assess the quality of the service before or even after it is purchased. For example, if a person engages a lawyer to undertake litigation, which is ultimately unsuccessful, it can be difficult for the consumer to know whether the legal services were poorly delivered or that the case was inherently difficult to win. These problems are compounded by the fact that many consumers are very infrequent consumers of professional services and therefore do not have repeat purchases to assess quality. Moreover, the consequences of purchasing poor professional services can be very significant. The service may represent a large expenditure for the consumer. Also a defective service (eg, a faulty operation) can risk serious and irreversible harm: where there are questions of safety, governments will often intervene to protect consumers even in the consumers are fully aware of the risks. Finally, the legal protections available for poor quality service are often unavailable in practice because of the difficulties, costs and delays of litigation and in many cases legal protections cannot reverse the original harm (eg, damage to health as a result of faulty medical treatment).[1]

The case for regulation is bolstered in practice by the character of the regulation of professional services itself which further limits choice and may inhibit the development of some market mechanisms discussed below which would otherwise address some of the problems adverted to above. Hence there seems to be a *prima facie* case for some regulation of the professions.

However, before concluding that the case for professional regulation is fully justified it would be necessary to consider whether the market deficiencies above could be at least partly overcome by corrective market mechanisms. For example, when there are problems concerning a deficiency of information in a market some mechanisms spring in to being that help overcome them, eg, information brokerage services; provision of published information that helps evaluate quality; low cost dispute settlement mechanisms where there are compensation issues etc.

In addition, the possibility that there may be regulatory failure needs to taken into account and weighed up against the possible benefits. In the case of the professions regulation often has a highly anticompetitive element and as a result a high cost for all consumers. In other cases they may not work well. It is often unclear that professional regulation would be warranted when these costs are taken into account. Milton Friedman, in his classic study *Capitalism and Freedom*,[2] concluded that the costs of regulating the medical

---

[1] A Fels, *et al,* 'Occupational Regulation' in G Amato and L Laudati, (eds), *The Anticompetitive Impact of Regulation* (London, Elgar, 2001) 104–15.

[2] M Friedman, *Capitalism and Freedom* (Chicago, University of Chicago Press, 1962).

profession greatly outweighed its benefits and argued for a completely deregulated market in medicine (other than that doctors be required to display their qualifications at their place of work).

So the tentative conclusion must be that there may well be a case for some regulation of some aspects of some of the professions to deal with the problem of information asymmetry but it could be outweighed by its costs. In particular there is a danger that even if some degree of regulation is justified in practice it may go too far or be of the wrong kind.

III. Forms of Regulation

There are a number of forms of regulation of professional markets. Most inhibit competition. They do so in two broad ways: through their effects on the structure of the relevant professional market; and on the market conduct of professional practitioners.

Structural regulation of professional markets include those forms of regulation which:

- Define and reserve a field of activity exclusively for licensed or certified or accredited professional practitioners eg, paid advocacy in the courts for lawyers; dentistry for dentists.
- Separate the market functionally into discrete professional activities (including those performed by accredited specialists such as insolvency practitioners in the field of accounting, barristers (as distinct from solicitors) in the field of advocacy, and the various classes of specialist practice in the medical profession (not to mention the separation of medical and paramedical activities).
- Impose restrictions on the ownership and organisation of professional practices eg, certain practices cannot be performed by corporations but only by sole practitioners or perhaps in some cases by partnerships.
- Regulate entry into the market. These entry restrictions can take a variety of forms:

  Registration requires practitioners to register to be able to provide a particular service. Requirements for registration can include appropriate educational qualifications and/or membership of professional bodies. In addition, candidates for registration may need to pass probity tests or satisfy the criteria to be a 'fit and proper' person. Registration schemes can be run by government agencies or by self-regulating industry bodies. In Australia registration schemes apply to regulate entry into a range of occupations such as law, accounting and health services.

Certification or accreditation is usually administered by a certification body responsible for keeping a 'list' of those practitioners who have reached a certain level of competency or meet other standards. These schemes are usually non-legislative and fostered by industry bodies. However, whereas certification indicates the achievement of a certain level of expertise or competency, a non-certified practitioner may also be able to provide similar services. For example, certified practising accountants (CPA) are distinguished from those accountants who have not completed the additional study required to become a CPA.

Licensing is similar to registration in the sense that the grant of a licence to practice an occupation is often dependent on formal qualifications, approved training periods, or general probity tests. However, licensing can restrict entry into an occupation and place restrictions on the range of activities that an individual can carry out. Licences can be issued by government agencies or by industry licensing boards. In Australia licences to practise have been traditionally associated with many occupations, including construction and manufacturing, engineering trades and agricultural industries as well as lawyers, accountants and other service professionals. For most occupations the license to practice has been valid only within the jurisdiction in which the license was granted. An additional license has been required to practice in another State or Territory but 'mutual recognition' policies are changing this.

Negative licensing is an approach where individuals are generally entitled to practice but can be prohibited from practising if they have committed some form of offence deemed serious enough to warrant exclusion from the industry. Negative licensing imposes lower barriers to entry than licensing.

Entry Restrictions and Performance Based Regulation. It is commonly stated that performance based regulation focused on outputs is generally to be preferred to prescriptive regulations which control inputs. This is because input controls tend to be more restrictive of innovation and competition. For example, it is usually better in environmental regulation to specify permissible levels of emissions rather than specify a particular technology (ie, an input) that must be used in a production process. The idea is that the performance based regulation allows firms to discover the best, or invent a better, means to achieve the emissions target which may not necessarily be the technology chosen by the regulator. In the case of professional regulation, entry barriers are more in the nature of input controls than performance based criteria. To the extent that this is justified, it should be because performance based criteria would not provide adequate protection to consumers due to a significant risk that unqualified persons would not be able to systematically provide services that would reach reasonable performance criteria and that the risk to consumers of sub standard service was very high.

Conduct regulations include those which: i) limit the fees which professionals may charge or require application of fees scale for particular professional services; ii) prohibit certain kinds of advertising, promotion or solicitation of business by professional practitioners; and iii) specify professional and ethical standards to be observed by, and disciplinary procedure to apply to, professional practitioners. In practice, the application and enforcement of these standards can be used with considerable anticompetitive effect, for example, instances where price cutting is concluded to be unethical.

There can be significant international dimensions to regulation of professions. For example, there may be restrictions on entry by foreign professionals such that they may not be recognised even though they are qualified practitioners in their home country or state. Also, in some case, foreign organisations may not be allowed to practise. This gives rise to an important policy agenda item—issues surrounding mutual recognition of qualifications obtained in one country (or area of a country) in another part of the world (or even in the same country).

IV. Australia

Prior to 1974 questions concerning the impact of the regulation of the professions on competition were largely ignored. When the Trade Practices Act was introduced in 1974 it had relatively little effect on the professions. This was because of the limited constitutional reach of the Commonwealth (or national) government. The Trade Practices Act initially only applied to corporations or persons engaged in interstate trade or commerce. Moreover, some national or local laws that authorised anticompetitive conduct also overrode the provisions of the Trade Practices Act. Hence the initial impact of the Act on the professions was quite minor.

In 1988–89 the Trade Practices Commission announced that it would conduct a research study of the impact on competition of professional regulation in Australia.

The TPC produced in December 1990 a discussion paper on *'Regulation of professional markets in Australia: issues for review'*. The discussion paper contained the following observation:

> In Australia the professions are subject to a diversity of government and self-regulation arrangements which vary considerably between individual professions. In many cases, the regulatory arrangements for particular professions vary between the individual States and Territories.

> The traditional justification for regulation of the professions has been the protection of consumers through measures to maintain the quality of services and the competence and integrity of their providers. It is being recognised increasingly, however, that such regulation is not without cost to consumers and the community. To the extent that it restricts competition, the service choices available to consumers may be limited, the incentive to innovate and contain costs may be reduced and prices may be inflated as a result.
>
> From the community's perspective, as well as that of the professions themselves, it is therefore important to be able to identify both the benefits and the costs of existing regulatory measures and to assess, as far as possible, for individual professions whether those regulations provide net benefits for consumers after taking account *of any costs resulting from restrictions on competition.*[3]

Subsequently, the TPC conducted studies and issued final reports on the accountancy profession in July 1992; the architects in September 1992; and the legal profession in March 1994. A snapshot of the TPC's views is as follows:

Regarding Accountancy:

> The accountancy profession in Australia is not subject to the same degree of regulation as other professions. This report concludes that, on the whole, regulation of the accountancy profession does not overly impede competitive activity within the various markets in which accountants operate. Nevertheless, a number of areas raise the concern that the effects on competition of some of the present regulatory arrangements go beyond that necessary to serve the public interest.[4]

Regarding Architecture:

> The market for building design services is generally competitive. It appears that in recent years the share of the market traditionally serviced by architects has been eroded through competition from other service providers. The competitive nature of the market has been particularly evident under the current economic conditions that have severely depressed building activity.
>
> The Commission concludes that the architectural profession's regulatory arrangements do not generally inhibit competitive activity in the market for building design services. In the light of the issues raised during the Commission's study a number of changes to current regulatory arrangements have been proposed by some State and Territory architects boards and by the RAIA. The Commission welcomes these proposed changes. It considers they will reduce the anticompetitive potential of those regulations, without having any adverse effects on the interests of consumers of architectural services.
>
> The RAIA's regulations were considered by the Commission during its authorisation of these arrangements in 1984 when the Institute amended its rules to lessen or remove their anticompetitive effect. The Commission does not consider the

[3] Regulation of professional markets in Australia: Issues for review—A discussion paper.

[4] Trade Practices Commission, Study of the professions—Final Report—July 1982: Accountancy, p 2.

RAIA's current self-regulatory arrangements are anti-competitive and it does not propose to review the authorisation granted in 1984 at this time.[5]

Regarding Law:

The Australian legal profession is heavily over-regulated and in urgent need of comprehensive reform. It is highly regulated compared to other sectors of the economy and those regulations combine to impose substantial restrictions on the commercial conduct of lawyers and on the extent to which lawyers are free to compete with each other for business. As a result, the current regulatory regime has adverse effects on the cost and efficiency of legal services and their prices to business and final consumers.

The legal profession plays an important role in the provision of justice for the Australian community under the law and it also has an important part to play in the day-to-day operations of business and in the affairs of households and individuals. The services of legal practitioners make an important contribution to the lives of ordinary Australians, for example, in the areas of housing, finance, personal injury, wills and probate and family law. Legal services also contribute to the establishment and expansion of businesses and to transactions between businesses and with their customers. The cost and efficiency of legal services therefore have a direct impact on the efficiency of business and the living standards of many consumers.

Reform of the extensive system of regulation applied to the legal profession is an important part of the agenda for micro-economic reform and the development of a national approach to competition policy. Inefficiencies in the provision of legal services will be passed on as costs incurred by downstream users including businesses exposed to international competition and final consumers. Thus, reforms which are focused on increasing competition and efficiency will have positive ramifications for users of legal services and for the economy as a whole.[6]

And

The Commission has examined the public interest arguments advanced in support of regulations which constrain the commercial behaviour of the legal profession against the public costs they impose by inhibiting competition and efficient service provision and has reached the overall conclusion that many of the regulations cannot be justified on public interest grounds. It therefore recommends comprehensive reform of those regulatory arrangements in each Australian State and Territory with the objective of exposing legal practitioners to more effective competition and of obliging them in that way to provide more efficient and competitively priced services to the business sector and the Australian public.

The regulations applied to the legal profession go far beyond the regulatory arrangements applied to any other sector of business, and to most other professions. The Commission considers that, by inhibiting market forces and competitive pressures and by discouraging innovation, the regulatory arrangements applied to the profession contribute to inefficiency in the organisation of legal practice and in

[5] Trade Practices Commission, Study of the Professions—Final Report of September 1992: Architects, (2002) p ix.

[6] Trade Practices Commission, Study of the Professions—Final Report of March 1994: Legal, (2004) p 3.

> the delivery of services. These inefficiencies will be reflected in the costing and pricing of legal services.
>
> The Commission has not been persuaded that these rules and regulations result in benefits to the public which more than offset the costs imposed by their anti-competitive effects. There are sound public interest reasons for ensuring that lawyers practice according to high professional and ethical standards and contribute to the maintenance of a judicial and legal system of high standing. The Commission considers, however, that those public interest objectives should be pursued directly through ethical and professional rules and disciplinary arrangements, rather than by imposing restrictions on the normal commercial and market behaviour of lawyers.[7]

Each of the above reports contained recommendations for detailed changes in professional regulation. In particular, the report on the legal profession made very detailed proposals for change. These included:

- The Trade Practices Act should apply in full to the legal profession. Any anti-competitive regulations concerning the legal profession should be repealed.
- The Commonwealth Government should take the necessary action within its own jurisdiction to implement pro-competitive reforms.
- All states and territories should automatically recognise lawyers accredited in other jurisdictions in Australia.
- All governments should open up the supply of legal services to appropriate qualified non-lawyers to the maximum extent that is consistent with the public interest and there should be no necessary presumption that any area of legal work should be reserved to lawyers without scrutiny.
- There should be mechanisms to determine what work needed to be reserved for lawyers.
- An appropriate body should work on issues about the reservation of legal work for lawyers; appropriate standards of education, training and accreditation for lawyers and non-lawyers providing legal services.
- The need for any additional consumer safeguards for accredited non-lawyers.
- Reform of regulations that limit competition.
- The artificial separation of different parts of the profession eg, between solicitors and barristers should be removed.
- Any practices of the legal profession (eg, Bar rules) that provide for a division of the profession into separate branches should be stopped.
- To the extent that specialist accreditation schemes have merit, as they often do, they could be promoted providing they are were not used to restrict entry into specialist areas and providing unaccredited specialists have the freedom to practice and advertise in specialty areas as long as this is not misleading nor deceptive. Various safeguards were called for here.

---

[7] *Ibid*, pp 6–7.

- Rules which impose restrictions on the ownership and organisation of legal practices should be removed or reformed to allow lawyers the freedom to choose the most efficient business and management arrangements. Further detailed recommendations were made about multi-disciplinary practices and corporation franchising, as well as the sole practitioner rule of the Bar.
- Restrictions on barrister, solicitors and non-lawyers combining their services should be removed.
- Subject to adequate freeing up of entry, the fees scales should be removed as they were seen to have adverse effects on competition and efficiency. They should be replaced by methods involving publication of market information about fees and a number of other devices to make the market better informed.
- There should be improved fee taxation.
- Any professional rules prohibiting discounting below fee scales to be dropped.

The reports and recommendations were influential. Many, but not all, of the recommendations have been implemented

The Trade Practices Commission (later merged into the Australian Competition and Consumer Commission) did not do any report on the medical profession. This was partly because it was thought better to devote resources to enforcing the law in the medical profession. Also, many of the general issues were almost inseparably linked with much broader questions concerning health policy and the health system.

V. Reform since the 1990s

During the 1990s a number of major reforms were made to Australian competition policy. In 1991 the Commonwealth, State and Territory governments agreed that anticompetitive behaviour was unacceptable in all areas of business unless it could be demonstrated publicly and independently to be in the public interest. They also decided that the scope of competition policy should extend from the prohibition of anticompetitive behaviour by businesses to the review of all laws and regulations that restricted competition to determine if they were in the public interest, and if they were in the public interest whether the public interest objectives could be achieved in less anticompetitive manner.

An independent committee of inquiry chaired by Professor Fred Hilmer reported on the implementation of these principles in August 1993. It cited a 1990 Trade Practices Commission discussion paper to the effect that data for 1987–88 suggested that five occupational groups alone—lawyers, accountants, engineers, architects and real estate agents—accounted for nearly 2% of

Australia's GDP. It observed that: 'The professions clearly comprise an important sector of the economy, and their services are a significant cost to many businesses which compete internationally.'[8]

This number would be much higher if the medical profession were added.

The report also observed that the principal reason for the partial exclusion of the professions from the Act was a constitutional limit unrelated to the status of the professions. It noted that the scope of the exemption depended largely on the legal form of business which varies widely across professions.

'The overall result is patchy and difficult to justify on public policy grounds.'[9]

The first important reform under the National Competition Policy was the extension of the Trade Practices Act to apply universally to all forms of business activity undertaken in Australia. Accordingly, for the first time the Act applied in full to the professions.

The second reform was that all laws and regulations that restricted competition whether at national or state level were subjected to an independent transparent review to remove those restrictions unless it could be demonstrated that each restriction was in the public interest and that the restriction was the least restrictive way of achieving the public interest objectives. This led to reviews of most professions.[10]

Third, during this period a much more substantial effort than in the past was made to address issues concerning recognition of qualifications gained in one part of Australia or New Zealand for use in another part of Australia or New Zealand. It was agreed in principle that there would be mutual recognition of qualifications gained in any part of Australia or New Zealand by all other parts of Australia and New Zealand.[11]

VI. The Australian Competition and Consumer Commission (ACCC) and the Professions since 1995

The Trade Practices Act applied in full to the professions from November 1995.

This meant that there is now a prohibition on anticompetitive agreements including price-fixing agreements between competitors, and primary boycotts

---

[8] *National Competition Policy*—Report by the Independent Committee of Inquiry, August 1993, the Australian Government Publishing Service, at p 135.

[9] *Ibid*, p 135.

[10] This review process is not considered in any detail in this paper.

[11] This experiment is not considered further in this paper. However, there is a full review of it in Productivity Commission *Evaluation of the Mutual Recognition Schemes* (research report), Canberra, Australia, 2003.

agreed by competitors; misuse of market power; anticompetitive exclusive dealing; and anticompetitive mergers. As with all other parts of Australian business it is possible in principle to obtain authorisation in advance for anti-competitive behaviour that would otherwise be in breach of the Act if it can be demonstrated that there is a sufficient benefit to the public. The law is backed by legal remedies including injunctions, damages actions, fines and other appropriate orders. It is also possible for individual parties to take individual action against other parties for breaches of the Trade Practices Act without the ACCC being involved, that is the private right of action also applies.

When the 1995 reforms were enacted, the Commission's initial approach was to focus heavily on intensive education for the professions about their rights and obligations under the Trade Practices Act.

They involved publicity, publications, seminars, speeches and were supplemented by an extensive education program undertaken by private sector law firms and professional associations.

In the early years the Commission received some complaints about alleged collective boycotts, particularly of country hospitals by doctors located in those towns. Those doctors wanted higher pay and they told hospitals that they would not work there (that is they engaged in a collective boycott) unless they received pay increases.

The Commission issued various warnings and indicated that it would consider court action if necessary. This generally put a halt to the boycotts that the Commission had received complaints about.

While these educational efforts have proceeded continuously since 1995 the Commission has been active in enforcing the law as well as adjudicating on authorisation applications.

The next step occurred when in 1998 the Commission took successful action against the Australian Society of Anaesthetists and four anaesthetists from the state of New South Wales. It successfully alleged that unlawful agreements were reached by anaesthetists at three private hospitals to introduce a $25 per hour charge for being 'on-call'. (Being 'on-call' meant that an anaesthetist, although not on site, was available for emergency and after hours anaesthetic services at the hospitals.) The Commission also successfully alleged that certain anaesthetists reached an unlawful agreement to tell the administrators at one of the private hospitals that unless the hospital agreed to pay for the supply of 'on-call' services those anaesthetists would not supply such services. The Commission also successfully alleged that there were other broader agreements about the introduction of a $25 per hour 'on-call' charge. In particular it found that the New South Wales Society as a whole made these unlawful agreements.

The Commission was not opposed in principle to there being 'on-call' charges. Its concern was simply that it was unlawful for competitors to reach an agreement on these charges. This case might well have been settled without recourse to the courts but there was stiff resistance from the New South Wales Society to any suggestion that the law had been broken or that there should be any sanctions or even undertakings. This provided the Commission with an excellent opportunity to test the law in court. As a result the Commission took the matter to court which upheld the validity of the Commission's concerns, concluded that there was unlawful behaviour and imposed injunctions and various other orders.

In this case this Commission did not seek penalties as it was the first enforcement action against medical professionals following the competition policy reforms. However, a breach of the undertakings to the court would put the specialists or the association at risk of contempt of court.

The next step was the imposition of penalties. In July 2000 the Commission instituted proceedings in the Federal Court against the Western Australian branch of the Australian Medical Association and the private health company Mayne Nickless Ltd alleging that they were involved in price-fixing and other anticompetitive conduct in breach of the Trade Practices Act 1974. These breaches occurred during negotiations involving the above parties pursuant to the establishment of new arrangements concerning the Joondalup Health Campus. After extremely protracted out of court negotiations the Australian Medical Association (AMA) eventually pleaded guilty and the court accepted a joint proposal from the ACCC and the AMA that there should be a fine of around $250,000 for the AMA including fines of around $10,000 each for the Executive Director and the former President of the AMA in Perth.

This case established a clear precedent that professional bodies and their leaders could be fined for breaches of the Trade Practices Act.

A curious feature of this case was that the other party to the agreement, Mayne Nickless, contested the allegations and a couple of years later was successful in persuading the court that it was not guilty of being involved in any unlawful price-fixing agreement. It would take us too far afield to discuss how the court reconciled the two decisions.

Another important and controversial case concerned gynaecologists in the small country town of Rockhampton, Queensland. There were several gynaecologists in this town who had a (lawful) agreement that they would look after each other's patients in the event that any one of them was absent or unable to attend to their own patients for any reason. This was called a roster agreement. However, one of the gynaecologists decided to make an agreement with a private health insurance company the effect of which was that his patients with such insurance would pay nothing at all if they were in hospital (normally under private health insurance there is a fee of about $A800, for treatment in a hospital even though there is private insurance). Some of the other gynaecologists were unhappy with this arrangement and informed the doctor that they were no longer prepared to look after his patients when he was absent. (The Commission later successfully alleged this was an unlawful collective boycott). As a result the doctor had to inform all of his patients that he had been forced to abandon the private health insurance arrangement. He advised them in writing (very conveniently from the ACCC's point of view) that instead of paying nothing for their stay in hospital his patients would have to pay about $A800.

The Commission investigated and successfully litigated in court obtaining refunds of $A800or so to the two hundred or so affected patients. This was the cause of considerable controversy. The Australian Medical Association in particular led a vigorous campaign arguing that there were already shortages of doctors in many country towns and this would exacerbate them. The Australian Medical Association argued that it should be exempt from the law. Eventually the Commonwealth government established an independent inquiry but it concluded there should be no such exemption.

VII. Authorisation of Anticompetitive Behaviour

Besides these enforcement actions, there have been a number of applications to the Australian Competition Tribunal for authorisation of anticompetitive behaviour.

In 1998, for example, the South Australian and Rural Medical Association applied to the Commission for authorisation to collectively negotiate and give effect to a Fee for Service Agreement for the remuneration of visiting medical officers treating public patients in South Australian rural public hospitals.

South Australia has 65 rural hospitals ranging from some with only one doctor to others with 25–50. There are very few resident specialists in rural SA and hospitals arrange periodic visits by particular specialists to cover their needs. Emergency support for complicated matters is arranged by flying 'recovery' teams from Adelaide or by airlifting patients to Adelaide. A major issue in the South Australian rural medical system is trying to attract doctors. In mid–1998, it was estimated that that the system was short by 30–40 doctors.

In a determination dated 31 July 1998 the Commission indicated that it considered that the Fee for Service Agreement had anti-competitive effects because it acted as a price floor for all hospitals in South Australia. Hospitals in regions that have little trouble attracting doctors would have had to pay the same rate for medical services as those in regions that have difficulty.

While the Commission agreed that the provision of medical services provides many public benefits, it was not convinced that the Fee for Service Agreement was the only method that would produce them. The Commission did, however, recognise that the South Australian Health Commission and the AMA and its members had established collective negotiation techniques.

In light of the fact that doctors carrying on their professional businesses in SA without incorporating were not subject to the *TPA* until July 1996, the Commission indicated that it recognised some public benefit in allowing the parties to phase in a less regulated system. Accordingly, the parties were given about 18 months to terminate the system.

1. Australian Society of Anaesthetists

On 8 October 1999 the Commission dismissed an application for authorisation lodged by the Australian Society of Anaesthetists (ASA) to undertake negotiations with health funds regarding rates and conditions on behalf of its members. The ASA also wished to be able to inform its members as to whether the ASA considered any standard form agreement (including rates of payment) arising from the negotiations to be fair and reasonable. It would make clear that the final decision rested with the individual anaesthetist and that he/she retained the right to negotiate individually.

The Commission was of the view that:

- The proposed conduct was likely to lead to an agreement in relation to minimum prices at a State level. The Commission considered a price agreement to be one of the most serious anti-competitive practices. In this case, it considered that substantial weighting should be given to the detriment arising from the likely price fixing effects of the proposal.
- While the ASA claimed that anaesthetists do not compete with each other, the Commission's view was that, as alternative providers of anaesthesia services, anaesthetists were in competition with each other for the purpose of the Act. The development of certain new products know as 'no gap' or 'known gap' products would represent a public benefit. However, the Commission was not satisfied that the proposal would lead to such products being made available. The proposal to have negotiations conducted at a State level did not satisfy the Commission's concern with respect to equalising negotiating power. It remained of the view that the proposal had the potential to reverse the balance of negotiating power and not lead to a true equalisation of any imbalance that may exist. The Commission also had reservations concerning the effectiveness of the proposed barriers to the exchange of information given the corporate structure of the ASA.
- The ASA could provide guidance to its members on issues that needed to be addressed in their negotiations without conducting centralised negotiations through State Committees of Management. This would enable some of the concerns expressed about the possible introduction of US style managed care to be mitigated. The Commission was encouraged to note that anaesthetists were not as implacably opposed to contract as other sections of the medical profession seem to be.

2. Royal Australasian College of Surgeons (RACS)

A major new development in the application of competition law occurred in relation to surgeons. The Commission probed issues concerning entry in to the field of surgery.

The Commission investigated allegations that RACS' processes restricted entry to advanced medical and surgical training in breach of the Trade Practices Act.

The Commission investigation concentrated on RACS' role in determining how many trainees received advanced training in orthopaedic surgery and how it assessed overseas-trained specialists referred to RACS by the Australian Medical Council. The Commission formed the view that RACS' procedure and conduct might constitute a breach of some of the competition provisions of the Act and put this view to RACS, indicating that it was seriously considering prosecution.

On 24 November 2000, RACS applied for authorisation of its processes in:

- selecting, training and examining surgical trainees in each of the nine specialities in which it conducted training;[12]
- accrediting hospital posts as being suitable for training surgeons; and
- assessing the qualifications of overseas-trained practitioners.

A very far-reaching consideration of the application occurred: on 30 June 2003 the Commission granted authorisation to the surgeons to restrict entry to their profession but it changed very substantially the entry restrictions. The aim was to broaden the entry provisions, to link them to public interest economic criteria, to make them more transparent, and to give better appeal rights to dissatisfied applicants. The option of totally scrapping this system and replacing it with a government conducted selection process was considered but not adopted at this stage. It is something that is to be considered at a review of the system in a few years time.

The Commission also spent considerable time reviewing the way in which numbers of new entrants were determined from one year to the next. Until the 1990s there did not seem to be any explicit system concerning how many new entrants gained admission. But there were some signs that numbers were restricted partly by surgeons for anticompetitive reasons and partly by governments to keep supply down which in turn would, it was considered, keep medical costs down (based on the theory that in medicine supply determines demand). Around that time there was extensive publicity concerning the possibility that the then Trade Practices Commission, now the ACCC, would investigate the surgeons closed-shop. Not long after, the government

[12] The nine RACS specialties are: general surgery; cardiothoracic surgery; neurosurgery; orthopedic surgery; otolaryngology-head and neck surgery; pediatric surgery; plastic and reconstructive surgery; urology; and vascular surgery.

established a committee to make long term projections of the required work-force in different parts of the medical profession. It was understood that this would be a factor in the colleges' determination of how many admissions to their college there would be. In its recent authorization case the Commission spent some time reviewing the system and concluded that it was flawed in various ways. It sought a more professional and flexible approach to the determination of work force numbers and to the determination of the flow on effects for demand for new graduates.

VIII. Other Professions

The Commission has not been involved in any major litigation concerning restrictions on entry or other forms of anticompetitive behaviour by members of the legal Bar. It would be very interesting to see how the courts of Australia approach such activity.

The Commission, however, has taken some action against solicitors and estate agents and has found the courts willing to conclude that there had been breaches of the law by these professions.

An important outcome of all these cases is that it has been established that the Commission has jurisdiction over the professions for breaches of the Act. The professions have accepted this fact.

IX. Conclusion

This paper has noted the high degree of regulation of the professions. It notes, however, that the rationale for possible regulation does not necessarily warrant the battery of regulations imposed on the professions, many of which are self-serving and anticompetitive.

The paper notes that there seem to be two ways of dealing with issues. One is through action to enforce the Trade Practices Act by the ACCC. This has been occurring. The other is that in some instances anticompetitive restrictions have been imposed by governments reportedly in the public interest. There has been some attempt at dealing with this through the process of reviewing anticompetitive legislation but some issues remain. Mutual recognition of professional qualifications obtained in various parts of Australia and New Zealand has also added to competition. The future with regard to recognition of overseas qualifications is more mixed and complicated but there has been a significant anticompetitive element at work when decisions have been made in this field.

III

*William E Kovacic**

Competition Policy Research and Development, Institutional Interdependency, and the Future Work of Competition Agencies in the Professions

I. Introduction

Discussions about the performance of competition policy agencies often tend to dwell upon the prosecution of cases. The initiation and litigation of cases provide readily observable events for analysis by academics, practitioners, and journalists. To a large degree, enforcement actions—especially 'big' cases involving easily recognized respondents—commonly are assumed to be the proper measure of what a competition authority has done.[1]

In critical respects, the case-centric vision of competition policy is a painfully inadequate conception of what competition agencies should do. Taken on its own terms, the case-centric view of public competition policy accords excessive importance to spectacular matters involving easily recognized respondents and routinely undervalues the small case that makes big law.[2] Moreover, by lauding the enforcement official who files the enforcement action, the case-centric view of competition policy tends to overlook to what the cases actually accomplished. This is the equivalent of measuring the quality of an airline by the number and size of departing flights without devoting equal attention to how, when, and where the airplanes descend to earth.

Equally serious pathologies of case-centrism are its disregard for non-litigation policy instruments that are vital tools of policy development and investments that help determine the effectiveness of litigation programs, and its failure to appreciate the importance of investments in the institutional capability that is the essence of successful policymaking. Case-centrism treats advocacy—for example, the filing of comments on proposed legislation or administrative regulations—as the last refuge of the enforcement official who

* General Counsel, US Federal Trade Commission. The views presented here are the author's alone and not necessarily those of the US Federal Trade Commission or any of its members.

[1] See WE Kovacic, 'The Modern Evolution of US Competition Policy Norms' (2004) 71 *Antitrust Law Journal* 377.

[2] See TJ Muris, 'How History Can Inform Practice' remarks before the Fall Forum of the American Bar Association Section of Antitrust Law, Washington DC, November 2003, text available at http://www.ftc.gov.

lacks the fortitude or imagination to bring adequate numbers of cases. Even less than advocacy does the case-centrist respect an agency's commitment to invest in building that intellectual capital that informs the choice and execution of litigation and non-litigation interventions, alike.

The antidote to case-centrism is a better awareness of the determinants of effective competition policy. Recent developments in the academic literature and public policy display a growing recognition of the role that institutional design and capability play in shaping the quality of government competition programs.[3] The emerging institution-oriented perspective emphasizes the value of a multi-dimensional approach to policymaking in which the competition agency uses a diverse array of litigation and non-litigation policy instruments to address competition problems.[4] This perspective also recognizes the essential contribution that intellectual leadership makes in supporting policy development and encourages conscious, continuing agency investments in 'competition policy research and development' to achieve and sustain such leadership.[5]

This paper discusses the importance of investments in competition policy R&D to effective performance by competition agencies. It uses the example of modern US experience with the professions to demonstrate the benefits of institution building and the acceptance of a broad conception of competition policy that reaches beyond the prosecution of cases alone. A major theme of the paper is that investments in competition policy R&D provide vital analytical foundations for litigation and non-litigation interventions and can supply a valuable means for blunting political opposition that often arises to the application of competition policy in the professions. Competition agencies should be evaluated by their skill in applying litigation and non-litigation instruments. The hypothetical scorecard by which we measure competition agencies should count advocacy as no less important that cases and should grade agencies by their investments in competition policy R&D—the equivalent of a private firm's investment in the R&D that drives product development.

The paper approaches the topic in four parts. Part II describes arguments for exceptional treatment often advanced when competition policy is applied to the professions. Part III reviews the need for competition agencies to use a

---

[3] See WE Kovacic, 'Institutional Foundations for Economic Legal Reform in Transition Economies: The Case of Competition Policy and Antitrust Enforcement' (2001) 77 *Chicago-Kent L Rev* 265; WE Kovacic, 'Achieving Better Practices in the Design of Competition Policy Institutions' remarks before the Seoul Competition Forum 2004–Seoul, Republic of Korea, April 2004, text available at http://www.ftc.gov.

[4] See TJ Muris, 'Looking Forward: The Federal Trade Commission and the Future Development of US Competition Policy', remarks for the Milton Handler Annual Antitrust Review, New York, December 2002 (hereinafter 'Looking Forward'), text available at http://www.ftc.gov.

[5] The concept of 'competition policy research and development' and its contributions to building the institutional capability of competition agencies is introduced in Muris, 'Looking Forward' (2002), above n 4.

multidimensional strategy that employs litigation and non-litigation policy instruments. Part IV more fully defines the concept of competition policy R&D and describes how such activity is an essential ingredient of litigation and non-litigation programs. Part V considers the importance to a competition agency of formulating stronger institutional links with other government institutions whose decisions influence competition in the professions.

II. The Professions and Competition Policy: Arguments for Exceptionalism

Demands for exceptional treatment run throughout the history of competition policy in the United States. It is the rare industry that, on some occasion, neither has sought an outright exemption from antitrust oversight nor insisted that special circumstances demanded the application of demonstrably more permissive rules. No US competition official ever erred by overestimating the intensity and durability of the exceptionalist impulse.

Arguments for exceptional treatment occupy a particularly prominent place in the history of efforts to apply competition policy to accountants, attorneys, engineers, physicians, and other service providers often classified under the general rubric of the 'professions.' These arguments have two principal themes. The first is that competition will produce destructive results by inducing service providers to skimp on quality in circumstances in which inadequate attention to quality can have particularly harmful consequences for the consumer of the service.[6] Among other measures, price floors, restrictions on competitive bidding, and stringent qualification standards are said to be necessary to ensure the provision of sufficient quality.

A second, closely-related argument is that consumers of professional services ordinarily cannot assess the validity of representations made by service providers about the price or quality of their services. Given extreme asymmetries in the information possessed by service providers and consumers, respectively, consumers may be particularly prone to be misled by such representations—again, to their severe detriment. Many professional bodies have proposed or implemented strict controls on advertising to address this possibility.

In addition to claims about the dangers of competition in the supply of professional services, professional bodies and individual providers have

[6] This quality-related argument is not unique to the professions. Various other service industries—for example, the transportation sector—from time to time have sought to curb or eliminate antitrust oversight by arguing that competition inevitably endangers consumers by discouraging needed investments in quality.

raised a separate argument that concerns the institutional competence of enforcement agencies and courts responsible for administering competition laws. This view contends that competition authorities and courts lack the capacity to properly diagnose commercial practices in the professions and therefore are likely to condemn behaviour that is benign or pro-competitive. Thus, even when competition agencies profess to be sensitive to purported quality justifications for certain restrictions, they are said to be unable to make well-informed, accurate distinctions.

The professions have raised these substantive and institutional arguments for exceptional treatment in two fora. First, the arguments have been raised vigorously in the courts to oppose the application of competition policy rules to the behaviour of professionals and their trade associations.[7] The second arena is the legislative process at both the national and state levels. In a number of instances, success in litigation by the competition agencies in establishing the application of antitrust principles to the professions has elicited determined efforts by the affected groups to persuade legislators to provide partial or complete dispensations from antitrust oversight.[8]

Arguments about quality and institutional competence have figured prominently in judicial and legislative deliberations. Regardless of the forum in which they appear and regardless the form of their policy intervention (bringing cases or providing advice as a competition advocate), competition agencies must be able to address and overcome concerns about the quality effects of competition and about their own capacity. Courts and legislatures are likely to seek assurances that competition does not pose a hazard to quality and that the competition agencies know what they are doing.

III. The Multidimensional Nature of Competition Policy

As the discussion above suggests, impediments to competition in the professions take a number of forms. In some instances, the relevant activity consists

---

[7] Examples include *California Dental Association v Federal Trade Commission* 526 US 756 (1999); *Federal Trade Commission v Indiana Federation of Dentists* 476 US 447 (1986); *National Society of Professional Engineers v United States* 435 US 679 (1978).

[8] In the 1970s, the Federal Trade Commission sued the American Medical Association and barred the group from imposing restrictions on truthful advertising and from banning efforts by its members to solicit patients. *American Medical Association* 94 FTC 701 (1979) (finding liability), order enforced as modified, 638 F 2d 443 (2nd Cir, 1980), affirmed by an equally divided Supreme Court 455 US 676 (1982). During the appeal of the FTC's administrative decision finding liability, the US Congress gave serious consideration to measures to withdraw the FTC's jurisdiction over any profession (including the legal and medical professions) subject to state regulation. See WE Kovacic, 'Congress and the Federal Trade Commission' (1989) 57 *Antitrust Law Journal* 869, 896–97 (discussing measures to remove FTC's jurisdiction over the professions); WE Kovacic, 'The Federal Trade Commission and Congressional Oversight of Antitrust Enforcement' (1982) 17 *Tulsa Law Journal* 587, 666–77.

of purely private behaviour, such as a decision by a professional association to adopt an ethical code that directs its members to abide by price floors in offering their services. In other cases, the obstacle to competition is an existing national or state regulatory regime that governs entry, pricing, advertising, or other phenomena that affect the provision of the service. In still other instances, the vehicle at issue is a proposed legislative or regulatory measure that would eliminate or restrict the operation of competition rules.

The capacity to bring cases and litigate challenged restraints unmistakably is an important means for competition agencies to make competition policy in the professions. Many of the most important accomplishments of the US competition agencies in the past three decades or so have consistent of successful lawsuits. A competition policy program that lacks a credible commitment to bring lawsuits to challenge apparent misconduct is unlikely to be successful.

Litigation is necessary to effective policymaking involving the professions, but it is not sufficient. Because legislation and administrative regulation are key sources of policy in this area, an agency must be prepared to engage in advocacy before legislatures and other government bodies with regulatory authority. US experience also shows that the competition authorities can make extremely useful contributions through the issuance of guidelines and advisory opinions that address issues of concern to members of the profession.[9] The effective agency does not have a one-dimensional focus on litigation. Instead, it applies a multi-dimensional strategy that involves its skills as an enforcement body, a competition advocate, and an advisor to affected business operators.

IV. The Importance and Contributions of Competition Policy R&D

A competition agency can undertake any of the foregoing policy interventions skilfully and, ultimately, successfully without an adequate knowledge base. The purpose of competition policy R&D is to supply and sustain the requisite knowledge base. A strong competition policy R&D program not only informs the application of all of the agency's policy instruments, but it also establishes credibility in the eyes of judges, legislators, other government ministries, academics, and practitioners. The agency's knowledge base determines its ability to comprehend accurately the competitive significance of and

[9] For example, the US antitrust agencies have issued guidelines dealing with antitrust enforcement in the health care sector and have issued numerous advisory opinions concerning health care competition issues.

justifications for specific business phenomena and its capacity to speak persuasively to various government and non-government audiences who otherwise might doubt its competence to make policy in fields featuring considerable technical complexity.

A good competition policy R&D program has several elements. The first is the sponsorship of empirical research to test the effects of restrictions on competition in the professions. Empirical research facilitates the creation of what might be called 'economic precedents'—economic studies that demonstrate the validity of a hypothesis and, like legal precedents, can be invoked over time to support specific policy interventions.[10] The agency can develop an indigenous capability to perform the relevant empirical research or contract with external bodies, such as universities, to conduct studies. One noteworthy element of the research agenda ought to be the examination of the consequences of past enforcement decisions, both to prosecute and not to prosecute.[11] Retrospective assessments of enforcement choices are necessary to test the wisdom of past interventions and to guide future policy development.

Comparative study can supply an informative ingredient of an agency's empirical agenda. Differences in regulation among a jurisdiction's political subdivisions or across jurisdictions have created possibilities for side-by-side comparisons of the effects of different regulatory regimes involving the professions. Thus, a valuable by-product of the complexity inherent in regulatory decentralization and diversity is the opportunity to perform studies that identify superior practices and facilitate a voluntary process of opting in to superior approaches.

A second means to build the agency's knowledge base is to conduct hearings, seminars, and workshops to accumulate knowledge from informed outsiders.[12] An agency might invite academics to present the results of empirical or theoretical work and to help guide the formulation of the agency's own research agenda and to encourage academics to consider research programs that might be of interest to the competition policy community.[13] Or the agency could use hearings to obtain the current thinking of business operators within the profession about developments that bear upon the formula-

---

[10] See RS Bond, *et al*, 'Federal Trade Commission Staff Report on Effects of Restrictions on Advertising and Commercial Practice in the Professions: The Case of Optometry' FTC Bureau of Economics (presenting results of empirical study on impact of restrictions on competition in provision of optometry services) (1980); see also *PolyGram Holding, Inc* (Federal Trade Commission, 24 July 2003) (relying, *inter alia*, on research concerning effects of restrictions on competition involving provision of professional services), available at http://www.ftc.gov.

[11] See WE Kovacic, 'Evaluating Antitrust Experiments: Using Ex Post Assessments of Government Enforcement Decisions to Inform Competition Policy' (2001) 9 *George Mason L Rev* 843.

[12] For example in 2003, the Department of Justice and the Federal Trade Commission jointly held over 20 days of hearings on Competition and Consumer Protection in Health Care. A report based on the hearings will be issued later this year.

[13] See, eg, Federal Trade Commission, 'Empirical Industrial Organization Roundtable' (2001), available at http://www.ftc.gov.

tion of competition policy. Such proceedings also serve as a means to solicit the views of other government institutions whose decisions determine the competitive environment for the professions. The mere fact that the competition agency actively and regularly seeks to learn from external groups can help establish a reputation for openness and superior practice.

Collectively, the initiatives described here are the equivalent of capital investments that characterize successful firms in the private sector. Successful firms routinely invest in research to develop new products and to refine existing product lines. A competition agency seeking to have an effective role in the professions can do no less to build and extend its own knowledge base.

V. Accounting for Institutional Interdependencies

National competition authorities are becoming ever more aware that they do not make policy in isolation. In dealing with the professions and with other sectors, competition agencies routinely discover that their decisions are only a subset of government policymaking that shapes the competitive environment.[14] A major challenge of modern competition policy is for competition agencies to identify relevant interdependencies, to formulate policy proposals that account for the activities of other government bodies, and to build intergovernmental relationships that can facilitate competition agencies to engage in advocacy and otherwise inform government agencies about the competitive consequences of their decisions.

VI. Conclusion: Towards a Norm That Encourages Enhancements in Long-Term Capability

The competition agency that aspires to success in the professions or other areas of policy making must attend carefully to matters of institutional design and capability. In evaluating the performance of competition agencies, it is just as important to ask what an agency has done to improve its capability for the long-term as it is to ask what interventions it is undertaking today. US experience with competition policy in the professions indicates that a competition

[14] These and other interdependencies are explored in WE Kovacic, 'Toward a Domestic Competition Network' remarks before the American Enterprise Institute, April 2003, available at http://www.ftc.gov; CS Yoo, 'New Models of Regulation and Interagency Governance' (2003) *Michigan State Detroit College of Law L Rev* 701.

agency requires the ability to use a range of litigation and non-litigation policy instruments.

Essential to the successful application of all of these instruments is the competition policy agency's commitment to two important measures: the investment in competition policy research and development to build the agency's intellectual capital, and the development of intergovernmental relationships that recognize the role of various public institutions in shaping the competitive environment for professional services.

To undertake these measures, competition agency leadership must accept a norm that recognizes the importance of enhancements in long-term capability. Today's leaders must make investments whose returns may appear chiefly or entirely during the tenure of their successors. It is a common aphorism of Washington policy-making that government officials should focus first on picking the low-hanging fruit. We should be no less insistent that public officials spend time planting trees.

IV

Mark C Schechter and Christine C Wilson***

The Learned Professions in the United States: Where Do We Stand Thirty Years after *Goldfarb*?

I. Introduction

Competition is the central organizing principle of the American economy. This is not to say, however, that unfettered competition is ubiquitous. Significant volumes of commerce in the US remain subject to regulation. A number of industries deemed to be of significant national interest are closely regulated; in the name of consumer protection, professions and other occupations are subject to licensing requirements at the federal, state, and local levels.

Building on the work of those like Milton Friedman, Irwin Stelzer, and Alfred Kahn, a significant body of literature is devoted to promoting the benefits of deregulation in industry. These works advocate eradicating or substantially lessening bureaucratic control of the marketplace and, instead, permitting market forces to determine outcomes. In recent decades, the process of deregulation has lessened substantially the level of government involvement in several industries, including telecommunications, airlines, railroads, trucking, financial services, natural gas, and electricity.[1]

Similar literature exists with respect to the professions. Scholars and commentators have written extensively regarding the relative costs and benefits of occupational licensing, and many have promoted deregulation of the

---

* Mark C Schechter chairs Howrey Simon Arnold & White's Government Antitrust Practice Group. He joined the firm as a partner in June 1995, after serving for 18 years with the Department of Justice's Antitrust Division, where he last held the position of Deputy Director of Operations.

** Christine C Wilson is partner in the Antitrust/Competition Practice Group at O'Melveny & Myers. She served as Chief of Staff to Chairman Timothy J Muris of the Federal Trade Commission from 2001 to 2002. Prior to serving at the FTC, she was a member of Howrey Simon Arnold & White's Government Antitrust Practice Group. The authors gratefully acknowledge the assistance of Jane L Antonio in the preparation of this paper.

[1] Although the term deregulation implies the eradication of direct government intervention in an industry, the reality in the US with respect to many 'deregulated' industries is otherwise.

> When you think of deregulation it is tempting to assume the government has stepped aside entirely and allowed competitive forces to take over. . . . Sometimes, 'deregulation' is used to describe situations in which the pervasiveness of regulation has been reduced [rather than eliminated]. . . . Even with more 'deregulation', our economy is likely to continue to be highly regulated. Harrison (1997) 18.

professions. So, too, have the courts recognized that private restraints within the professions can generate harms to consumers. Based on this recognition, cases beginning with the 1975 US Supreme Court decision in *Goldfarb v Virginia State Bar*[2] make clear that the professions are not exempt from the antitrust laws.

Yet private restraints and government regulations exist in abundance within the professions in the US today. And, as testimony to the profits to be reaped, new private restraints are uncovered and new regulations are proposed frequently at both the federal and state levels. While these restrictions frequently are sought to be justified on the grounds of public health, safety, and consumer protection, their principal effect often may be to insulate incumbents from competition. Thus, despite *Goldfarb* and its progeny, the US experiences far from unfettered competition within its professions today. Left unattended, there is a risk that the professions will become more insulated from the welfare-enhancing effects of competition.

Both public and private restraints within the professions have received, and continue to warrant, the attention of competition authorities. Anticompetitive private restraints fruitfully can be addressed through aggressive antitrust enforcement. Both the federal and state antitrust authorities in the US have devoted resources to the cause. Public restraints, however, pose a different and more intractable issue. Many of these restraints are shielded from the application of the antitrust laws by the state action doctrine. Antitrust authorities can and should seek to address this issue by insuring that the state action doctrine is applied in a manner consistent with its arguably limited doctrinal foundations.

To complement these efforts, though, an active competition advocacy program is vital. Regulators frequently fail to consider market mechanisms when seeking solutions, and rational incumbents within the professions choose profitable rent-seeking activities. Consequently, it frequently falls to competition authorities to bring the market-oriented perspective to the table. By preaching the culture of competition to federal agencies, legislators, and state authorities, federal antitrust authorities can contribute significantly to consumer welfare. State attorneys general, too, can benefit consumers through counselling their state governments on the benefits of competition rather than regulation, and by assisting in the deregulation process.

Thus, while much remains to be done, there are many tools at the disposal of competition authorities to eliminate public and private restraints and promote competition within the professions.

---

[2] 421 US 773 (1975).

II. Defining the Problem

1. Professional Restraints Subject to Antitrust Scrutiny

Thirty years ago, the Supreme Court in *Goldfarb v Virginia State Bar* ruled that the antitrust laws are applicable to the 'learned professions.' In that case, the Supreme Court held that a county bar association's adoption of minimum fee schedules violated the Sherman Act. Footnote 17 of the *Goldfarb* opinion left open the possibility that the antitrust laws might be applied differently within the context of the professions, stating that the 'public service aspect, and other features of the professions, may require that a particular practice, which could properly be viewed as a violation of the Sherman Act in another context, be treated differently.'[3] Three years later, the Supreme Court in *National Society of Professional Engineers*[4] addressed the legality of an association's canon of ethics that effectively prevented competitive bidding by its members. The association asserted that the canon minimized the risk that competition would produce inferior engineering work that could endanger public safety. The Court characterized this reasoning as 'nothing less than a frontal assault on the basic policy of the Sherman Act.'[5] In several subsequent cases, footnote 17 of *Goldfarb* notwithstanding, the Supreme Court has applied the antitrust laws in a straightforward manner to anticompetitive conduct undertaken by physicians,[6] dentists,[7] and other professionals.

The US Supreme Court also has analyzed restrictions on professional speech under the First Amendment Commercial Speech Doctrine of the US Constitution. In this line of cases, the Supreme Court has given more weight to assertions that the markets for professional services possess special characteristics, including an information asymmetry between professionals and consumers of their services. Consequently, under this framework, the Supreme Court in some instances has upheld bans on advertising and solicitation so as to protect consumers and promote professionalism. In *Florida Bar v Went For It, Inc,* for example, the Court upheld a solicitation ban that prevented lawyers from contacting for 30 days anyone who had been injured, relatives of the injured person, or relatives of those who had died in accidents.[8]

---

[3] *Ibid,* 788–89, n 17.
[4] *Nat'l Soc'y of Prof'l Eng'r v United States* 435 US 679 (1978).
[5] *Ibid,* 695.
[6] *Arizona v Maricopa County Med Soc'y* 457 US 332 (1982).
[7] *FTC v Indiana Fed'n of Dentists* 476 US 447 (1986).
[8] *Florida Bar v Went For It, Inc* 515 US 618 (1995).

These two lines of cases collided in *California Dental Ass'n v FTC*. In *CDA*, the FTC challenged restrictions on price and quality advertising imposed by the code of ethics of the California Dental Association, a voluntary association of local dental societies in California. An administrative law judge,[9] the full Commission,[10] and the Ninth Circuit Court of Appeals[11] each held that the challenged restrictions violated the antitrust laws. The Supreme Court, however, found inappropriate the Ninth Circuit's application of an abbreviated rule of reason to assess the legality of the challenged restraints. Stating that 'a less quick look was required for the initial assessment of the tendency of these professional advertising restrictions,'[12] the Court remanded the case for further review. Commentators have cautioned against interpreting *CDA* too expansively, however, asserting that the opinion should be read merely to require all plaintiffs to provide an empirical basis for their assertions that challenged restraints harm consumers.[13]

Given the Supreme Court's holdings in *Goldfarb* and its progeny, one might expect to see a steady diminishing of professional restraints throughout the US. In fact, however, even a cursory examination of the professions reveals that potentially anticompetitive restraints within the learned professions are flourishing.

2. Despite *Goldfarb*, Restraints Persist: the Legal Profession as an Illustration

A brief review of restraints in the legal profession in the US, though none relate specifically to antitrust practitioners, is illustrative. Myriad regulations govern both entry into the legal profession and the conduct of attorneys in their practice of law. These restraints generally fall into two major categories: entry regulation and conduct regulation. Not surprisingly, observers have charged that these regulations harm consumers by artificially restricting the supply of attorneys and limiting competition among them.

The first category of government-imposed restraints—entry regulation—concerns the states' licensing of attorneys to practice law. Every state requires would-be attorneys successfully to complete a bar examination and a character and fitness review. In addition, all but a handful of states require bar applicants to have graduated from a law school accredited by the American

---

9 *In re California Dental Ass'n* 121 FTC 190, 195–283 (1996).

10 *Ibid*, 371–78.

11 *California Dental Ass'n v FTC* 128 F 3d 720 (9th Cir, 1997).

12 *California Dental Ass'n v FTC* 526 US 756, 781 (1999).

13 See, eg, Muris (2000) (stating that *California Dental Ass'n* 'will have been worthwhile' if the long run impact is to force plaintiffs to have an evidentiary basis for why competitor restraints harm consumers).

Bar Association. Entry regulation also encompasses the various statutes and court orders barring the unauthorized practice of law by non-lawyers. Although state supreme courts nominally are in charge of entry regulation in almost every state, they generally have delegated their authority to unified state bar associations or to a separate agency.

Conduct regulation controls the behaviour of lawyers once they are licensed. The regulations in this category include restraints on advertising, client solicitation, client referrals, statements concerning lawyer credentials, law firm affiliation, and fee regulations. All 50 states regulate lawyer conduct; most rely on some variation of the ABA's Rules of Professional Conduct or Code of Professional Responsibility.[14] Rules governing conduct generally are enforced through bar disciplinary authorities or separate administrative agencies of the state supreme courts.

Many practitioners and laymen take this level of regulation for granted, but history would appear to demonstrate otherwise. One commentator has observed:

> In the middle of the 19th century the legal market was virtually unregulated. Several states passed statutes allowing any registered voter to practice law, and the nominal requirements for bar entry in other states were not enforced. There was also no explicit regulation of attorney behaviour. Since this time we have seen steady growth in the regulation of the legal market. The first changes came in tightening bar requirements, and later in the adoption and enforcement of codes of legal ethics.[15]

Thus, he concluded, 'the rules that govern the legal market have grown exponentially in scope and changed in character; the legal market is now unquestionably regulated to a high degree.'[16]

In a recent article, Professor Leonard Brickman argued that a specific subset of the legal profession—tort liability contingency fee lawyers[17]—has received significant monetary benefits as a result of extensive regulation and restraints on competition.[18] Professor Brickman asserted that just as tort liability in the US has increased significantly during the last forty years, so too have lawyers' contingency fees. Indeed, he argued that the effective hourly rates of contingent fee lawyers far exceed those of their hourly rate counterparts (solace to antitrust lawyers), and that 'a top tier of contingent fee lawyers comprising approximately one-fourth to one-third of that bar routinely obtains effective hourly rates of thousands of dollars.' According to Professor Brickman, these astronomical earnings are attributable not to the

---

14 American Bar Association (2003).

15 Barton (2001) 429–30.

16 *Ibid*, p 431.

17 With few exceptions, US lawyers who litigate tort claims are engaged by their clients on a contingent fee basis. The lawyer retains a predetermined percentage of the plaintiff's monetary recovery if plaintiff's lawsuit is successful, but receives no remuneration if the plaintiff loses.

18 See Brickman (2003).

actual risk level of most contingent fee lawyers' portfolios of cases, but rather to a lack of competition in the market for these services.[19]

Professor Brickman sought to identify various structural impediments to competition, including significant search costs and asymmetrical information with regard to both the value of tort claims and the quality of lawyering services. The effect of these structural factors has been compounded, argued Professor Brickman, by the adoption of ethical restrictions that preclude alternative price mechanisms. For example, many commentators predict that efficient outcomes would arise if attorneys could compete to purchase the rights to clients' legal claims and prosecute them on their own behalf.[20] Ethical restrictions, however, prohibit attorneys to purchase tort claims and to bid for clients. Similarly, ethical restrictions prevent attorneys from providing financial assistance to their clients. Professor Brickman asserted that in the absence of this prohibition, 'lawyers would be expected to bid against each other through offers of financial assistance, based upon the anticipated value of the claim,' effectively forcing attorneys to divide rents with their clients.[21] Professor Brickman asserted that 'lawyers act collusively to maintain a uniform price,'[22] and that '[a]bsent these structural impediments and ethical restrictions, which are means of maintaining rents for members of the legal profession, it is likely that price competition in the market for tort claiming services would arise, thereby improving client welfare.'[23]

Professor Brickman is not alone in criticizing the body of regulations governing legal practice in the US. Many observers have expressed concerns about the 'mismatch' of purported goals underlying the regulations and the means by which those goals are sought to be achieved. For example, they question whether concerns about information asymmetry between attorneys and clients would be better served by abandoning restrictions on the flow of information about legal services embodied in advertising restraints, statements about lawyer credentials, and other conduct requirements.[24] Others question whether the purported goals underlying some current restraints are even desirable. For example, some question whether the maintenance of an elite system of law maintained by extensive accreditation and education requirements may do a disservice to clients who would prefer to choose

---

[19] Prof Brickman identified several indicia of the lack of competition in the relevant market, including a uniform price ranging from 33.3% to 50% of plaintiff's recovery depending on the jurisdiction; an absence of price advertising; the enormous increase in the effective hourly rates realized by tort lawyers during the last 40 years; and the historical derivation of the standard contingent fee, which he characterized as political rather than market-driven. Brickman (2003) 78–93.

[20] Brickman (2003) 117.

[21] *Ibid*, p 121.

[22] *Ibid*, p 127.

[23] *Ibid*, p 126.

[24] See Barton (2001).

between high-quality, high-priced legal services and more affordable, albeit lower-quality, legal counsel.[25]

As our purpose here is merely to reiterate that extensive regulations of the legal practice remain in place today in the US, we will leave detailed exploration of these criticisms to other fora. We find it sufficient to note that significant doubts have been raised about the need for many of the regulations currently in place, and that some observers have asserted that these regulations result more from the bar's desire to restrict supply and raise prices than from their desire to protect consumers and maintain professionalism.

3. Potentially Anticompetitive Restraints Persist in Other Professions

Other professions, too, are subject to extensive licensing requirements and competitive restraints. Physicians, dentists, architects, accountants, engineers, and myriad other professions are subject to entry and conduct regulations in states throughout the US.[26] While much of this regulation may be consistent with the antitrust laws, questions have been raised about both the need for such regulations and the ostensible justifications underlying their promulgation. Similarly, a review of the enforcement activities of the federal antitrust agencies in recent years underscores the extent to which private anticompetitive restraints permeate the professions. For example, the FTC has initiated at least 18 challenges against alleged price-fixing agreements among physicians since May 2002.[27]

Looking beyond the professions to occupations more broadly, a similar phenomenon is apparent. For example, a recent study of occupational licensing requirements in Arizona concludes that:

> In Arizona, occupational licensing requirements and regulations stifle competition, diminish quality of service, and drive up prices. Thousands of laws restrict entry into occupations for people wishing to become cosmetologists, barbers, African hair braiders, taxicab drivers, and street vendors. State agencies and occupational licensing boards act as gatekeepers, restricting competition and ensnaring entrepreneurs in thick layers of red tape.[28]

---

[25] Lao (2001) (asserting that ABA accreditation process should be overhauled).

[26] The breadth and depth of government intervention in the professions can be confirmed by a brief review of the professional licensing requirements imposed by the five most populous states (California, New York, Texas, Florida, and Illinois). The professional licensing regimes of these states are available on their web sites. *See* http://www.commerce.ca.gov/ttca/business/licensehandbook.pdf, http://www.*op*.nysed.gov/proflist.htm; http://www.tdh.state.tx.us/hcqs/plc/plcd.htm; http://www.myflorida.com/dbpr/pro/index.shtml; and http://www.dpr.state.il.us/proflist.asp.

[27] FTC (2004a) 7–17.

[28] Keller (2003) 1.

Another study found that:

> Nearly 1,000 occupations are regulated by the states. In 490 instances, individuals must secure licenses to engage lawfully in their professions. Occupations subject to licensing requirements range from the obvious—such as doctors and lawyers—to professions in which the need for regulations or restrictions on entry is not at all clear, such as bee keepers, lightning rod salesmen, shorthand reporters, fence installers, and septic tank cleaners. Barbers and beauticians are subject to licensing in all jurisdictions.[29]

These findings are consistent with earlier studies of occupational licensing.[30]

Unfortunately, the battle is not limited to eradicating existing restraints. New private restraints are discovered and challenged by the antitrust authorities with regularity. In addition, proposals for new public restrictions on competition within the professions appear frequently. For example, a number of proposals have been made in recent years at both the state and federal levels to provide antitrust exemptions for various types of price-setting by physicians and other health care providers. In the legal profession, several states recently have witnessed proposals to limit the ability of non-lawyers to compete with lawyers in residential real estate closings and re-financings.

In some instances, familiar restraints are occurring in a new environment. While e-commerce opens up possibilities for consumers, brick-and-mortar incumbents seek to insulate themselves from online competition. In testimony before the US House of Representatives,[31] for example, FTC staff explained that many mortgage brokers and providers of financial services now operate online and may be able to provide consumers with lower rates. In response to this phenomenon, a number of states have adopted regulations requiring companies to maintain in-state offices or in-state licenses if they offer residential mortgage loans. FTC staff observed that while these regulations may benefit consumers by limiting unscrupulous practices, they may also 'have the secondary effect of insulating local businesses from wider competition, or of allowing only national mortgage firms that already have physical offices in all states to sell online in all states.'[32] The FTC explored the topic of possible anticompetitive efforts to restrict competition on the Internet—including restraints among lawyers, opticians, and funeral directors—in a workshop held in October 2002.[33]

The costs imposed on consumers by occupational licensing regimes and restrictive business practices within the professions, although frequently difficult to quantify, can be substantial. Studies of the price effects of licensing in dentistry observe that restrictions in supply result in 4 to 15% price

---

29 Bolick and Legge (1991).
30 See, eg, Cox and Foster (1990).
31 US House of Representatives (2002a) 34–38.
32 *Ibid*, p 37.
33 For more information regarding this workshop, see Federal Trade Commission, 2002.

increases.[34] Another study found that the average eye exam and eyeglass prescription costs 35% more in cities with restrictive commercial practices for optometrists.[35] And measures considered by several states that would require borrowers to hire attorneys to represent them in real estate loan closings typically would increase costs to consumers by between $150 and $400.[36]

Certainly, proponents of these regulations and restraints proffer justifications and benefits that ostensibly offset the costs imposed on consumers. A growing body of literature suggests, however, that the justifications may be overstated or even unfounded, and the costs may far exceed the benefits. For example, the recent study of occupational licensing in Arizona concludes:

> Although regulatory boards and commissions are frequently defended on the grounds of alleged health or safety concerns, the principal effect of many occupational licensing schemes is to promote the vested interests of those already engaged in regulated professions, creating government-sanctioned cartels. To the extent that regulation adds marginal protections for consumers, those protections come at a significant price in lost productivity and lost economic dynamism. When government regulation is necessary, regulations should be highly circumscribed, easily understandable, and narrowly tailored to achieve legitimate goals such as preventing fraud.[37]

In a similar vein, the DOJ Antitrust Division Manual notes that regulations impose substantial costs on consumers, and 'should be permitted only on compelling evidence that competition cannot work or is inimical to some overriding social objective.'[38]

Even without substantial analysis, it is apparent that many existing regulations in the US would not meet this test. In Louisiana, for example, would-be retail florists must pass a state-mandated florist licensing exam before the government will permit them to practice floristry.[39] Grading of the exam is based upon subjective criteria;[40] applicants are graded by the same state-licensed florists with whom they hope to compete. Readers will not be surprised to learn that the pass rate for the exam is less than 50%. 'Cut flower dealers' who sell cut flowers either singly or in bunches are not subjected to exam requirements but are regulated nonetheless. They are forbidden from selling two different kinds of flowers together in the same bunch, and from placing flowers in a vase or other container; these activities would constitute

---

[34] *See* Cox and Foster (1990) 31; and Kleiner and Kudrle (2000).

[35] *See* Bond, *et al*, (1980).

[36] US Department of Justice and FTC (2001).

[37] Keller (2003).

[38] US Department of Justice (1998) Ch V, A1.

[39] For a description of the Louisiana statute and plaintiffs' lawsuit, see Institute for Justice.

[40] Grading of the practical portion of the exam is particularly subjective, with judges asked to evaluate whether the applicant's arrangements have the proper focal point, whether the flowers are spaced effectively, and whether the arrangement is in proportion to its container. *Ibid.*

flower arranging, which only licensed retail florists may do. In December 2003, in an attempt to have the state's florist licensing law declared unconstitutional, private litigants filed suit against the Louisiana Horticulture Commission.[41]

And in California, plaintiff hair stylists successfully challenged a cosmetology licensing regime under which African hair braiders were required to take 1600 hours of cosmetology training that did not include a single hour of hair braiding instruction, at an average cost of $7000. In contrast, California imposed far fewer training requirements on other occupations that affect public health and welfare much more directly. For example, the state required 22 hours of training for security guards with firearms, 110 hours for emergency medical technicians, and 1142 hours for paramedics. A federal district court judge observed that requiring African hair stylists to obtain the requisite training was 'wholly irrelevant to the achievement of the State's objectives'[42] and concluded that requiring plaintiffs to comply with the state's cosmetology regulations was unconstitutional. Similar regulations successfully have been challenged in other jurisdictions in the US, including Arizona and the District of Columbia.

Of course, there are far more mundane examples relating to regulations preventing the formation of new taxi companies so long as incumbent companies verify they can meet existing demand; prohibitions on private 'jitneys' that would compete with the bus service offered by local governments; statutes preventing shipments from out-of-state wineries directly to in-state consumers, while permitting shipments from in-state wineries to those consumers;[43] and prohibitions on construction waste hauling by companies other than those granted monopolies by local municipalities.

III. Vigorous Antitrust Enforcement Is Essential

In seeking to eradicate private anticompetitive restraints within the professions, the onus rests primarily upon competition agencies, which ideally serve as disinterested advocates for consumer welfare. Perhaps the most obvious, but not necessarily the most broadly effective, tool available to these author-

---

41 *Meadows v Odom*, No 03–CV–960 (MD La). The case is pending.

42 *Cornwell v Hamilton* 80 F Supp 2d 1101, 1118 (1999).

43 The US Supreme Court granted *certiorari* in three such cases on 24 May 2004. In these cases, the Court will decide whether a state's regulatory scheme that permits in-state wineries directly to ship alcohol to consumers but restricts the ability of out-of-state wineries to do so violates the dormant Commerce Clause of the US Constitution. *See Granholm v Heald*, No 03–1116, 2004 US LEXIS 3697 (US, 24 May 2004); *Michigan Beer & Wine Wholesalers Ass'n v Heald*, No 03–1120, 2004 US LEXIS 3698 (US, 24 May 2004); and *Swedenburg v Kelly*, No 03–1274, 2004 US LEXIS 3699 (US, 24 May 2004).

ities lies in the pursuit of vigorous antitrust enforcement. As the following overview of notable cases illustrates, the experience of the US in this area indicates that a combination of antitrust enforcement at the federal and state levels can address some of these anticompetitive restraints.

1. Antitrust Enforcement of Professional Restraints at the Federal Level

As alluded to in the previous discussion of the legal profession in the US, the law school accreditation process administered by the ABA's Section of Legal Education and Admissions to the Bar plays an integral role in supporting entry regulations into the field of law. Indeed, the ABA's law school accreditation process is the only one recognized by the US Department of Education, which carries implications for student loan availability. In addition, more than 40 states require bar applicants to graduate from an ABA-approved law school. For these and other reasons, obtaining accreditation from the ABA has been characterized as 'critical to the successful operation of a law school.'[44]

In 1995, DOJ filed suit against the American Bar Association alleging that it had violated Sherman Act Section 1 in its accreditation of law schools.[45] Specifically, the complaint alleged that the ABA restrained competition among professional personnel at ABA-approved law schools by fixing their compensation levels, fringe benefits, and working conditions, and by limiting competition from non-ABA approved schools through boycott activities. The complaint also alleged that the ABA permitted its accreditation process to be captured by legal educators, who have a direct interest in its outcome.

In language reminiscent of other criticisms of the ABA,[46] the Competitive Impact Statement bluntly stated that the ABA at times acted not as an accreditation body but rather as a guild that protected the interests of professional law school personnel.[47] In contrast, legitimate accreditation activities, noted

---

[44] Competitive Impact Statement, *US v Am Bar Ass'n*, (No 95–1211 (CR)) 60 Fed Reg 39,421, 39,424 (27 June 1995), available a*t* http://www.usdoj.gov/atr/cases/f1000/1034.htm.

[45] Complaint, *US v Am Bar Ass'n*, No 95–1211 (CR) (DDC), *at* http://www.usdoj.gov/atr/cases/f0200/0254.pdf (27 June 1995).

[46] See Vest (2000); and Shepherd and Shepherd (1998).

[47] Competitive Impact Statement, above n 44, at 39,425:

> These Standards, Interpretations, and their application have unreasonably restricted competition in the market for the services of professional law school personnel. The salary Standard and its application had the effect of ratcheting up law school salaries. The Standard relating to proprietary law schools erected an unnecessary barrier to competition from these schools, which often provide their professional staff with lower salaries and fewer amenities than do ABA-approved schools. The restrictions on enrolling graduates of non-ABA-approved schools, and on offering transfer credits for course work completed at those schools, were unreasonable restraints of trade aimed at deterring effective competition from law schools that are likely to pay less in salaries and benefits to their professional staffs.

the complaint, 'focus on assuring the quality of the educational program and providing consumers with information regarding the quality of the educational program.'[48] The ABA accreditation process had not limited its activities to assessing quality, but also had evaluated salaries, perquisites and other terms and conditions of employment.

The ABA entered into a consent decree prohibiting it from taking any action to fix the compensation levels and other terms of employment of law school employees, and from taking any action to limit competition from non-ABA approved schools.[49] In addition, the ABA agreed to revise its accreditation process so as to limit the influence of law school personnel in, and to increase the transparency of, the process. The consent decree further provided that the ABA must institute an antitrust compliance program and establish a Special Commission to determine whether further changes in the accreditation process were warranted.

In another case involving higher education, DOJ filed suit against eight Ivy League universities and the Massachusetts Institute of Technology.[50] The complaint alleged that beginning at least as early as 1980, the defendants conspired to restrict the amount of financial aid awarded to admitted undergraduate students. According to the complaint, the conspiracy deprived students receiving financial aid and their families of the benefit of free and open price competition, causing some of these students and their families to pay more for an undergraduate education than they otherwise would have.

All but one of the defendants, MIT, entered into a consent decree that prohibited the consenting defendants from continuing their conspiracy. The consent decree included provisions requiring the institutions independently to decide financial aid policies and independently to calculate financial aid awards to individual students. In addition, defendants also were required to establish a comprehensive antitrust compliance program.[51]

In another case relating to restraints in the legal profession, the FTC brought suit against a group of private lawyers who agreed not to accept court appointments to represent indigent criminal defendants until the

---

[48] Complaint, above n 45, at para 33.

[49] *US v Am Bar Ass'n* 934 F Supp 435 (DDC, 1996).

[50] See Competitive Impact Statement, *US v Brown Univ* (No 91–CV–3724), 56 Fed Reg 26,156 (6 June 1991).

[51] The Antitrust Division litigated its case against MIT in federal court. The district court entered judgment in favour of the Division, holding that the agreement among the universities constituted price fixing. Due to the non-profit status and educational mission of the defendants, however, the court declined to apply the *per se* rule of illegality and instead applied an abbreviated version of the rule of reason. *US v Brown Univ* 805 F Supp 288 (ED Pa, 1992). The Court of Appeals held that the district court was correct when it concluded that non-profit institutions were covered by the Sherman Act and that the challenged practices implicated 'trade or commerce' within the meaning of Sherman Act S 1, but that it erred when it decided the case under an abbreviated rule of reason analysis, thereby giving short shrift to the procompetitive and social welfare justifications for the challenged practices. The Court of Appeals reversed and remanded, directing the district court to analyze the challenged conduct under a full scale rule of reason analysis. See *US v Brown Univ* 5 F 3d 658 (3rd Cir, 1993).

District of Columbia increased the lawyers' compensation. The US Supreme Court found that this boycott constituted a naked restraint of trade.[52] The Court concluded that the social justifications proffered in defence of the boycott—that the District of Columbia purchases the lawyers' services because it has a constitutional duty to provide representation to indigent defendants, and that the quality of representation may improve when rates are increased—did not make the agreement any less unlawful.

Also rejected by the Court was defendants' assertion that its conduct was protected as free speech by the First Amendment of the US Constitution because it sought to vindicate constitutional rights. The Court observed that '[n]o matter how altruistic the motives of the respondents may have been, it is undisputed that their immediate objective was to increase the price that they would be paid for their services.'[53] This type of economic boycott, ruled the Court, did not fall within the scope of earlier precedent protecting a non-violent, politically motivated boycott designed to effectuate rights guaranteed by the US Constitution.[54]

2. Antitrust Enforcement of Professional Restraints by the State Attorneys General

The State Attorneys General also have challenged private restraints among professionals. In a seminal case, the State of Arizona filed a complaint against two county medical societies and two foundations for medical care that the medical societies had organized. The foundations established the schedule of maximum fees that participating doctors agreed to accept as payment for services performed for patients insured under plans approved by the foundations. The State of Arizona alleged that the maximum fee agreements constituted unlawful price-fixing in violation of Sherman Act Section 1.

Before the Supreme Court, defendants asserted that *per se* treatment of the challenged conduct was inappropriate because doctors rather than non-professionals were parties to the price-fixing agreements.[55] The Court observed that the defendants did not argue, as had the defendants in *Goldfarb* and *Professional Engineers*, that the quality of the professional services offered by the foundations' participating doctors was enhanced by the price restraint. As the challenged agreements were not premised on public service or ethical norms, there was no basis for distinguishing the medical profession from any other provider of goods or services.[56] The Court likewise rejected

---

52 *FTC v Superior Court Trial Lawyers Ass'n* 493 US 411 (1990).

53 *Ibid*, p 427.

54 See *NAACP v Claiborne Hardware Co* 458 US 886 (1982).

55 *Arizona v Maricopa County Med Soc'y* 457 US 332, 349 (1982).

defendants' assertion that *per se* treatment was inappropriate because the judiciary had little antitrust experience in the health care industry, noting that 'the Sherman Act, so far as price-fixing agreements are concerned, establishes one uniform rule applicable to all industries alike.'[57] Finally, the Court rejected defendants' assertion that *per se* treatment was inappropriate because alleged procompetitive justifications for the conduct had been offered, stating that the 'anticompetitive potential inherent in all price-fixing agreements justifies their facial invalidation even if procompetitive justifications are offered for some.'[58] Having rejected these assertions, the Court held that the challenged agreements constituted *per se* violations of Section 1 of the Sherman Act.

In a more recent case, In re *Disposable Contact Lens Antitrust Litigation*,[59] thirty-two state AGs and a consumer class brought suit alleging anticompetitive conduct by eye care professionals and contact lens manufacturers. The complaint alleged that practitioners, acting through their trade associations, conspired with contact lens manufacturers to restrict or eliminate the supply of replacement disposable contact lenses available to so-called alternative channels of distribution, including mail order companies and pharmacies. In addition, the practitioners allegedly undertook to limit consumers' ability and opportunity to purchase contact lenses from alternative channels by restraining consumer access to the prescriptions or work orders needed to obtain replacement contact lenses.

The complaint alleged that through their actions, defendants restricted or eliminated the supply of contact lenses to alternative channels, thereby inhibiting their growth. Consequently, consumers allegedly paid more for contact lenses purchased from eye care professionals and alternative channels, and consumers experienced a lower level of convenience than they had come to expect from the alternative channels, because the distributors' sources of supplies were uncertain and covert. Defendant contact lens manufacturers and the American Optometric Association eventually settled the lawsuit, agreeing to provide a total recovery package for plaintiffs worth almost $100 million and to refrain from attempts to limit competition from alternative distribution channels.

---

[56] *FTC v Superior Court Trial Lawyers Ass'n* 493 US 411 (1990).

[57] *Ibid*, p 349–51.

[58] *Ibid*, p 351.

[59] In re *Disposable Contact Lens Litigation*, MDL Docket No 1030 (MD Fla).

IV. Competition Advocacy Is also Essential

As the preceding discussion illustrates, antitrust enforcement can serve as one tool in eliminating anticompetitive restraints within the learned professions. Antitrust litigation, however, is lengthy, costly, and unlikely to remedy or deter a persistent landslide of new private restraints. Moreover, the reach of the antitrust laws is not boundless: the state action doctrine shields many restraints from scrutiny under the antitrust laws.[60] In the United States, the state action doctrine limits the scope of the antitrust laws by providing that otherwise illegal conduct will be immune from challenge under the antitrust laws if it is in furtherance of a 'clearly articulated' state policy and is 'actively supervised' by the state.

Over the long run, antitrust enforcement authorities can address this issue by insuring that the state action exemption 'remains true to its doctrinal foundation of protecting the deliberate policy choices of sovereign states, and is otherwise applied in a manner that promotes competition and enhances consumer welfare.'[61] A recently released FTC staff report concludes that in the US, the doctrine 'has become unmoored from its original objectives . . . and is frequently invoked to protect private commercial efforts with no relation to state policy.'[62] In an attempt to rein in overbroad interpretations that may result in consumer harm, the FTC's state action report recommends several clarifications to the doctrine, including more rigorous application of the 'clear articulation' and 'active supervision' requirements.[63]

Even then, however, some category of restraints still will fall beyond the scope of antitrust enforcement. In these cases, a second approach—competition

---

[60] Outgoing FTC Chairman Timothy J Muris has noted that rational firms are likely to prefer governmentally imposed restraints to private agreements in restraint of trade. In a speech before the Fordham Annual Conference in 2003, Chairman Muris stated:

> In many ways, public restraints are far more effective and efficient at restraining competition. Unlike private restraints, there is no need to maintain backroom secrecy or to incur the costs of conducting a covert cartel. Public restraints can be open and notorious. Public restraints are also a more efficient means of solving the entry problem. Rather than ceaselessly monitoring the marketplace for new rivals, a firm can simply rely on a public regime that, for example, provides for only a limited number of licenses. Perhaps the clearest advantage of public restraints is that they frequently include a built-in cartel enforcement mechanism. While cheating often besets private cartels, public cartels suffer from no such defect. Cheaters, once identified, can be sanctioned through government processes. (Muris, 2003, 2.)

[61] *Ibid*, p 15.

[62] FTC (2003b).

[63] FTC (2003c).

advocacy—is vital.[64] Antitrust authorities can make a major contribution to consumer welfare by persuading legislators and regulatory bodies to adopt a more market-oriented perspective. They can advocate deregulation in those instances in which regulation is unnecessary, and urge reliance on market mechanisms to fashion more efficient regulatory schemes when regulation is deemed necessary.

1. Competition Advocacy at the Federal Level

In remarks delivered at the inaugural meeting of the International Competition Network in 2002, FTC Chairman Timothy J Muris observed that competition advocacy is essential to creating a 'culture of competition.'[65] In identifying ways to encourage greater competition, Chairman Muris acknowledged enforcement as an important tool, but observed that other tools 'may be better or more effective, especially when governments are making major policy changes that fundamentally will reshape the competitive landscape.'[66] He expounded upon the concept of competition advocacy:

> Competition policy is more than enforcement—it is a way of organizing our economy. In this sense, competition policy is a form of regulation that competes with other regulatory structures, many of which are hostile to free markets. For this reason, competition policy must become more aggressive in competing with other forms of regulation. As competition advocates, we should support the philosophy of competition policy at every opportunity and in every forum. In executive councils, before national and local legislatures, and through public opinion, we should increase our efforts to produce the evidence and rhetoric necessary to defend the marketplace.[67]

As will be discussed in greater detail below, the FTC has a lengthy history of competition advocacy, particularly within the medical and legal professions.

DOJ historically also has viewed competition advocacy as an important aspect of its mission. Chapter 5 of the Antitrust Division Manual is devoted completely to a discussion of this topic. The Manual states that '[i]n addition to enforcing the antitrust laws, the Antitrust Division also acts as an advocate for competition, seeking to promote competition in sectors of the economy that are or may be subject to government regulation.'[68] The goals of the Division's advocacy program are fourfold:

---

[64] Yet another route that has been employed lies in challenging state laws and regulations as unconstitutional under the Commerce Clause of the US Constitution, which preserves free trade among the states. US Constitution art. I, para 8. A state law that discriminates on its face against interstate commerce will be invalidated by the courts.

[65] Muris (2002).

[66] *Ibid.*

[67] *Ibid.*

[68] US Department of Justice, 1998, Ch V, A1.

(1) To eliminate unnecessary and costly existing regulation;
(2) To inhibit the growth of unnecessary new regulation;
(3) To minimize the competitive distortions caused when regulation is necessary by advocating the least anticompetitive form of regulation consistent with the valid regulatory objectives; and
(4) To ensure that regulation is properly designed to accomplish legitimate regulatory objectives.[69]

The goal expressed by the Division is 'to promote reliance on competition rather than on government regulation wherever possible under the circumstances and to ensure that necessary regulation is well designed to achieve its objectives.'[70]

The Division's Manual also provides guidance regarding the analytical model that it employs when analyzing the need for new or continued regulation.

> [T]he Division attempts to focus attention on the comparative benefits of free competition, on the one hand, and the proposed method of regulation, on the other, by asking several basic questions:
>
> (1) What are the costs or disadvantages of free competition in the market or industry at issue?
> (2) If the regulatory scheme is an existing one, has regulation fulfilled its purpose; and, do the underlying economic and social conditions justifying regulatory interference with the marketplace still exist?
> (3) What are the costs and benefits associated with the existing or proposed regulatory scheme?
> (4) If existing regulation is to be eliminated, what are the necessary elements of a transition from regulated to a competitive, unregulated market?
> (5) If regulation is appropriate, is the particular regulatory scheme well-tailored to achieve its purpose?
>
> Asking these questions requires those who favour regulation to demonstrate that the benefits to the public of regulation outweigh its anticompetitive effects; that such benefits cannot be achieved by some less anticompetitive alternative; and that, where regulation is needed, it be wisely crafted to accomplish its objectives with no unintended consequences.[71]

When these showings cannot be made, concludes the Manual, 'the case for regulatory reform, up to and possibly including the elimination of regulation, is compelling.'[72]

The competition advocacy activities of the federal agencies assume many forms. Both DOJ and the FTC interact with numerous federal agencies; provide testimony on legislative initiatives; undertake studies of various

[69] *Ibid.*
[70] *Ibid,* §B.
[71] *Ibid,* §A1.
[72] *Ibid.*

industries and hold hearings on relevant topics; and intervene in regulatory agency proceedings. Some examples of these activities are explored below. Although not all of the examples relate directly to restraints within the professions, they nonetheless serve to illustrate the manner in which intervention by the federal antitrust authorities may promote greater reliance on market mechanisms.

2. Interaction with Other Federal Agencies

The Antitrust Division has played an active role in the airline industry since Congress enacted the Airline Deregulation Act of 1978. In addition to undertaking various enforcement actions for airline matters falling within its jurisdiction, DOJ also provides both formal and informal guidance to the Department of Transportation on airline matters falling within that agency's jurisdiction. For example, DOJ has filed comments in various DOT proceedings, including the review of proposed international airline alliances, rulemakings concerning computer reservations systems, and rulemakings concerning the allocation of slots at high-density airports. During the years when DOT possessed merger review authority, DOJ also provided comments to DOT on proposed airline mergers.

In addition, DOJ has played an integral role in the implementation of the Telecommunications Act of 1996.[73] Section 271 of that statute provides that a Bell Operating Company may not provide in-region long distance services until it demonstrates to the Federal Communications Commission that it has met legal requirements designed to open the local telecommunications markets in a particular state to competition. In considering whether to approve a company's application for long distance authority in a particular state, the FCC must consult with the DOJ and give 'substantial weight' to its assessment.[74]

DOJ also provides market-oriented guidance to the Department of Agriculture (*eg,* consultation on studies that USDA has conducted regarding competition-related aspects of agricultural markets), the Federal Aviation Administration (*eg,* comments on alternative policy options for managing capacity at LaGuardia Airport and proposed extension of lottery allocation), the Federal Energy Regulatory Commission (*eg,* comments on the notice of proposed rulemaking on regional transmission organizations), the Federal Maritime Commission (*eg,* comments on Section 6(g) of the Shipping Act of 1984), the Federal Communications Commission (*eg,* comments on the proposed acquisition of Hispanic Broadcasting Corporation by Univision

[73] Telecommunications Act of 1996, Pub L No 104–4, 110 Stat 56 (1996).
[74] *Ibid* para 271(d)(2)(A).

Communications Inc.), the Federal Reserve Bank (*eg,* comments on the Federal Reserve Bank's Interpretive and Compliance Guide to the Anti-Tying Restrictions of Section 106 of the Bank Holding Company Act Amendments of 1970), and the Securities and Exchange Commission (*eg,* comments on proposed option market linkage plans by stock exchanges).[75]

In a speech in 2003 before the Fordham Annual Conference on International Antitrust Law and Policy, Chairman Muris addressed the importance of working with other federal agencies to promote competition.[76] During the course of these interactions, observed Chairman Muris, the FTC has encouraged its colleagues in other agencies to adopt rules that incorporate principles of competition. The FTC has provided a competition perspective to the Food and Drug Administration (*eg,* comments on direct-to-consumer advertising of pharmaceutical products), the Federal Energy Regulatory Commission (*eg,* comments on revisions to market-based rate tariffs and authorizations), and the Environmental Protection Agency (*eg,* comments on boutique fuel regulations).[77]

3. Congressional Testimony on Legislative Initiatives

On numerous occasions during the last several years, the FTC has testified before the US Congress regarding the likely anticompetitive impact of proposed antitrust exemptions that would permit physicians and other health care providers to engage in collective bargaining with health plans.[78] The proposed exemptions have arisen in an era of sweeping changes in the health service markets precipitated by the efforts of private employers and government health care programs to address rapidly increasing health care costs. Physicians and other health care providers have asserted that, in this environment, antitrust exemptions are necessary to promote the quality of patient care and to place physicians, dentists, pharmacists, and other health care professionals on a more level playing field when negotiating with powerful health plans.

Relying on the expertise that it has obtained through dozens of enforcement actions in the health care industry, the FTC consistently has opposed Congressional legislation that would exempt health care providers' collective negotiation of rates and other contractual elements from antitrust liability. Historically, the agency's objections have focused on two major points. First,

---

[75] DOJ's submissions to federal agencies are available at http://www.usdoj.gov/atr/public/comments/comments.htm.

[76] Muris, 2003.

[77] The FTC's submissions to other federal agencies are available at http://www.ftc.gov/be/advofile.htm.

[78] *See* US House of Representatives (2000b); US House of Representatives (1998); and US House of Representatives (1996).

the FTC has asserted that an antitrust exemption for physician collective bargaining would authorize price-fixing by physicians and other health service providers, which could be expected to generate increased consumer costs and decreased consumer access to care. Second, the FTC has argued that while this type of exemption likely would not improve the quality of patient care, there are other, more effective means of addressing quality of care issues that do not sacrifice the benefits of a competitive marketplace.

Similarly, DOJ in recent years has offered testimony before the US Congress urging the repeal of antitrust exemptions and the deregulation of regulated industries, and discouraging the enactment of additional regulations that would inhibit the functioning of market forces. To name just a few examples, officials from DOJ have testified in favour of removing the antitrust exemption for ocean carriers from the Shipping Act of 1984;[79] in opposition to the efforts of the US Postal Service to expand the scope of the statutory protections afforded by the Private Express Statutes, and to erect restrictions on competition in international mail services;[80] and in favour of efforts to deregulate the electricity industry while taking into account competitive issues that will arise in a restructured market.[81]

4. Studies of Regulated Industries

The agencies also advance the culture of competition by holding hearings and undertaking studies of regulated industries. As an independent expert agency and a deliberative body, the FTC is particularly well-suited to conduct such activities. One recently released FTC staff report explores possible barriers to e-commerce with respect to disposable soft contact lenses. The FTC staff report acknowledged that there are significant health issues concerning the use and sale of contact lenses, but concluded that requiring online companies to obtain professional licenses to sell replacement contact lenses is likely to raise prices and reduce convenience to consumers without substantially increasing health protections already provided by existing prescription requirements and general consumer protection laws. Based on this conclusion, the report recommends that policymakers rescind, or refrain from adopting, requirements that Internet sellers have a professional license to sell replacement contact lenses.[82]

During the period from February to September of 2003, the FTC and DOJ co-sponsored a series of hearings on the implications of competition law and policy for health care financing and delivery. During the course of several

[79] US House of Representatives (2002b).
[80] US House of Representatives (2000a); and US House of Representatives (1999a).
[81] US House of Representatives (1999b).
[82] FTC (2004b).

months in 2002, the agencies co-hosted another set of hearings to explore how best to manage the issues that arise at the intersection of antitrust and intellectual property law and policy.[83]

5. Comments to State Governments

State policymakers sometimes ask the federal antitrust authorities to comment upon the likely competitive consequences of proposed legislation or regulations. In recent years, for example, the Antitrust Division and the FTC repeatedly have counselled against the adoption of restraints by state bar associations and state legislatures that would inhibit non-lawyers from competing against lawyers. One notable area of activity in which lawyers have sought to limit competition concerns real estate closings; this area has become a significant battleground between lawyers and lay closers. The issue has arisen in part because of the increased presence of online mortgage brokers, which frequently rely on non-attorneys at closings. Competition between attorneys and lay closers can result in cost savings and greater convenience for consumers.

Feeling the pressure, bar associations and state supreme courts in several states have considered measures that would render real estate closings the sole province of attorneys. In numerous instances, the federal antitrust authorities have counselled state authorities to reconsider these measures.[84] One recent example in this area illustrates the positive impact that the federal agencies can have.

In 2001, the North Carolina State Bar adopted two ethics opinions that required the physical presence of lawyers at all real estate refinancing[85] and residential real estate purchase closings.[86] The opinions effectively prevented consumers from using the services of less expensive or more convenient lay closers or paralegals working under the supervision of an attorney. In a joint letter to the Ethics Committee of the North Carolina (NC) State Bar,[87] the FTC and DOJ observed that these measures likely would increase the closing costs of NC consumers by $150 to $400, and decrease consumers' convenience by preventing them from using lay closers more likely to conduct closings on evenings and weekends. The FTC and DOJ emphasized that the

[83] The FTC subsequently released a report containing recommendations regarding the manner in which the patent system can maintain a proper balance with competition law and policy. See FTC (2003a).

[84] See, eg, US Department of Justice and FTC (2003b); US Department of Justice and FTC (2003a); US Department of Justice and FTC (2002b); US Department of Justice and FTC (1999); and US Department of Justice and FTC (1997).

[85] North Carolina State Bar Ethics Committee (2001a).

[86] North Carolina State Bar Ethics Committee (2001b).

[87] US Department of Justice and FTC (2001).

opinions made no showing of harm to consumers from lay settlements that would justify these reductions in competition.

The DOJ/FTC joint letter was effective in raising red flags regarding the anticompetitive effects of the opinions. An investigatory hearing was scheduled to explore the concerns raised by the federal antitrust authorities; staff of the FTC provided testimony at the hearing. Two additional ethics opinions subsequently were proposed, one that would permit lawyers to delegate real estate closing tasks to their employees working under their supervision,[88] and one that would authorize lay closers to perform the ministerial functions of real estate closings if they refrained from providing legal advice.[89] A joint letter from the FTC and DOJ urged adoption of both opinions, which would 'allow North Carolina consumers to enjoy the fruits of competition between attorneys and non-lawyers: lower prices and more choices in how and when closing services are provided.'[90] The new opinions were adopted in early 2003.

As discussed above, the FTC on a number of occasions has testified before the US Congress in opposition to proposed federal legislation that would permit physicians and other health service providers collectively to negotiate fees and other aspects of their contracts with health plans. The FTC's advocacy efforts in this area extend beyond proposals at the federal level. In addition, the FTC has expressed similar concerns about bills before state legislatures. Specifically, FTC staff has submitted comments regarding various types of proposed antitrust exemptions for health care providers to the state legislatures of Alaska,[91] Ohio,[92] Texas,[93] and Washington,[94] and to the District of Columbia Office of Corporation Counsel. In a similar vein, FTC staff has provided comments to state authorities in North Dakota[95] and Vermont[96] regarding the likely anticompetitive effects of proposed antitrust exemptions for cooperative agreements among hospitals and other health care providers. The FTC and DOJ have submitted many other comments to state authorities, as well.[97]

6. *Amicus* Filings

The federal agencies can use *amicus* briefs to encourage the use of market mechanisms and limit the scope of regulatory licensing requirements. In one

88 North Carolina State Bar Ethics Committee (2003a).

89 North Carolina State Bar Ethics Committee (2003b).

90 US Department of Justice and FTC (2002a).

91 Simons and Cruz (2002) (commenting on Alaska Senate Bill 37); and Cruz (2002).

92 Brennan and Cruz (2002) (commenting on Ohio House Bill 325).

93 Baer (1999) (commenting on Texas Senate Bill 1468).

94 Brennan, Cruz and Harwood (2002) (commenting on Washington House Bill 2360).

95 Wise (1993) (commenting on North Dakota Senate Bill 2295).

96 Wise (1994).

97 A complete list of the FTC's submissions to state authorities is available at http://www.ftc.gov/be/advofile.htm. DOJ's submissions to state authorities are available at http://www.usdoj.gov/atr/public/comments/comments.htm.

recent instance, the FTC filed an *amicus* brief in a case involving a state board that sought to invoke one of the FTC's consumer protection rules as justification for a state licensing requirement.[98] The case was brought by an Internet-based casket manufacturer who filed suit against the Oklahoma State Board of Embalmers and Funeral Directors. The suit alleged that Oklahoma's Funeral Services Licensing Act (FSLA),[99] which provides that only holders of funeral director and funeral establishment licenses may sell funeral service merchandise in Oklahoma, violates the Commerce Clause of the US Constitution. Given the extensive training and infrastructure prerequisites required to obtain the licenses, Internet-based casket retailers effectively are precluded from selling caskets to Oklahoma residents. The Board asserted that the challenged provisions were designed to protect Oklahoma's consumers from overreaching sales tactics, and in fact advanced the same goals as the FTC's Funeral Rule.

In its *amicus* brief, the FTC clarified that the Funeral Rule was adopted, in part, to permit consumers to purchase caskets and other funeral merchandise from third parties who are not funeral directors. The FTC asserted in its brief that the FSLA does not promote consumer choice, but instead 'forces consumers to purchase caskets from funeral directors. Whatever ends the FSLA can be said to be advocating, it is not advancing the ends of the FTC's Funeral Rule.' The FTC's brief further observed that by insulating the funeral service industry in Oklahoma from competition, the FSLA's requirements would deny Oklahoma consumers the benefits of competition from alternative forms of casket retailing, resulting in higher prices and fewer choices.

The district court declined to rule on the Commerce Clause challenge and ruled against plaintiffs on their other constitutional challenges.[100] Under this test, the court concluded that '[c]onsumer protection is a legitimate goal of Oklahoma public policy and licensure is one rational way in which the State may choose to serve that goal, despite the impact of that choice on other public policy interests such as increased competition in the marketplace.'[101] Courts in three other states, however, have struck down similar laws.[102]

---

[98] Memorandum of Law of *amicus* Curiae the Federal Trade Commission, *Powers v Harris* (No CIV–01–445–F) *at* http://www.ftc.gov/os/2002/09/ok *amicus*.pdf (29 Aug 2002).

[99] Okla. Stat. tit. 59, para 395.1–396.28(2004).

[100] *Powers v Harris*, No CIV–01–445–F, 2002 US Dist LEXIS 26939 (WD Okla, 2002).

[101] *Ibid,* n 55. Despite its ultimate ruling, *dicta* indicates that the court questioned whether the challenged FSLA provisions protect consumers, and whether a consumer shopping on-line for a casket at the time of a family member's death was as vulnerable as suggested by the State. Based on the available evidence, the court speculated that consumers might well be served 'by a little less protection and a little more access to open competition,' and that 'the actual motivation for enactment of the challenged legislation was in all likelihood, far less altruistic than the rationales proffered now.' *Ibid,* p 57–58. Despite its doubts, the court found that the necessary showings had been made under the relevant analytical framework, thereby requiring the court to uphold the challenged licensing requirements.

[102] See *Craigmiles v Giles* 110 F Supp 2d 658 (ED Tenn, 2000), aff'd *Craigmiles v Giles* 312 F 3d 220 (6th Cir, 2002); *Casket Royale v Mississippi* 124 F Supp 2d 434 (SD Miss, 2000); and

With the similar motive of preventing the displacement of the antitrust laws, DOJ filed an *amicus* brief with the Second Circuit Court of Appeals in the *In re: Stock Exchange Options Trading Antitrust Litigation.*[103] Plaintiffs alleged that the defendant stock exchanges conspired to restrict the listing and trading of particular options to one exchange at a time in violation of Sherman Act Section 1. If it existed, the alleged agreement also would violate a rule promulgated by the Securities and Exchange Commission. The district court held that the Securities Exchange Act of 1934 impliedly repealed the Sherman Act with respect to the listing and trading of options on securities exchanges regulated by the SEC, and granted the defendants summary judgment on the implied repeal issue.[104]

In its *amicus* brief, DOJ asserted that the lower court had erred. Implied repeal of the antitrust laws is disfavoured and must be found only when and to the extent necessary to make a federal regulatory program work as Congress intended, argued DOJ. Here, where the challenged conduct violates both the federal antitrust laws and the relevant SEC rule adopted pursuant to the federal securities laws, no finding of implied repeal was required to make the securities laws work. A panel of the Second Circuit Court of Appeals affirmed the lower court's ruling with respect to the implied repeal issue, holding that '[t]he appropriateness of an implied repeal does not turn on whether the antitrust laws conflict with the current view of a regulatory agency; rather it turns on whether the antitrust laws conflict with an overall regulatory scheme that empowers the agency to allow conduct that the antitrust laws would prohibit.'[105] Noting that the panel's decision was the first ever to hold the Sherman Act impliedly repealed as to alleged conduct affirmatively prohibited by agency rule, DOJ petitioned the Second Circuit to grant rehearing en banc.[106]

7. Litigation to Clarify/Limit the Scope of the Regulatory Regime

The Antitrust Division Manual observes that antitrust enforcement efforts can be employed to insure that a regulatory scheme does not shield a broader

---

Peachtree Caskets Direct Inc v State Board of Funeral Service of Georgia, No 1: 98–CV–3084–MHS (ND Ga, 9 Feb 1999).

[103] Brief *amicus* Curiae of the United States Urging Reversal In Support of Appellants, *In re Stock Exch. Options Trading Antitrust Litig.* (No 01–7371), *at* www.usdoj.gov/atr/cases/f8700/8715.htm (July 7, 2001).

[104] In re Stock Exch Options Trading Antitrust Litig 2001–1 Trade Cas (CCH) ¶73,186 (SDNY, 2001).

[105] *Miller v Am Stock Exch (In re Stock Exch. Options Trading Antitrust Litig)* 317 F 3d 134, 149 (2nd Cir, 2003).

[106] Brief for the United States as *amicus* Curiae in Support of Petition for Rehearing En Banc, *In re Stock Exch. Options Trading Antitrust Litig* (No 01–7371), *at* www.usdoj.gov/atr/cases/f200700/200758.htm (10 February 2003).

category of anticompetitive activity than is necessary or intended. For example, the DOJ successfully litigated a case that established that mergers between ocean carriers were not subject to Federal Maritime Commission approval and antitrust immunity under Section 15 of the Shipping Act.[107]

8. Advocacy in the International Arena

The US promotes the adoption and enforcement of competition laws by foreign jurisdictions. The spread of antitrust regimes brings with it certain dangers, however, including the possibility that jurisdictions new to antitrust enforcement will employ their nascent antitrust laws to promote other goals, such as industrial policy and protectionism. Thus, in the international arena, the US employs competition advocacy to promote vigorous antitrust enforcement well-grounded in sound principles and practices.

The importance of the topic of competition advocacy further is reflected in the work of international organizations, including the International Competition Network. One DOJ official observed that one of the primary goals underlying the formation of the ICN 'was to promote greater convergence . . . around sound competition principles by working together, and with stakeholders in the private sector, to develop best practice recommendations for antitrust enforcement and competition advocacy that could then be implemented voluntarily by the member agencies.'[108] In fact, one of the ICN's first working groups was created to address the topic of competition advocacy.

V. Competition Advocacy by the State Attorneys General

The state attorneys general have a significant contribution to make in the area of competition advocacy, as well. Susan Creighton, Director of the FTC's Bureau of Competition, discussed the comparative advantages of the state attorneys general in the formulation of state regulatory policy in 2003.[109] She identified three ways in which state attorneys general are uniquely positioned to advance competition policy within their jurisdictions:

(1) as principal legal counsel to the state, the state AG is well-positioned to provide counsel on the potential competitive ramifications of proposed

[107] *United States v RJ Reynolds Tobacco Co* 416 F Supp 316 (DNJ, 1976).
[108] Kolasky (2002) 8.
[109] Creighton (2003).

regulatory measures and the ways in which they may interface with other statutory regimes, including the antitrust laws;

(2) the state AG is intimately familiar with the policy objectives and goals of state regulatory policy, and therefore able to suggest ways in which regulatory measures can be tailored to meet those objectives while accommodating competition policy to the extent possible; and

(3) the state AG has the advantage of proximity to state boards and the consumers they serve.

In addition, she observed that the state AGs are well-positioned to supervise the implementation of regulatory regimes in a manner that is consistent both with the state's objectives and the supervisory requirements of the state action doctrine.

A review of the recent advocacy efforts of the state attorneys general reveals that they, like the federal antitrust agencies, engage in a variety of activities on several fronts.[110] Within the last decade, they have submitted *amicus* briefs in eight Supreme Court cases involving antitrust issues that ultimately were decided on the merits. In addition, they have submitted countless other *amicus* briefs relating to antitrust issues in federal and state courts throughout the nation. The advocacy efforts of the state attorneys general also include numerous submissions to state and federal legislatures and regulatory bodies.

VI. Conclusion

Thirty years after the US Supreme Court's holding in *Goldfarb v Virginia State Bar*, public and private restraints within the professions abound. The antitrust enforcement and competition advocacy efforts of the federal and state competition authorities can be taken as a positive sign. Relentless forces are at work, however, both to undermine and to outrun the efforts of the competition authorities. First, members of the professions possess a significant financial incentive to implement restraints—both public and private—that will inhibit competition among incumbents and limit entry by would-be competitors. Second, to accommodate the federalist structure of the US, the state action doctrine permits state and local governments to choose to displace competition. Finally, federal, state, and local governments generally seem more enamoured of the cause of restraints in the professions, cloaked, as they usually are, as measures to protect public health, safety, and

[110] A list of competition advocacy efforts by the state attorneys general undertaken through various mechanisms can be found at http://www.abanet.org/antitrust/committees/state-antitrust/advocacy.html#acb.

welfare.

Against this backdrop, and given the apparently voluminous number of restraints currently inhibiting competition within the professions today, greater effort by competition authorities seemingly is warranted. Moreover, even in the best of cases, when anticompetitive restraints or unnecessary regulations are abolished, the job of the competition authorities is not complete: continued oversight of deregulation efforts and competitive practices within the professions plays a vital role in insuring that competition can flourish.

V

*Mario Siragusa**

Critical Remarks on the Commission's Legal Analysis in its Report on Competition in Professional Services

I. Introduction

In this paper, I wish to provide some comments on the Commission Communication titled 'Report on Competition in Professional Services', published on 9 February 2004 (the 'Report'). Similar comments are contained in the paper that the Council of the Bars and Law Societies of the European Union will soon provide to the Commission and that my partner Giuseppe Scassellati Sforzolini has helped to draft. In particular, this paper focuses on the Commission's analysis of the Community legal framework within which the allegedly restrictive State or professional bodies' regulations have to be analysed.

Preliminarily, I would like to note that the approach *vis-à-vis* professional regulations adopted in the Report is not entirely consistent with what the Commission itself has recently proposed in its draft framework Directive on services in the internal market.[1] The draft Directive provides, for example, that advertising by regulated professions 'must comply with professional rules which relate, in particular, to the independence, dignity and integrity of the profession, as well as to professional secrecy, in a manner consonant with the specific nature of each profession'[2] thereby clearly acknowledging that advertising by members of the liberal professions requires regulation. More importantly, the draft Directive encourages the drawing up, at Community level, of codes of conduct for regulated professions concerning advertising and rules of professional ethics aimed at ensuring independence, impartiality and professional secrecy,[3] thus showing a generally more favourable attitude than the Report with regard to regulation by professional bodies.

With more specific regard to the Commission's competition law analysis, I believe that the Report contains a number of statements and suggestions

* Cleary Gottlieb Steen & Hamilton, Rome, Italy.

[1] Commission Proposal for a Directive of the European Parliament and of the Council on services in the internal market, available http://www.europa.eu.int/eur-lex/en/com/pdf/2004/com2004_0002en01.pdf.

[2] See Art 29 of the draft Directive.

[3] See Art 39 of the draft Directive.

which do not appear to be fully in line with the European Courts' case law, in particular with certain important recent developments. Furthermore, the Commission has not addressed at least one significant issue in the Report, ie, the potential application of Article 86(2) EC to members of the professions.

II. Liability of Members of the Professions under EC Competition Rules

1. The Commission Analysis of the '*Wouters* Exception'

In my view, the Report seeks to minimise the impact of the *Wouters* judgment where the Court of Justice (the 'Court') set forth the law concerning the application of Article 81 EC of the Treaty self-regulation by a bar. Indeed, when analysing what it calls the '*Wouters* exception', the Commission states that, in that judgment, the Court held that not every agreement between undertakings or every decision of an association of undertakings which restricts competition necessarily infringes Article 81(1) EC. Indeed, in the *Wouters* case, there was no infringement of Article 81(1) EC because the professional regulation at stake, despite being inherently restrictive of competition, 'was necessary for the proper practice of the profession, as organized in the Member State concerned' (paragraph 75).

In the Commission's view, one prong of the test that the Court established in order to assess whether a given professional regulation falls within the scope of, and thus infringes, Article 81(1) EC, is whether the effects restrictive of competition of such regulation do not 'go beyond what is necessary in order to ensure the proper practice of the profession'. This statement, quoted from the *Wouters* judgment,[4] must be read together with the Commission's invitation to EU professional bodies to review the restrictions contained in their existing rules and regulations considering, *inter alia*, 'whether there are no less restrictive means to achieve' the desired objective (paragraphs 93 and 94).

I think, however, that the defining feature of the *Wouters* judgment is precisely the Court's recognition of a margin of discretion of bar associations in deciding what they deem appropriate and necessary to protect the proper practice of the profession in their respective Member States.[5]

First, the Court clearly stated that the fact that less restrictive rules may be applicable in certain Member States does not mean that a more restrictive

[4] Case C–309/99 *Wouters, Savelbergh, Price Waterhouse Belastingadviseurs v Algemene Raad van de Nederlandse Orde van Advocaten* [2002] ECR I–1577.

[5] *Wouters*, para 105 and 108.

rule in force in another Member State infringes EC competition law.[6] This is because, as acknowledged by the Court, in the absence of specific Community rules in the field, each Member State remains in principle free to regulate the exercise of the legal profession within its territory. As a consequence, different Member States may consider different core values as being necessary for the proper exercise of the profession—and/or different means to protect them—and accordingly professional regulations may significantly differ from one Member State to another.[7]

In *Wouters*, for example, the Court found that the approach in the Netherlands was to consider the following duties necessary to ensure the proper practice of the legal profession: (i) the duty to act on behalf of the client in complete independence and in the client's sole interest; (ii) the duty to avoid all conflicts of interest; and (iii) the duty to observe strict professional secrecy. There were no comparable duties imposed on accountants in the Netherlands.[8] Thus, the fact the multi-disciplinary partnerships of lawyers and accountants are allowed in some Member States was not relevant to assess whether the Dutch Bar regulation prohibiting such partnerships fell within the scope of Article 81(1) EC since the analysis must be carried out having regard to the national context (*eg,* in *Wouters*, to the legal regimes by which members of the Bar and accountants are respectively governed in the Netherlands).

In light of the above, frequent statements made by the Commission in the section of the Report analysing the main categories of allegedly restrictive regulations, to the effect that such restrictions have been removed or relaxed in certain Member States and that this might mean that there are less restrictive alternatives to achieve the desired results, should not be read as meaning that 'more restrictive' regulations in other Member States may be considered contrary to EC competition law.

Having said this, it is true that certain statements in *Wouters* indicate that a professional regulation falls outside the scope of Article 81(1) EC if: (i) its restrictive effects do not go beyond what is necessary to ensure the proper practice of the legal profession, as perceived in the Member State in question; and (ii) there are no less restrictive means.

However, the crucial point in *Wouters* is that the assessment of whether professional regulations fulfil these conditions is substantially deferred to professional bodies. Indeed, the language of the Court clearly indicates that bar associations enjoy a margin of discretion to decide what is appropriate and necessary to protect the proper practice of the profession, in light of their respective national legal context and of the prevailing perceptions of the

[6] *Wouters*, para 108.
[7] *Wouters*, para 99.
[8] *Wouters*, paras 100 to 103.

profession in their respective Member State.[9] In other words, in my view, the *Wouters* judgment stands for the principle that, since they are better placed to fully evaluate whether a restrictive professional regulation is necessary to protect the core values of the legal profession, bar associations must retain the power to opt for the solution (which need not necessarily be the least restrictive) that they deem most appropriate to this end.

Therefore, I believe that it would be contrary to the *Wouters* judgment—to use EC competition rules to unduly limit this necessary margin of discretion through a mechanical application of a 'less restrictive means' test.

2. The Potential Application of Article 86(2) EC

In his opinion in the *Wouters* case,[10] Advocate General Léger held that Article 86(2) EC applies to lawyers practicing in the Netherlands. As we all know, this Article allows undertakings which are entrusted with the operation of services of general economic interest—conditions the Advocate General considered satisfied by members of the Dutch Bar—to be subject to competition rules only to the extent that the application of such rules does not obstruct the performance of the task assigned to them. The Advocate General concluded that the Dutch Bar regulation prohibiting multi-disciplinary partnerships between lawyers and accountants fell within the scope of Article 81(1) EC, without prejudice to the application of Article 86(2) EC. He added that the latter might apply to the Dutch Bar regulation if that measure is necessary in order to safeguard lawyers' independence and professional secrecy, but that it was for the national court to determine whether that was the case.[11] Although the Court declined to address the issue in its judgment, the position of Advocate General Léger is of significant interest. The only cursory reference to Article 86 in the Report is in the introduction where the Commission states that since it 'finds that important progress can be made using other mechanisms, it does not at this stage explore the potential use of Article 86 EC'. I think that it is unfortunate that the Commission decided not to address this issue in a communication whose main purpose is to set out the Commission's thinking on the application of competition rules to professional services in the EU.

---

[9] *Wouters*, para 108, where the Court states that 'the Bar of the Netherlands *is entitled to consider* that the objectives pursued by the 1993 Regulation cannot, having regard in particular to the legal regimes by which members of the Bar and accountants are respectively governed in the Netherlands, be attained by less restrictive means' (emphasis added); and para 107 where it concludes that '[A] regulation such as the 1993 Regulation *could therefore reasonably be considered to be necessary* in order to ensure the proper practice of the legal profession, as it is organised in the Member State concerned' (emphasis added).

[10] Opinion of Advocate General Léger of 10 July 2001, [2002] ECR I–1577.

[11] Opinion, paras 155 to 201.

III. Liability of Member States

1. The Absence of a Public Interest/Proportionality Test in the Case Law of the Court on Member States' Liability under Articles 3(1)(g), 10(2) and 81(1) EC

In the section concerning Member State liability, the Commission states that:

> [A] proportionality test would seem appropriate to assess to what extent an anti-competitive professional regulations [sic] truly serves the public interest. For this purpose it would be useful that each rule had an explicitly stated objective and an explanation [of] how the chosen regulatory measure is the least restrictive mechanism to effectively attain the stated objective (paragraph 88).

This statement constitutes the basis of the invitation, contained in Section 6.1 of the Report, to the Member States' regulatory authorities to review national legislation or regulations and, in particular, to consider (i) whether the existing restrictions pursue a clearly articulated and legitimate public interest objective; (ii) whether they are necessary to achieve that objective; and (iii) whether there are no less restrictive means to achieve this.[12]

In this regard, it must be noted that in the case law concerning Member States' liability under Articles 3(1)(g), 10(2) and 81(1) EC, there is *no mention* of the need of State measures to pursue legitimate public interest objectives, as measured by an authority other than the Member State legislator, and to be proportional to the achievement of those objectives. As clearly stated by the Court in *Arduino*,[13] pursuant to this case law, although Article 81 EC is, in itself, concerned solely with the conduct of undertakings and not with laws or regulations emanating from Member States, that provision, read in conjunction with Article 10(2) EC, 'none the less requires the Member States not to introduce or maintain in force measures, even of a legislative or regulatory nature, which may render ineffective the competition rules applicable to undertakings'.[14] In particular, the Court has consistently held that Articles 10(2) and 81(1) EC are infringed where a Member State requires or favours the adoption of agreements, decisions or concerted practices contrary to Article 81 EC or reinforces their effects, or where it divests its own rules of the

---

12 See para 93. See also the Executive Summary of the Report where the Commission states '[W]here a State delegates its policy-making power to a professional association without sufficient safeguards, that is *without clearly indicating the public interest objectives to respect*, without retaining the last word and without control of the implementation, the Member State can also be held liable for any resulting infringement' (emphasis added).

13 Case C–35/99 *Manuele Arduino, third parties Diego Dessi, Giovanni Bertolotto and Compagnia Assicuratrice Ras SpA* [2002] ECR I–1529.

14 *Arduino*, para 34.

character of legislation by delegating to private economic operators responsibility for taking decisions affecting the economic sphere.[15]

Therefore, if a Member State's measure has one of the effects described above, it infringes Articles 3(1)(g), 10(2) and 81(1) EC irrespective of whether it pursues a legitimate public interest objective—the existence of which should in any case be presumed for State legislation or regulation—and whether it is proportional to its achievement. Conversely, if the Member State's measure does not have any of the effects mentioned above, it is not contrary to Articles 3(1)(g), 10(2) and 81(1) EC even if, hypothetically, it does not pursue a legitimate public interest or it is not proportional to its achievement.

In conclusion, it is clear, in my view, that there is currently *no basis* in EC competition law for the public interest/proportionality test proposed by the Commission at paragraph 88 of the Report and that, likewise, Member States are not under any duty to amend their existing restrictive regulations in order to comply with such a test.

Based on the above, it is also worth noting that the possible 'non-proportionality' of a State measure could not lead the competent national competition authority to disapply it. Indeed, in its recent *CIF* judgment,[16] often quoted by the Commission in the Report, the Court stated that national competition authorities have an affirmative duty to disapply national measures contrary to EC competition rules, but has *not* elaborated a new substantive test to determine when a national measure is contrary to Articles 3(1)(g), 10(2) and 81(1) EC. In this respect, the Court referred to the above-mentioned established case law concerning the obligation of each Member State to abstain from introducing or maintaining in force measures, including of a legislative or regulatory nature, that may render ineffective the Treaty competition rules applicable to undertakings. As already mentioned, this case law does not provide for the public interest/proportionality test proposed by the Commission.

2. The Test Established by the Court in *Arduino*

In the section analysing Member States' liability, the Commission also comments on the *Arduino* judgment. In particular, it states that in that case 'the participation of the professional association in fee-setting was limited to proposing a draft tariff and the competent minister *had the power to amend*

---

[15] See Case 267/86 *Van Eycke* [1988] ECR 4769, para 16; Case C–185/91 *Reiff* [1993] ECR I–5801, para 14; Case C–153/93 *Delta Schiffahrts- und Speditionsgesellschaft* [1994] ECR I–2517, para 14; Case C–96/94 *Centro Servizi Spediporto* [1995] ECR I–2883, para 21; and Case C–35/96 *Commission v Italy (customs agents' tariff)* [1998] ECR I–3851, para 54.

[16] Case C–198/01 *Consorzio Industrie Fiammiferi* (CIF) [2004] ECR I–8055.

the tariff, and therefore there was no challengeable delegation to private operators' (paragraph 86, emphasis added). Consequently, the Commission states that among the Member States' measures or practices which can be challenged under Articles 3(1)(g), 10(2) and 81(1) of the Treaty, there are, *inter alia*, 'practices whereby the authorities of a Member State are only entitled *to reject or endorse the proposals of professional bodies* without being able to alter their content or substitute their own decisions for these approvals' (paragraph 87, emphasis added).

In this regard, I believe that the Commission's description of both the facts of the *Arduino* case and of the Member States' measures which are challengeable under Articles 3(1)(g), 10(2) and 81(1) EC based on the *Arduino* judgment, is ambiguous and leaves room for an interpretation not in line with the Court's case law.

The system under scrutiny in *Arduino* was the compulsory tariff for fees of members of the bar in Italy. Under Italian law, legal fees are determined by a scale setting the minimum and maximum fees chargeable by lawyers for their services. This scale is adopted by the Italian Minister for Justice on the basis of drafts prepared by the *Consiglio Nazionale Forense* (the National Council of the Bar, the 'CNF'), a body composed of lawyers elected by their peers. Furthermore, the Minister is assisted by two public bodies, the *Consiglio di Stato* and the *Comitato interministeriale dei prezzi* whose opinions he must obtain before he can approve the tariff.

In *Arduino*, the Court concluded that by adopting the system described above, the Italian State had not divested its own rules of the character of legislation by delegating to private economic operators responsibility for taking decisions affecting the economic sphere and thus was not liable under Articles 3(1)(g), 10(2) and 81(1) EC. In particular, the Court argued that the Italian State had not waived its power to make decisions in the last resort because the CNF is only responsible for producing a draft tariff which, as such, is not compulsory. Indeed, without the Minister's approval, the draft tariff does not enter into force and the earlier approved tariff remains applicable. Accordingly, as the Court stated, 'the Minister has the power to *have the draft amended by the CNF*' (emphasis added).[17]

Therefore, contrary to what the Commission states in the Report, in *Arduino* the authority of the Member State, *ie,* the Minister of Justice, did not have 'the power to amend the tariff' and was formally only 'entitled to reject or endorse' the CNF's proposal. However, the Court deemed that, by refusing to approve the draft tariff with the consequence that the old tariff remained applicable, the Minister can prompt the CNF to amend its draft along the lines he indicates. This circumstance was considered sufficient by

[17] *Arduino*, para 41.

the Court to conclude that the Italian State had not waived its power to make last resort decisions.[18]

On the contrary, based on the position adopted by the Commission in the Report, one might conclude that a State mechanism such as the one at stake in *Arduino* should be considered contrary to Articles 3(1)(g), 10(2) and 81(1) EC. Therefore, either the Commission is proposing a new test to assess the compatibility of State measures with EC competition law, which departs from the established case law of the Court, in which case it should state this explicitly, or it should consider modifying the language used in the Report in order to bring it into line with the Court's jurisprudence.

[18] The Court also gave weight to the circumstance that the Italian State had retained the power to review the implementation of the tariff. Indeed, under Italian law, fees are to be settled by the courts, having regard to the seriousness and number of issues dealt with. Fees must remain within the limits set by the scale; however in certain exceptional circumstances and by duly reasoned decision, the court may depart from the limits set by the scale.

Bibliography

1. Publications:

Ahrens D. (2002): "Der europäische Rechtsanwalt zwischen Rechtspflege und Dienstleistung", 115 *Zeitschrift für zivilprozess* 281.

Akerlof G. A. (1970): "The Market for 'Lemons': Quality Uncertainty and the Market Mechanism", 84 *Quarterly Journal of Economics* 488.

Akermann T. (1997): *Art. 85 Abs. 1 EGV und die rule of reason*, Forschungsinstitut für Wirtschaftsverfassung und Wettbewerb, Köln.

Albors-Llorens A. (2002): *EC Competition Law and Policy,* Willan Publishing, Cullompton Portland.

Amato G. and Laudati L., eds. (2001): *The Anticompetitive Impact of Regulation*, Hart Publishing, Oxford and Portland, Oregon.

American Antitrust Institute (2000): *Converging Professional Services: Lawyers Against The Multidisciplinary Tide*, available at http://www.antitrustinstitute.org/books/multidisc.cfm.

Ariño Gutierrez M. (2004): "Competition Law and Pluralism in European Digital Broadcasting: Addressing the Gaps", 54 *Communications and Strategies* 97.

Arruñada B. (1992): "Profesionales del monopolio", 14 *Revista de Economía* 95.

Arruñada B. (1999a): *The Economics of Audit Quality: Private Incentives and the Regulation of Audit and Non-Audit Services*, Kluwer International, Boston and Dordrecht.

Arruñada B. (1999b): "The Provision of Non-Audit Services by Auditors: Let the Market Evolve and Decide", 19 *International Review of Law and Economics* 513.

Arruñada B. (2000): "Audit Quality: Attributes, Private Safeguards and the Role of Regulation", 9 *The European Accounting Review* 205.

Arruñada B. (2001): "Las farmacias y el paso de los siglos", 5 *Revista de Administración Sanitaria* 119.

Arruñada B. (2003): "Property Enforcement as Organized Consent", 19 *Journal of Law, Economics and Organization* 401.

Arruñada B. (2004): "Quality Safeguards and Regulation of Online Pharmacies", 13 *Health Economics* 329.

Arruñada B. and Andonova V. (2004a): "Market Institutions and Judicial Rule-Making", in Ménard C. and Shirley M. M., eds., *Handbook of New Institutional Economics*, Springer Norwell, Massachusetts.

Arruñada B. and Andonova V. (2004): "Cognition, Judges and Market Order", *Economics and Business Working Paper Series* No. 768, July 2004, Universitat Pompeu Fabra, Department of Economics and Business, available at www.econ.upf.es/ cgi-bin/onepaper?768.

Ayres I. and Braithwate J. (1992): *Responsive Regulation: Transcending the Deregulation Debate*, Oxford University Press, Oxford.

Bachmann G. (2003): "Der 'Deutsche Corporate Governance Kodex': Rechtswirkungen und haftungrisiken", 56 *Wertpapiermitteilungen* 2137.

Baer W. (1999): *Letter to the Honorable Rene O. Oliveira, Texas House of Representatives*, available online at http://www.ftc.gov/be/v990009.htm.

Baggott R. and Harrison L. (1986): "The Politics of Self-Regulation: The Case of Advertising Control", 14 *Policy and Politics* 143.

Bahlmann K. (1982): "Der Grundrechtsschutz in der EG", 17 *Europarecht* 1.

Baquero Cruz J. (2002): *Between Competition and Free Movement: The Economic Constitutional Law of the European Community,* Hart Publishing, Oxford and Portland, Oregon.

Barton B. (2001): "Why Do We Regulate Lawyers? An Economic Analysis of the Justifications for Entry and Conduct Regulation," 33 *Arizona State Law Journal* 429.

Basedow J. (1995): "Zielkonflikte und Zielhierarchien im Vertrag über die Europäische Gemeinschaft", in Due O., Lutter M. and Schwarze J., eds., *Festschrift für Ulrich Everling*, Vol. I, Nomos, Baden-Baden, 54 *et seq*.

Becker G. S. and Stigler G. J. (1974): "Law Enforcement, Malfeasance, and Compensation of Enforcers", 3 *Journal of Legal Studies* 1.

Berle A. A. and Means G. C. (1982): *The Modern Corporation and Private Property*, Transaction Publishers, Somerset, New Jersey.

Blair R. D. and Rubin S. (1980): *Regulating the Professions*, Lexington Books, Lexington, Massachussets.

Böge U. (2004): Speech delivered on the occasion of the Opening Session of the *Seoul Competition Forum 2004*, Seoul, 20 April 2004.

Bolick C. and Legge D. (1991) "Challenging Barriers to Economic Opportunity: *Uqdah v. Board of Cosmetology*," Institute for Justice, Washington DC—paper available at www.ij.org/cases/economic/uqdah.shtml.

Bordoni L. (2001): "Issue Paper", report of the proceedings of the Working Group Manufacturing "Consumer Goods Industry", Conference on *The E-conomy in Europe*, Brussels, 1–2 March 2001 (http://europa.eu.int/comm/enterprise/events/e-economy/doc /manufacturing2_paper.pdf).

Bourgeois J. and Bocken J. (2005): "Guidelines on the Application of Article 81(3) of the EC Treaty or How to Restrict a Restriction", 32 *Legal Issues of Economic Integration* 111.

Brennan J. and Cruz R. (2002): *Letter to Representative Dennis Stapleton, Chairman of the Insurance Committee of the Ohio House of Representatives*, available at http://www.ftc.gov/os/2002/10/ohb325.htm.

Brennan J., Cruz R. and Harwood C. A. (2002): *Letter to Representative Brad Benson, Ranking Minority Member of the Financial Institutions and Insurance Committee of the Washington House of Representatives*, available at http://www.ftc.gov/be/v020009.pdf.

Brickman L. (2003): "The Market for Contingent Fee-Financed Tort Litigation: Is It Price Competitive?," 25 *Cardozo Law Review* 65.

Brown D. J. (2003): "The Competition Bureau's Information Bulletin on the Regulated Conduct Defence: Observations from the Astral/Telemedia Case", 21 *Canadian Competition Record* 43.

Button K. and Flemming M. (1992): "The Effects of Regulatory Reform on the Architectural Proffession In the United Kingdom', 12 *International Review of Law and Economics* 95.

Calkins S. (2000): "California Dental Association: Not A Quick Look But Not The Full Monty", 67 *Antitrust Law Journal* 495.

Carr J. L. and Matthewson G. F. (1990): "The Economics of Law Firms: A Study in the Legal Organization of the Firm", 33 *Journal of Law and Economics* 307.

Christensen-Szalanski J. J. and Willham C. F. (1991): "The Hindsight Bias: A Meta-Analysis", 48 *Organizational Behavior and Human Decision Processes* 147.

Cohen J. R. (1996): "Het domein geherdefinieerd", 76 *Advocatenblad* 233.

Creighton S. (2003): "A Federal-State Partnership on Competition Policy: State Attorneys General as Advocates," Address Before the National Association of Attorneys General 2003 Antitrust Seminar, available at http://www.ftc.gov/speeches/other/031001naag.htm.

Cruz R. (2002): "The Threat of Consumer Harm Resulting from Physician Collective Bargaining Under Alaska Senate Bill 37," Prepared Remarks Before the Committee on Labor and Commerce, Alaska House of Representatives, available online at http://www.ftc.gov/be/hilites/cruz020322.htm.

D'Attorre G. (2004): "Una 'ragionevole' concorrenza: Il ruolo della 'rule of reason' dopo la riforma del diritto antitrust comunitario", 31 *Giurisprudenza Commerciale* I-80.

Darby M. R. and Karni E. (1973): "Free Competition and the Optimal Amount of Fraud", 16 *Journal of Law and Economics* 67.

Deards E. (2002): "Closed shop versus one-stop shop: the battle goes on", 27 *European Law Review* 618.

Deckert M. R. (2000): "Some Preliminary Remarks on the Limitations of European Competition Law", 8 *European Review of Private Law* 173.

Deneke V. (1956): *Die freien Berufe*, Friedrich Vorwerk Verlag, Stuttgart.

Dingwall R. and Fenn P. (1987): "A Respectable Profession? Sociological and Economic Perspectives on the Regulation of Professional Services", 7 *International Review of Law and Economics* 51.

Dreher M. (2004): "Kartellrechtscompliance in der Versicherungswirtschaft", *Versicherungsrecht* 1.

Dreher M. and Thomas S. (2004): "Rechts- und Tatsachenirrtümer unter der neuen VO 1/2003", 54 *Wirtschaftsrecht und Wettbewerb* 8.

Drinker H. (1953): *Legal Ethics*, Columbia University Press, New York.

Edward D. (2001): "Recent Case Law of the European Court of Justice", in Schwarze M., ed., *Europäisches Wettbewerbsrecht im Wandel*, Nomos, Baden-Baden, 51 *et seq*.

Edward D. (2002): "Competition and National Rule-making", in von Bogdandy A., Mavroidis P. and Mény Y., eds., *European Integration and International Co-ordination, Studies in Transnational Economic Law in Honour of Claus-Dieter Ehlermann*, Kluwer Intl., The Hague/London/New York, 2002, 136 *et seq*.

Ehlermann C-.D. (1993): "Concurrence et professions libérales: antagonisme ou compatibilité?", 36 *Revue du Marché Commun et de l'Union europeéne* 136.

Ehlermann C.-D. (2000): "The Modernisation of EC Antitrust Policy: A Legal and Cultural Revolution", 37 *Common Market Law Review* 537.

Ehlermann C.-D. and Atanasiu I., eds. (2001): *European Competition Law Annual 2000: The Modernisation of EU Competition Law* Hart Publishing, Oxford and Portland, Oregon.

Ehlermann C-D. (1994): "Developments in Community Competition Law Procedures", 1 *EC Competition Policy Newsletter* 2.

Eichele K. and Happe E. (2003): "Verstoßen die BORA und die FAO gegen das europäische Kartellrecht", 17 *Neue Juristische Wochenschrift* 1214.

Eilmansberger T. (2005): "How to Distinguish Good from Bad Competition under Article 82 EC: In Search of Clearer and More Coherent Standards for Anti-competitive Abuses", 42 *Common Market Law Review* 129.

Emmerich V. (2001): *Kartellrecht*, 9th edition, Beck Juristischer Verlag, München.

Engel C. (2003): "A Constitutional Framework for Private Governance", 5 *German Law Journal* 197.

Fama E. F. and Jensen M. C. (1983a): "Separation of Ownership and Control", 26 *Journal of Law and Economics* 301.

Fama E. F. and Jensen M. C. (1983b): "Agency Problems and Residual Claims", 26 *Journal of Law and Economics* 327.

Feldstein P. J. (1988): *Health Care Economics*, 3rd edition, Wiley, New York.

Fels A., Parker D., Compley B. and Beri V. (2001): "Occupational Regulation", in Amato G. and Laudati L., eds., *The Anticompetitive Impact of Regulation*, Edgar Elgar, London, 104 *et seq*.

Fikentscher W. (2001): "Das Unrecht einer Wettbewerbsbeschränkung: Kritik an Weißbuch und VO-Entwurf zu Art. 81, 82 EG-Vertrag", 51 *Wirtschaft und Wettbewerb* 446.

First H. (1979): "Competition In the Legal Education Industry (II): An Antitrust Analysis", 54 *New York University Law Review* 1049.

Fischhoff B. (1975): "Hindsight ? Foresight: The Effect of Outcome Knowledge on Judgment under Uncertainty", 1 *Journal of Experimental Psychology: Human Perception and Performance* 288.

Fitzsimmons J. A. and Sullivan R. S. (1982): *Service Operations Management*, McGraw-Hill, New York.

Forrester I S. and Norall C. (1984): "The Laicization of Community Law: Self-Help and the Rule of Reason: How Competition Law Is and Could be Applied", 21 *Common Market Law Review* 11.

Forrester I. (1995): "Competition Structures for the 21st Century", in Hawk B., ed., *International Antitrust Law and Policy 1994*, *Annual Proceedings of the Fordham Corporate Law Institute*, Juris Publ., New York.

Forrester I. (2001): "The Reform of the Implementation of Articles 81 and 82 Following Publication of the Draft Regulation", 28 *Legal Issues of Economic Integration* 173.

Forrester I. and Norall C. (1984): "The Laicization of Community Law: Self-Help and the Rule of Reason: How Competition Law Is and Could be Applied", 21 *Common Market Law Review* 11.

Fox E. M. (2004): "State Action In Comparative Context: What If *Parker v. Brown* Were Italian?", in Hawk B., ed., *2003 Fordham International Antitrust and Policy* 463.

Friedman M. (1962): *Capitalism and Freedom*, University of Chicago Press, Chicago.

Frowein J. A. (1981): "Eigentumsschutz in Europarecht", in Grewe W. et al., eds., *Festschrift für H. Kutscher*, Nomos, Baden-Baden, 189 *et seq*.

Gambardella A., Orsenigo L. and Pammolli L. (2000): "Global Competitiveness in Pharmaceuticals: A European Perspective", Report Prepared for the Directorate-General Enterprise of the European Commission, available at http://pharmacos.eudra.org/F2/pharmacos/docs/Doc2000/nov/comprep nov2000.pdf.

Gavalda C. and Parleani G. (2002): *Droit des affaires de l'Union européenne*, Litec, Paris.

Gerber D. J. (1998): *Law and Competition in Twentieth Century Europe: Protecting Prometheus*, Oxford University Press, Oxford.

Gifford D. J. and Kudrle R. T. (2003): "European Union Competition Law and Policy: How Much Latitude for Convergence with the United States?", 48 *The Antitrust Bulletin* 727.

Gilson R. J. and Mnookin R. H. (1985): "Sharing Among the Human Capitalists: An Economic Inquiry into the Corporate Law Firm and How Partners Split Profits", 37 *Stanford Law Review* 313.

Goldman C. S. and Bodrug J. (2004): *Competition Law of Canada*, Juris Publishing, New York.

Goyder D. (2003): *EC Competition Law*, Oxford University Press, Oxford.

Grabitz E. (1990): "Über die Verfassung des Binnenmarktes", in Baur J., Hopt K. and Mailänder K., eds., *Festschrift für Ernst Steindorff zum 70. Geburtstag am 13 März 1990,* Verlag Walter de Gruyter, Berlin/New York, 1233 *et seq*.

Grabitz E. and Hilf M. (2002): *Das Recht der Europäischen Union*, Loseblatt-Kommentar in vier Bänden, Vol. 2 (Art. 249).

Grabosky P. and Braithwaite J. (1986): *Of Manners Gentle: Enforcement Strategies of Australian Business Regulatory Agencies*, Oxford University Press, Oxford.

Gyselen L. (1989): "State Action and the Effectiveness of the EEC Treaty's Competition Provisions", 26 *Common Market Law Review* 33.

Gyselen L. (1994): "Anti-Competitive State Measures under the EC Treaty: Towards a Substantive Legality Standard", 19 *European Law Review* 55.

Gyselen L. (2002): "The Substantive Legality Test under Article 81–3 EC Treaty—Revisited in Light of the Commission's Modernization Initiative", in von Bogdandy A., Mavroidis P. and Mény Y., eds., *European Integration and International Co-ordination, Studies in Transnational Economic Law in Honour of Claus-Dieter Ehlermann*, Kluwer Intl., The Hague/London/New York, p. 197.

Gyselen L. (2003): "Anti-Competitive State Measures Under the EC Treaty: Towards a Substantive Legality Standard", *European Law Review* special issue on "Competition Law Checklist 1993" 55.

Gyselen L. (2004): "De Vlaamse balies, multidisciplinaire samenwerking en EG-mededingingsrecht: prelude tot het arrest van het Hof van Cassatie", in *Liber Amicorum Jean-Pierre de Bandt*, Bruylant, Brussels, 95 *et seq*.

Harrison J. L., Morgan T. D. and Verkuil P. R. (1997): *Regulation and Deregulation: Cases And Materials*, West, Eagan Minnessotta.

Hatzopoulos V. G. (2002): "When Lawyers Ignore Competition or State and Semi-state Measures in the Light of Community Competition Rules after the *Arduino* and *Price Waterhouse* Judgments", 50 *Nomiko Vima* 863.

Hawk B., ed. (1999): *International Antitrust Law and Policy 1998*, *Annual Proceedings of the Fordham Corporate Law Institute*, Juris Publ., New York.

Henssler M. and Prütting H. (1997): *BRAO-Kommentar*, Auflage, München.

Herrmann H. (1984): *Interessenverbände und Wettbewerbsrecht,—Ein deutsch-amerikanischer Vergleich zum Recht der unberechtigten Verfahrenseinleitung, Selbstbeschränkungsabkommen und Wettbewerbsregeln*, Nomos, Baden-Baden.

Herrmann H. (1989a): "Comment", 153 *Zeitschrift für das gesamte Handelsrecht* 596.

Herrmann H. (1989b): "Recht freier Berufe", in Sahner H., Herrmann H. and Trautwein H.-M., eds., *Zur Lage der freien Berufe: Niedersachsen im Vergleich zur Bundesrepublik*, Vol. 1, Univ. Lüneburg, Lüneburg, 299 *et seq*.

Herrmann H. (1996): *Recht der Kammern und Verbände Freier Berufe in der Europäischen Union und den USA*, Nomos, Baden-Baden.

Herrmann H. (2003a): "Normstrukturen des europaweiten De-Regulierungstrends und Kartellrecht", text available at http://europa.eu.int/comm/competition/liberalisation/conference/speeches/harald_herrmann_powerpoint.pdf.

Herrmann H. (2003b): "New Economy und Recht freier Berufe", 3 *Forum: Neues Wirtschaftsrecht* 120.

Herrmann H. (2004): *Deutsches und europäisches Unternehmens- und Gesellschaftsrecht*, IF Verlag, Ahrensdorf.

Hesse K. (1999): *Grundzüge des Verfassungsrechts der Bundesrepublik Deutschland*, Auflage, Heidelberg.

Hirschmann A. O. (1979): *Exit, Voice and Loyalty. Responses to Decline in Firms, Organizations and States*, Harvard University Press, Cambridge, Massachusets.

Hommelhoff P. and Schwab M. (2001): "Staatsersetzende Privatgremien im Unternehmensrecht", in *Festschrift für Heinrich Wilhelm Kruse*, Schäffer-Poeschel/O. Schmidt, Stuttgart /Köln, 693-.

Hommelhoff P. and Schwab M. (2003): "Regelungsquellen und Regelungsebenen der Corporate Governance", in Hommelhoff P., Hopt P. J. and von Verder A., eds., *Handbuch Corporate Governance*, Schäffer-Poeschel/O. Schmidt, Stuttgart/Köln, 59–.

Hossenfelder S. and Lutz M. (2003): "Die neue Durchführungs VO zu den Artt. 81 und 82 EG-Vertrag", 53 *Wirtschaft und Wettbewerb* 118.

Idot L. (2001): "A French Point of View on the Radical Decentralisation of the Implementation of Article 81(1) and (3)", in Ehlermann C.-D. and Atanasiu I., eds., *European Competition Law Annual 2000: The Modernisation of EU Competition Law*, Hart Publishing, Oxford and Portland, Oregon, p. 336.

Idot L. (2002): "Avocats et droit de la concurrence : La rencontre a eu lieu . . .", 5 *Europe* 5.

Idot L. (2003): "Le nouveau système communautaire de mise en œuvre des articles 81 et 82 CE (Règlement 1/2003 et projets de textes d'application)", 39 *Cahiers de Droit Européen* 283.

Immenga U. (2001): "Coherence: A Sacrifice of Decentralisation?", in Ehlermann C.-D. and Atanasiu I., eds., *European Competition Law Annual 2000: The Modernisation of EC Antitrust Policy*, Hart Publishing, Oxford and Portland, Oregon, 355-.

Immenga U. and Mestmäcker E.-J. (1992): *GWB. Kommentar zum Kartellgesetz*, Beck Juristischer Verlag, München.

Jähnke P. (1988): "Rechtliche Vorgaben einer künftigen Neuregelung des anwaltlichen Standesrechts", 12 *Neue Juristische Wochenschrift* 1888.

Jenny F. (1998): "The Objectives of Competition Policy", in C.-D. Ehlermann and L. Laudati, eds., *European Competition Law Annual 1997: Objectives of Competition Policy*, Hart Publishing, Oxford and Portland, Oregon, 29-.

Joerges C. *et al.* (1988): *Die Sicherheit von Konsumgütern und die Entwicklung der Europäischen Gemeinschaft*, Nomos, Baden-Baden.

Joliet R. (1967): *The Rule of Reason in Antitrust Law: American, German and Common Market Law*, Martinus Nijhoff, The Hague.

Keller T. (2003): "Burdensome Barriers: How Excessive Regulations Impede Entrepreneurship in Arizona", Policy Report No. 185, Goldwater Institute, available online at http://www.goldwaterinstitute.org/pdf/materials/378.pdf.

Kennish T. and Bolton J. (2003): "The Regulated Conduct Defence: Time for Legislative Action," 21 *Canadian Competition Record* 52.

Keppenne J.-P., Lagondet F. and van Raepenbusch S. (2003): "Chronique de jurisprudence: Année 2002", 39 *Cahiers de Droit Européen* 433.

Kieninger E. M. (2002): *Wettbewerb der Privatrechtsordnungen im Europäischen Binnenmarkt*, Mohr Siebeck Verlag, Tübinger.

Kilian M. (2003): "Was will uns das Bundesverfassungsgericht sagen?", 65 *Anwaltsblätter* 256.

Klein B. and Leffler K. (1981): "The Role of Market Forces in Assuring Contractual Performance", 89 *Journal of Political Economy* 615.

Kleine-Cosack M. (2004): *Das Werberecht der rechts- und steuerberatenden Berufe*, 2nd edition, Auflage, Freiburg.

Kleine-Kosack M. (2003): "Freie Berufe auf dem Prüfstand", text available at http://www.rae.hibaco.de/anwaelte/Bruessel.pdf.

Kleiner M. and Kudrle R. (2000): "Does Regulation Affect Economic Outcomes?: The Case of Dentistry", 43 *The Journal of Law & Economics* 547.

Kolasky W. (2002) "Global Competition Convergence and Cooperation: Looking Back and Looking Ahead," Address at the American Bar Association Fall 2002 Forum, available online at http://www.usdoj.gov/atr/public/speeches/200442.pdf.

Kommers D. and Waelbroeck M. (1986): "Legal Integration and the Free Movement of Goods: The American and European Experience", in Cappelletti M., Seccombe M. and Weiler J., eds., *Integration Through Law*, Vol. I: *Methods, Tools and Institutions*, Book 2: *Forces and Potential for a European Identity*, Walter de Gruyter, Berlin, 197-.

Kon S. (1982): "Article 85, Para. 3: A Case for Application by National Courts", 19 *Common Market Law Review* 541.

Korah V. and O'Sullivan D. (2002): *Distribution Agreements under the EC Competition Rules*, Hart Publishing, Oxford and Portland, Oregon.

Korah V. (2000): *An Introductory Guide to EC Competition Law and Practice*, Hart Publishing, Oxford and Portland, Oregon.

Korah V. (2002): "Rule of Reason: Apparent Inconsistency in the Case Law Under Article 81", 1 *Competition Law Insight* 24.

Kovacic W. E. (1982): "The Federal Trade Commission and Congressional Oversight of Antitrust Enforcement," 17 *Tulsa Law Journal* 587.

Kovacic W. E. (1989): "Congress and the Federal Trade Commission," 57 *Antitrust Law Journal* 869.

Kovacic W. E. (2001a): "Evaluating Antitrust Experiments: Using Ex Post Assessments of Government Enforcement Decisions to Inform Competition Policy," 9 *George Mason Law Review* 843.

Kovacic W. E. (2001b): "Institutional Foundations for Economic Legal Reform in Transition Economies: The Case of Competition Policy and Antitrust Enforcement," 77 *Chicago-Kent Law Review* 265.

Kovacic W. E. (2003): "Toward a Domestic Competition Network", remarks before the American Enterprise Institute, April 2003, available at http://www.ftc.gov.

Kovacic W. E. (2004a): "Achieving Better Practices in the Design of Competition Policy Institutions", remarks before the Seoul Competition Forum 2004—Seoul, Republic of Korea, April 2004, text available at http://www.ftc.gov.

Kovacic W. E. (2004b): "The Modern Evolution of U.S. Competition Policy Norms," 71 *Antitrust Law Journal* 377.

Kraakman R. H. (1986): "Gatekeepers: The Anatomy of a Third-Party Enforcement Strategy", 2 *Journal of Law, Economics and Organization* 53.

Kuijpers M., Noailly J. and Vollaard B. (2005): *Liberalization of the Dutch Notary Profession: Reviewing its Scope and Impact* CPB Netherlands Bureau for Economic Policy Analysis, Discussion Paper No. 93/Sept. 2005.

Lao M. (2001) "Discrediting Accreditation?: Antitrust and Legal Education," 79 *Washington University Law Quarterly* 1035.

Lazear E. P. (1979): "Why Is There Mandatory Retirement?", 87 *Journal of Political Economy* 1261.

Leland H. E. (1979): "Quacks, Lemons and Licensing: A Theory of Minimum Quality Standards", 87 *Journal of Political Economy* 1328.

Lenaerts K. and Gerard D. (2004): "Decentralisation of EC Competition Law Enforcement: Judges in the Frontline", 27 *World Competition* 313.

Levitt T. (1972): "Production Line Approach to Services", *Harvard Business Review* 41.

Levitt T. (1976): "The Industrialization of Services", *Harvard Business Review* 63.

Lorz R. A. (2002): "Die Erhöhung der verfassungsgerichtlichen Kontrolldichte gegenüber", 26 *Neue Juristische Wochenschrift* 169.

Love J. H. and Stephen F. H. (1996): "Advertising, Price and Quality In Self-Regulating Professions: A Survey", 3 *International Journal of the Economics of Business* 227.

Love J. H., Stephen F. H., Gillanders D. D. and Paterson A. A. (1992): "Spatial Aspects of Deregulation In the Market for Legal Services", 87 *Regional Studies* 1328.

Löwe H. (1988): "Werbung im künftigen Berufsrecht für Rechtsanwälte", 50 *Anwaltsblätter* 545.

Lueck D., Olsen R. and Ransom M. (1995): "Market and Regulatory Forces in the Pricing of Legal Services", 7 *Journal of Regulatory Economics* 63.

Lutter M. (2002): "Die Erklärung zum Corporate Govewrnance Kodey gemäß § 161 AktG", 166 *Zeitschrift für das gesamte Handelsrecht* 523.

Manzini P. (2002): "The European Rule of Reason—Crossing the Sea of Doubt", 23 *European Competition Law Review* 392.

Manzini P. (2003): "I parafernali del giudizio antitrust: Regola della ragionevolezza, restrizioni accessorie, divieto 'per se'", 30 *Giurisprudenza Commerciale* II-285.

McCullough J. T. (1984): "The Continuing Search for Greater Certainty: Suggestions for Improving US and EEC Antitrust Clearance Procedures", 6 *Northwestern Journal of International Law and Business* 803.

Mestmäcker E.-J. (1999): "Versuch einer katellpolitischen Wende in der EU. Zum Weißbuch der Kommission über die Modernisierung der Vorschriften zur Anwendung der Artt. 85 und 86 EGV a.F. (Artt. 81 und 82 EGV n.F.)", 17 *Europäische Zeitschrift für Wirtschaftsrecht* 523.

Mestmäcker E.-J. and Schweitzer H. (2004): *Europäisches Wettbewerbsrecht*, 2nd edition, Beck Verlag, München.

Miller J. (1985): "The FTC and Voluntary Standards: Maximizing the Net Benefits of Self-Regulation", 4 *Cato Journal* 897.

Monti G. (2002): "Article 81 EC and Public Policy", 39 *Common Market Law Review* 1057.

Monti M. (2003): "Comments and Concluding Remarks", sppech at the Conference on Professional Regulation, European Commission, Brussels, October 2003.

Monti M. (2003): "Competition in Professional Services: New Light and New Challenges", speech given before the Bundesanwaltskammer, Berlin, 21 March 2003.

Monti M. (2004): "A Reformed Competition Policy: Achievements and Challenges for the Future", Center for European Reform, Brussels, 28 October 2004, available at http://europa.eu.int/comm/competition/speeches.

Monti M. (2004): "Pro-Active Competition Policy and the Role of the Consumer", speech given at the European Competition Day, Dublin, 29 April 2004.

Mortelmans K. (2001): "Towards Convergence in the Application of the Rules on Free Movement and on Competition?", 38 *Common Market Law Review* 613.

Müller-Graff P.-C. (2004): "L'économie de marché concurrentielle comme principe constitutionnel commun dans l'Union européenne", in *Études en l'honneur de Jean-Claude Gautron, Les dynamiques du droit européen en début de siècle,* Editions Pédone, Paris, 479 *et seq*.

Muris T. J. (2000): "*California Dental Association v. Federal Trade Commission*: The Revenge of Footnote 17," 8 *Supreme Court Economic Review* 265.

Muris T. J. (2002): "Creating a Culture of Competition: The Essential Role of Competition Advocacy," speech given before the International Competition Network, Panel on Competition Advocacy and Antitrust Authorities, available online at http://www.ftc.gov/speeches/muris/020928naples.htm.

Muris T. J. (2002): "Looking Forward: The Federal Trade Commission and the Future Development of U.S. Competition Policy", remarks for the Milton Handler Annual Antitrust Review, New York, December 2002, text available at http://www.ftc.gov .

Muris T. J. (2003): "How History Can Inform Practice", remarks before the Fall Forum of the American Bar Association Section of Antitrust Law, Washington DC, November 2003, text available at http://www.ftc.gov.

Muris T. J. (2003): "State Intervention/State Action—A U.S. Perspective," speech before the 2003 Fordham Annual Conference on International Law & Policy, available online at http://www.ftc.gov/speeches/muris/fordham031024.pdf.

Murphy D. (2004): *The Structure of Regulatory Competition*, Oxford University Press, Oxford, New York.

Murphy K. M., Schleifer A. and Vishny R. W. (1991): "The Allocation of Talent: Implications for Growth", 106 *Quarterly Journal of Economics* 503.

Nahuim R. and Noailly J. (2005), *Competition and Quality in the Notary Profession*, CPB Netherlands Bureau for Economic Policy Analysis, Discussion Paper No. 94/Sept. 2005.

Nelson P. (1970): "Information and Consumer Behavior", 78 *Journal of Political Economy* 311.

Nickel D. (1980): "Zum Grundrechtsdefizit der EG", 12 *Zeitschrift für Rechtspolitik* 161.

Noll P. (1973): *Gesetzgebungslehre*, Rowohlt, Hamburg.

O'Leary S. and Fernández-Martín J. M. (2002): "Judicially-Created Exceptions to the Free Provision of Services", in Andenas M and Roth W.-H., eds., *Services and Free Movement in EU Law*, Oxford University Press, Oxford, 163 *et seq*.

Ogus A. (1995): "Rethinking Self-Regulation", 15 *Oxford Journal of Legal Studies* 97.

Ogus A. (2000): "Self-Regulation", in Bouckaert B. and de Geest G., eds., *Encyclopedia of Law and Economics*, Edward Elgar, Aldershot.

Oliver P. (1996): *Free Movement of Goods in the European Community*, 3rd edition, Sweet & Maxwell, London.

Olsen R. N. (2002): "The Regulation of the Medical Professions', in Bouckaerts B. and De Geest G., eds., *Encyclopaedia of Law and Economics*, Vol. III: Regulation of Contracts, Edward Elgar, Aldershot, 1018 *et seq*.

Olson M. (1965): *The Logic of Collective Action*, Harvard University Press, Cambridge.

Parker C. (2002): *The Open Corporation. Effective Self-Regulation and Democracy*, Cambridge University Press, New York.

Paterson I., Farmer L., Stephen F. H. and Love J. (1988): "Competition and the Market for Legal Services", 15 *Journal of Law and Society* 361.

Paterson I., Fink M. and Ogus A. (2003): *Economic Impact of Regulation in the Field of Liberal Professions in Different Member States*, Institute for Advanced Studies, Vienna, January, available at http://europa.eu.int/comm/competition.

Petersen C. E., ed. (1971): *The Rules of Work of the Carpenters' Company, of the City and County of Philadelphia*, The Pyne Press, Princeton.

Poiares Maduro M. (1999): "Striking the Elusive Balance Between Economic Freedom and Social Rights In the EU", in Alston P., ed., *The EU and Human Rights*, Oxford University Press, Oxford, 451 *et seq.*

Posner R. A. (1995b): "What Do Judges Maximize", in *Overcoming Law*, Harvard University Press, Cambridge, Massachusets.

Posner R. A. (2004): "Antitrust in a Transatlantic Context", speech delivered in Brussels, Belgium, 7 June 2004.

Quinn J. (1982): "Multidisciplinary Services and Preventive Regulation", in Evans R. and Trebilcock M. J., eds., *Lawyers and the Consumer Interest: Regulating the Market for Legal Services*, Butterworths, Toronto.

Reich N. (1994): "The November Revolution of the European Court of Justice: *Keck*, *Meng* and *Audi* Revisited", 31 *Common Market Law Review* 459.

Rekaiti P. and van den Bergh R. (2000): "Cooling-Off Periods in the Consumer Laws of the EC Member States. A Comparative Law and Economics Approach", 23 *Journal of Consumer Policy* 371.

Ringleb H.-M., Kremer T., Lutter M. and von Werder A. (2003): *Deutscher Corporate Governance Kodex. Kommentar*, Kodex-Kommentar, Beck, München.

Rizzo J. A. and Zeckhauser R. J. (1992): "Advertising and the Price, Quantity and Quality of Primary Physician Services", 28 *Journal of Human Resources* 381.

Römermann V. and Wellige K. (2002): "Rechtsanwaltskartelle—oder: Anwaltliches Berufsrecht nach den EuGH-Entscheidungen Wouters und *Arduino*", 57 *Betriebs-Berater* 633.

Scassellati Sforzolini G. and Rizza C. (2003): "La tensione fra regole di concorrenza comunitarie e regole professionali e deontologiche nazionali", 30 *Giurisprudenza Commerciale* II-8.

Schinnick E. and Stephen F. H. (2000): "Professional Cartels and Scale Fees: Chiselling on the Celtic Fringe?", 20 *International Review of Law and Economics* 407.

Schmid C. U. (2000): "Diagonal Competence Conflicts between European Competition Law and National Regulation: A Conflict of Laws Reconstruction of the Dispute on Book Price Fixing", 8 *European Review of Private Law* 155.

Schmidt K. (2003): "Umdenken im Kartellverfahrensrecht", 58 *Betriebs-Berater* 1237.

Schneider H. (1991): *Gesetzgebung*, 2nd edition, CF Müller, Heidelberg.

Schroeter J. R., Smith S. L. and Cox S. R. (1987): "Advertising and Competition in Routine Legal Service Markets: An Empirical Investigation", 36 *Journal of Industrial Economics* 49.

Shapiro C. (1983): "Premiums for High Quality Products as Returns to Reputations", 98 *Quarterly Journal of Economics* 659.

Shapiro C. and Stiglitz J. E. (1984): "Equilibrium Unemployment as a Worker Discipline Device", 74 *American Economic Review* 433.

Shepherd G. and Shepherd W. (1998): "Scholarly Restraints? ABA Accreditation and Legal Education," 19 *Cardozo Law Review* 2091.

Simons J. and Cruz R. (2002): *Letter to the Honorable Lisa Murkowski, Chair, House Labor and Commerce Committee, Alaska House of Representatives*, available online at http://www.ftc.gov/be/v020003.pdf.

Siems M. (2005): *Die konvergeuz der Riechtssysteme im Recht der Actionäre*, Mohr Siebeck, Tübingen 2005.

Siragusa M. (1998): "Rethinking Article 85: Problems and Challenges in the Design and Enforcement of the EC Competition Rules", in Hawk B., ed., *International Antitrust Law and Policy 1997, Annual Proceedings of the Fordham Corporate Law Institute* Juris Publ., New York, 276 *et seq.*

Söllner A. (2001): "Kundenbindung", in Diller H., ed., Vahlens Großes Marketing Lexikon, Auflage, München.

Stephen F. H. (1994): "Advertising, Consumer Search and Prices in a Professional Service Market", 26 *Applied Economics* 1177.

Stephen F. H. (2004): "The Market Failure Justification for the Regulation of Professional Service Markets and the Characteristics of Consumers", University of Strathclyde, Glasgow, July 2004.

Stephen F. H. and Love J. (2000): "Regulation of the Legal Profession", in Bouckaert B. and de Geest G., eds., *Encyclopedia of Law and Economics*, Edward Elgar, Aldershot, 987 *et seq.*

Stephen F. H., Love J. and Paterson I. (1994): "Deregulation of Conveyancing Markets in England and Wales", 15 *Fiscal Studies* 102.

Strobel W. (1988): "Der Markt anwaltlicher Dienstleistungen", 50 *Anwaltsblätter* 307.

Stürner R. and Bormann J. (2004): "Der Anwalt—vom freien Beruf zum dienstleistenden Gewerbe", 18 *Neue Juristische Wochenschrift* 1481.

Stuyck J. (1999): "Libre circulation et concurrence: les deux pilliers du marché commun", in Dony M. and de Walsche A., eds., *Mélanges en hommage à Michel Waelbroeck*, Vol. II, Bruylant, Brussels, 1477 *et seq.*

Sunstein C. R. (2003): *Why Societies Need Dissent—Oliver Wendell Holmes Lectures*, Harvard University Press, Cambridge, Massachusetts.

Teubner G. (1978): *Organisationsdemokratie und Verbandsverfasasung:* Rechtsmodelle Fr Politisch Relevante Verbaende, Mohr, Tübingen.

Teulings C. N., Bovenberg A. L. and van Dalen H. P. (2003): *De calculus van het publieke belang*, The Hague.

The Shorter Oxford English Dictionary on Historic Principles, 3rd edition, Clarendon Press, Oxford (1988).

Tizzano A. (2002): "Note sulla recente giurisprudenza della Corte comunitaria", 7 *Il Diritto dell'Unione Europea* 535.

Todino M. (1998): "Le norme comunitarie di concorrenza nei poteri dell'Autorità garante della concorrenza e del mercato", 12 *Diritto del Commercio Internazionale* 751.

Triantafyllou D. (1976): *Vom Vertrags- zum Gesetzesvorbehalt*, Nomos, Baden-Baden.

Tullock G. (1975): "The Transitional Gains Trap", 6 *The Bell Journal of Economics and Management Science* 671.

Tzouganatos D. (2001): *Exclusive and Selective Distribution Agreements in Free and Unfair Competition Law*, Athens [in Greek].

Ulmer P. (2002): "Der Deutsche Corporate Governance Kodex", in *Zeitschrift für das gesamte Handelsrecht,* Verlag Recht und Wirtschaft, Frankfurt am Main, 150-.

van den Bergh R. (1999): "Self-Regulation of the Medical and Legal Professions: Remaining Barriers to Competition and EC Law" in Bortolotti B. and Fiorentini G., eds., *Organized Interests and Self-Regulation*, Oxford University Press, Oxford, 89 *et seq.*

van den Bergh R. (2000): "Towards an Institutional Legal Framework for Regulatory Competition", 53 *Kyklos* 435.

van den Bergh R. (2004): *Towards Efficient Self-Regulation in Markets for Professional Services*, Erasmus University Press, Rotterdam.

van den Bergh R. and Faure M. (1991): "Self-Regulation of the Professions in Belgium", 11 *International Review of Law and Economics* 165.

van der Esch B. (1994): "Loyauté fédérale et subsidiarité à propos des arrêts du 17 novembre 1993 dans les affaires *Meng*, *Ohra* et *Reiff*", *Cahiers de Droit Europeen* 523.

van Gerven G. (2004): "The Application of Article 81 in the New Europe", in Hawk B., ed., *Annual Proceedings of the Fordham Corporate Law Institute, International Antitrust Law and Policy 2003*, Juris Publ., New York, 429 *et seq*.

van Houtte B. (1982): "A Standard of Reason in EEC Antitrust Law: Some Comments on the Application of Parts 1 and 3 of Article 85", 4 *Northwestern Journal of International Law and Business* 497.

Vázquez Albert D. (2002): *Derecho de la Competencia y Ejercicio de las Profesiones*, Thomson Aranzadi, Madrid.

Venit J. (2003): "Brave New World: The Modernization and Decentralization of Enforcement under Articles 81 and 82 of the EC Treaty", 40 *Common Market Law Review* 545.

Verouden V. (2003): "Vertical Agreements and Article 81(3) EC: The Evolving Role of Economic Analysis", 71 *Antitrust Law Journal* 525.

Vest H. (2000): "Felling the Giant: Breaking the ABA's Stranglehold on Legal Education in America", 50 *Journal of Legal Education* 494.

Vesterdorf B. (2002): "Recent Developments in the Case Law of the ECJ and the CFI in the Field of Competition Law", in Baudenbacher C., ed., *Neueste Entwicklungen im europäischen und internationalen Kartellrecht, Neuntes St. Galler Internationales Kartellrechtsforum 2002*, Helbing & Lichtenhahn, Basel/Genf/München, 106 *et seq.*

von der Groeben H., Thiesing J. and Ehlermann C.-D., eds. (1998): *Kommentar zum U-/EG-Vertrag*, 4th edition, Vol. 4., Nomos, Baden-Baden.

von Werder A. (2003): "Ökonomische Grundfragen der Corporate Governance", in Hommelhoff P., Hopt P. J. and von Verder A., eds., *Handbuch Corporate Governance*, Schäffer-Poeschel/O. Schmidt, Stuttgart/Köln, 3 *et seq.*

Vossestein A. J. (2002): Commentary on *Wouters* and *Arduino*, 39 *Common Market Law Review* 841.

Waddington I. (1992): "Medicine. The Market and Professional Autonomy", in Conze W. and Kocka J., eds., *Bildungsbürgertum im 19. Jahrhundert Bildungssystem und Professionalisierung in internationalen Vergleichen*, 2nd edition, Part I, Klett-Cotta, Stuttgart, 388 *et seq* .

Waelbroeck M. (1987): "Antitrust Analysis under Article 85(1) and Article 85(3)", in Hawk B., ed., *North American and Common Market Antitrust and Trade Laws 1987, Annual Proceedings of the Fordham Corporate Law Institute*, Juris Publ., New York.

Wagner A. (2003): "Der Systemwechsel im Kartellrecht: Gruppenfreistellungen und. Übergangsproblematik", 49 *Wettbewerb in Recht und Praxis* 1369.

Watts R. L. and Zimmerman J. L. (1979): "The Demand for and Supply of Accounting Theories: The Market for Excuses", 54 *The Accounting Review* 273.

Watts R. L. and Zimmermann J. L. (1986): *Positive Accounting Theory*, 2nd edition, Prentice-Hall, Englewood Cliffs, New Jersey.

Weatherill S. (1999): "Recent Case Law Concerning the Free Movement of Goods: Mapping the Frontiers of Market Deregulation", 36 *Common Market Law Review* 51.

Wesseling R. (1999): "The Commission White Paper on Modernisation of EC Antitrust Law: Unspoken Consequences and Incomplete Treatment of Alternative Options", 20 *European Competition Law Review* 420.

Whish R. (2000), "National Courts and the White Paper: A Commentary", in: *The Modernisation of EC Competition Law: The Next Ten Years*, CELS Occasional Paper No. 4, Cambridge.

Whish R. (2003): *Competition Law*, 5th edition, Sweet and Maxwell, London.

Whish R. and Sufrin B. (1987): "Article 85 and the Rule of Reason", 7 *Yearbook of European Law* 1.

Williamson O. E. (1983): "Credible Commitments: Using Hostages to Support Exchange", 73 *American Economic Review* 519.

Wineburgh M. (2004): "Are Clinical Social Workers An Endangered Species?", 35 *The Clinician* 1.

Wise M. (1994): *Remarks Before the Joint Committee on the Public Interest in Competitive Practices in Health Care of the Vermont Legislature*, available online at http://www.ftc.gov/be/v950001.htm.

Witt P. (2000): "Corporate Governance im Wandel", 69 *Zeitschrift Führung und Organisation* 159.

Yoo C. S. (2003): "New Models of Regulation and Interagency Governance," *Michigan State Detroit College of Law Law Review* 701.

Zalmanowitz B. (2003): "Competition Bureau Releases Information Bulletin on the Regulated Conduct Defence", 21 *Canadian Competition Record* 39.

Zwick S. (2001): "Médecines sans Frontières: A Dutch Dotcom that Fills Prescriptions for its Neighbors Challenges Germany's Strict Regulations", *Time* Europe, June 8 2001, available at http://www.time.com/time/europe/biz/column/0,9868,101418,00.html.

Zywicki T. J. (2003): "Competition Policy and Regulatory Reforms: Means and Ends", sppech available at http://www.ftc.gov/speeches/other/031120zywickijapan speech.pdf.

2. Official studies, reports, etc.:

American Bar Association, Center for Professional Responsibility (2003): *Annotated Model Rules of Professional Conduct*, 5th edition, Center for Professional Responsibility, Washington DC.

Australian Government Publishing Service (1993): *National Competition Policy—Report by the Independent Committee of Inquiry*, August 1993.

Australian Trade Practices Commission (1992): *Study of the professions—Final Report—July 1982—Accountancy.*

Australian Trade Practices Commission (2002): *Study of the Professions—Final Report ' September 1992 ' Architects.*

Australian Trade Practices Commission (2004): *Study of the Professions—Final Report—March 1994—Legal.*

Autoritá Garante della Concorrenza e del Mercato (1997): *Indagine conoscitiva IC15—Settore degli ordini e dei collegi professionali*, full text (in Italian) available at http://www.agcm.it.

Bond R. S. *et al.* (1980): *FTC Staff Report on Effects of Restrictions on Advertising and Commercial Practice in the Professions: The Case of Optometry*, FTC Bureau of Economics, Washington DC.

Canadian Bureau of Competition (1996): *Notes for a presentation on behalf of the Director of Investigation and Research to the Manitoba Public Utilities Board re: Review of Natural Gas Supply Procurement, Transportation and Storage Functions of Centra Gas Manitoba Inc. and Review of Guidelines for Acceptable Conduct Between Centra Gas Manitoba Inc. and Affiliated Companies*, July 9, 1996.

Commissie Monitoring Notariaat (2003): *Eindrapport Periode 1999–2003*, The Hague, available at http://www.justitie.nl/Images/11 21107.pdf.

Cox C. and Foster S. (1990): "The Costs and Benefits of Occupational Regulation," FTC Bureau of Economics, Washington DC.

Dutch Ministry of Economic Affairs (2002): *Crystal-clear: more insight into transparency*, available at www.ez.nl.

Dutch Ministry of Economic Affairs (2003): *Delivery on Demand. Demand-driven public services provision in practise,* available at www.ez.nl.

Dutch Ministry of Economic Affairs (2004a): *Pamphlet on the Liberal Professions*, The Hague, The Netherlands, available at www.ez.nl.

Dutch Ministry of Economic Affairs (2004b): Public interests and market regulation in the liberal professions, The Hague, The netherlands, available at www.ez.nl.

Dutch Ministry of Economic Affairs and Dutch Ministry of Social Affairs and Employment (2004): *Choosing for Growth: Prosperity for Now and Later*, The Hague, The Netherlands.

Dutch Scientific Council for Government Policy (2000): *Het borgen van publiek belang*, The Hague, The Netherlands.

European Commission (1995): *25th Report on Competition Policy.*

European Commission (2000): *30th Report on Competition Policy.*

European Commission (2002): *32nd Annual Report on Competition Policy*, para. 206.

European Commission (2002): *Report from the Commission to the Council and to the European Parliament on the State of the Internal Market for Services*, COM (2002)441 final of 30.07.2002.

European Commission (2004): *Report on Competition in the Professional Services*, COM(2004) 83 final.

European Commisssion (1998): *28th Report on Competition Policy.*

FTC (2001): *Empirical Industrial Organization Roundtable*, available at http://www.ftc.gov.

FTC (2002): *Possible Anticompetitive Efforts to Restrict Competition on the Internet*, available online at http://www.ftc.gov/opp/ecommerce/anticompetitive/index.htm.

FTC (2003a): *To Promote Innovation: The Proper Balance of Competition and Patent Law and Policy*, available at http://www.ftc.gov/os/2003/10/innovationrpt.pdf.

FTC (2003b): "Staff Report Recommends Clarifications of the Antitrust State Action Doctrine", available online at www.ftc.gov/opa/2003/09/stateaction.htm.

FTC (2003c): *Report of the State Action Task Force: Recommendations to Clarify and Reaffirm the Original Purposes of the State Action Doctrine To Help Ensure That Robust Competition Continues to Protect Consumers*, available online at http://www.ftc.gov/os/2003/09/stateactionreport.pdf.

FTC (2004a): *FTC Antitrust Actions in Healthcare Services and Products, Bureau of Competition, Health Care Products and Services Division*, available online at http://www.ftc.gov/bc/hcupdate0404.pdf.

FTC (2004b): *Possible Anticompetitive Barriers to E-Commerce: Contact Lenses*, available online at www.ftc.gov/os/2004/03/040329clreportfinal.pdf.

FTC (2004c): Improving Health Care: A Dose of Competition: A Report by the Federal Trade Commission and the Department of Justice, available at http://www.ftc.gov/opa/2004/07/healthcarerpt.htm.

FTC, Office of Policy Planning (2003): *Report of the State Action Task Force: Recommendations to Clarify and Reaffirm the Original Purposes of the State Action Doctrine to Help Insure that Robust Competition Continues to Protect Consumers*, available at http://www.ftc.gov/os/2003/09/stateactionreport.pdf.

INDECON (2003): *Assessment of Restrictions on the Supply of Professional Services*, report prepared for the Irish Competition Authority, Dublin.

Knowledge Centre for Regulation Issues (2004): *Key to the Calculus of the Public Interest*, The Hague, The Netherlands, available at www.marktordening.nl.

Law Society (2002): *Findings From the Law Society's 2001 Business Survey*, London.

Legal Services Review (2004): *Report of the Review of the Regulatory Framework for Legal Services in England and Wales*, available at http://www.legal-services-review.org.uk/content/report/index.htm.

Mergers and Monopolies Commission (1970): *A Report on the General Effect on the Public Interest of Certain Restrictive Practices so far as they prevail in relation to the Supply of Professional Services*, Cmnd 4463, HMSO.

National Competition Law Section of the Canadian Bar Association (2003): *Submissions on the Competition Bureau Information Bulletin on the Regulated Conduct Defence*.

North Carolina State Bar Ethics Committee (2001a): *Formal Ethics Opinion 4,* available at www.ncbar.com/eth op/ethics sel.asp?ID=632&LIST=number&BACK='ethics o. asp'.

North Carolina State Bar Ethics Committee (2001b): *Formal Ethics Opinion 8*, available at www.ncbar.com/eth op/ethics sel.asp?ID=634&LIST=number&BACK='ethics o.asp.

North Carolina State Bar Ethics Committee (2003a) Formal Ethics Opinion 9, available online at www.ncbar.com/eth op/ethics sel.asp?ID=655.

North Carolina State Bar Ethics Committee (2003b): *Authorized Practice Advisory Opinion 2002–1*, available at www.ncbar.com/eth op/ethics sel.asp?ID=656.

OECD (1999): *Round Table on Competition Law and Policy*, Paris.

OECD (2004): *Economic Survey—Netherlands 2004*, Paris, available at www.oecd.org/infobycountry/.

OFT (2001): *Competition in the professions: A Report by the Director General of Fair Trading*, London.

OFT (2004): *Consumer Codes Approval Scheme: Core Criteria and Guidance*, London, available at http://www.oft.gov.uk/business/codes.

Productivity Commission (2003): *Evaluation of the Mutual Recognition Schemes* (research report), Canberra, Australia.

SEO Amsterdam Economics (2003)ç *Do it yourself? Stock-Taking Study of Self-Regulation Instruments*, Amsterdam.

SOU (1998): *Läkemedel i vård och handel: om en säker, flexibel och samordnad läkemedelsförörjning (betänkande)* (SOU 1998:28), Fritzes offentliga publikationer, Stockholm.

US Department of Justice (1998): *Antitrust Division Manual*, 3rd ed., available at http://www.usdoj.gov/atr/foia/divisionmanual/ch5.htm#a1.

US Department of Justice (1999): *Letter to Board of Governors, Kentucky Bar Association*, available at http://www.usdoj.gov/atr/public/comments/3943.pdf.

US Department of Justice and FTC (1997): *Letter to Supreme Court of Virginia*, available at http://www.usdoj.gov/atr/public/comments/3967.pdf.

US Department of Justice and FTC (2001): *Letter to the Ethics Committee of the North Carolina State Bar*, available at http://www.usdoj.gov/atr/public/comments/9709.htm.

US Department of Justice and FTC (2002a): *Letter to the Ethics Committee of the North Carolina State Bar*, available at http://www.usdoj.gov/atr/public/comments/11438.pdf.

US Department of Justice and FTC (2002b): *Letter to the Rhode Island House of Representatives*, available at http://www.usdoj.gov/atr/public/comments/10905.pdf.

US Department of Justice and FTC (2003a): *Letter to the Rhode Island House of Representatives*, available online at http://www.usdoj.gov/atr/public/comments/200901.pdf.

US Department of Justice and FTC (2003b): *Letter to the Standing Committee on the Unlicensed Practice of Law of the Georgia State Bar*, available at http://www.usdoj.gov/atr/public/comments/200857.pdf.

US House of Representatives (1996): "Concerning H.R. 2925, 'Health Care Reform Issues: Antitrust, Medical Malpractice Liability, and Volunteer Liability'": Hearing Before the House Committee on the Judiciary, 104th Congress, prepared statement of Robert Pitofsky, available online at http://www.house.gov/judiciary/148.htm.

US House of Representatives (1998): "Concerning H.R. 4277, 'The Quality Health-Care Coalition Act of 1998'": Hearing Before the House Committee on the Judiciary, 105th Congress, prepared statement of Robert Pitofsky, available online at http://www.house.gov/judiciary/10193.htm.

US House of Representatives (1999a): "Concerning H.R. 22: 'The Postal Modernization Act of 1999'", Hearing Before the Subcommittee on Postal Service, House Government Reform Committee, 106th Congress, prepared statement of Donna E. Patterson, available online at http://www.usdoj.gov/atr/public/testimony/2285.htm.

US House of Representatives (1999b): "Electricity Restructuring: Hearing Before the House Committee on the Judiciary," 106th Congress, prepared statement of A.

Douglas Melamed, available online at http://www.house.gov/judiciary/mela0728.htm.

US House of Representatives (2000): "International Postal Policy: Hearing Before the Subcommittee on Postal Service, House Government Reform Committee," 106th Congress, prepared statement of Donna E. Patterson, available online at http://www.usdoj.gov/atr/public/testimony/4291.pdf.

US House of Representatives (2002a) "State Impediments to E-Commerce: Consumer Protection or Veiled Protectionism?", Hearing Before the Subcommittee on Commerce, Trade, and Consumer Protection of the House Committee on Energy and Commerce, 107th Congress, prepared statement of Ted Cruz, available online at http://energycommerce.house.gov/107/action/107-130.pdf.

US House of Representatives (2002b): "Concerning H.R. 1253: 'The Free Market Antitrust Immunity Reform Act of 2001' ", Hearing Before the House Committee on the Judiciary, 107th Congress, prepared statement of Charles James, available online at http://www.house.gov/judiciary/james060502.htm.

van den Heuvel J., Lackner I. and Verkerk H. (2004): *Public Interests and Market Regulation in the Liberal Professions*, report to the Dutch Ministry of Economic Affairs, The Hague, The Netherlands.

World Bank (2004): *Doing Business in 2004: Understanding Regulation*, Washington DC and Oxford University Press, Oxford.

3. EC Legislation:

Amended Proposal for a Directive of the European Parliament and of the Council on the recognition of professional qualifications (presented by the Commission pursuant to Article 250 (2) of the EC Treaty), COM(2004)317 of 20.04.2004.

Commission Guidelines on the Application of Article 81(3) of the Treaty, OJ C 101 [2004].

Commission Directive 70/50/EEC of 22 December 1969 based on the provisions of Article 33 (7), on the abolition of measures which have an effect equivalent to quantitative restrictions on imports and are not covered by other provisions adopted in pursuance of the EEC Treaty, OJ L 13 [1970].

Commission Guidance on the effect on trade concept contained in Articles 81 and 82 of the Treaty, OJ C 101 [2004].

Commission Notice—Guidelines on the Applicability of Article 81 of the EC Treaty to Horizontal Cooperation Agreements, OJ C 3 [2001].

Commission Notice on cooperation within the Network of Competition Authorities, OJ C 101 [2004].

Commission Notice on informal guidance relating to novel questions concerning Articles 81 and 82 of the EC Treaty that arise in individual cases (Guidance Letters), OJ C 101 [2004].

Commission Notice on the Co-operation between the Commission and the Courts of the EU Member States in the Application of Articles 81 and 82 EC, OJ C 101 [2004].

Commission Notice on the Handling of Complaints by the Commission under Articles 81 and 82 of the EC Treaty, OJ C 101 [2004].

Commission Proposal for a Council Regulation on the Implementation of the Rules on Competition Laid Down in Articles 81 and 82 of the Treaty and Amending Regulations (EEC) No 1017/68, (EEC) No 2988/74, (EEC) No 4056/86 and (EEC) No 3975/87 ("Regulation Implementing Articles 81 and 82 of the Treaty"), COM(2000) 582 final, OJ C 365E [2000].

Commission Regulation 773/2004 of 7 April 2004 Relating to the Conduct of Proceedings by the Commission Pursuant to Articles 81 and 82 of the EC Treaty, OJ L 123 [2004].

Common Position adopted by the Council with a view to the adoption of a Directive of the European Parliament and of the Council on the recognition of professional qualifications, of 21.12.2004, available at http://europa.eu.int/comm/internal market/qualifications/future en.htm#20050511.

Council Directive 77/249/EEC of 22 March 1977 to facilitate the effective exercise by lawyers of freedom to provide services, OJ L 1 [1994].

Council Directive 77/452/EEC of 27 June 1977 concerning the mutual recognition of diplomas, certificates and other evidence of the formal qualifications of nurses responsible for general care, including measures to facilitate the effective exercise of this right of establishment and freedom to provide services, OJ L 353 è1990].

Council Directive 77/453/EEC of 27 June 1977 concerning the coordination of provisions laid down by Law, Regulation or Administrative Action in respect of the activities of nurses responsible for general care, OJ L 341 [1989].

Council Directive 78/1026/EEC of 18 December 1978 concerning the mutual recognition of diplomas, certificates and other evidence of formal qualifications in veterinary medicine, including measures to facilitate the effective exercise of the right of establishment and freedom to provide services, OJ L 353 [1990].

Council Directive 78/1027/EEC of 18 December 1978 concerning the coordination of provisions laid down by Law, Regulation or Administrative Action in respect of the activities of veterinary surgeons, OJ L 431 [1989].

Council Directive 78/686/EEC of 25 July 1978 concerning the mutual recognition of diplomas, certificates and other evidence of the formal qualifications of practitioners of dentistry, including measures to facilitate the effective exercise of the right of establishment and freedom to provide services, OJ L 353 [1990]

Council Directive 78/687/EEC of 25 July 1978 concerning the coordination of provisions laid down by Law, Regulation or Administrative Action in respect of the activities of dental practitioners, OJ L 206 [2001].

Council Directive 80/154/EEC of 21 January 1980 concerning the mutual recognition of diplomas, certificates and other evidence of formal qualifications in midwifery and including measures to facilitate the effective exercise of the right of establishment and freedom to provide services, OJ L 353 [1990].

Council Directive 80/155/EEC of 21 January 1980 concerning the coordination of provisions laid down by Law, Regulation or Administrative Action relating to the taking up and pursuit of the activities of midwives, OJ L 341 [1989]

Council Directive 85/384/EEC of 10 June 1985 on the mutual recognition of diplomas, certificates and other evidence of formal qualifications in architecture, including measures to facilitate the effective exercise of the right of establishment and freedom to provide services, OJ L 384 [1990].

Council Directive 85/432/EEC of 16 September 1985 concerning the coordination of provisions laid down by Law, Regulation or Administrative Action in respect of certain activities in the field of pharmacy, OJ L 201 [2001].

Council Directive 85/433/EEC of 16 September 1985 concerning the mutual recognition of diplomas, certificates and other evidence of formal qualifications in pharmacy, including measures to facilitate the effective exercise of the right of establishment relating to certain activities in the field of pharmacy, OJ L 353 [1990].

Council Directive 89/48/EEC of 21 December 1988 on a general system for the recognition of higher-education diplomas awarded on completion of professional education and training of at least three years' duration, OJ C 192E [2003].

Council Directive 93/13/EEC of 5 April 1993 on Unfair Terms in Consumer Contracts, OJ L 95 [1993].

Council Directive 93/16/EEC of 5 April 1993 to facilitate the free movement of doctors and the mutual recognition of their diplomas, certificates and other evidence of formal qualifications, OJ L 206 [2001].

Council Regulation (EC) No 1/2003 of 16 December 2002 on the implementation of the rules on competition laid down in Articles 81 and 82 of the Treaty, OJ L 1 [2003].

Council Directive 92/51/EEC of 18 June 1992 on a second general system for the recognition of professional education and training to supplement Directive 89/48/EEC, OJ L 51 [1992].

Directive 1999/42/EC of the European Parliament and of the Council of 7 June 1999 establishing a mechanism for the recognition of qualifications in respect of the professional activities covered by the Directives on liberalisation and transitional measures and supplementing the general systems for the recognition of qualifications, OJ L 42 [1992].

Directive 97/7/EC of the European Parliament and of the Council of 20 May 1997 on the protection of consumers in respect of distance contracts, OJ L 144 [1997].

Directive 98/5/EC of the European Parliament and of the Council of 16 February 1998 to facilitate practice of the profession of lawyer on a permanent basis in a Member State other than that in which the qualification was obtained, OJ L 77 [1988].

E-Europe: An Information Society For All, Communication on a Commission Initiative for the Special European Council of Lisbon, COM(1999) 687 final, available at http://europa.eu.int/information_society/eeurope/news_library/pdf_files/initiative_en.pdf.

E-Europe: An Information Society For All. Objective 3—Stimulate the use of Internet: Accelerating e-commerce, available at http://europa.eu.int/information_society/eeurope/index_en.htm.

European Parliament and Council Directive 2001/95/EC of 3 December 2001 on General Product Safety, OJ L 11 [2002].

European Parliament and Council Directive 97/55/EC of 6 October 1997 Amending Directive 84/450/EEC Concerning Misleading Advertising so as to Include Comparative Advertising, OJ L 290 [1997].

European Parliament and Council Directive 97/7/EC of 20 May 1997 on the Protection of Consumers in Respect of Distance Contracts, OJ L 144 [1997].

European Parliament and Council Directive 98/27 of 19 May 1998 on Injunctions for the Protection of Consumers' Interests, OJ L 166 [1998].

Proposal for a Directive of the European Parliament and of the Council on the recognition of professional qualifications, COM(2002)119(01) of 7.03.2002.

Proposal for a Directive of the European Parliament and of the Council on Services in the Internal Market, COM(2004)2 final of 5.03.2004.

White Paper of 28 April 1999 on Modernisation of the Rules Implementing Articles 85 and 86 of the EC Treaty, COM(1999) 101 final, OJ C 132 [1999].
White Paper on Completing the Internal Market, COM (85)310 of 14.06.1985.